Engaged Persuasion in a Post-Truth World

Engaged Persuasion in a Post-Truth World

Stephen K. Hunt • Kevin R. Meyer
Illinois State University

Bassim Hamadeh, CEO and Publisher
Todd R. Armstrong, Publisher
Sara Watkins, Developmental Editor
Michelle Piehl, Senior Project Editor
Abbey Hastings, Production Editor
Trey Soto, Licensing Specialist
Natalie Piccotti, Director of Marketing
Kassie Graves, Senior Vice President of Editorial
Jamie Giganti, Director of Academic Publishing

Printed in the United States of America.

Brief Contents

Contents

Engaged Persuasion Activity and Engaged Persuasion Research Boxes

Engaged Persuasion Activities

Engaged Persuasion Research

Preface

We are thrilled to present this new textbook that introduces students to persuasive principles, research, and theories. The text covers the dynamics of persuasion, including important source, receiver, and message components, while also explaining the effects of persuasive communication on receivers' attitudes, values, beliefs, and behaviors. As a result, students learn numerous personal, professional, and social benefits that stem from a better understanding of persuasive communication. For example, students will become sensitized to the fact that they have been and will continue to be bombarded with attempts to influence them for the rest of their lives. The text examines the application of persuasive communication concepts and theories to students' lives in multiple contexts in campus, residence, workplace, classroom, and online communities.

The text integrates several important themes that differentiate it from other books on the market. Several chapters contain applications of contemporary persuasion theory and research to the *post-truth era*. The post-truth era reflects the reality that many receivers of persuasion place more emphasis on personal beliefs and emotional appeals than on objective facts and rational argument. The term received a great deal of attention following the 2016 presidential election but has applications far beyond political communication. As many communication scholars have argued, the post-truth era is marked by the difficulty of maintaining communities of rational discourse and holds important implications for the functioning of our democracy. This textbook breaks new ground in persuasion by exploring research examining the origins of post-truth persuasion, how claims are disseminated, as well as strategies for producing and consuming persuasive messages in a post-truth world. Ultimately, we believe that it is essential that students possess this knowledge as a means of curbing the destructive effects of outrage discourse, political polarization, and stagnation in policymaking.

The text also explores the profound *influence of new digital and social media* on persuasive communication. As we are all aware, individuals are increasingly turning to the internet and social media to communicate, consume, produce, and distribute messages on a wide variety of topics. Simply put, online persuasive communication is ubiquitous, and students should learn how message construction, reception, and dissemination in online environments differs from face-to-face persuasion. As a result, the text introduces students to the most recent research available on new media, technology, and persuasion.

The text is also unique in that it includes prompts to help students envision how they can use persuasive communication to become *civically engaged* and advance the *common good* through social movements, communication campaigns, small-group decision making, and persuasive advocacy. The text will help prepare students to communicate effectively as citizens in a democracy and to avoid being victimized by manipulative and deceptive messages and viral deception. Several scholars have made the case that communication faculty are well positioned to promote civic learning (Denton, 2017; Hunt et al., 2016; Hunt et al., 2009; Palczweski et al., 2012). Importantly, training in persuasive communication can play a significant role in encouraging students' future civic and political engagement (i.e., while civic engagement is a pronounced characteristic of this textbook, the book also addresses more traditional ways in which studying communication can benefit students' lives).

One significant benefit of incorporating these themes is that students will become *more informed and critical consumers of persuasive messages.* In addition, a better understanding of persuasive communication will go a long way toward enhancing students' efforts to persuade others. This text introduces students to a wide variety of empirically tested persuasive concepts and theories that will aid them in every facet of their lives—from influencing friends and family, to resisting the persuasive attempts of others, to using their knowledge of persuasive communication to become an active citizen in our democracy.

Perhaps most importantly, as we worked to complete this text, we could not avoid thinking about why it is so essential now that those in higher education work to equip students with persuasion knowledge and skills. Our nation is facing multiple, simultaneously occurring pandemics of systematic racism, COVID-19, and misinformation. How might persuasion theory and research be used to dismantle systematic racism? Can persuasion theory and research inform the way health officials communicate about COVID-19? How might an understanding of the ways persuasive misinformation spreads help us mitigate its impacts, reduce political polarization, and restore democracy? Throughout this book we encourage readers to think about how persuasion theory and research can be applied to understand and address these issues in order to advance the common good.

Overview of the Book

Overall, the core of the textbook we have written is the theories that are currently employed by persuasion practitioners and scholars as well as contemporary research studies demonstrating the current state of a subject (e.g., through meta-analyses). It is certainly a textbook that emphasizes the current state of persuasion scholarship rather than the historical background. There is far more available content on persuasion than could be covered in what might reasonably be fit into a semester-long course. Each of us who teaches a persuasion course knows the struggle between balancing a desire to cover how persuasion affects a variety of other specific subjects (e.g., advertising campaigns, persuasion in mass media and film, rhetorical and historical roots traced to ancient Greece and Rome) and knowing that we are limited by the finite time that we can devote to each subject during class meeting times. Thus, as all persuasion textbooks must, we have made choices about the content we believe is most useful to students today. The focus on engaged persuasion and civic engagement informed many of these choices. Our approach blends social scientific studies, rhetorical perspectives, and qualitative data as well as findings related to topic areas within advertising, relational communication, mass media, and the like in an integrated fashion within each chapter rather than covering those topics within individual stand-alone chapters.

The organizational pattern of this textbook is based on the philosophical premise that students first need to be exposed to the definition of persuasion and the ethical implications of persuasion used in a negative manner. As such, the material is organized as follows:

- Chapter 1 introduces students to the definition and scope of persuasion as well as models of persuasion.
- Chapter 2 covers ethical persuasive communication and introduces students to persuasion in a post-truth era.
- Chapter 3 introduces students to using persuasion for the common good, which is a theme continued throughout the rest of the text.
- Chapter 4 examines the application of persuasion to campaigns and social movements.
- Chapter 5 introduces students to the role that attitudes play in persuasive communication as well as the attitude-behavior relationship.
- Chapter 6 covers persuasive message construction.
- Chapter 7 covers source characteristics and persuasion. Covering message before source is unique for a persuasion textbook, but this approach helps students understand persuasion fully before analyzing the ways messages are constructed and received. Addressing source before message characteristics is problematic because it assumes a linear process of persuasive communication.
- Chapter 8 introduces students to compliance-gaining techniques and sequential persuasion.

- In Chapter 9, students learn about message processing theories and research.
- Chapter 10 covers important variables related to the reception of persuasive messages.
- Chapter 11 introduces theories vital to understanding how receivers react and respond to persuasive messages.
- Chapter 12 covers language and nonverbal persuasion.
- Appendix A is particularly useful for instructors who require students to deliver persuasive public speeches and/or group discussions. Our discussion of group presentations is novel in that we provide strategies for facilitating group-led discussions of persuasion content.
- Appendix B will help students grasp persuasion research and theory by providing familiarity with the nature of scientific inquiry, research design, and theory building.

Features of the Textbook

There are several features of this textbook designed to aid student learning. Each chapter features **learning objectives, check your understanding review questions, chapter summaries**, and a **list of key terms** that help students gain a common content knowledge base through the text from which the instructor can build to higher levels of learning in classroom discussions.

Each chapter also contains **engaged persuasion research and activity side boxes.** These side boxes present novel applications of research and engage students in critical thinking about course concepts. For example, in Chapter 4 students are asked to play the role of a communication consultant and design a persuasive health campaign. This activity helps students apply persuasion theory and research to a health campaign promoting vaccinations.

The text covers many of the traditional social scientific theories of persuasion, such as cognitive dissonance theory, inoculation theory, and dual process models of persuasion, but it also covers important humanistic, philosophical, and rhetorical approaches (e.g., Toulmin's argument model, forms of rhetorical proofs, and rhetoric of social movements), thus offering students a compelling blend of different metatheoretical approaches. In addition, the text incorporates the **latest persuasion scholarship** and **relevant and updated examples** that makes the content relevant to students. The examples in the text make important applications of persuasion theory and research to numerous areas, including political communication, organizational communication (e.g., marketing, PR, and advertising), public speaking, culture, and media.

For adopting instructors, the **ancillaries and engaged learning activities** include chapter outlines; experiential activities; sample assignments and evaluations; instructional strategies for student engagement, including reading objectives and higher order discussion prompts; chapter by chapter list of potential media that facilitates application and transfer of course content; printable activities and handouts; suggestions for assessing student participation both in and out of class; reading review quizzes; and a test bank. Additionally, accompanying the text is an **Active Learning** program for enhanced student engagement. Please refer to the Active Learning notice in the front matter of this textbook for more information about how to access the Cognella Active Learning platform and material. For more information about adopting this textbook for your classroom, please contact adopt@cognella.com.

Overall, the text is written in a manner so that instructors can spur meaningful class discussions and facilitate experiential group projects that apply textbook concepts to multiple contexts. In writing this text, we provide a concise presentation of the principles, skills, and theories of persuasive communication that will motivate students to read and promote engagement with material.

Acknowledgments

We are grateful to have had the opportunity to write this textbook. We have learned a great deal as we explored the fascinating extant literature related to persuasive communication in a wide array of important contexts. We are especially appreciative of the opportunity to advocate for engaged persuasion used to advance the common good. Given the dynamics of the post-truth era, our democracy needs informed and ethical persuaders now more than ever.

We are also extremely grateful to Todd Armstrong, Michelle Piehl, and everyone at Cognella Academic Publishing who believed in and supported our work from the beginning.

We appreciate all individuals who served as reviewers for this book. Your comments and suggestions ultimately made this a much stronger project.

Stephanie J. Coopman (San José State University)

Abbe S. Depretis (Temple University)

Heidi E. Hamilton (Emporia State University)

Jeffrey H. Kuznekoff (Miami University)

Angela McGowan-Kirsch (State University of New York at Fredonia)

Tim McKenna-Buchanan (Manchester University)

Richard Murphy (McKendree University)

Steve Rains (University of Arizona)

Samantha J. Shebib (Utah State University)

Stephanie Eisenberg Todd (Chabot College)

Finally, our colleagues at Illinois State University and our families provided the support and encouragement needed to see this project to completion. You know who you are and you absolutely rock!

ACTIVE LEARNING

This book has interactive activities available to complement your reading.

Your instructor may have customized the selection of activities available for your unique course. Please check with your professor to verify whether your class will access this content through the Cognella Active Learning portal (http://active.cognella.com) or through your home learning management system.

CHAPTER 1

Scope of Persuasive Communication

Chapter Objectives

After reading this chapter, you should be able to:

- List and describe the benefits of studying persuasion
- Define persuasive communication
- List and define the aims of studying persuasion
- Understand the components of the Elaboration Likelihood Model and the Heuristic Systematic Model
- Identify and define the core principles of Cialdini's model of persuasion

In our daily activities we are bombarded with persuasive messages. From advertising on mass and social media to our interpersonal interactions, we are constantly exposed to attempts to change or reinforce our attitudes, values, beliefs, and behaviors. On the other hand, we routinely attempt to influence others and gain compliance through persuasive attempts of our own. Without question, persuasion is a central feature of virtually every aspect of human communication and is found wherever we find people communicating. As you will see throughout this text, scholars have developed a great number of empirically tested persuasive techniques, strategies, and theories than can help you become an effective producer and consumer of persuasive messages. This chapter provides key definitions, introduces students to the study of persuasive communication, and outlines the general goals of persuasion.

Benefits of Studying Persuasion

There are numerous reasons that you should become more familiar with persuasion research and theory. You have been and will continue to be bombarded with attempts to influence you for the rest of your life. Take a look around your campus, residence, workplace, and classroom for examples of persuasive communication. As you left your residence for class today, you likely encountered people on campus who solicited you for something. As you sit in the classroom, you are probably surrounded by flyers advertising study abroad opportunities, student organization activities, credit cards, and the like. As you listen to your instructor and classmates, you are being persuaded—even if indirectly—to adopt a particular view of the world. As you scroll through your social media feeds, you are saturated with advertisements for a whole range of products. And all this is only a simple thumbnail sketch of the ways that others attempt to persuade you on a daily basis. Thus, understanding academic research and theory on persuasion provides a number of personal, professional, and social benefits.

Personal Benefits

Studying persuasion offers us many personal benefits. You probably have already developed your own personal theories about how to persuade others and to respond to the persuasive attempts of others. You likely test these lay theories in different situations, adapting them as you learn from experience. However, there is a limit to what you can learn from experience alone. Clearly, there are times when you should not rely on this learning-from-experience approach. Think about the potentially severe implications of making a mistake when attempting to purchase a home or car. Such a mistake could cost you hundreds or even thousands of dollars. Similarly, the use of ill-informed compliance-gaining strategies could have negative implications for your interpersonal relationships. Being a wiser consumer of persuasive messages stimulates our ability to think independently and critically about the messages we encounter. Relatedly, we are less likely to be duped and more prone to make decisions that align with our interests and positions if we understand how communicators we encounter use persuasive strategies in attempts to influence us. The result is that we are more likely to be satisfied with the decisions we make when we can identify persuasive attempts and reach independent conclusions of our own freewill. Finally, improving your persuasive communication skills will help you become more confident in developing, presenting, and defending persuasive arguments.

Professional Benefits

Studying persuasion affords you a host of professional benefits. Think for a moment about the ways that persuasion is related to your professional success. Do people generally accept your ideas? Are you able to effectively advocate for the resources you need to be successful? Are you able to communicate to others what you have to offer? Often, our professional success, ability to accomplish tasks, and career advancement hinge on our ability to influence others. Whether you are working with customers, public audiences, coworkers, or supervisors,

FIGURE 1.1 Persuasion operates in social groups when we influence others.

Engaged Persuasion Activity: Advantages of Persuasion

Already, in your experiences, you have probably figured out that your ability to persuade others varies based on the situation or context, those you are attempting to persuade, the particular topic or persuasive message of concern, and a variety of other factors. Think of a time when another person was successfully able to persuade you. Perhaps it was a satellite TV salesperson, political pollster, nonprofit representative seeking a donation, or a coworker? Now, think of a time when another person's attempt to persuade you failed. What factors differed in those situations? And what advantages or disadvantages resulted from those communicative encounters for the other person? Next, consider whether persuasive individuals reap greater benefits in personal, professional, and social contexts. Certainly, most people are persuasive in certain situations. However, some individuals appear to be more persuasive in a variety of situations. What benefits do these more persuasive individuals (who are frequently successful at persuasion) seem to accrue in personal, professional, and social situations?

you frequently need to influence others to achieve objectives that benefit others while also advancing your professional career. Employers often list communication, group and teamwork, problem solving, and critical thinking among the skills they most covet in prospective employees. Arguably, persuasion lies at the heart of these skills. Understanding persuasive strategies also helps us to craft messages effectively as well as consume and dissect the messages we encounter. Furthermore, persuasion helps us to communicate effectively, work competently in groups, solve problems, and think critically.

Social Benefits

Studying persuasion has many social benefits. Consider the social benefits that effective persuaders gain with friends, family, colleagues, classmates, and acquaintances. Typically, these benefits rely on your ability to effectively articulate your perspective, influence and network with others, and reach mutually beneficial agreements. As you will learn in Chapter 3, developing your understanding of persuasion will also help you become a more effective and engaged participant in our democracy. For example, you can use your knowledge of persuasion to help identify problems in your community and propose solutions. In fact, it is hard to imagine that any positive social change would be possible without persuasion. Persuasion is essential to public campaigns, social movements, collective action, and the broader functioning of democracy. In short, persuasion is the vehicle for civic engagement. Now more than ever it is critical to study persuasion as we are exposed to a plethora of increasingly complex persuasive messages that reach us quickly and may mislead us through devious and subtle strategies.

Defining Persuasive Communication

Definitions ought to tell you what something is as well as what something is not. In other words, good definitions are clear about what is included and what is excluded; they set parameters around a term to demarcate the ground covered by the term. Parameters might permit more narrow or broad interpretations of the term. Either way, though, definitions provide reasonable limits that distinguish what something is from what something is not. Defining something is a speech act, with the goal of altering or fixing the meaning of a term for use in future discourse (Walton, 2005). Thus, definitions serve to spur constructive communication and are subject to further revision (Walton, 2005).

For purposes of this textbook, we will define persuasion in brief terms, unpack the concepts included in that definition, and explain the various levels of persuasion. **Persuasive communication** is the process of employing symbolic communication to create, alter, reinforce, or extinguish an audience's attitudes, values, beliefs, or behaviors in a given situation. While this definition may seem fairly straightforward and concise, it is necessary to unpack the assumptions and limiting criteria inherent in our definition.

First, a process involves a series of steps. Thus, for instance, process means that persuasion does not stop when a persuader sends a message; we must account for the message reception and effects. Second, symbolic communication refers to the verbal and/or nonverbal cues used by the persuader. Like communication more broadly, persuasion involves the use of symbols.

Third, the persuasive process can occur at all the various levels of communication. More specifically, persuasion involves one or more communicators. It is possible for one to persuade oneself, such as in the case of intrapersonal communication. While the boundary between self-persuasion and persuasion involving others might appear fuzzy given that we could ask an existential question about whether anything is truly *self*-persuasion and devoid of outside influences, we do recognize that individuals might persuade themselves without the intentional and conscious involvement of other communicators (e.g., talking yourself into one more slice of cake). Of course, persuasion also occurs in interpersonal, small group, public speaking, and mass communication contexts.

Relatedly, we ought to mention the role of discourse and dialogue that occurs at some of these levels of communication. Discourse is inherently persuasive (Condit, 1997), as is dialogue (Walton, 2005). Does this mean, however, that when we engage in any discourse or dialogue that we are acting as persuaders? To the extent that discourse and dialogue can influence others, or even ourselves, we are potential persuasive agents when we converse with others. So where does the term "rhetoric" come in? Walton (2005) notes that "any kind of persuasion tends to be seen as rhetorical, or even as subjective" (p. 177).

Fourth, our definition recognizes the agency of the communicators involved in a persuasive situation. Our definition takes a receiver-oriented approach since persuasion is perceived, either consciously or subconsciously, by an audience. Not all audiences will perceive a persuasive communication attempt or message in the same way. Another way to think about the role of agency in persuasion is to consider that the communicators at least perceive intention to be a part of the process. Thus, we would say that persuasion is an intentional act.

Fifth, although one might argue that fate guides human decisions and behaviors more than freewill, we contend that persuasion necessarily involves at least the perception of freewill during communicative interactions. In persuasion, the receiver has freewill and "the receiver's participation is fundamental to achieving the persuader's expected result" (Nettel & Roque, 2012, p. 60). Our contention that persuasion involves freewill means that there is conscious awareness on the part of the receiver that persuasion, or at least an attempt to persuade, is happening.

Sixth, persuasive acts are influence attempts. Attitudes, values, beliefs, and/or behaviors can be created, altered, shifted, or changed in a different direction or further reinforced, entrenched, or bolstered. Thus, persuasion can be thought of as either an agent of change or an agent of the status quo (e.g., the present system or state of being). For instance, if your friend tells you she is considering quitting her job and you convince her this is a good idea because you think she is miserable at work and has plenty of other employment prospects, you are persuading her to make a change. On the other hand, if you convince her to stay with her present employer because you suggest things will get better and the income is good, you are persuading her to maintain her status quo.

Relatedly, we ought to consider where meaning resides when defining persuasion. Like communication generally, persuasion typically involves reaching

FIGURE 1.2 Civic engagement is persuasion for the common good.

FIGURE 1.3 Peaceful protests are an example of persuasion for the common good.

a shared meaning among the interactants involved in persuasive communication. To say that meaning is shared is to say that meaning is co-constructed among the participants involved.

Next, it is imperative for us to distinguish and define several terms we will continue to use throughout this textbook to explain the boundaries of persuasion: engaged persuasion, ethical persuasion, and fringe persuasion (e.g., subliminal, manipulation, propaganda, coercion, intimidation, torture, and indoctrination). When we say **engaged persuasion**, we are referring to the definition of persuasion we outlined above. In our view, the core of persuasion can be characterized as engaged persuasion. Engaged persuasion is aimed at advancing the common good. However, engaged persuasion must also be ethical. Thus, **ethical persuasion** also refers to the definition of persuasion we outlined above. On the other hand, **fringe persuasion** is quite distinct. Persuasion should be distinguished from manipulation (Nettel & Roque, 2012) and other fringe elements of the persuasive landscape (e.g., subliminal, propaganda, coercion, intimidation,

Engaged Persuasion Research: Peaceful Persuasive Protests

Burnell and Reeve (1984) explicate the positive justification for persuasion as a peaceful political process. For instance, they point to picketing as an unobjectionable and nonthreatening behavior that does not intimidate. In this respect, they distinguish persuasion from power or authority, indoctrination, manipulation, torture, and coercion, based on the good faith of the persuader. While they acknowledge that good faith is difficult to identify, it contributes a moral dimension to persuasion. Interestingly, they note that persuasion does not need to be successful. "The process of persuasion entails 'coming to have reasons'" (Burnell & Reeve, 1984, p. 400). They also explain that while persuasion might exist within bargaining, it should definitionally exclude bargaining. For Burnell and Reeve, persuasion is the process of getting another to believe, accept, or reject something through the presentation of reasons and consequences of various alternatives one would not otherwise believe, accept, or reject.

Engaged Persuasion Research: Misinformation in Breaking News Stories

Rich and Zaragoza (2016) investigated how news reports of unfolding events that include misinformation continue to influence audience perceptions. They tested how corrections to misinformation might reverse the effects of the initial reports including misinformation in the minds of audiences. The results indicate that, despite corrections, audiences "continue to rely on the discredited information" (Rich & Zaragoza, 2016, p. 62). Corrections were not as effective in countering misinformation that was implied as they were in countering explicit misinformation. The researchers reasoned that implied information was more resilient to correction because it tends to be integrated and connected to the news story to a greater extent than explicit misinformation.

torture, and indoctrination). Some claim that persuasion lies between convincing and manipulation (Spahn, 2012). Future chapters will tease out the elements and implications of fringe persuasion; but, for now, we want to make it clear that fringe persuasion is not the same as the engaged and ethical persuasion we will refer to as the central focus of our exploration in this textbook.

In sum, then, our definition of persuasion includes engaged and ethical persuasion while excluding fringe persuasion. Our very choice of using the term "fringe persuasion" represents an acknowledgment that there are communicative acts that would otherwise seem to be persuasion attempts but must be separated due to the negative implications of these acts. For instance, we regard misinformation, deception, subliminal messages, propaganda, coercion, intimidation, torture, and indoctrination as falling into this category of fringe persuasion. Certainly, these elements of fringe persuasion share some characteristics in common with what we label persuasion. However, fringe persuasion does not

FIGURE 1.4 Example of a protest speaker using persuasion to advocate for the common good.

share all the characteristics of persuasion that we detailed above. Furthermore, our use of the terms "engaged" and "ethical" to describe persuasion helps to distinguish how persuasion is a positively balanced and socially responsible communicative act, whereas fringe persuasion is negatively balanced and typically at odds with individual rights and choices or the common good.

Aims of Persuasion

As simplistic as it might sound, persuasion is considered to be a measure of one's ability to influence others. When we influence others, we are persuading them by creating, reinforcing, altering, or changing their attitudes, values, beliefs, and/or behaviors. Consequently, it is necessary to unpack what each of these concepts mean in practical terms and examine how scholars have conceptualized these terms.

Attitudes

In many ways, the study of attitudes has dominated contemporary scholarship on persuasive communication (Ajzen, 2001). An **attitude** consists of positive or negative evaluations of some object (e.g., person, issue, or oneself; Petty et al., 1994). In other words, attitudes represent global evaluations of objects along dimensions like good–bad, harmful–beneficial, and pleasant–unpleasant. "I like Jeep Wranglers," "I hate work," and "Gun control is terrible!" are all examples of attitudes since these statements express an evaluation of some object.

Model of Dual Attitudes

This definition may lead you to conclude that individuals develop one, and only one, attitude toward any given object. However, attitudes are more complex than that. According to Wilson et al. (2000), when attitudes change, the new attitude overrides but may not entirely replace the old one. The model of dual attitudes posits that people often hold dual attitudes, "which are different evaluations of the same attitude object, one of which is an automatic, implicit attitude and the other of which is an explicit attitude" (Wilson et al., 2000, p. 102). As an example, consider a scenario in which a European American is raised in a racist family and therefore adopts a prejudiced attitude toward African Americans. Later in life this person may come to adopt a more egalitarian attitude that rejects prejudice. Instead of replacing the initial racist attitude, Wilson et al. suggest that the individual now has two attitudes toward African Americans—a habitual negative evaluation and a more recent positive attitude. The implications of this model for predicting behavior change are discussed in more detail in Chapter 5.

This discussion might also lead you to consider how engaged persuasion could be used to counter racist attitudes. Ibram X. Kendi is a professor of history and the founding director of the Antiracist Research and Policy Center at American University. Kendi (2019) defines an antiracist individual as one who supports "antiracist policy through their actions or expressing an antiracist idea" (p. 13). Kendi (2019) notes that addressing systemic racism requires all of us to acknowledge and understand how widespread and problematic racism is in the status quo:

> Our world is suffering from metastatic cancer. Stage 4. Racism has spread to nearly every part of the body politic, intersecting with bigotry of all kinds, justifying all kinds of inequities by victim blaming; heightening exploitation and misplaced hate; spurring mass shootings, arms races, and demagogues who polarize nations; shutting down essential organs of democracy; and threatening the life of human society with nuclear war and climate change. (p. 234)

Kendi (2019) argues further that to eliminate racial inequality, individuals must identify systematic racism and use their advocacy skills to eliminate racist policies and ensure that new racist policies are not instituted. Kendi also argues that all citizens need to be equipped with the knowledge, critical thinking, and information literacy skills necessary to sustain a healthy antiracist body politic. Indeed, throughout this text we will highlight examples of how engaged persuasion can be employed to foster meaningful participation in our democracy in order to address some of the most vexing issues of our time. Similarly, the images we incorporate in this text, like the opening photograph and many of the figures in this chapter, bring engaged persuasion to life, demonstrating how it can be used to address issues like racism and advance the common good.

Functions of Attitudes

What specific functions do attitudes serve? The Functional Theory of Attitudes developed by Katz (1960) outlines four functions of attitudes and stipulates that messages that target the reason why an individual possesses an attitude on the subject (i.e., the function of the attitude) will be more effective than if the persuader targets a different function. Initially, attitudes may serve an ego-defensive function. Katz noted that attitudes are held because they help people protect themselves, and they can serve as means of rationalizing undesirable beliefs or behaviors. For example, Katz (1960) argued that having deep feelings of inferiority may lead some to "project those feelings onto some convenient minority group and bolster our egos by attitudes of superiority toward this underprivileged group" (p. 172).

FIGURE 1.5 Persuasion aims to change, alter, or reinforce attitudes. Attitudes are sometimes displayed through facial expressions, as the woman in this photo does, but can also be concealed.

Attitudes may also serve a value-expressive function. This function allows individuals to express their unique values. For example, an individual who has a passion for electric vehicles because their use represents a commitment to environmental sustainability has an attitude that serves the value-expressive function. If you were attempting to persuade an individual based on this function, you would obviously need to know which specific value the attitude serves to develop a compelling message.

Attitudes can also fulfill a knowledge function. According to Katz (1960), people seek knowledge to make sense out of a chaotic and ever-changing world. Attitudes can provide the frames of reference we need to operate in the world. Katz also argued that efforts to change attitudes that serve a knowledge function will be most successful if they demonstrate that the target's current attitudes are inadequate to account for new and changing situations.

Finally, Katz (1960) noted that attitudes can serve a utilitarian function. These attitudes help us remember which objects in our environment bring rewards and which bring pain. For example, you may develop favorable attitudes toward a particular political party because you believe that the party will best advance your financial situation. When targeting individuals whose attitude serves a utilitarian function, Katz would suggest a message strategy that communicates how the change will help the target satisfy their desires and goals.

Extant research strongly supports the position that persuaders should seek to match their appeals to the functions of the attitudes that receivers hold. In fact, Carpenter's (2012) meta-analysis of functional theory research demonstrates that "attitude matching may often produce stronger effects than employing inoculation theory, cognitive dissonance, and the elaboration likelihood model" (p. 447).

Are there times when it might be more persuasive to mismatch persuasive arguments with recipients' attitude functions? Research by Petty and Wegener (1998) suggests that mismatching persuasive arguments with attitudinal functions may be most persuasive if the only available arguments are weak and easy to counterargue. They conclude that message recipients might "engage in greater scrutiny of content that matches the functional basis of their attitudes than content that does not match" (Petty & Wegener, 1998, p. 237). As a result, persuaders should evaluate both the attitudinal functions of target audiences and the strength of their persuasive arguments and seek to match when possible.

Values

Values are defined as abstract goals that individuals use as guiding principles in their lives (Maio & Olson, 1998; Rokeach, 1973). Fairness, liberty, justice, and equality are examples of values. Because we attach significant importance to values, we will vigorously defend them. Rokeach (1968) argued that values occupy central positions in our networks of attitudes and beliefs. Indeed, the work of several scholars reveals that studying the rankings and ratings of the importance of values can predict a broad range of attitudes and behaviors (Maio et al., 1996; Rokeach, 1968, 1973). For example, scholars have demonstrated that emancipative and secular values predict prosocial behaviors, like donations to charities (Kistler et al., 2017); existence values (i.e., valuing personal stability, health, and survival) predict mate retention behaviors (Lopes et al., 2017); and adolescent future values (i.e., family responsibility, personal responsibility, autonomy, civic responsibility, and hedonistic privilege) predict adult social roles, civic behaviors, and alcohol use (Finlay et al., 2015).

How do values derive their strength? According to research by Maio and Olson (1998), most values do not derive their strength from cognitive support. In other words, people rarely reflect on the reasons supporting their values. Instead, values operate like cultural truisms in that they are widely shared and very rarely questioned by most people. Think about debates that you consume in the media regarding issues like affirmative action. It is common for coverage of those issues to feature hotly contested debates over which specific policies should be implemented. However, there is very little debate in our society about the desirability of equal opportunity as a value. Values are resilient because people attach strong feelings to them, and they are often "taught as moral absolutes during socialization" (Maio & Olson, 1998, p. 308).

What are the implications of values for persuasion? Maio and Olson (1998) argue that the provision of cognitive support can help to strengthen values and ultimately affect related attitudes and behaviors. In other words, by "strengthening values, large networks of value-relevant attitudes might be affected" such that they influence attitudes and behaviors (Maio & Olson, 1998, p. 309). For example, when considering whether to volunteer for a nonprofit organization, people might be more willing to do so if they are given strong, compelling reasons to support the value of community responsibility. Providing cognitive support for values might also make individuals more resistant to attempts to change their values. This could also make individuals less vulnerable to the influence techniques of groups like cults that aim to change values.

FIGURE 1.6 The Black Lives Matter sign placed on this statue of President Abraham Lincoln is an example of engaged persuasion which is peaceful and does not damage property.

Beliefs

As Petty and Cacioppo (2018) note, **beliefs** include information that an individual has about other people, objects, and issues. Beliefs are more cognitive in nature than attitudes and reflect our subjective probabilities about the world (Fishbein & Ajzen, 2010). In other words, beliefs reflect an individual's acceptance that a particular statement is true.

Belief Formation

Individuals form beliefs about the world through observation, consumption of information, and inference. Observational beliefs are based on direct observations that we make. For example, an individual may develop the belief that working out regularly has positive health effects by observing another person's workout routine. Observational beliefs can be especially resilient, as we rarely question the validity of our senses (Fishbein & Ajzen, 2010). However, such beliefs may weaken over time as we forget our initial information or encounter contradictory information.

Informational beliefs are formed on the basis of information we consume and accept from outside sources. Such sources are virtually limitless and include television and radio, social media, print publications, friends, and coworkers (Fishbein & Ajzen, 2010). For example, you may encounter an advertisement on Facebook for a new fishing lure that promises to catch enormous bass and form the belief that using that lure will empower you to do the same.

Finally, individuals form inferential beliefs through a process of inference, relying on other relevant beliefs (Fishbein & Ajzen, 2010). For example, you might discover that studying very hard for a midterm exam in a particular class improved your grade and infer that studying diligently in other classes will significantly boost your overall grade point average.

Relationship Between Beliefs and Behaviors

Beliefs are related to behaviors in several important ways. According to Fishbein and Ajzen (2010), the following types of beliefs play a particularly important role in our behaviors: behavior, injunctive normative, descriptive normative, and control. Behavioral beliefs involve an assessment that performing a behavior will lead to some outcome (e.g., belief that working out more will improve my health). Injunctive normative beliefs are "subjective probabilities that particular referents prescribe or proscribe performance of a behavior" (Fishbein & Ajzen, 2010, p. 221). Descriptive normative beliefs involve an assessment of the likelihood that referents are or are not performing a behavior. Finally, control beliefs reflect an individual's assessment that specific factors can enhance or impede performance of a behavior. Beliefs are likely to influence our behaviors to the extent that we believe the behavior will have a positive outcome (behavioral beliefs), that relevant others in our social network believe that we should engage in the behavior (injunctive normative beliefs) and engage in the behavior themselves (descriptive normative beliefs), and our positive assessment that we can perform the behavior (control beliefs). All of these components of beliefs will be discussed in great detail in Chapter 5.

Belief Perseverance Dynamics

It is important to note that beliefs are not facts and are often not true. Flynn et al. (2017) define **misperceptions** as "factual beliefs that are false or contradict the best available evidence in the public domain" (p. 128). Individuals can hold many misperceptions about a wide range of topics. For example, Flynn (2016) found that over 1 in 5 Americans hold misperceptions about topics like universal background checks, changes in debt and deficit, the federal tax burden, and time limits on welfare benefits. In addition, a significant number of Americans reject widespread scientific evidence that the earth's climate is warming (McCright & Dunlap, 2011). Pockets of Americans also erroneously believe that childhood vaccines are linked to autism (Funk et al., 2017).

Logically, then, we might suspect there is a relationship between beliefs and the spread of persuasive misinformation as well as one's susceptibility to fake news. If people hold misperceptions, as Flynn et al. (2017) described, then we would reasonably suspect that those people are more likely to spread misinformation to others. To the extent that individuals truly believe the misinformation they spread to others, that misinformation may come across as quite persuasive. Likewise, if people hold misperceptions, we might reasonably expect they will be more susceptible to fake news since the fake news appears to confirm or reconcile with their belief misperceptions.

How do we correct false beliefs? Many might assume that simply presenting individuals with the facts (e.g., data demonstrating the planet is warming) would cause targets of this persuasive information to alter their beliefs. However, the **information deficit fallacy** stipulates that the assumption that more information will correct misperceptions is false and cautions that providing corrective information may even backfire (Nyhan & Reifler, 2012). Why is this the case? One explanation can be found in literature exploring the perseverance of beliefs. Belief perseverance research indicates that when information is "encoded in memory, it can be very difficult to eliminate its effects on subsequent attitudes and beliefs" (Nyhan & Reifler, 2012, p. 3). Research also suggests that individuals who perceive themselves to be highly experienced are especially prone to **belief perseverance dynamics.** Staats et al.'s (2018) study demonstrates that "feelings of expertise can lead to escalation of commitment after receiving negative news" (p. 821). The implications of belief perseverance dynamics for persuasion will be discussed throughout this textbook.

Engaged Persuasion Research: Political Affiliation and the Effectiveness of Fact-Checking

How rational are we when we consume persuasive information about political candidates? According to Jarman (2016), the answer depends on our political affiliation and the political party of the candidate. Specifically, Jarman examined the role of political affiliation and the type of fact-check criticism (e.g., whether or not the candidate's statement was shown to be true after fact-checking) on evaluation of President Obama's statement that immigration reform would not provide amnesty to undocumented persons living in the United States. Jarman found that partisanship significantly undermines the effectiveness of fact-checking. In other words, Democrats and Republicans did not change their partisan evaluations of President Obama's statement when presented with corrective information. As Jarman (2016) notes, "Merely exposing the public to 'facts' is not enough to significantly change their opinion" (p. 14).

Behaviors

Thus far, we have discussed concepts that may be difficult to observe: attitudes, values, and beliefs. After all, people are not always open about disclosing their attitudes, values, and beliefs. Behaviors, on the other hand, are far more observable or known in most circumstances. It is also easier for someone to tell us what they think we want to hear with regard to their attitudes, values, and beliefs, whereas we might observe them behaving in ways that run contrary to those reports. Behaviors, therefore, offer persuasion scholars an arguably more concrete and objective understanding of human interaction and communication. Ultimately, though, we may need to persuade others to change their attitudes, values, and beliefs before we can change their behaviors.

Ajzen and Fishbein (1977) propose that **behaviors** consist of four elements. The first element reflects the action performed (e.g., smoking or skateboarding). The second element refers to the target toward which the action is directed (e.g., cigarette or skateboard). The third element is the context in which the action is performed. Is the action performed on campus or at a public park? The final element, according to Ajzen and Fishbein, is time. Did this action occur at noon or midnight? By considering all of these elements together, we have a complete picture of the specific behavior in question. Based on the examples in this section, the person could be smoking a cigarette on campus at noon. Alternatively, the person could be riding a skateboard in a public park at midnight. As you will see in Chapter 5, effectively predicting the relationship between attitudes and behaviors depends on the extent to which the attitude measure corresponds to the action, target, context, and time elements of the behavior.

One logical question in your mind, at this point, might be "How can we persuade people to change their behavior?" The answer to this question initially lies in a matter of isolating exactly what you wish to change. For instance, you can target persuasive messages at a single behavior or at a range of (or category of) behaviors. Do you wish to convince someone to stop smoking? Or do you wish to convince someone to adopt a range of heathier behavioral practices? A second consideration would be how you wish to measure behavioral change. For example, would you consider your persuasion successful if someone promises to quit smoking? Their declaration that they intend to cease smoking is what we would call behavioral intention. One's **behavioral intention** is an indication of what they are projecting their future behavior will be. Since future behavior cannot be observed or measured, behavioral intentions may be the best available predictor of future behavior. Or would consider your persuasion to be successful only if you are able to observe such a behavioral change? We could observe a known smoker not smoking, perhaps over several observational periods, and conclude that they have indeed followed through with their pledge to stop smoking. However, it is unlikely that we would be able to collect enough observational data to conclude that we are certain they have stopped smoking. Thus, observations of behavior are rather limited in terms of the scope of conclusions we can make based on those observations.

Future chapters in this textbook will delve deeper into behaviors, behavioral intentions, and the relationship between attitudes, values, and beliefs to those behaviors. In upcoming chapters, the theories and research studies we will explore will further explain these connections.

Dual Process Models of Persuasion

So how do we process the persuasive messages we encounter? There are two dual process models that explain how individuals process persuasive messages. The **Elaboration Likelihood Model** (ELM), developed by Richard E. Petty, a social psychologist at the Ohio State University, and John Cacioppo, a social neuroscientist at the University of Chicago, and the **Heuristic Systematic Model** (HSM), developed by Shelly Chaiken, a social psychologist at New York University, share some similarities, in that each is a dual process model and propose similar routes for two types of cognitive processors: central route or systematic processing and peripheral route or heuristic processing (Chaiken & Maheswaran, 1994). However, ELM and HSM differ in their terminology and theoretical constructs. Glockner and Witteman (2010) contend that **dual process models** make clear delineations between deliberative and intuitive information processing, judgment, and decision making but fail to further differentiate within those categories.

Elaboration Likelihood Model

According to the ELM, changing an individual's attitude and understanding requires the receiver to be motivated to exert cognitive effort to think about and process the message (Robert & Dennis, 2005). ELM holds that there are two routes to changing attitudes, the central and the peripheral routes. Petty et al. (1983) explain that the **central route** to attitude change stems from careful scrutiny of information and weighing of the pros and cons related to message itself, whereas the **peripheral route** holds that attitude change results from simple inferences made about positive and negative cues attendant to the message. In other words, "The basic tenet of ELM is that different methods of inducing persuasion may work best depending on whether the elaboration likelihood of the communication situation (i.e., the probability of message- or issue-relevant thought occurring) is high or low" (Petty et al., 1983, p. 137). High elaboration likelihood leads to the central route, while low elaboration likelihood leads to the peripheral route. Individuals using central processing exert a great deal of cognitive effort evaluating information. Indeed, attitude change driven by thoughtful consideration and processing tends to be more enduring over time and predictive of future behavior (Petty et al., 1993). Peripheral processers adhere to simple acceptance or rejection cues, so they are not affected by argument quality. "Arguments that pass through the central route will result in enduring, resistant, and predictable behavior changes, while arguments that pass

Engaged Persuasion Activity: Message Processing

Imagine that you are in charge of convincing two different audiences to purchase and implement a new software program that will run all the human resource (HR) processes for your company. The new software package can handle employee applications, hiring paperwork, tax forms, employee timesheet recording, and benefits packages. You happen to know your audience consists of two different groups of cognitive processers. In a meeting next week, you will be making your pitch to the HR workers in your company. The HR workers will have to use the software daily, so you reason that they will pay careful attention to the details and functions of the software. In other words, you suspect the HR workers will be central processers. The following week, you will present your pitch to the company executives, who you know care less about the software package details and functions than they do employee satisfaction and expenses. Thus, you reason that the executives will be peripheral processers. Assuming you have only 15 minutes to make your pitch and that your suspicions about the two groups' cognitive processing of your message is on target, how will you craft two different messages to pitch the new software program to each group?

through the peripheral route will only result in temporary, susceptible, and unpredictable behavior changes" (Robert & Dennis, 2005, p. 12). Social projection explains how individuals who elaborate deeply assess the task difficulty facing others, because individuals who deeply elaborate are more prone to apply their own ratings of task difficulty to the tasks facing others (Krispenz et al., 2016).

Repetition-Frequency Model

Building on the principles of the ELM, the Repetition-Frequency Model of persuasive communication, depicted in Figure 1.7, shows that repeated exposure

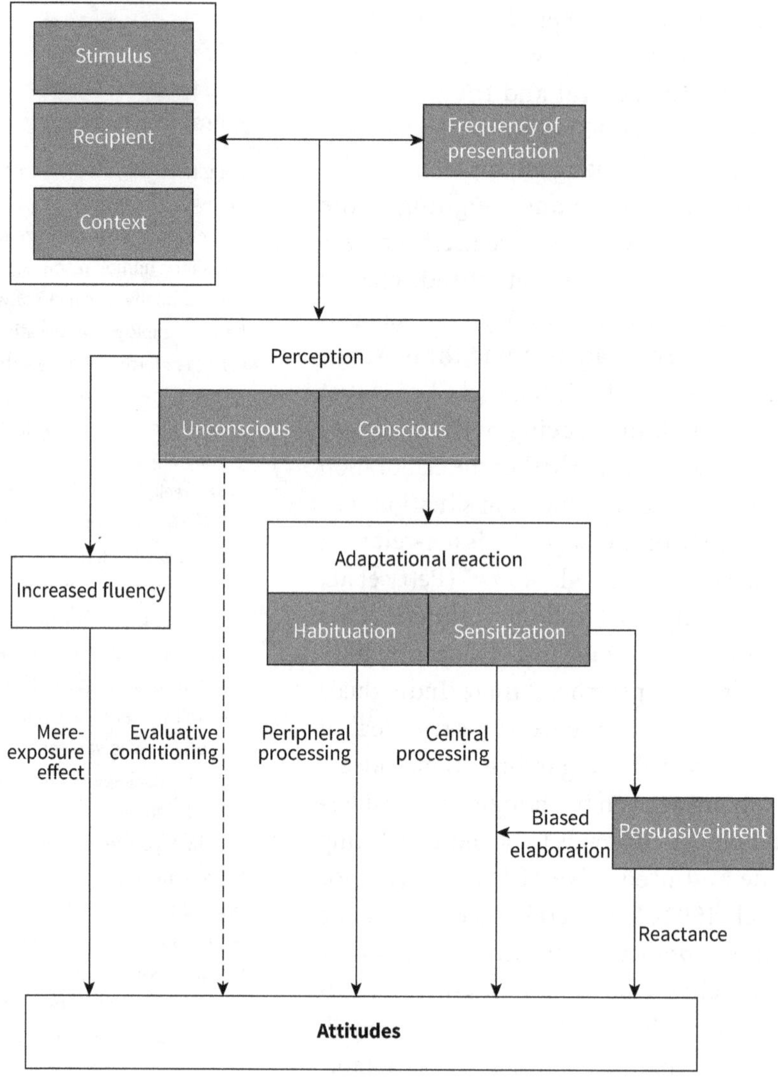

FIGURE 1.7 Repetition-Frequency Model of persuasive communication (Koch, 2017).

leads to positive attitudes toward a persuasive stimulus; but the model outlines several possible paths based on the degree of repetition (Koch, 2017). Notice that the solid lines in Figure 1.7 suggest direct paths, whereas the dashed lines indicate indirect paths. For instance, when frequency is consciously perceived, the resulting paths are direct, whereas unconscious perception of repetitive exposure to the persuasion stimuli leads indirectly to attitudes. Also notice that central and peripheral processing, which we learned about in the ELM, are included in this model. According to Koch, repeated exposure to a message can result in persuasion, and the frequency of repetition determines if the message is perceived consciously or unconsciously. If the repeated exposure is consciously perceived, it may lead to peripheral processing via habituation, or it may lead to central processing via sensitization (Koch, 2017). He elaborates by explaining:

> If the recipient perceives the stimulus consciously, this can lead to habituation to the stimulus and to peripheral processing; alternatively, the recipient can become sensitized to the stimulus, which can result in central processing and perceiving the stimulus as a persuasive attempt. Moreover, mere-exposure effects can also have an influence on the perception of the stimulus, independent of the other paths described. (Koch, 2017, p. 220)

Mere-exposure effects are not necessarily weaker (Koch, 2017). "High presentation frequency tends to foster the conscious perception of the stimulus" (Koch, 2017, p. 233), which triggers either the habituation or sensitization path.

Heuristic Systematic Model

Similar to the ELM, the HSM theorizes that receivers of persuasive messages process messages differently. Specifically, HSM posits that two message processing modalities exist: heuristic and systematic. Individuals can even use both modalities to make attitude judgments (Trumbo, 2002). HSM explains that a person's need for information (Kahlor et al., 2003) or "desire for accurate and sufficient information is a strong motivation for processing" (Griffin et al., 2002, p. 706). The **sufficiency principle** in HSM reasons that individuals require sufficient information to change attitudes or behaviors, but heuristic processors do not require as much information as systematic processors do to reach sufficiency. Overall, the sufficiency principle stipulates that receivers strive to acquire just enough information to make a decision, but no more or less. Motivation (Trumbo, 1999) and interest (Kahlor et al., 2003) predict systematic processing. "Deeper, more systematic processing of risk information is positively related to evaluation strength, attitude strength, and the number of strongly held behavioral beliefs" (Griffin et al., 2002, p. 705). Generally speaking, individuals who use heuristic processing employ fewer cognitive resources and exert less cognitive effort when evaluating messages than do individuals who use systematic processing (Griffin et al., 2002). Naturally, people follow a principle of least effort, wherein they default to heuristic processing for most messages. In these instances, heuristic processing may rely on trusted spokespeople, statistics, or message length (Griffin et al., 2002). When available evidence is ambiguous, heuristic processing can bias systematic processing (Chaiken & Maheswaran, 1994). Some findings suggest that persuasive health campaigns utilizing narratives as evidence lead to heuristic processing of messages (Winterbottom et al., 2008). HSM can be applied to persuasive messages concerning health communication, environmental issues, and risk perception (Trumbo, 2002) as well as political campaigns, media framing, agenda setting, and the spiral of silence (Neuwirth et al., 2002).

Cialdini's Model of Persuasion

Robert Cialdini is regent's professor emeritus of psychology and marketing at Arizona State University and is among the most cited scholars of research on persuasion and influence. Cialdini's (2009) model of persuasion rests on the assumption that humans engage in several fixed-action patterns of behavior that can be triggered through relatively simple influence techniques. According to this approach, we live in a fast-paced and complicated world and often default to **judgmental heuristics** (i.e., mental shortcuts) when making decisions. Cialdini's model outlines the following principles of influence: reciprocation, consistency and commitment, social proof, liking, authority, and scarcity. An overview of this model and defense strategies can be found in Table 1.1.

Reciprocation

Cialdini (2009) notes that the **principle of reciprocation** holds that "we should try to repay, in kind, what another person has provided us" (p. 19). For example, if someone does a favor for you, this norm indicates that you are obligated to the future repayment of that favor (Goei et al., 2007). The norm of reciprocity is powerful and deeply embedded in cultures around the world. Research has shown the principle of reciprocation to be persuasive across many contexts and settings, including as a means to boost tipping behavior in hospitality contexts (Seiter & Weger, 2014), facilitating negotiations involving financial implications (Blanchard et al., 2016), boosting purchase intentions (Dahl et al., 2005), increasing intentions to become an organ donor (Guttman et al., 2016), and increasing the willingness of consumers to communicate personal data (Happ et al., 2016). This principle also explains the effectiveness of the **free sample technique** where consumers feel compelled to purchase goods and services in response

TABLE 1.1 Cialdini's Model of Persuasion and Defense Strategies

Principle	Definition	Defense Strategies
Reciprocation	We are obligated to repay the things that others provide us.	Accept initial favors, concessions, or gifts of others, but be prepared to redefine them as unethical compliance attempts if the evidence later supports such a conclusion.
Consistency and Commitment	We strive to be consistent with what we have done in the past.	Identify situations where consistency and commitment are being used to influence you to act in a way you do not want to act. If you do commit to something, question whether you would make the same decision again if you could go back in time given what you know now.
Social Proof	We determine what is correct by modeling the behavior of others.	Be mindful of instances when social evidence has been purposefully falsified (e.g., in the marketing of products). Be cognizant of the impact of chaos in our hectic lives. Learn to be skeptical of the social response instinct. Recognize that the actions of similar others should not form the sole basis for our decisions.
Liking	We prefer to say yes to people we know and like.	You should be vigilant about circumstances in which undue liking is produced. This requires that you question why you feel yourself liking a persuader more than you should under the circumstances.
Authority	People generally obey authorities and defer to experts.	Carefully evaluate the persuasive attempts of experts, and ask yourself the following questions: Is the authority knowledgeable on the topic? Is the authority trustworthy? Does the authority have your best interests in mind?
Scarcity	Opportunities seem more valuable when they are less available.	Be cognizant of the arousal stimulated by scarcity appeals. Slow down, and carefully consider the merits of scarcity appeals in the decision-making process.

to a perceived need to reciprocate for receiving a free sample (Kolyesnikoa & Dodd, 2009). Finally, the principle of reciprocity explains the effectiveness of the **door-in-the-face** (DITF) compliance-gaining strategy. The DITF technique involves making an extreme request, that likely will be rejected, followed by a legitimate concession that results in a subsequent request for that which is truly desired (Cialdini & Goldsmith, 2004; Schindler & Reinhard, 2015). The goal of this sequential request strategy is that the request recipient will reciprocate the concession by complying with the second request. We will discuss sequential request strategies in much greater detail in Chapter 8.

Consistency and Commitment

Cialdini (2009) defines the **principle of consistency** as the desire to be consistent with what we have said and done in the past. He notes further that the influence of consistency can be enhanced through commitment. For example, if you can get a target of persuasion to make a commitment, especially one that is public, you will have set the stage for future compliance. Once an individual takes a stand, there is a natural tendency to behave in ways that are consistent with that stand.

A great deal of research supports the effectiveness of consistency and commitment. For example, Demarque et al. (2013) found that participants who received a proenvironmental persuasive message followed by a request to help create a new slogan for an environmental group were substantially more likely to agree to a larger request to spend hours staffing a booth for the organization at an upcoming event compared to the group of participants who were not asked to make an initial, small commitment. Importantly, consistency and commitment explain the effectiveness of the **foot-in-the-door** (FITD) technique where an initial small request is followed by a larger, related request. As with the DITF technique, we will discuss the FITD strategy in greater detail in Chapter 8.

In a meta-analysis of 19 studies of commitment in environmental research, Lokhorst et al. (2013) identified several factors that heighten the effectiveness of commitment. First, the commitment strategy is effective when used in combination with other interventions like hypocrisy, high cost, and feedback. This finding is consistent with research by Wichmann et al. (2016) who found that simply consulting the target by asking for advice or help on how to improve the plan can yield more commitment. Second, Lokhorst et al. note the importance of keeping the commitment salient. In other words, persuasive targets should receive feedback on the behaviors they are performing and be reminded of their commitment.

Third, practitioners may produce longer lasting commitments if they activate personal norms (Lockhorst et al., 2013). Consider, for example, a campaign designed to persuade targets to use alternative forms of transportation. It is likely that a percentage of the target audience of this campaign will hold favorable attitudes toward decreased automobile use. Practitioners can activate these attitudes and norms through various media to make the targets more likely to commit to the desired behavior of using alternative forms of transportation.

Fourth, activating social norms can boost the effectiveness of commitment. In other words, getting a target to commit with a group of similar others may be more effective than an individual commitment. Fifth, labeling the targets as "the kind of people who would perform this behavior" instead of more general characteristics like "good people" can enhance commitment. Sixth, Lockhorst et al. (2013) argue that it is essential to clearly communicate the details of the commitment. Targets need to know how, when, and where the desired behavior will be performed. Finally, the results of this meta-analysis suggest that it is much easier for individuals to maintain adherence to a commitment if they enjoy the behavior.

Social Proof

The **principle of social proof** states that we determine what is correct behavior by modeling the behavior of others. In other words, we view a particular behavior as appropriate in a given situation to the extent that we see others performing it. The principle of social proof is widely used in society. For example, producers of situation comedies use canned laughter to increase the humorous responses of audiences. Bartenders place a few dollars in their tip jars at the beginning of their shift to give the impression that others view tipping as appropriate. Further, as Cialdini (2009) notes, the advertising we consume often features appeals about the "fastest growing" or "largest selling" products. According to Cialdini, uncertainty and similarity are two factors that can strengthen the persuasive effect of social proof.

Uncertainty

Initially, we are particularly vulnerable to social proof in conditions of high uncertainty. Cialdini (2009) uses the term pluralistic ignorance to refer to the tendency of individuals to rely on the behaviors of others to decide how to act in emergency situations. Unfortunately, this ignorance can manifest in bystander inaction, where groups of individuals mistakenly interpret an emergency (e.g., an individual experiencing a heart attack on the sidewalk) as a nonemergency. Further, we are most likely to encounter uncertainty in urban areas because (1) cities are clamorous and rapidly changing environments; (2) cities are more populous, and individuals are therefore more likely to be with others when encountering an emergency situation; and 3) people who live in cities typically know a small percentage of fellow residents compared to those who live in small towns. As a result, individuals who live in cities are more likely to be in a group of strangers when encountering an emergency situation. Of course, it is much easier to go along with the crowd when we lack access to trusted referents.

Similarity

Similarity also influences the effectiveness of social proof. In short, we are more prone to social proof when observing the behavior of others we perceive to be similar to us. As an example, research by Hilmert et al. (2006) demonstrates that we develop more positive opinions of the music recommendations of similar others and more negative opinions of the music recommendations of dissimilar others. These findings have been replicated in a wide range of contexts, including the persuasiveness of narratives (de Graaf, 2014), performance of virtual teams (van der Land et al., 2015), effectiveness of campaigns to boost environmental conservation (Goldstein et al., 2008), building rapport and boosting compliance in high-stakes police interviews (Goodman-Delahunty & Howes, 2016), and influencing scientists to communicate with the general public (Hu et al., 2018).

Liking

According to Cialdini (2009), the **principle of liking** stipulates that we are more prone to the persuasive attempts of people we like. Further, the following factors have been shown to cause liking: physical attractiveness, similarity, compliments, contact and cooperation, and conditioning and association.

Physical Attractiveness

The extant literature contains many studies suggesting a positive association between physical attractiveness and liking. For example, research has shown that we automatically assign favorable traits, like talent, kindness, and honesty, to those we perceive to be attractive (Langlois et al., 2000). The effects of attractiveness may be attributable to a **halo effect**, where one positive characteristic of a person dominates the way that person is viewed by others. Research by Palmer and Peterson (2016) suggests that physical attractiveness often functions as such a characteristic.

Similarity

Beyond physical attractiveness, research clearly demonstrates that we like people we perceive to be similar to us (Alves et al., 2016; Bruchmann et al., 2018; Burger et al., 2004; Collisson & Howell, 2014; Hampton et al., 2019; Wróbel et al., 2015). Further, Cialdini (2009) notes that the effect of similarity on liking holds true "whether the similarity is in the area of opinions, personality traits, background, or lifestyle" (p. 148). Of course, persuaders often attempt to manipulate perceptions of similarity through dress, experiences, backgrounds, interests, vocal style, mood, and other factors. As a consumer of persuasive communication, you should carefully evaluate the authenticity of attempts to influence you through perceived similarity.

Compliments

Several studies demonstrate that simple compliments facilitate liking and increase compliance. For example, compliments have been found to significantly increase tipping behavior in the contexts of hairstyling salons (Seiter & Dutson, 2007) and restaurants (Seiter & Weger, 2010). Further, Cavazza and Guidetti (2018) found that audiences evaluate political candidates who flatter them in speeches more positively than candidates who do not use flattery. Similar effects have been found for candidates who compliment their political opponents (Cavazza, 2016). Although Cialdini (2009) suggests that compliments boost compliance by facilitating liking, it is important to note that some research demonstrates a direct effect of compliments on compliance, independent of liking (Grant et al., 2010).

Contact and Cooperation

According to Cialdini (2009), we generally like things and individuals we perceive to be familiar. For example, extant research provides some support for the argument that contact with others increases familiarity that is positively associated with liking (Biernat, 1990; Monahan et al., 2000); however, contact may not always produce liking. Can you think of situations in which working with others caused you to like them less? According to Cialdini, contact and exposure to a person or object under unpleasant conditions can create frustration and conflict leading to less liking.

Cialdini (2009) asserts that the answer to the potential problems of contact is cooperation. He points to research in education suggesting that cooperative learning has been shown to be effective in reducing prejudice and increasing liking. Indeed, over 1,200 studies across several decades demonstrate that cooperative learning is effective (Johnson & Johnson, 2009). Further, cooperative learning has been shown to increase liking and acceptance of stigmatized social groups (Desforges et al., 1991). More specifically, research by André et al. (2011) shows that cooperative learning increases acceptance of disabled mainstreamed students by their peers. However, research also suggests that cooperative learning is most effective when the groups are truly cooperative rather than competitive (Montoya & Pittinsky, 2011) and when the tasks assigned are authentic (Buchs et al., 2011).

Conditioning and Association

The **principle of association** indicates that we like people and objects that are linked to positive things. Cialdini (2009) notes further that the principle is general, governing our reactions to both positive and negative connections. For example, research indicates that we dislike bearers of bad news even when they are not the cause of the bad news (Lott & Lott, 1965; Manis et al., 1974). Additional support for the power of association can be found in research on celebrity endorsements. Linking the positive characteristics of celebrities to the products they promote has been shown to be an effective strategy to increase sales (Spry et al., 2011; Tantiseneepong et al., 2012). Similarly, research demonstrates that the association of humor with products can increase persuasion (Strick et al., 2009). Cialdini also suggests that the principle of association explains the success of the luncheon technique where people like the things they experience while eating. Much like classical conditioning, the positive reaction to food is transferred to other things through association.

Authority

The **principle of authority** states that people generally obey authorities and defer to the recommendations of experts. Much of the research in obedience studies springs from the work of famed psychology professor Stanley Milgram. Milgram was particularly interested in the obedience demonstrated by Nazis during the Holocaust. In fact, he was appalled by the claim by many who faced trial for their crimes that they were merely following orders. Milgram begin this research assuming that Americans would not demonstrate the same the kind of obedience he observed in Nazi Germany.

In one study, Milgram (1963) instructed subjects that they were participating in a memory test designed to explore the extent to which pain, delivered in the form of electrical shocks for making mistakes, would improve learning. However, the true aim of the research was to assess how far participants were willing to go in delivering shocks to others. Participants were assigned to roles as "teachers," while research confederates severed as "learners." Importantly, no real shocks were delivered. When participants pulled the shock switches, the learners merely acted as if they were being shocked.

Milgram (1963) also had another research confederate serve as an "experimenter" who directed participants through the experiment. Participants were instructed to start by delivering a shock of 15 volts for mistakes. The shock increased by 15 volts for each of the following mistakes, up to a maximum shock of 450 volts. When the learners expressed unwillingness to continue, the experimenter responded with one of the following prods: (a) Please continue, (b) the experiment requires that you continue, (c) it is absolutely essential that you continue, and (d) you have no other choice, you must go on.

So how far were participants willing to go? Keep in mind that participants could hear the learner pounding on the wall in the next room once the shock level reached 300 volts. Also, Milgram (1963) described in detail that participants experienced intense emotional disturbance and profuse sweating and trembling. Further, when the shock exceeded 350 volts, the learner made no sound at all, implying that the learner was seriously hurt. Despite experiencing intense emotional distress, two thirds of the participants pulled every one of the 30 shock switches! Milgram offered an obedience to authority explanation for this behavior. In other words, participants were simply unable to defy the commands of perceived authorities.

Recent research provides a more nuanced view of the persuasiveness of authority. For example, Wall et al.'s (2019) research demonstrates that individuals who score high on measures of neuroticism, social inhibition, and negative affectivity are likely to obey authorities more than those who score high on measures of Machiavellianism and psychoticism. In addition, Bègue et al. (2015) found that disobedience is associated with political orientation such that those on the political left are less obedient than those on the political right. Further, Jung and Kellaris's (2006) research shows that perceived credibility moderates the influence of authority on attitude change. Their study also highlights important cultural differences in that participants in high power distance cultures where obedience is prized are more deferential to authority than members of low power distance cultures. Finally, to maximize the influence of authority, research by Gaube et al. (2020) suggests that the persuasive message of the authority must fit the context in which it is delivered. They found that a sign with a persuasive message from a doctor urging people to practice good hand hygiene was a good fit in the context of a hospital. The same sign may not be as persuasive in other contexts. We will return to the use of appeals to authority when we discuss source characteristics in Chapter 7.

Scarcity

According to Cialdini (2009), the **principle of scarcity** stipulates that "opportunities seem more valuable to us when they are less available" (p. 200). What makes appeals to scarcity so effective? Initially, we invoke a simple heuristic that things that are difficult to obtain are better than things that are easy to obtain (Lynn, 1991). Another explanation for the effectiveness of scarcity can be found in the literature on Psychological Reactance Theory presented in Chapter 11. Scarcity triggers reactance as it threatens and limits our freedoms. Further, the reactance we experience causes us to want the items or goods and services more.

It is important to recognize that not all scarcity appeals are equally persuasive. Aguirre-Rodriquez (2013) examined the persuasiveness of demand-related (e.g., limited availability due to high demand) versus supply-related (e.g., limited availability of supplies) scarcity appeal ad messages. In addition, this study explored the persuasive effects of message specificity for supply-related (SRS) and demand-related (DRS) scarcity appeals. Aguirre-Rodriguez (2013) employed the following specificity manipulations:

> Specific SRS appeal: "Only 500 households per zip code can claim a coupon. Due to restricted supply, this offer's availability is limited!"

> Nonspecific SRS appeal: "A maximum number of households per zip code can claim a coupon. Due to restricted supply, this offer's availability is limited!"
>
> Specific DRS appeal: "Over 500,000 have already responded to this offer. Due to popular demand, this offer's availability is limited!"
>
> Nonspecific DRS appeal: "Thousands have already responded to this offer. Due to popular demand, this offer's availability is limited!" (p. 376)

Overall, Aguirre-Rodriquez (2013) found that SRS messages are less likely to activate persuasion knowledge than DRS messages. In other words, consumers are less likely to carefully scrutinize SRS messages via central processing, as they recognize them as an attempt to inform rather than an attempt to persuade. Similarly, and consistent with the ELM, specific messages were less persuasive than nonspecific messages. According to Aquirre-Rodriguez, specific messages stimulated careful processing of the message content while nonspecific messages were processed as peripheral cues.

In a series of seven studies, Kristofferson et al. (2017) identified aggression as a possible dark side of scarcity appeals. In the first study, Kristofferson et al. found that consumers exposed to scarcity responded more aggressively than consumers exposed to a control advertisement. Interestingly, the authors operationalized aggression as firearm shooting behavior and found that exposure to scarcity led to participants firing significantly more bullets than those in the control condition. In a real consumption context, the second study demonstrated that participants exposed to scarcity appeals physically assaulted a vending machine significantly more than participants in the control condition. The third study in this series revealed that exposure to scarcity appeals led to increased levels of testosterone among participants. The fourth study demonstrated that exposure to scarcity led participants to perceive others as competitive threats to obtaining the desired product. The fifth and sixth studies provided further support for the argument that scarcity causes consumers to view others as a competitive threat. Finally, the last study demonstrated that the aggressive reaction to scarcity appeals occurs when the message limits product quantity but not time. We will discuss persuasive appeals based on scarcity of time in greater detail in Chapter 12.

Summary

In this chapter, we explained the benefits of studying persuasive communication and defined persuasion while articulating the connection to engaged and ethical persuasion. Importantly, we discussed how persuasion differs from fringe persuasion, such as manipulation, propaganda, subliminal, coercion, intimidation, torture, and indoctrination. In addition, we covered the four concepts that persuasion aims to affect: attitudes, values, beliefs, and behaviors. We also explored two dual process models for understanding how receivers process persuasive messages: ELM and HSM. We will return again to ELM and HSM in Chapter 9. Finally, we introduced you to the major components of Cialdini's model of persuasion.

The next chapter addresses the ethical ramifications of persuasion in the post-truth era while juxtaposing ethical persuasion with coercion, deception, and propaganda—or the dark side of persuasion.

Check Your Understanding Review Questions

1. What are the various benefits of studying persuasive communication?
2. What are attitudes, values, beliefs, and behaviors? And how do these constructs differ from one another?
3. How is persuasion defined? What do we mean by engaged persuasion? What characteristics constitute persuasive communication? How is persuasive communication different from coercion, propaganda, and deception?
4. What is a dual process model of persuasion?
5. How does the Elaboration Likelihood Model explain persuasion?
6. How does the Heuristic Systematic Model explain persuasion?
7. What similarities do ELM and HSM share?
8. Define the six principles (reciprocation, commitment and consistency, social proof, liking, authority, and scarcity) in Cialdini's model of persuasion.

Key Terms

attitudes (p. 9)
behavioral intention (p. 16)
behaviors (p. 15)
belief perseverance (p. 15)
beliefs (p. 13)
dual process models (p. 17)
Elaboration Likelihood Model (p. 16)
engaged persuasion (p. 7)
ethical persuasion (p. 7)
fringe persuasion (p. 7)
Heuristic Systematic Model (p. 16)
persuasive communication (p. 5)
sufficiency principle (p. 19)
values (p. 12)

Credits

Fig. 1.0: Copyright © 2020 by PDBVerlag. Reprinted with permission.

Fig. 1.1: Copyright © 2016 by Alexis Brown. Reprinted with permission.

Fig. 1.2: Copyright © 2020 by H. F. E. & CO. Reprinted with permission.

Fig. 1.3: Copyright © 2020 by Lemon Ruan. Reprinted with permission.

Fig. 1.4: Copyright © 2017 by Vlad Tchompalov. Reprinted with permission.

Fig. 1.5: Copyright © 2018 by Mark Pan4ratte. Reprinted with permission.

Fig. 1.6: Copyright © 2020 by Hybrid. Reprinted with permission.

Fig. 1.7: Thomas Koch, from "Again and Again (and Again): A Repetition-frequency-model of Persuasive Communication," *Studies in Communication and Media*, vol. 6, no. 3, p. 229. Copyright © 2017 by Thomas Koch.

CHAPTER 2

Ethical Implications of Persuasion

Chapter Objectives

After reading this chapter, you should be able to:

- List and describe the ethical guidelines for persuasive communication
- Understand the dark side of persuasive communication, including coercion and propaganda
- Describe the theories used to study deception in persuasive interpersonal communication
- Distinguish deception from ethical persuasion
- Understand the influence of the post-truth era on persuasive communication

This chapter addresses the ethical ramifications of persuasion in the post-truth era while juxtaposing ethical persuasion with coercion, deception, and propaganda—or what *Star Wars* fans might call the dark side of persuasion. Individuals who are capable of utilizing persuasive tactics to influence the attitudes, behaviors, values, and beliefs of others should be diligent about following ethical guidelines. While it might seem natural to think about persuasion as a tool for getting what you want and influencing others to do what you want them to do, we must be careful about how we attempt to persuade others and cognizant of the effects that our communication has on other individuals as well as society more broadly.

Ethical Guidelines

Issues of ethics are inherent to human communication. The term **ethics** refers to the study of what ought to be the grounds for determining right and wrong human behavior and the commitment to do what is right (Johannesen et al., 2008). In other words, ethical communicators are aware of ethical guidelines and principles and behave accordingly. Persuaders should practice ethical communication.

FIGURE 2.1 Theranos CEO and founder, Elizabeth Holmes.

When unethical persuasion occurs, we are often left wondering if the costs are really worth it. For instance, the founder and CEO of Theranos, Elizabeth Holmes, proclaimed as the world's youngest self-made female billionaire, announced that the company had developed a revolutionary, cheap new method of blood testing (McLean, 2018). Holmes stated publicly that Theranos's technology could test for hundreds of diseases from a simple pinprick of blood. This technology, according to Holmes, would save millions of lives and fundamentally change the world. However, the testing devices that Holmes touted were based on technology that had yet to be invented. The testing that Theranos did was completed using existing blood testing technology purchased from third parties. As a result, it is alleged that she engaged in massive deception in order to raise more than $700 million from venture capitalists and investors. Later, when it was revealed that the company lied, Holmes was indicted on federal wire fraud charges by the Securities and Exchange Commission, and the company was dissolved in September 2018 (McLean, 2018). This stark example demonstrates the potential negative implications of unethical persuasive communication.

Is persuasion inherently unethical? We agree with Walton (2001) who argues that "there is nothing inherently fallacious or deceptive about persuasion in itself" (p. 128). In other words, persuasion, like communication generally, is a tool that can be used for good or evil. This means that in assessing the ethics of persuasive communication, we must consider the ways that the persuader's motives color the means. For example, using a fear appeal to coerce or blackmail another is clearly unethical. However, instructors might use fear appeals appropriately to dissuade students from committing acts of academic dishonestly, like plagiarism (Sprinkle et al., 2006). According to Baker and Martinson (2001), the persuasive end "must be formulated in a way that places an emphasis on respect for those to whom particular persuasive communication efforts are directed" (p. 158).

Engaged Persuasion Activity: Escalation of Deception in Organizations

Unfortunately, the Theranos example discussed in this chapter is not unique. In recent years, similar scandals have rocked several high-profile organizations. Fleming and Zyglidopoulos (2007) developed a model that describes how deception escalates through organizations like Theranos. The following are the elements of their model: initial deception (the initial lie told by an individual or group), ease of further deception (the extent to which lies can continue to be told without detection), severity of deception (the initial lie requires a series of subsequent cover-up lies that progressively increase in severity), pervasiveness of deception (lying begets lying, which spreads through the organization), and amplification through organizational complexity (complex organizations are often marked by low transparency, which facilitates deception). If these elements are not checked by other moderating variables, the model stipulates that deception will escalate through the organization eventually resulting in its demise. This research helps explain how companies like Theranos can be infected and ultimately destroyed by deception. Check out an ABC radio podcast and preview of a *Nightline* documentary about the Theranos case, called "The Dropout" (https://abcnews.go.com/Business/nightline-documentary-podcast-dropout-story-elizabeth-holmes-theranos/story?id=60365362). Then apply Fleming and Zyglidopoulos' model to the Theranos case.

Approaches to Communication Ethics

Arnett et al. (2006) provide a thorough review of the literature related to communication ethics. Ronald C. Arnett, a communication professor at Duquesne University, and colleagues examined the evolution of communication ethics scholarship and outlined the following six approaches: democratic communication ethics; universal-humanitarian communication ethics; codes, procedures, and standards in communication ethics; contextual communication ethics; narrative communication ethics; and dialogic communication ethics.

Democratic communication ethics refers to the functioning of democracy and commitment to advance the common good. As Arnett et al. (2006) note, this perspective "privileges the communicative process of argumentation and debate, which presupposes the existence of rationality that in practice encourages good decision-making" (p. 73). Arnett et al. also note that the democratic approach is rooted in evidence, social responsibility, free speech, open debate, and reasoned opinion.

Advocates of the universal-humanitarian communication ethics approach articulate universal principles that should guide human behavior. As Arnett et al. (2006) note, this approach "presupposes value-laden terms about a 'good' life that can be rationally made visible, ever connected to an *a priori* conception of the good, the beautiful, and the responsible" (p. 75). This approach to communication ethics is rooted in public morality, creativeness, and identification of transcendent ideals.

Arnett et al. (2006) also discuss codes, procedures, and standards that govern ethical communication. "Codes, procedures, and standards both prescribe (presuppose) and publicly proclaim communicative limits and constraints (public procedure)" (Arnett et al., 2006, p. 75). An excellent example of this approach can be found in the National Communication Association's (NCA) Credo for Ethical Communication. NCA is the national academic organization within the United States for communication scholars. NCA promotes the discipline of communication and holds an annual convention where the latest scholarship is presented. The credo, adopted by the NCA Legislative Council (2017), reads:

> Questions of right and wrong arise whenever people communicate. Ethical communication is fundamental to responsible thinking, decision making, and the development of relationships and communities within and across contexts, cultures, channels, and media. Moreover, ethical communication enhances human worth and dignity by fostering truthfulness, fairness, responsibility, personal integrity, and respect for self and others. We believe that unethical communication threatens the quality of all communication and consequently the well-being of individuals and the society in which we live. Therefore we, the members of the National Communication Association, endorse and are committed to practicing the following principles of ethical communication:
>
> - We advocate truthfulness, accuracy, honesty, and reason as essential to the integrity of communication.
> - We endorse freedom of expression, diversity of perspective, and tolerance of dissent to achieve the informed and responsible decision making fundamental to a civil society.

- We strive to understand and respect other communicators before evaluating and responding to their messages.
- We promote access to communication resources and opportunities as necessary to fulfill human potential and contribute to the well-being of individuals, families, communities, and society.
- We promote communication climates of caring and mutual understanding that respect the unique needs and characteristics of individual communicators.
- We condemn communication that degrades individuals and humanity through distortion, intimidation, coercion, and violence, and through the expression of intolerance and hatred.
- We are committed to the courageous expression of personal convictions in pursuit of fairness and justice.
- We advocate sharing information, opinions, and feelings when facing significant choices while also respecting privacy and confidentiality.
- We accept responsibility for the short- and long-term consequences for our own communication and expect the same of others.

The contextual communication ethics perspective outlines different communication standards for different audiences and cultures. In other words, a "given context gives birth to temporal standards appropriate for guiding communication ethics in that situation" (Arnett et al., 2006, p. 76). This approach privileges the contingent nature of communication, communication environment, situational ethics, and culturally embedded norms of conduct.

The narrative communication ethics perspective presumes that "culture functions as an implicit story supported by a web of communicative practices that orchestrate communicative behavior by guiding and delimiting communicative possibilities for a people" (Arnett et al., 2006, p. 78). Unlike the universal-humanitarian approach, narrative communication ethics do not presume the existence of universal truths. Instead, narrative ethics outline good stories that advance good reasons in the process of persuasive communication.

The dialogic communication ethics approach assumes an "embedded communicative agent" using narrative to give "birth to a given set of social practices, virtues, and understandings of the 'good' that are carried forth in dialogue" (Arnett et al., 2006, p. 79). This approach privileges responsive communication, interpersonal negotiation, relationships, and respectful communication. This approach also presumes that new ideas emerge as individuals negotiate differences in perspectives through communication. Dialogic ethics recognizes that many different approaches to communication exist. Communicators who subscribe to this approach are willing to engage with and learn from others who hold competing perspectives.

TARES Test for Ethical Persuasion

How can we best assess what constitutes ethical persuasion? Baker and Martinson (2001) propose the TARES test for ethical persuasion that achieves a moral end. The five principles of the TARES test consist of (a) truthfulness (of the message and content), (b) authenticity (integrity and sincerity of the one doing the persuading), (c) respect (for the one being persuaded and not violating their rights or interests), (d) equity (fairness of the appeal being used to persuade), (e) and social responsibility (or concern about the common good). See Figure 2.2 for a visual depiction of the five TARES principles. Notice that the five principles are centered about a dashed pentagram, which we could think of as the persuader since the sender of the persuasive message is arguably in control of each the five principles. Baker and Martinson (2001) argue that communicating "false, misleading, or deceptive information in a serious circumstance, from a moral philosophy perspective, does wrong because to do so perverts the very purpose of speech (communication)" (p. 154). Distrust of persuasion professionals, such as advertisers, promotional campaigns spokespeople, and public relations practitioners, often arises because an audience can sense that they are being manipulated in ways contrary to their own interests (Baker & Martinson, 2001). Thus, the TARES test establishes "prima facie duties" that define "the

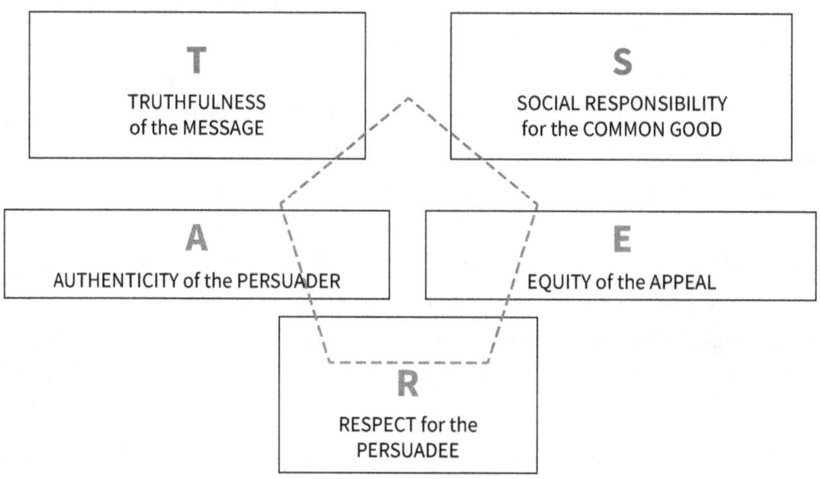

FIGURE 2.2 The TARES test: Five principles for ethical persuasion (Baker & Martinson, 2001).

moral boundaries of persuasive communications and serves as a set of action-guiding principles directed toward a moral consequence in persuasion" (Baker & Martinson, 2001, p. 159). Persuaders should adhere to these duties at all times (Baker & Martinson, 2001). "Although professional persuasion is a means to an immediate instrumental end (such as increased sales or enhanced corporate image), ethical persuasion must rest on or serve a deeper, morally based final (or relative last) end" (Baker & Martinson, 2001, p. 172).

Ethics and Online Information

Beyond face-to-face settings, ethical considerations come into play when we produce and consume persuasive information online. Think for a moment about questions of ethics that surrounded the 2016 presidential election. Many people around the word were shocked to learn that Cambridge Analytica (a British political consulting firm) was able to unethically use personal data from a personality quiz administered on Facebook to target users to influence them to vote for a particular candidate (see Figure 2.3). Examining the image carefully, we might consider the first three steps to represent a multivariate psychological profile. With all the information depicted in the first three steps, we might speculate that particular types of advertising would not only be more personalized but would also be more persuasive. As Cerejo (2018) notes, this was a prime example of "black hat design, a deceptive use of persuasion tactics, combined with unethical use of personal information" (para. 1).

The Cambridge Analytica hack is just one example of unethical persuasive communication that you might encounter on the internet. According to the 2017 Internet Crime Report produced by the Federal Bureau of Investigation

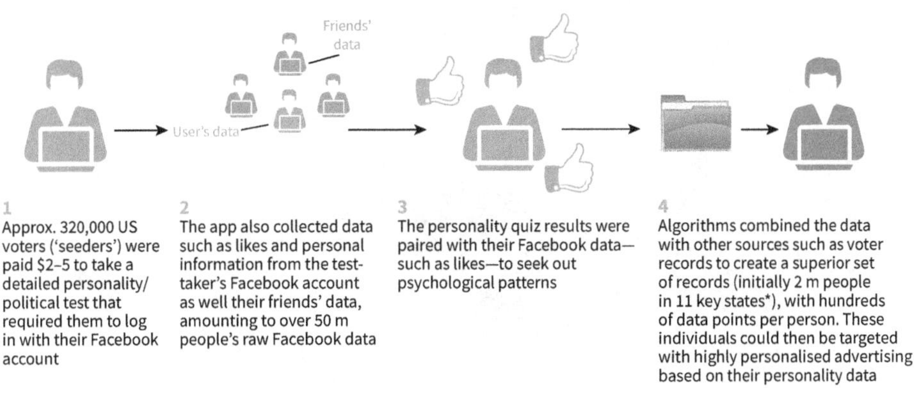

FIGURE 2.3 Cambridge Analytica: How 50 million Facebook records were hacked (*The Guardian*, 2018).

(FBI), some of the hot topics for 2017 included business email compromise (i.e., fraudsters compromise legitimate business emails to steal funds or personally identifiable information), ransomware (i.e., malware designed to make critical data and/or systems inoperable until a ransom is paid), and technology support fraud (i.e., criminals claim to provide support in an attempt to defraud individuals and gain access to their devices). The FBI estimates that they receive over 800 internet crime complaints each day, and those crimes resulted in $1.42 billion in victim losses in 2017.

Ethics and Mobile Technology

Beyond the internet, the proliferation of new technologies, including smart devices, wearable technology, augmented reality, and artificial intelligence, offer ever-present opportunities for persuasion. As Cerejo (2018) notes, these technologies provide for moments of high impact persuasion given that they make it "easy to know a user's location, context, time, routine, and give them the opportunity to take action" (para. 12). For example, you might receive an offer on your smart watch from a coffee shop located just a few blocks away. According to Spahn (2012), these types of persuasive technologies raise ethical questions that straddle the line between manipulation and influence. "Many technologies, that try to bring about behavior change, can be seen as attempts of 'manipulation' or even 'coercion' rather than 'persuasion'" (Spahn, 2012, p. 641). Although persuasion is typically thought of as a nonmediated human speech

FIGURE 2.4 Lego figures using coercion.

act, persuasive technologies can be powerful persuaders, and humans can assign agency to inanimate objects (Spahn, 2012).

Cerejo (2018) offers several ethical guidelines that designers and users should consider when creating and using persuasive technology, including beneficence and nonmaleficence (do no harm), fidelity and responsibility (being aware of the responsibilities to intended and unintended users), integrity (promoting truthfulness in the design of products), justice (designs should benefit both creators and users), and respect for users' rights and dignity (these rights include privacy and confidentiality). The next section of this chapter explores the dark side of persuasive communication.

Dark Side of Persuasive Communication

Not all persuasive attempts represent engaged persuasion for the common good, or even ethical persuasion. Some persuasive communication is what we call fringe persuasion, in the sense that there are characteristics in common with what we would consider more of the core of persuasion. However, fringe persuasion differs in substantive and important ways. The use of coercion and propaganda are examples of fringe persuasion.

Coercion

How does persuasion differ from coercion? Your initial instinct might lead you to the conclusion that persuasion and coercion differ substantially and that **coercion** is almost always unethical. Indeed, most people would likely agree with Fârte (2016) that doxastic coercion, or the "exertion of force with the aim of getting people to believe or not to believe something," is dramatically different than evidential persuasion (p. 51). From this view, coercion involves the invocation of some threat to force the target to act as the coercer desires. Further, it is true that many ways (e.g., threating physical violence) of coercing others are dangerous, damaging, and unlawful (Anderson, 2017).

In contrast, Anderson (2017) argues that authorized coercion may be necessary for the maintenance of well-ordered societies and appropriate as a strategy to "keep the bloody minded and recalcitrant from harming others" (para. 1). Anderson (2017) proposes a number of factors that should be considered in evaluating the ethics of coercion, including "why and how it is used, who uses it, against whom, in what circumstances, and what other means were possible instead" (para. 82).

Rather than relying on coercion, Thaler and Sunstein (2009) advocate for utilizing **nudges**, a form of libertarian paternalism, in policymaking to push people to make better choices or actions that are seen as desirable to those individuals and/or society at large. Nudges are sometimes referred to as choice architecture. Importantly, they explain that nudging is an ethical influence strategy because targets retain substantive freedom of choice and the ability to resist the influence attempt. For instance, a company might make payroll deductions or contributions to their employees' retirement accounts the default choice upon initial hiring. In other words, employees would need to opt out of the retirement savings plan rather than opting in. The reasoning here would be that it is in the employees' best interests to set aside a portion of their paychecks right from the beginning of their employment so that they are financially prepared to retire when the time comes.

Although there are clearly circumstances in which nudging can constitute ethical persuasion, Hausman and Welch (2010) warn that "nudges are not necessarily intended to benefit those whom they nudge" (p. 125). They further contend that some nudges are paternalistic because they are intended to benefit the individuals being nudged, while others are not. "There may be something more insidious about shaping choices than about open constraint" (Hausman & Welch, 2010, p. 131). In other words, making choices for citizens—even to their benefit—is paternalism. "The decision-making abilities of citizens are flawed and might not be significantly diminished by concerted efforts to exploit these flaws, an organized effort to shape choices still appears to be a form of disrespectful social control" (Hausman & Welch, 2010, p. 134). They also argue that government actions and policies along these lines run the risk of being abused.

> Coercion is often justified, and shaping sometimes a better alternative than coercion, but rational persuasion is the ideal way for government to influence the behavior of citizens. Although the force of rational persuasion is limited, and actual persuasion is rarely purely rational, only rational persuasion fully respects the sovereignty of the individual over his or her own choices. (Hausman & Welch, 2010, p. 135)

Hausman and Welch (2010) conclude by stating that "systematically exploiting non-rational factors that influence human decision-making, whether on the part of the government or other agents, threatens liberty, broadly conceived, notwithstanding the fact that some nudges are justified" (p. 136).

This section makes it clear that persuasion and coercion are not polar opposites, as the two concepts do overlap. However, the concepts depart in a few important ways. As our definition makes clear in Chapter 1, persuasion does not involve the use of threats or intent to harm others. Also, the purest forms of persuasive communication respect the free will and choice of the targets of influence. As we noted earlier in this chapter, evaluations of ethics must consider the motives of the persuader.

Propaganda

FIGURE 2.5 Example of propaganda using Uncle Sam to recruit for the military.

Black (2001) explains that most common definitions of **propaganda** conceptualize it as control, manipulation, and perhaps even coercion that dehumanizes the targets of propaganda through a power imbalance between the propagandist and the audience. For instance, Jowett and O'Donnell (2019) define propaganda as "the deliberate and systematic attempt to shape perceptions, manipulate cognitions, and direct behavior to achieve a response that furthers the desired intent of the propagandist" (p. 7). Ultimately, though, Black suggests that some messages that might be perceived as propaganda should be considered more neutrally and ought not be value-laden. In fact, Jowett and O'Donnell (2019) concur that propaganda, "in the most neutral sense, means to disseminate or promote particular ideas" (p. 2). While propaganda employs the strategies of persuasion, its purpose differs (Jowett & O'Donnell, 2019). Black seems to recommend that not all propaganda should be deemed self-serving. In other words, he argues that some communication that might fit the characteristics of propaganda are not unduly propagandistic in the negative sense. Still, he does note that democracies need to avoid mass media messages that encourage unconscious and uncritical consumption by audiences. Thus, informed audiences should understand how propagandistic messages are structured so they can become "sophisticated" consumers who are able to respond effectively to "truth claims" and preserve the "public welfare" (Black, 2001, p. 132). The structural characteristics of propaganda include an emphasis on authority figures instead of empirical evidence, the incorporation of unverified or even unverifiable claims, a fixed view of the subject matter, a single cause as opposed to alternative causes, a warped sense of the flow of time, and conflict as opposed to cooperation (Black, 2001).

Fawkes (2007) acknowledges that some public relations professionals and theorists are reluctant to embrace the topic of persuasion or "admit that public relations is sometimes synonymous with propaganda" (p. 327). She further explains that several prominent models of ethics, including the TARES test explained earlier in this chapter, that public relations scholars have applied to

FIGURE 2.6 Propaganda can appeal to patriotism.

their profession eschew the term persuasion, advise avoiding it altogether, and perceive it to be inherently unethical. To an extent, Fawkes reasons that criticisms leveled against the public relations field, such as it undermining democracy and stifling or distorting debate, have resulted in the reluctance to embrace the term "persuasion." Yet, she observes that "advocacy is essentially persuasive" (Fawkes, 2007, p. 320). Certainly, there are differences between ethical persuasion and propaganda; but, in certain contexts, both terms may be viewed in a negative light. Our position is that ethical persuasion enhances democracy through constructive advocacy and is distinct from negative connotations of propaganda.

To better understand the implications of propaganda for democracy, we turn to the 2020 presidential election. Joe Biden won the popular vote by more than seven million votes and he claimed 306 electoral college votes to Trump's 232. Despite this decisive outcome, President Trump is still contesting the outcome at the time we are writing this, weeks after the election was decided. Trump has advanced several arguments about the election, including conspiracy theories that Democrats used an algorithm to change how machines recorded votes and that votes were tabulated outside of the United States. He has also advanced false attacks on mail-in voting and false claims that the election was rigged. Although these claims have been dismissed as baseless in numerous court cases, the objective of this propaganda appears to be to sew confusion and persuade the public that the election result is in doubt. Christopher Krebs, who led Trump's Cybersecurity and Infrastructure Security Agency, has debunked all of these claims and argued that the 2020 election was the most secure in our nation's history. Importantly, President Trump fired Krebs shortly after he made that pronouncement.

According to Rauch (2020), Trump's strategy is based on a new model of propaganda. Researchers at the Rand Corporation argue that this model, deemed the **firehose of falsehood**, is based on information warfare techniques employed by the Russian government to use "high numbers of channels and messages and a shameless willingness to disseminate partial truths or outright fictions" (Paul & Matthews, 2016, p. 1). The model is persuasive because the first impressions formed by exposure to the falsehoods are resilient and repetition of the messages leads to familiarity, which leads to message acceptance. So how might this rhetorical strategy impact American democracy? Rauch (2020) argues that Trump's goal is to "undermine legitimate authorities, polarize and fracture society, and open the door to cynicism and demagoguery" (para. 8). Ultimately, this strategy disorients the public and makes them more distrustful of others and our institutions, which weakens democracy and threatens the integrity of our electoral system.

Importantly, the implications of this type of propaganda do not stop at mere mistrust of public institutions. On January 6, 2021, President Trump talked to supporters in Washington, DC, and urged them to march on the U.S. Capitol. His supporters did just that, and five people were killed, and dozens more were injured in the assault. In fact, the FBI is warning the public of upcoming armed attacks on state capitols across the country as well as additional attacks on the U.S. Capitol. According to Synder (2021), the argument that Trump was denied a win in 2020 by massive fraud is not a problematic, big lie simply because it defies reason and demands belief in conspiracy theories. Instead, Synder (2021) contends that the claim constitutes a destructive big lie "because it reverses the moral field of American politics and the basic structure of American history" (para. 20). Synder argues further that 4 years of Trump's lies and propaganda has contributed to the demise of democracy and the rise of pre-Fascism. Synder (2021) concludes that America will not "survive the big lie just because a liar is separated from power. It will need a thoughtful repluralization of media and a commitment to facts as a public good" (para. 41). We will return to the ethical implications of post-truth persuasion in a later section of this chapter.

FIGURE 2.7 Detecting deception means spotting lies.

Deception in Persuasive Interpersonal Communication

Levine (2014) defines **deception** as "intentionally, knowingly, and/or purposely misleading another person" (p. 379). Importantly, while some deception may involve preplanning, "a sender may only recognize the deceptive nature of their communication after completing the deceptive utterance" (Levine, 2014, p. 379). It is also important to establish that deceptive communication is inherently persuasive. Miller (1983) argues that "deceptive communication is a general persuasive strategy that aims at influencing the beliefs, attitudes, and behaviors of others by means of deliberate message distortion" (p. 99). Numerous theories have been developed to explain deceptive communication. The next sections of this chapter explore the Four Factor Model, Interpersonal Deception Theory, Information Manipulation Theory, and Truth Default Theory.

Four Factor Model

According to Zuckerman et al. (1981), the **Four Factor Model** stipulates that attempted control, arousal, felt emotion, and cognitive processing play significant roles in deceptive communication.

The attempted control factor refers to the effort made by liars to control the way in which deceit is leaked via nonverbal cues (Monahan, 2014). Zuckerman and Driver (1985) argue that attempted control may yield three cues to deception. First, the deceptive behavior may appear too planned. Second, the liar may attempt to be "too persuasive, presenting a too slick and/or exaggerated performance" (Zuckerman & Driver, 1985, p. 131). Finally, people cannot monitor all aspects of their behavior, and when lying, there may be discrepancies between their verbal and nonverbal messages. Ekman and Friesen's (1974) sending capacity hypothesis addresses the difficultly individuals may experience when attempting to control nonverbal leakage. The hypothesis posits that people are much more aware of their facial behavior when they lie than their body movement. As a result, deceptive communicators attempt to carefully control facial behavior and unintentionally leak deception cues through observable body behavior (e.g., fidgeting of hands or feet).

The second factor in this model stipulates that people experience arousal as they tell lies that manifests in observable nonverbal behaviors like pupil dilation, eyeblinks, voice pitch, speech errors, and speech hesitations.

The third factor in this model is felt emotion. As Zuckerman and Driver (1985) note, deception is associated with negative emotions like guilt and anxiety. Liars are said to experience guilt about engaging in deception and significant anxiety about the prospect of getting caught. The experience of anxiety can be leaked through communication behaviors like less pleasant facial expressions and negative verbal content (Zuckerman & Driver, 1985). In order to separate themselves from the negative emotions of the lies they tell, deceivers may also employ fewer self-references in the messages they communicate.

The final factor in this model is cognition. According to this approach, lying requires significant cognitive effort, which affects speech patterns and other nonverbal behavior. In other words, this model assumes that it is much more difficult to lie than to tell the truth. According to Zuckerman and Driver (1985), "The more complex nature of lie telling may result in longer latencies, more frequent hesitations, and increase in pupil dilation, and fewer illustrators" (p. 133). Further, if telling lies requires more cognitive work than telling the truth, you might also expect deceptive communicators to have fewer things to say and to offer irrelevant information as a stopgap.

Are highly motivated deceivers more persuasive than their lesser motivated counterparts? DePaulo and Kirkendol (1989) claim they are not. Specifically, they note that the motivational impairment effect posits that liars experience significant arousal (e.g., stress and guilt) during deception that unintentionally spills out through nonverbal communication (e.g., blushing and fidgeting) when they interact with others. According to this view, the more "motivated deceivers are to succeed, the harder it is for them to control nonverbal evidence of deception and appear credible to their targets" (Kelley, 2014, p. 682).

Although several studies support the motivational impairment effect, virtually all of this research has been conducted in face-to-face settings where receivers are able to monitor the nonverbal behaviors of deceivers. More contemporary research explores the role that motivation plays in deceptive computer-mediated communication (CMC). For example, Hancock et al. (2010) propose that motivation may actually enhance deception in CMC. The motivational enhancement effect stipulates that deceivers will be more successful in CMC environments because CMC messages do not include observable nonverbal behavior, and motivated liars "may take advantage of the editability and increased time available for planning in text-based CMC" (Hancock et al., 2010, p. 338). Their results support the motivational enhancement effect, as text-based CMC senders were the most successful deceivers in their study.

Interpersonal Deception Theory

The Four Factor Model describes the factors that go into the production of deceptive communication but stops short of examining deception in the context of interpersonal interactions. Buller and Burgoon (1996) developed **Interpersonal Deception Theory** (IDT), which positions deception as an interactional process. The first assumption of IDT is that all parties to any communication simultaneously send and receive messages. IDT also assumes that we actively and continuously assess the credibility of those with whom we communicate. As Judee Burgoon (2009), a communication scholar at the University of Arizona, notes, "Gauging another's truthfulness is an implicit part of all human encounters" (p. 552). Further, IDT proposes that deception entails strategic or deliberate management of information, behavior, and image. Information management includes attempts of a speaker to control the verbal contents of a message. Behavior management "refers to efforts to control accompanying nonverbal behaviors to suppress any telltale signs of deceit and to appear 'normal'" (Burgoon, 2009, pp. 552–553). Finally, image management includes efforts to maintain credibility if caught in a lie. Communicators who handle these three classes of strategic actions well can produce a "believable communication performance" (Burgoon, 2009, p. 553). However, other "nonstrategic, or unintentional, behaviors—such as signs of nervousness, fear, or excessive behavioral control—may also occur, producing unnatural behavior, damaging performances, and undermining credibility" (Burgoon, 2009, p. 553).

The Four Factor Model and IDT share several common assumptions. As Levine and McCornack (2014) note, both approaches share predictions that "honest people behave differently from liars; that (consequently) cues exist that can usefully distinguish truths from lies; and that deception cues are explainable in terms of various psychological mediating states such as emotions, anxiety, arousal, cognitive efforts, and/or strategic efforts to appear honest" (p. 434). As a result, both the Four Factor Model and IDT can be thought of as cue theories. In contrast, the two theories we discuss next, Information Manipulation Theory and Truth Default Theory, are non-cue theories in that neither theory addresses nonverbal behaviors associated with emotions, arousal, cognitive effort, or the desire to appear honest.

Information Manipulation Theory

How do individuals manipulate the information they provide in conversations in order to deceive others? According to **Information Manipulation Theory** (IMT), deceptive messages derive from violations of conversational norms. Steven A. McCornack (1992), a communication scholar from Michigan State University, argues that we generally assume that people will be cooperative and truthful in conversation. However, speakers sometimes intentionally violate conversation norms in an attempt to produce deceptive messages. These violations can concern the quantity of the information communicated (e.g., the speaker does not provide all relevant information), the quality of the information communicated (e.g., what the speaker communicates is not at all true), the manner of communication (e.g., the speaker provides vague and ambiguous information), and the relevance of the information communicated (e.g., the speaker provides information that is not at all germane to the conversation). Individuals can covertly violate any or all of these norms in attempts to deceive others. As McCornack notes, the strength of IMT is that it allows communication scholars to identify and isolate specific features of messages that can be manipulated to deceive others. Table 2.1, based on McCornack's research, presents examples of deceptive messages.

TABLE 2.1 Information Manipulation Theory: Exploring Deceptive Messages

Conversational Norms	Examples of Deceptive Messages
Quantity Violation	Failure to provide all the relevant information
Quality Violation	Communicating information that is untrue
Manner Violation	Providing vague and ambiguous information
Relevance Violation	Provides information that is not germane

Although the original IMT was successful in influencing communication scholars to investigate deceptive discourse as a multidimensional construct, it was not without limitations. McCornack et al. (2014) note that IMT was not a theory, as no "formal, testable, falsifiable propositions were posited" (p. 351). In addition, no explanation "was offered regarding the production mechanism underlying information manipulation" (McCornack et al., 2014, p. 351). According to McCornack et al. (2014), Information Manipulation Theory 2 (IMT2) overcomes these limits and stipulates the following:

> The single strongest determinant of whether or not someone will deceive is the nature of the information they possess in working and long-term memory. When people possess information that they deem too problematic to disclose, they will deceive. Contrastively, in situations where little personal, relational, or professional costs are attached to disclosing information, people will tell the truth. In either case, the driving force behind such behaviors is the nature of the possessed information, or more precisely, its practical, contextual goodness-of-fit. (p. 370)

As you can see, IMT2 builds on IMT by proposing a specific mechanism that triggers deceptive communication—problematic information. Individuals may retain problematic information for any number of reasons, including past problematic behavior. As McCornack et al. (2014) note, instead of assuming that deception complicates people's lives, IMT2 "suggests that people living complicated, dysfunctional lives are compelled to deceive as the most efficient solution to their self-induced problems" (pp. 370–371). Alternatively, people may work in professions, like politics, that place them in situations where revealing their true feelings may have significant professional consequences, and they feel compelled to be less than honest to protect their livelihood.

Is it cognitively harder to deceive others than to tell the truth? IMT2 dismisses the notion that deception always requires more cognitive effort than truth telling. To illustrate this, think about whether it would be easier to recall from memory exactly what you were doing at 6:34 p.m. CST on January 21, 2011, or to simply tell a lie about what you were doing. IMT2 proposes that deception requires less cognitive effort than truth telling because "false information is readily deployable from working memory and the truth isn't; the truth is difficult to retrieve from long-term memory; and/or the truthful information is impossible to contextually package in a face- and relationship-management fashion" (Levine & McCornack, 2014, p. 436).

Two experiments conducted by Clementson (2018) revealed that voters consider dodging an interview question to be deceptive behavior by politicians. However, huge distinctions were uncovered based on the identification of the voter with the politician. Specifically, voters evaluating politicians of an opposing party found dodges to be more deceptive behavior, while voters of the same party affiliation as the politician did not consider the politician as any more or less deceptive. "Susceptibility to deception depends on whether voters identify with a politician" (Clementson, 2018, p. 531). Thus, voters who identify with a politician are less discerning of and more vulnerable to deception, while those who do not identify with a politician are less vulnerable. "If voters do not identify with a politician, then a dodge will convey that the politician is more deceptive" (Clementson, 2018, p. 539).

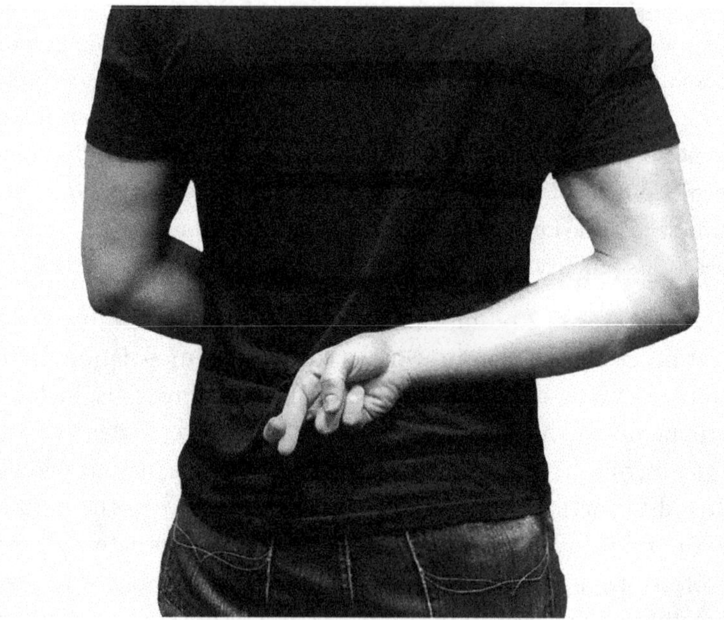

FIGURE 2.8 Crossing fingers behind one's back is the embodiment of deception.

Truth Default Theory

Truth Default Theory (TDT) assumes that when "humans communicate with other humans, we tend to operate on a default presumption that what the other person says is basically honest" (Levine, 2014, p. 378). However, this orientation to assuming that others are truthful leaves us vulnerable to deceit. According to Levine (2014):

> There are times and situations when people abandon the presumption of honesty, and the theory describes when people are expected to suspect a lie, when people conclude that a lie was told, and the conditions under which people make truth and lie judgments correctly and incorrectly. The theory also specifies the conditions under which people are typically honest and the conditions under which people are likely to engage in deception. (p. 379)

TDT is logically consistent with the assumptions of IMT2; however, "whereas IMT2 is primarily a theory of deceptive discourse production, TDT is focused more on credibility assessment and deception detection accuracy and inaccuracy" (Levine, 2014, p. 379). Levine outlines several propositions of TDT. For example, TDT proposes that most people are honest most of the time and that the vast majority of lies are told by a few prolific liars. TDT also proposes that "deception is reserved for situations where honesty would be ineffectual, inefficient, and/or counterproductive in goal attainment" (Levine, 2014, p. 386). In other words, individuals are strategic in their approach to using deceptive communication and will resort to it when telling the truth would not allow them to realize their goals. TDT further stipulates that people have a threshold for believing that others are honest. However, certain triggers may cause this threshold to be crossed forcing us to abandon the truth-default state. These trigger events can include projected motives for deception, behaviors that are perceived to be associated with deception, incoherence in the structure of message content, or information from a third party warning of deception. Importantly, deception judgments do not always occur at the time of deception, as we often suspect and uncover lies long after the fact. Further, TDT proposes that we are most likely to detect deception either through "(a) subsequent confession of the deceiver or (b) by comparison of the contextualized communication content to some external evidence or preexisting knowledge" (Levine, 2014, p. 386).

These propositions make it clear that TDT refutes earlier theories of deception that presume that liars "leak emotional states through facial expressions, liars exhibit or can be induced to exhibit various nonverbal indications of cognitive effort or arousal, and/or liars engage in various other strategic and nonstrategic behaviors indicative of lying" (Levine, 2014, p. 382). More recent research has called into question the ability of humans to detect lies through this kind of nonverbal leakage. In fact, in a meta-analysis of 206 documents and almost 25,000 judges, Bond and DePaulo (2006) found that deception detection accuracy is slightly better than chance regardless of factors like training, age, communication media employed, and experience. TDT suggests that we are better able to detect deception based on contextualized communication content or through a confession.

In deception research, consistency is distinguished conceptually as either coherence or correspondence. While coherence means that claims cannot contradict one another, correspondence requires that descriptions correspond with empirical facts. A series of four experiments by Blair et al. (2018) found that correspondence is the criterion that judges often use to separate deceivers from truth tellers. Participants in these experiments judged truthful statements as corresponding to trusted information and expected truthful confessors to be able to recall and describe empirical facts. "As statements became less consistent, they were perceived to be less truthful" (Blair et al., 2018, p. 495). However, a single inconsistent detail was not found to signal deception. Instead, the data suggested that participants judged correspondence with empirical facts, much like police do in the course of investigations, as the ultimate measure of truthful communication. Ultimately, Blair et al. concluded that coherence is only used as a criterion when correspondence cannot be applied.

Detecting Deception

How obvious is deception to observers? The answer really depends on our ability to detect deception. Normally, skillful deceptive communicators who are high self-monitors appear truthful and are able to control and monitor their behavior (Stiff et al., 1994). However, those trained to detect deception may notice deceptive behaviors that may slip past lay audiences. A former Central Intelligence Agency (CIA) interrogator, Phil Houston, remarked that he'd never seen an interviewee as deceptive as Brett Kavanaugh when he gave testimony before the United States Senate Judiciary Committee (Al-Sabai, 2018). The former CIA interrogator noted that Kavanaugh's testimony in response to accusations of sexual assault vividly displayed plentiful indicators of deceptive behavior: persistent evasion of answers to questions, blistering attacks of particular senators, and rigorous attempts to influence audience perceptions (Al-Sabai, 2018).

In a study that merged IDT and **Dyadic Power Theory** (DPT), Dunbar et al. (2014) examined how power and dominance impacted the detection of deceptive communication. In this particular experiment, deceivers were asked to promote a weaker resume of a friend in a hiring decision. The deception was that deceivers did not divulge that the weaker resume was a friend of theirs. One of the key findings was that, regardless of their power relative to a deceiver, individuals are susceptible to deception. "Deceptive partners easily deceived truthful individuals in all power categories" (Dunbar et al., 2014, p. 869). Overall, deceivers were incredibly successful at misleading other research participants 84% of the time. Dominance, which translated to greater perceptions of credibility, was an effective means of compliance gaining for deceivers, especially those who are in a weaker position than the partners they need to convince (Dunbar et al., 2014). Interestingly, "deception seems to grant the deceiver informational power because the deceiver knows and understands reality and yet misrepresents it to others" (Dunbar et al., 2014, p. 869).

In one experiment, 10 students were asked to tell either a truth or lie about their opinions on either the death penalty or smoking in public (Frank et al., 2004). These truths and lies were then videotaped and shown to participants who were randomly assigned to either an individual or small group condition. The findings revealed that "small group judgments were more accurate than individual judgments when judging deceptive but not truthful communication" (Frank et al., 2004, p. 45). In other words, the results echoed other research that indicates individuals are bad lie detectors and struggle with identifying when they are being deceived, whereas small groups are better able to detect deceptive communication. This means that individuals are prone to a **truth bias** wherein they are not able to detect deceptive communication. Fortunately, small group deliberation and decision making appears to be one means of correcting for truth bias and accurately identifying deceptive communication. Groups "were significantly more critical of sender messages than individuals working alone" (Frank et al., 2004, p. 54). Interestingly, though, both individual participants and those in the small group condition faired nearly as well with identifying

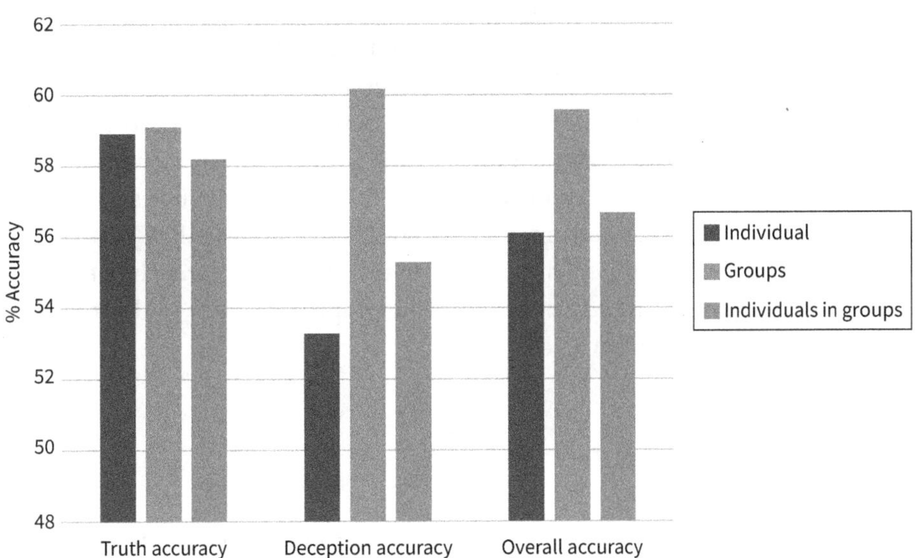

FIGURE 2.9 Detection accuracy by group condition (Frank et al., 2004).

when they were being told the truth. Finally, the researchers speculated that CMC might also assist in detecting deceptive communication. See Figure 2.9 for a breakdown of the results. The most striking data featured in the bar graph is that groups fared much better than individuals at detecting lies or falsehoods. In fact, individuals appear to be extremely poor lie detectors. However, as the graph shows, being able to consult with group members actually leads to better deception detection than truth detection.

Problematizing Deception Research

As the previous sections demonstrate, there is an ongoing debate among communication scholars conducting deception research regarding important variables such as cognitive load and the role that cues play in deception detection. Beyond that debate, scholars have identified a number of problems with the state of deception research. Levine and McCornack (2014) describe some of these concerns in the following terms:

> As several large-scale meta-analyses have made clear, a startling truth about deception research is that theory-inconsistent findings are the norm rather than the exception. But rather than sparking a wholesale questioning of theories and underlying assumptions, scholars instead have adapted their theories to be nonfalsifiable. No matter what the findings, they always either are embraced as "confirmation" or dismissed as methodological artifacts. (p. 432)

Gerlach et al.'s (2019) recent meta-analysis of dishonesty research reveals similar methodological concerns across 565 studies. As consumers of persuasion scholarship, we think it is vital that you understand the boundaries of these kinds of debates about persuasion theory and research. Although the debates may make it seem like the conclusions of some lines of research are inconclusive, it is important that you appreciate how these debates advance science and our understanding of persuasion. Ultimately, these debates allow scholars to refine theory and develop new hypotheses to test. In that regard, the next several years hold substantial promise for the development of our understanding of deceptive communication.

Persuasion in a Post-Truth Era

Several scholars have noted that the post-truth era holds significant implications for ethics and persuasive communication. Oxford University Press (2017) named post-truth the word of the year in 2016 and defined it as "relating to or denoting circumstances in which objective facts are less influential in shaping public opinion than appeals to emotion and personal belief" (para. 1). The term came to popularity in the wake of the 2016 presidential election and represents the concerns that many have about the state of truth in our society given the "massive dissemination of blatant lies, new forms of propaganda and deception facilitated by the digital revolution, public opinion completely unsupported by facts, and publics uninterested in the fact-grounded truth and relatively impermeable to correction" (Waisbord, 2018, p. 19).

Does the post-truth era really represent a new, unique era of communication? There is no question that deliberate distortion, **fake news**, and alternative facts have long been part of American life. Indeed, deliberate deception "aimed at profiting from people's ignorance and misinformation is as old as rhetoric and persuasion" (Waisbord, 2018, p. 19). So what exactly is new about the post-truth era? Post-truth represents a fundamental shift in the conditions for public communication and persuasion that are required for truth-telling. Specifically, **post-truth persuasion** "denotes the absence of conditions in the public sphere for citizens to concur on objective and processual norms to determine the truth as verifiable statements about reality" (Waisbord, 2018, p. 20). We now exist in a communication environment in which a substantial percentage of the "populace is living in an epistemic space that has abandoned conventional criteria of evidence, internal consistency, and fact-seeking" (Lewandowsky et al., 2017, p. 360).

Engaged Persuasion Research: Fake Election News Stories

Silverman's (2016) research found that the top-performing fake election news stories on Facebook generated significantly more engagement than the top stories from legitimate news outlets in the final 3 months of the 2016 U.S. presidential campaign. Specifically, the 20 top-performing fake election stories generated 8,711,000 shares, reactions, and comments on Facebook. In contrast, the 20 top-performing legitimate stories yielded 7,367,000 shares, reactions, and comments on Facebook. This research sheds light on the prevalence and impact of persuasive misinformation on the 2016 campaign.

If people dislike the media, are they more likely be fooled by a fake headline? A collaborative research initiative led by researchers at Arizona State University and the University of Texas at Austin found that several factors predict how susceptible one is to believing news that really is fake (Chen et al., 2018). Those with more education, including graduate degrees, and income were better able to identify fake news, whereas those with negative attitudes toward the media, including Republicans, were less able to spot fake news stories (Chen et al., 2018). To help the public, students, and educators better identify fake news, the researchers have created a series of resources concerning best practices on their website (https://newscollab.org/best-practices/).

Lewandowsky et al. (2017) note that four aspects uniquely mark post-truth persuasion. First, post-truth persuasion is often designed to create a sense of uncertainty about whether any facts are knowable at all. In other words, persuaders empower audiences to choose their own reality and to question information that contradicts their attitudes and beliefs. Second, post-truth arguments are often employed to distract the public from unwanted information or unpopular policy actions. Third, in the post-truth world, anyone can be turned into a friend or a foe at any time. Finally, post-truth persuasion is self-perpetuating. As we noted in Chapter 1, belief preservation techniques can be activated making them harder to change. In fact, some research indicates that efforts to change beliefs that are based on misinformation may backfire and end up strengthening beliefs (Nyhan & Reifler, 2010).

Put simply, the rise of the internet and other factors have unleashed a set of tools that allow individuals to disseminate lies to wide, public audiences. The fact that so many falsehoods are spread via the internet is especially concerning given that 68% of U.S. adults indicate that they receive their news from social media (Matsa & Shearer, 2018). In the post-truth world, it is very difficult to facilitate fact-based discussions about reality. Indeed, taken to the extreme, post-truth persuasion presumes that "facts and rigor do not matter, that all truth-telling is wrong, and that subjective beliefs are sufficient proof of reality" (Waisbord, 2018, p. 21). The post-truth era stands in stark contrast to the democratic communication ethics frame discussed earlier in this chapter. Recall that this perspective privileges fact-based, rational debate. The goal for communicators operating within the boundaries of democratic ethics is to advance the common good through informed decision making. In contrast, many of our current political leaders model deception and lying, and falsifying "reality is no longer about changing people's beliefs, it is about asserting power" (Lewandowsky et al., 2017, p. 361).

Importantly, access to new digital communication is not limited to large government organizations or massive corporations. This flattening of communication opens the door for cynical profiteers to take advantage of gullible, uninterested, and less savvy consumers of persuasive misinformation. To make matters worse, highly partisan individuals are more than willing to share misinformation with others in their social networks. As a result, uninformed citizens "casually reproduce false information produced by news organizations, politicians, companies, and fellow

Engaged Persuasion Activity: Persuasion in a Post-Truth World

In 2017, the Stanford Social Innovation Review published an article titled "Persuasion in a 'Post-Truth' World." The authors of this article argue that social sector organizations must reshape their approach to persuasion to reach their target audiences in a post-truth era. For this Engaged Persuasion Activity, visit the Stanford Social Innovation website and read the article (https://ssir.org/articles/entry/persuasion_in_a_post_truth_world). Do you agree with the conclusions the authors reach? Are the persuasive tactics they advocate reasonable? Can these strategies be used in other contexts (e.g., for profit, interpersonal, political, etc.) beyond the nonprofit sector?

citizens" (Waisbord, 2018, p. 23). As you will learn in later chapters, biased processing, selective perception, and confirmation bias work together to help spread persuasive misinformation. Unfortunately, these factors also make it very difficult to correct misinformation.

Kavanagh and Rich (2018) refer to this new era as **truth decay,** which is a set of four related trends: (a) widespread disagreement about facts and interpretations of data, (b) a blurring of the distinction between fact and opinion, (c) the increasing persuasiveness of opinion over fact, and (d) declining trust in previously respected sources of information. Kavanagh and Rich also argue that the consequences of truth decay include the erosion of civil discourse, political paralysis, alienation of individuals from civic and political institutions, and policy uncertainty. The relationships between the drivers, trends, and consequences of truth decay are presented in Figure 2.10. If we were to examine Figure 2.10 with

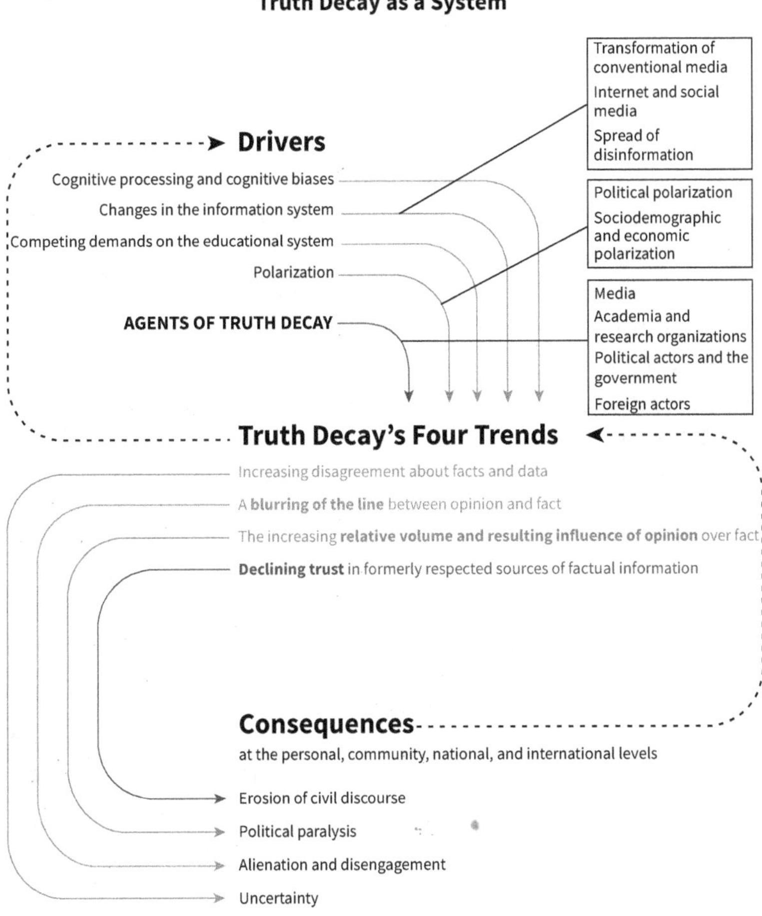

FIGURE 2.10 Drivers, trends, and consequences of truth decay (Kavanagh & Rich, 2018).

American politics from 2016–2021 in mind, we could think of many examples of these trends and consequences. However, we might also conclude that the consequences shown in this figure are incomplete. The divisiveness and polarization in American politics have resulted in even more severe consequences, as demonstrated by the insurrection and attempted coup on January 6, 2021, when Trump incited his followers to march to the capitol building and disrupt the counting of electoral college votes.

What would cause individuals to accept falsehoods spreading through the post-truth world? One explanation can be found in research exploring counterfactual thinking. **Counterfactual thinking** is the process of imagining alternative outcomes when reflecting on past events (Wang & Yang, 2011). Effron (2018) found that counterfactual thoughts, which means thinking that events would have occurred differently if circumstances had been different, can result in people excusing falsehoods told by politicians. Interestingly, he also discovered that if one's political preferences aligned with the politician telling the falsehood, people were willing to excuse the unethical behavior, judge the politician as moral, and oppose punishment. Because counterfactual thoughts lead us to mentally reverse a falsehood with ambiguous information, the behavior seems less unethical. Conversely, if one's political preferences did not align with the politician telling the falsehood, then people were more likely to be skeptical of the counterfactual thoughts. In other words, according to Effron (2018), "Counterfactual thoughts can amplify partisan differences in judgments of alleged dishonesty," thus heightening political polarization (p. 279). Effron reasons that the rise of social media and the post-truth world risk increased effects of counterfactual thoughts. To blunt the effects of counterfactual thoughts, Effron suggests warning people about such persuasive attempts and inoculating them with weakened counterfactual arguments. Ultimately, he warns that counterfactual thoughts threaten ethical standards for persuasion:

> Partisans may not ignore facts, but readily excuse falsehoods based on weak justifications. We should thus be wary of our ability to imagine alternatives to reality. When leaders we support encourage us to consider how their lies could have been true, we may hold them to laxer ethical standards. (Effron, 2018, p. 743)

Counterfactual thinking also applies to consumer behavior (Wang & Yang, 2011). Crawford and McCrea (2004) found that attitudes toward social issues bias counterfactual thoughts which, in turn, predict attitudes that are polarized. They concluded that biased attitudes reinforced initial attitudes and make "one less susceptible to unwanted persuasion" (Crawford & McCrea, 2004, p. 72).

This section may leave you wondering what could be done to address the problems of the post-truth era. Interestingly, a group of behavioral scientists have developed the Pro-Truth Pledge (PTP) designed to persuade signees to adopt research-informed methods for evaluating the persuasive information they produce and consume (see https://www.protruthpledge.org/ to take the pledge). To be clear, the PTP stipulates that any statement against the truth violates the pledge, including directly lying, lying by omission, or otherwise misrepresenting the truth. Built on the foundation of choice architecture, the PTP "encourages signees to celebrate both others and themselves for retracting incorrect statements and updating their beliefs toward the truth" (Tsipursky et al., 2018, p. 276). Early efforts to assess the efficacy of the PTP give us reason to be optimistic about the ability to combat the ills of the post-truth era. Tsipursky et al.'s (2018) research demonstrates a "statistically significant increase in alignment with the behaviors of the pledge, both on one's own profile on Facebook and when interacting with other people's posts and in groups" (p. 282). Tsipursky et al.'s PTP can be found in Table 2.2.

Beyond efforts like the PTP, we strongly believe that the techniques for combating post-truth ills can be found in the research and theories presented in this book. For example, this text will help you become a savvier consumer of persuasive misinformation as you learn about motivated reasoning theory, tests of evidence, argumentation, and credibility, among many other persuasion theories and concepts. Our goal is that you will acquire the knowledge and skills necessary to produce truthful and ethical persuasive communication. Ultimately, we agree with Lewandowsky et al. (2017) that the problems associated with post-truth persuasion can only be assuaged when the public possesses the motivation to become well-informed producers and consumers of persuasive information.

Engaged Persuasion Activity: Conspiracy Theories in Narrative Fiction

Do fictional shows and movies that address conspiracy theories persuade viewers? Nera et al. (2018) conducted two studies to explore whether fictional narratives persuade viewers about conspiracy theories. In their studies, they used clips from *The X-Files* television series that showed the character Mulder giving voice to conspiracy theories. While other research has indicated that narratives produce a strong persuasive effect by reducing viewers' resistance to persuasion, which is consistent with the Extended Elaboration Likelihood Model (E-ELM), the findings in Nera et al.'s studies failed to reveal any persuasive effect. In fact, exposure to *The X-Files* episode actually decreased conspiracist beliefs among participants, which suggests a possible boomerang effect. In other words, exposure to a strong conspiracy narrative did not provoke greater endorsement of conspiracist beliefs among participants. The results, however, did suggest that participants who were more predisposed to believe real-world conspiracy theories accepted the fictional narrative as plausible and realistic. Can you think of a reason why *The X-Files* manipulation used in Nera et al.'s studies might have produced unique results? Are there other fictional narratives you can think of that endorse or portray conspiracy theories? Do you think conspiracy theories shown in fictional narratives are effective at spreading such perspectives among viewers predisposed to believe real-world conspiracy theories as well as other viewers in general?

TABLE 2.2 The Pro-Truth Pledge

I Pledge My Earnest Efforts To:
Share the truth
Verify: fact-check information to confirm it is true before accepting and sharing it
Balance: share the whole truth, even if some aspects do not support my opinion
Cite: share my sources so that others can verify my information
Clarify: distinguish between my opinion and the facts
Honor the truth
Acknowledge: acknowledge when others share true information, even when we disagree otherwise
Reevaluate: reevaluate if my information is challenged, retract it if I cannot verify it
Defend: defend others when they come under attack for sharing true information, even when we disagree otherwise
Align: align my opinions and my actions with true information
Encourage the truth
Fix: ask people to retract information that reliable sources have disproved even if they are my allies
Educate: compassionately inform those around me to stop using unreliable sources even if these sources support my opinion
Defer: recognize the opinions of experts as more likely to be accurate when the facts are disputed
Celebrate: celebrate those who retract incorrect statements and update their beliefs toward the truth

Source: "The Pro-Truth Pledge." Copyright © by Intentional Insights. Reprinted with permission.

Summary

This chapter explored the dark side of persuasion by distinguishing ethical from unethical persuasion as well as juxtaposing persuasion with concepts such as coercion, propaganda, and deception. Clearly, separating the positive aspects of persuasion from seemingly similar, yet disturbing and negative, concepts is essential. We further problematized the notion of ethical persuasion by situating persuasion in the post-truth era, which presents emerging and unique challenges for those who consume, produce, and study persuasion. While this chapter dealt with the dark side of persuasion, the next chapter covers the positive contributions of engaged persuasion by focusing on civic engagement, campaigns, social movements, and group decision making.

Check Your Understanding Review Questions

1. What distinguishes ethical persuasion from unethical persuasion?
2. How do the various approaches to communication ethics differ?
3. How does coercion differ from ethical persuasion? Do you think that nudges are coercive?
4. In what ways does propaganda differ from persuasion?
5. Is deception distinct from persuasion? And how do the various theoretical approaches to deception differ?
6. Why is studying and understanding persuasion critical in the post-truth era? How do social media platforms and political ideology affect social movements?
7. How can post-truth persuasion and fake news be effectively countered?

Key Terms

coercion (p. 39)
counterfactual thinking (p. 56)
deception (p. 44)
Dyadic Power Theory (p. 50)
ethics (p. 32)
fake news (p. 53)
Four Factor Model (p. 44)
Information Manipulation Theory (p. 46)
Interpersonal Deception Theory (p. 45)
nudges (p. 39)
post-truth persuasion (p. 53)
propaganda (p. 41)
truth bias (p. 51)
Truth Default Theory (p. 49)

Credits

Fig. 2.0: Copyright © 2020 by Unrated Studio. Reprinted with permission.

Fig. 2.1: Copyright © by TechCrunch (CC BY 2.0) at https://commons.wikimedia.org/wiki/File:Theranos_Chairman,_CEO_and_Founder_Elizabeth_Holmes_speaks_onstage_at_TechCrunch_Disrupt_at_Pier_48_on_September_8,_2014_(14996937900).jpg.

Fig. 2.2: Sherry Baker and David Martinson, from "The TARES Test: Five Principles for Ethical Persuasion," *Journal of Mass Media Ethics*, vol. 16, no. 2/3, pp. 160. Copyright © 2001 by Lawrence Erlbaum Associates.

Fig. 2.3: Adapted from *The Guardian*, "Cambridge Analytica: How 50m Facebook Records Were Hijacked," theguardian.com. Copyright © 2018 by The Guardian.

Fig. 2.3a: Copyright © 2012 Depositphotos/bioraven.

Fig. 2.3b: Copyright © 2013 Depositphotos/RealVector.

Fig. 2.3c: Copyright © 2011 Depositphotos/creatOR76.

Fig. 2.4: Copyright © 2017 by slon_pics. Reprinted with permission.

Fig. 2.5: Source: https://commons.wikimedia.org/wiki/File:Unclesamwantyou.jpg.

Fig. 2.6: Source: https://unsplash.com/photos/o_ez64ErEbQ.

Fig. 2.7: Copyright © 2016 by OpenClipart-Vectors. Reprinted with permission.

Fig. 2.8: Copyright © 2016 by tswedensky. Reprinted with permission.

Fig. 2.9: Mark Frank, et al., from "Individual and Small Group Accuracy in Judging Truthful and Deceptive Communication," *Group Decision and Negotiation*, vol. 13, p. 51. Copyright © 2004 by Springer Nature.

Fig. 2.10: Adapted from Jennifer Kavanagh and Michael Rich, *Truth decay: An Initial Exploration of the Diminishing Role of Facts and Analysis in American Public Life*, p. xvii. Copyright © 2018 by RAND Corporation.

CHAPTER 3

Using Persuasion for the Common Good

Chapter Objectives

After reading this chapter, you should be able to:

- Understand the relationship between persuasion and civic engagement
- Explain the four approaches to educating students for civic engagement
- Understand the factors that influence group dynamics
- Describe how social proof and group polarization affect persuasion
- Understand the consequences of social loafing and the strategies to reduce its effects

The argument that civic and political disengagement is a serious concern worthy of the attention of those in higher education is well documented (Beaumont et al., 2006; Colby et al., 2003; Galston, 2003; Hunt, 2010; Hunt et al., 2009; Spiezio et al., 2005; Stroup et al., 2013). Beaumont et al. (2006) argue persuasively that "although college students and recent graduates continue to be more involved in politics and public life than their less educated peers," these groups also show "low levels of political participation, whether measured relative to prior generations or according to theoretical standards of participatory democracy" (p. 250). Fortunately, by studying persuasion theory and research and acquiring the skills to become a more effective producer and consumer of persuasive messages, you will also become better equipped to participate as an active member of our democracy. This chapter covers the positive contributions of engaged persuasion by focusing on persuasion as a vehicle for civic engagement. Also, given that small groups are the building blocks for larger civic engagement activities like persuasive campaigns and social movements, this chapter will introduce you to persuasion and small group decision making.

Persuasion and Civic Engagement

The principle objective of this chapter is to introduce you to the role that persuasive communication plays in advancing the common good. As you work through the material in this chapter, we hope you gain a better understanding of your own civic agency and you start to think about how your growing knowledge of persuasion can be used to advance the causes and issues you feel are important to your community (i.e., the common good). Harry C. Boyte (2009), founder and codirector of the Center for Democracy and Citizenship based at Augsburg College, defines **civic agency** as the "capabilities of people and communities to solve problems and to generate cultures that sustain such agency" (p. 3). Toward that end, this chapter will ask you to consider questions such as the following: What is a citizen? Why is active citizenship important? What is the relationship between civic engagement and persuasion? Before examining approaches to civic engagement and exploring the ways that persuasive communication can be used to advance the common good, it is critical to understand the types and importance of citizenship.

Approaches to Citizenship

What does it mean to be an active citizen in a democracy? Most dictionary definitions of citizenship address aspects such as the legal status of residents within a country, social conduct, patriotism, nationalism, and community membership;

however, citizenship involves much more than these elements. As you might imagine, there are differences between younger and older generations in this country in beliefs about what "counts" as citizenship (Dalton, 2009). And there are significant disagreements about what citizenship means within generations. For example, in their research exploring high school students' perceptions of citizenship, Kahne et al. (2003) found that students' definitions of citizenship vary widely. These discrepancies can make it difficult for individuals to find common ground on the topic and hinder efforts to develop educational programs that produce active citizens. Fortunately, Westheimer and Kahne (2004) advance this conversation by outlining the following three types of citizens: personally responsible, participatory, and justice oriented. The personally responsible citizen is honest and law abiding. Such citizens do what is expected of them and respond to community issues that require action when called on to do so. The participatory citizen goes a step further and actually assumes leadership roles in the community. Specifically, participatory citizens play active roles in government and community organizations. The justice-oriented citizen openly questions and challenges existing rules and regulations when they do not produce positive results for the community. Justice-oriented citizens also seek to determine the root causes of problems in their communities and use civic and policy structures to change government institutions and other organizations that are not effective. Table 3.1, based on Westheimer and Kahne's research, provides additional information about the three types of citizens.

TABLE 3.1 Types of Citizens

Personally Responsible	Participatory	Justice Oriented
Law abiding	Active in community organizations	Challenges the status quo
Works and pays taxes	Knows how government works	Seeks out and addresses injustice
Volunteers	Knows strategies for getting things done	Knows how to use social movements to accomplish goals

Although some would advocate that individuals in our democracy should seek to develop the skills necessary for justice-oriented citizenship on just about every issue, we agree with Zukin et al. (2006) who acknowledge that we live in a pluralistic society with many diverse interests, talents, skills, and preferences for engaged citizenship. As a result, they advocate that individuals should develop the skills, knowledge, and motivation to be able to comfortably move along this continuum of engagement and be able to use the skills of justice-oriented citizenship when necessary. The types of citizens outlined by Westheimer and Kahne (2004) offer a useful framework for understanding the topic; however, their typology was developed prior to the proliferation of new digital means of communication made possible by the internet. In the next section, we look at how the digital age has influenced the way communication scholars approach citizenship.

Wells (2015) describes a communication divide between legacy ways of expressing citizenship and new digital tools that allow for remote interaction. He argues that government and nongovernmental organizations often stifle active digital citizenship through their use of the web and social media that he claims reproduces a "twentieth-century, mass media approach to engaging citizens much more than they embrace the participatory and networked norms of digital media" (Wells, 2015, p. 5). This gap is problematic because it does not align with the engagement styles of the youth in this country who prefer to engage in private and flexible activities and who look for opportunities that "lend themselves to self-expression and the production and maintenance of identity through expression and communication" (Wells, 2015, p. 38). Wells (2015) describes two distinct civic information styles that reflect the way that individuals consume and act on civic information:

> In sum, what we have established are two quite different notions of the role of communication in civic action: for the dutiful style, communication is largely a precursor to civic action that takes place separately; when communicative activity takes place, it tends to be officially targeted and strategically directed. In contrast, for the actualizing style, civic actions are always permeated with communication practices, and the distinction between the two is impossible to draw. Further, civic communicative activities frequently have important expressive components, allowing the communicator to express aspects of their identity alongside what may be instrumental attempts to influence the opinions of networked publics. (p. 56)

The research conducted by Wells (2015) clearly indicates that "there are profound differences in how younger and older citizens see communication's relationship to politics" (p. 55). The engagement style preferred by older, dutiful citizens include actions like emailing a public official, writing media outlets, and interacting with others in traditional, institutional arenas. On the other hand, the engagement preferences of younger, actualizing citizens include sharing civic information with friends, posting political information on social media, and establishing connections to candidates and civic leaders through digital media (e.g., friending candidates on Facebook so they show up in their news feed). As Wells (2015) notes, actualizing citizens also interact with others in traditional, formal civic settings; however, "members of the contemporary young generation holding actualizing preferences tend, more so than their elders, to look for civic information experiences in which participation, networked information seeking and sharing, and expressive opportunities for action are present" (p. 56).

FIGURE 3.1 Civically engaged citizens.

Approaches to Civic Engagement

Now that you have a better understanding of the nature of citizenship, we turn our attention to a discussion of how citizenship is enacted through civic engagement. Importantly, scholars have developed numerous definitions and approaches to civic engagement and civic education. As Barbara Jacoby (2009), a senior consultant at the Do Good Campus at the University of Maryland, notes, "There are probably as many definitions of civic engagement as there are scholars and practitioners concerned with it" (p. 5). We adopt a very broad definition of civic engagement and consider it an umbrella term for several approaches, including service learning, political engagement, and democratic engagement (for a more detailed discussion of various civic engagement frames, see Hunt & Woolard, 2016, and Woolard, 2017). As you will see in the sections that follow, each of these approaches relate to ways those in higher education teach students to be civically engaged. Each approach also holds assumptions about the kind of activity that students should be involved in to acquire the skills, knowledge, and motivation required for civic agency.

Civic Engagement

Jacoby (2009) defines **civic engagement** as "acting upon a heightened sense of responsibility to one's community" (p. 9). More specifically, Goldner and Golan (2017) note that civic engagement "refers to the ways in which individual and collective actions aimed at identifying and addressing issues of public concern are undertaken to improve conditions for others and/or help shape a community's future" (p. 692). Civic engagement includes a broad range of civic actions, including taking an active role in the political process, participation in public life, alleviating public problems through democratic means, developing social responsibility, and assuming leadership and membership roles in community organizations (Jacoby, 2009; Saltmarsh & Hartley, 2011). In a novel study exploring undergraduate students' definitions of engagement, Richards-Schuster et al. (2019) found that students considered the following actions as examples of civic engagement: paying attention to the news, attending activist meetings, volunteering, contacting elected representatives, voting, and donating money to a group or cause.

Service Learning

Service learning is a "form of experiential education in which students engage in activities that address human and community needs together with structured opportunities intentionally designed to promote student learning and development" (Jacoby, 1996, p. 5). Within the context of higher education, service learning typically involves hands-on encounters with community organizations (e.g., service in a local food bank or homeless shelter), a link to course curriculum, and reflection on the service experience, and these experiences are structured to foster civic agency and community involvement (Steiner & Watson, 2006). Although service learning has emerged as one of the most popular approaches to educating for citizenship in higher education, it is not without criticism (Hunt & Woolard, 2016). Many service learning critics have argued that this approach is rarely structured to equip students with the political and policy skills needed to secure meaningful change in their communities. Robinson (2000) summarizes this criticism in the following terms:

> As a whole, service learning advocates are decidedly apolitical, profoundly leery of any association with "justice advocacy," and all too willing to channel students into narrowly defined, direct-service, therapeutic activities with professional organizations and to caution students against involving themselves in conflict-ridden movements that carry the possibility of social transformation. (p. 607)

Critics of service learning acknowledge that having students volunteer in the community is good for the community. However, they argue this approach merely puts Band-Aids on the problems faced by our communities, stopping short of developing permanent solutions to these problems. This criticism has led scholars to advocate for educating students with the political knowledge, skills, and motivation to be politically engaged.

Political Engagement

Political engagement includes direct participation in electoral politics, such as "voting, participating in campaigns or political parties, contacting elected officials, running for office, and the like" (Colby et al., 2007, p. 29). Colby et al. (2007) outline the components of political engagement in the following terms:

FIGURE 3.2 Informed citizenship means addressing issues through constructive debate, reasoning and evidence, and thoughtful argumentation—as this protest sign demonstrates.

> Preparation for informed citizenship should include some understanding of political institutions, processes, and issues, and it should include long-term interests, habits, and commitments that support at least a basic level of knowledge and engagement. It should also include the abilities to acquire and evaluate political information, to formulate and express opinions about important political issues, including those who have quite different views. Although these capacities can all be developed through informal as well as formal means, it would be hard to argue that people who lack them are well educated. (p. 277)

Proponents of political engagement argue that volunteerism and service learning approaches are problematic because "while civic participation may be connected to politics in some ways, there are limits to this connection, and it would be a mistake to assume that it can substitute for more explicitly political engagement" (Zukin et al., 2006, p. 199). Zukin et al. (2006) also argue that "while civic engagement may also be political in a sense, and may even lead to certain kinds of political engagement, there remain numerous reasons to be concerned about the relative lack of direct involvement in the political realm of Americans in general, and younger generations in particular" (p. 200). A more detailed overview of the legacy (based on Colby et al.'s research) and digital skills (Pew Research Center, 2018) for political engagement can be found in Table 3.2.

As you think about the relationship between persuasion and political engagement, consider our discussion of systematic racism in Chapter 1. Many of the photographs in this textbook show groups of protesters using persuasion to advocate for political change. As Kendi (2019) argues, this type of political engagement is necessary to uncover racist policy and replace it with antiracist policy

TABLE 3.2 Skills for Political Engagement

Legacy Skills	Digital Skills
• Work together with someone or some group to solve a problem in the community where you live. • Contact or visit a public official—at any level of government—to ask for assistance or to express your opinion. • Contact a newspaper or magazine to express your opinion on issue or issue a press release detailing your issue. • Call in to a radio or television talk show to express your opinion on an issue. • Attend a speech, informal seminar, or teach-in about politics. • Take part in a protest, march, or demonstration. • Sign a written or email petition about a political or social issue. • Work with a political group or for a campaign or political office. • Boycott something because of conditions under which the product is made or because you dislike the conduct of the company that produces it. • Buy a certain product or service because you like the social or political values of the company that produces it. • Work as a canvasser going door to door for a political candidate or cause.	• Join a group on social media that shares an interest in a cause. • Use digital media to encourage others to take actions on important issues. • Use the internet to look up information on local protests/rallies. • Change your profile picture to show support for a cause. • Use hashtags related to a political/social issue. • Use digital media to get elected officials to pay attention to issues or influence policy decisions. • Use digital media to create sustained movements for social change. • Use digital media as a venue to express your political opinions. • Use digital media to give a voice to underrepresented groups. • Use digital media to hold powerful people accountable. • Use digital media to highlight important issues that may not get a lot of attention.

designed to eliminate racial inequality. We will discuss many other connections between persuasion, civic and political engagement, and advancing the common good throughout this text.

Democratic Engagement

Although efforts to educate students for active citizenship have proliferated across higher education, some critics have argued the movement has stalled in the last 10 years. Like criticism aimed at service learning, pundits have posited that most of the civic education efforts in this country focus on service and volunteerism rather than proactive work to solve the problems facing our communities. Saltmarsh and Hartley (2011) take this criticism one step further, noting that institutions of higher education too often view their communities as passive receivers of student volunteers rather than experts who could effectively partner with higher education to address problems in our communities. To correct this problem, Saltmarsh and Hartley (2011) claim that the "movement must not only strive to encourage civic impulses and actions among students, it must assume a joint responsibility with the communities with which it works to confront problems and to enact change through every democratic means possible" (p. 4). The term they use for this approach is democratic engagement. According to Hunt and Woolard (2016), **democratic engagement** is:

> Based upon reciprocity and co-creation of knowledge. From this perspective, community members and organizations and those affiliated with institutions of higher education have shared authority for knowledge production. In addition, students, faculty, and members of the community work collaboratively to address community problems. (p. 545)

Proponents of democratic engagement embrace service learning, civic engagement, and political engagement when these efforts are tied intentionally to democratic community partnerships. The next section of this chapter explores the links between persuasion and civic engagement.

Persuasion as a Vehicle for Civic Engagement

So what is the relationship between civic engagement and persuasive communication? Put another way, why are we discussing civic engagement in a textbook about persuasive communication? Hunt et al. (2016) argue that communication scholars and students are uniquely positioned to foster civic agency and engagement, as meaningful participation in our democracy rests on the foundation of communication competence. In terms of persuasion specifically, Hunt et al. (2016) note that "in order to engage in political persuasion, students must have the verbal and argumentation skills needed to clearly articulate a position" (p. 120). Also, in her seminal study examining the effects of higher education on students' civic

FIGURE 3.3 Voting is a form of democratic engagement, and letting others know you have voted (as these stickers do) can encourage others to be democratically engaged.

engagement, Hillygus (2005) found that the best predictor of future civic and political engagement was training in communication. Hillygus (2005) goes so far as to conclude that her findings "suggest that an educational system geared towards developing verbal and civic skills can encourage future participation in American democracy" (p. 41). In other words, learning the skills of communication, generally, and persuasion, specifically, can go a long way to preparing you for future civic engagement. Palczewski et al. (2012) affirm the critical role of training in communication and persuasion in preparing students for active citizenship, arguing that true civic engagement:

> Occurs when human communication generates new areas for discussion, when people are willing to accept the risk of being wrong (and accept correction of their views), when people affirm a commitment to engage one another in discourse, and when creative forms of communication create social connections among individuals. (p. 14)

Finally, Denton (2017) summarizes the relationship between persuasion and civic engagement when he argues that the essence of politics is persuasive communication that forces us to "interpret, evaluate, and to act. Communication is the vehicle for human action" (p. xv). The preceding scholars draw very clear connections between persuasion and civic engagement. Think about it—how would you develop a public health campaign without persuasion? How you would build, launch, and sustain a social movement without persuasion? How would you elect candidates for political office without persuasion? Also, reconsider the skills for political engagement listed in Table 3.2. How many of those skills rely on persuasive communication? Virtually all of them! Quite simply, persuasion is the vehicle for civic engagement.

Civic Engagement in a Post-Truth Era

Before proceeding, we want to address a few features of our current political environment that you are likely to encounter as you become more civically engaged. Fortunately, the knowledge you are developing in this course is especially timely given the nature of our current political climate. Unfortunately, as we noted in Chapter 2, we are living in what some scholars have dubbed a post-truth era characterized by a rejection of common standards for determining the truth, extreme political polarization, and an abundance of divisive discourse. This era presents several challenges to persuasion scholars, educators, and students. Initially, as Semetko and Tworzecki (2018) note, the line between fact and opinion is blurred in the world of post-truth politics and citizens are:

> Ensconced in "information bubbles" courtesy of individually-tailored news feeds delivered to them by social media platforms, are not likely to

> encounter either authoritative corrections to deliberately spread falsehoods, or indeed any other information inconsistent with their tastes, sensibilities, and political commitments. (p. 444)

Why would individuals intentionally spread persuasive misinformation? Bøggild et al. (2020) examined the ways citizens transmit political information through interpersonal communication. Their research revealed a transmission bias where political information that does not match an individual's beliefs and ideology is transmitted with greater error than information that matches their beliefs and ideology. Communicating information in this way helps to reinforce their existing beliefs and maintain cohesiveness and cooperation with groups of similar others. Bøggild et al. (2020) conclude that the transmission bias "may make citizens vulnerable to manipulation through fabricated conspiracy theories and other types of misinformation" (p. 15). In other words, individuals will transmit conspiracy theories and misinformation especially if the content matches their political view of the world.

In this era, persuasive misinformation spreads rapidly through our online social networks, reaching massive audiences. Bakir and McStay (2018) define fake news as those stories that are "either wholly false or containing deliberately misleading elements incorporated within its content or context" (p. 154). Bakir and McStay (2018) claim that the rise of fake news is the logical outcome of the following factors:

> The financial decline of legacy news; the news cycle's increasing immediacy; the rapid circulation of misinformation and disinformation via user-generated content and propagandists; the increasingly emotionalized nature of online discourse; and the growing number of people financially capitalising on algorithms used by social media platforms and internet search engines. (p. 158)

All of these factors contribute to a communication environment that can be difficult to navigate without the information and media literacy skills required to scrutinize the persuasive information we encounter.

FIGURE 3.4 News in the post-truth era can make it seem like the world is on fire.

To make matters worse, polarizing persuasive communication dominates our conversations about civics and politics. In his book on divisive discourse, Zompetti (2018) notes that this polarization permeates our conversations about the most important social and cultural issues of the day, including issues such as gun rights, freedom of speech, religion, immigration, and race. According to Zompetti, this extreme polarization and divisive discourse turns many people off to talking about politics and ultimately undermines our democracy. Importantly, his solutions for moving beyond divisive discourse include developing the knowledge and skills required for competent persuasive communication discussed throughout this text.

In addition, the way persuasive political messages are composed can contribute to political polarization. For example, Jang (2018) conducted a series of experiments to examine the effects of reading news accounts of tragic cases of mass shootings. The findings suggested that fear appeals used in shooting stories resulted in polarization along party lines. Specifically, a boomerang effect was observed wherein Republicans strengthened their objections to gun control and increased their support for open-carry laws. The practical implication, for gun control advocates, is that using mass shootings as a persuasive tool in campaigns advocating gun control might unexpectedly polarize the issue along partisan lines and further entrench existing positions regarding gun control.

Research also shows that we are commonly exposed to outrageous persuasive communication through the television, radio, online blogs, and newspapers we consume. Sobieraj and Berry (2011) define **outrage discourse** as persuasive communication designed to "provoke visceral responses (e.g., anger, righteousness, fear, moral indignation) from the audience through the use of overgeneralizations, sensationalism, misleading or patently inaccurate information, ad hominem attacks, and partial truths about opponents" (p. 20). Their research indicates that political pundits and commentators on the left and the right use the tools of outrage (e.g., insulting language, name calling, mocking, and sarcasm) to attract niche audiences. Outrage discourse simultaneously shocks audiences and flatters them for their moral and intellectual superiority given their ability to "see through the manipulative smoke, mirrors, and buffoonery offered by the other side" (Sobieraj & Berry, 2011, p. 36).

Of course, polarizing political discourse is found in abundance in online environments. As Entman and Usher (2018) note, the ways "people communicate with each other in groups, families, and organizations, how people assimilate culture, how networks are structured and weighted, and how actors draw rhetorical power are profoundly impacted by digitalized media" (p. 307). Research by Anderson et al. (2018) demonstrates that exposure to uncivil and divisive discourse fuels polarization and creates a **nasty effect** where those exposed to uncivil user comments online develop more negative perceptions of the media sources that house the comments. Beyond the nasty comments we encounter when consuming the news online, research suggests that excessive use of social media increases political polarization (Hong & Kim, 2016). We will examine this research in greater detail in other chapters of this book, but suffice it to say that we live in a highly polarized political climate.

All of the factors discussed in this section have contributed to the rise of negative partisanship, which represents a large negative shift in affect toward the opposing party among supporters of both major parties (Abramowitz & Webster, 2018). In other words, members of parties unify around a shared hatred of the opposing party rather than a shared sense of purpose or political ideology. Abramowitz and Webster argue that negative partisanship is problematic for American democracy because it hampers the lawmaking process and causes citizens to lose trust in governing institutions.

Engaged Persuasion Activity: Exploring the Digital Polarization Initiative

In 2017, the American Democracy Project (ADP; see http://www.aascu.org/ADP/) launched the Digital Polarization Initiative (#DigiPo). The objective of this initiative is to build student web literacy as they participate in a cross-institutional project to fact-check news stories that appear in our social media feeds. For this Engaged Persuasion Activity, visit the #DigiPo website (https://www.digipo.io/wiki/help/index.htm) and peruse a few of the stories posted there. Do you think this initiative is an effective approach to combating the spread of fake news and political polarization? How do we continue to combat these problems without destroying the democratic potential of the web?

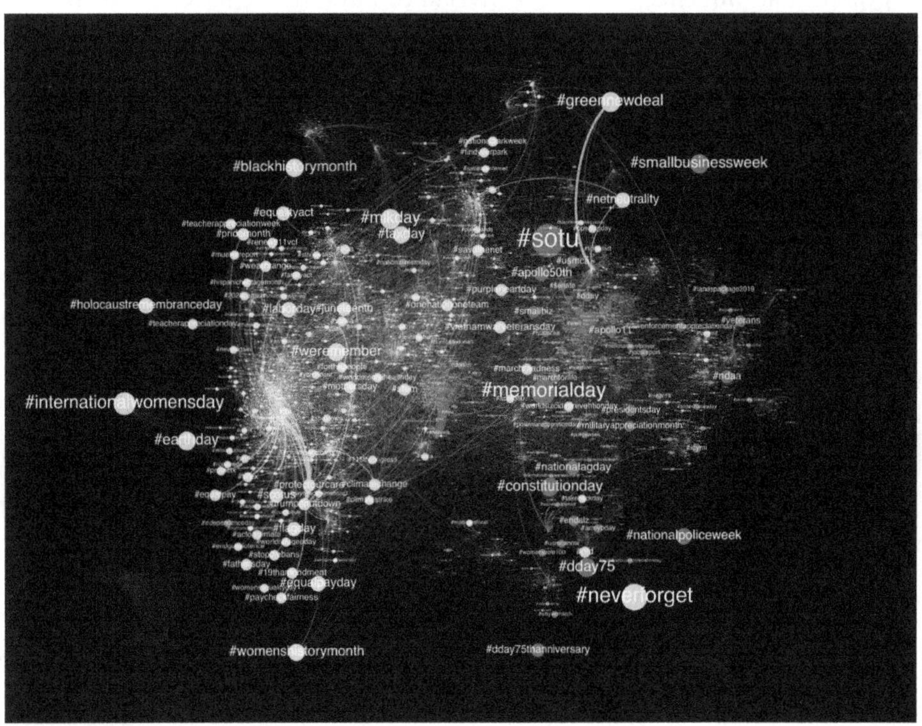

FIGURE 3.5 Social network analysis snapshot visualizing the digital polarization of how U.S. senators had used hashtags in 2019 (Nathan Carpenter, Social Media Analytics Command Center at Illinois State University, 2019).

One significant reason that people default to divisive persuasion is that they do not have the persuasive communication skills necessary to engage in civil discourse. Our hope is that by learning about persuasion, you will become a more informed and skilled producer and consumer of persuasive discourse and, in so doing, will look for opportunities to become civically engaged. Given that small groups are the building blocks of society, the next section of this chapter explores the persuasive dynamics of small group decision making.

Persuasion and Group Decision Making

We often believe that our decisions are our own, that we make individual choices. Do we truly make our own decisions, though? Or are the decisions we make actually influenced by others? If you really think about the decisions you make, your attitudes, beliefs, and values, or even your behavior, it is not difficult to trace the influence that others—and groups of other individuals—have on us. The groups we belong to, and the groups that we encounter, influence us in ways that we might not always be conscious of. Thus, understanding how groups influence us is critical to self-awareness. And, of course, we often participate in groups that influence others in a myriad of ways. As we have already noted, groups are the building blocks for persuasive campaigns and social movements.

FIGURE 3.6 Group members influence one another when the deliberate, dialogue, discuss, or make decisions. When we make points and support those points, as the speaker in this group appears to be doing, we influence other group members.

Consequently, it is important that we understand how groups operate to improve our understanding of how we are persuaded as well as our chances of successfully persuading others. Groups not only influence individual members' behavior but also influence the collective action of a group.

Understanding Influence Dynamics in Groups

Groups are complex, and several factors influence their performance. From the perspective of persuasive communication for the common good, three factors deserve special attention. First, online communication environments alter some of what we know about how group influence functions in face-to-face settings. Second, and of vital relevance to many efforts attempting to facilitate the common good, the political ideology of individuals must be considered if we wish to change another's attitudes or behaviors. Third, storytelling during group deliberations is one means of bridging differences among perspectives even for those engaged in a disagreement.

Online Communication and Influence in Groups

First, let us examine how online communication may alter influence dynamics in groups. The increasing multitude of electronic communication tools available to us further complicate how we, as individuals, must understand the influence others have on us. Likewise, technological means of communication provide us, as members of groups, opportunities to influence others. Thus, we need to consider how we might best influence others through technological communication. When we are attempting to enhance the common good, whether as part of a social movement or other civic engagement effort, we would be well-served to consult research that indicates which strategies and approaches work effectively—and which do not. For example, experimental research by Guadagno et al. (2013) found that online communication can be used successfully when it is based in social validation. The process of **social validation** online means that we can see that others have either supported or rejected an idea. Most social media platforms and other means of electronic communication make it quite easy for us to see how others have reacted. Thus, for example, when we go online and see that others have volunteered for a cause or supported an idea, we are more likely to volunteer ourselves. In fact, the effect of social validation was found to be much more influential than the likeability of the communicator attempting to recruit others' help (Guadagno et al., 2013), which means we pay more attention to how other audience members have responded than we do to the messenger.

Political Ideology and Influence in Groups

Second, we would be well-served to recognize how political ideology affects influence processes in groups. For instance, the **political ideology** of a group member as well as the overall ideological composition of the group impact the outcomes of group deliberation. Gastil et al. (2008) studied 57 zero-history groups who were asked to deliberate over public issues topics. In addition to discovering that group deliberation enabled participants to distinguish conservative and liberal policy approaches, these researchers uncovered a disturbing pattern. Specifically, conservative participants "reacted against" groups in which a greater number of group members aligned with liberal ideology (Gastil et al., 2008, p. 38). In other words, a **repulsion effect** occurred wherein conservatives who were outnumbered were driven further toward conservative ideology, thus entrenching conversative viewpoints on public policy issues. On the other hand, no repulsion effect was found for liberal group members. Meanwhile, those with moderate political ideologies were found to convert to left-leaning policy aproaches "when a higher proportion of group members were liberal" (Gastil et al., 2008, p. 38). On a separate note, the researchers concluded that group members regard deliberation as an effort to reduce differences in viewpoints and find a common ground to achieve the common good. This means that although groups respond favorably to group deliberation, political ideology can influence outcomes in directions that might be contrary to expectations. Cohen (2003) likewise found that "attitudes toward a social policy depended almost exclusively upon the stated position of one's political party" (p. 808), even overwhelming the reactions to the content of the policy and ideological beliefs. Essentially, "groups

FIGURE 3.7 Groups with diverse members do better at avoiding polarization than homogeneous groups.

affect attitudes by shaping perceptions of objects in the social world" (Cohen, 2003, p. 819). More problematically, the influence of political party affiliation "did not bias information processing as much as it posited the very information to be processed" (Cohen, 2003, p. 820). In other words, partisan affiliations change how people perceive information.

Narratives and Influence in Groups

Third, stories play a vital role in group deliberation. How many times have you been in a group discussion and noticed yourself or others telling stories? We actually do it quite often during group interactions. Black (2008) theorized that stories, or narratives, help group members "appreciate each other's perspectives" and "negotiate the tension between self and other" (p. 96). So narratives can enable us to appreciate the viewpoints of others and consider positions that differ from ones we hold. Although narratives do not always lead to dialogic moments, when they do there exists the potential for group members—even those involved in a disagreement—to "build their commitment to the public good by identifying ways in which they are connected" (Black, 2008, p. 96). Thus, narratives offer the potential to bridge differences among group members. Black (2008) posited that narratives enable perspective taking because they reflect the narrator's values and worldviews while drawing "listeners into the story world, thus helping listeners understand the storyteller's perspective in ways that rational argumentation does not" (p. 106). In other words, narratives may succeed where traditional forms of debate or discussion do not.

Conformity and Social Proof

Groups can function as sources that encourage conformity and wield a great deal of social influence over us. The conformity that groups foster in us can certainly work in counterproductive ways, as instances of cults and, to a lesser extent, cliques demonstrate. Yet conformity does serve an essential function for groups. In part, our **conformity** arises from social proof. As we noted in Chapter 1, Cialdini (2001) explains that **social proof**, or the power of peers to influence us, means that "people follow the lead of similar others" (p. 75). Some evidence exists to indicate that the influence of social proof varies across cultures. For instance, highly collectivist cultures are more swayed by social proof, whereas highly individualistic cultures are swayed more by commitment and consistency in their decisions (Cialdini et al., 1999). Still, social proof matters a great deal even within individualistic cultures.

We might be prone to think of our online behaviors as being somewhat individualized and devoid of group influences. However, many online platforms permit us to see the reactions of other individuals. Whether we see the comments

Engaged Persuasion Research: Social Proof and Science Communication

Scientists play a critical role in shaping public understanding of issues like sustainability, climate change, and environmental behaviors. However, some scientists may be reticent to engage in public dialogue about their research for a variety of reasons. Hu et al.'s (2018) research explored the use of social proof as a means of persuading Chinese scientists to engage in public communication about their climate change research. Based on their field experiment, Hu et al. found that social proof (i.e., information about peer engagement in science communication) significantly increased scientists' participation in science communication. Hu et al. (2018) conclude that "simple 'nudges' can trigger a substantial increase of scientist participation and effort making in public engagement" (p. 1050).

and reactions at the bottom of an online news article, the star ratings and reviews for a hotel, the number of upvotes on Reddit, or the likes and other vanity expressions on social media accounts, such as Facebook, Twitter, or Instagram, we are usually quite aware of how other online visitors have reacted to the content we are viewing. For example, likes are a form of paratextual social proof in social media platforms and can diminish negative reactions to advertising recognition (Seo et al., 2018). As such, the ability to view and investigate the online reactions of others serves as a means of establishing social proof about the content we are searching.

Also, recall our discussion of post-truth persuasion in Chapter 2. Research indicates that social proof can negatively influence social media users' sharing of false information. According to Tsipursky et al. (2018), those who see others sharing misinformation will be more likely to "share viral deception themselves, as that person's actions provide him with an implicit permission to do so" (p. 276). Tsipursky et al.'s Pro-Truth Pledge (PTP) addresses this problem by having signees commit to standards of truthful and ethical behavior.

How many times have you stayed in a hotel room and found a sign or note from the hotel asking you to be environmental conscious and reuse your towels, if possible? Are those messages effective? Well, one team of researchers conducted two field experiments to show that using provincial norms in the same setting, or in this case hotel room, as the guests was more effective than general appeals for guests to be environmentally conscious (Goldstein et al., 2008). Specifically, they discovered that a message such as "The majority of guests in this room reuse their towels" spurred greater participation in a towel reuse program (Goldstein et al., 2008, p. 472). Have you ever checked out the reviews on a hotel before booking a stay? As it turns out, there is a difference in how social proof may influence decisions to choose compared to decisions to reject alternatives. For instance, when hotel ratings are good, the total number of reviews matter, whereas the number of reviews has no effect when ratings are negative (Gavilan et al., 2018).

Conventionally, social proof is regarded as a powerful and lasting influence over individuals' preferences since we rely on the opinions of others in determining our own positions, and we desire to remain cognitively consistent by sticking with those preferences over time. However, in a study of all NASDAQ stock market firms over a 7-year period, some limitations of social proof were uncovered (Rao et al., 2001). More specifically, Rao et al. confirmed that initial adoption decisions are swayed by the heuristic of social proof, but only in the short term. The findings demonstrated that stock market firms regularly experience post-decision regret and then reverse course. Thus, the researchers concluded that social proof functions as "a double-edged sword: it is easy for decision makers to use, but precisely because it is easy to use, it leads to errors and decision reversals" (Rao et al., 2001, p. 521). Importantly, the results of this study contradict the conception of social proof as easily able to dupe people since decision "abandonment implies that actors discover and correct mistakes" (Rao et al., 2001, p. 522). In other words, the influence of social proof may be short-lived.

Does it matter who the social proof comes from? Do we care more about what similar others think, say, or do? By and large, in-group members are more influential than out-group members, although out-group members can be as persuasive when individuating information enhances the perception of them being heterogeneous (Wilder, 1990). In other words, when out-group members are viewed as voices distinct from other out-group individuals, their messages are better received by a member of an in-group. Practically speaking, although members of our own circles wield greater influence over us, we are more prone to listen to those outside our circles if we perceive them to be unique voices among the out-group crowd. Of course, we are quick to acknowledge how others are affected by social influence processes but are reluctant to recognize the effect on ourselves. While we generally tend to believe that violence and negative media content has a greater impact on others than ourselves, which is known as a third-person effect, some evidence exists to suggest that group processes and in-group norms with salient group members may reduce this third-person effect (Duck et al., 1999).

So is social proof effective? And does it matter who the social proof comes from? Dillard et al. (2007) found that the perceived effectiveness of campaign messages leads to actual effectiveness, which they operationalized as behavioral intention. Their results held up in five experiments testing fear appeals or threats as well as PSAs, leading them to conclude that perceived-message effectiveness is a viable persuasive strategy in its own right. The methodology they employed in the fifth study demonstrated that descriptive norms from unknown others, rather than those within one's reference group, were effective. Thus, broadly employed social proof appeared to sway behavioral intentions. Levine and Boster (2001) found that "message effectiveness varies as a function of social power" (p. 28). More precisely, powerful individuals were found to wield more social power, with corresponding increases in message effectiveness, compared to low-power individuals and those being nice.

Group Performance and Decision Making

Do we tend to make better decisions when working in a group compared to when we work individually? What causes some individuals to slack when working in a group? The answers to these questions are critical to understanding group performance and decision making and can be found in literature exploring group polarization and social loafing.

Group Polarization

Harvard University law professor Cass Sunstein's (2002) review of **group polarization**, a phenomenon wherein deliberating groups make a decision that is more extreme in the direction of group members' prediscussion preferences, revealed that polarization occurs with statistical regularity. Once people hear what other group members believe, "they adjust their positions" through social comparison "in the direction of the dominant position" (Sunstein, 2002, p. 179). Exposure to persuasive arguments of other group members lead individuals, who otherwise might tend to seek middle positions, to support more extreme positions since the arguments articulated during deliberation will be expressed with less inhibition. It can even "amplify religious impulse[s]" (Sunstein, 2002, p. 183). Sunstein also described the dangers of enclave deliberation, in which like-minded individuals are inundated with exposure to similar viewpoints leading to extremism and fanaticism. Members of outgroups are particularly prone to polarization in extreme, even violent, directions, "fueling and amplifying their outrage" and "producing cascade effects" when "walled off from competing views" (Sunstein, 2002, pp. 191, 195). Interestingly, though, groups will depolarize if they are composed of opposing subgroups relatively equal in membership. Heterogeneous groups, or those of diverse and representative membership, can also guard against the risks of group polarization (Sunstein, 2002).

More recently, in contrast, Bail et al. (2018) found that "social media sites contribute to political polarization by creating 'echo chambers' that insulate people from opposing views about current events" (p. 1). In that particular study, the team of researchers from Duke University, Brigham Young University, and New York University recruited frequent Twitter users and randomly assigned them to treatment conditions wherein those who aligned with the Democratic Party were exposed to Twitter bot messages exposing conservative viewpoints, and vice versa (i.e., Republican participants were exposed to messages from liberal Twitter bots). See Figure 3.8 for the research design employed by Bail and colleagues in their study. Upon closer inspection, the research design appears to be extremely effective at permitting us to isolate the reason for any attitude changes noted in the posttest. Notice that the study used pretests and posttests for both the control and experiment groups with Republicans as well as Democrats. Thus, any changes in political attitudes from the pretest to the posttest would be reasoned to be caused by exposure to the treatment or experimental condition. Additionally, any differences between Republicans and Democrats in their posttest attitudes would suggest party affiliation has differential effects on changes in political attitudes.

The results of Bail et al.'s (2018) study echo some of the previous research we have covered in this chapter but provide important updates that are especially relevant given the increasing prevalence of social media usage. "Republicans who followed a liberal Twitter bot became substantially more conservative posttreatment" (Bail et al., 2018, p. 1). Meanwhile, "Democrats exhibited slight increases in liberal attitudes after following a conservative Twitter bot, although these effects are not statistically significant" (Bail et al., 2018, p. 1). So while we might think that exposing people to opposing viewpoints would lead them to become more open-minded, this study demonstrates the opposite effect. Rather than reducing political polarization, exposing frequent Twitter users to messages with

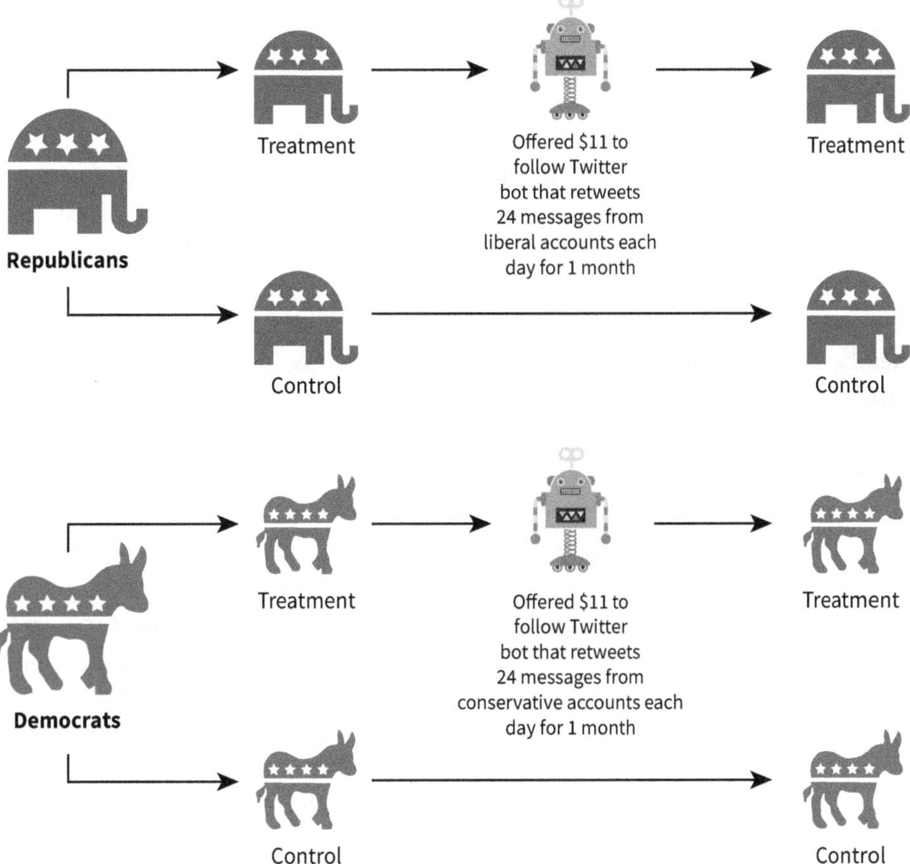

FIGURE 3.8 Research design for partisan backfire effects on Twitter (Bail et al., 2018).

opposing views produced backfire effects by expanding partisan differences. Bail et al. (2018) concluded that "attempts to introduce people to a broad range of opposing political views on a social media site such as Twitter might be not only be ineffective but counterproductive—particularly if such interventions are initiated by liberals" (p. 5). We will discuss backfire effects in much greater detail in Chapter 9.

Social Loafing

Many of our most important tasks can only be accomplished through collective work in groups. It is likely that you have worked in many groups at this point in your life (e.g., sports teams, committees, bands, group projects as part of class, etc.). Also, you probably have experienced working with others who fail to contribute their fair share of work to the group. Karau and Williams (1993) refer to this phenomenon as **social loafing** and define it as the "reduction in motivation and effort when individuals work collectively compared with when they work individually or coactively" (p. 681). Importantly, research demonstrates that social loafing is most likely to occur when the members of the group are strangers, the task to be performed is easy and of low personal relevance, and when everyone in the group is working on the same task (Jackson & Harkins, 1985). As you might expect, social loafing can have a damaging impact on certain aspects of the performance of the group (Karau & Williams, 1993). Despite social loafing, groups are often able to achieve synergy through social compensation. The social compensation effect occurs when group members compensate for and do the work the social loafer failed to do, which helps the group outcome. In other words, groups can still achieve positive results and experience synergy because other members compensate for the social loafer. Nevertheless, the experience of dealing with a social loafer can lead to feelings of group hate wherein members approach future group situations with negative memories of prior group experiences.

Importantly, social loafing is not confined to face-to-face group tasks. In fact, Suleiman and Watson (2008) argue that loafing may be more prevalent in virtual teams because members are physically dispersed and may feel less identifiable. Yeow et al. (2006) found that social loafing occurs often in groups working online. Yeow et al. argue that low participation among loafers indicates that they do not think their contributions will affect the outcome of the group and that their individual contributions are inconsequential. Küçük (2010) also found that individuals in virtual groups report loafing because they perceive others were posting enough that they had no need to contribute. As a result, individuals may choose to remain silent if they think others will post sufficient information. As Amichai-Hamburger et al. (2016) note, participants in online groups who loaf typically "feel less accountability to the group and consequently do not participate as much as they would have, if the onus of participation was on them alone" (p. 27).

Why is social loafing so prevalent in small groups? Scholars have developed several explanations for this phenomenon. For example, **Social Impact Theory (SIT)** posits that the workload imposed on individuals decreases as the size of the group increases (Latané et al., 1979). In other words, SIT advances a many-hands-make-light-work explanation for social loafing. As Latané et al. (1979) explain, increasing the number of others who are the targets for group tasks reduces the "pressures on each individual because the impact is divided among the group members" (p. 830).

Other explanations for social loafing are less benign. For example, the free ride effect stipulates that individuals will not contribute equitably to the group if they think they can reap the rewards of group work and avoid getting caught slacking off. As Albanese and Van Fleet (1985) note, free riders seek to obtain the benefits of group membership but do not "bear a proportional share of the costs of providing the benefits" (p. 244).

Scholars have also advanced explanations for social loafing in situations where all members of the group receive the same level of rewards regardless of their individual level of performance. Specifically, a sucker effect may be observed when people "fear that others in the group will benefit from an individual's efforts" (Schnake, 1991, p. 43). Put simply, people generally do not want to play the role of a sucker in a group by contributing to group work when others are not contributing equitably. As Jackson and Harkins (1985) explain, "When one's partner is hardly working, one would be a 'sucker' to make up for it by working hard" (p. 1205).

The **Collective Effort Model (CEM)** posits that social loafing occurs when individuals in a group perceive that their work will not be rewarded or that they will not accomplish their individual goals (Karau & Williams, 1993). Karau and Williams (1993) further explain how these variables influence individual performance in the following terms:

> The relative value of these outcomes depends on a number of factors, including the meaningfulness and intrinsic value of the task, the task's importance to the individual or group,

Engaged Persuasion Research: Strategies for Decreasing Free Riding in Group Assignments

You have likely experienced free riders in past group assignments. What can be done to discourage free riding in such contexts? Shak (2016) sought to answer this question by exploring undergraduate students' perceptions of free riding. As you would expect, most of the participants in her study indicated that college group work was very susceptible to incidents of free riding. Students in this study offered the following suggestions for combating the problem: The group should impose a reasonable penalty on free riders, members of the group should directly confront free riders with the problems that slacking present to group performance, group members should inform the instructor of free riding incidents, and group members should clearly communicate responsibilities to all members and establish time lines for the completion of individual work. Shak (2016) also argues that instructors should "specify the necessary steps to be taken should the free-riding issue rear its ugly head so that prompt actions can be taken to correct the problem before it is too late" (p. 410).

> the degree to which the individual is dispositionally predisposed to view collective outcomes as important, and the degree to which the outcome provides information relevant to the individual's self-evaluation. (p. 684)

In sum, the CEM proposes that social loafing occurs when individuals think that their effort will not lead to valued outcomes for themselves and/or the group.

Beyond the strategies offered by the students in Shak's (2016) study (see "Engaged Persuasion Research: Strategies for Decreasing Free Riding in Group Assignments"), what can be done to combat social loafing? Karau and Williams (1993) offer the following suggestions:

> Providing individuals with feedback about their performance or the performance of their work group, monitoring individual performance or making such performance identifiable, assigning meaningful tasks, making tasks unique such that individuals feel more responsibility for their work, enhancing the cohesiveness of work groups, and making individuals feel that their contributions to the task are necessary and not irrelevant might all serve, under some conditions, to reduce or eliminate social loafing. (p. 700)

Albanese and Van Fleet (1985) also add that assigned tasks should be at least moderately difficult to deter free riding. Finally, in their research exploring feedback in group assignments, Brooks and Ammons (2003) found that an "evaluation system that provides feedback on specific criteria at both early and multiple points during a group project can reduce free-rider problems" (p. 271).

Summary

Can persuasion be used to affect positive changes in society? Our contention is that the answer to that question is a resounding *yes*. There is little doubt that engaged persuasion plays a critical role in helping influence individuals to adopt positive behaviors and improve their lives. While Chapter 2 addressed the darker side of persuasion, this chapter dealt with persuasion as a force for good. In this chapter we discussed persuasion as a tool for civic engagement and examined the role of engaged persuasion in group decision making. In fact, much of our hope for a better society lies in utilizing persuasion not for ourselves or our own interests but for the good of others. Civic engagement represents one type of persuasive activity that aims to improve the lives of others and strengthen a democratic society.

The next chapter introduces you to the role that persuasive communication plays in public campaigns and social movements.

Check Your Understanding Review Questions

1. What role does persuasion play in a democratic society and the development of democratic citizens?
2. What is civic engagement, and how does it relate to the common good?
3. What does it mean to be a civically engaged citizen?
4. How does persuasion impact civic engagement?
5. How and why do groups influence us?
6. Why are conformity and social proof persuasive?
7. What is group polarization, and how does it affect decision making?
8. How do political ideology and electronic communication affect our reactions to group influences?
9. What are the strategies for reducing social loafing in groups?

Key Terms

Credits

CHAPTER 4

Persuasive Campaigns and Social Movements

Chapter Objectives

After reading this chapter, you should be able to:

- Understand the factors that impact the effectiveness of persuasive campaigns
- Understand the implications of the post-truth era for political campaigns
- Describe how persuasive principles and theories can be applied to inform political, health, and public awareness campaigns
- Identify and define the theoretical constructs of the Health Belief Model
- Explain the persuasive goals of social movements

The previous chapter described the relationship between persuasive communication and civic engagement. In this chapter, we explore how persuasion can be used as a tool in public campaigns and social movements to advance the common good. Throughout this chapter we intentionally highlight theories and contemporary research studies that are especially pertinent to those who wish to understand, study, and practice persuasion for the common good. However, we are intentionally not providing a comprehensive or historical breakdown of these subjects. In other words, although there are many types of persuasive campaigns, we are purposefully focusing on the types of campaigns that illustrate engaged persuasion that can positively affect society.

Persuasive Public Communication Campaigns

According to Rice and Atkin (2009), **persuasive public communication campaigns** represent intentional efforts to influence attitudes and behaviors in large audiences within a specific time frame using media messages in several channels with the intent of benefiting individuals and society. In addition, Atkin and Rice (2013) note that campaign designers analyze the situation and establish goals "leading to the development of a coherent set of strategies and implement the campaign by creating informational and persuasive messages that are disseminated via traditional mass media, new technologies, and interpersonal networks" (p. 3). Persuasive campaigns are also characterized by an identifiable start and end date and a clearly articulated target audience (Woodward & Denton, 2018). As you might imagine, persuasive campaigns can be created around a wide variety of topics; however, this section provides an overview of how persuasion can be incorporated into large communication campaigns related to politics, health, and public awareness.

Political Campaigns

As we noted in Chapter 3, the essence of politics is human interaction and persuasion. Political campaigns are ubiquitous in the United States. In fact, it has been estimated that we elect over 500,000 officials at local, state, and national levels, which accounts for a great deal of persuasive communication through political campaigns (Lawless, 2011). In many ways, political campaigns constitute the lifeblood of democracy (Benoit, 2017). Communication scholars have applied numerous theories to political campaign communication, including Agenda Setting Theory (Lou et al., 2019), Framing Theory (de Vreese, 2004), and Politeness Theory (Daily et al., 2017); however, a full review of all of these approaches is beyond the scope of this chapter. In this section, we focus on two approaches (Functional Theory and Uses and Gratifications Theory) that highlight the production and consumption of persuasive political communication. We also examine political campaigns in a post-truth era.

Functional Theory

Do political campaigns truly influence voting behavior? Believe it or not, this question has received significant debate. Functional Theory offers an approach to understanding the impact of political campaign messages. According to William Benoit (2017), a communication scholar at the University of Alabama at Birmingham, **Functional Theory** positions "candidate statements in a political campaign as functional, or as a means to an end: obtaining sufficient votes to win the office sought in the campaign" (p. 5). Functional Theory has been employed to examine persuasive campaign messages in a variety of contexts, including television spots (Benoit & Compton, 2014), presidential debates (Benoit & Harthcock, 1999), candidacy announcement speeches (Benoit, 2014), nominating convention keynote speeches (Benoit et al., 2000), and campaign messaging on social media (Borah, 2016).

Functional Theory is grounded in five assumptions about the nature of campaigning. First, the theory posits that voting is a comparative act. As Benoit (2017) argues, candidates do not need to persuade voters that they are perfect, but they must "appear—and it is important to always keep in mind the fact that political campaigns are all about voters' perceptions—preferable to their opponents" (p. 5). Second, candidates must create persuasive messages that highlight differences between themselves and their opponents. Although they do not need to disagree with opponents on every issue, candidates must differ enough in order to win at the ballot box. A third assumption of Functional Theory is that we "learn about candidates and their positions through political messages disseminated by a variety of sources including candidates, their supporters, the news media, and special interest groups" (Benoit, 2017, p. 6). Fourth, Functional Theory proposes that candidates establish their superiority to opponents through acclaims (messages that support the candidate's strengths), attacks (messages that highlight an opponent's weaknesses), and defenses (messages that refute attacks directed at a candidate). Finally, Functional Theory assumes that political campaign discourse can address policy (what the candidate has done or will do in office) and character (who they are) issues. Research demonstrates that acclaims are more common than attacks (especially in primary elections) and that:

> Policy is more common than character, character is more frequent than policy in primaries compared with general campaigns, candidates are more likely to acclaim than attack on general goals and ideas, and journalists stress character and attacks more than the candidates themselves. (Benoit, 2017, p. 14)

In a recent study, Benoit (2019) extended Functional Theory to an analysis of presidential campaign posters (1828–2012). Beyond printed and spoken words, Benoit argues that visual symbols play a significant role in a variety of persuasive political campaign messages, including television advertisements, webpages, social media, and posters. In his examination of posters, Benoit found, consistent with previous research, that acclaims were more common than attacks. Interestingly, the research demonstrates that candidates used posters to discuss character more than policy. Benoit speculates that visual elements may be better suited to addressing character rather than policy.

FIGURE 4.1 James A. Garfield 1880 campaign poster.

An example of one of the posters Benoit (2019) analyzed can be found in Figure 4.1. The poster from James A. Garfield's presidential campaign in 1880 depicts him as a farmer using a scythe, displaying honesty, ability, and patriotism. As you can see, Garfield uses the tool to cut snakes representing calumny, falsehood, fraud, malice, defamation, hatred, and venom. According to Benoit, this image illustrates acclaims and attacks on character.

Uses and Gratifications Theory

Uses and Gratifications Theory is another popular approach for explaining the effects of political campaign communication on voters. Blumler and McQuail (1969) developed this theory in their work exploring the political information-seeking motivations of voters. **Uses and Gratifications Theory** posits that the effects of exposure to political communication on voters depends on their needs and motivations.

McLeod and Becker (1981) outline five basic assumptions of Uses and Gratifications Theory. First, the theory assumes that the audience plays an active role in consuming communication. Second, an individual's use of media or other channels of communication is goal-oriented. Third, consumption of communication fulfills several needs ranging from escape to education. Fourth, individuals know and can articulate their reasons for using specific communication channels. Fifth, uses and gratifications are derived from communication content, exposure, and the context in which the exposure occurs. Although it was originally proposed as a means of understanding mass communication, Rubin and Rubin (1985) argue that Uses and Gratifications Theory can be applied to all communication channels, including interpersonal communication.

In terms of political communication, specifically, voters may seek information for political reasons (voting guidance), surveillance (keeping up with the issues), and excitement/entertainment (seeing which party or candidate wins the election; Blumler & McQuail, 1969). In addition, Kaye and Johnson's (2002) research reveals four reasons individuals consume politically-oriented internet sites, including those mentioned by Blumler and McQuail as well as social utility (talking about politics with others).

Uses and Gratifications Theory has been used to understand how political supporters consume information about candidates for office through social media. In their analysis of political candidate profiles on MySpace, Ancu and Cozma (2009) found that the profiles "gratify visitors' need for social interaction with other candidate supporters, as well as information-seeking and entertainment needs" (p. 576). Ancu and Cozma articulate two practical implications for persuasive political campaigns based on their findings. First, they argue candidates for office can use social networking sites (SNSs) to effectively disseminate campaign information, especially to young voters. Second, SNSs can be employed to enhance political engagement if users are provided the opportunity to satisfy social interaction needs (i.e., allow user-generated content like comments, solicit visitor feedback, and facilitate peer-to-peer communication).

Park et al. (2009) administered a survey to 1,715 college students to examine Facebook users' gratifications and the relationship between those gratifications and future offline political engagement. Park et al. found that college students join Facebook groups to obtain information about activities, socialize with friends, seek status, and find entertainment. Their research also demonstrates that users who seek political information online are more likely to participate in offline political activities. For example, respondents reported using Facebook to organize political events, meetings, and parties on campus. Park et al. (2009) conclude that their findings demonstrate the potential of SNSs for "drawing young adults' attention to societal concerns and uniting the young generation as active participants in society" (p. 733).

More recently, Lariscy et al. (2011) employed Uses and Gratifications Theory to examine generational differences in internet-based political information-seeking. Unsurprisingly, they found that young people are more likely to seek information online (and to consider such behavior as political participation) than their older counterparts. This finding is consistent with the research by Wells (2015) discussed in Chapter 3 indicating that young people prefer an actualizing civic information style, including seeking information online and interacting with others through social media.

Political Campaigns in a Post-Truth Era

Beyond these theoretical approaches, it is critical that we consider how the contemporary political climate influences persuasion in campaigns. Many scholars have attempted to characterize distinct eras of political campaign persuasion. As Semetko and Tworzecki (2018) note, the first era of political campaigning (from the birth of the nation through the 1950s) was characterized by communication through print, radio, whistle-stop tours, and doorstep canvassing. The second era (from the 1950s through the mid-1980s) featured heavy reliance on network television and witnessed the professionalization of political campaigns. In this era, persuaders became increasingly savvy in their approach to winning votes, and campaigns became dramatically more expensive. The third era (from the late 1980s to the late 1990s) was characterized by narrowcasting of campaign messages through direct mail and more precisely targeted television advertising.

According to Semetko and Tworzecki (2018), several "interrelated developments have transformed election campaigns and, taken together, have ushered in a new, fourth, era of political communication" (p. 443). This post-truth era can be distinguished by three major developments. First, the rise of "big data" means campaigns now have access to a massive amount of information about voters and the tools necessary to deploy this information. Second, individuals are now more likely to consume news on social media than other channels, like print and television. These platforms provide an outlet for participation in democracy but also diminish the "fact-checking and gate-keeping roles once played by elites, giving free and very visible reign to falsehood, incivility, and outright hate speech" (Semetko & Tworzecki, 2018, p. 443). The third major development in the fourth era of political communication is the globalization of campaigning. While this entails the replication of strategies used in the United States around the world, it also highlights the influence of nondemocratic countries in U.S. elections. According to the director of the National Security Agency, Admiral Michael Rogers, hacking by the Russian government in our 2016 presidential election represented a "conscious effort by a nation-state to attempt to achieve a specific effect" (cited in Corn, 2016, para. 1). In other words, the Russian government

Engaged Persuasion Research: Political Campaigns and Late Night Political Comedy

Warner et al.'s (2018) experimental research found that while both political comedy and campaign attack advertising altered attitudes toward Donald Trump during the 2016 presidential election and indirectly decreased intentions to vote for him, those effects applied mainly to those high in need for cognition. Additionally, the persuasive impact of political comedy was undermined when paired with attack ads. Thus, political campaigns may want to avoid running attack ads during political comedy shows such as *Late Night with Seth Meyers*, which was used as the stimuli in Warner et al.'s experiment. These findings echoed previous research indicating that the effects of comedy are less likely to diminish over time, which provides some evidence for a sleeper effect with political humor. Finally, "comedy and ads can influence evaluations of the target and alter vote intentions" (Warner et al., 2018, p. 16).

intervened in an attempt to affect the outcome of our election and decrease American's confidence in our democratic infrastructure.

The effects of the post-truth era on political campaigns are not limited to the United States. Lilleker and Liefbroer (2018) examined the effects of post-truth campaigns on the 2016 referendum on membership in the European Union (i.e., Brexit) and the subsequent 2017 general election in the United Kingdom. Overall, they found that voters based their decisions on peripheral cues rather than deeply processing campaign messages. During interviews, participants in the study were unable to provide detailed, rational explanations for their positions. Instead, participants merely recounted sound bites from the campaigns. Lilleker and Liefbroer (2018) advance the following observations about post-truth political campaigns:

> However, if the drift is towards a reliance on intense emotional reactions incurred by the juxtaposition of simple images presenting the case for each side, then we are moving to a situation where election outcomes will be increasingly informed by simple and slick marketing, by the claim that appears believable, made by the person deemed trustworthy, but without a clear evidence base for making those decisions. (p. 363)

Ultimately, such campaigns risk undermining democracy by decreasing trust in political institutions and facilitating decision-making based on emotion rather

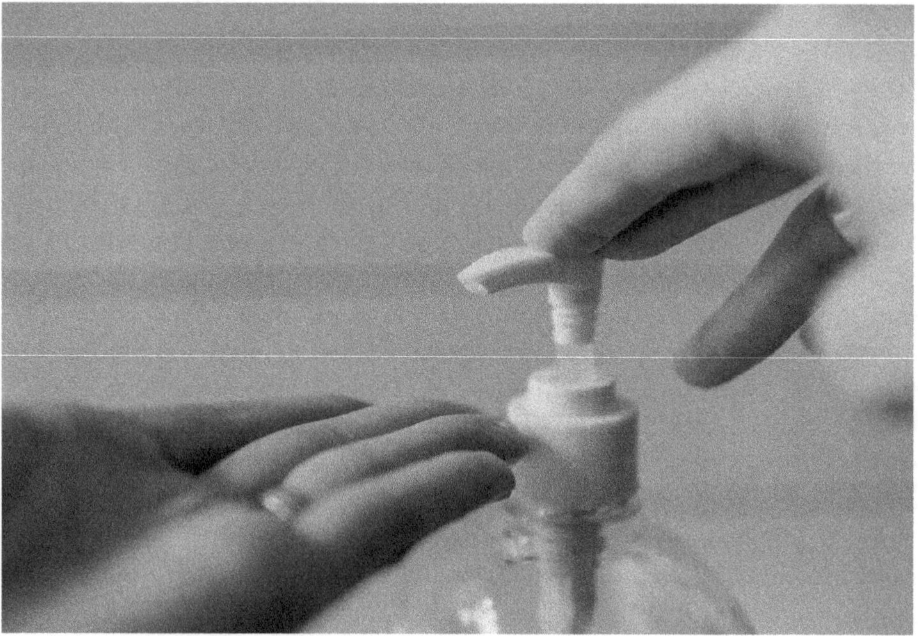

FIGURE 4.2 Encouraging the use of hand sanitizer is an example of a persuasive health campaign.

than rational argument and critical thinking. As noted in Chapter 3, these developments heighten the importance of honing your persuasion skills to become a more critical consumer of persuasive political communication. The next section of this chapter examines the use of persuasion in public health campaigns.

Health Campaigns

Health campaigns are an increasingly important means of educating and persuading particular target audiences as well as the public at large. There is likely a very long list of the persuasive health campaigns you have encountered. According to Snyder et al. (2004), the behaviors commonly targeted in health campaigns include commencement of desirable new behavior, prevention of undesirable new behavior, and cessation or reduction of undesirable old behavior. Whether through television, print, radio, online, or other media, you have encountered messages that urge you to quit smoking, become an organ donor, brush and floss regularly, drink responsibly and not drive while under the influence, see your physician for annual cancer screenings or other preventative care, exercise regularly, avoid sugary foods, not text while driving, and so on. How many others can you recall? Clearly, we encounter numerous persuasive messages that center around healthy behavior or medical issues. But how effective are these messages? Certainly, the causes seem worthy and the aims appear to be ones we can get on board with. So are you exercising regularly, avoiding sugary foods, and flossing? Have you become an organ donor? Despite all the good intentions behind these messages and, perhaps, our general agreement that these are worthy ambitions, why is it that we are still not doing all those behaviors we have been told lead to a healthier lifestyle? Could it be, at least in part, how the message was constructed and relayed to us?

FIGURE 4.3 Meditation is an example of a health belief.

Framing Persuasive Health Messages

One important aspect of persuasive health campaigns is the framing of the message content. For instance, using metaphors to frame message content is common, but perhaps not effective. Landau et al. (2018) randomly assigned research participants to one of three experimental messages about skin cancer. While messages employing metaphors have the potential to aid health prevention efforts, the study revealed that metaphors can backfire when they "perpetuate counterproductive beliefs about health risks and the importance of a given prevention behavior" (Landau et al., 2018, p. 147). Thus, although metaphors have the ability to translate complex health information into concrete and digestible terms, messages employing metaphors can also create more harm if they are not chosen wisely and solidly rooted in theory (Landau et al., 2018).

Other examples of message framing include the use of humor to counter myths as well as the choice between privileging either narrative or statistical information. In the case of organ donation campaigns, narrative messages that utilize humor to counter common myths about organ donation have been shown to be effective (Weber et al., 2006). In contrast, statistical information and sad messages were not as effective (Weber et al., 2006). Of note, the researchers speculated that "humorous messages increase persuasion by affecting mood, by making receivers more agreeable, and by interfering with the ability to construct counterarguments" (Weber et al., 2006, p. 83). When testing the effects of a public service announcement (PSA) about organ donation, White and Dillon (2000) discovered that people will more critically scrutinize a PSA message after they have been told that others have either positively or negatively evaluated the same message. Reinhart and Anker (2012) found that individuals exposed to organ donation PSAs that emphasized recipient narratives were more interested in the message than PSAs that emphasized donor-focused appeals. Furthermore, individuals who perceived the organ donation PSAs to threaten their freedom of choice were less swayed by the PSAs and more prone to experience psychological reactance.

Humor, of course, can be subjective. Consider the PSA in Figure 4.4, for instance. On its surface, this PSA appears to be a humorous message encouraging audiences to drink responsibly. Notice, though, that the color pink is used to depict the individual with a head in the PSA. When one of the authors of this textbook showed this PSA to his classes, both male and female students consistently noted the color pink and interpreted it as meaning that women need to, unfairly, keep their heads about them and moderate consumption, while males are not charged with similar responsibility. In this case, students speculated that the PSA was engaging in a form of victim blaming. Rather than being humorous, then, the message came across as discriminatory. What do you think?

Extended Parallel Process Model and Reactance Theory

Persuasive health campaigns firmly rooted in theoretical frameworks are generally effective. Two theories that will be explored in greater detail in later chapters hold relevance for persuasive health campaigns. First, the **Extended Parallel Process Model** (EPPM), which examines how **fear appeals** are coupled

FIGURE 4.4 Example of a humorous public service announcement about responsible drinking.

with **efficacy statements**, sheds light on how messages ought to be constructed to spur behavioral changes. Second, **Psychological Reactance Theory** examines how messages that threaten perceived freedoms or choices can trigger **boomerang effects** that flaunt desired behavioral outcomes. "Reactance is best understood as an intermingling of negative cognition and anger" (Dillard & Shen, 2005, p. 160). Researchers concerned with investigating the effectiveness of persuasive health messages have employed both theories to understand how individuals react to health campaigns. Controlling language in health promotion messages aimed at young adults is counterproductive, as it can trigger psychological reactance and fails to result in behavioral changes advocated by such campaigns (Miller et al., 2007). However, concrete and direct language coupled with postscripts that restore freedom help to avoid the boomerang effects described by psychological reactance theory, attract greater attention, and enhance persuasiveness for young audiences (Miller et al., 2007).

Research on health communication messages has also shown that fear appeals can arouse perceptions that one's freedom is threatened, whereas efficacy statements can reduce threats to freedom (Quick et al., 2017). Interestingly, fear messages that avoid triggering psychological reactance can lead to favorable attitudes toward the recommended health behavior (Quick et al., 2017). The language used in persuasive health messages bears careful scrutiny. Dogmatic language is found to threaten freedom and is unpersuasive to all audiences (Quick & Stephenson, 2008). Of course, not all audiences respond similarly in all situations. High sensation seekers, who engage in risky behaviors and have a need for arousing messages, are not threatened by vivid language with certain persuasive messages—such as the skin cancer dangers from not using sunscreen—whereas high sensation seekers did perceive vivid language about the need to exercise to be threatening (Quick & Stephenson, 2008). In fact, the topic of the persuasive health campaign can produce differing results in how recipients process those messages (Dillard & Shen, 2005). Of note, though, is that high sensation seekers do not favor messages that combine dogmatic language with vivid language and respond through a vicious boomerang effect (Quick & Stephenson, 2008). Reactance, which may be driven by and communicated through anger in response to perceived freedom threatening messages, appears to be triggered less by cognition than by emotions (Quick & Stephenson, 2008).

Health Belief Model

Another theoretical framework used in persuasive health campaigns, the **Health Belief Model** (HBM), offers further guidance. "Applying constructs of the HBM can be valuable tools in health promotion planning" (Guilford et al., 2017, p. 261). More precisely, we can categorize the constructs of the HBM into two general categories: threat perception and behavioral evaluation (Hartley et al., 2018; Rosenstock et al., 1988). Threat perception includes the perceived susceptibility to and the perceived severity of the health risk, while behavioral evaluation includes "*potential benefits and barriers* [emphasis added] of adopting the health behavior" (Hartley et al., 2018, p. 16). As research on the HBM has developed over the years, two other constructs were added: cues to action and self-efficacy (Hartley et al., 2018). For instance, Rosenstock et al. (1988) advised adding self-efficacy, which refers to an individual's belief that they are capable of engaging in the recommended health corrective, as an independent variable to the Health Belief Model. Table 4.1, based on Hartley et al.'s and Rosenstock et al.'s research, provides explanations for each construct with the HBM.

TABLE 4.1 Health Belief Model's Theoretical Constructs

Construct	Definition
Perceived Susceptibility	Perceived likelihood or risk of the health problem
Perceived Severity	Beliefs regarding the seriousness or consequences of the health problem
Perceived Benefits	Beliefs about the advantages of following the recommended health behavior
Perceived Barriers	Potential obstacles preventing one from engaging in the recommended health behavior
Cues to Action	Cues one may encounter that encourage participating in the recommended health behavior
Self-Efficacy	Belief one is capable of participating in the recommended health behavior

The HBM has been applied to a variety of persuasive campaigns aimed at improving women's health behavior. Education efforts rooted in the HBM can improve women's knowledge and attitudes regarding preconception care prior to pregnancy and childbirth (Fazeli et al., 2018). Training based on the HBM has been shown to increase women's knowledge as well as other model indicators and prepare women to adopt osteoporosis prevention behaviors (Shobeiri et al., 2016). The HBM has also been used to reduce unnecessary C-sections by encouraging women in developing countries to prefer vaginal childbirth (Dadipoor et al., 2017). In a study examining adherence to cystic fibrosis treatment, HBM variables accounted for 50% of the variance in children's adherence and 38% of parents' adherence (Dempster et al., 2018). More specifically, barriers emerged as the most crucial variable for children, while cues to action were most important for parents (Dempster et al., 2018). Breast cancer self-examinations can be influenced by employing HBM constructs in persuasive health campaigns in the United States (Guilford et al., 2017). In Ghana, HBM was able to explain 68.9% of the variance in women's behavior with breast cancer protection (Tweneboah- Koduah, 2018). In fact, the study in Ghana found statistically significant relationships between all the HBM variables and women's breast cancer protection behaviors, with the exception of severity.

Investigations addressing a plethora of other health topics have also lent support for the HBM. In a study of pest control using the HBM, perceived benefits and barriers as well as severity predicted intentions to adopt intervention measures, whereas perceived susceptibility and health motivation did not (Lipman & Burt, 2017). Persuasive appeals from those within one's personal network tend to be crucial. Peachey et al. (2016) found that certain constructs from the HBM were able to predict the use of helmets by skateboarders. Specifically, their data showed that cues to action from friends, family, and parents as well as lower perceptions of danger predicted helmet use. Meanwhile, vanity and discomfort concerns were associated with nonwearers. Of note, attention to media cues to action differed substantially between wearers and nonwearers. In the end, the researchers concluded that safety and danger are not effective message foci, while distribution of information or pledge cards from peers may diminish vanity concerns.

Some studies have suggested that the HBM has drawbacks. For instance, Sas-Nowosielski et al. (2016) found that the HBM only partially and weakly predicted changes in physical activity of older adults, leading them to doubt the utility of the full model. While the research team discovered that self-efficacy and perceived barriers were useful predictors, benefits, susceptibility, severity, and dangers were not. In the study discussed earlier about treatment adherence for children with cystic fibrosis, the HBM produced significant results for only three of the eight treatments examined and showed differences in health beliefs

Engaged Persuasion Activity: Working as a Communication Consultant for a Persuasive Health Campaign

A nonprofit organization (NPO) hires you as a communication consultant for a persuasive campaign they intend to implement in the coming months. The campaign revolves around encouraging parents to vaccinate their children against various diseases per the recommendations of the American Medical Association. The NPO is armed with a wealth of facts about the benefits of vaccination. However, the NPO is concerned about how to craft their message in a way that will also persuade antivaxxers and counter their arguments against vaccinations. The NPO expects a detailed report that will guide their message construction and dissemination. They do not need you to be an expert on vaccinations, but they do need you to provide advice on how to best reach their varied target audiences effectively. Fortunately, you are familiar with the theories and research studies covered in this chapter. Immediately, you think about how social media might be used—as well as other communication channels. You also wonder about antivaxxer demographics and if there is a connection between the tendency to succumb to antivaxxer beliefs and political ideology. The antivaxxers remind you of a social movement in certain ways, while the NPO's campaign sounds like some of the civic engagement efforts you have read about. There is little doubt in your mind that the NPO is attempting to embark on a persuasive health campaign, so the theories and research studies in that area will be very helpful in crafting your report. Finally, you suspect that the different groups involved with this vaccination issue mean that scholarship on group dynamics and influence will offer important insights. You would like to provide a series of perhaps 10 recommendations firmly rooted in persuasion theory and research to the NPO by the end of the week. What recommendations will you make?

of children and parents (Dempster et al., 2018). Thus, the HBM is far from a one-size-fits-all solution for persuasive health campaigns.

One study addressing influenza vaccination behavior argued that findings supported integrating motivation variables of Self Determination Theory with the HBM (Fall et al., 2018). In particular, the combination of autonomous motivation and self-efficacy were significant predictors of intention, which, in turn, predicted 51% of the variance in vaccination behavior (Fall et al., 2018). On the other hand, Hartley et al. (2018) recommend a new model that integrates the Theory of Planned Behavior with the HBM to examine exercise-related injury prevention.

So, overall, how effective are health campaigns at changing knowledge and behavior? Anker et al.'s (2016) meta-analysis of 51 studies demonstrates clear effects of mass-mediated health campaigns compared to controls. Specifically, their study revealed a weighted mean effect size of 9% for knowledge change and 5% for behavior change. This study has significant implications for designers of persuasive health campaigns. In terms of knowledge change, Anker et al. argue that their findings show that health campaigns are particularly effective when targeting receivers with little experience or awareness of the topic. In terms of considerations for behavior change, the authors note that campaign designers should carefully consider the desired behavior of the target, assessment of the design of the campaign, and the experience the target audience has with the topic.

Another important concern for designers of persuasive health campaigns is message fatigue. Kim and Cohen (2017) define message fatigue as an "aversive motivational state of being exhausted and bored by overexposure to similar, redundant messages over an extended period of time" (p. 10). In a study exploring anti-obesity messages, Kim and So (2018) found that message fatigue predicts psychological reactance and inattention to the message. Importantly, inattention was found to negatively predict intentions to adopt the behaviors recommended in the anti-obesity messages. Given the prevalence of exposure to health messages, Kim and So recommend that campaign designers should practice caution and look for creative ways to grab the attention of the target audience.

Public Awareness Campaigns

According to Bouder (2013), public awareness campaigns represent a "comprehensive effort that includes multiple components (messaging, grassroots outreach, media relations, government affairs, budget, etc.) to help reach a specific goal" (para. 4). Such campaigns cover just about any social issue you can imagine from the environment to child welfare to nuclear nonproliferation and everything in between. Public awareness campaigns can be differentiated based on their primary goals. For example, individual behavior change campaigns "strive to change in individuals the behaviors that lead to social problems or the behaviors that will improve individual or social well-being" (Coffman, 2002, p. 6). On the other hand, public-will campaigns attempt to create "public will that will motivate public officials to take policy action" (Coffman, 2002, p. 7). In other words, public-will campaigns focus less on the individual performing the behavior and more on the political and policy processes needed to create systemic behavioral change.

Awareness Culture

As the previous section made clear, a variety of factors influence whether or not public awareness campaigns will be effective. According to Atkin and Rice (2013), campaigns may attain only minimal impact because of "meager dissemination budgets, unsophisticated application of theory and models, and poorly conceived strategic approaches" (p. 15). Importantly, campaigns that stop at raising awareness without spurring action are highly problematic. Hill and Thompson-Hayes (2017) describe the limitations of awareness only campaigns in the following terms:

> (1) Awareness campaigns have been oversaturated—and sometimes overcommercialized—to the point of being ineffective and perhaps counterproductive; (2) the scholarship surrounding awareness has been misunderstood, misapplied, and even ignored; and (3) educators and practitioners should move beyond awareness as an end goal in public health campaigns. (p. 7)

For Hill and Thompson-Hayes (2017), the Ice Bucket Challenge that swept the internet by storm in 2014 is a prominent example of the limitations of awareness campaigns. Without question, the Ice Bucket Challenge reached millions of social media users and shattered previous fundraising efforts in support of ALS (also known as Lou Gehrig's disease). Although the origins of the Ice Bucket Challenge are hotly contested (Levin, 2014), the basic idea was to challenge someone to make a large donation to the ALS Association (ALSA) or to "post a video of a bucket of ice water being dumped on his or her head and submit a smaller donation to ALSA" (Hill & Thompson-Hayes, 2017, p. 22). The Ice Bucket Challenge generated millions of dollars in donations in support of ALS research. So what is the problem with that? For Hill and Thompson-Hayes (2017), the problem is that persuasive campaigns dictated by viral memes and celebrities contribute to an awareness culture "whereby rather than seeking out meaningful causes, people wait until they are amused or entertained enough to join in" (p. 25). In such a culture, people don't participate unless they are in the spotlight themselves. And most problematically, "while awareness might seem innocuous, there is some evidence that it actually leads to familiarity and a great acceptance of the behavior in question" (Hill & Thompson-Hayes, 2017, p. 8). In other words, rather than leading to the behavior change that campaign designers seek, awareness campaigns may make people less likely to engage in the recommended behaviors.

Commitment-Communication Model

As an alternative to awareness only campaigns, Hill and Thompson-Hayes (2017) propose that persuaders use the **Commitment-Communication Model** (CCM) to guide campaign development. The CCM posits that getting the public to commit to solve a problem depends on the following variables:

> (1) attempts to get others to recognize there is a problem and heightened sensitivity to messages about the problem, (2) ongoing attempts to seek information and become educated on the problem, and (3) participation in efforts to alleviate and solve problems. (Hill & Thompson-Hayes, 2017, p. 112)

Put simply, the CCM stipulates that to create meaningful change, designers of public awareness campaigns must persuade the public to commit to and participate in solving the problem.

Commitment is at the core of this model, but the variables of recognition involvement, knowledge seeking and education, and participation are also important. **Recognition involvement** refers to the degree to which individuals view a problem "as needing to be addressed and is based on perceived level of personal salience and involvement" with the problem (Hill & Thompson-Hayes, 2017, p. 113). As you can see, this variable extends well beyond mere awareness of the problem. Knowledge seeking and education refers to the degree to which "individuals seek knowledge about and become educated" on a problem (Hill

& Thompson-Hayes, 2017, p. 114). Finally, participation refers to the degree to which "people participate in specific activities, including communication activities, in order to solve or alleviate" the problem identified by the campaign (Hill & Thompson-Hayes, 2017, p. 115). Participation may include providing social support, donating to a cause, fundraising, or other activities organized by the campaign.

Communication also plays a vital role in this model, as messages are disseminated through mass media, social media, and interpersonal networks. As Hill and Thompson-Hayes (2017) note, the variables in the CCM are "constructed through communication, and communication is the process by which movement occurs throughout the model and links the dependent variable, commitment, with the independent variables" (p. 117). Taken together, the components of the CCM offer campaign designers practical insights regarding the identification of target audiences, setting clear and realistic

Engaged Persuasion Research: Message Design in Public Awareness Campaigns

Extant research demonstrates that public awareness campaigns ought to carefully consider the message strategies they employ. For instance, personality-based persuasive message strategies can be effective means of reaching target audiences. Hirsh et al. (2012) found that targeting persuasive advertisements to the Big Five personality traits (extroversion, agreeableness, conscientiousness, neuroticism, and openness/intellect) is successful in augmenting the impact of the message. Additionally, awareness campaigns that employ fear appeals may affect multiple audiences. For example, direct fear appeals about rape have been shown to be persuasive in motivating women to indicate intentions to enroll in self-defense classes as well as motivating men to indicate intentions to encourage women to enroll (Morrison, 2005).

FIGURE 4.5 Mobilizing for social change.

goals, identifying key communication channels, and monitoring public discourse about the subject of the campaign.

Persuasion and Social Movements

Persuasive campaigns can be an effective means of advancing the common good and may even spur the development of social movements. In this section we define social movements and outline their major persuasive goals.

Defining Social Movements

Social movements are complex collective entities. According to Stewart et al. (2012), to be defined as a **social movement**, entities must meet the following criteria: organization (they are composed of identifiable leaders and followers who are at least minimally organized to accomplish tasks), uninstitutionalized (they are not part of established orders or governing systems of the status quo), large in scope (e.g., geographic area, life span, participants, etc.), promote or oppose changes in societal norms and values (e.g., voting rights, police-community relations, equal pay, etc.), encounter opposition in a moral struggle (members believe they have a moral obligation to advance their vision of the common good), and, finally, social movements rely primarily on persuasion rather than violence, coercion, or bargaining to achieve their goals. Now that we have a

FIGURE 4.6 The Occupy Wall Street movement in 2011 fought against economic inequality.

better understanding of the definition of social movements, we next consider their persuasive goals.

Persuasive Goals of Social Movements

Persuasion is a critical feature of all social movements. As Stewart et al. (2012) note, social movements ultimately seek to fulfill the following six persuasive functions: transform perceptions of reality, alter self-perceptions of protestors, legitimize the social movement, prescribe courses of action, mobilize followers for action, and work to sustain the social movement. These functions are achieved through persuasive communication. How effectively a social movement employs persuasion is often the key to their success. Historically, successful social movements (e.g., women's suffrage, civil rights, and various labor and environmental movements) have utilized engaged persuasion effectively. Today, though, social movements operate in a digital age and an increasingly polarized political landscape. Consider contemporary examples of social movements, including Black Lives Matter (BLM), #MeToo, Occupy Wall Street (OWS), Pro- and Anti-Choice, #Ferguson, Arab Spring, and #Resist or The Resistance. Movements today certainly reflect a willing embrace of communication technologies and social media to facilitate mobilization while still emphasizing traditional strategies and tactics employed by social movements of the past.

Transforming Perceptions of Reality

Initially, it is important to understand that social movements engage in attempts to influence perceptions of reality. As Stewart et al. (2012) note, social movements must "make people aware that the generally accepted view of social reality fostered by political, social, religious, educational, legal, literary, and media institutions is false and something must be done about it" (p. 50). Consider some of the contemporary social movements mentioned in the introduction to this section. Levine (2019) notes that movements like BLM and climate activism "do not merely advocate specific policies but attempt to fundamentally transform society, from white supremacy to racial equity, or from carbon-dependence to global sustainability" (p. 9).

In addition, Stewart et al. (2012) argue that movements accomplish this by altering people's perceptions of the past, present, and future. In terms of transforming perceptions of the past, Woodward and Denton (2014) argue that movements "must challenge accepted ways of viewing historical events and people in order to emphasize the severity of a problem and the need for drastic action" (p. 246). Social movements use a variety of strategies to alter perceptions of the present. For example, leaders may rename or redefine an event (e.g., the pro-life movement refers to a fetus as a baby and abortion as murder) and provide information that counters facts offered by those in power (Woodward & Denton, 2014). Finally, social movement leaders must provide a utopian vision of the future.

Wouters's (2019) examination of the persuasive strategies used in the BLM movement demonstrates that members transformed perceptions of reality and increased support and identification with the movement by displaying diversity of membership, advancing the worthiness of the cause, and through sheer numbers of those participating in protests (i.e., social proof).

Altering Self-Perceptions of Protestors

Social movements face significant persuasive challenges in overcoming the power of institutions and bureaucracy in the status quo. Therefore, Stewart (1999) argues that the "ego function is a necessary ingredient in the rhetoric of any collective effort that challenges powerful, entrenched institutions and inevitably brings down the wrath of these institutions and their sympathizers upon the collective heads of protestors" (p. 92). In other words, movements need to bolster the egos of members to prepare them to take on the status quo. Many of the persuasive messages movements "perpetuate an us-versus-them perspective while also increasing feelings of belonging, identity, respect, and power that are not possible if someone is not a member of the movement" (Zompetti et al., 2013, p. 245).

The specific persuasive strategies that members of movements employ depend on whether they are self- or other-directed. Stewart et al. (2012) note that self-directed movements are "created, led, and populated primarily by those who perceive themselves to be dispossessed and are struggling primarily for their personal freedom, equality, justice, and rights" (p. 58). In contrast, other-directed movements are "created, led, and populated primarily by those who do not perceive themselves to be dispossessed and are struggling for the freedom, equality, justice, and rights of others rather than selves" (Steward et al., 2012, pp. 58–59). As Stewart's (1999) research demonstrates, persuaders in self-directed movements tend to position themselves as exploited and oppressed. Persuaders in other-directed movements do not portray themselves as victims. Instead, they focus on what they are protesting because their sense of self derives from the fight rather than individual identity (Stewart, 1999). The key differences between these persuasive strategies, based on Stewart's research, are further outlined in Table 4.2.

Legitimizing the Movement

Stewart et al. (2012) note that legitimizing the movement is the primary goal of movements, the most significant challenge to institutions in the status quo, and the most difficult barrier to overcome. They also argue that legitimizing social movements involves the persuasive functions of conferring the right to

TABLE 4.2 Persuasive Strategies for Bolstering Egos

	Self-Directed Movements	Other-Directed Movements
Key Arguments	Address the sexual, racial, ethnic, sexual orientation, and class groups to which they belong. Argue they are exploited by evil oppressors.	Argue they are the people who dare to speak out and demonstrate for the good of others. They do not argue they are personally exploited.
Members' Views of Self	Innocent and blameless victims. They feel persecuted for who they are.	Members take pride in being singled out because they represent a threat to victimizers.
Persuasive Strategies	Members rely on the rhetoric of self-pity, self-defense, and self-preservation.	Persuasive efforts focus on the morality of fighting on behalf of victims and emphasizes how good members are.

exercise influence and the process of retaining legitimacy once it is conferred. As Francesconi (1982) notes, acquiring and retaining legitimacy are inherently persuasive given the "implicit requirement of rationality attached to its legitimacy, a rationality of good reasons" (p. 50). In other words, members of social movements must persuade others, through good, persuasive reasons, that the movement is legitimate, has the right to exercise authority, and they seek to "identify with fundamental societal norms and values to transport themselves from the margins of society to the centers where legitimacy resides" (Stewart et al., 2012, p. 65).

Social movements rely predominantly on coactive and confrontational persuasive strategies to acquire legitimacy. Coactive persuasion establishes that the movement is "similar to the social order in important ways—legal, law-abiding, supporter of traditions, moral—and therefore worthy of a degree of legitimacy" (Stewart et al., 2012, p. 68). As you might imagine, protestors cannot rely on coactive strategies alone, as they are often seeking to change the institutions and social order in some way. As a result, Stewart et al. (2012) argue that **confrontational persuasion** is "necessary to break the rhetorical stalemate by bringing institutional legitimacy into question and enabling the social movement to transcend the social order in perceived legitimacy" (p. 69). Confrontational persuasion can include nonviolent resistance and civil disobedience (e.g., strikes, boycotts, and demonstrations) as well as militant confrontational strategies (e.g., disruptions, assaults on property, and verbal violence). Ultimately, confrontational persuasion sets social movements apart from institutions in the status quo by demonstrating that existing institutions are illegitimate and in need of change.

Social movement leaders also use the internet and social media to establish legitimacy and draw attention to their cause. According to Tufekci (2014), social and digital media help protestors capture public attention, evade censorship efforts, and coordinate protest events. Given that legacy media (e.g., television and radio) are "no longer the gatekeepers of information, public attention is more easily captured through citizen-driven information dispersion" (LeFebvre & Armstrong, 2018, p. 11). Also, the speed of information dispersion through social media allows social movement leaders to respond quickly to threats from the police, government, and other actors (LeFebvre & Armstrong, 2018). Finally, social media are said to democratize social movement persuasion given that they provide a way for citizens to broadcast their concerns and express themselves, and these platforms make the general public less reliant on elites for information (LeFebvre & Armstrong, 2018).

Although the #MeToo movement began in 2006, it gained a global audience when #MeToo went viral on Twitter in 2017. In their analysis of more than 2,000 #MeToo tweets, Schneider and Carpenter (2020) found that social media provided an ideal platform for the movement to gain attention. Further, their research showed that the hashtag provided users with the opportunity to disclose their past experiences with sexual assault and receive social support and validation.

Prescribing Courses of Action

A critical persuasive task that social movements confront is defining specific actions that must be taken to address the problems they are concerned with. In short, prescribing courses of action involves selling the social movement's ideology (Stewart et al., 2012). Zald (2000) defines social movement ideology as the "belief systems defending and attacking current social relations and the social system" (pp. 3–4). Put another way, Platt and Williams (2002) claim that ideology represents a "symbolic perspective regarding desired social conditions; it is an assemblage of ideas about the construction of activities and circumstances oriented to achieve interests and life experiences in an idealized past, present, and future" (p. 333). As this definition implies, ideologies drive social movement members to craft messages that describe the "movement's focus/exigence; identifies the locus of blame (individual, institutional, principles) for the exigence; codifies its beliefs, values, and positions on issues germane to the exigence; and presents a plan to solve the serious problem the exigence caused" (Zompetti et al., 2013, pp. 244–245).

Sorochan (2016) examined the ideology of the Occupy Wall Street (OWS) movement. Although many members of OWS were attracted to the movement because of their concerns about capitalism and greed, those concerns did not form the movement's core ideology. According to Sorochan (2016), it was democratic participation that was advanced as the "ultimate value regardless of whether it contributed to building democratic power oriented toward an egalitarian transformation of capitalism or undermining it" (pp. 23–24). Further, participation served as a way of challenging hegemonic forces in the status quo and advancing

FIGURE 4.7 The Black Lives Matter movement opposes police brutality and race-based violence.

the cause of class struggle. Ultimately, this focus on participation may have undermined the ability of OWS members to effectively engage in change and policy making. As Sorochan (2016) notes, the result of this ideology was a "lack of shared political principles, an overemphasis on organizational structure as the key to equity, and antirepresentational attitudes" (p. 38).

Mobilizing for Action

Movements must mobilize members and other constituents to address the problem; however, mobilizing individuals to join a social movement is not easy. As Stewart et al. (2012) note, ideals of individualism, belief in U.S. institutions, and fear of agitators dissuade many Americans from attending rallies and formally joining social movements.

Although there are a variety of strategies to mobilize followers, Platt and Williams (2002) note that leaders often "attempt to foment crises, thereby mobilizing participation. They also knowingly assert divergent information to different groups to encourage them to construct alternate but circumstantially relevant ideologies in order to mobilize them" (p. 337). In addition, LeFebvre and Armstrong (2018) assert that leaders may turn to social media to mobilize followers for both online and offline participation:

> Because social media platforms allow for speedy information dissemination and low cost forms of communication, they have been utilized by many

> groups hoping to mobilize citizens for physical engagement in protest events. Additionally, social media platforms serve as an outlet to those unable to uninterested in participating in physical protests allowing them to remain engaged with the subject of those protests and their broader social implications. (p. 12)

In fact, contemporary social movements would be remiss to ignore the reach that social media platforms can provide. Yet movements today must also contend with a political landscape that is becoming increasingly polarized. Thus, social movements need to heed ideological beliefs among the various audiences to which their messages are targeted as well as audiences not targeted directly by those messages—but who are likely to receive and respond to such messages. Put another way, "It is important to recognize that ideology can mobilize different segments of society with varying structural interests, each group with overlapping yet distinct ideological outlooks, to participate in a single organization" (Platt & Williams, 2002, p. 338).

Consider recent efforts to mobilize individuals for the March for Our Lives demonstrations in 2018. Estimates suggest that over 800,000 people, mostly students and young people, participated in the rally in Washington, DC, alone. Impressively, there were hundreds of similar demonstrations in the United States and around the world. According to Carty and Reynoso Barron (2019), the demonstrations reflected the Never Again Movement, which seeks to "call out politicians to go beyond 'thoughts and prayers' rhetoric after mass shootings and to actually change the gun laws" (p. 385). The Never Again Movement is perhaps the first to aggressively take on the National Rifle Association (NRA). While these demonstrations offer a powerful example of mobilizing individuals for action, much work remains to sustain the movement.

Sustaining the Movement

Social movements have life cycles, and leaders must continually work to sustain operations. Persuasion plays a vital role in justifying setbacks and delays and maintaining the viability and visibility of the movement. In terms of setbacks, Stewart et al. (2012) explain that movement leaders must explain them as well as any "lack of meaningful achievements or victories, why agreements with institutions remain unfulfilled or ineffective, and why target dates come and go without visible results" (p. 80). Social movement leaders also use persuasion to maintain the visibility of the movement. Stewart et al. (2012) discuss a few of the persuasive strategies movements use in the following terms:

> They try to remain visible through every means imaginable: billboards, bumper stickers, stickerettes, buttons, T-shirts, jewelry, uniforms and

> items of clothing, famous women paper dolls, coloring books, playing cards, Christmas cards, dial-a-message, and websites. They may select new symbols. They may use street newspapers, journals, and the Internet to communicate directly with members because commercial media ignore the movement or are perceived—correctly, research shows—to treat it unfairly. (p. 83)

Given setbacks and delays, emotional burnout of members, the constant need to fundraise, and many other factors, social movements face serious challenges to their viability. As a result, leaders rely on persuasion to bolster the morale of members, utilize legacy and digital media to assert the relevance of the cause to multiple audiences, and demonstrate that victory is inevitable if members remain faithful to the cause.

Summary

Persuasive campaigns are another area in which communicators attempt to positively influence the attitudes and behaviors of others. And social movements frequently aim to advocate for issues or causes that advance the common good. Those who care about such concerns would do well to study theories and research about persuasion. Whether you wish to help others or influence their behavior, persuasion provides the vehicle through which you can do so effectively. Using relevant theory and research as a guide will assist you in being more successful in your persuasive efforts.

The next chapter introduces you to the role that attitudes play in persuasion and outlines the key theories for predicting behavioral responses to persuasive messages.

Check Your Understanding Review Questions

1. What are the various types of persuasive campaigns?
2. Why is persuasion important in effective campaigns?
3. How do Functional Theory and Uses and Gratifications Theory inform the way individuals produce and consume persuasive political communication?
4. What are the constructs of the Health Belief Model?
5. How can the Commitment-Communication Model (CCM) be employed to guide the development of persuasive public awareness campaigns?

6. Why is persuasion critical for social movements?
7. How do social media platforms and political ideology affect social movements?

Key Terms

Commitment-Communication Model (p. 100)
confrontational persuasion (p. 105)
Extended Parallel Process Model (p. 94)
Functional Theory (p. 88)
Health Belief Model (p. 96)
persuasive public communication campaigns (p. 87)
Psychological Reactance Theory (p. 95)
recognition involvement (p. 100)
social movement (p. 102)
Uses and Gratifications Theory (p. 89)

Credits

Fig. 4.0: Copyright © 2019 by PatricioHurtado. Reprinted with permission.
Fig. 4.1: Source: https://www.loc.gov/pictures/resource/cph.3b50191/.
Fig. 4.2: Copyright © 2020 by Kelly Sikkema. Reprinted with permission.
Fig. 4.3: Copyright © 2019 by Madison Lavern. Reprinted with permission.
Fig. 4.4: Source: https://courses.lumenlearning.com/clinton-marketing/chapter/reading-advertising/.
Fig. 4.5: Copyright © 2017 by StockSnap. Reprinted with permission.
Fig. 4.6: Copyright © by Mike Fleshman (CC BY-SA 2.0) at https://commons.wikimedia.org/wiki/File:Occupy_Wall_Street_March_2012_foreclosure_banner.jpg.
Fig. 4.7: Copyright © 2020 by Ehimetalor Akhere Unuabona. Reprinted with permission.

CHAPTER 5

Theories Predicting Behavior

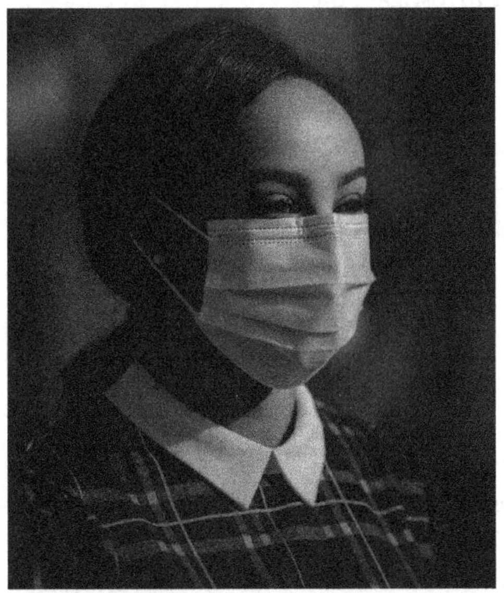

Chapter Objectives

After reading this chapter, you should be able to:

- Define attitude and behavior
- Understand the difference between attitudes and behavior
- Explain the relationship between attitudes and behaviors
- Understand the components of the theories of reasoned action and planned behavior as well as the reasoned action approach
- Know the implications of the theories of reasoned action and planned behavior as well as the reasoned action approach for persuasion and behavioral interventions
- Understand the components of Attitude Accessibility Theory

In this chapter, we will explore the role that attitudes play in persuasion and take a deep dive into the key theories predicting behavioral responses to persuasive messages (the attitude-behavior relationship). How can we predict behavior? Or, put another way, what factors predict behavior? That is the central issue around which the theoretical models addressed in this chapter revolve and has been the focus of an enormous amount of persuasion research (Petty et al., 1997). In one regard, you might think that behavior is so complicated that predicting it seems nearly impossible. And you would be right that it is complicated and, indeed, difficult to predict. So why try? Well, to truly understand how people respond to persuasive messages, we must investigate the factors that predict behavior as well as their antecedents. Okay, so why do we care about doing that? Ultimately, persuaders are interested in changing behavior, whether we want to change our own behavior (e.g., I want to exercise more or eat healthier in the coming year) or the behavior of others (e.g., we want bystanders to intervene and report sexual assault incidents on college campuses, or we want to increase compliance with campus nonsmoking policies). As a result, if we want to change behavior, then it is imperative for us to explore how our behaviors are formed and the factors that predict behavior.

Theory of Reasoned Action

Next, we want to direct your attention to a few of the most influential and widely researched theories about the attitude-behavior relationship. First up is a theory developed by social psychologists Martin Fishbein and Icek Ajzen. The **Theory of Reasoned Action** (TRA) examines the factors, or variables, that predict behavior. A meta-analysis is a study of other studies that pools the data sets of multiple studies to determine what we know across a line of research, which makes a meta-analysis more informative than a single-shot study. Two early meta-analyses of studies employing the TRA found strong support for the predictive utility of the TRA and for **behavioral intention** in determining actual behavior (Sheppard et al., 1988). In other words, the TRA posits that behavioral intentions lead to actual behaviors. Thus, we should be concerned about what predicts behavioral intention if we ultimately want to understand, affect, or predict behavior. A large body of research has produced data supporting the TRA. In fact, Sheppard et al. (1988) found that the TRA "has strong predictive utility, even when utilized to investigate situations and activities that do not fall within the boundary conditions originally specified for the model," such as activities involving an explicit choice among alternatives (p. 338).

Attitude Toward the Behavior

General dispositions, or attitudes, are poor predictors of behaviors in specific situations (Ajzen, 1991). Thus, the TRA includes one's attitude toward the specific

FIGURE 5.1 Awareness events for organ donation can help to create positive attitudes and subjective norms, which Wong and Chow (2017) found to be important influences on intentions to register to donate organs.

behavior in question. Behavioral beliefs influence **attitude toward the behavior** (Ajzen, 1991). Moreover, the TRA is concerned with “people’s attitude toward personally performing the behavior—that is, their positive or negative evaluation of their performing the behavior in question” (Fishbein & Ajzen, 2010, p. 20). Thus, attitude reflects an individual’s favorable or unfavorable disposition toward personally performing a specific behavior (Fishbein & Ajzen, 2010; Kruglanski et al., 2015). Consequently, it makes sense to discuss the role of attitude within the context of a specific behavior.

Consider, then, a qualitative study using focus group discussions about organ donation conducted by Wong and Chow (2017). Organ donation is a popular subject of research in both persuasion and health communication. And it is one where behavioral intention is especially important. Signing up or registering to be an organ donor is typically a fairly simple process in most locales; however, studies have shown that it is equally important for potential donors to make their intentions known to family members, significant others, and friends, as one’s survivors must also know one’s wishes. Wong and Chow discovered that the university students in Hong Kong who took part in the focus group discussions, not unlike younger individuals in many other countries, had not discussed their views on organ donation with their family, significant others, and friends. Moreover, while they personally supported the idea of organ donation and said their parents would also think positively about organ donation, they also tended to assume that their parents may be disturbed by going through such a consent process for their own child. Thus, the focus group participants were hesitant to discuss their attitudes toward organ donation with those closest to them, which can be problematic if laws where one lives require surviving family to consent to the donation of the deceased person's organs. Applying the TRA, Wong and Chow discovered that comments in the focus groups supported the importance of attitudes and subjective norms in the organ donation process. Of particular note, the investigators determined that "attitude involves both cognitive nature (such as cursing vs. blessing) as well as affective nature (such as unhappy vs. happy)" (Wong & Chow, 2017, p. 295). The university students from Hong Kong expressed positive thoughts about and acceptance of organ donation, but their attitudes became mixed when thinking about how the organ donation process, upon their death, might impact their family in terms of emotions, decision-making stress, and memories.

While not addressed in the initial TRA model, recent research has raised questions about attitudes and how they are formed. For example, do attitudes toward a behavior suggest anything about our goals? Kruglanski et al. (2015) point out that goals drive behaviors because attaining goals is accomplished through behaviors. Thus, attitudes or liking alone may not produce wanting, and wanting does not lead to goal commitment or behavior; only attitudes coupled with goals will lead to behaviors seeking goal attainment (Kruglanski et al., 2015). "Liking must be transmuted into wanting, wanting must evolve into a goal, the goal must

FIGURE 5.2 Protests supporting Black Lives Matter help shape attitudes and subjective norms regarding racism and police brutality.

be momentarily dominant, and the specific behavior must be chosen as means of goal pursuit" (Kruglanksi et al., 2015, p. 598). Can we predict attitudes? Expected outcome and political belief emerged as good predictors of attitude in a study examining e-participatory democracy in Nigeria (Oni et al., 2017).

Subjective Norm

Think about the image presented in Figure 5.2. What role might others play in an individual making a decision to participate in a protest? Injunctive normative beliefs, or—as we discussed in Chapter 1—what we think others think we should do, are determinants of subjective norms. Fishbein and Ajzen (2010) define **subjective norm** as the perception that those who are important to the individual in question wish, expect, or recommend the individual to either engage in or refrain from a specific behavior. Although the original TRA model explained and measured subjective norm as an **injunctive norm**, Fishbein and Ajzen (2010) now "recommend a measure of social norms that incorporates both

FIGURE 5.3 Messages encouraging donations often emphasize positive social norms. In this image, a number of diverse individuals can be seen raising their hands in support of an issue, which can serve to shape perceptions of social norms.

injunctive and descriptive norms" (p. 152). To fully appreciate this development, we should recognize that Fishbein and Ajzen (2010) regard injunctive norms as our perceptions of "what important others think we should do," while **descriptive norms** refer to our perceptions that "others have done, are doing, or are likely to do" (p. 151). Ultimately, they have concluded that subjective norm should be considered one's perception of the social norm, which necessarily includes both injunctive and descriptive norms.

In fact, recent studies have supported the ability of descriptive norms to predict behavioral intention and, ultimately, behavior. This path from descriptive norms to behavioral intentions is known as the Theory of Normative Social Behavior, which a study about indoor tanning by Carcioppolo et al. (2017) supported. They found that perceived descriptive norms predicted 46% of the variance in behavioral intentions. Interestingly, their data did not show a significant relationship between injunctive norms and behavioral intention.

Recall the study of organ donation intentions among university students in Hong Kong that Wong and Chow (2017) conducted. Their focus group data reinforced the importance of subjective norm in determining intentions to become organ donors. In particular, however, the comments of focus group participants emphasized the vital role that family (especially parents), friends, and respected others play in influencing their views about organ donation. Because parents emerged as the most prominent group influencing the students, Wong and Chow (2017) recommended that persuasive health campaigns switch "the focus to parents and encourage them to initiate discussion with their children" (p. 297). Remember that the focus group participants generally expressed positive attitudes toward organ donation but worried that their parents would be disturbed by the process. In this case, it seems that subjective norms might override attitudes toward the behavior. Despite expressing that their parents thought positively about organ donation, as did the students, the focus group participants worried that their loved ones would find it difficult to deal with the emotions of consenting to the donation of their own child's organs. Thus, the students were apparently reluctant to discuss organ donation with their parents. Wong and Chow's suggestion that campaigns focus on encouraging parents to

Engaged Persuasion Research: Social Media Affects Social Norms

How does the social media age affect perceptions of social norms? A study examining the impact that the number of views on a YouTube video made on perceptions of social norms found evidence to answer this question (Spartz et al., 2017). In the study, perceptions of social norms about the importance of climate change increased when there were a greater number of views of a YouTube video on the subject. The researchers, thus, concluded that "people can indeed be influenced by informational cues in social media environments" (Spartz et al., 2017, p. 11). In this particular case, study participants exposed to a YouTube video about climate change with a high number of views reported greater perceived importance of climate change to Americans. In other words, social media channels that allow us to see how many others have viewed the same content affect our perceptions of social norms.

discuss organ donation with their children does seem to be a good way to correct potential misperceptions of subjective norms.

Behavioral Intention

Behavioral intention is a central factor in the TRA. The stronger one's intention to perform a behavior is, the better behavioral intention will be at predicting actual behavior (Ajzen, 1991). Fishbein and Ajzen (2010) describe behavioral intention as "a readiness to perform the behavior" (p. 21). Underlying behavioral intention is an estimate of how likely or probable a person believes it is that they will engage in or perform a given behavior (Fishbein, 2008). A person's motivation to carry out a behavior is an essential component of their intention (Eagly & Chaiken, 1993). Intentions are the single best predictor of behavior, yet intentions do not always lead to behavior in cases where individuals are unable to act on their intentions (Fishbein, 2008).

According to the TRA, "When the behavior/situation affords a person complete control over behavioral performance, intentions alone should be sufficient to predict behavior" (Ajzen, 1991, p. 185). In fact, behavioral intentions are able to accurately predict actual behavior (Sheppard et al., 1988). Attitudes toward the behavior and subjective norm are independent antecedents of behavioral intention. Behavioral intention is considered an "immediate antecedent" of actual behavior because "people are expected to carry out their intentions when the opportunity arises" if they have "a sufficient degree of *actual* control over the behavior" (Ajzen, 2002, p. 665). Behavioral intentions, however, "do not always lead to successful enactment of the behavior" and prior meta-analyses indicate that only 38% of the variance in behavior can be explained by behavioral intention (Conner & Armitage, 1998, p. 1450). Researchers want to be able to account for as much variance as possible in the dependent variable they are measuring. Although, more recent meta-analyses have found the correlation between behavioral intention and behavior to range from .44 to .56 (Fishbein, 2008). A correlation of 1.00 would be a perfect correlation, so correlations of .44 to .56 are actually fairly good in social scientific research.

Theory of Planned Behavior

As an extension of the TRA, the **Theory of Planned Behavior** (TPB) adds the variable of perceived behavioral control to the theoretical model, which means all the TRA variables we just discussed are maintained in the TPB (see Figure 5.4). Look at Figure 5.4, and imagine that the box labelled "perceived behavioral control" is removed; then the figure would be the TRA rather than the TPB.

The addition of a single variable might not seem like a large difference, but when you consider Figure 5.4 carefully and think about the dashed line leading from perceived behavioral control to behavior, you can recognize that this new variable can add to the predictive power of behavioral intent or operate entirely separately from intent—which means the ramifications of this single variable are huge. The TPB "places the construct of self-efficacy belief or perceived behavioral control within a more general framework of the relations among beliefs, attitudes, intentions, and behavior" (Ajzen, 1991, p. 184). The combination of behavioral intention and perceived behavioral control, then, is able to predict a substantial proportion of the variance in actual behavior. "At its core, the TPB is concerned with the prediction of intentions" (Ajzen, 2011, p. 1115). The TPB is one of the most influential and frequently cited models for predicting behavior, with several meta-analyses suggesting that it predicts intentions and behavior at levels close to the theoretical limit (Ajzen, 2011).

The words "reasoned" and "planned" make it sound as if our behavior is carefully considered. Critics as well as some supporters of the two theories point this out. Both the TRA and TPB "can be considered as deliberative processing models, as they imply that individuals make behavioral decisions based on careful consideration of available information" (Conner & Armitage, 1998, p. 1430). Although, Fishbein and Ajzen (2010) claim they have never held the position that people must be rational and deliberate decision-makers. In fact, Ajzen (2011) explains that neither the TRA nor the TPB assume that people are rational actors or that they always make decisions based on accurate information; instead, people may act on incomplete or inaccurate information when forming beliefs and may base decisions on perceptions that rely on faulty or irrational premises.

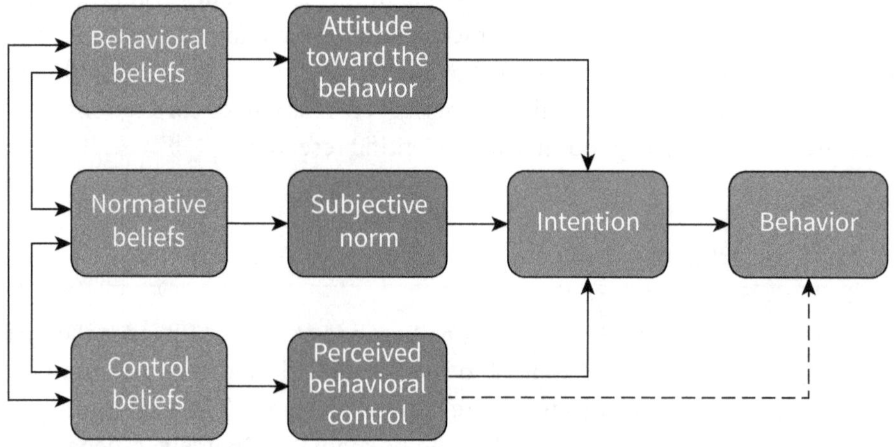

FIGURE 5.4 Theory of Planned Behavior (Hrubes et al., 2001).

"Intentions and behavior follow reasonably from these kinds of considerations, often spontaneously without much cognitive effort" (Ajzen, 2012, p. 24).

Perceived Behavioral Control

The concept of **perceived behavioral control** encompasses the ability, or behavioral control, one perceives to have over one's behavior. Ajzen (1991) defines perceived behavioral control as "people's perception of the ease or difficulty of performing the behavior of interest" (p. 183). It is the perception of one's behavioral control, or their expectations about being capable of performing a behavior given available resources and their ability to overcome obstacles they encounter (Ajzen, 2002; Fishbein & Ajzen, 2010; Albarracin et al., 2001), that is important to grasp. For Fishbein and Ajzen (2010), "perceived behavioral control reflects both internal and external factors that may facilitate or impede performance of a given behavior" (p. 177). For instance, while you might have control over what you eat, whether or not you will change your dietary habits largely depends on how in control of your nutritional consumption you perceive yourself to be. If you perceive your dietary habits to be difficult to control due to having a job that means you are on the road traveling quite often, then you may perceive situational factors to be more in control than you are of your food options. Or, if you are back home for the holidays, you might perceive your eating habits to be tough to control when your family and friends are providing the food options.

Ajzen (2002) compares perceived behavioral control to the concept of perceived self-efficacy, which is how effectively one believes they can execute behaviors. In other words, perceived behavioral control represents one's confidence in their ability to perform a behavior. Of course, Ajzen (2002) points out that realistic perceptions of our behavioral control are necessary. This means that all the confidence in the world that I can become an astronaut will not make it so. Thus, when one does not have complete **volitional control** (meaning conscious control), measuring perceived behavioral control, as the TPB does, provides better predictions of actual behavior than the TRA model is able to provide (Ajzen, 1991).

Measurements of perceived behavioral control should include survey items that tap into self-efficacy and controllability, or the locus of control, which multiple factor analyses have shown to be the two dimensions of perceived behavioral control (Ajzen, 2002). More recently, Fishbein and Ajzen (2010) have relabelled the dimensions of perceived behavioral control as capacity (e.g., self-efficacy) and autonomy (e.g., controllability). The degree of control people have over their behaviors is best considered on a continuum, from easily controlled behaviors, like brushing your teeth in the morning, to those that are more difficult to execute, such as becoming an astronaut (Eagly & Chaiken, 1993). In the end, the addition of

> **Engaged Persuasion Activity: Organ Donation**
>
> Using the components of the TPB, create an outline of a persuasive campaign to encourage organ donation. What would your message need to include? What would the campaign need to know or measure among your target audience to effectively predict their likelihood to become organ donors? How will you go about measuring each of the variables included in the TPB?

perceived behavioral control that the TPB adds to the TRA provides "a more comprehensive model that applies to behaviors that require skills and resources and thus do not occur merely because people decide to act" (Eagly & Chaiken, 1993, p. 189).

Attitudes toward the behavior, subjective norm, and perceived behavioral control are "three conceptually independent determinants" of behavioral intention (Ajzen, 1991, p. 188). Favorable attitudes toward the behavior and subjective norms with respect to the behavior, coupled with greater perceived behavioral control, will more strongly and positively predict behavioral intention (Ajzen, 1991). Control beliefs underlie and provide the basis for perceptions of behavioral control (Ajzen, 1991). "Because many behaviors pose difficulties of execution that may limit volitional control, it is useful to consider perceived behavioral control in addition to intention" (Ajzen, 2002, pp. 665–666). Can adding a measure of perceived behavioral control allow researchers to better predict behavior? Ajzen (2002) argues that "a measure of perceived behavioral control can serve as a proxy for actual control and contribute to the prediction of the behavior in question" (p. 666).

FIGURE 5.5 Engagement can lead to behavior change.

Perceived behavioral control can both indirectly, via behavioral intention, and directly predict behavior (Ajzen, 2002; Fishbein & Ajzen, 2010). Past behavior can influence perceptions of behavioral control. More specifically, if a person has performed a behavior in the past, then the likelihood they will perceive having control over that behavior is greater (Albarracin et al., 2001). It is also possible for behavioral interventions to increase perceptions of behavioral control (Albarracin et al., 2001), possibly by instilling confidence about controlling one's behavior in the target audience.

Predicting Behavior

In 1991, Azjen noted that "the large number of studies" on the TRA and TPB "have clearly established the utility of the distinctions by showing that the different constructs stand in predictable relations to intentions and behaviors" (p. 199). Since 1991, plenty more empirical research on the TRA and TPB have been conducted, with additional evidence supporting the theories. Ajzen (1991) explains that the TPB is able to accurately predict and account for a large proportion of the variance in actual behavior, which is supported by a large body of empirical studies. Beck and Ajzen (1991) found the TPB to accurately predict dishonest actions, specifically shoplifting, lying to get out of assignments, and, especially, student cheating on tests.

More recently, however, these reasoned action models, as they are called, have also received their fair share of criticism, and some have even called to retire the reasoned action models. So let's consider a few of the criticisms levied against the TRA and TPB.

Based on "a number of studies showing past behavior to be the best predictor of future behavior," some contend that cognition models such as the TRA and TPB are not better at predicting future behavior, which is certainly true with habitual processes (Conner & Armitage, 1998, p. 1436). Beck and Ajzen (1991) observed that "there is considerable consistency in dishonest behaviors over time, and that this consistency is not fully reflected in the constructs of the theory of planned behavior" (p. 300). In response, Ajzen (1991) argued that past behavior provides a test of sufficiency of the TPB. "Repetition of behavior should lead to enhanced perceptions of control" (Conner & Armitage, 1998, p. 1437). And past behavior contributes to the predictions of behavioral intention and actual behavior once all the TPB variables are accounted for (Conner & Armitage, 1998). Alone, past behavior adds approximately 2% of the variance accounted for in actual behavior to the TPB, a relatively small contribution (Azjen, 1991).

Recall our discussion of the model of dual attitudes discussed in Chapter 1. According to Wilson et al. (2000), this model holds significant implications for the attitude-behavior relationship in that it is dependent on the type of attitude (implicit or explicit) the individual holds and the type of behavior (implicit or explicit) in question. In other words, they caution that the "same individual can have both an implicit attitude and an explicit attitude, which predict different kinds of behavior" (Wilson et al., 2000, p. 121). The implication is that the TRA and TPB do not account for different kinds of behavioral reactions.

How well do the TRA and TPB fair based on the empirical evidence? There has certainly been some criticism of the models, but there is overall support for the models across the research literature. Ogden (2003) reviewed 47 research studies published in four health psychology journals over a 5-year period. She concluded that TRA and TPB, along with the Health Belief Model and Protection

Motivation Theory, cannot be tested and might alter cognitions and behaviors rather than describing them. Furthermore, she concluded that study results did not support predicted relationships, were not subject to tests of falsification, and were true by definition but not observation. Azjen and Fishbein (2004) defend the reasoned action models, which include both TRA and TPB, against Ogden's attacks by pointing to meta-analyses that find strong support for the models. For instance, Armitage and Conner's (2001) meta-analysis of 185 previous studies showed that TPB accounted for 39% of the variance in behavioral intention and 27% of the variance in behavior. Specifically, Azjen and Fishbein contend that measures are valid, which means accurate in the language of quantitative research methods, and that the model accounts for a substantial proportion of variance in both behavioral intention and behavior. Statistically speaking, the greater the variance accounted for, the better the ability to predict or explain. While they admit that individual studies may fail to provide support, the body of research as a whole is consistent with the theoretical models.

Conner and Armitage (1998) argued that most studies of the TRA and TPB were based on correlational data and self-report data, failing to test causal claims about behavioral predictions. "There is evidence to suggest that the TPB only provides an account of the determinants of behavior when both motivation and opportunity to process information are high" (Conner & Armitage, 1998, p. 1452). More recently, Sniehotta et al. (2014) called for the retirement of the TPB. In so doing, they pointed to longitudinal studies and experimental evidence that fail to support the predictive validity of the TPB. In response, Armitage (2015) contends that the lack of experimental studies does not justify retiring the TPB. Armitage and Conner's (2001) later meta-analysis also provided a range of support for and insight into the TPB. For instance, they found that perceived behavioral control "accounted for significant amounts of variance in intention and behaviour, independent of theory of reasoned action variables" (Armitage & Connor, 2001, p. 471). The variance accounted for was 11% higher when studies employed self-report measures as opposed to objective measures or observations. Consistent with prior meta-analyses, Armitage and Conner (2001) found support for the TPB's ability to predict intention as well as behavior (with medium to large effect sizes), some evidence of discriminant validity, and concluded that TPB is more effective than TRA since perceived behavioral control "adds—on average—6% to the prediction of intention, over

Engaged Persuasion Research: Hunting Intentions

The TPB has been studied in a variety of specific contexts to determine if the theoretical model supports behaviors in these particular situations. For instance, Hrubes et al. (2001) examined hunting behaviors. Their results indicated that behavioral intentions about hunting predicted the frequency of self-reported past hunting behaviors. The researchers also found that attitudes, subjective norms, and perceived behavioral control influenced hunting intentions. However, perceived behavioral control did not, meaning that hunting is a matter of volitional control.

and above attitude and subjective norm" (p. 486). In other words, perceived behavioral control is able to both directly and indirectly influence behavior, making it a helpful addition to the TRA. However, the meta-analysis indicated that "self-efficacy should be the preferred measure of 'perceived control' within the TPB" (Armitage & Connor, 2001, p. 488).

Designing Interventions

The TPB is helpful to scholars seeking to understand the effects of persuasion on behavior and to practitioners seeking to implement behavioral interventions (Ajzen, 1991). In essence, the root of the TPB is in examining behavioral determinants, any one of which could serve as a point of attack for interventions seeking to change behavior (Ajzen, 1991). When individuals have complete volitional control over a specified behavior, the TRA would suffice, whereas the TPB and accounting for perceived behavioral control can address instances "in which people may lack complete volitional control over the behavior of interest" (Ajzen, 2002, p. 666; see also Fishbein & Ajzen, 2010).

One of the strongest contributions of the reasoned action approach to predicting behavior is that it offers guidance to persuasive campaigns in constructing and targeting behavioral interventions. "Behavioral prediction has important implications for behavioral change interventions" (Fishbein & Ajzen, 2010, p. 407). Whether we wish to persuade others to engage in a desired behavior, or want others to stop performing an undesirable behavior, the reasoned action approach highlights the role of behavioral intention and perceived behavioral control, as well as their antecedents, in our efforts. The reasoned action models also incorporate attitudes and beliefs into the prediction of behavior, meaning that three of the four aims of persuasion we discussed in Chapter 1 are present (i.e., attitudes, beliefs, and behaviors). Meanwhile, values serve as background variables by indirectly influencing beliefs and attitudes (Ajzen, 1991; Hrubes et al., 2001).

The TPB has influenced the successful design and evaluation of a multitude of behavior change interventions (Ajzen, 2012). A TPB-inspired, print-based persuasive campaign aimed at increasing student compliance with a campus tobacco-free policy demonstrated positive behavioral changes in response to the campaign (Record et al., 2017). Based on the campaign results, the researchers recommended encouraging voluntary compliance, theory-driven campaigns and prior focus group testing. As Ajzen (2012) contends, "Behavior change interventions must accomplish two major objectives: they must motivate individuals to perform the behavior, and once this has been accomplished, they must ensure that the behavior will be carried out" (p. 22).

Given what we discuss about WEIRD populations (meaning Western, educated, industrialized, rich, and democratic; Rad et al., 2018) in Appendix B, we must be cautious about one-size-fits-all interventions. Behavioral interventions may be successful in one culture but not in another (Fishbein, 2008). Thus, persuasive messages and behavioral interventions ought to be pretested with the target population carefully before a persuasive campaign is fully implemented (Fishbein, 2008).

While theories predicting behavior and behavior change are certainly helpful, Fishbein (2008) acknowledges that they do not provide us guidance about how to design persuasive messages or behavioral interventions that can successfully change or reinforce beliefs. He bemoans the inability of research on persuasive communication to explain the factors that lead to someone either accepting or rejecting an argument or particular piece of information. Other chapters in this textbook will address these concerns.

Those designing interventions certainly need to know which TPB constructs to target in their persuasive messages and campaigns. While each construct or variable plays a more or less influential role in predicting behavior, and some differences have emerged in studies related to particular behaviors, "these constructs may work together synergistically to produce change" (Montanaro et al., 2018, p. 757). In other words, interventions ought not to target only certain constructs; in fact, it can be quite difficult to affect one construct without affecting others (Montanaro et al., 2018). In their study of risky sexual behavior, Montanaro et al. found that interventions aimed at all four constructs (e.g., attitudes, norms, perceived behavioral control, and intentions) produced the greatest changes in behavior. They concluded that "all four constructs in the TPB potentially need to be targeted in order to create change" and that "interventions focusing on attitude change alone would be uniquely unsuccessful at reducing risky sexual behavior" (Montanaro et al., 2018, p. 766). Chang (1998) also found that attitude toward the behavior and subjective norm were not as independent from other theoretical constructs as the reasoned action approaches hypothesize.

FIGURE 5.6 Social media and mobile technology play crucial roles in persuasion.

Integrating Social Media

As we have discussed in prior chapters, social media can play a crucial role in persuasion, sometimes altering the messaging strategies needed or affecting how persuasive messages are processed. Using the TPB, Namkoong et al. (2017) implemented an interactive antismoking campaign on social media. Their findings showed that increased media use played a vital role in changing students' "attitudes and perceived social norms about smoking behaviors, and eventually reducing smoking intention" (p. 41). Overall, the study contributed to the body of evidence supporting the ability of the TPB to predict behavioral intention. The study investigated the mediating role of interactive media use in a persuasive health campaign. More specifically, though, interactive social media demonstrated indirect effects mediated by descriptive norms, played a unique role in mediating intervention effects on attitudes, and increased internet use thereby directly effecting attitudes. One noteworthy insight emerged: "As the treatment-group participants used the Internet more frequently to develop campaign ideas, they experienced greater influence on their own attitudes toward smoking behaviors" (Namkoong et al., 2017, p. 47). Consequently, the researchers stressed the practical implications of using social media to reach young adults and using social network sites or interactive media as a means of persuasion. Implementing the antismoking campaign on social media encouraged students "to play active roles in developing campaign ideas, which influenced their communicative behaviors and eventually their attitudes toward the issue of the campaign" (Namkoong et al., 2017, p. 47).

Another interesting study, using the TPB framework and new media platforms, proved effective in promoting bystander intervention and reducing campus sexual assault (Sundstrom et al., 2018). The study compared persuasive messages employing print-only messages with those integrating social media (see Figure 5.7). Although the A and B conditions do not include pictures or students or hashtags, notice that they do include QR codes—so perhaps a bit of a mix between traditional media and technology. Meanwhile, we may also want to consider that the students in the C and D conditions appear to be different genders, which fits the specific messages they are holding up in the images. If the researchers had used the same rather than different genders in conditions C and D, do you think that would have had an impact? While the printed flyers with QR codes proved to be effective, with 44% of participants preferring them, the social media enhanced messages using QR codes and hashtags were particularly successful in producing favorable attitudes toward the message among participants as well as enhancing behavioral intentions. More specifically, participants exposed to the messages in Figure 5.7 reported more favorable attitudes about intervening if they saw a sexual assault occurring as well as greater intention to intervene to prevent sexual assault. Participants who viewed the messages in Figure 5.7 also reported thinking that others would support their decision to intervene, thus suggesting more favorable social norms. "Students preferred all forms of new media, in combination, over traditional media. In order to reach college students, the use of new media is critical" (Sundstrom et al., 2018, p. 1148). In this case, the TPB was able to predict bystander intervention behavior.

Of course, online communication and new media are not helpful in changing all behaviors. In one study of mothers with young children, that followed the reasoned action approach we will cover in greater detail later in this chapter, McKeever and McKeever (2017) found "a significant, direct, negative association between time spent online and breastfeeding intentions" (p. 1059). More specifically, more time spent on motherhood websites resulted in lower reported intentions to breastfeed young children for a full year after childbirth. Additionally, attitudes, norms, and perceived behavioral intentions did not follow theoretically described roles in the process and "were unable to explain the unique contribution

(a)

(b)

(c)

(d)

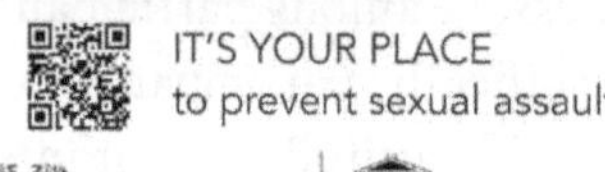

Printed campaign material examples. This figure illustrates (a, b) text-only campaign messages, and (c, d) student-led social media white board posters.

FIGURE 5.7 The *It's Your Place* campaign (Sundstrom et al., 2018) examined how new media platforms could influence behavioral intentions of college students to intervene when they see sexual assault, which is an example of the Theory of Planned Behavior.

of time spent on motherhood-specific websites in predictions intentions" to breastfeed (McKeever & McKeever, 2017, p. 1063). The researchers thus recommend that "health communicators may need to meet mothers here they are—and that may mean meeting them online" (McKeever & McKeever, 2017, p. 1063).

TRA or TPB

So is it better to use the TRA or the TPB? The answer depends on the type of control an individual has over a given behavior and whether perceived behavioral control will provide additional predictive input about a given behavior. In a study examining 10 different behaviors representing varying degrees of control over the behavior, Madden et al. (1992) found "that inclusion of perceived behavioral control enhances the prediction of behavioral intention and behavior," particularly if the behavior is problematic with regard to control (p. 3).

When behaviors are under volitional control, the TRA model is all that is needed. For instance, in a meta-analysis of 96 data sets concerning condom use, both the TRA and TPB demonstrated strong predictive capabilities; however, because perceived behavior control fared better when studies measured past behavior as compared to future behavior, the effect of perceived behavioral control on condom use was statistically small (Albarracin et al., 2001). In the case of condom use, therefore, the TRA model seems to perform better than the TPB.

On the other hand, a meta-analysis of 72 studies examining physical activity showed that while both the TRA and TPB exhibited good fit to the data, the TPB's perceived behavioral control augmented by self-efficacy accounted for more variance in both physical activity intentions and behavior (Hagger et al., 2002). Another meta-analysis of 56 studies applying the TPB to health-related behaviors found that "intention remained the most important predictor, but in half of the studies reviewed perceived behavioral control significantly added to the prediction" (Godin & Kok, 1996, p. 87). Likewise, a meta-analysis of 31 studies demonstrated that the TPB was superior to the TRA in predicting exercise behavior (Hausenblas et al., 1997). Although the researchers concluded that their meta-analysis data showed that "the theory of reasoned action is a good theory" and that "its extension, the theory of planned behavior, is an even better theory" (Hausenblas et al., 1997, p. 47), the reality is that the specific behavior of interest as well as the ability of perceived behavioral control to predict unique variance actually determines whether the TRA or TPB is the better approach. Chang (1998) concluded that the TPB was better than the TRA at predicting immoral and unethical behavior (e.g., illegal copying of software). He further discovered that perceived behavioral control was better than attitude at predicting behavioral intention, in part because the TRA fails to account for resources and opportunity in predicting unethical behavior.

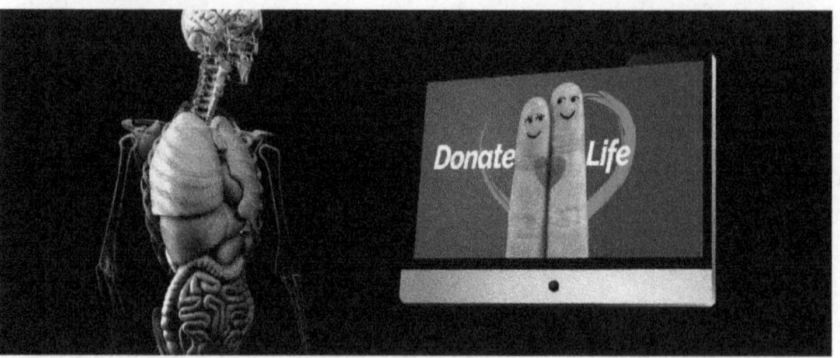

FIGURE 5.8 Organ donation campaign.

The Reasoned Action Approach

"A reasoned action approach to the explanation and prediction of social behavior assumes that people's behavior follows reasonably from their beliefs about performing a behavior" (Fishbein, 2008, p. 835). Consequently, behavioral intention is the single best predictor of behavior according to the **reasoned action approach** (Fishbein, 2008). The reasoned action approach extends the TPB by dividing each of the constructs (attitude toward behavior, perceived norm, and perceived behavioral control) into two subcomponents (McEachan et al., 2016). Thus, the key distinction between the TPB and the reasoned action approach lies in the subcomponents, or antecedents.

A meta-analysis of the reasoned action approach, which included 62 studies, found that the various subcomponents demonstrated utility in predicting and understanding health behaviors, with only autonomy failing to emerge as a significant predictor (McEachan et al., 2016). The meta-analytic data discovered direct effects for experiential attitude and descriptive norm on behavior as well as "the lack of direct effect on intention or behavior for autonomy" (McEachan et al., 2016, p. 606). Furthermore, the data demonstrated the value of the subcomponents in understanding predictors of health behaviors. "Although less parsimonious than the TPB," the reasoned action approach's subcomponents offer "unique insights into the determinants of health behaviors" (McEachan et al., 2016, p. 608).

So, how can we best predict behavior? Well, as with most questions concerning persuasion, the answer is it depends. To clarify, from the perspective of the reasoned action approach, which encompasses both the TRA and TPB, Fishbein and Ajzen (2010) explain:

> Under certain conditions, attitudes tend to carry more weight than perceived norms or perceived control whereas under other conditions, perceived control or perceived social norms may become more important.

> Similarly, whereas the behavior of some individuals is influenced more by normative than attitudinal considerations, the behavior of other individuals is influenced primarily by attitudinal factors. (pp. 217–218)

As a whole, the TRA and TPB have persisted for more than 4 decades of academic research and garnered a great deal of empirical support. As Fishbein and Ajzen (2010) conclude:

> Attitudes, perceived social norms, and perceived behavioral control—when considered simultaneously, are found to account for a considerable proportion of the nonrandom variance in intentions, and intentions and perceived control are found to explain a sizable proportion of the variance in behaviors. This is true across a wide variety of behaviors in many different behavioral domains. (p. 408)

Some scholars have proposed adding identity as a subcomponent to the reasoned action framework in various ways as a background variable; yet, a study by Paquin and Keating (2017) testing competing models of integrating identity into the framework failed to yield support to the notion of including identity. Their findings "call into question the basis for considering identity as an additional predictor of behavioral intention" (Paquin & Keating, 2017, p. 61).

One of the latest formulations of the reasoned action approach (see Figure 5.9) is the Integrative Model of Behavioral Prediction. Does Figure 5.9 look vaguely familiar? That is because all the variables included in Figure 5.4, which we examined earlier in this chapter, are also present here. However, you will notice that Figure 5.9 now includes a large set of background influence variables in the left-hand column as well as two additional variables that influence how behavioral intention impacts behavior. Notice that the integrative model is not as parsimonious, or simple, as the TPB, but it is more comprehensive. As Fishbein (2008) explains, the integrative model of behavioral prediction maintains all the variables included in the TRA and TPB but also accounts for background influences, descriptive as well as injunctive norms, and actual control (e.g., skills and abilities as well as environmental factors). Using the integrative model of behavioral prediction to test message strategies promoting healthy sleeping behavior among college students, one study found that while attitudes and perceived behavioral control were the best predictors of intentions and behavior, control beliefs about stress and time management demonstrated promise (Robbins & Niederdeppe, 2015). Wang (2020) employed the integrative model to explore predictors of organ donation intentions in China. Results demonstrated that self-efficacy, subjective norms, and anticipated guilt had moderate to strong relationships with donor registration intentions.

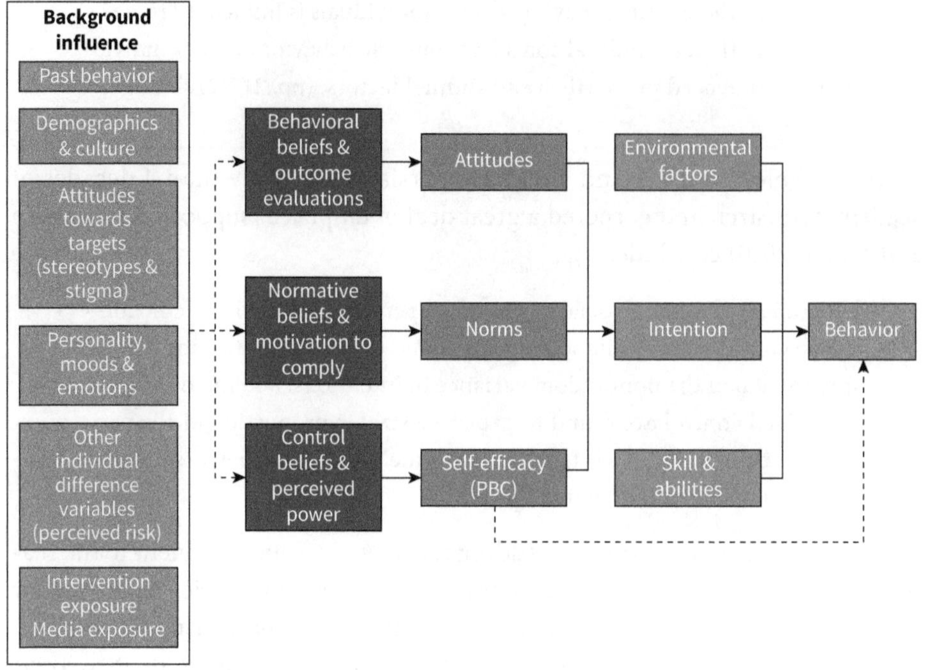

FIGURE 5.9 A Reasoned Action Approach (Fishbein, 2008).

Attitude Accessibility Theory

Are there times when you do not take a reasoned approach when deciding how to behave? Consider an evening after a long day of classes. Starving, you suddenly recall the slogan "I'm loving it," and an image of the golden arches pops into your mind. In the next moment, you head to McDonald's to grab dinner. According to Fazio (1990), in this scenario your positive attitudes toward McDonald's are readily accessible. In fact, the central premise of Attitude Accessibility Theory is that attitudes will influence behavior to the extent that they can be activated at the time a decision needs to be made. Importantly, research by Rocklage and Fazio (2018) demonstrates that the "more an attitude is based on emotion, the more accessible it is in memory, particularly for positive attitudes" (p. 516).

Over the years, research in this area has sought to uncover the nature of the attitude-behavior relationship, the conditions under which attitudes predict behavior, and the processes that allow attitudes to guide behavior. According to Schuette and Fazio (1995), the **Motivation and Opportunity as Determinants of Behavior (MODE) Model** stipulates that attitudes guide behavior through one of two processes—"a fairly spontaneous process based on the automatic activation of a relevant attitude or a more effortful, deliberative process involving careful consideration of the available information" (p. 704).

According to the MODE model, two prerequisites must be met for spontaneous processing to influence behavior. First, the attitude toward the object must be activated from memory. Second, the attitude must serve as a filter, coloring the way the individual views the object. This kind of processing lies in stark contrast to the processing proposed by the reasoned action approach. Importantly, Fazio and colleagues do not deny the claim that individuals sometimes think very carefully and critically about their attitudes toward behaviors. Instead, the MODE model seeks to integrate spontaneous and reasoned processing in the same framework. As Schutte and Fazio (1995) note, "Preexisting attitudes will govern people's judgments and behavior—unless the individuals are motivated to engage in deliberative processing and given sufficient opportunity to do so" (p. 705).

Research supports the efficacy of Attitude Accessibility Theory in a wide range of contexts. Attitude accessibility has been shown to confer resistance to persuasion through inoculation. Pfau et al. (2003) found that inoculation treatments elicit attitude accessibility, which bolsters attitude strength. Attitude strength then fosters resistance to the influence of counterattitudinal messages. We will discuss Inoculation Theory in more detail in Chapter 9.

Attitude accessibility also explains the persuasiveness of advertising. Berger and Mitchell (1989) assigned participants to one of four experimental conditions designed to assess their perceptions of marketing materials for new candy bars. In the direct experience condition, participants tasted the candy bars. In the single repetition condition, participants viewed an advertisement for each candy bar. In the two multiple-repetition conditions, participants were shown the same ads three or four times. The results indicated that repeated exposure to ads produced attitudes that were "just as accessible from memory and held with as much confidence as attitudes formed on the basis of direct behavioral experience" (Berger & Mitchell, 1989, p. 277). Further, findings revealed that highly accessible attitudes were highly predictive of future behavior.

Attitude Accessibility Theory can also be applied to health communication campaigns. For example, Rhodes et al. (2008) examined the role attitude accessibility plays in smokers' processing of antismoking public service announcements (PSAs). Participants in this study viewed several PSA types communicating social disapproval of smoking, regulation of smoking to reduce secondhand exposure, the dangers of environmental tobacco smoke exposure, and attacks on the tobacco industry. The findings demonstrated that the accessibility of tobacco-related attitudes caused smokers to process the antismoking messages centrally. More importantly, these accessible attitudes "set the stage for defensive processing leading to rejection to the message" (Rhodes et al., 2008, p. S230). In other words, the antismoking ads backfired for smokers. In terms of the implications for health campaigns that seek to reduce smoking, Rhodes et al.

suggest that designers should avoid messages that may be perceived as biased by smokers. Instead, messages should be employed to encourage receivers to think about important people in their social circles who do not want them to smoke.

Scholars have also applied Attitude Accessibility Theory to the context of beer consumption. Initially, Descheemaeker et al. (2014) note that alcohol consumption can lead to a host of negative health and interpersonal outcomes. Further, they argue that better understanding the relationship between attitudes toward alcohol and consumption can lead to the development of prevention and treatment strategies. With that in mind, they conducted an experiment to assess attitude accessibility and beer consumption. Using low alcohol beer, they presented participants with three pitchers of beer, three pitchers of water, and a cup. The behavioral measures were the amount of beer poured and consumed subtracted by the amount of water poured and consumed. Participants also completed measures of their attitudes toward beer. The results showed that attitudes toward beer were predictive of the amount of beer poured and consumed for participants whose attitude toward beer was highly accessible but not for participants who had low or moderate levels of attitude accessibility.

Finally, Attitude Accessibility Theory sheds light on some of the health and stress concerns that students face as they transition to college. Fazio and Powell (1997) hypothesized that first-year students who enter college knowing what they like and dislike about academic issues should experience better health in this setting compared to students who have not developed such attitudes. In this study, participants completed a set of measures assessing their academic interests as well as their physical and mental health. In order to measure the impact of attitude accessibility over time, participants completed the same measures 2 months later. Fazio and Powell found that attitude accessibility moderated the relationship between stress and health on all measures. Specifically, they found that students with more accessible attitudes toward academics "do not appear to have been as adversely affected by the stressors they were experiencing" (Fazio & Powell, 1997, p. 433). The authors conclude that students who enter college knowing what they like and dislike about academics (e.g., courses, majors, types of classes, and other academic activities) are better able than their peers who do not have accessible attitudes to focus their mental and emotional resources on coping effectively with stress.

Summary

In this chapter, we have taken a deep dive into a few of the most prominent and widely researched theories about behavior change. Specifically, we learned about the TRA, TPB, and the reasoned action approach to predicting behavior.

At the beginning of this chapter, we said that, as students of persuasion, we are interested in behavior because we sometimes want to change our own behavior or the behavior of others. Understanding the theory behind behavior change and the variables that predict behavior is crucial for persuasion practitioners. If we use theory and empirical findings to guide the design and implementation of interventions aimed at changing behavior, we stand a far better chance of successfully persuading target audiences than we do otherwise. We also learned how important it is to predict behavioral intention if we ultimately want to change actual behavior. Finally, we explored the conditions under which spontaneous processing may affect behaviors when attitudes are readily accessible.

The next chapter elucidates the methods of constructing persuasive messages, including persuasive argument construction and appeals.

Check Your Understanding Review Questions

1. What is the attitude-behavior relationship?
2. How does behavioral intention lead to behavior?
3. What variables and their antecedents predict behavioral intention?
4. How does the theory of reasoned action differ from the Theory of Planned Behavior?
5. What does the reasoned action approach add to the TRA and TPB?
6. How can persuasive interventions be designed and implemented to be successful in changing behavioral intention and behavior?
7. Why is perceived behavioral control important in predicting behavioral intention and behavior?

Key Terms

attitude toward the behavior (p. 113)
behavioral intention (p. 112)
descriptive norms (p. 116)
injunctive norms (p. 115
MODE Model (p. 130)
perceived behavioral control (p. 119)
reasoned action approach (p. 128)
subjective norm (p. 115)
Theory of Planned Behavior (p. 117)
Theory of Reasoned Action (p. 112)
volitional control (p. 119)

Credits

Fig. 5.0: Copyright © 2020 by Gift Habeshaw. Reprinted with permission.

Fig. 5.1: Copyright © 2019 Depositphotos/RobertoGalan.

Fig. 5.2: Copyright © 2020 by Corey Young. Reprinted with permission.

Fig. 5.3: Copyright © 2016 Depositphotos/Rawpixel.

Fig. 5.4: Daniel Hrubes, Icek Ajzen, and John Daigle, from "Predicting Hunting Intentions and Behavior: An Application of the Theory of Planned Behavior," *Leisure Sciences*, vol. 23, no. 3, p. 166. Copyright © 2001 by Taylor & Francis Group.

Fig. 5.5: Copyright © 2020 by Alex Motoc. Reprinted with permission.

Fig. 5.6: Copyright © 2019 by Daniel Korpai. Reprinted with permission.

Fig. 5.7: Beth Sundstrom, et al., from "It's Your Place: Development and Evaluation of an Evidence-Based Bystander Intervention Campaign," *Health Communication*, vol. 33, no. 9, p. 1144. Copyright © 2017 by Taylor & Francis Group.

Fig. 5.8: Copyright © 2019 by geralt. Reprinted with permission.

Fig. 5.9: Martin Fishbein, from "A Reasoned Action Approach to Health Promotion," *Medical Decision Making*, vol. 28, no. 6, p. 13. Copyright © 2008 by Sage Publications.

CHAPTER 6

Constructing Persuasive Messages

Chapter Objectives

After reading this chapter, you should be able to:

- List and describe the components of the Toulmin Argument Model
- Explain the differences between gain- and loss-framed messages
- List and define the various types of persuasive appeals
- Understand how to optimally mix types of appeals to maximize persuasion
- Explain the components of the Extended Parallel Process Model
- Articulate the relationship between fear appeals and self-efficacy

How exactly are persuasive messages constructed? This chapter elucidates the methods of constructing persuasive messages, including persuasive argument construction, types of supporting materials, framing of persuasive messages, and types of persuasive appeals. Additionally, the Toulmin Argument Model and the Extended Parallel Process Model are two important parts of our discussion in this chapter. We have situated persuasion as a process of influence in previous chapters. Thus, you may be wondering why we are now talking about argumentation in relation to constructing persuasive messages. Well, let's throw that question back at you. How likely do you think it is for people to be influenced or persuaded by a message that is poorly constructed or has recognizable gaps in argumentation? Generally speaking, most audiences can recognize when persuasive messages lack sound argumentation. Also, consider that persuasive attempts may often come across, or be perceived, as argumentative. Have you ever tried to persuade a friend to try something they have not previously tried? A typical conversation of this nature might involve reluctance or resistance on your friend's part, which likely prompts you to incorporate persuasive appeals to convince your friend they will like it if they just try it. As you try your best persuasive pitch, your friend may say something like "Stop arguing with me." Does your friend have a point? Is persuasion argument? And does argumentation play a role in how we construct and support persuasive messages?

The answers to these questions are nuanced. In cases of rational argumentation where neither side is wrong, the role of argumentation "is to persuade rather than to prove, demonstrate or refute" (Bench-Capon, 2003, p. 429). Thus, some types of argumentation are persuasive. Nevertheless, the aims of persuasion and argumentation differ (Nettel & Roque, 2012). So how and where does persuasion and argumentation overlap? "There are argumentative discourses without persuasion and persuasive discourses without argumentation" (Nettel & Roque, 2012, p. 55). In other words, they do overlap, as in a Venn diagram, but are distinct constructs. Persuasive argumentation lies where there is overlap between argumentative and persuasive discourses (Nettel & Roque, 2012).

The Toulmin Argument Model

Think about the last time you had a robust conversation with someone about a controversial issue. How did you present your arguments? What kinds of evidence did you use to support your claims? How did you respond to the objections of others? What types of appeals did you find most effective? These questions address the core elements of effective arguments. Unfortunately, the term "argument" evokes negative connotations for many people. In the context of persuasive communication, we use the term argument to refer to the process of advancing claims supported by qualified evidence and sophisticated reasoning.

Argumentativeness refers to a focus on the content or issues, which means it is a positive characteristic to possess. So the next time someone tells you that you are being argumentative, keep in mind that the term itself in academic literature does not have the same negative connotation you have just been accused of exhibiting. Meanwhile, verbal aggression refers to a focus on attacking the person rather than the issues, which means that being verbally aggressive is a negative behavior.

As we noted in Chapter 1, many of the approaches to understanding persuasion discussed in this text are grounded in the social scientific tradition. Influenced by the fields of psychology, social psychology, sociology, and communication (among others), the social scientific approach to persuasion seeks to uncover the variables in senders or receivers of messages, or the messages themselves, that will more likely lead to a positive outcome of the attempt to persuade. An additional goal of the social scientific approach is to generalize the findings of research to other representative populations and contexts. In this chapter, we begin with a logical/philosophical approach to argumentation that outlines the major components of persuasive arguments. You will see that this model is also consistent with the social scientific research in argumentation and persuasion.

The **Toulmin Argument Model** was developed by British philosopher Stephen E. Toulmin (2003). Our slightly modified version of his model, represented in Figure 6.1, contains six elements: claims, evidence, evidence credibility statements, warrants, qualifiers, and rebuttals. An understanding of these elements and how they work together will help you become a more critical producer and consumer of persuasive arguments.

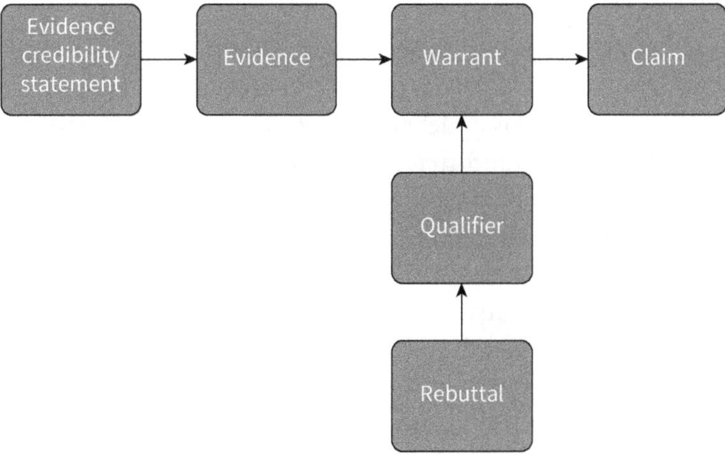

FIGURE 6.1 Toulmin Argument Model.

Claims

A **claim** represents the assertion or point that a persuader advocates. Generally, we advance claims of fact (claims that address whether something is true or not), value (claims that concern whether some action is right or wrong, moral or immoral, just or unjust, etc.), or policy (claims that concern what specific actions should or should not be taken). Consider the following claim regarding the cancellation of student loan debt:

> Cancellation of all student loan debt would significantly benefit the U.S. economy.

What are your initial impressions of this claim? Is this a claim of fact, value, or policy? As it is written, this statement advances a claim of fact. You should also note that the claim by itself is not persuasive. The claim could be bolstered if it were supported by credible evidence.

It is certainly possible to become confused about what type of claim is being advanced. To grasp this confusion, simply imagine a scenario wherein an acquaintance makes what appears to be a claim of fact (indeed, they probably believe it is a claim of fact) that is really a claim of value. We discuss claims of fact, value, and policy in much greater detail in Appendix A.

Evidence

In our version of Toulmin's model, **evidence** is employed to substantiate a persuader's claim and can take several forms, including statistics, analogies, facts, examples, testimony, and narrative. Consider the following evidence:

> Cancellation of all student loan debt would increase annual gross domestic product (GDP) in the U.S. by $22 billion and decrease the unemployment rate. (Steinbaum, 2018)

Is this appropriate evidence to support the claim that cancellation of all student loan debt would significantly benefit the U.S. economy? The evidence does establish the positive implications of debt cancellation for GDP and unemployment.

It is critical to understand that several factors combine to influence the overall persuasiveness of evidence, including the perceived credibility of the persuader, message delivery, and the persuader's familiarity with the evidence. In a meta-analysis of research on testimonial assertion evidence, Reinard (1998) found that evidence has relatively little impact when it is included in a speech that is delivered poorly, when the audience is familiar with the topic, and when the data presented are inconsistent with individuals' initial attitudes.

In examining the literature regarding the effectiveness of evidence, Reynolds and Reynolds (2002) note that it is most persuasive when recipients are aware of the evidence, it is processed centrally rather than peripherally, and it is judged as legitimate. A meta-analysis by Stiff (1986) also demonstrates that evidence is more effective when receivers process it centrally. Research further indicates that evidence is more likely to change attitudes and beliefs when it is plausible and novel rather than something the receivers have already heard several times before (Morely & Walker, 1987). Finally, research by Hunt (1972) suggests the use of evidence can increase the persuasiveness of low-credibility sources. Another way to strengthen the persuasiveness of evidence is by using evidence credibility statements.

Engaged Persuasion Research: Exploring the Persuasiveness of Narrative Evidence in the Climate Change Debate

In the case of climate change, narrative messages have been found to be persuasive across the political spectrum due to the ability of climate change stories to be relatable and engaging (Sangalang & Bloomfield, 2018). In other words, information about climate change presented in a narrative format is persuasively appealing to audiences of all political ideologies (Sangalang & Bloomfield, 2018). According to the study's authors, the most effective type of narrative was one that was sad, relayed clear moral values, was situated in the past, and was realistic. Thus, the researchers concluded that "narratives are an effective way to communicate social and political issues, such as climate change" (Sangaland & Bloomfield, 2018, p. 594).

Evidence Credibility Statements

Competent persuaders have the burden of demonstrating that the evidence they use to bolster their claims derives from credible sources. **Evidence credibility statements** are brief statements that establish the quality of the information you use to support your claims. Indeed, research indicates that such statements bolster the effectiveness of evidence by calling attention to and establishing the legitimacy of the evidence you employ (Kim et al., 2012; Reynolds & Reynolds, 2002). Consider the following evidence credibility statement for the quote presented in the last section:

> In a 2018 report posted on the New Deal blog, Dr. Marshall Steinbaum (Ph.D. in economics from the University of Chicago), who is a Fellow and Research Director at the Roosevelt Institute, concludes that cancellation of all student loan debt would increase annual GDP in the U.S. by $22 billion and decrease the unemployment rate. (Steinbaum, 2018)

Does the fact that you now know the source of the evidence is from a person who has a doctorate in economics from the University of Chicago and who also serves as a research director at a prestigious institute influence your perception of the quality of the evidence presented? Research suggests that the use of evidence credibility statements establishes the trustworthiness of the evidence you cite and has the added benefit of enhancing your perceived credibility (O'Keefe, 1998).

Warrants

According to Toulmin (2003), a **warrant** provides the justification and reasoning to connect the evidence with the claim. In short, a warrant provides receivers with an explanation of how the evidence supports the claim and demonstrates that making the mental leap from one to the other is logical and rational. In other words, if we can articulate how the evidence is consistent with and supports the claim we make, then the warrant is germane and fits. On the other hand, if the evidence fails to support or echo the claim, then the warrant falls apart. Research by Munch et al. (1993) demonstrates that warrants enhance the receiver's comprehension and acceptance of the conclusion of the argument. Consider the following example:

> *Claim:* Cancellation of all student loan debt would significantly benefit the U.S. economy.
>
> *Evidence:* Cancellation of all student loan debt would increase annual gross domestic product (GDP) in the U.S. by $22 billion and decrease the unemployment rate. (Steinbaum, 2018)
>
> *Warrant:* Growth of the U.S. economy is good.

In this example, the persuader links the claim (cancellation of all student loan debt would significantly benefit the U.S. economy) and the data (the report from Dr. Steinbaum) through the unstated principle that most Americans view economic growth positively. Examining the argument on face value, the evidence does warrant the claim that cancellation of student loan debt would benefit the U.S. economy.

Is it better to state the warrant explicitly or to allow the audience to implicitly draw their own conclusions? The answer to this question depends on several factors. Initially, persuaders often rely on enthymematic arguments. An enthymeme is an argument containing an unstated assumption that is provided by the receiver of the persuasive argument. In the example provided above, the warrant (growth of the U.S. economy is good) is implied.

Extant research provides insights about the effectiveness of message explicitness. Allowing the audience to draw their own conclusions has been shown to be effective in certain contexts, such as product advertising (Kardes et al., 1994). However, more recent research suggests that explicit conclusions are more persuasive in narrative contexts (e.g., television, movies, and literature) and persuasive speeches, as they provide clear directions to receivers (Dillard, 2014). However, some audience members may perceive explicit conclusions as pushy, preferring to draw their own conclusions (Martin & Strong, 2016).

A closer inspection of the literature in this area provides a nuanced picture of the advantages and disadvantages of implicit and explicit conclusions, as scholars consider factors related to the relevance of the content and the cognitive styles of receivers. For example, Sawyer and Howard's (1991) research demonstrates that implicit conclusions are most effective when messages are personally relevant to receivers. In addition, individuals who like to think deeply about issues (i.e., they score high on a measure of need for cognition, NFC) tend to prefer enthymematic arguments (Martin et al., 2003). On the other hand, those who are low in NFC hold more positive attitudes toward explicitly concluded messages (Kao, 2007).

Of course, it is important to recognize that members of the audience may not agree with the warrant. In such cases it is important that persuaders provide additional data supporting the validity of the warrant. Returning to our running example in this chapter, it may be necessary to provide additional support for the warrant that economic growth is good. This kind of backing is most necessary when the warrant is weak and/or contested.

Qualifiers

When advancing a persuasive argument, it is important that you avoid using terms like "always" or "never." **Qualifiers** reflect the fact that argumentation is not an exact science. In other words, qualifiers express the degree of certainty you have in the claims you advance. As Toulmin discovered, your credibility with the audience will suffer if you use absolute terms—especially in cases where the audience is aware of exceptions to your claims. In addition, acknowledging your degree of certainty safeguards against the appearance that you are taking an unreasonable position on the topic.

Let's take another look at the running example we have been discussing in this chapter. Can you think of any situations in which cancellation of student loan debt might not benefit the U.S. economy? Put another way, how significantly would this policy influence the economy? Would adding $22 billion to the GDP make much of a difference considering that the current U.S. GDP is approximately $19.4 trillion? Also, would debt cancellation significantly lower unemployment? Ultimately, even Dr. Steinbaum (2018) acknowledges that this proposal would be modestly stimulative to the U.S. macroeconomy. As a result, we suggest qualifying the original claim using the following terms:

> Cancellation of all student loan debt would modestly benefit the U.S. economy.

Why are qualifiers so important to persuasion? As Crowley and Hoyer (1994) note, qualifiers create a disincentive for message recipients to generate further counterarguments to the position advocated by the persuader. Petty and Cacioppo (2018) also note that qualifiers can function to inoculate the audience against future arguments presenting the opposite position.

Rebuttals

Given the nature of persuasive communication, it is highly likely that you will encounter receivers who are hostile to your argument. **Rebuttals** are responses to arguments that run counter to our positions or claims. To better understand how rebuttals work, it is first necessary to examine the literature regarding message sidedness.

Communication scholars distinguish between one- and two-sided messages. A **one-sided message** presents arguments in favor of the speaker's position on the issue. **Two-sided messages** present arguments in favor of the speaker's position as well as counterarguments to the position. Allen (1998) further distinguishes between two-sided refutational and nonrefutational messages. Two-sided refutational messages present counterarguments to the speaker's position followed by a strong rebuttal to the counterarguments. On the other hand, two-sided nonrefutational messages present the speaker's position and counterarguments to the position without a rebuttal.

So which message strategy is most effective? Both Toulmin (2003) and Allen (1998) agree that the two-sided message with rebuttal is most effective, followed by one-sided messages. As you might expect, the two-sided message with no rebuttal is the least persuasive. Meyer et al. (2010) refer to the process of anticipating and rebutting counterarguments as preemptive argumentation. They note that by "anticipating objections and providing counterarguments to those objections, speakers are better able to present a complete argument," which is stronger than a one-sided argument (Meyer et al., 2010, p. 9). Importantly, while we might be tempted to raise counterarguments that are weak and easily defeated (i.e., what we would call a straw person logical fallacy), ethical and effective rebuttals address and respond to the strongest and most likely counterarguments the opposition might raise in response to our position. Consider the following example of a two-sided refutational message:

> While the data presented here demonstrate that cancelling all student loan debt would produce modest benefits for the U.S. economy, some argue that action is not necessary because student loan debt is not actually burdening the economy. However, Dr. Steinbaum's (2018) analysis directly refutes this claim and shows that the student loan crisis not only burdens the economy but disproportionately affects Black graduates. As Dr. Steinbaum notes, although higher education is commonly thought to be the best route to economic and social mobility, "the racialized pattern of the student debt crisis demonstrates how structural barriers to opportunity stand in the way of individual efforts. Insisting that student debt is not a problem amounts to denying this reality."

Like qualifiers, rebuttals have been shown to increase persuasion by disincentivizing further counterarguing (Crowley & Hunter, 1994). Rebuttals also make receivers less susceptible to future attempts of presenting the opposite position through inoculation (Petty & Cacioppo, 2018). As Areni (2003) notes, arguments that have compelling qualifiers and rebuttals "should be stronger than corresponding arguments that lack these key propositions, provided message recipients have a predisposition to counter-argue the fundamental claim" (p. 361).

It should be clear after reading this chapter that formulating an effective argument requires you to research multiple perspectives related to the position you advocate. Also, effective argumentation requires you to carefully analyze your audience and refute any counterarguments they hold to your position. Further, developing an effective argument requires that you avoid fallacies that occur when a persuader relies on unsound reasoning or evidence. A sample of common fallacies of reasoning can be found in Table 6.1.

TABLE 6.1 Sample Fallacies of Reasoning

Fallacy	Definition	Example	Explanation
Ad Hominem	Involves an attack against the character of a person making an argument rather than the argument itself.	Donald's arguments against voting reform don't matter because he is a faculty member. He is just a lackey to the university, so we can't believe what he says.	In this case, the persuader is attempting to divert attention away from the argument and toward Donald's character. On its face, this attack has no bearing on the argument.
Appeal to Authority	Arguments that presume that a statement is true because it came from an authority.	Professor of Communication Stephen Hunt says that the Nonproliferation Treaty is necessary to limit nuclear proliferation.	Appeals to authority become problematic when the person referenced is not an authority on the topic or when the person is situated in some circumstance that undermines their credibility (e.g., they are being compensated to make the argument). In this case, Professor Hunt's expertise in communication likely does not position him to be an expert in nonproliferation.
Appeal to Tradition	This fallacy stipulates that an argument is correct on the basis that it is consistent with past tradition.	Charging students for parking is the right way to go because we've always done it that way.	This fallacy rests on the assumption that the old ways of doing things are correct. However, circumstances may have changed, rendering traditional ways of doing things moot.

(continued)

Fallacy	Definition	Example	Explanation
Bandwagon	This fallacy presumes that something is correct, good, or true because many other people agree with it or are doing it.	Recent polls suggest that the vast majority of Americans oppose COVID-19 mitigation guidelines. Obviously, we must end all mitigation efforts and open the economy back up.	As we noted in Chapter 1, appeals to social proof can be very effective. However, acting on the basis of social evidence may lead to poor decision making. In this case, it may be more important to reference the guidance of health experts than to rely on polling data.
False Dilemma	This fallacy occurs when a persuader asserts that a complicated question has only two answers when more actually exist.	Either you support the president's immigration policy or you are anti-American.	This clearly presents a false dilemma, as one could be opposed to a specific policy and simultaneously support the country. This kind of argument is problematic, as it is designed to keep the receiver from considering other alternatives.
Red Herring	Persuaders commit the red herring fallacy when they introduce irrelevant information into an argument in order to draw attention away from the real issue under discussion.	Senator Freed has argued that I don't agree with President Trump's strategy in the Middle East. However, everyone knows that Senator Freed accepted money from companies doing business in that region. Clearly, it's time for a new start.	In this example, the speaker diverts attention away from Middle East policy by introducing information about Senator Freed's business interests.
Slippery Slope	This fallacy occurs when a speaker claims that some event must inevitably follow from another down a steep slope to disaster.	If we don't take action to sanction North Korea now, they will continue to develop their nuclear program leading to nuclear war in the next 5 years.	In this example, the speaker references a chain of events that lead to nuclear war. As a consumer of slippery slope arguments, you should carefully consider the evidence offered for each step in the chain of events.
Straw Person	This fallacy occurs when a persuader substitutes another person's argument with an exaggerated or distorted version of the argument.	Ja Tavia has argued that we should mandate mask wearing. What she's really saying is that we should eliminate personal freedom and accept university-imposed fascism.	In this example, the speaker clearly mischaracterizes Ja Tavia's position. The intent here is to replace Ja Tavia's argument with a claim that can easily be defeated.

Persuasive Argumentation in a Post-Truth Era

As we noted in Chapter 2, the post-truth era is characterized by a rejection of common standards for determining the truth, extreme political polarization, and divisive and uncivil discourse. We noted further in Chapter 3 that social media fosters the creation of echo chambers that shield us from information that might counter our existing attitudes, beliefs, and values (Semetko & Tworzecki, 2018). Vasile (2018) refers to the abundance of post-truth in argumentation as the Műnchausen effect. In psychiatry, this syndrome refers to people who exaggerate or create symptoms of illness to get attention or sympathy. In communication, Vasile (2018) defines the Műnchausen effect as the "intentional distortion of truth (by means of elliptical and erroneous argumentation, a.s.o) for the sake of persuasion, or propaganda or any other form of social influence" (p. 62). Given this environment of post-truth, fake news, and alternative facts, you might question whether rational argumentation and critical thinking is even possible.

We certainly do believe that reasoned argument is possible in the current environment. In fact, you could argue that it is more important and necessary now than ever before. We also agree with Walters and Stout (2019) that learning the argument model is a critical means for producers of persuasion to push back against post-truth by changing the "starting point for how people process important decisions. It is possible to separate fact from fiction and we can work toward clearer understanding in an objective reality" (p. 4). Reznitskaya and Wilkinson (2017) note that students of virtually all ages can develop an understanding of the importance of acknowledging diverse perspectives, building coherent arguments, and incorporating valid and logical reasons and evidence.

Although the argument model presented in this chapter provides a mechanism to develop persuasive and fallacy-free arguments, it is important to note that post-truth communication is not simply a concern for producers of persuasion. Consider the following argument advanced by Wight (2018):

> Post-truth resides not in the realm of production, but in the realm of reception. If lies, dissembling, spinning, propaganda and the production of bullshit have always been part and parcel of politics, then what has changed is how publics respond to them. (p. 22)

This interpretation is consistent with the definition of post-truth we offered in Chapter 2, which stipulates that "objective facts are less influential in shaping public opinion than appeals to emotion and personal belief" (Oxford University Press, 2017, para. 1). As a result, learning argumentation skills will not only make you a better producer of persuasion but will also equip you to be a savvy consumer of arguments. So why is it so important that we develop the skills of argumentation and ethical persuasion? As Walters and Stout (2019) conclude, argumentation, critical thinking, and a "commitment to civil discourse are all necessary for

Engaged Persuasion Activity: Applying the Argument Model to the COVID-19 Crisis

On March 25, 2020, New York Governor Andrew Cuomo conducted a press conference in which he presented an argument for more federal help to address the COVID-19 crisis. For this engaged persuasion activity, view Governor Cuomo's press conference (https://www.youtube.com/watch?v=k2khIjJuLHI), and answer the questions that follow. Did Governor Cuomo effectively use all the components of the argument model in this press conference? What key counterarguments did he address, and how did he respond to them? Was the evidence he cited credible and persuasive? Were the visuals he presented persuasive, and did they add to the strength of the argument? In 2021, several allegations, ranging from harassment to sexual assault, emerged against Governor Cuomo. Looking back, do these allegations influence your perceptions of how he handled the COVID-19 crisis? Why or why not? Overall, how persuasive was Governor Cuomo's argument?

the continued success of our democratic form of government" (p. 4). The remaining sections of this chapter discuss persuasive appeals that can be incorporated into arguments.

Framing Persuasive Messages

The most frequently studied type of framing effect in persuasion involves participants' evaluations of the outcomes of two alternative options that either emphasize gain or loss. Tversky and Kahneman's (1981) seminal study in this area had participants respond to an Asian Disease Problem (ADP). Specifically, participants were told that the United States is preparing for the outbreak of an unusual Asian disease, which is expected to kill 600 people. Imagine you were a participant in this research and received the prompts below.

> If Program A is adopted, 200 people will be saved.
>
> If Program B is adopted, there is a one-third probability that 600 people will be saved and a two-third probability that no people will be saved.

Which option would you choose in this scenario? In Tversky and Kahneman's (1981) study, 72% of participants selected the certain option—Program A. Another group of participants were presented with the same ADP scenario but received different response options.

> If Program C is adopted, 400 people will die.
>
> If Program D is adopted, there is a one-third probability that nobody will die and a two-third probability that 600 people will die.

Interestingly, 78% of the participants in this condition selected the uncertain option—Program D. What are the differences between these two groups? The first set of options were presented using positive framing while the second set were presented using negative framing. In the persuasion literature, scholars refer to these as gain-framed (positive) and loss-framed (negative) messages.

According to Salovey et al. (2002), **gain-framed messages** typically "present the benefits that are accrued through adopting the behavior" (p. 392). In contrast, **loss-framed messages** usually "convey the costs of not adopting the requested behavior" (Salovey et al., 2002, p. 392).

Message framing literature is grounded in Prospect Theory, which posits that individuals are more risk-averse in terms of potential gains and more risk-seeking when they face losses (Kahneman & Tversky, 1979). As Wirtz et al. (2015) note, people like to protect what they already have and are "less willing to take a risk if taking that risk means they may lose something good" (p. 182). Prospect Theory also stipulates that people will take greater risks if they believe they will experience a loss, particularly if they think the risky option will mitigate the potential loss.

At first glance, this literature seems to support the conclusion that people are generally more motivated by what they stand to lose when making a decision rather than what they stand to gain. In fact, the framing effects literature does indicate modest effect sizes for the tendency of people to make risk-averse choices when presented with positive frames and risk-seeking choices when presented with negative frames (Kühberger & Gradl, 2013). Overall, the literature on message framing presents a mixed bag of results. For example, recent meta-analyses of framing effects in health communication have demonstrated that gain-framed messages are statistically more persuasive than loss-framed messages; however, the effect sizes in these studies were so small that the advantage of gain-framed messages is practically insignificant (O'Keefe & Jensen, 2007, 2009).

As a result, communication scholars working in this area have begun exploring variables that moderate framing effects. For example, Nan (2012) examined differences in the effectiveness of framing based on whether participants were present minded (individuals who focus on immediate, short-term outcomes in their decision making) or future minded (individuals who consider long-term consequences when making a decision). Nan found that loss-framed messages were more persuasive than gain-framed messages for present-minded participants. Message framing had no impact on the attitudes or behavioral intentions of participants who were future minded. This research suggests an advantage for loss-framed messages for individuals who tend to focus on the immediate, short-term implications of their decisions.

Mann et al. (2004) examined the effectiveness of gain- and loss-framed messages for arguments promoting flossing based on participants' approach/avoidance orientation. Individuals who have an approach orientation tend to be highly responsive to positive and reward cues. On the other hand, individuals who take an avoidance orientation are more responsive to punishment or threat cues. Mann et al.'s findings revealed that gain-framed messages were more persuasive for approach-oriented participants. Also, loss-framed messages were found to be significantly more persuasive for avoidance-oriented participants. In fact, Mann et al. (2004) note that the "individuals who reported the healthiest flossing behavior in this study were avoidance-oriented individuals who were given a loss-framed article" (p. 333).

Scholars have also examined how mood affects the way individuals process persuasive messages. According to Wegener et al. (1994), individuals in a positive mood respond best to gain-framed messages when the message states that adoption of the recommendations will make positive outcomes likely or when adoption makes negative consequences unlikely. Alternatively, more recent research in this area suggests those in a good mood actually respond better to loss-framed messages (Wirtz et al., 2015). Wirtz et al. argue that when people are in a good mood, they tend to pay more attention to personally relevant, loss-framed information. More research is needed to clarify the moderating effects of mood on the effectiveness of gain- and loss-framed messages.

Persuasive Appeals

When constructing persuasive messages, communicators have a variety of persuasive appeals at their disposal. This section covers some of the most common logical and emotional appeals that have been studied by communication scholars.

Appeals to Logos, Ethos, and Pathos

As far back as ancient Greece, Aristotle was theorizing about three modes of persuasion he termed logos, ethos, and pathos (Aristotle, 1960). According to Aristotle, logos (or **logical appeal**) relies on evidence and reasoning. Ethos refers to the receiver's perception of the communicator's credibility, including an assessment of the communicator's competence, character, and goodwill. Finally, pathos (or **emotional appeal**) targets the feelings of receivers.

Logos

The term "logos" refers to a persuader's use of rational proof. Although rational proof can take a number of forms, we will limit our discussion in this section to inductive and deductive reasoning.

When employing inductive reasoning, advocates begin with specific instances or cases and formulate a valid generalization or conclusion from them. In other words, inductive reasoning moves from the particular to the general. Consider the following example:

> Theranos engaged in unethical business practices.
>
> Halliburton engaged in unethical business practices.

> Philip Morris engaged in unethical business practices.
>
> Therefore, unethical business practices are common in the United States.

Does this argument provide enough examples to warrant the conclusion that unethical business practices are common in the United States? When using inductive reasoning, it is critical that persuaders avoid jumping to conclusions bases on a small number of examples. Consider the following argument:

> My brother has no interest in civic engagement.
>
> My cousin has no interest in civic engagement.
>
> None of my friends are interested civic engagement.
>
> Therefore, young people have no interest in civic engagement.

Although exaggerated, this argument clearly illustrates a hasty generalization—a fallacy of reasoning that occurs when the conclusion offered is based on insufficient evidence. Beyond conducting research to uncover additional examples to support the conclusion, what other strategies could the persuader employ to strengthen the argument? Following the argument model discussed in this chapter, one strategy could be to qualify the conclusion. For example, the persuader could discuss the percentage of youth who have no interest in civic engagement rather than jumping to the conclusion that no youth have an interest in civic engagement. Also, inductive arguments should rely on cases or example that are typical, representative, and timely.

Unlike inductive reasoning, deductive reasoning begins with a generalization and moves logically to an application to a specific case. Consider the following deductive argument:

> Killing people is always immoral.
>
> The death penalty involves killing people.
>
> Therefore, the death penalty is always immoral.

This example follows the classic form of deduction by starting with a major premise (killing people is always immoral), moving to a minor premise (the death penalty involves killing people), and ending with a conclusion (the death penalty is always immoral). Aristotle labeled this full version of a deductive argument a syllogism. The syllogism is a common form of persuasive argument and can be highly effective when the conclusion is logically derived from premises that are true.

As noted earlier in this chapter, persuaders often do not present the entire syllogism. Recall than an enthymeme presents a truncated version of a syllogism and relies on receivers to draw the conclusion. The research cited earlier demonstrates that enthymemes are most persuasive when persuaders and their targets share similar knowledge, values, and experiences related to the position being advocated. However, enthymemes may be less effective when you share little in common with the audience or for targets who prefer explicit conclusions.

Ethos

Think of a speaker you have observed recently whom you perceived to be highly credible. Are those perceptions of the speaker something that they possess, or does credibility reside in your cognitions as the receiver of the message? Most communication scholars agree that source credibility is a perception that resides in the mind of the receiver. Indeed, O'Keefe (2002) defines **credibility** as "judgments made by a perceiver (e.g., a message recipient) concerning the believability of a communicator" (p. 181). As a result, persuaders are only as credible as their receivers perceive them to be. Although we will discuss source credibility in much greater detail in Chapter 7, this section will provide a preliminary overview of the components of credibility, including expertise, trustworthiness, and goodwill.

Expertise refers to the receiver's perceptions of the communicator's intelligence, competence, and overall knowledge related to the position advocated. **Trustworthiness** refers to the receiver's perception of the communicator's character, honesty, and sincerity. Finally, **goodwill** reflects the extent to which an

FIGURE 6.2 Appeal to emotion.

audience perceives that the communicator has their best interests in mind. In general, extant research suggests that we are more likely to accept the message recommendations of sources we perceive to be highly credible, and we tend to discount the recommendations of those we perceive to be less credible (Petty & Cacioppo, 2018).

Engaged Persuasion Research: The Power of Metaphorical Messages to Persuade

Messages employing metaphors have greater persuasive impact than literal messages (Van Stee, 2018). The use of metaphorical messages is more persuasive because metaphors provide interpretive frames that influence actions, capture attention, reduce counter-arguments, stimulate elaboration, and help organize information (Van Stee, 2018). The effect of metaphorical messages is particularly heightened when they are presented visually and exhibit high familiarity (Van Stee, 2018).

Pathos

The term "pathos" refers to appeals to emotion. As will be clear in the upcoming sections of this chapter, persuaders can appeal to a broad range of emotions, including fear, pity, guilt, and pride. Research substantiates that emotional appeals can operate as powerful persuasive tools (Miceli et al., 2006). For example, a persuader might attempt to arouse anger in an effort to influence a message recipient to evaluate a particular policy negatively. Alternatively, a persuader interested in motivating action (e.g., to donate money to a charitable cause) might use an appeal targeting pity or guilt.

Humorous Appeals

Without question, we are bombarded by **humorous appeals** in virtually every facet of life. As Beard's (2005) review of the use of humor in American advertising in the last 100 years reveals, advertising is saturated with humorous appeals. If you watch the Super Bowl, it probably will not surprise you to learn that over 70% of the advertisements rely on humor (Gulas et al., 2010). Humorous appeals are also found in health care settings. For example, Lippert and Hunt (2005) found that those living in long-term care facilities use humor to confront the rigors of old age and institutional care. In fact, humorous interactions with staff were found to enhance perceptions of the communication climate and quality of care received. Humorous content also plays a significant role in politics and political campaigns (Becker, 2014). From shows like *Saturday Night Live*, hilarious headlines featured in *The Onion*, user content and memes posted on social media, and political advertising, we are exposed to a tremendous amount of politically entertaining content.

Humor is fundamentally a function of communication. As Meyer (2000) notes, "Communication is a key factor in nearly all theories of humor because of its resulting from a message or interaction perceived by someone" (p. 311). Integrating the research on humor is challenging because it is an umbrella term that

FIGURE 6.3 Environmental message with a humorous appeal.

includes numerous related concepts (Warren et al., 2018). For example, scholars use the term to refer to a joke, psychological state associated with amusement, and/or an individual difference in the tendency or need to amuse others. In this section we discuss the theoretical frameworks and effects of humorous appeals as well as recommendations for the use of humor in persuasive communication.

Persuasive Effects of Humor

Despite its prevalence, scholars have struggled to conclusively document the persuasive effects of humor. As Walter et al. (2018) observe, scholarship in this area has been "notorious for producing inconsistencies between different theoretical mechanisms that attempt to explain its effects" (p. 344). For example, one line of thinking indicates that humor facilitates persuasion by drawing attention to messages (Weinberger & Gulas, 1992). On the other hand, Relief Theory posits that "humor stems from the relief experienced when tensions are engendered and removed from the individual" (Meyer, 2000, p. 312). This theory also proposes that tension reduction facilitates liking of the source.

Yet another approach, the Discounting Cue Hypothesis, suggests that humor facilitates persuasion by reducing critical argument scrutiny. In other words, it requires significant cognitive effort to process humorous messages, so we are less likely to counterargue when exposed to humor (Young, 2008). Similarly, Cognitive Appraisal Theory suggests that humor puts individuals in a good mood leading them to appraise message recommendations more favorably (Kuiper et al., 1995).

Finally, scholars have sought to explain the effects of humor on perceptions of the source of the message. For instance, Lyttle (2001) found that the use of self-effacing humor enhances perceptions of source credibility. In addition, Wanzer et al. (1996) found that humorous sources are perceived as more socially attractive and popular than nonhumorous sources. In contrast, Eisend (2009) found that humor negatively influences perceptions of source credibility in the context of advertising. Also, Lammers et al. (1983) found that humor is associated with a sleeper effect where participants' ratings of source credibility improved over time as they disassociated the source from the message. Lammers et al. (1983) conclude that humorous appeals may be more persuasive than serious appeals because "they stimulate, in the long term, the generation of cognitive responses which are predominately favorable" (p. 182).

Recommendations For the Use of Humor in Persuasion

A recent meta-analysis of 89 humor studies provides new clarity for this body of research and offers practical advice for persuaders. First, Walter et al.'s (2018) findings clarify that the persuasive effects of humor are not restricted to educated, younger audiences as had been suggested in prior research (Eisend, 2011). In other words, this meta-analysis did not produce unique effect sizes for student samples. This suggests that humor can be persuasive across a wide range of ages.

Second, Walter et al.'s (2018) research shows that issue involvement and message relevance interact to influence the persuasiveness of humor. Specifically, "highly-involved individuals tend to be persuaded more from humor when it is related to the persuasive message" (Walter et al., 2018, p. 362). The use of unrelated humor with highly involved individuals proved to be less persuasive. In addition, the meta-analysis revealed that humor works better for low-involved individuals; however, "persuasive messages that use unrelated humor are not penalized to the same extent as using unrelated humor to persuade highly-involved individuals" (Walter et al., 2018, p. 362).

Third, this research shows that there is a ceiling for the persuasive effects of humor. More specifically, "the effects of humor on persuasion are governed by an inverted U-shaped pattern that peaks at moderate levels of perceived humor and then gradually decreases when the humorous message becomes 'too funny'" (Walter et al., 2018, p. 362). The authors reason that too little humor might not be sufficient to capture attention, while too much humor might overwhelm the information processing capacity of receivers.

Fourth, the meta-analysis reveals differences in humor style. Specifically, the use of parody was found to exert a positive effect, while the results for satire were mixed. Walter et al. (2018) posit that satire may be less persuasive as it relies on ambiguous humor that "impedes persuasion, as it leaves much more room for selective perception and individual interpretation" (p. 363).

Taken together, this research offers four important insights for persuaders who wish to use humorous appeals: (1) The effects are not restricted to a particular age, (2) humorous appeals are more effective when the humor is related to the persuasive message, (3) persuaders should use a moderate amount of humor when trying to persuade others, and (4) ambiguous humor use decreases persuasion.

Guilt Appeals

Guilt appeals are common in social marketing campaigns seeking to promote prosocial behavior around issues like health and the environment. Tangney et al. (2007) define guilt as a negative emotion caused by the perception of negative consequences associated with the self. Therefore, **guilt appeals** seek to elicit feelings of guilt in receivers and stress the personal responsibility of the individual to engage in the recommended behavior (e.g., avoid binge drinking, donate to a charity, recycle more, etc.).

Research has demonstrated the effectiveness of guilt appeals in a wide variety of contexts, including promoting responsible drinking (Duhachek et al., 2012), enhancing emergency preparedness (Turner & Underhill, 2012), and stimulating intentions to donate to charitable organizations (Lwin & Phau, 2014). For example, one study has demonstrated that the intention to donate to charities is positively related to guilt arousal (Hibbert et al., 2007). Positive affective evaluations about the charity as well as favorable beliefs about the charity enhanced guilt arousal (Hibbert et al., 2007). Seemingly, then, messages that use guilt appeals are effective in this instance. However, the study also discovered that participants who perceived the message to be manipulative and were skeptical of the advertising tactics employed were less likely to experience guilt arousal. Paradoxically, though, perceptions of manipulative intent resulted in increased intentions to donate. Thus, "the manipulative intent effect has a divergent twofold

Engaged Persuasion Research: Are Sex Appeals More Effective Than Other Persuasive Appeals?

Although sex appeals are common in advertising, few scholars have isolated specific factors that make them more effective than other persuasive appeals, like humor. To address this issue, Das et al. (2015) conducted two experiments examining the combined persuasive effects of different levels of pleasure (moderate, high) and arousal (moderate, high) for sexual and nonsexual ads. Their results demonstrate that sexual appeals only outperform nonsexual appeals under certain conditions. Specifically, their "findings show that sexual content enhanced ad persuasiveness under conditions of moderate pleasure and high arousal" (Das et al., 2015, p. 417). These findings shed new light on the advertising mantra "Sex sells." Specifically, this research shows that there is nothing particularly special about sex appeals compared to other persuasive appeals. Ultimately, if persuasive ads evoke feelings of pleasure, appeals to sex work but not any better than any other persuasive appeal.

impact. Although it inhibits guilt arousal and therefore donation intention indirectly, this is ameliorated to some extent by its ability to enhance donation intention directly (although the latter effect is weaker)" (Hibbert et al., 2007, p. 738).

Recent research has revealed that the motive of the persuader moderates the persuasive effects of guilt appeals. Turner et al. (2018) compared participants' reactions to guilt appeals from for-profit and nonprofit sponsors. They found that commercially-oriented, high-intensity guilt appeals were not persuasive. However, participants developed more positive brand attitudes when they received high-intensity guilt appeals from a nonprofit sponsor. Unlike participants in the for-profit condition, those in the nonprofit condition reported increases in liking and persuasiveness as guilt intensity increased. This research clearly demonstrates that the motives color the means, especially when persuaders employ appeals to guilt.

Engaged Persuasion Research: The Use of Guilt and Virtual Reality to Promote Charitable Giving

Many nonprofits struggle with developing persuasive strategies to enhance giving. New research by Kandaurova and Lee (2019) suggests that virtual reality (VR) may help charitable organizations stimulate monetary gifts and volunteering. Specifically, Kandaurova and Lee investigated the effects of VR on empathy, guilt, responsibility, and donation of time and money. Participants in this study watched a prosocial video about a charitable organization on Oculus Rift (VR condition) or on a 14-inch laptop. Those who viewed content on the VR platform reported significantly higher levels of empathy, responsibility, and intention to donate money and volunteer their time compared to those who viewed the content on the laptop. The use of VR was also found to increase participants' self-reported levels of guilt and social responsibility, leading to higher intentions to volunteer.

It is important to note that, although researchers often use the terms interchangeably, there are important differences between guilt and shame. One of the most important differences between these concepts is that when people feel guilt, they often focus on the behaviors that caused the guilt. However, when people experience shame, they tend to focus on themselves exclusively, ignoring their behaviors. As Tangney et al. (2007) explain, when individuals experience guilt, they regret what they have done and are more concerned about future behavior. When individuals experience shame, they regret who they are and are more concerned about the past. Importantly, appeals that elicit shame may cause receivers to feel anger and make them less likely to change their behaviors (Boudewyns et al., 2013). As Boudewyns et al.'s research demonstrates, shame-free guilt appeals are far more persuasive than high-intensity guilt appeals that evoke shame. Key differences between guilt and shame appeals are further illustrated in Figures 6.4 and 6.5 (these ads served as the stimuli in the research conducted by Boudewyns and colleagues). Though the differences in these figures might be difficult to spot initially, closer inspection reveals that the A through D answer options for each question prompt contain critical language variations. In Figure 6.4, the guilt message, the language in the answer options is less personal, direct, or attacking than in the other figure. In fact, one could argue that the wording in the shame message, Figure 6.5, could be read as name calling since it attacks the character of the person who gave their partner an STD and labels them.

Beyond the research described previously, there is a dark side to the use of appeals that arouse negative emotions in people. As Antonetti and Baines (2015) note, the use of guilt highlights receivers' past failures. As a result, the use of this appeal might cross the threshold of ethical persuasion by causing receivers to

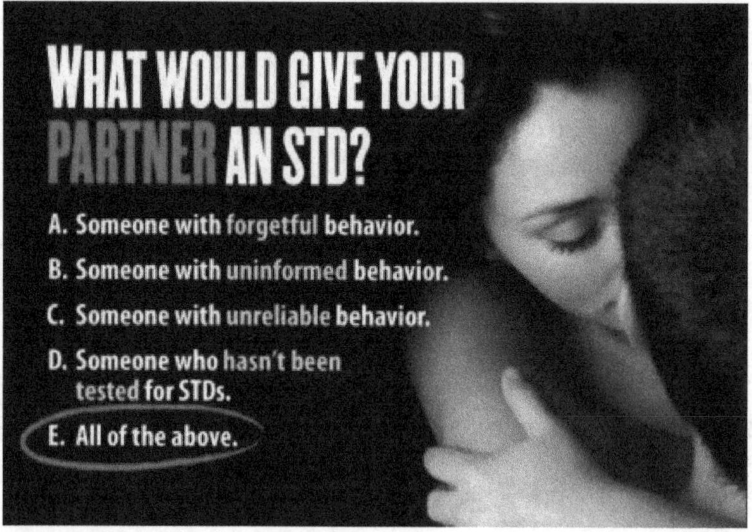

FIGURE 6.4 Sample guilt appeal from the Boudewyns et al. (2006) study.

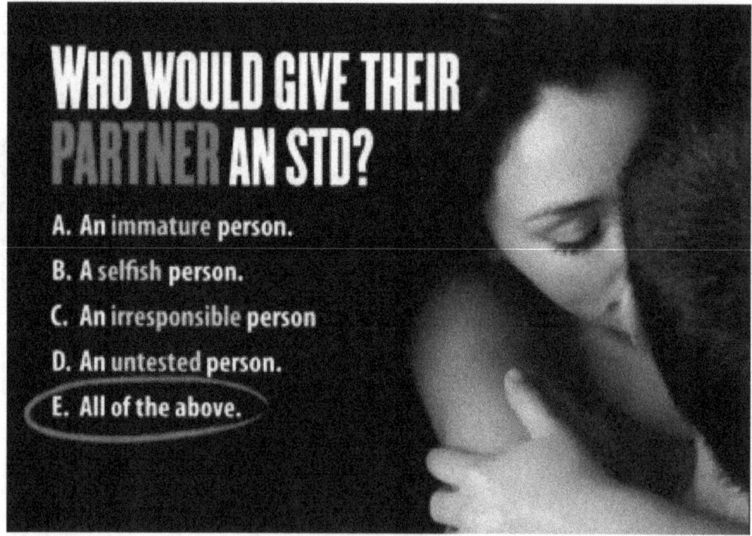

FIGURE 6.5 Sample shame appeal from the Boudewyns et al. (2006) study.

experience excessive guilt. In addition, excessive guilt might cause receivers to perceive the source as less credible, especially if they perceive the source has manipulative intent (Antonetti & Baines, 2015). This is consistent with Chang's (2011) research indicating that very strong guilt appeals can backfire and cause receivers to generate negative responses to the source of the message.

Overall, the extant literature suggests that guilt appeals are most persuasive when (a) a moderate amount of guilt is used (Chang, 2011); (b) text-based messages are accompanied by images (Antonetti et al., 2018); (c) receivers of guilt appeals feel a sense of personal responsibility and empathy for others (Basil et al., 2006; Boudewyns et al., 2006); and, finally, (d) high-intensity guilt appeals are accompanied by efficacy information (i.e., information that shows the target can perform the desired action; Boudewyns et al., 2006).

Fear Appeals

The **Extended Parallel Process Model** (EPPM) developed by Kim Witte (1992), a communication scholar at Michigan State University, posits that **fear appeals** coupled with efficacy statements lead to behavioral changes. Fear appeals are designed to scare or threaten us into doing what a persuasive message recommends, whereas efficacy statements tell us that we can take actions to avoid the problem described in the message (Witte, 1992). Importantly, Witte explained that statements can be either high or low in efficacy and that perceived efficacy can be broken down into either beliefs about self-efficacy or response efficacy. Meanwhile, fear appeals can be divided into beliefs about perceived threat susceptibility or severity (Witte, 1992). "Quite often fear appeals are employed in efforts to convince people to change 'for their own good'" (Dillard, 1994, p. 314). According to the EPPM, "When both perceived threat and perceived efficacy are high, danger control processes are initiated" (Witte, 1992, p. 338). Notice that Witte acknowledges that fear may lead to message rejection but also acknowledges that fear appeals can lead to cognitions about a perceived threat that result in message acceptance. If fear appeals are used effectively and coupled with messages high in efficacy, then positive behavioral changes result (Witte, 1992). Messages that elicit high levels of fear and are coupled with low efficacy, however, result in message rejection (Lewis et al., 2013; Olson et al., 2020; Witte, 1992). See Figure 6.6 for a visual representation of the EPPM. As you examine the image, recall that fear appeals alone lead to very different responses as compared to when fear appeals are coupled with efficacy statements. Although the arrows in this figure may initially appear to be confusing, keep in mind that the aim is to trigger danger control since the message will be more persuasive and accepted. If fear control is triggered, then the message will be rejected. Thus, an examination of Figure 6.6 would lead us to conclude that efficacy is essential.

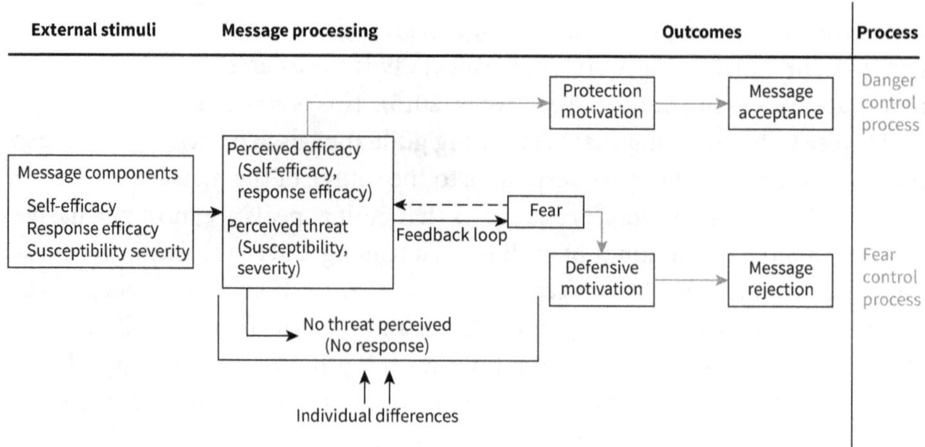

FIGURE 6.6 The Extended Parallel Process Model (Witte, 1992).

The EPPM has attracted a great deal of attention among researchers and practitioners alike. "EPPM has advanced our understanding of how fear appeals operate and continues to generate questions for research in risk messaging" (Maloney et al., 2011, p. 206). In fact, "Fear appeals are a widely accepted method of persuasion" (Maloney et al., 2011, p. 216), and "in the 20 years since its inception, the EPPM has been shown to be a valid framework for understanding why fear-based persuasion may succeed or fail" (Lewis et al., 2013, p. 97). The body research employing the EPPM has lent support to many of the theoretical propositions. For instance, studies investigating topics as diverse as computer security have found that fear appeals about online security risks, when combined with efficacy statements about password guidelines, have increased compliance among users (Mwagwabi et al., 2018).

In a quite different study investigating messages aimed at preventing the spread of genital warts, researchers found that fear appeals create strong perceptions about fear and threat, thus motivating action, and act as powerful persuasive devices (Witte et al., 1998). In addition, the researchers discovered that messages high in perceived efficacy were critical in guiding participants toward protective health responses. Health campaigns need to first make the target audience feel susceptible to a severe health threat and then perceive efficacy in a manner that permits them to believe they are capable of taking preventative actions that will control the danger (Witte et al., 1998). Thus, fear appeals must be paired with high-efficacy statements. Weak efficacy perceptions will result in failure to take corrective action or, worse yet, may backfire in the sense that the target audience may deny the threat, react negatively, or respond defensively to the message (Witte et al., 1998). In other words, "If it appears that low efficacy perceptions cannot be adequately addressed in a public health campaign, then practitioners should avoid the use of fear appeals in that campaign" (Witte et al., 1998, p. 583).

Affect and the EPPM

How important are feelings and emotions in fear appeal messages? Dillard (1994) explains that "fear might either augment or diminish the amount of cognitive capacity available for message processing. Furthermore, fear might enhance or inhibit motivation to engage in message analysis" (p. 315). Lewis et al. (2013) found that "irrespective of emotional appeal type, high levels of threat and efficacy enhanced message outcomes via maximizing acceptance and minimizing rejection" (p. 84). More specifically, Lewis et al. (2013) found:

> When addressing a serious health issue, a message must ensure that the target audience identifies the threat as relevant and severe and perceives that there are strategies that they can use to reduce/avoid the threat. Furthermore, that there must be consideration of the fact that message rejection and acceptance are two likely, competing responses influencing a message's persuasiveness. (p. 97)

While fear is associated with message acceptance, other feelings or affects can lead to the acceptance (e.g., sadness or surprise) or rejection (e.g., anger or puzzlement) of a persuasive message (Dillard et al., 1996). Indeed, affect and persuasion are related (Dillard, 1994). Interestingly, happiness was unrelated to message acceptance (Dillard et al., 1996). What feelings fear appeals generate should be considered when constructing persuasive campaigns, as Dillard et al. (1994) observed:

> Some affects facilitate persuasion, whereas others inhibit it. These knowledge claims become relevant to health campaigns to the extent that campaigns design and produce messages that arouse feelings in message recipients. Fear appeals, such as those used in AIDS/HIV campaigns, do much more than scare people; they evoke a variety of affective responses that have separate and unique effects on persuasion. To construct effective public health messages, campaign designers must begin to give explicit attention to the affective outcomes of their persuasive appeals. (p. 68)

Hope is an important emotion in the processing of fear appeal messaging. In a two-study design, Nabi and Myrick (2018) discovered significant interactions between hope and self-efficacy in predicting behavioral intentions, specifically claiming that the persuasive success of fear appeals is heightened when participants experience feelings of hope. "One might have a more negative attitude toward a behavior yet still be motivated to perform it when feeling hopeful about a desired outcome" (Nabi & Myrick, 2018, p. 9). Moreover, high efficacy combined with hopeful feelings were found to predict behavioral intentions, which suggests that the relationship between cognitions and emotions is recursive (Nabi & Myrick, 2018). In the studies, hope produced a stronger effect on, and uniquely explained variance in, behavior intention as compared to fear. In conclusion, Nabi and Myrick (2018) recommend:

> Rather than simply letting people know what they can do (response-efficacy) and assuring them that they can do it (self-efficacy), which may spark hope on their own, it could be valuable to also encourage audiences to *feel* that engaging in the recommend behavior will lead to desired outcomes to increase the amount of hope that audiences experience. (p. 10)

Through the context of campus sexual assault, Morrison and McCornack (2015) investigated other-directed persuasive fear appeals. More specifically, they asked college men to think of a significant other and then read a fear appeal message concerning sexual assault against women. "Men experienced fear for the women they care about, primarily recalled threatening message information, and were motivated to speak with women regarding the protective message recommendations" (Morrison & McCornack, 2015, p. 103). As a result, the researchers argue that susceptibility can be thought of as a social or interactional variable rather than merely an intrapersonal one. Thus, concern for the well-being of another can be evoked through fear appeals even when the target audience is not directly susceptible, resulting in a motivation to protect others by implementing recommended actions highlighted in the efficacy statements (Morrison & McCornack, 2015). Interestingly, their data revealed that both feelings and cognitions play a role in recalling fear appeal messages, which calls into questions some of the EPPM's original assumptions. Remember that the EPPM stipulates two separate processes (see Figure 6.6): fear control leading to emotional and maladaptive responses and danger control leading to cognitive and adaptive responses. Thus, the findings that both feelings and cognitions can be simultaneously involved in the process seems to contradict the separate and linear paths charted by the EPPM.

FIGURE 6.7 United Nations COVID-19 stay-at-home message.

Meta-Analyses of the EPPM

Does the EPPM hold up to meta-analytic scrutiny? Witte and Allen (2000) conducted a meta-analysis that demonstrated support for the EPPM hypotheses. Specifically, they found that strong fear appeals inducing perceived severity and susceptibility when coupled with high-efficacy messages were persuasive, resulting in message acceptance and producing behavioral changes. Conversely, strong fear appeals paired with low-efficacy risk create defensive responses. So while Witte and Allen confirmed that fear appeals motivate adaptive danger control actions, they may result in either message acceptance or maladaptive fear control actions, like reactance or defensive responses. Overall, stronger fear appeals (e.g., vivid language and gruesome pictures) are more persuasive, and fear appeals produce weak but reliable effects on attitudes, intentions, and behaviors (Witte & Allen, 2000). Meanwhile, weak fear appeals may backfire and trigger defensive responses "if target audiences do not believe they are able to effectively avert a threat" (Witte & Allen, 2000, p. 606). Thus, "A persuader should promote high levels of threat and high levels of efficacy to promote attitude, intention, and behavior changes" (Witte & Allen, 2000, p. 604). Ultimately, producing high-efficacy perceptions is the single most important takeaway for practitioners.

A different meta-analysis, which examined studies investigating the effect of fear appeals, found "that threat only had an effect under high efficacy" and "efficacy only had an effect under high threat" (Peters et al., 2013, p. S8). In other words, the interaction effect revealed by the meta-analysis indicates the effect of a threat depends on the level of efficacy. No effects were found when either threat was low or efficacy was low (Peters et al., 2013). Disturbingly, the meta-analysis was only able to find six studies that directly tested the effects of EPPM using sound methodology (Peters et al., 2013). However, the researchers concluded that there is reason to suspect that threat under low efficacy conditions may lead to less healthy behaviors, meaning that the persuasive message may backfire (Peters et al., 2013). Thus:

> If an intervention developer is not very certain that either the population is high in response *and* self-efficacy, or that a given relevant intervention will manage to considerably increase response *and* self-efficacy, threatening communications should be avoided (in fact, the significant main effect of efficacy and the strong effect of efficacy under high threat that were found in the current meta-analysis suggest that a focus on efficacy is a better bet in any case). (Peters et al., 2013, p. S24)

For instance, cigarette warning labels employing fear appeals rather than efficacy statements could actually increase smoking behavior among current smokers (Peters et al., 2013).

After reviewing 60 years of research on fear appeals, Ruiter et al. (2014) concluded that the experimental evidence argues against using threatening health messages while the support for threatening messages is justified by weak scientific data. Fear appeals can even produce counterproductive effects (Ruiter et al., 2014). Ruiter et al. (2014) synthesize the findings of six different meta-analyses by contending that "coping information aimed at increasing perceptions of response effectiveness and especially self-efficacy is more important in promoting protective action than presenting threatening health information aimed at increasing risk perceptions and fear arousal" (p. 63). The meta-analyses supported strengthening self-efficacy, promoting response efficacy, and raising awareness of susceptibility but did not support messages with emotional tones that heightened threat severity (Ruiter et al., 2014). Like Peters et al. (2013), Ruiter et al. found only six studies that provided high quality experimental data to support the use of fear appeals and the EPPM. In the end, Ruiter et al. (2014) cautioned:

> By focusing primarily on threat severity, the evidence on fear appeals is not translated into the design of health messages. Current evidence shows that information about the severity of possible negative consequences from risk behavior may prompt defensive responses. These counterproductive responses may be avoided by providing instruction on how to successfully implement the recommended actions as well as convincing people that they are personally susceptible to the threat. (p. 68)

In practice, the problem is that specific instructions about corrective health actions is rarely combined with fear appeals—meaning that the efficacy statements are low (Ruiter et al., 2014). Further, Meadows et al. (2020) compared health messages sent via social media from the Centers for Disease Control (CDC) to messages sent on the same platform by state health departments. The authors found that the CDC's Facebook posts were more likely to include severity, susceptibility, self-efficacy, and response efficacy than those posted by state health departments. They

Engaged Persuasion Activity: Crafting a Fear Appeal Message

Witte's (1992) EPPM and supporting research tells us that fear appeals should evoke fear by indicating the severity and susceptibility of the threat while including high-efficacy statements. You and a group of your fellow students have been recruited to create a campus campaign that convinces students to avoid texting while driving. Quite easily, your group has found statistics about the prevalence and dangers of texting and driving, including several news stories, testimonials, and unsavory pictures of resulting accidents and fatalities. Now, your task is to craft a persuasive message that employs the best practices recommended in the theory and research concerning fear appeals and the EPPM. What will you include in the message campaign? What will you exclude? How will you test your message with target audiences to verify that it is effective?

encourage message designers to craft persuasive health messages that are guided by theories like the EPPM.

Future Directions for the EPPM

"Have there been any revisions to the EPPM?" you might ask. So (2013) proposes a revision of Witte's EPPM, which she calls the extended-EPPM or E-EPPM. Specifically, the E-EPPM incorporates both affective and cognitive aspects (e.g., anxiety and fear) while also positing that monitoring and blunting coping style moderate further information seeking (So, 2013). "Empirical research examining the effects of fear appeal messages has provided mixed support" for the EPPM (So, 2013, p. 76). Thus, the addition of anxiety in E-EPPM is noteworthy. "For risk communication effort to induce protection motivation, individuals must first perceive the portrayed threat to be serious and possible. This cognition is postulated to evoke fear and anxiety, which, in turn, activate the coping appraisal process" (So, 2013, p. 80). Message acceptance therefore depends on adequate efficacy information being provided, such that high levels of self-efficacy and response efficacy are perceived (So, 2013). If efficacy is low, though, blunters will reject the message; monitors, meanwhile, will seek further information to increase their efficacy and may ultimately accept the message (So, 2013). Consequently, E-EPPM "suggest that the health messages should be equipped to facilitate further information seeking by suggesting ways of obtaining more information (e.g., hotline, websites)" (So, 2013, p. 81). In other words, persuasive messages should contain information sufficient to help various audiences "form adequate levels of efficacy beliefs" (So, 2013, p. 81). The E-EPPM also calls for audience segmentation since not all individuals need the same information and respond differently to information. For instance, individuals high in knowledge on the topic may be satisfied with efficacy-only messages.

On a separate note, it is possible that responses to fear appeal messages may involve variables not accounted for in the EPPM. In her doctoral dissertation, Rulffes (2017) failed to uncover support for the EPPM hypotheses but did find that cognitive dissonance predicts message acceptance or rejection. While the study remains unpublished, the idea of exploring how dissonance affects responses to fear appeal messages is intriguing.

The classroom setting is an interesting one in which to test the EPPM hypotheses. For instance, while instructional communication research generally sides against using threats or antisocial compliance-gaining strategies, Sprinkle et al. (2006) found that instructor threats when coupled with high efficacy could produce positive changes. One reason why the classroom provides an interesting context in which to study fear appeals lies in the nuances and complexity of the classroom environment and the teacher–student relationship. Sprinkle et al. discovered that, compared to use of fear alone, the use of fear paired with

FIGURE 6.8 Appeals to youth persuade by making people feel younger. In this photo, the youth's exuberant attitude may make us feel younger.

high-efficacy statements was more effective in achieving positive outcomes for student affective learning, motivation, affect for the course, and out-of-class communication with the instructor. However, the efficacy-alone condition emerged as the superior compliance-gaining strategy (Sprinkle et al., 2006). In this case, high-efficacy statements by instructors produced more favorable outcomes with students. On the other hand, Sprinkle et al. acknowledge that there are times and situations in which instructors need to evoke fear and use threats, for instance, to discourage plagiarism and emphasize the serious consequences of engaging in academic dishonesty. They do caution that instructors should be trained to use fear appeals appropriately by pairing threats with high-efficacy messages.

Evaluating the Persuasive Effects of Appeals

There are numerous other appeals that are beyond the scope of this chapter, including ingratiation, pride, freedom, patriotism, honor, and youth. If you think about it, virtually any human emotion can serve as the basis for a persuasive appeal.

The research covered in this chapter may lead you to question which appeals are most effective. Research by Hornik et al. (2017) provides an answer, at least in the context of advertising. Hornik et al. conducted a meta-analysis of past advertising appeals research. Meta-regression was employed to examine variability in effect sizes across seven persuasive appeals (sex, humor, comparative, metaphor, fear, gain-framed, and two-sided). Their results demonstrate that emotional appeals led by sex and humor were more persuasive than fear and rational appeals. However, year of publication and media type were found to moderate the persuasive effects of ads. Specifically, emotional appeals were more effective on television and more impactful in recent studies. A summary of the appeals included in this study can be found in Table 6.2.

TABLE 6.2 Hierarchy of Persuasive Appeals

Appeal	Valence	Frame	Dependent Variable	Effect Size
Humor	Positive	Emotional, pleasure, satire, wit, relief, positive mood	Ad Liking Attitude	0.38** 0.35**
Sex	Positive	Emotional, physiological arousal, sensation, fantasy, dreams, self-esteem	Ad Liking Attitude	0.22** 0.19**
Comparative	Positive/negative	Rational, relative advantage, high performance, better value, wisdom, independence	Ad Liking Attitude	0.15** 0.19**
Metaphor	Positive	Rational/emotional, indirect messaging, maturity, sophistication	Ad Liking Attitude	0.15** 0.13**
Fear	Negative	Emotional, anxiety, tension, danger, threat	Ad Liking Attitude	0.12** 0.16**
Gain-framed	Positive	Rational, personal gains, long-term advantage	Ad Liking Attitude	0.11* 0.14**
Two-sided	Positive	Rational, logical inferences, certainty, positive evaluation	Ad Liking Attitude	0.09* 0.11

Note: *$p < 0.05$, **$p < 0.01$.

Importantly, persuasive appeals can also be used in combination. For example, Yoon and Tinkham (2013) examined the combined use of humor and fear. Their study demonstrates that these appeals can be mixed effectively based on the involvement level of the target audience. They note that issue involvement may be inherently low for some audiences (e.g., risks of high blood pressure for

FIGURE 6.9 Combination appeals might use fear and humor in conjunction. In this photo, the upraised utensils and serious facial expression could instill fear while the colors and setting could be read as simultaneously humorous.

younger audiences) or inherently high (e.g., risks of high blood pressure for elderly males). Yoon and Tinkham's (2013) results indicate that when issue involvement is low, the "audiences may be better persuaded with nonhumor with low threat intensity or humor with high threat intensity" (p. 39). The opposite is true for those who are highly involved in the issue—the "targets may be better persuaded with humorous, low-threat-intensity or nonhumorous, high-threat-intensity" messages (Yoon & Tinkham, 2013, p. 39). As this research demonstrates, humor can be employed to offset the emotions generated by fear appeals.

Engaged Persuasion Activity: Persuasion via Technology?

There are researchers working on computational persuasion who are teaching artificial intelligence (AI) to persuade humans and change our behavior by understanding how to argue with humans (Hunter, 2018). The possible applications of persuasion through AI could range from mundane, everyday uses—such as our personal technological devices persuading us to exercise—to potentially more far-reaching decisions—such as AI that influences who we hire, how we respond to emergency situations, or where we invest our money. Certainly, we rely on technology quite a lot these days; and this trend is only likely to continue. Thus far, however, we are not accustomed to having the technology we use argue with us. What are the possible benefits and drawbacks that you can foresee from developing AI that can argue with and persuade humans?

Summary

This chapter addressed the construction of persuasive messages. By examining the argumentative structure and properties of persuasion as well as the various types of persuasive appeals, we have a better idea of not only how to construct a sound persuasive message ourselves but also how to interpret and deconstruct messages we encounter. Knowing the Toulmin Argument Model and the Extended Parallel Process Model are two musts for scholars of persuasion.

The next chapter covers the factors that affect how the source of a persuasive message is perceived and offers several strategies for bolstering and enhancing credibility.

Check Your Understanding Review Questions

1. What are the components of the Toulmin Argument Model? How do these components function together?
2. How is argumentation related to persuasion?
3. What are the various types of persuasive appeals? Which appeals are effective in particular situations?
4. How do the components of the Extended Parallel Process Model function?
5. What is the difference between fear control and danger control processes?
6. How does the strength of self-efficacy affect the way fear appeals are processed?
7. What is the difference between gain-framed and loss-framed messages? Which is more effective?

Key Terms

claims (p. 138)
emotional appeals (p. 148)
evidence (p. 138)
evidence credibility statements (p. 139)
Extended Parallel Process Model (p. 157)
fear appeals (p. 157)
guilt appeals (p. 154)
humorous appeals (p. 151)
logical appeals (p. 148)
qualifiers (p. 141)
rebuttals (p. 141)
Toulmin Argument Model (p. 137)
warrants (p. 139)

Credits

Fig. 6.4: Vanessa Boudewyns, et al., from "Shame-Free Guilt Appeals: Testing the Emotional and Cognitive Effects of Shame and Guilt Appeals," *Psychology and Marketing*, vol. 30, no. 9, p. 825. Copyright © 2013 by John Wiley & Sons, Inc.

Fig. 6.5: Vanessa Boudewyns, et al., from "Shame-Free Guilt Appeals: Testing the Emotional and Cognitive Effects of Shame and Guilt Appeals," *Psychology and Marketing*, vol. 30, no. 9, p. 824. Copyright © 2013 by John Wiley & Sons, Inc.

Fig. 6.6: Erin K. Maloney, Maria K. Lapinski, and Kim Witte, from "Fear Appeals and Persuasion: A Review and Update of the Extended Parallel Process Model," *Social and Personality Psychology Compass*, vol. 5, no. 4, p. 207. Copyright © 2011 by John Wiley & Sons, Inc.

Fig. 6.7: Copyright © 2020 by United Nations COVID-19 Response. Reprinted with permission.

Fig. 6.8: Copyright © 2020 by Annie Spratt. Reprinted with permission.

Fig. 6.9: Copyright © 2017 by Alex Iby. Reprinted with permission.

CHAPTER 7

Source Characteristics and Persuasion

Chapter Objectives

After reading this chapter, you should be able to:

- Understand the definition of source credibility and identify its dimensions
- Explain the conditions under which source credibility functions to enhance or impair persuasion
- Understand how Image Repair Theory can be used to understand source credibility following reputation damage
- Describe the implications of the post-truth era for judgments of source credibility
- Articulate the strategies for enhancing and repairing source image and credibility

If we asked you to identify a charismatic speaker, many would likely list former President Barack Obama. Indeed, President Obama was admired by many and described as a cool and charismatic leader and communicator (Bligh & Kohles, 2009). But what specific characteristics and traits are associated with charisma, and how does it influence persuasion? Levine et al. (2010) attempted to answer this question by asking research participants to define charisma. Participants in their study associated several characteristics with charisma, including strength, charm, confidence, and humor. They also indicated that charismatic leaders demonstrate the ability to listen to, empathize with, and understand others. Of course, participants also suggested charismatic leaders have excellent interpersonal and public speaking skills. The variability in responses support Levine et al.'s conclusion that there is little consensus among scholars about how to define and measure charisma. Although some strides have been made in recent years in operationalizing and measuring charisma (Tskhay et al., 2018), most persuasion scholars have focused their attention on understanding a related source characteristic—credibility.

When you ponder the role that source characteristics have in persuasive messages, a few questions should leap to mind. Is source credibility as important as the content of the message in facilitating persuasion? What are the primary dimensions of source credibility? What are the strategies for bolstering source credibility? If you commit an act that causes damage to your reputation and/or credibility, what are the strategies for repairing your image? These are the central questions that we seek to answer throughout this chapter. As you will see, there are often not simple answers to these fundamental questions; however, you will learn that source credibility often plays a substantial role in persuasive communication. We begin this chapter with a definition of source credibility and explore its primary dimensions. From there, we examine an array of research that teases out the conditions under which source credibility works most effectively to enhance persuasion. We also explore the implications of the post-truth era for receivers' assessments of source credibility. Finally, we conclude the chapter with a review of strategies for enhancing and repairing credibility.

Source Credibility

The concept of credibility, or ethos, dates back to the ancient Greeks. The social scientific study of credibility received a significant boost in the 1940s and 1950s from esteemed social psychologist Carl Hovland and his colleagues who developed the attitude change and research project at Yale University (Hovland et al., 1953; Hovland et al., 1949). As we noted in Chapter 5, **credibility** refers to the "judgments made by a perceiver (e.g., a message recipient) concerning the believability of a communicator" (O'Keefe, 2002, p. 181). Since Hovland's pioneering research in the area, scholars have examined the persuasiveness of source credibility in numerous contexts, including marketing (Eisend, 2004), classroom communication (Finn et al., 2009; Moore & Richards, 2019), information foraging (Schweiger & Cress, 2019), intentions to use emergency contraception (Wagner et al., 2018), journalists' perceptions of online information (Vergeer, 2018), online advertising (Wang et al., 2018), political communication (Pressgrove & Kim, 2018), and perceptions of risks associated with climate change (Dong et al., 2018). Overall, the research in this area demonstrates that a high credible source induces more persuasion than a low credible source (Pornpitakpan, 2004); however, there are some exceptions as we will discuss throughout this chapter. Importantly, credibility is created, sustained, and altered through communication.

We also noted in Chapter 5 that credibility is a receiver-based construct. In other words, perceptions of credibility reside in the minds of receivers and are not "owned" by the source. For example, President Donald Trump may be perceived as a brilliant political outsider by some and as a politically incompetent leader by others. As you can see, sources are only as credible as receivers perceive them to be.

Dimensions of Source Credibility

Over the years, scholars have explored numerous dimensions of source credibility. For example, Berlo et al. (1969) examined the dimensions of competence, trustworthiness, and dynamism. Whitehead (1968) argued that credibility consists of four dimensions: trustworthiness, competence, dynamism, and objectivity. In his early research, McCroskey (1966) focused on authoritativeness and character. There is now widespread agreement among scholars that a credible communicator is one who is perceived to be an expert, is regarded as trustworthy, and who displays goodwill toward receivers (Perloff, 2017).

FIGURE 7.1 Dr. Anthony Fauci.

Expertise

Expertise refers to the receiver's perceptions of the communicator's intelligence, competence, and overall knowledge related to the position advocated. In a meta-analysis of credibility studies, Wilson and Sherrell (1993) found that expertise has a stronger effect on persuasion than other dimensions like similarity and attractiveness. They reason that "expertise may be more relevant to the decision task facing the subject and thereby produce a stronger effect on persuasion because of the cognitive nature of the message" (Wilson & Sherrell, 1993, p. 109).

Do you recognize the person in Figure 7.1? This is Dr. Anthony Fauci who emerged as a prominent infectious disease expert during the COVID-19 pandemic. Are such medical experts persuasive? Importantly, communication scholars have examined perceptions of credibility when messages about public health issues are consumed via social media. For example, Lin et al. (2016) examined how individuals evaluate the source credibility of tweets and retweets based on noncontent attributes, including authority cues (e.g., cues that designate the source as an official authority), identity cues (e.g., tweets from the user's peers), and bandwagon cues (e.g., cues that others think the information in the tweet is reliable). Tweets from an official government site without any retweets were perceived to be the most credible. At least in the context of communicating information about public health issues through Twitter, Lin et al.'s research suggests that information expressing the expertise of the source is likely to be viewed as most persuasive.

Trustworthiness

Trustworthiness refers to the receiver's perception of the communicator's character, honesty, and sincerity. Research by McGinnies and Ward (1980) demonstrates that a trustworthy communicator is more persuasive than an untrustworthy communicator, regardless of expertise. Further, in a study exploring celebrity endorsements of an airline, Wang and Scheinbaum (2018) found that highly involved customers were more persuaded by source attractiveness and trustworthiness, whereas low-involvement customers focused only on source trustworthiness. Wang and Scheinbaum also found that the source's expertise and attractiveness did not influence low-involvement participants' attitudes toward the brand or perceived brand credibility. These studies suggest that trustworthiness may be more important than expertise in some contexts and for some types of receivers.

Goodwill

Goodwill reflects the extent to which an audience perceives that the communicator has their best interests in mind. Further, goodwill communicates caring through understanding (knowing another's perspective and needs), empathy (identification with another's feelings), and responsiveness (being attentive to the communication attempts of others; McCroskey & Teven, 1999). As McCroskey and Teven explain, goodwill is a means of widening the channel of communication between the sender and receiver. Goodwill has been shown to have significant

FIGURE 7.2 This speaker at a Black Lives Matter rally would be perceived as trustworthy if the audience believes they are honest and sincere. Trustworthiness can be more important than expertise in establishing credibility.

implications for persuasion in several contexts. For example, in the context of health communication, Quaschning et al. (2013) found that doctors who were perceived as caring generated higher patient satisfaction and treatment acceptance than those who were perceived as less caring.

In the context of the classroom, instructor goodwill has been found to be positively related to several student learning outcomes. As Finn et al.'s (2009) meta-analysis reveals, teachers who display goodwill toward their students are "likely to enhance their students' interest in the course, their involvement in classroom activities and assignments, and ultimately their learning" (p. 531). See Table 7.1 for the items commonly used to measure the dimensions of source credibility.

TABLE 7.1 Items Commonly Used to Measure the Dimensions of Source Credibility

Expertise	• Intelligent / Unintelligent • Trained / Untrained • Expert / Inexpert • Informed / Uninformed • Competent / Incompetent • Bright / Stupid

(continued)

Trustworthiness	• Honest / Dishonest • Untrustworthy / Trustworthy • Honorable / Dishonorable • Moral / Immoral • Ethical / Unethical • Genuine / Phony
Goodwill	• Cares about me / Doesn't care about me • Has my interests at heart / Doesn't have my interests at heart • Not self-centered / Self-centered • Concerned with me / Unconcerned with me • Sensitive / Insensitive • Understanding / Not understanding

As the preceding sections demonstrate, determining which of these dimensions is most important to persuasion depends on several factors, including the topic, context, medium of communication, and other factors. In addition, it is important to realize that these dimensions may interact and work together to influence receivers. For example, Ismagilova et al.'s (2019) meta-analysis of the effects of source credibility on consumer behavior reveals that expertise, trustworthiness, and perceived similarity work together to influence perceived electronic word of mouth (eWOM) usefulness, intention to purchase, and information adoption.

It is also important to note that source credibility is a dynamic construct that changes over time. One example of this can be found in the changing perceptions of individuals who disclose they are gay. In 2002, Russ et al. conducted a study to explore the influence of instructor sexual orientation on perceptions of teacher credibility. In this study, the same male instructor presented a lecture on cultural influences to 154 undergraduate students enrolled in an introductory communication course. In each class, the instructor kept his delivery cues and content of the lecture consistent. However, the instructor's sexual orientation was systematically manipulated. During half of the lectures, the instructor subtly referred to his opposite-sex partner three times. In the other half of the lectures, the instructor subtly referred to his same-sex partner three times. Russ et al. found that students perceived the gay teacher as significantly less credible than the straight teacher. Students also reported learning significantly less from the gay instructor compared to the straight instructor.

Interestingly, Russ et al.'s (2002) study was replicated by Boren and McPherson in 2018. Using the same procedures as the 2002 study, Boren and McPherson found that students did not rate gay instructors lower in credibility and learning compared to straight instructors. In fact, their findings showed that students rated the gay instructor significantly higher on the goodwill dimension of credibility than the straight instructor. Boren and McPherson point out that many cultural and legal conditions changed significantly in the 16 years between the two studies. For example, same sex marriage was legalized, and other legal protections for gay and lesbian individuals increased significantly over that time period. The dramatically different findings of these two studies also reflect the fact that our attitudes regarding homosexuality have changed significantly in recent years. For example, Brown (2017) notes that in 2016, 63% of Americans said that homosexuality should be accepted compared to 51% in 2006. Taken together, these two studies vividly illustrate the dynamic nature of source credibility.

Research Related to Source Credibility

Now that you have a better understanding of the definition of source credibility, it is important to explore the extant research in this area. Our review of the literature in this area is not exhaustive, but it will equip you with the knowledge and theory necessary to begin assessing the optimal conditions under which credibility can be used to enhance persuasion.

FIGURE 7.3 When issue involvement is high individuals focus on central message cues, as appears to be the case for the individuals in this photo.

Issue Involvement

The dual process models (i.e., the Elaboration Likelihood Model and the Heuristic Systematic Model) we discussed in Chapter 1 provide further insight into the persuasiveness of source credibility. Scholars using the ELM and HSM often stipulate that credibility is most persuasive when receivers are not engaged in effortful and critical evaluation of the persuasive message. For the ELM, scholars have argued that credibility operates as a peripheral cue. Similarly, scholars employing the HSM often posit that credibility functions as a simple decision-making rule (heuristic).

Stiff's (1986) meta-analysis of research on issue involvement and message processing supports this view. Specifically, Stiff found that participants in the low involvement category process few central or peripheral cues. In other words, these individuals care so little about the topic that they do not process the persuasive messages or attendant cues. In contrast, highly involved individuals care so much about the issue that they focus almost exclusively on the central message cues. Source credibility was found to be most persuasive for moderately involved individuals who were motivated to process both central and peripheral cues. As Stiff (1986) notes, the "effect of source credibility increased up to a point, beyond which further increases in involvement produced decreases in the effect of source credibility on attitudes" (pp. 86–87).

Importantly, Tormala and Petty (2004) found that when receivers are engaged in highly elaborative thinking and they resist the persuasive attempt, they are more likely to reject the recommendations of a highly credible source. Tormala and Petty argue that in such circumstances, the presence of a highly credible source makes receivers more confident in their initial attitude than they were before hearing the persuasive message.

In contrast, recent research by McDermott and Lachlan (2020) demonstrates that source credibility may operate as a central cue in some circumstances. These scholars employed the ELM to examine processing routes used by audiences to evaluate image repair messages for the National Rifle Association (NRA) following the Columbine and Sandy Hook school shootings and the New England Patriots football team following the Spygate and Deflategate cheating scandals. They found that audiences who hold extreme views and who are intensely ego involved are less likely to engage in central processing that might challenge closely held beliefs. In other words, these receivers did not engage in thinking critically about the message out of fear that it might challenge their beliefs, or they felt they already had the information needed to make a decision on the issue. Alternatively, source credibility may function as a central cue for those who hold less extreme positions. Their results support the claim that "source credibility might have a greater relationship with central processing than peripheral processing" (McDermott & Lachlan, 2020, p. 344).

Prior Attitudes and Knowledge

Kumkale et al.'s (2010) meta-analysis examined the effects of source credibility based on participants' prior attitudes and knowledge. They hypothesized that source credibility would be most persuasive when participants have no prior knowledge or attitudes related to the topic. Kumkale et al. (2010) concluded that "reliance on source credibility is most marked when people not only lack a prior attitude, but also the opportunity to form a new one based on prior knowledge of an issue" (p. 10). One of the implications of this research is that persuaders must rely on strategies beyond source credibility with audiences who are knowledgeable about the topic. In other words, source credibility generally functions effectively to help form attitudes but less effectively in changing attitudes.

Importantly, Kumkale et al. (2010) acknowledge that there may be situations where highly knowledgeable individuals would be influenced by source credibility. For example, "People who want to be accepted by the group to which a communication source belongs may find the opinion of the source to be highly relevant to their current goals" (Kumkale et al., 2010, p. 10). As a result, such individuals may rely on the recommendations of the source even if they hold prior attitudes and knowledge that contradicts the recommendations.

Counterattitudinal Advocacy

Is credibility more persuasive when the source is advocating a position you agree with or when the source is advocating a position that is counter to yours? According to Clark and Evans (2014), low credible sources are most persuasive when the position advocated is counterattitudinal and the arguments presented are weak. On the other hand, high source credibility was found most persuasive when participants in their study received pro-attitudinal messages supported by strong arguments.

Clark and Evans (2014) hypothesized that these differences are likely a result of different motives that are triggered by counter- and pro-attitudinal messages. Specifically, the **Discrepancy Motives Model** (DMM) stipulates that when individuals encounter counterattitudinal messages, they are motivated to defend their existing opinion by counterarguing and refuting the message (Clark & Wegener, 2013). As a result, "Recipients may ultimately feel more confident in their counterarguing

Engaged Persuasion Research: Source Credibility and Acceptance of Consumer-Generated Media on Travel Sites

Assuming that you book some of your vacations online, how much attention do you pay to the images and other consumer-generated media (CGM) posted by other travelers? According to research by Ayeh (2015), CGM posted by travelers perceived to be highly credible is very persuasive. Ayeh (2015) tested participants' reactions to CGM posted on TripAdvisor and found that "online travelers are more favourably disposed towards the use of CGM for travel planning when they believe that CGM is from credible travelers" (p. 178).

FIGURE 7.4 Protesters opposing systemic racism.

thoughts when they later learn that the source is low rather than high in credibility" (Clark & Evans, 2014, p. 1034).

In contrast, DMM proposes that when individuals encounter pro-attitudinal information, they are more motivated to bolster or strengthen their views. In this situation, credibility facilitates bolstering, as receivers are more likely to trust favorable information that is communicated by a highly credible source. This conclusion is also consistent with the research by Tormala and Petty (2004) who found that highly involved receivers respond to counterattitudinal persuasion from highly credible sources by becoming more certain in their initial attitudes.

Source Certainty

Does the certainty of the source influence receivers' perceptions of credibility? According to Price and Stone (2004), source confidence operates as a heuristic cue communicating that the source is knowledgeable, competent, and correct. At first glance, this claim makes sense. We are more likely to perceive a highly certain source as more credible than a source who appears uncertain in the positions they advocate.

However, Karmarkar and Tormala's (2010) research departs from the confidence heuristic and suggests that nonexpert sources induce greater persuasion when expressing certainty, while expert sources induce greater persuasion by expressing uncertainty. This research is predicated on an **Informational Incongruity Assumption** "whereby incongruent expertise and certainty information would violate expectations, stimulate involvement, and foster persuasion as long as message arguments were strong" (Karmarkar & Tormala, 2010, p. 1044). In other words, nonexpert sources violate the expectations of receivers by expressing certainty in the positions they advocate, while expert sources violate expectations by expressing uncertainty in those positions. These expectancy violations lead to persuasion because they grab the attention of receivers and heighten their involvement and interest in the message. Importantly, Karmarkar and Tormala's research demonstrates an opposite effect when the message arguments are weak. In such cases, incongruity between the expertise of the source and perceived confidence works to highlight the deficiencies of weak arguments and therefore decreases persuasion and perceptions of source credibility.

Source Attributions

Attribution theory posits that receivers of persuasive messages are skeptical and actively develop explanations for why communicators advocate certain positions (Kelley, 1973). Eagly et al. (1978) advance this approach, noting that receivers attribute communicators' statements on positions to different factors. For example, if you were told that you were going to hear a speech about academic debate by a member of your school's debate team, you would likely assume that the speaker would advocate for the benefits of participating in the activity. Ultimately, these attributions significantly influence receivers' perceptions of source credibility.

According to Eagly et al. (1978), receivers look to identify two kinds of bias when processing messages. First, **knowledge bias** refers to a receiver's belief that a communicator has a biased view of an issue. This bias can be based on factors internal or external to the source. For example, receivers may infer that the source holds certain attitudes or beliefs on the basis of source characteristics like personality traits, gender, ethnicity, or age. Similarly, receivers may perceive that the source is biased based on external factors like how well read the source is on the topic. As Eagly et al. (1978) note, such external factors "may lead observers to infer that a communicator's sampling of information relevant to particular issues and events is nonrepresentative" (p. 425). In other words, receivers may determine that the source has not carefully considered all perspectives on the issue.

Second, **reporting bias** refers to the belief that the source is unwilling to report or disclose certain points of view on an issue. Again, this belief can be based on attributes of the source (e.g., the source is overly polite and does not want to offend the audience) as well as situational variables (e.g., the source does not want to advocate positions that they perceive the audience to be hostile to). Ultimately, knowledge and reporting biases damage source credibility and dramatically reduce persuasion.

What happens when speakers advocate positions that violate the expectations and attributions of the audience? According to Eagly et al. (1978), receivers may assume that a "particularly compelling external reality caused the communicator to override the personal or situational pressure that the recipient initially regarded as the most likely influence on the communicator's position" (p. 425). In other words, audiences may perceive sources to be more credible and persuasive when they advocate positions that violate knowledge and reporting norms.

Of course, there are limits to the persuasive effects of violations of reporting norms. If the source's advocacy is consistent with the attitudes, values, and beliefs held by the audience, the source is likely to be viewed as credible. Sources that violate reporting norms and advocate positions that are inconsistent with the attitudes, values, and beliefs of the audience are likely to be viewed negatively. This is particularly true when audiences hold strong attitudes with wide latitudes of rejection. The implications of strong attitudes for persuasion will be discussed in greater detail in Chapter 10.

Timing of Source Identification

Scholars have explored how the timing of source credibility information affects receivers' attitudes and perceptions of the source. O'Keefe's (1987) meta-analysis of the timing literature found that high credibility sources are most persuasive when introduced before the message content. In contrast, O'Keefe's study revealed that low credibility sources were most persuasive when introduced following the message content. O'Keefe (1987) concludes that timing source information appropriately (before for the high-credibility source and after for the low-credibility source) "more than doubles the success rate (from 32% to 68%)" (p. 71). These results are consistent with research by Allen et al. (2002) indicating that the "greatest effect for credibility is observed when the information is provided prior to the message" for high credible sources (p. 53).

More recent research in this area has examined how timing of source information affects the attitudes of individuals who engage in highly elaborative processing of persuasive information. Tormala et al. (2007) examined timing effects for receivers who engaged in highly elaborative processing of persuasive messages. Their results demonstrated that when the source was identified before the message, receivers generated more positive thoughts about the position advocated. When the source was identified after the message, receivers became more confident in their attitudes toward the position advocated. However, Tormala et al. also found that argument quality plays a key role in the persuasiveness of source credibility. Specifically, their research shows that when elaboration is high and the arguments presented are weak, "source credibility will have a reverse effect on attitudes such that increasing credibility undermines persuasion" (Tormala et al., 2007, p. 550). They reason that the presence of weak arguments negatively violates receivers' expectations that expert sources should advance strong arguments.

Engaged Persuasion Research: Persuasion in 140 Characters

Do you perceive persuasive information you encounter on social network sites like Twitter to be as credible as legacy news sources? Wasike (2017) set out to examine this question using an experimental design that assessed the framing of pro- and anti-gun-control arguments following the Sandy Hook school shooting in Newtown, Connecticut. Wasike found that participants perceived pro-gun-control frames to be more persuasive than anti-gun-control frames by the college student sample. College students also indicated that information transmitted by online news articles was more credible and persuasive than those transmitted via Twitter. This study makes a unique contribution to the credibility literature by comparing participants' perceptions of social media sites to more traditional news outlets.

Sleeper Effect

Many studies of source credibility operate from the assumption that the influence of a persuasive message is greatest immediately after the communication and loses impact over time (Priester et al., 1999). In contrast, the sleeper effect posits that messages from low credibility sources become more persuasive over time. Greenwald et al. (1986) define the **sleeper effect** as a "delayed persuasive impact following a communication accompanied by a discounting cue (i.e., information indicating that the communication is untrustworthy)" (p. 217).

Importantly, Kumkale and Albarracín's (2004) meta-analysis of the sleeper effect in persuasion research demonstrated the effect was more likely to be observed when the message arguments and discounting cue had a strong initial impact. In addition, increases in persuasion were stronger when the message recipients had higher motivation to think about the content of the message and received the discounting cue after the message.

How does the sleeper effect result in increased persuasion over time? In their early research, Hovland et al. (1949) proposed the **Dissociative Cue Hypothesis** to explain why messages from low credibility sources become more persuasive over time. This hypothesis stipulates that the immediate impact of a message is reduced when it is associated with a disclaimer, counterattitudinal message, or negative information about the source. According to this explanation, as time passes, the message is dissociated from the discounting cue and thus becomes more persuasive. In other words, receivers may find that the reasons for discounting the message from a low credibility source initially become less accessible in memory over time. In a meta-analysis of sleeper effect research, Allen and Stiff (1989) found support for the dissociative model and noted that attitude change is "caused by retention of information in the message while the source is no longer associated with the information" (p. 423).

Alternatively, scholars have proposed a **Differential Decay Hypothesis** to explain the sleeper effect. This perspective holds that a sleeper effect is observed when the message and discounting cue have a similar initial influence on attitudes; however, the cue decays more quickly than the message (Pratkanis et al., 1998).

It is important to note that researchers have sought to explore different types of sleeper effects. The absolute sleeper effect occurs when attitude change increases over time when research participants are exposed to a discounting cue compared to a control group (Cook et al., 1979). Put simply, the absolute sleeper effect occurs when messages from a low credibility source become more persuasive over time. On the other hand, the relative sleeper effect occurs when messages from both high and low credible sources lose favor over time; however, messages from high credible sources become less persuasive faster than messages from low credible sources (Pratkanis et al., 1998). An illustration of the absolute and relative sleeper effects can be found in Figure 7.5.

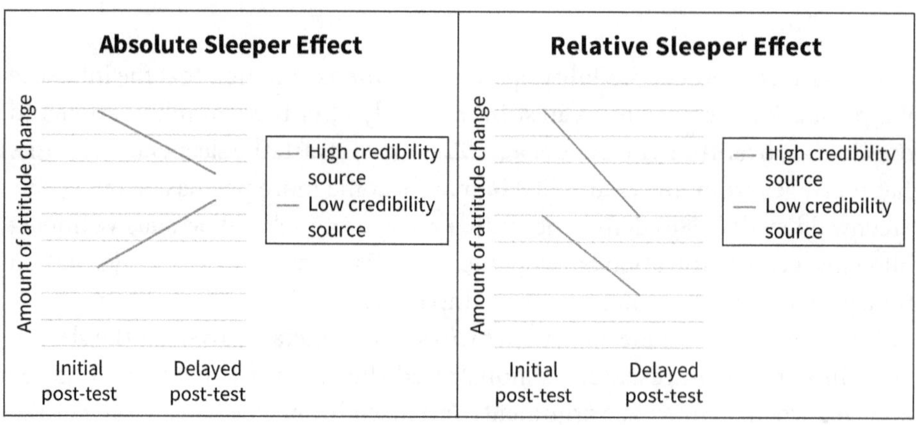

FIGURE 7.5 Models of the absolute and relative sleeper effects.

Research on the sleeper effect has produced mixed results. For example, Schulman and Worrall's (1970) replications of early sleeper effect studies failed to find a positive change in attitudes for the group receiving the discounting cue. Similarly, a series of failed experiments led Gillig and Greenwald (1974) to conclude that the sleeper effect did not exist. Also, scholars have questioned the conditions under which the effect could be observed outside of tightly controlled laboratory settings. Shadish et al. (2002) went so far as to conclude that "the circumstances under which this effect occurs turn out to be quite limited and unlikely to be of any general interest" (p. 19).

Despite these mixed results, a recent study by Foos et al. (2016) demonstrated support for the classic absolute sleeper effect in the context of advertising. Foos et al. had participants evaluate advertisements for a fictional gluten-free pizza. Participants in the discounting condition received the following cue after seeing the advertisement:

> The health claims of Ciao's gluten-free pizza are unsubstantiated, and have never been tested by nutritionists. In fact, adopting a gluten-free lifestyle can result in nutrition deficiencies and even weight gain. Furthermore, customers have complained about the lack of flavor of Ciao's pizza. (Foos et al., 2016, p. 22)

As you might imagine, participants in this study who received the discounting cue reported an initial negative attitude toward the pizza. However, the delayed posttest revealed an absolute sleeper effect in that participants' attitudes became more favorable to the pizza over time. Moreover, the results of this study provide support for the Dissociative Cue Hypothesis given that the increase in attitudes over time in the group that received the discounting cue "implies that the discounting cue is less accessible than the message topic in the delayed posttest" (Foos et al., 2016, p. 24). Further, Foos et al. argue that their study demonstrates the relevance of sleeper effect research in real world contexts like online advertising. Finally, this study demonstrates that the absolute sleeper effect is more likely to be observed when the discounting cue follows, rather than precedes, the message.

Taking research in the area one step further, Albarracín et al. (2017) introduced a new kind of sleeper effect where delayed increases in persuasion occur for weak messages associated with credible sources. Albarracín et al. conducted three experiments that showed when attention was focused on the communicator, there was a sleeper effect for the source. On the other hand, their research demonstrated that when attention of the recipients was focused on the message arguments, a traditional sleeper effect was observed. In other words, persuasion increased over time when strong arguments were presented by a noncredible source. The fact that they demonstrated a sleeper effect for the source shows there are situations where source credibility is very important. In fact, the salience of credibility is likely higher in situations where personal contact with source matters more than the arguments they advocate. As Albarracín et al. (2017) conclude, "Credibility may sometimes be the only piece of information that endures the passage of time" (p. 179).

Engaged Persuasion Research: The Sleeper Effect and Negative User Comments on Online News Articles

Numerous studies have explored the effects of user comments on readers' attitudes and evaluations of news articles. In a novel study, Heinbach et al. (2018) applied the sleeper effect to online news environments and found that negative user comments function as discounting cues that decrease the initial persuasive impact of news articles. Their results revealed a relative sleeper effect where the persuasiveness of the article containing positive user comments decayed over time while remaining constant for participants who received negative user comments. These results have significant implications for the role that user comments play in the formation of attitudes and opinions of online news consumers. As Heinbach et al. argue, if the negative user comments are civil and rational, they may work to facilitate online deliberation and suppress the spread of misinformation. Alternatively, uncivil and nonrational negative user comments may facilitate the spread of misinformation and hamper the deliberative process.

Source Credibility in a Post-Truth Era

As we noted in Chapter 2, we have witnessed a fundamental shift in the conditions for persuasion that are required for truth-telling in recent years. In the post-truth era, many communicators place less emphasis on evidence and fact-seeking (Kavanagh & Rich, 2018; Lewandowsky et al., 2017). In addition, we discovered in Chapter 3 that our political discourse is marked by outrage and extreme polarization making it difficult for many to engage in productive debate about the most pressing issues facing our democracy. We also noted that social media facilitates the spread of persuasive misinformation and establishes echo chambers that limit our exposure to information that contradicts our attitudes

FIGURE 7.6 These protesters at a public march reflect the challenges for persuasion in the post-truth era, specifically the need for truth-telling or speaking truth to power.

and beliefs. To make matters worse, we noted in Chapter 1 that belief perseverance dynamics make it very difficult to alter misperceptions we hold and that merely providing corrective information may backfire. As Boudry and Braeckman (2012) note, our human "belief engine" is susceptible to a number of influences, including confirmation bias, because of "its proficiency at rationalization and ad hoc reasoning, its valuation of an appearance of objectivity, and its motivation for cognitive dissonance reduction" (p. 359). Also recall the research we discussed in Chapter 1 indicating that perceived credibility moderates the influence of authority and expertise on attitude change (Jung & Kellaris, 2006). In other words, individuals follow the advice of experts they perceive to be credible and may ignore the advice from those they find lacking in credibility. Without question, these dynamics have significant implications for how receivers of persuasive information evaluate source credibility.

Nichols (2017) explores the implications of our current communication environment for credibility in his work on the death of expertise. According to Nichols, although we now have access to more information than any other time in human history, the information age has fueled narcissism, which cripples public debates. In other words, many participants in our democracy have convinced themselves that it is unnecessary to pay attention to experts, as the internet and social media provide them sufficient information to make decisions on their own. In this context, the death of expertise is "fundamentally a rejection of science and dispassionate rationality, which are the foundations of modern civilization" (Nichols, 2017, p. 5).

What makes this situation particularly troubling for Nichols (2017) is that many people vastly overestimate their competence on a range of topics and confidently spread misinformation. According to the **Dunning-Kruger effect**, people often hold overly favorable views of their abilities in many intellectual domains (Kruger & Dunning, 1999). Further, Kruger and Dunning's research reveals that unskilled and incompetent people are often so confident in their beliefs that they lack the ability to recognize they are incompetent. As Nichols (2017) notes, this research suggests that the least-competent people "were the least likely to know they were wrong or to know that others were right, the most likely to fake it, and the least able to learn anything" (p. 46). This claim is consistent with Hall and Raimi's (2018) research indicating that individuals highly confident in their beliefs were the "least likely to recognize their own knowledge shortcomings, but also the least likely to remedy them" (p. 303).

The death of expertise has serious implications for our democratic republic. Nichols (2017) argues that when trust between citizens and experts collapses, they become warring factions. When that happens, "democracy itself can enter a death spiral that presents an immediate danger of decay either into rule by the mob or toward elitist technocracy" (Nichols, 2017, p. 216). Additionally, as individuals turn away from education and civic engagement, they become "less capable citizens, and the cycle continues and strengthens" (Nichols, 2017, p. 217).

We outlined several strategies to address the problems of the post-truth era in Chapter 2 that may also be effective in overcoming the death of expertise. For example, a better understanding of persuasion research and theory will help you become an educated consumer and producer of persuasive information. In addition, this knowledge will help build civic agency and enhance your capacity to become civically engaged. This is an essential step to break the vicious cycle discussed by Nichols (2017) because when citizens are not engaged, "experts will give up talking to them and instead rely on their positions in the policy world to advocate for their own solutions" (p. 225).

Also, recall the Pro-Truth Pledge (PTP) that we discussed in Chapter 2. The authors of the PTP argue that it combats the Dunning-Kruger effect by compelling signees to "recognize the opinions of those who have substantially more expertise on a topic than myself as more likely to be accurate in their assessments" (Tsipursky et al., 2018, p. 276). Ultimately, we agree with the contention advanced by Hunt et al. (2009) that our nation desperately needs a "new generation of savvy critical thinkers that know how to access, use and evaluate information, and how to use their communication skills for the common good" (p. 23).

Strategies for Enhancing and Repairing Source Credibility

Recall our discussion of Theranos CEO Elizabeth Holmes in Chapter 2. Holmes used deceptive techniques to raise over $700 million for a blood-testing technology that did not exist. When investors and the public became aware of the fraud, it severely damaged her credibility and tarnished the image of her company. Though Theranos no longer exits, the experience provides a vivid example of actions that can damage credibility and points to the need to know how to respond to such incidents. In fact, many individuals, corporations, nonprofit organizations, governmental agencies, and other institutions find themselves in situations where they must act to repair their image. This final section of the chapter provides an overview of image repair theory and offers several strategies for bolstering credibility.

Image Repair Theory

Managing reputation is a critical concern for persuaders. As William Benoit (2015), a communication scholar and creator of Image Repair Theory, notes, threats to our image can arise as a result of four factors. First, we compete with others for limited resources (e.g., money, time, space, etc.), and complaints can arise when resources are not distributed equitably. Second, circumstances not under our control can arise, leading to complaints. Third, as human beings, we make mistakes that can upset others. For instance, when Michael Vick, then the quarterback for the Atlanta Falcons (see Figure 7.7), was convicted on charges related to dogfighting, many fans and nonfans were upset. Fourth, people have different goals and objectives that can come into conflict, leading to complaints.

Individuals turn to persuasion when their image is threatened. Specifically, Benoit's **Image Repair Theory** (IRT) offers five broad categories of image repair strategies that persuaders can employ to respond to a crisis: denial, evasion of responsibility, reducing offensiveness of the event, corrective action, and mortification.

FIGURE 7.7 Michael Vick.

Denial

Benoit (2016) notes that one option for repairing image is simply to deny that the act occurred or that the accused committed it. Alternatively, individuals may attempt to shift the blame to provide a target for hostile audiences and establish who committed the act.

Evasion of Responsibility

Those accused of wrongdoing who cannot deny the offensive act may resort to evasion of responsibility through scapegoating (e.g., claim the wrongful act was simply a response to another wrongful act committed by another person) or defeasibility (e.g., claim that the accused lacked information or the ability to control the situation). Further, individuals may seek to evade responsibility by claiming that the offensive act occurred accidently. Finally, the accused could argue that the offensive act was done with good intentions. As Benoit (2016) notes, "People who do bad while trying to do good are usually not held as accountable as much as those who intend to do bad" (p. 22).

Reduce Offensiveness

Rather than deny or evade responsibility, accused individuals may seek to "reduce the perceived offensiveness of that act" (Benoit, 2016, p. 22). This image repair category consists of the following six strategies: bolstering, minimization, differentiation, transcendence, attacking one's accuser, and compensation (see Table 7.2 for examples of each of these strategies).

TABLE 7.2 Strategies to Reduce the Perceived Offensiveness of Actions

Strategy	Definition	Example
Bolstering	An attempt to strengthen the audience's positive affect toward the accused.	Individual highlights their positive characteristics or past good deeds.
Minimization	An attempt to minimize the negative feelings evoked by the act.	Individual argues that the act is not as bad as it first appeared.
Differentiation	An attempt to distinguish the act from other similar, but more offensive, actions.	Individual argues that, in comparison, the act in question is much less offensive than other actions.
Transcendence	An attempt to place the act in a more favorable context.	The accused could reframe the context by arguing that other, more important, values justify the act.
Attacking One's Accuser	The accused directly attacks their accuser.	The accused could argue that attacker lacks credibility and cannot be believed.
Compensation	The accused offers to reimburse the victim to nullify negative feelings generated by the act.	The accused offers a monetary reimbursement to the victim.

Corrective Action

Individuals who pursue corrective action promise to solve any problems arising from their behavior. In other words, corrective action involves "restoring the state of affairs existing before the objectionable action or promising to take action to prevent the recurrence of the offensive act" (Benoit, 2016, p. 23). Importantly, individuals may offer corrective action without confessing or apologizing.

Mortification

The final strategy for image repair in Benoit's (2015) IRT is mortification. Individuals who employ this strategy confess to committing the wrongful act and ask for forgiveness. Benoit also notes that individuals can couple mortification with corrective action.

Research suggests that corrective action is the most effective image repair strategy (Benoit, 2106; Cos et al., 2016; Gribas et al., 2016). For example, Benoit's research suggests that corrective action was viewed by participants as the single most effective strategy based on liking of the source, perceived offensiveness (corrective action was perceived as least offensive), and punishment deserved (participants perceived that sources using corrective action deserved the least punishment). In addition, Arendt et al. (2017) meta-analysis showed that corrective action had a high success rate (57%) across the 110 IRT studies they reviewed. As Arendt et al. note, corrective action was successful in a broad range of contexts, including high profile sports teams and athletes, product recalls, and responses to natural disasters. Further, in a survey of 800 public relations professionals, Ferguson et al. (2018) found that participants ranked corrective action as the most effective crisis response strategy. Beyond corrective action, participants in Benoit's (2016) study also found accident, mortification, compensation, and denial as acceptable image repair strategies. However, Benoit's (2016) data suggest that "people do not want to hear others attack their accuser, minimize the charges, claim they were provoked, or shift the blame" (p. 30).

Enhancing Your Credibility

As you consider strategies to bolster your credibility, keep in mind that it is a multidimensional construct. Think carefully about the ways you demonstrate your expertise on the topic while also communicating trustworthiness and goodwill. In addition, consider the following strategies for enhancing your credibility.

- *Consider audience involvement and knowledge.* It is important to account for how involved and knowledgeable your audience is on the positions you advocate and make adjustments accordingly. Remember that credibility is most persuasive when audience members are moderately involved (Stiff, 1986) and have no prior knowledge on the topic (Kumkale et al., 2010).
- *Develop strong and compelling arguments to support your case.* The argument model presented in Chapter 6 provides a template for developing compelling, persuasive arguments. It is important to recognize that research supports the claim that relying on appeals to expertise while presenting weak arguments can be problematic. In fact, Bohner et al. (2002) found that high source expertise can actually backfire when weak arguments are presented. Tormala et al. (2006) also found that when

persuasive messages contain weak arguments, high credibility sources produced less persuasion than low credibility sources. Bohner et al. reason that providing weak arguments violates receivers' expectations for experts and leads to more negative thoughts and less persuasion. As a result, we encourage you to employ the argument model to develop the strongest and most persuasive arguments possible.

- *Cite credible evidence to support your claims.* As we noted in Chapter 6, another strategy for bolstering your credibility is to cite credible evidence to support your persuasive arguments. The literature establishes that evidence is most persuasive when recipients are aware of the evidence, it is processed centrally rather than peripherally, and it is judged as legitimate (Reynolds & Reynolds, 2002; Stiff, 1986). Research further suggests the use of evidence can increase the persuasiveness of low credibility sources (Hunt, 1972). Beyond merely citing evidence, research suggests that the use of explicit evidence credibility statements demonstrates that your evidence is trustworthy and enhances your perceived credibility (O'Keefe, 1998).
- *Limit knowledge and reporting bias.* Given the assumptions of Attribution Theory, it is important that persuaders limit knowledge and reporting bias. Following the argument model presented in Chapter 6 will aid you in identifying and responding to potential counterarguments to your positions. In addition, the argument model requires that you qualify your claims, which limits perceptions of bias.
- *Emphasize similarity with your audience.* Another strategy to enhance your credibility and persuasiveness is to emphasize similarity between you and your audience. We like people we perceive to be similar to us, and this holds true "whether the similarity is in the area of opinions, personality traits, background, or lifestyle" (Cialdini, 2009, p. 148). As a result, demonstrating similarity between you and your audience will make them more amenable to your recommendations.
- *State your qualifications.* Remember that expertise is an important dimension of source credibility. It is especially important to establish your expertise when communicating with an audience unfamiliar with you and your experience. Also, recall research by Allen et al. (2002) indicating that you should establish your credibility before presenting the persuasive message.
- *Avoid exaggerating your record.* Research indicates that persuaders should be very careful about exaggerating or misrepresenting their achievements. Cobb et al. (2013) examined receivers' reactions to political figures when positive information about them is discredited. This research revealed a punishment effect where receivers negatively adjusted their attitudes

toward political figures after learning the positive information attributed to those figures was false. For Cobb et al., the implications of this are clear—persuaders who exaggerate or misrepresent their achievements risk a serious backlash if receivers learn the accomplishments are false. Importantly, the punishment effect holds even if the persuader is not the one responsible for the misrepresentation.

- *Establish trust and demonstrate goodwill.* As noted in this chapter, it is often not enough to simply demonstrate your expertise on the topic. Audiences will also evaluate your trustworthiness and expect you to act with their interests in mind. Therefore, you should look for opportunities to show your audience how compliance with your requests will directly benefit them.
- *Prepare carefully and practice your pitch.* It should go without saying that you should take the time to carefully research and practice any persuasive speech you give. Research in this area is clear—your audience is more likely to find you credible and persuasive if the message is well delivered, plausible, and contains persuasive examples and evidence (Slater & Rouner, 1996).
- *Utilize corrective action if you need to repair your image.* Finally, if you find yourself in a situation where you need to repair your image, extant research strongly suggests that corrective action is the most persuasive strategy. As IRT stipulates, people generally do not appreciate attempts to get out of trouble by attacking accusers, minimizing the charges, or attempting to shift blame. Individuals are likely to be more successful by accepting responsibility and communicating a plan to correct any harms that arose from the persuader's actions. Corrective action also involves presenting a plan to avoid future misbehavior.

Engaged Persuasion Activity: Negative Political Ads

We are bombarded by negative political ads in virtually every election cycle. Research by Lariscy and Tinkham (1999) demonstrated that viewers of negative ads experience a sleeper effect where the ads become more persuasive over time. They argue that the persuasive impact of these ads can last through election day. For this Engaged Persuasion Activity, view a negative political ad on a website like the Political TV Ad Archive (https://politicaladarchive.org/) or the Annenberg Public Policy Center's fact-check site (https://www.factcheck.org/). Was the ad you viewed credible and persuasive? Why, or why not? What specific negative tactics did the ad employ? Given the literature on source credibility and image repair, what should a candidate who has been attacked do to counter the damage?

Summary

In this chapter, we defined source credibility and examined its primary dimensions. In addition, we explored some of the fundamental research related to credibility to distill some of the conditions under which credibility works best to facilitate persuasion. Finally, we discussed strategies for repairing image and enhancing credibility.

The next chapter addresses how persuasive messages are effectively designed to influence the behaviors of others. While previous chapters examine the dynamics of messages that influence receivers' attitudes, values, and beliefs, compliance-gaining perspectives explore how individuals craft persuasive messages to get others to do what we want them to do.

Check Your Understanding Review Questions

1. What are the primary dimensions of source credibility, and what role do they play in fostering persuasion?
2. Is source credibility a static concept, or do our assessments change over time?
3. How do issue involvement and prior knowledge influence receivers' evaluations of source credibility?
4. Define knowledge and reporting bias. How can you use Attribution Theory to enhance your credibility?
5. What is the sleeper effect, and what does research suggest about its relevance to persuaders?
6. In what ways does the post-truth era complicate assessments of expertise?
7. What are the major strategies for repairing image and enhancing your credibility?

Key Terms

Attribution Theory (p. 179)
credibility (p. 170)
Differential Decay Hypothesis (p. 181)
Discrepancy Motives Model (p. 177)
Dissociative Cue Hypothesis (p. 181)
Dunning-Kruger effect (p. 184)
expertise (p. 171)
goodwill (p. 172)
Image Repair Theory (p. 186)
Informational Incongruity Assumption (p. 178)
knowledge bias (p. 179)
reporting bias (p. 179)
sleeper effect (p. 181)
trustworthiness (p. 172)

Credits

Fig. 7.0: Copyright © by Daniel Schwen (CC BY-SA 4.0) at https://commons.wikimedia.org/wiki/File:Obama_Biden_rally_3.jpg.

Fig. 7.1: Source: https://commons.wikimedia.org/wiki/File:Anthony_Fauci_on_April_16,_2020_face_detail,_from-_White_House_Coronavirus_Update_Briefing_(49784743606)_(cropped).jpg.

Fig. 7.2: Copyright © 2020 by Taylor Turtle. Reprinted with permission.

Fig. 7.3: Copyright © 2018 by heylagostechie. Reprinted with permission.

Fig. 7.4: Copyright © 2020 by Alex Motoc. Reprinted with permission.

Fig. 7.5a: Based on ideas from Thomas D. Cook, et al., "History of the Sleeper Effect: Some Logical Pitfalls in Accepting the Null Hypothesis," *Psychological Bulletin*, vol. 86, no. 4. Copyright © 1979 by American Psychological Association.

Fig. 7.5b: Based on ideas from Anthony R. Pratkanis, et al., "In Search of Reliable Persuasion Effects: III. The Sleeper Effect Is Dead: Long Live the Sleeper Effect," *Journal of Personality and Social Psychology*, vol. 54, no. 2. Copyright © 1988 by American Psychological Association.

Fig. 7.6: Copyright © 2020 by Chris Henry. Reprinted with permission.

Fig. 7.7: Copyright © by Ed Yourdon (CC BY-SA 2.0) at https://commons.wikimedia.org/wiki/File:Michael-Vick_Jets-vs-Eagles-Sept-3-2009_Post-Game-Interview.jpg.

CHAPTER 8

Compliance-Gaining Techniques and Sequential Persuasion

Chapter Objectives

After reading this chapter, you should be able to:

- Understand approaches to compliance-gaining research
- Identify and explain the five bases of power
- Understand compliance-gaining design logics and goals
- Articulate the limitations of compliance-gaining research
- Understand and describe various strategies for ordering persuasive messages

This chapter addresses how persuasive messages are effectively designed to influence the behaviors of others. While previous chapters examined the dynamics of messages that influence receivers' attitudes, values, and beliefs, compliance-gaining perspectives explore how individuals craft persuasive messages to get others to do what we want them to do. In other words, compliance-gaining techniques are rarely intended to create, alter, reinforce, or extinguish an audience's attitudes, values, or beliefs. Instead, they are designed to change a target's behavior. Accordingly, Wheeless et al. (1983) defined **compliance gaining** as the "communicative behavior in which an agent engages so as to elicit from a target some agent-selected behavior" (p. 111). What is the best way to get others to comply with our requests? When should we make persuasive requests? How do our personal goals influence the persuasive strategies we use? Is there a sequence or strategy for making such requests? While these questions certainly oversimplify the matter, the content in this chapter does, indeed, present research that answers those questions and others.

Early Approaches to Compliance Gaining

If we think about persuasion as influencing others, then we ought to consider how persuaders attempt to gain the compliance of others. Compliance entails acquiescence to an explicit or implicit request (Cialdini & Goldsmith, 2004). Thus, compliance implies that the influence of others leads to our compliance with their requests. When requesters, those who make the persuasive request, construct messages, those messages are aimed at a target, or the person who is the receiver of the request. The persuasive attempt is successful if the target complies with the request. Cialdini and Goldsmith point out that we are aware that we are expected to respond to compliance-gaining requests in desired ways. In other words, we are conscious that a response is expected, and we know how it is we are expected to respond. Persuaders are trying to achieve conformity from target audiences; if they gain our compliance, then we are conforming to their wishes. Moreover, compliance functions under a norm of reciprocity. The norm of reciprocity holds

FIGURE 8.1 Example of symbols representing multiple bases of power.

that we feel an obligation to return unsolicited favors from others (Liang et al., 2013). To understand how compliance gaining works, we must first discuss **power**.

Power Bases

Some of the earliest studies in this area sought to understand how persuaders use power to gain compliance. French and Raven (1959), who were social psychologists, identified five bases of power: reward, coercive, referent, legitimate, and expert. Table 8.1 provides an overview of the five **power bases**. After reviewing the table, consider Figure 8.1 as you read about each power base. Which bases of power are present in the photo? Reward and coercive power are the most seemingly self-explanatory of the power bases. Reward power refers to ability to bestow rewards or acknowledgement or reinforce behaviors of others. Coercive power can be thought of as the ability to punish those who do not comply with requests. Often, supervisors possess both reward and coercive power in that they may be able to issue raises or demote subordinate employees. Expert and legitimate power are also not extremely difficult to comprehend. Expert power stems from the knowledge or expertise one possesses with regard to a given subject. Legitimate power refers to the power that comes with a certain title, position, or status. When discussing

TABLE 8.1 Five Power Bases

Power Bases	Description
1. Reward	Power to bestow recognition, rewards, or reinforcement
2. Coercive	Power to punish, condemn, or withhold privileges
3. Referent	Power given by others who identify with or follow the person with referent power
4. Legitimate	Power that comes with titles, positions, or status
5. Expert	Power that comes with specialized knowledge, expertise, or information

FIGURE 8.2 Activists exercising prosocial power.

climate change, a scientist with a doctorate degree in climatology would be perceived to be an expert on the subject. Also, an instructor is considered a legitimate authority figure in the classroom simply because they have the title of teacher. Legitimate authority can also come with titles, such as chairperson, or status symbols, such a doctor wearing a white lab coat. Referent power, on the other hand, is the one power base that a person cannot attain of their own accord. This is because referent power refers to how others identify with and are willing to follow someone they perceive to have referent power. While those with referent power may also share other power bases, they do not have to possess other power. We follow referent powers because we like them and identify with them. In short, we take our cues from them even if they hold no other power over us.

According to Mottet et al. (2006), some bases of power are more influential than others. Prosocial bases of power, such as expert, referent, and reward power, tend to be more effective at enhancing motivation and yielding long-term influence (i.e., internalization). In contrast, antisocial bases of power, such as legitimate and coercive power, are less effective and yield short-term influence (i.e., compliance).

Levine and Boster's (2001) experiment demonstrated that the effectiveness of compliance message attempts varied based on social power. More specifically, they discovered that power and message behavior interact to moderate compliance. The more powerful partner did better at gaining compliance during the bargaining experiment.

Grant et al. (1994) found that receivers' willingness to comply was greater when they rated communication satisfaction higher. They also discovered that negative sanctions produced the lowest estimates for willingness to comply. For instance, threats, guilt messages, and warnings were not effective, whereas positive, prosocial messages such as altruism were highly effective. Thus, "a persuader who quickly resorts to a severe, or intense strategy, especially one involving negative sanctions, may actually reduce compliance" (Grant et al., 1994, p. 107). Also, the relational distance, or

Engaged Persuasion Research: Compliance Gaining and Civic Engagement

Activists have been found to employ a broad range of both prosocial and antisocial compliance-gaining strategies (Cameron et al., 2003). More specifically, Cameron et al. found that activists utilized prosocial strategies (i.e., direct requests and hinting) as well as antisocial strategies (i.e., debt, warning, thought manipulation, threat, aversive simulation, and deceit). While activists were likely to report beginning with prosocial strategies, they admitted using multiple strategies to achieve their goals. Cameron et al. explained this finding as consistent with a lower ethical threshold. Interestingly, their data did not reveal significant effects for biological sex or argumentativeness, but verbal aggressiveness was a significant predictor of a lower ethical threshold. One implication is that "if we want to increase those involved in community decisions and civic engagement, knowing that activists use a broader range of strategies may be helpful in training others to participate in policy decision-making processes" (Cameron et al., 2003, p. 279).

FIGURE 8.3 Early struggles with compliance gaining.

intimacy level, did not affect receivers' willingness to comply. Further, the use of aggressive compliance-gaining strategies, with both romantic and nonromantic partners, has independently been found to relate to perceptions of how parents, peers, and parasocial partners use these same strategies (Cvancara et al., 2016). Parents emerged as the strongest predictor in nonromantic relationships, while peers were the most influential role model in romantic relationships.

The pique technique, which involves making an unusual request and will be covered in greater detail in Chapter 10, is effective at increasing compliance rates (Lee & Feeley, 2017).

Compliance-Gaining Typologies

Imagine you want to persuade a friend to go see a movie you really want to see. What specific persuasive techniques would you employ to gain your friend's compliance? What messages would you construct based on these techniques? In early compliance-gaining research, scholars from a variety of disciplines set out to answer these questions by developing typologies of compliance-gaining behaviors and messages.

Typology of Compliance-Gaining Techniques

In 1967, Gerald Marwell and David Schmitt, sociologists at the University of Wisconsin, created a taxonomy of 16 compliance-gaining tactics. In order to develop this typology, Marwell and Schmitt distributed a questionnaire and asked participants to rank their likelihood of using various techniques in four situations: requesting a promotion from a supervisor, encouraging a child to study more, selling encyclopedias door-to-door, and convincing a roommate to tutor you. This study is important as it served as a catalyst for a host of additional compliance-gaining studies; however, we will note some of the important limitations of this approach later in this chapter. Marwell and Schmitt's framework is presented in Table 8.2.

TABLE 8.2 16 Typology of Compliance-Gaining Behaviors

Technique	Message	Example
1. Promise	If you comply, I will reward you.	You offer to increase an employee's salary for working additional hours.
2. Threat	If you do not comply, you will be punished.	You threaten to fire an employee for not working additional hours.
3. Positive Expertise	If you comply you will be rewarded because of "the nature of things."	You argue that working additional hours will position the employee to advance in the organization.
4. Negative Expertise	If you do not comply you will be punished because of "the nature of things."	You argue that the employee will not be able to advance in the organization without working additional hours.
5. Liking	Persuader is friendly and messages are designed to get the target in a good frame of mind to facilitate compliance.	You attempt to be as friendly and positive as possible to get the employee in a good frame of mind before making the request.
6. Pre-Giving	Persuader rewards the target before requesting compliance.	You raise the employee's salary and then ask that they work additional hours.
7. Aversive Stimulation	Persuader punishes the target, making cessation contingent on compliance.	You forbid the employee from using the breakroom until they agree to work more hours.
8. Debt	You owe me compliance because of past favors.	You point out that you bent over backwards to get the employee this job and that they owe you as a result.
9. Moral Appeal	You are immoral if you do not comply.	You tell the employee that it is morally wrong not to help the company by putting in more hours.
10. Positive Self-Feeling	You will feel better about yourself if you comply.	You tell the employee that they will feel proud by working more hours.

(continued)

Technique	Message	Example
11. Negative Self-Feeling	You will feel worse about yourself if you do not comply.	You tell the employee that they will feel ashamed if they do not work more hours.
12. Positive Altercasting	A person with "good" qualities would comply.	You tell the employee that since they are mature and devoted to the company, they should naturally want to work more hours to help the company.
13. Negative Altercasting	Only a person with "bad" qualities would not comply.	You tell the employee that only a loafer would not want to work more hours.
14. Altruism	I need your compliance badly, so do it for me.	You tell the employee that you really want them to advance in the company and wish they would work more hours.
15. Positive Esteem	People you value will think better of you if you comply.	You tell the employee that their family would be extremely proud of them for working more hours.
16. Negative Esteem	People you value will think worse of you if you do not comply.	You tell the employee that their family will be very disappointed in them for not working more hours to help the company.

Source: Adapted from Gerald Marwell and David R. Schmitt, "Dimensions of Compliance-Gaining Behavior: An Empirical Analysis" *Sociometry*, vol. 30, no. 4, pp. 357-358. Copyright © 1967 by American Sociological Association.

It should be clear that Marwell and Schmitt's (1967) typology aligns well with French and Raven's power bases. For example, rewarding and punishing activity parallel reward and coercive power. Further, tactics based on expertise are grounded in expert power. Similarly, activation of personal commitments aligns with referent power while activation of impersonal commitments is similar to legitimate power. Marwell and Schmitt (1967) concluded that an individual's compliance-gaining style reflects the "extent of each power-resource possessed by the individual" and the individual's willingness to utilize that power (p. 364).

Importantly, a listener's compliance may depend on many factors. For instance, the nonverbal behaviors of the requester, the proximity of the requester to the target, and the persuasive vocal tone all influence compliance (Chidambaram et al., 2012).

Typology of Behavior Alteration Techniques and Messages

Instructional communication scholars have developed typologies of compliance-gaining strategies used by instructors and students. A series of studies, and the resulting typologies, provide a lens for understanding these persuasive strategies (Golish & Olson, 2000; Kearney et al., 1984, 1985; McCroskey et al.,

1985; Plax et al., 1986; Richmond et al., 1987; Roach, 1991). In particular, Kearney et al. (1985) created a typology of Behavior Alteration Techniques (BATs) and corresponding Behavior Alteration Messages (BAMs). They define BATs as the specific tactics persuaders use to gain compliance. In contrast, BAMs refer to the actual verbal messages that persuaders produce. Kearney et al.'s study was conducted in two phases. In phase one, the scholars distributed the following question to 177 college students enrolled in various communication courses:

> People try to get other people to do things they may not want to do. The other person usually thinks and often asks, "Why should I do this?" Give us the most common answers you'd give to this question, such as, "It'll be good for you," or "You will lose a lot if you don't." (Kearney et al., 1985, p. 22)

After the messages were generated, students were grouped and asked to categorize their responses. As with previous compliance-gaining typologies, BATs and BAMs can be classified as prosocial, antisocial, or neutral. Kearney et al.'s typology can be found in Table 8.3.

TABLE 8.3 Typology of Behavior Alteration Techniques (BATs) and Messages (BAMs)

BATs	BAMs
Reward From Behavior	You will enjoy it. You will be rewarded if you do what I ask. Doing this for me will make you happy.
Reward From Others	Others will think highly of you if you do what I ask. Others will like you if you do what I ask. Others will respect you if you do what I ask.
Punishment From Source	I will punish you if you don't do what I ask. I will make life miserable for you if you don't comply. I will continue doing bad things to you if you don't comply.
Referent-Model	This is the way I always do it. People who are like me do this. People you respect do this.
Legitimate-Higher Authority	Do it. I'm just telling you what I was told. It's a rule. I have to do and so do you.
Guilt	If you don't do what I ask, others will be hurt. If you don't do what I ask, others will be unhappy.
Reward From Source	I will reward you if you do what I ask. I will continue to reward you if you comply.
Normative Rules	Everyone else does it. We voted, and the majority rules. All of your friends are doing it.
Personal Responsibility	It is your responsibility to comply. There is nobody that can do this. People are depending on you to comply.

(continued)

BATs	BAMs
Expert	From my experience, it is a good idea. From what I have learned, it is what you should do.
Punishment From Behavior	You will be punished if you don't comply. You will be hurt if you don't comply.
Self-Esteem	You will feel good about yourself if you comply. You are the best person for the job.
Debt	You owe me this. You promised to do it.
Personal Relationship—Negative	I will dislike you if you don't comply. I will lose respect for you if you don't comply.
Altruism	If you do this it will help others. Others will benefit if you comply.
Personal Relationship—Positive	I will like you better if you comply. I will think more highly of you if you comply.
Duty	Your groups needs the job done. Our group depends on you.
Legitimate-Personal Authority	Do it because I told you so. You have to do it. It's required. You don't have a choice.

Source: Adapted from Patricia Kearney, et al., "Power in the Classroom III: Teacher Communication Techniques and Messages," *Communication Education*, vol. 34, no. 1, p. 23. Copyright © 1985 by Taylor & Francis Group.

In the second phase of this study, an instrument based on the categories developed in phase one was distributed to 204 elementary and secondary teachers enrolled in graduate courses in instructional communication. The teachers were asked to indicate how often they used each BAT to gain the compliance of their students. Teachers reported using seven BATs in classroom management: reward from behavior, reward from source, personal responsibility, expert, self-esteem, altruism, and duty.

How do students respond to the compliance-gaining efforts of teachers? According to Hildenbrand and Houser (2020), students' responses may depend on their learning orientation. Students who attend college with a primary objective to earn good grades are categorized as grade oriented. In contrast, students who attend college with a primary focus on gaining knowledge for the sake of learning new information are categorized as learning oriented. Hildenbrand and Houser found that grade-oriented students were more willing to comply with antisocial BATs, while learning-oriented students were more willing to comply with prosocial BATs.

Scholars have also sought to identify the BATs and BAMs students use to persuade instructors. For example, Golish (1999) found that students use both verbal and nonverbal BATs when seeking the compliance of instructors. In addition, students reported relying on group persuasion (e.g., "As a class we decided that we need another week to prepare for the exam") to gain the compliance of instructors. Golish also found that students reported using antisocial BATs and BAMs (e.g., "This discussion will reflect poorly on your course evaluations") as a last resort when prosocial influence attempts failed. Interestingly, Kussart et al. (2007) found that students in learning communities reported using more BATs, including antisocial BATs, compared to students who were not enrolled in learning communities. How do teachers respond to the compliance-gaining efforts of students? Sidelinger et al. (2012) found that instructors were more likely to comply when they reported liking their students.

Variables like gender and biological sex also play a role in the kinds of compliance-gaining tactics persuaders employ. Baker et al. (2005) found that "males and females differ in their use of power to influence others" (p. 23). More specifically, men employed aggressive persuasion tactics more often, while women relied on emotional strategies more often. The researchers concluded that men may feel they have greater power than women do in the classroom. Beyond the classroom, Dallinger and Hample (1994) found that men report using more antisocial strategies, while women report using more person-centered strategies. In medicine, male physicians have been found to use direct orders to gain compliance (e.g., adherence to treatment regimens) with female patients (Levesque & Li, 2016).

FIGURE 8.4 Pro-social requests for help will be more effective than anti-social threats when the persuader thinks the request will be resisted. Mood and nonverbals, such as those in this photo, might make us suspect the request will be resisted.

Researchers have also examined differences in compliance-gaining based on biological sex in the context of information we encounter via social media. The rapid proliferation of social media has resulted in vast amounts of personal information potentially being available to advertisers, marketers, or other would-be persuaders. As a result, they often know more about us than we do about them. In a study that tested whether an asymmetrical information distribution (i.e., a situation in which the persuader knows a great deal about the receiver but not vice versa), Stefanone et al. (2015) found that persuaders do benefit from asymmetrical information in that they are more successful at getting receivers to comply with requests after a mere 10-minute online conversation. They also found that conversational style improved compliance. Stefanone et al. found that men were significantly more likely to comply with requests when the persuader held an asymmetrical information advantage, whereas women tended to comply regardless of condition.

Understanding the Persuasive Situation

To gain another's compliance entails a persuasive process. Without question, many situational variables influence the compliance-gaining strategies we employ. As Cody et al. (1980) observed, "One cannot ignore the role of the environment as a determinant of message strategy selection" (p. 132). Further, Cody et al.'s (1983) research identified seven situational dimensions of compliance gaining: personal benefits, intimacy, rights, resistance, dominance, situational apprehension, and relational consequences. Each of these dimensions is explored in greater depth in Table 8.4.

TABLE 8.4 Situational Dimensions of Compliance Gaining

Situational Dimension	Definition	Example
Personal Benefits	The extent to which the persuader believes the strategy will benefit the self or others.	You select strategies you perceive will produce the greatest benefits.
Intimacy	The level of emotional attachment one has to others in the persuasive situation.	Because of your concern for maintaining your relationships, you use different compliance-gaining strategies with your friends than strangers.
Rights	The extent to which the persuader believes the request is justified or warranted.	You may perceive that complaining about the amount of homework assigned in your classes is justifiable, while complaining about another student's physical appearance is not.
Resistance	The extent to which the persuader thinks the request will be resisted.	You decide that a prosocial request for help will generate less resistance than an antisocial threat.
Dominance	The level of power the persuader has in the relationship.	Given power differences, you use more prosocial strategies with your boss than employees who work for you.

(continued)

Situational Dimension	Definition	Example
Situational Apprehension	The persuader's perception of apprehension in the situation.	You use fewer threats in situations you find highly apprehensive.
Relational Consequences	The degree to which a compliance-gaining strategy will have long- or short-term consequences for the relationship.	You avoid threatening your relational partner to maintain the viability of the relationship.

Beyond the work of Cody et al., several scholars have found that the situational dynamics of interpersonal relationships influence compliance gaining (see Boster & Smith, 1984, for a review of the research in this area). For example, Miller et al. (1977) found that individuals have a broader array of compliance-gaining options with intimate partners compared to nonintimate partners. They reasoned that persuaders' knowledge of intimate partners allows them to tailor their compliance-gaining efforts to specific desires, wants, and needs. They also found that the selection of compliance-gaining techniques depended on the persuader's perception of whether the situation carried long- or short-term consequences.

Is it better to gain compliance efficiently, or is gaining compliance effectively more important? The answer likely depends on the persuasive situation. In studying hints, threats, suggestions, and promises, Kellermann and Shea (1996) argued that the efficiency and effectiveness of compliance-gaining requests have distinct outcomes. They found direct requests to be efficient ways to gain compliance, while threats were not efficient.

Compliance-Gaining Design Logics

According to O'Keefe (1988), individuals employ different compliance-gaining strategies based on beliefs they hold about the process of communication. Put simply, individuals hold different definitions of communication that manifest in a range of ways of constructing and consuming persuasive messages. O'Keefe describes three systems of belief, or **message design logics** (MDL), about communication: expressive, conventional, and rhetorical. A comparison of these approaches can be found in Table 8.5.

Expressive Design Logic

Individuals with the expressive design logic beliefs view language as a medium for expressing thoughts and actions. Such communicators view messages solely as a means for making one's thoughts and actions known to others. Expressive

TABLE 8.5 Message Design Logics

MDL	Belief About Communication	Function of Message	Importance of Context
Expressive	Language is a medium for expression.	Self-expression.	Little attention is devoted to context.
Conventional	Communication is a cooperative game played by established social rules.	Secured a desired outcome.	Communication is context dependent.
Rhetorical	Communication is the creation of social selves and contexts.	Negotiate social consensus and relationships.	Communication processes create context.

communicators tend to be succinct, open, and honest and assume that words have common definitions that are broadly understood. Importantly, individuals who subscribe to the expressive approach often fail to recognize that communication can be used for other ends; therefore, they speak rather bluntly and tend to dump their thoughts and feelings into the conversation. A person operating from this perspective might say something like: "Look, I can't handle this situation anymore. Why do you keep doing this to me? Just go away!" As you likely inferred, the expressive approach is the least sophisticated message design logic.

Conventional Design Logic

Individuals with the conventional design logic belief view communication as a game that is played cooperatively according to established rules and procedures. This view subsumes the expressive approach but adds that the "propositions one expresses are specified by the social effect one wants to achieve rather than the thoughts one happens to have" (O'Keefe, 1988, p. 86). In other words, conventional communicators express themselves in a way that is appropriate to the social situation in which they are communicating. An individual operating from this design logic might say something like the following:

> When you didn't complete the last assignment, you offered a ton of excuses. When you enrolled in this class, the rules regarding late work were clearly explained. This is the second time that I've mentioned to you that assignments must be turned in on time. In the future, please be sure to get all assignments to me by the date they are due.

Given their focus on the social situation, conventional communicators are aware of the effects of overly expressive messages and may alter their communication to achieve desired goals. Compare the messages displayed in Figures 8.5

FIGURE 8.5 COVID-19 message with apology.

and 8.6 explaining that supplies are limited due to COVID-19. Keeping conventional design logic in mind, consider how the messages differ and how customers might react to the two messages.

Rhetorical Design Logic

According to O'Keefe (1988), individuals who embrace the rhetorical design logic believe that "communication involves the creation and negotiation of social selves and situations" (p. 87). As a result, the process of communication involves coordination and negotiation. Further, rhetorical message producers place a great deal of importance on interpersonal harmony and consensus and prefer to

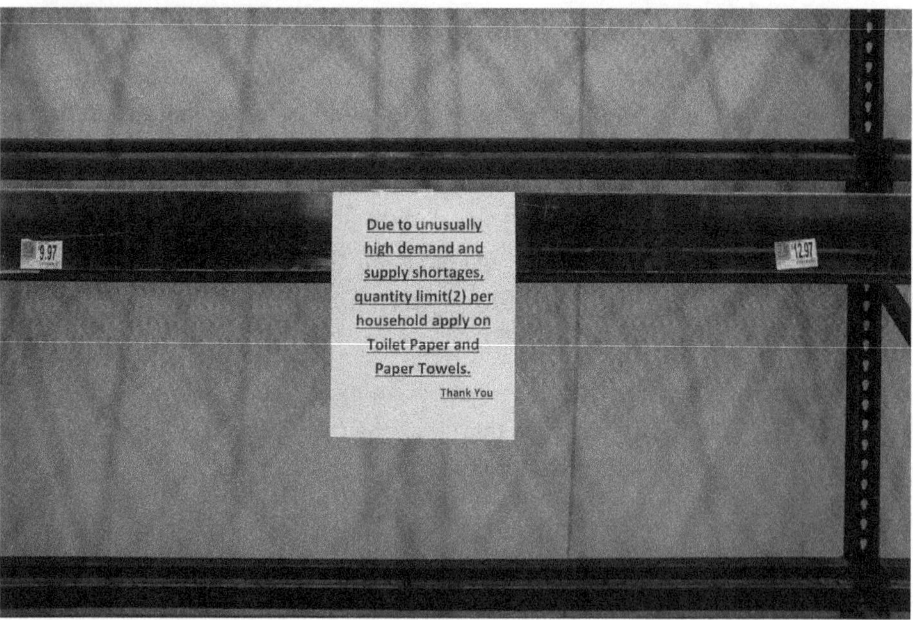

FIGURE 8.6 COVID-19 message with thank you.

use rational arguments. A communicator following this MDL might make the following argument:

> Things have gone so well that we have a week left to work on this group project. It's in pretty good shape, but it could use some polishing. Why don't we use the next week to see if everyone can improve their part?

Clearly, rhetorical persuaders are often proactive in seeking harmony and building consensus. This design logic takes skill to execute and O'Keefe (1988) argues that it requires the most cognitive complexity.

Research generally supports the conclusion that messages grounded in a rhetorical design logic are rated as more effective, competent, and persuasive than messages based in the expressive or conventional approaches (Barton & Stein, 2017; Lambert & Gillespie, 1994; O'Keefe & McCornack, 1987; Scott et al., 2013). However, scholars have failed to demonstrate support for the rhetorical approach over other design logics in the context of friendship and romantic relationships (Hullman, 2004; Hullman & Behbehani, 2018).

Engaged Persuasion Research: Message Design Logics and Organizational Change

Implementing change in any organization requires a carefully planned communication strategy. One important factor is consideration of how organizational stakeholders respond to proposed change. For example, it is important to consider the kinds of persuasive message design logics employees utilize in response to organizational change. Barbour et al. (2013) examined the messages respondents in their study produced in response to a hypothetical organizational change scenario. They found that participants elected to use more sophisticated message design logics when communicating with someone they perceived to have high status. Participants also employed more sophisticated design logics when communicating about change they perceived to be organizationally local. Further, the researchers found that intensity of beliefs mediated relationships between message sophistication and attitude toward the proposed change. As Barbour et al. (2013) noted, "As favorability becomes stronger, the relationship with sophistication leveled off. Support for change was positively related to message sophistication, but only to a point" (p. 371). Taken together, these findings provide important insights for anyone navigating organizational change.

Compliance-Gaining Goals

Persuasion scholars have also examined the goals of communicators seeking to gain compliance. Wilson and Kunkel (2000) defined compliance-gaining goals as the reasons why a source seeks to alter a target's behavior. Importantly, Wilson and Kunkel (2000) noted that communicators "interpret compliance-gaining episodes based on their understanding of specific goals" (p. 197). As Dillard et al. (1989) noted, these goals bracket the communication situation. Put another way, these goals frame a target's thinking about the communication situation as the individual seeks to understand what is motivating the source's use of particular compliance-gaining strategies.

In her extensive review of literature in this area, Kellermann (2004) identified several common compliance-gaining goals, including providing guidance, getting advice, obtaining a favor, obtaining information, moving relationships forward, ending relationships, and fulfilling obligations. As you can see, these goals vary significantly in their negative affect potential. For example, the goal of ending a relationship with a partner may result in negative feelings of rejection. In contrast, the goal of providing guidance to another may increase the target's positive impressions of the sender.

Cai and Wilson (2000) applied Politeness Theory to examine how sources give reasons, communicate approval, and exert pressure in compliance-gaining situations. According to Brown and Levinson (1987), Politeness Theory posits that communicators are motivated to maintain positive and negative face. Positive face involves one's desire to be liked, approved of, and appreciated. In contrast, negative face involves one's desire to maintain autonomy and freedom. Cai and Wilson argued that politeness theory is particularly helpful in understanding how persuaders identify threats to their face by combining their knowledge of the rules governing compliance requests with their understanding of the specific influence goals being pursued.

Cai and Wilson's (2000) study focused on two compliance-gaining situations—asking a favor and requesting that a favor be repaid. In addition, they examined the influence of culture by comparing participants from the United States and Japan. Overall, their findings suggest that individuals associate similar face threats with the influence goals of asking a favor and enforcing repayment. However, their findings revealed several important cultural differences. For example, the goal of the compliance-gaining request had a stronger effect on participants' desire to support the target's negative face (e.g., participants' desire to avoid imposing too much on the target) for the U.S. sample compared to the Japanese sample. On the other hand, the same goal exerted more influence on participants' desire to support the target's positive face (e.g., making sure that the target doesn't look or feel bad) for the Japanese sample.

Cai and Wilson (2000) concluded that individuals across cultures generally prefer to express approval for the target and refrain from using strong pressure when asking favors or seeking to enforce obligations. However, the means by which persuaders express approval and avoid pressure may vary significantly by culture.

Given the research on goals, do persuasive requests need to present compliance-gaining goals that appropriately match or fit the means used by the requester? Empirical evidence indicates that donation amounts and compliance are higher when the compliance-gaining context fits the goals, meaning that the verbal presentation of goals primes targets for compliance (Shaw et al., 2017).

Problematizing Compliance-Gaining Research

Hundreds of articles, book chapters, and conference presentations have been generated since the publication of Marwell and Schmitt's (1967) compliance-gaining typology. As work in this area progressed, scholars became more and more concerned that the reliance on reactions to hypothetical scenarios and the overuse of college students in samples was not generalizable to complex, real world compliance-gaining situations. As Stiff and Mongeau (2016) noted, communication scholars concluded that "studies of hypothetical compliance-gaining situations lacked the ecological and predictive validity necessary to gain much understanding of persuasion in naturally occurring interpersonal situations" (p. 262).

Another potential problem with this line of research is social desirability bias. In other words, when presented with a list of compliance-gaining behaviors, participants may select prosocial or neutral compliance-gaining techniques because they perceive that admitting they use antisocial techniques would make them look bad to others. In fact, a study by Dillard (1998) seriously undermined the validity of the message selection approach. Dillard had participants rate their likelihood of using particular compliance-gaining techniques in a way that was consistent with prior message selection studies. However, he then observed participants in actual compliance-gaining situations and found no relationship between their ratings and actual behavior. As the next section of this chapter demonstrates, scholars have largely abandoned the message selection paradigm and have opted to study actual behavior.

Engaged Persuasion Research: Compliance in the Context of Health Communication

Wrench and Booth-Butterfield (2003) found a positive relationship between the humor orientation of physicians and compliance-gaining strategies. More specifically, physicians who rated higher in humor orientation were more prone to employ a plethora of compliance-gaining strategies to enhance patient compliance. Additionally, increased communication about compliance gaining led to higher patient satisfaction as well as more positive ratings of physician credibility. The practical implication, therefore, is that medical schools would be well served to teach future physicians to incorporate humor into their communication with patients. By integrating humor, physicians will then be more able to enhance patient compliance with treatment regimens.

Sequential Persuasion

How persuasive requests are sequenced makes a difference in gaining the compliance of receivers. If the man in the opening photo of this chapter offered you a free red balloon and then asked for a favor, would you be inclined to comply with a subsequent request? Even young children learn quite early to sequence their persuasive requests. For instance, a child may first lead with a question they feel the parent will easily agree to before making a larger request.

Innately, then, we sense that sequencing our persuasive attempts may lead to greater success. See Table 8.6 for an overview of the four most commonly discussed **sequential persuasion** tactics.

TABLE 8.6 Four Most Common Types of Sequential Persuasion

Sequential Persuasion Tactic	Example
1. Foot-in-the-Door Tactic	Make a small request, then follow with a larger and related request
2. Door-in-the-Face Tactic	Make an extreme request, then follow with a more reasonable target request
3. That's-Not-All Tactic	Follow an initial offer by immediately sweetening the deal
4. Lowball Tactic	Seek commitment to an initial offer, then follow with less favorable terms

Foot-in-the-Door Tactic

With the **foot-in-the-door** (FITD) **tactic**, an initial request for something small and minimally invasive is made. After securing compliance with the small request, the persuader makes a larger, related request. The foot-in-the-door technique operates on the premise that people desire consistency (Cialdini & Goldsmith, 2004). The reasoning here is that if I can get you to say to yes to a small request or two, you will be likely to respond affirmatively when I next make a larger request. Our self-perception is that we are consistent, so we desire to make decisions that are consistent with our prior decisions. For instance, I might ask you to loan me a few office supplies for a project I am working on. This simple, small request is easy enough for you to comply with. Then, when I return to ask for you to even more supplies so I can finish the project, you may feel that the only cognitively consistent response is to agree once again.

Evidence even suggests a strong FITD effect when requests are made by robots, thus indicating that FITD is effective even when requests are technologically generated (Lee & Liang, 2019). In fact, 70% of targets who complied with the robot's initial request also complied with a larger subsequent request. These findings suggest that FITD can be explained by consistency and commitment. Lee and Liang also found the FITD effect to operate independently of source credibility.

Door-in-the-Face Tactic

The **door-in-the-face** (DITF) **tactic** involves making an extreme request, that likely will be rejected, followed by a legitimate concession that results in a subsequent request for that which is truly desired (Cialdini & Goldsmith, 2004). The idea is that the request recipient will reciprocate the concession by complying with the second request. In other words, if I ask for something big that I suspect you will say no to, then when I follow with a second request I really care about, you are less likely to decline. For example, if what I really want you to do is agree to volunteer an hour of your time at a charity event, my initial request might be for you to volunteer 20 hours. The 20-hour request is more extreme, so when I remove that from the table and follow up with the 1-hour request, it will seem to you as if you are getting off easy. Plus, you may feel bad that you turned down the 20-hour request for such a noble cause, so donating a single hour of your time seems the least you can do. Research is split regarding the effectiveness of this tactic as well as the moderating factors, such as feelings of guilt that may arise from turning down the initial request, that might be at play (Cialdini & Goldsmith, 2004). Think of the child who asks a parent to buy an expensive toy in the store. The child appears to really want the expensive toy and to be crushed when the parent says no. Now, the child asks the parent if they will at least buy a less expensive toy. What will happen in this scenario? Will the parent feel guilty about having turned down the more expensive request and now cave to the less expensive request?

Through a series of three experiments, Feeley et al. (2017) found that DITF worked as a result of reciprocal concessions. The researchers also speculated that the request context may moderate DITF effects. In other words, when DITF works effectively it likely does so because targets of requests are reciprocating the favor provided by the requester when the requester essentially bargains or negotiates a lower offer. Importantly, "The larger the concession undertaken on the part of the message sender, the greater the effect size in terms of intentions to help or assist the sender in relation to a prosocial cause" (Feeley et al., 2017, p. 118). Thus, when requesters make greater concessions, targets feel obliged to comply.

Cantarero et al.'s (2017) study discovered that DITF effectiveness depends on targets' preference for consistency, or their desire for consistency in their own and others' behaviors. When preference for consistency was low, meaning targets preferred change and unpredictability, the DITF effect was stronger. In other words, after refusing the initial request, those low in preference for consistency showed a higher probability to comply with the subsequent request.

That's-Not-All Tactic

Persuaders using the **that's-not-all tactic** make an initial request but immediately follow that request by sweetening the deal before the receiver has a chance to respond (Cialdini & Goldsmith, 2004). By sweetening the deal, the persuader might reduce the cost of a product or increase the benefits associated with compliance. If I try to sell you a product and immediately throw in a bonus product for no additional money, you may be more likely to agree to the purchase. The seller, in this situation, appears to be generous since they sweeten the deal. Thus, the reasoning behind this tactic is that we will respond favorably to such generosity by being generous ourselves and acquiescing to the request. And we tend to like receiving bonus items because it seems like a better deal to us. When bonus items are thrown into the deal, our perception of the initial item is enhanced.

Lowball Tactic

The **lowball tactic** plays upon people's desire to act in a manner consistent with their prior, public commitments (Cialdini & Goldsmith, 2004). The lowball tactic first seeks commitment in response to an initial, favorable offer and subsequently makes a request with less favorable terms (Pascual et al., 2016). It is the second request, the one with less favorable terms, that is the target request.

Let us imagine that we are general managers for professional baseball teams. If I were to initially offer to trade you a player from my team that you wanted for your team in exchange for a player from your team that you did not mind parting with, you might agree to a straight-up swap of the players. Using the lowball tactic, that is exactly what my initial offer would suggest. However, once I get you to agree in principle to trading Player A for Player B, I would then come back with a revised offer. For instance, I would remind you that you already agreed to swap the players but then inform you that I also need a late-round draft pick thrown in. The terms of this revised trade are not as favorable to you, but since you have already committed to swapping the players, you now feel obliged to acquiesce. There is a perfect example of this scenario in a scene from the 2011 movie *Moneyball* where the Oakland A's general manager Billy Beane (portrayed by Brad Pitt) trades players with another team and then, when the other team's general manager calls back to agree to the deal, Pitt's character immediately requests that the other team also pay to stock the A's clubhouse soda machine. While the additional terms might only amount to a minor alteration of the initial offer, the terms are certainly less favorable. Car salespeople are known to employ the lowball tactic frequently. See "Engaged Persuasion Activity:

Engaged Persuasion Activity: The Ethics of the Lowball Tactic

In some countries, such as France, the lowball tactic is illegal and covered by consumer protection laws. Pascual et al. (2016) point out that the ethical question at the heart of the matter is that lowballing is essentially lying by omission. Do you think that lowballing is unethical? If one team is able to get a second team to commit in principle to a player trade but then proposes additional terms when it comes time to make the deal final, is that unethical? What are the arguments for and against the ethics of lowballing in this situation? Now, let us imagine that you are purchasing a new vehicle. The salesperson asks if you are committed to making the purchase so that the paperwork can be drawn up. You agree, but then the salesperson comes back and says that the deal you committed to comes with a couple additional terms as stipulated in the paperwork you must sign to get your new vehicle. Would you feel that you have been treated ethically? What are the arguments for and against the ethics of lowballing in this situation?

The Ethics of the Lowball Tactic" for a discussion of the ethical ramifications of lowballing.

Meta-analysis evidence has supported the efficiency of the lowball tactic and shown that commitment appears to be a reasonable explanation of why the tactic works (Pascual et al., 2016). The meta-analysis results also show that a delay is essential between the initial commitment and the additional terms. The delay could provide time for the target to feel more committed to their initial decision (Pascual et al., 2016).

Other Sequential Techniques

Now that we have covered the four most commonly discussed sequential persuasion techniques, we want to call your attention to a few other sequential persuasion tactics that research has shown to hold promise.

In a meta-analysis of 42 studies about the "**but you are free**" (BYAF) **tactic**, which involves informing the persuasive target that they are free to refuse the request, Carpenter (2013) found BYAF to be effective at gaining compliance for a variety of requests, whether prosocial or self-serving. However, the meta-analysis revealed that the effectiveness of BYAF diminished if the request was not made immediately afterwards. Later research about the BYAF technique has relabelled it the **evoking-freedom** (EF) **tactic** to reflect any variation of the phrase "You are free to refuse" (Samson-Secrieru & Carpenter, 2017). One reason the EF request, which the target is at least somewhat aware of due to the phrasing, works is that the requester is perceived as friendly (Samson-Secrieru & Carpenter, 2017). However, evidence suggests that the technique effectively increases compliance not because it is considered polite but because it preserves the freedom of the target and, thus, prevents a reactance response (Carpenter & Pascual, 2016). In other words, it does not threaten the freedom of the target. Consequently, health communication practitioners should consider these results. Specifically, persuasive health messages relayed in both mediated public service announcements as well as by physicians during interpersonal encounters with patients should employ the technique to reduce reactance (Carpenter & Pascual, 2016).

The **dump-and-chase** (DAC) **tactic** involves strategic persistence. In other words, the technique involves making repeated request of a target until they comply. If a target initially refuses, the persuader asks the target to explain why compliance is not an option. The persuader then advances counterarguments to the target's reasons for noncompliance and asks for compliance again. Two experiments by Boster et al. (2009) demonstrated that the DAC technique is more effective at generating greater compliance than both the door-in-the-face and foot-in-the-door techniques. Thus, persistence is a promising means of gaining compliance, whether the request is prosocial or self-serving (Boster et al., 2009).

FIGURE 8.7 This United Nations COVID-19 message emphasizing how every contribution counts is an example of the LPC technique.

The **legitimization of paltry contributions** (LPC) **tactic** involves adding the phrase "Even a penny helps" to a direct message request, which activates the target's sense of social responsibility as well as feelings of duty and obligation (Shaw et al., 2017). In a series of three field experiments in Poland, the technique was shown to increase the probability of donations to charity (Dolinski et al., 2005). When accompanied by dialogue between the requester and target, the technique was even more successful with participants in the experiments. In a meta-analysis of 13 studies utilizing the LPC technique, Bolkan and Rains (2017) found that LPC significantly increases compliance compared to control messages. However, their meta-analysis also discovered that LPC can result in smaller individual donation amounts and overall solicitation campaign totals that are similar to control conditions. "Although LPC messages may increase compliance rates, they might simultaneously serve to reduce the amount that is donated" (Bolkan & Rains, 2017, p. 991). Thus, Bolkan and Rains concluded that, in some cases, solicitation campaigns might be better off if they do not employ LPC since there is a risk that large donations may be forfeited. Why does this meta-analysis matter? College and university advancement offices often emphasize that any donation amount helps. While these efforts to build university endowments are often successful at encouraging more alumni to become first-time donors, this meta-analysis suggests that overall fundraising totals may not end up being significantly different, and there is the risk that otherwise large donations may be reduced in size.

The **foot-in-the-hand** (FITH) **tactic** involves requesting money while the requester is holding a few coins in one hand (Gueguen, 2015). In a series of three experiments, Gueguen's results demonstrated the effectiveness of FITH. In the first study, the mere presence of coins in the requester's hand increased compliance compared to a control condition in which no coins were present. When coins in the requester's hand were accompanied by a reason for the request, in the second study, or a statement that the request was close to reaching their goal, in the third study, compliance continued to increase. Gueguen concluded that the effects, while moderate, indicated stronger correlation with compliance than other techniques such as FITD, DITF, BYAF, and LPC.

The **"just-one-more"** (JOM) **tactic**, which involves variations of the phrase "I just need one more person to help" and creates the impression that the compliance of the target is more valuable than others who have been approached, has been shown to be effective at gaining compliance (Carpenter, 2014). The caution with the JOM approach is that it should not be used deceptively in situations in which the target is not actually the last participant the requester needs to reach their goal, as doing so raises ethical concerns and endangers long-term relationships with targets (Carpenter, 2014).

The **disrupt-then-reframe** (DTR) **tactic** involves employing a small disruption, such as asking for 100 pennies rather than saying one dollar, followed by a direct reframing of the request, such as noting that 100 pennies is a bargain. Through a series of four studies, Davis and Knowles (1999) demonstrated that DTR was effective at influencing targets to make a purchase from a charitable organization. Importantly, the studies found that the small disruption needs to precede the direct reframing to be effective. DTR works because the disruption interrupts resistance to the persuasive attempt while the reframing provides an additional incentive to support a charitable cause (Davis & Knowles, 1999). The researchers suspected that "if the unusual request increased mindfulness, it would diminish the effectiveness of any reframing message that was offered" (Davis & Knowles, 1999, p. 198).

Engaged Persuasion Research: Sequential Love Priming

In a field experiment, Lamy et al. (2015) had an undergraduate female request a late note for her class from metro employees in Paris, France, by priming them with feelings of love. The undergraduate female first explained that she was late because of an encounter with a hospitalized grandmother or a favorite celebrity star. If this implicit priming of love failed, the undergraduate female then used explicit priming by adding the statement "It's someone I love so much!" Sequential love priming, which is speculated to disrupt initial processing of a request, was found to increase compliance with the request when the priming was explicit as compared to a control condition. Implicit priming, however, did not enhance compliance.

Summary

In this chapter, we discussed compliance gaining, the five power bases, message design logics, compliance-gaining goals, and sequential persuasion techniques. Each of these topics are pivotal to understanding how requesters attempt to gain the compliance of their targets. To the extent that persuasive communication attempts aim to get a target to comply with a request or make a donation, understanding these topics and how targets respond to such persuasive tactics is essential.

The next chapter details theories critical to understanding how receivers process persuasive messages cognitively. Importantly, the chapter examines both sides of the message processing coin by exploring how individuals process messages actively as well as strategies that can be used to make receivers less susceptible to persuasion.

Check Your Understanding Review Questions

1. What does compliance gaining mean?
2. How does power relate to and affect compliance gaining?
3. In what ways do the expressive, conventional, and rhetorical message design logics differ?
4. What is the norm of reciprocity?
5. How do the five bases of power differ?
6. How do sequential persuasion techniques work?
7. In what ways do the sequential persuasion techniques differ?
8. Why are each of the sequential persuasion techniques effective?

Key Terms

compliance gaining (p. 194)
door-in-the-face tactic (p. 210)
dump-and-chase tactic (p. 213)
evoking-freedom tactic (p. 213)
foot-in-the-door tactic (p. 210)
lowball tactic (p. 212)
message design logics (p. 204)
power (p. 195)
power bases (p. 195)
sequential persuasion (p. 210)
that's-not-all tactic (p. 211)

Credits

CHAPTER 9

Message Processing Theories and Research

Chapter Objectives

After reading this chapter, you should be able to:

- Understand the Elaboration Likelihood Model of persuasion
- Understand the Heuristic Systematic Model of persuasion
- Explain Social Judgment Theory and its related components
- Describe Inoculation Theory and understand how to apply it to a variety of contexts
- Understand how forewarning can be used to bolster resistance to persuasion

How do we think about persuasive messages we encounter? This chapter details theories critical to understanding how receivers cognitively process persuasive messages. But are there times when we react to persuasive messages with negative cognitions? Yes, our thoughts are sometimes about resisting the persuasive message. Importantly, this chapter examines both sides of the message processing coin by exploring how individuals process messages actively as well as strategies that can be used to make receivers less susceptible to persuasion. More specifically, the theories addressed in this chapter that explore how people actively process messages include the dual process models and Social Judgment Theory. Meanwhile, Inoculation Theory explores how receivers can be less susceptible to persuasive influence attempts.

Dual Process Models of Persuasion

You were already introduced to the **Elaboration Likelihood Model** (ELM) and the **Heuristic Systematic Model** (HSM) in Chapter 1, where we focused on a brief overview of the **dual process models.** In this chapter, we will delve into other key aspects of each dual process model as well as the relevant research. Dual process models theorize that people process persuasive messages through differing cognitive processes. As you will recall, both ELM and HSM posit that receivers cognitively process persuasive messages through one of two routes or processes. While ELM and HSM use different terminology, both models suggest that we do not process all persuasive messages in the same manner. Although there are distinctions between ELM and HSM that we will explore in greater detail later in this chapter, let us begin by recognizing that each dual process model is concerned with attitude formation and change. In some cases, our attitudes develop and change based on careful scrutiny, comparison of information, and cognitive effort. In other words, we really think about and mentally wrestle with the

FIGURE 9.1 Dual process models posit dual routes to persuasion.

persuasive message. In other cases, though, we focus more on cues presented in the persuasive message and devote as few cognitive resources as possible to thinking about it. Thus, at the most basic level, both ELM and HSM describe how we may either expend a great deal of cognitive energy or as little cognitive energy as necessary when making a judgement about the persuasive message.

Elaboration Likelihood Model

As Petty et al. (1983) explained, ELM contends that receivers cognitively process messages through either the central or the peripheral route. The central route involves careful scrutiny of information related to message itself, while the **peripheral route** involves simple inferences made about the cues attendant to the message (Petty et al., 1983). These routes to attitude change are considered to be distinct, meaning that receivers will process persuasive appeals through one of these routes. How much message elaboration, which is another way of saying involvement, a receiver engages in can vary. High elaboration likelihood leads to the central route because receivers are more involved with the message. In other words, the message may be relevant to them or the consequences may more directly affect them, which motivates the receiver to expend cognitive effort to engage with the message and cognitively elaborate on it (Petty et al., 1983). Meanwhile low elaboration likelihood leads to the peripheral route since receivers default to being **cognitive misers** who are not involved with the message and are less likely to engage cognitively with it (Petty et al., 1983).

If you were actively in the market for a new car and planning to make a purchase soon, you would be more likely to attend to vehicle advertisements. After all, the advertisements are relevant to you, and you are more involved in the issue. Thus, you would process the advertisements through the central route. More specifically, you would be likely to elaborate on the information presented and expend cognitive resources thinking about the vehicles depicted in the advertisements. If you are not in the market for a new car and not planning to purchase one in the near future, however, it is more likely that you will process the advertisement through the peripheral route. After all, the message is not as relevant to you, and you are not as involved. Thus, you would be a cognitive miser and elaborate less on the message. Now, imagine what would catch your attention in the advertisements. A central processor would elaborate more on the information presented, think carefully about the facts and information presented, and focus on the details provided. You might pay special attention to the gas mileage estimates, the price tag, and the incentives offered. However, a peripheral processor would elaborate less, consider the advertisements less relevant, and expend less cognitive energy pondering the specific details provided. You might pay more attention to how the vehicle looks, the color of the car, or the music in the advertisement. You would be drawn more to the peripheral cues rather than the information central to making a purchasing decision.

It is important for us to recognize that people do not always follow only one of the routes. For instance, you might use the central route for certain messages but the peripheral route for other messages. In other words, people will do both types of processing, although they will default to one of the routes for a given message. For persuasive messages that are repetitive, or perhaps those with which receivers are already familiar, people tend to prefer peripheral processing (Koch, 2017). Hemispheric electroencephalogram activity may be linked to attitudes and cognitions (Cacioppo et al., 1982), which suggests that we can potentially see how messages are processed through physiological measures. The manner in which the message is presented may also matter. As Slater and Rouner (2002) explain, ELM suggests that narrative messages can enhance persuasion by suppressing counterarguments when the message content is counterattitudinal. However, one limitation is that ELM does assume the conscious perception of a message, so it fails to account for strong persuasive effects from unconsciously perceived stimuli (Koch, 2017).

FIGURE 9.2 ELM is able to explain processing of mediated communication.

How well does ELM apply to online and electronic communication? Disparate research studies indicate that ELM is able to explain processing of mediated messages quite well. One study, for instance, examining crowdfunding on Kickstarter confirmed ELM tenets by showing that potential funders who possess greater motivation and ability to make careful evaluations tended to process funding appeals centrally, while inexperienced and first-time funders relied on peripheral cues (Allison et al., 2017). Another study examined how social media fits ELM. The results of that study suggested that the quality of information on social media is processed through the central route, while peripheral processing includes the source credibility of social media as well as the reputation of social media (Zha et al., 2018). Even searching for information using digital libraries can be explained using ELM. Information quality, processed through the central route, and sources credibility and reputation, processed through the peripheral route, predict digital library usage for obtaining information (Zha et al., 2016). Finally, contrary to the original propositions and findings of ELM, one study investigating how website design impacts online persuasion found that highly knowledgeable users were more persuaded by peripheral cues, while users with low prior knowledge relied on central cues (Cyr et al., 2018). For example, one specific finding revealed that pictures of other users on a website, which is considered a peripheral cue, were persuasive to more knowledgeable users. The researchers, thus, concluded that "the routes to online persuasion are more tangled and complex than first expected" (Cyr et al., 2018, p. 818).

How much empirical data is there to support the ELM? A meta-analysis, which combined the findings from 134 previous studies, by Carpenter (2015) confirmed the hypotheses of dual process models that strong arguments are more persuasive than weak ones and that messages processed centrally are more persuasive than messages processed peripherally. Thus, this meta-analysis largely supported the claims of ELM. Individual studies, however, may reveal differences in particular situations. For instance, a study examining peer-to-peer lending found that central as well as peripheral routes significantly affected the decision making of lenders (Han et al., 2018). Still, we should always give special weight to meta-analytic data, as this technique combines multiple studies conducted over a period of time.

Heuristic Systematic Model

Like ELM, HSM is a dual process model of persuasion that posits that receivers use either heuristic or systematic processing when encountering persuasive messages. Heuristic processing in HSM is similar to the peripheral route in ELM, while systematic processing in HSM is similar to the central route in ELM. People who process messages heuristically use less cognitive effort and resources than those who use systematic processing (Griffin et al., 2002). Since most people will devote the least effort needed to process most messages, they typically default to heuristic processing. Heuristic processing entails a reliance on trusted spokespeople, statistics, or message length to make attitude changes (Griffin et al., 2002). "Heuristic processing implies that people have formed or changed their attitudes by invoking heuristics such as 'experts can be trusted,' 'majority opinion is correct,' and 'long messages are valid messages'" (Chaiken & Maheswaran, 1994, p. 460). In a sense, heuristic processing is "comparatively effortless" and often follows rules of thumb (Neuwirth et al., 2002, p. 321). On the other hand, "Systematic processing implies that people have formed or updated their attitudes by actively attending to and cognitively elaborating persuasive argumentation" (Chaiken & Maheswaran, 1994, p. 460). People who scrutinize persuasive messages carefully, compare information, and are motivated to evaluate the message are using systematic processing (Trumbo, 1999).

Remember those advertisements for new vehicles you encountered? If you are planning to make a purchase soon, you are more likely to process the message systematically and scrutinize the information presented. If you are not searching for a new ride, though, you are more likely to process the advertisements heuristically and focus on the spokesperson in the advertisement or the awards the new vehicle has won. Now, imagine how long those advertisement will stay in your thoughts. The systematic processor may continue thinking about the information or vehicles even after the commercial ends. Meanwhile, the heuristic processor is likely finished thinking about the car as soon as the commercial is over (unless, of course, that song playing in the background gets stuck in your head!). "If people process a message quickly, their understanding of its contents will likely be much more superficial than if they process that same message systematically" (Kahlor et al., 2003, p. 355). High interest in the message content is also associated with systematic processing (Kahlor et al., 2003).

In comparison, heuristic judgments tend to be less stable than judgments made systematically (Trumbo, 2002). Importantly, HSM holds that people process persuasive message through either heuristic or systematic processing, or a combination of the two. Consequently, we should highlight that both types of processing may be used in response to the same persuasive message. "Individuals may use both processing modes as they work to make a judgment" (Trumbo, 2002, p. 368). In other words, people use one of the two types of processing, depending on the message, and may even use both types of processing for the same message. Under certain conditions, such as when message content is ambiguous, heuristic processing can bias systematic processing (Chaiken & Maheswaran, 1994) because people may be prone to revert to previous scripts or cues for similar messages when processing ambiguous messages.

There are two factors that determine motivation, according to HSM: accuracy motivation and information sufficiency (Trumbo, 2002). People are motivated to form and change attitudes that reconcile with the relevant facts and information. Thus, people are motivated to discover information when they perceive they do not possess sufficient information upon which to make an attitude judgment. The need for sufficient information is known in HSM as the **sufficiency principle.** "Sufficiency entails a trade-off between minimizing processing effort and achieving a suitable level of confidence about judgments made" (Neuwirth et al., 2002, p. 322).

One recent area of research utilizing HSM deals with risk. HSM is useful for understanding how people process persuasive messages differentially based on their perceptions of risk (Trumbo, 2002). Receivers often are called upon to make judgments in response to persuasive messages. These judgments might entail attitude formation, attitude change, or decision making in response to the message. When judgments are deemed to hold less risk, people are prone to employ heuristic processing (Trumbo, 1999).

How do social media platforms and online resources affect information processing? Metzger et al. (2010) found that, despite the wealth of online resources available to research issues, people rely on group-based social media tools to process issues heuristically. Specifically, "Rather than systematically processing information, participants routinely invoked cognitive heuristics to evaluate the credibility of information and sources online" (Metzger et al., 2010, p. 413). In certain respects, then, when message processing in an online environment occurs,

FIGURE 9.3 Using online resources may lead to heuristic processing.

or simply when individuals have access to social media and online resources, audiences may respond more heuristically than systematically. In the absence of online resources, of course, we would expect HSM to function normally, wherein audience members would process persuasive messages either heuristically or systematically depending on their need for information. However, Metzger et al.'s findings suggest that having social media and other online resources on hand may result in more heuristic processing than we might otherwise expect.

Social Judgment Theory

Social Judgment Theory, developed by social psychologists Carolyn Sherif, Muzafer Sherif, and Carl Hovland, highlights the role that strong attitudes play in the ways we process persuasive messages. According to Ajzen (2001), strong attitudes are thought to be "relatively stable over time, to be resistant to persuasion, and to predict manifest behavior" (p. 37). The aim of Social Judgment Theory is to predict the direction and extent of attitude changes based on the positionality of the persuasive message in relation to one's current attitude (Sherif & Hovland, 1961; Sherif & Sherif, 1967). Most research on Social Judgment Theory takes a quantitative approach to analyzing judgments (Hall & Oppenheimer, 2015; Unsworth et al., 2015). Thus, receivers make judgments about a message based on their existing **anchor point**, or stance on a particular issue or message (Asemah & Nwammuo, 2017). As you can see, Social Judgment Theory posits that people

FIGURE 9.4 March to encourage science funding and acceptance of scientific analysis in politics.

do not evaluate persuasive messages simply on the merits of the arguments communicated. Instead, people evaluate messages based on their existing attitudes, the argument presentation, and the position of the argument in relation to their existing opinions about the issue (Rumble et al., 2017). Ego involvement causes receivers to be more resistant to persuasion (Park et al., 2007).

Latitudes of Acceptance, Noncommitment, and Rejection

According to Social Judgment Theory, one's attitude can be plotted in a series of zones or latitudes: the latitude of acceptance, latitude of noncommitment, and latitude of rejection (Karlsen & Aardal, 2016). In other words, these latitudes can be found along an attitude continuum (Park et al., 2007). Ideas that one finds acceptable fall within the latitude of acceptance, while ideas one finds unacceptable fall within the latitude of rejection; and the latitude of noncommitment encompasses ideas one has no opinion about (Asemah & Nwammuo, 2017). Consider how the march for science shown in Figure 9.4 aimed messages depicted in their signs toward politicians. Would these messages be accepted or rejected by politicians? Does the answer to that question depend on the anchor points of individual politicians? "If the advocated position is close to the initial position of the receiver, it is assumed that this position falls within the receiver's latitude of acceptance. As a result, the receiver is likely to shift in the direction of the advocated position (assimilation)" (Dykstra et al., 2015, para. 9). Of course, persuasion effectiveness can vary, depending on certain factors. As Park et al. (2007) explain:

> The width of these attitudes varies across individuals and attitude topics. For some people and some attitudes, the latitude of acceptance is relatively wide and the latitude of rejection is relatively small. For such people and attitudes, successful persuasion is more likely to occur. For other people and attitudes, however, persuasion is more likely to fail because they have a narrow latitude of acceptance and a wide latitude of rejection. (p. 83)

How can knowledge of these latitudes be useful to persuaders? Recent research by Ruth and Rumble (2019) demonstrates how consumers evaluate persuasive messages about genetically modified (GM) food. Specifically, Ruth and Rumble sought to describe the latitudes of acceptance, rejection, and noncommitment for Florida residents who hold positive and negative attitudes toward GM food. Table 9.1 presents a summary of their findings for respondents who held negative attitudes toward GM food. As you can see, they found that individuals most aligned with the position that GM food can cause cancer strongly rejected the arguments indicating that "GM foods are safe for human consumption," "GM food has increased the food available for me to purchase," and "GM food can

TABLE 9.1 Latitudes of Acceptance, Rejection, and Noncommitment for Those Holding Negative Attitudes Toward GM Food

Statement that Most Aligned with Personal Attitude	Latitudes of Acceptance, Rejection, and Noncommitment for the Following Statements							
	GM food can cause cancer in humans.	GM food contributes to the prevalence of antibiotic resistant bacteria.	Potential risks of GM food related to health have not been adequately studied.	GM foods might be riskier to consume than traditional food.	GM foods are safe for human consumption.	GM food has increased the food available for me to purchase.	GM food can provide me with improved nutrition compared to traditional food.	GM food can be used to increase the safety of certain foods.
GM food can cause cancer in humans.		49.8%	60.1%	71.8	56.3%	36.8%	52.5%	46.2%
Potential risks of GM food related to health have not been adequately investigated.	46.3%	43.7%		67.7%	53.5%	39.7%	39.9%	42.2%

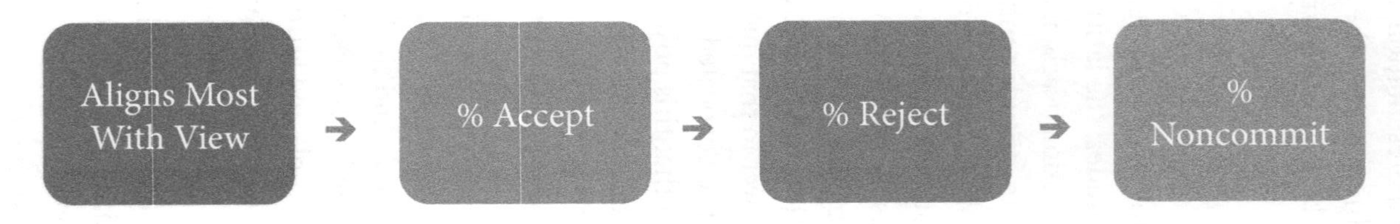

Source: Adapted from Taylor K. Ruth and Joy N. Rumble, "Consumers' Evaluations of Genetically Modified Food Messages," *Journal of Applied Communications*, vol. 103, no. 1, p. 10. Copyright © 2019 by New Prairie Press.

provide me with improved nutrition compared to traditional food." In comparison, participants most aligned with the position that the risks of GM food have not been adequately investigated reported noncommitment to most of the positive messages about GM food.

The latitudes of acceptance, rejection, and noncommitment for participants whose attitudes were favorable to GM food are presented in Table 9.2. As you can see, participants in this group who aligned with the position that GM foods are safe for human consumption strongly rejected statements indicating that "GM food can cause cancer in humans" and "GM foods might be riskier to consume than traditional food." Participants who aligned with the argument that GM food can be used to increase the safety of certain foods expressed noncommitment to the negative statements about GM food.

Furthermore, it is important to consider targeting messages that fall within the latitude of noncommitment. According to findings by Rumble et al. (2017), "There is a large group of individuals who can be persuaded by the messages with high levels of non-commitment" (p. 9). For example, in one study that investigated how a social norms campaign aimed to reduce drinking behaviors among students at Michigan State University, the researchers created messages based on survey data about the average number of drinks the typical students consumed (Smith et al., 2006). Since Social Judgment Theory predicts that messages falling within the latitude of noncommitment are more effective, the research deployed messages that incorporated information about the average number of drinks students consumed and then measured student perceptions of these norms. Smith et al. (2006) concluded that "changes in latitudes will produce changes in attitudes" (p. 148). They also noted that "the boundaries of latitudes vary over time, across populations, and between types of norms" (Smith et al., 2006, p. 150).

Consider the example of political party affiliation. Karlsen and Aardal (2016) explain that "the ideological pre-dispositions of a voter, that is, his or her political values, will decide which parties will be included in the latitude of acceptance and which parties will be rejected" (p. 263). While a particular political party might be preferred, several parties may be evaluated favorably within the latitude of acceptance (Karlsen & Aardal, 2016). In other words, if you prefer the Democratic party, the Libertarian Party may also fall within your latitude of acceptance.

Contrast and Assimilation Effects

An **assimilation effect** occurs when the positionality of the persuasive message is relatively close to the advocated position of the receiver, whereas a **contrast effect** will occur if the persuasive message and the receiver's stated position are far apart—which can help to explain the effects of polarization (Jager, 2017). Contrast effects help explain how messages that fall within one's latitude of

TABLE 9.2 Latitudes of Acceptance, Rejection, and Noncommitment for Those Holding Favorable Attitudes Toward GM Food

Statement that Most Aligned with Personal Attitude	Latitudes of Acceptance, Rejection, and Noncommitment for the Following Statements							
	GM food can cause cancer in humans.	GM food contributes to the prevalence of antibiotic resistant bacteria.	Potential risks of GM food related to health have not been adequately studied.	GM foods might be riskier to consume than traditional food.	GM foods are safe for human consumption.	GM food has increased the food available for me to purchase.	GM food can provide me with improved nutrition compared to traditional food.	GM food can be used to increase the safety of certain foods.
GM foods are safe for human consumption.	48.3%	51.6%	52.4%	31.8%		69.4%	72.8%	75.4%
GM food can be used to increase the safety of certain foods.	57.6%	58.3%	48.3%	57.8%	53.5%	48.7%	56.5%	

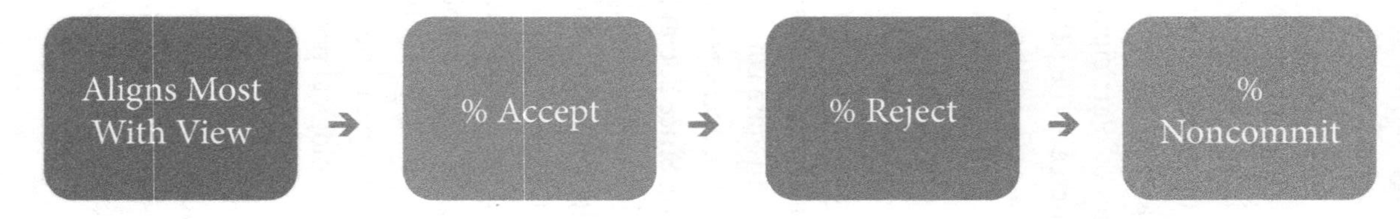

Source: Adapted from Taylor K. Ruth and Joy N. Rumble, "Consumers' Evaluations of Genetically Modified Food Messages," *Journal of Applied Communications*, vol. 103, no. 1, p. 10. Copyright © 2019 by New Prairie Press.

rejection fail to result in behavior change (Asemah & Nwammuo, 2017). People who hold strong opinions about an issue will tend to reject nearly all arguments that are inconsistent with their opinion (Sherif et al., 1965). In other words, it is extremely difficult to change the mind of someone who already holds a strong opinion about an issue, as those with strong opinions or who are ego involved are less likely to assimilate messages that contradict their existing strong opinions (Rumble et al., 2017). Park et al. (2007) found evidence, in certain conditions, to support the Social Judgment Theory prediction that when ego involvement is high, people will be more resistant to persuasion. "As involvement increases, latitudes of acceptance and noncommitment shrink and the latitudes of rejection expand" (Park et al., 2007, p. 83).

Social Judgment Theory even has implications for advertising messages. For instance, Asemah and Nwammuo (2017) contend that Social Judgment Theory explains what motivates consumers to purchase a product and connects those motivations to consumer attitudes regarding the advertisement, company, celebrity spokespersons, and products and services. "People compare messages with their pre-existing attitudes and make evaluations about the message based on their anchors on this topic or messages" (Asemah & Nwammuo, 2017, p. 76).

Strong Attitudes

Social Judgment Theory is particularly useful for understanding strong attitudes. Think for a moment about issues that you are especially passionate about. Perhaps you have formed strong attitudes about religion, abortion, gun control, or sports. Regardless of the issue, extant research is clear that strong attitudes are important. According to Krosnick et al. (1993), **strong attitudes** are characterized by attributes like extremity (the attitude deviates significantly from neutrality), intensity (strong emotional reactions are affiliated with the attitude), certainty (we are convinced the attitude is correct), importance (we care deeply about the issue), and accessibility (the attitude is easily accessed from memory). Strong attitudes are also very stable, highly resistant to change, and serve as a guide to behavior. As you might imagine, strong attitudes are accompanied by large latitudes of rejection.

Wang Erber et al. (1995) provide five reasons for why strong attitudes are so resilient. First, strong attitudes are networked with other beliefs and values, which insulates them to change. For example, changing an individual's religious beliefs would require changing a host of other related attitudes, values, and beliefs as well. Second, people are likely more knowledgeable about the issues they are passionate about, which makes them resistant to counterarguments. Third, we tend to associate with others that share our attitudes, and people in our social circle help us maintain our attitudes. Fourth, as Krosnick et al. (1993)

also note, strong attitudes are easily accessed from memory, which means they can be activated quickly when we confront crosscutting information. Fifth, Wang Erber et al. (1995) argue that "people with strong attitudes are likely to attend to and seek out information relevant to the topic, arming them with still more arguments with which to resist attempts to change their minds" (p. 438).

To illustrate how strong attitudes influence behaviors like voting and policy preference, DeSante and Smith (2020) examined the relationship between attitudes toward the racial status quo and emotional reactions to racism. Specifically, they created a multidimensional measure of racist attitudes that tapped into participants' fear of people of other races, acknowledgement of institutional racism, and racial empathy. Examining data from the 2016 presidential election, they found that supporters of Donald Trump were more "fearful of other races, the least angered about racism, and least likely to agree that whites have advantages based on the color of their skin" compared to those who supported Hillary Clinton (DeSante & Smith, 2020, p. 645). The measure of racial attitudes also similarly predicted White individuals' preferences on issues like welfare, interracial marriage, and perceived need to address racial inequality.

Strong attitudes permeate our personal relationships, workplaces, and online interactions, and they contribute to the extreme polarization that dominates our political discourse. Given their importance, it is essential to understand strategies for changing strong attitudes. Initially, you should understand that attempts to talk through differences with highly opinionated people may backfire. As Wojcieszak (2012) notes, individuals with strong attitudes "perceive more disagreement than others do, react with negative emotions to political debates, polarize against dissimilar views, and are mobilized to various actions" (p. 240). As a result, advocating positions that fall within the receiver's latitude of rejection will not result in persuasion. Instead, look for common ground, and start with instances where both sides agree. In addition, you can leverage the positive attitudes of similar others who can serve as a role model and persuade through social proof. You might also reinforce the values of fairness and perspective-taking and argue to the receiver that it would be inconsistent not to consider alternative perspectives. Finally, you can employ the argument model discussed in Chapter 6 to construct strong arguments supporting

Engaged Persuasion Activity: Strong Attitudes and Post-Truth Persuasion

Social Judgment Theory makes it clear that we develop strong attitudes around many political issues. In fact, this theory explains why people may be susceptible to persuasive misinformation and highly reluctant to change their minds. Social Judgment Theory also explains why our nation is so polarized at the moment. In other words, research in this area exposes many of the underlying mechanisms of persuasion in a post-truth era. Given the research on strong attitudes, what strategies would you recommend for overcoming extreme polarization? What other persuasion research or theories could be applied to this problem? Is it even possible for Americans to reach common ground on hotly contested political issues?

your case for attitude change. Ultimately, you should recognize that changing strong attitudes is a difficult and time-consuming process. You will need to utilize several reinforcing persuasive strategies and expect that change will occur in stages.

Bolstering Resistance to Persuasion

Thus far, we have mostly discussed persuasion as a means of changing another person's mind, as in their attitudes, values, or perceptions, or changing their behavior. However, there may be situations in which we do not want the other person to change. Instead, we may want to reinforce their existing attitudes, values, perceptions, or behaviors. Accordingly, persuasion can also be used to bolster existing states in audiences and help them resist others' attempts to get them to change. Imagine, for instance, that you want to persuade your team to resist outside influence attempts. In this case, you may not want your teammates to change; you may simply want your teammates to resist others' attempts to get them to change.

Persuasive Inoculation

Inoculation Theory contends that small doses, or exposure, to a message can help people build immunity to the message and learn to resist being persuaded by

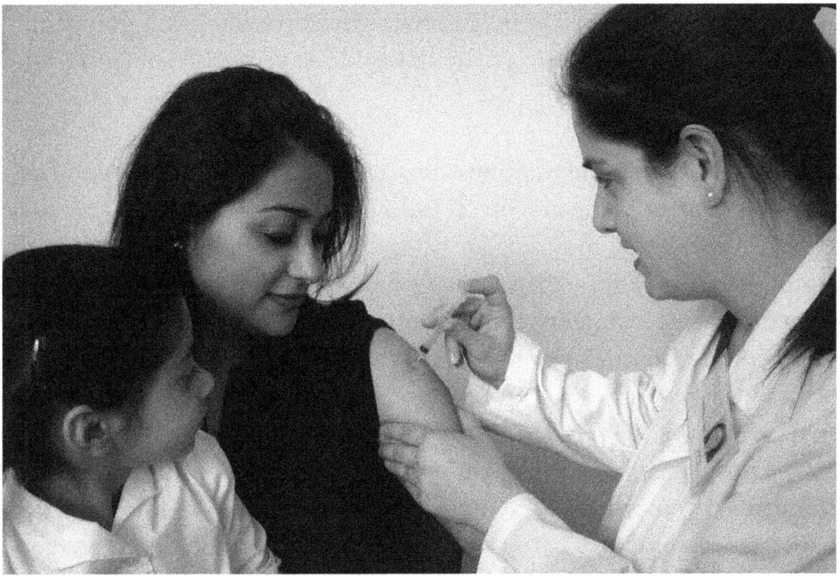

FIGURE 9.5 Receiving an inoculation means getting a weakened dose of the virus.

such messages. "Inoculation theory explains how persuasive messages can confer resistance to subsequent persuasive attacks, much like a medical inoculation confers resistance to subsequent viral attacks" (Compton & Kaylor, 2013, p. 94). Similar to how a weakened virus helps produce antibodies to fend off stronger antigens in the future, inoculation messages motivate a resistance process whereby exposure to a weakened argument contrary to one's current attitudinal position can produce refutations that help an individual ward off stronger future attacks (Compton, 2016; Ivanov et al., 2018; McGuire & Papageorgis, 1962). In this sense, Inoculation Theory is an intriguing and distinct theory of persuasion because it is all about how to resist persuasive message attempts. Thus, it is a theoretical framework to protect people from challenges to their current beliefs or attitudes (Jackson et al., 2017). In other words, social psychologist William McGuire's Inoculation Theory is about how to best confer resistance behavior to a target audience (Banas & Rains, 2010) and prevent persuasion (Banas & Miller, 2013). Often referred to as a grandfather theory, inoculation is supported by over 5 decades of research studies. "The primary objective of inoculation theory is to yield positive transformations to achieve healthier human environments" (Matusitz & Breen, 2013, p. 464). Inoculation messages "present weakened versions of oppositional arguments to motivate a process of resistance—a process that strengthens attitudes (or beliefs, or opinions) prior to encountering stronger attacks" (Compton & Kaylor, 2013, p. 94). Parents may find themselves utilizing this strategy when trying to prepare their children to deal with peer pressure. For instance, if parents want to teach their child to say "no" to friends when offered a cigarette, the parents may prepare the child to say "no" in hypothetical situations that are smaller in scale. In other words, parents attempt to stimulate their child's defenses by exposing them to weakened versions of potential attacks.

Refutational Preemption

Of course, parents often find they must also get the child's attention by convincing them there is a threat in the first place. Indeed, including an explicit forewarning prior to the inoculation message has been found to sufficiently generate threat (Compton & Ivanov, 2012). Threat simply means recognizing that one's existing belief is vulnerable to counterattitudinal attacks, which are attacks or arguments than run counter to one's existing beliefs. Inoculation messages equip target audiences with responses to refute counterattacks, a process known as refutational preemption. "Preemption may be so crucial because it creates frames or schema for perceiving subsequent messages" (Banas & Miller, 2013, p. 200). Thus, inoculation messages serve to protect "attitudes before they are attacked or challenged" (Compton, 2016, p. 1). While both the refutational preemption and the explicit forewarning generate threat, "having people consider their perceived threat levels during an inoculation treatment message seems to boost their threat levels and resistance" (Compton, 2016, p. 10). Even simply asking people to ponder their potential vulnerability can boost threat and bolster resistance to attacks on their positions (Compton & Ivanov, 2012).

Freedom-Threatening Language

It is important to note that inoculation forewarnings, as well as the subsequent appeals included in the inoculation messages, should avoid using language that is highly freedom threatening. Richards et al. (2017) discovered that elaborated inoculation can trigger psychological reactance, while limited inoculation can decrease reactance if the subsequent appeals are less freedom threatening. Thus, "Inoculation has the potential to facilitate or buffer reactance depending on the level of threat communicated in inoculation forewarnings and in subsequent persuasive health appeals" (Richards et al., 2017, p. 890). While Richards et al. tested the inoculation treatments advocating for reduced consumption of soda and alcohol, their conclusions could speak more generally to other inoculation messages. These results contradict conventional understanding of how threat functions in an inoculation message because "less elaborated inoculation messages that minimize threat can reduce reactance, whereas elaborated messages that enhance threat can increase reactance" (Richards et al., 2017, p. 896). See Figure 9.6 for more detail. Notice that the lines on the graph depicted in Figure 9.6 cross over, thus reflecting an interaction effect. In other words, the graph shows that the level of freedom-threatening language interacts with the presence or absence of inoculation to produce varying levels of reactance. More specifically, we could read this graph as suggesting that inoculation backfires when the level of freedom-threatening language is high. Put another way, "when threat is high, inoculation is at best ineffective and at worst counterproductive," leading to exacerbated reactance (Richards et al., 2917, p. 899). As a result, inoculation messages ought to be composed using language that avoids threatening freedom. A couple years prior, Richards and Banas (2015) found that inoculations could be employed to successfully mitigate psychological reactance that could lead to undesirable health behaviors if the forewarning informed participants about the possibility of reactance occurring. By warning participants that self-generated cognitions about feeling threatened could occur, the forewarning was able to reduce reactance that otherwise might lead to negative behaviors. Alternatively, Niederdeppe et al. (2014) argue that highlighting threats to personal freedom, posed by the counterattitudinal attacks, can strengthen inoculation treatments. Similarly, Miller et al. (2013) found that psychological reactance can be employed in the inoculation message (by explaining that one's freedoms may be threatened by the counterattitudinal attack) to augment refutational preemption, motivate intensified resistance, and spur counterarguing. Thus, their results indicate that enhancing forewarnings with reactance inducing concerns about threats to

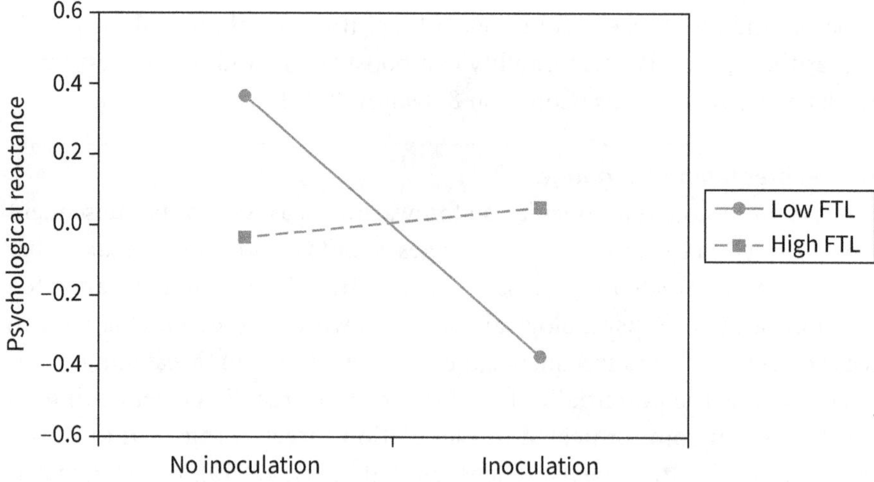

FIGURE 9.6 Interaction effect of inoculation and freedom-threatening language (Richards et al., 2017).

freedom in the inoculation message can create a booster effect for resistance by redirecting the receiver's reactance response toward the counterattitudinal attack.

Inoculation Research

In a meta-analysis examining 41 studies testing the effectiveness of inoculation theory with over 10,000 participants, Banas and Rains (2010) found mixed support for inoculation messages. On the one hand, inoculation messages consistently outperformed supportive messages as well as no-treatment control messages in fostering resistance to attitude change. On the other hand, refutational-same and refutational-different preemptions were both effective in reducing attitude change. Predictions about threat, time delay, and involvement were not shown to have significant relationships to increased resistance in the meta-analysis. Most disturbingly, the meta-analysis did not find a significant relationship between perceived threat and resistance. Banas and Rains (2010) concluded that "inoculation is an effective method for instilling resistance to attitude change; however, more work is needed to clarify the various 'nuances' of the process of inoculation" (p. 305). A later study by Banas and Richards (2017) indicated that motivational threat, which is not as reliant on fear or anxiety, was more effective in triggering resistance than the traditional conceptualization of threat.

Specific studies have yielded findings that demonstrate the potential of Inoculation Theory and how it functions in particular situations. Inoculation Theory has demonstrated the ability to reduce undesirable health behaviors (e.g., alcohol, drug, and tobacco use), inappropriate sexual behaviors, and susceptibility to sarcastic attack messages (Clyne et al., 2020) and may possibly even prevent prisoner recidivism (Matusitz & Breen, 2013), skin cancer (Matusitz & Breen,

2013), susceptibility to attacks on the First Amendment (Parker et al., 2020), or susceptibility to misinformation and fake news (Robson, 2019). One study, by Jackson et al. (2017), even used inoculation messages to help students successfully reduce public speaking anxiety. In a study of adolescents' resistance to peer pressure about alcohol consumption, Godbold and Pfau (2000) found that normative messages that lowered estimations of peer acceptance of alcohol use were effective at increasing resistance to peer pressure. Participants were shown commercials immediately after viewing public service announcements (PSAs). They were resistant to peer pressure to use alcohol immediately and, also, 2 weeks later. Additionally, inoculation messages can be an effective means of providing a "blanket of protection" pre-crisis and even enhancing "the ability of individuals to cope with the aftermath of a crisis" (Ivanov et al., 2016, p. 381). Moreover, inoculations can combat initial feelings, in a crisis situation, of helplessness or distress (Ivanov et al., 2016). Inoculations to negative press about a corporate crisis can confer resistance in consumers (Kim, 2013). The blanket of protection provided by inoculations has even been found to extend to providing cross-protection for a range of attitudes that are related but untreated (Parker et al., 2016). This cross-protection works by "providing practice in refuting counterarguments and protecting one's attitude" (Parker et al., 2016, p. 64). In a study comparing loss-framed to gain-framed inoculation messages, the loss-framed messages did a better job of protecting investors' initial beliefs about keeping their investments in the stock market during times of financial crisis and preventing belief slippage (Dillingham & Ivanov, 2015). "Using loss frame language could boost generated resistance, thus strengthening the overall effect of inoculation treatments" (Dillingham & Ivanov, 2015, p. 120).

Of course, inoculation is only effective if it is capable of helping individuals later resist attacks. In other words, if parents hope to prevent their children from caving to peer pressure to consume alcohol, they may provide children with inoculation messages. As soon as the child is away from their parents and with their peers, however, the inoculation message must still work to be truly effective. According to Ivanov et al. (2017), "Inoculation messages can help promote resistance to counterattitudinal attacks" (p. 105). In fact, inoculation messages presented to participants with initially neutral or opposing attitudes produced attitude changes

Engaged Persuasion Activity: Deconstructing Persuasive Misinformation

Cook et al. (2018) argued that Inoculation Theory can be applied to inoculate individuals against persuasive misinformation relating to climate change. The core of their argument stipulates that training people with advanced argumentation and critical thinking skills should facilitate the identification of logical fallacies and ultimately lead them to reject misinformation. Think back to the argument model presented in Chapter 6. Do you think training in argumentation is an effective approach to combating the spread of persuasive misinformation? Beyond climate change, could this method be effectively applied to other topics, like vaccination and evolution?

in response to counterattitudinal attacks, thus moving in the direction advocated by the inoculation message. Ivanov et al. (2017) concluded that inoculation can protect against persuasion and reduce postattack slippage: "Inoculation messages may serve to shape neutral attitudes toward a topic and change those attitudes that are opposing" (p. 121). The data demonstrated that inoculation was better at protecting those individuals with initially desirable attitudes as well as shifting the attitudes of those with initially neutral or opposing attitudes in the direction of the desired attitude change; and inoculation messages protected participants from attack-induced slippage. Another study by Banas and Miller (2013) demonstrated that "brief inoculations can inhibit attitude change to comparatively longer persuasive messages" (p. 198). However, Niederdeppe et al. (2014) found that, while inoculations were effective in the short term at changing policy beliefs about the source of counterattitudinal attacks, the inoculation messages failed to produce sustained resistance over the long term.

Resisting peer pressure is one thing, but you might suspect that a child's close friends may be another matter entirely. Indeed, you would be correct that interpersonal relationships and social networks are important. Ivanov et al. (2015) examined the role that postinoculation talk may play in the inoculation process and found that interpersonal processes can help inoculate people to resist attacks. In their study, Ivanov et al. discovered that postinoculation talk, where participants may talk with each other to seek reassurance and advocacy after an inoculation message, was helpful in spreading the process of resistance to attacks. Those who were inoculated were found to be more likely to share materials included in the inoculation message and discuss topics related to the issue. In other

Engaged Persuasion Research: Metainoculation

Banas and Miller (2013) randomly assigned 312 college student participants to one of three groups: control, inoculation, and metainoculation. All groups were shown a 9/11-truth conspiracy theory film, *Loose Change: Final Cut*. The inoculation and metainoculation groups were exposed to material prior to viewing the film, however. The inoculation group received a one-page written message that inoculated them with facts about the topic and conspiracy theories, whereas the metainoculation group also received a message about how inoculation messages themselves function prior to the fact-based inoculation message. In the metainoculation group, the message warned participants that there were people who would try to change how they think about an issue, explained how inoculation messages work, warned them that inoculation messages could manipulate their attitudes, and encouraged them to make up their own minds after hearing from both sides. Thus, the metainoculation message itself consisted of a generic caution targeting the nature of inoculation messages themselves. The findings from Banas and Miller's experiment revealed that the fact-based inoculation message was the most effective condition in resisting the illogical and emotionally charged conspiracy theory presented in the film. Interestingly, the metainoculation treatment reduced the efficacy of the fact-based inoculation treatment. In other words, metainoculation diminishes the impact of subsequent inoculation messages. "Inoculation messages may reduce resistance to inoculation treatments themselves" (Banas & Miller, 2013, p. 189). The metainoculation group still resisted the film's attacks better than the control group, however, so the efficacy of the fact-based inoculation was not completely eliminated.

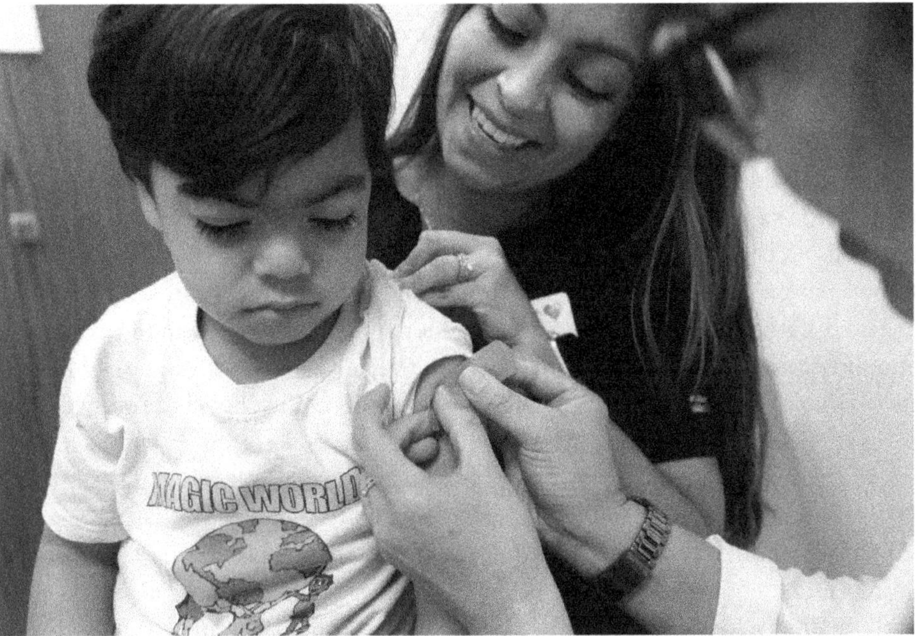

FIGURE 9.7 Like the child receiving a flu shot in this photo, inoculation messages can create a blanket of protection.

words, discussions with friends and others following inoculation can result in stronger inoculation effects. Thus, postinoculation talk can serve to both advocate and reassure, spreading the process of inoculation or resistance among one's social network (Ivanov et al., 2015). The results also lent support to findings of previous studies that inoculation messages protect recipients against arguments not addressed in the specific inoculation message.

Using Inoculation Theory to Combat Misinformation in a Post-Truth Era

We have noted throughout this text that the post-truth era poses several dangers to the functioning of democracy and policymaking. In recent years, scholars have turned to the application of Inoculation Theory to protect individuals from persuasive misinformation in several contexts. For example, van der Linden et al. (2017) found that public attitudes about climate change can be inoculated against misinformation. Specifically, their research revealed inoculation messages can protect individuals from attacks suggesting that no scientific consensus exists on the issue of climate change. Additional research by Maertens, Anseel, et al. (2020) as well as Williams and Bond (2020) also supports the claim that providing information about scientific consensus and an inoculation treatment can help combat misinformation about climate change.

In addition to inoculation, Cook et al. (2017) found that activating participants' critical thinking and argumentation skills made them less susceptible to relying on judgmental heuristics when evaluating misinformation. In other words, making receivers aware of the flaws in the argumentation used in messages containing misinformation can go a long way to making them more critical consumers of persuasion. Cook et al. (2017) argue that "generally-framed inoculations could potentially neutralize a number of misleading arguments that employ the same technique or fallacy" (p. 15). For example, much information exists about child immunizations and various vaccines, which can be confusing to new parents. Yet, most physician recommended immunizations and vaccines are no different from a flu shot in their general purpose. Have you received a flu shot previously, like the child in Figure 9.7, to guard against flu season? Most of us would pay little attention to misinformation about flu shots because we have been armed with information about their purpose and efficacy.

In a novel application of Inoculation Theory, Roozenbeek and van der Linden (2019) created an online news game that inoculates players against persuasive misinformation. The game, titled *Bad News*, was released in 2018. Players of the game enter a virtual environment complete with a simulated social media ecosystem. They experience fake posts, images, and other content that they use to gain followers and spread misinformation. Roozenbeek and van der Linden's pilot study revealed that the process of active inoculation induced by the fake news game significantly reduced participants' perceived reliability and persuasiveness of misinformation. A follow-up study by Maertens et al. (2020) also revealed that participants found fake news headlines less reliable than before they played the game. Further, the effects of the inoculation treatment were found to last for several weeks. Similarly, Roozenbeek et al. (2020) found that the *Bad News* game improved participants' ability to spot misinformation but did not make them more skeptical of real news. You can play the *Bad News* game yourself at its website (https://www.getbadnews.com).

Forewarning of Persuasive Intent

The **Strength Model of Self-Control** posits that self-control is a finite resource and that acts of self-control result in short-term reductions in subsequent self-control in related and unrelated areas (Baumeister et al., 2007). Self-control is a conscious and deliberate form of self-regulation (Baumeister et al., 2007). These areas could include drinking, eating, financial spending, sexual behavior, critical thinking, interpersonal behavior, or decision making (Baumeister et al., 2007). The short-term impairments, otherwise known as ego depletion, mean that our self-control may be depleted or expended—just as we might tire from physical activity. In this case, though, it is our mental resources that tire. The argument is that our mental resources get depleted when we work hard to regulate our behavior. Thus, ego depletion weakens willpower. Just as we might experience muscle fatigue, our self-control can also weaken over time or in response to repeated tests of our self-control—similar to how you might turn down a cookie when initially offered it but may cave when repeatedly offered cookies.

Fortunately, Baumeister et al. (2007) explain that psychological interventions can improve our self-control or willpower. In other words, just as physical exercise can build our muscle strength and enable us to endure greater future physical activity, exercising mental self-control can build our capacity to exercise greater self-control in the future. An example of this might be your friend who has a weakness for spending money when shopping. While your friend might be quite good at controlling their spending when eating out, they may have a particular proclivity for buying new clothes. Even when you witness your friend exercising good self-control and passing up a new outfit, you know they will eventually breakdown and buy new clothing they do not really need. Recently, however, since running up a large credit card debt, your friend has been better at resisting the urge to purchase new clothes (mostly because the limit on their credit card has been maxed out). After this period of regulating their spending, you notice your friend seems to have turned a new leaf and is able to resist purchasing more often even though their credit account is now in good standing.

Planning requires mental work, similar to self-control, while wants and desires come much more easily (Sjastad & Baumeister, 2018). But planning requires mental effort, is future directed, and helps us obtain our long-term goals. Certainly, people vary in their level of self-control. Those who exhibit high levels of self-control engage in more planning, while those lower in self-control may experience more ego-depletion and, thus, less planning (Sjastad & Baumeister, 2018). Remember your friend who is fond of shopping for clothes? If your friend has low self-control, they are less likely to plan and save their money for a future purchase. After all, "people with poor self-control do not like to plan" and tend to avoid the effort that planning requires (Sjastad & Baumeister, 2018, p. 139).

However, forewarnings about impending attempts to influence us can help us to conserve willpower and enhance our ability to self-regulate our behavior (Janssen et al., 2010). **Forewarning** works to help us conserve mental resources until we need them later (Janssen et al., 2010). "Resisting persuasion involves active self-regulation" (Janssen et al., 2010, p. 911), but resisting persuasion depletes our willpower resources. More specifically, Janssen et al. (2010) found that forewarnings are effective because they not only reduce our compliance with the influence attempt but also because they lead us to generate more counterarguments against the influence attempt. In their experiment, Janssen et al. discovered that participants who were forewarned of an impending influence attempt fared better than those who were not forewarned. Thus, forewarning triggers us to conserve willpower so that we can better resist influence at a later time. If I warned you that cookies would be available and that our host would repeatedly offer us cookies, you might stand a better chance of exercising self-control and refusing the cookies! In other words, external interventions such as forewarnings may help us resist persuasion.

After conducting a meta-analysis of relevant studies, Benoit (1998) concluded that "forewarning an audience to expect a persuasive message tends to make that message less persuasive" regardless of which type of forewarning is presented, and regardless of whether a delay has occurred between the forewarning and the influence attempt (p. 146). Prior to Benoit's meta-analysis, a delay was believed to be important to bolster resistance to subsequent persuasive attempts (Hass & Grady, 1975). Forewarnings concerning topics with which people are involved or have immediate outcomes produce defensive reactions that bolster initial attitudes. In two subsequent meta-analyses, Wood and Quinn (2003) found that "resistance emerged from careful scrutiny of relevant information whereas agreement emerged from more superficial analysis" in cases where little thought was required and people's identities were threatened (p. 135). More specifically, "Warnings generated resistance by biasing people's thoughts about the issue in the appeal, in contrast to the reactions of those who received a message with no warning" (Wood & Quinn, 2003, p. 135). Chen et al. (1992) found recipients demonstrated greater resistance to influence attempts when their involvement with the message topic was high, the topic was important to them, and they were not cognitively distracted. Conversely, recipients low in topic involvement were more swayed by the message overall. Jacks and Devine's (2000) results found that recipients to whom the topic was of high importance were extremely resistant to influence attempts regardless of forewarning or delay, whereas those to whom the topic was low in importance were most resistant when forewarned and provided time to engage in anticipatory counterarguing prior to the influence attempt.

A variety of other research studies on forewarning have produced interesting results. For instance, some studies have examined forewarnings and relationships. Wagner (2011) found that partners in romantic relationships experienced

Engaged Persuasion Research: Protecting the Elderly From Telemarketing Scams

Scheibe et al. (2014) ran a field experiment to determine if forewarning would protect consumers who had been victimized by telemarketing scams in the past. The majority of their 145 participants were older consumers, who happen to be the demographic that telemarketers commonly prey upon. The findings indicated that forewarning "reduced unequivocal acceptance" of both the same mock scam as well as an entirely different mock scam (Scheibe et al., 2014, p. 272). Consumers who received forewarning of the exact same telemarketing scam were better able to refuse the scam, as compared to those who received forewarning of a different scam. However, the different scam forewarning did not lose effectiveness over time, at either the 2-week or 4-week period, while the same scam warning did. The research team reasoned that consumers exposed to the same scam message recognized the fraudulent offer and followed the advice to refuse it, although, over time, may remember the message content but forget that it is fraudulent. Consumers exposed to a different scam message may have been better at remembering they should doubt and be skeptical of similar scam offers.

greater psychological reactance when messages included forewarning. Leon et al.'s (2003) results showed that forewarnings of deception induced cautiousness about attractiveness when participants viewed online photographs of the opposite sex. "Forewarned participants rated target photos as less attractive, and were less likely to report a desire to chat online or date the target individual" than were control group participants who were not forewarded about online deception (Leon et al., 2003, p. 52). Several studies have examined forewarning about advertisements. Compared to participants who were forewarned, those who were primed with persuasive intent were better able to resist advertisements in an experiment conducted by Fransen and Fennis (2014). In an experiment conducted by Rozendaal et al. (2016), children ages 8–10 responded well to forewarnings about the manipulative intent of television commercials but did not respond as effectively to forewarnings about commercial intent of advertising. Lee (2010) found that forewarnings about advertiser's intentions were effective at generating "resistance to persuasion even among individuals with positive prior brand attitudes who are expected to have less resistance to persuasion" (p. 234). In short, forewarnings led audiences to react negatively toward the persuasive intent of the advertisement. Another study examined how readers engage with texts. Kamalski et al. (2008) found that coherence markers, which are lexical cue phrases or connectives, can raise the awareness of readers that an author is trying to influence them, which causes readers to build up resistance to persuasion. Readers could easily recognize subjective markers as persuasive attempts and were thus able to resist persuasion. Objective markers were found to be more persuasive, as readers integrated that information rather than resisting.

Summary

This chapter covered several persuasion theories as well as other strategies that people use to cognitively process persuasive messages. The dual process models, ELM and HSM, as well as Social Judgment Theory address how people think about and process persuasive messages. The dual process models indicate that people can process messages through scrutinizing details (the central route in ELM and systematic processing in HSM) or by attending to simple cues (the peripheral route in ELM and heuristic processing in HSM). Social Judgment Theory suggests that the distance between a persuasive message position and our existing anchor point determine whether we accept, reject, or are noncommitted to the message. This chapter also examined how we can resist persuasive message attempts. Inoculation Theory explains that small doses of a message that runs counter to our existing position can help bolster our immunity to such messages by generating counterarguments.

The next chapter unpacks research about the reception of persuasive messages and effects of those messages on individual receivers.

Check Your Understanding Review Questions

1. What are the similarities and differences between ELM and HSM?
2. How does the sufficiency principle and the idea of cognitive misers determine which route or processing people use to cognitively process messages?
3. What are the differences among the three latitudes (latitude of acceptance, rejection, and noncommitment) explained in Social Judgment Theory?
4. How do assimilation and contrast effects work in Social Judgement Theory?
5. How is Social Judgment Theory useful in understanding strong attitudes?
6. What insight does Inoculation Theory offer about how we can teach people to resist persuasive influence attempts?
7. Do inoculations provide a blanket of protection and cross-protection on related issues?
8. What is metainoculation?
9. How does forewarning function in the strength model of self-control?

Key Terms

anchor point (p. 224)
assimilation effect (p. 227)
cognitive misers (p. 219)
contrast effect (p. 227)
dual process models (p. 218)
Elaboration Likelihood Model (p. 218)
forewarning (p. 239)
Heuristic Systematic Model (p. 218)
Inoculation Theory (p. 231)
Social Judgment Theory (p. 224)
Strength Model of Self-Control (p. 238)
strong attitudes (p. 229)
sufficiency principle (p. 223)

Credits

CHAPTER 10

Receiving Persuasive Messages

Chapter Objectives

After reading this chapter, you should be able to:

- List and describe the demographic variables related to persuasion
- Understand how various psychological states and traits influence the reception of persuasive messages
- Define priming effects and the pique technique
- Understand the ways that mood affects reception of persuasive messages
- Understand Motivated Reasoning Theory and its applications for how receivers process persuasive messages

This chapter unpacks research about the reception of persuasive messages and effects that persuasive messages have on receivers. Initially, it is vital for persuaders to understand how individual characteristics, such as demographic variables as well as psychological factors, affect the reception of persuasive messages. Additionally, persuaders should examine how the presentation of messages affects receivers. Do unusual persuasive requests generate greater compliance by receivers? In other words, can we pique the attention of receivers? And is it possible to prime receivers to comply with persuasive requests? Third, we need to examine how a receiver's mood and emotions affect responses to persuasive messages. Finally, this chapter will address Motivated Reasoning Theory to better understand how receivers process persuasive messages and whether they process messages through biased processing designed to protect their existing attitudes and beliefs. This latter question is particularly important when considering how receivers process messages in the post-truth era.

Individual Characteristics and Persuasion

Is it fair to begin with the assumption that not all receivers will process the same message in a similar fashion? Could various groups of receivers with unique characteristics respond differently to the same persuasive message? Certainly,

FIGURE 10.1 Individuals of different ages and races converse in public. Demographic variables such as age and race influence the persuasion process.

we would expect that demographic differences among receivers may contribute to how they respond to such messages. Might the individuals conversing in Figure 10.1 respond to persuasive messages based in part on their the perspective in relation to demographic variables such as age and race? Three **demographic** variables—age, gender, and culture—are particularly important to consider.

Demographic Variables

Age

How does age influence the process of persuasion? Consider the relationship between age and susceptibility to persuasion through advertising. According to Wilcox et al. (2004), children in the United States are exposed to nearly 40,000 commercials every year. As you might imagine, extant research indicates that youth under the age of 8 are especially susceptible to advertising. According to Oates et al. (2002), children under the age of 8 recognize the messages in advertising but lack the ability to discern persuasive intent. Instead, such children think the advertisements are there to inform them. Further research by Oates et al. (2003) shows that some children are not advertising literate until they reach 10 years old.

Orji et al. (2015) examined the influence of age on participants' susceptibility to the strategies in Cialdini's (2009) model of persuasion (i.e., scarcity, liking, reciprocation, commitment, social proof, and authority). Orji et al. showed that adults (participants over the age of 35) found commitment significantly more persuasive than younger adults (participants between the ages of 18 and 25). In addition, results demonstrated that younger adults found scarcity to be significantly more persuasive than older adults. No differences were found between the groups for any of the other persuasive strategies in Cialdini's model. The authors conclude that emotional appeals that emphasize what persuasive targets stand to lose should be effective for younger adults. In terms of older adults, Orji et al. (2015) suggest that "persuasive approaches that require users to make any kind of commitment such as those that require users to set a daily or weekly goal and compare achievement with set goals should be emphasized" (p. 156).

The literature we have reviewed so far shows that youth are more susceptible to persuasion than older adults. Interestingly, research by Eaton et al. (2009) demonstrates a curvilinear relationship between age and susceptibility to persuasion. In other words, middle-aged adults are the least susceptible to persuasion. One reason for this is that "those in midlife disproportionately hold positions of power in the workplace" (Eaton et al., 2009, p. 1656). Put another way, midlife adults internalize powerful role norms appropriate to the positions they hold, develop strong attitudes, and thus become more resistant to attitude change. In addition, research by Spotts (1994) indicates that age-related declines in cognitive ability affect motivational variables in the Elaboration Likelihood Model such as need for cognition. Therefore, older adults tend to engage in more peripheral processing of persuasive messages than younger adults.

The findings of Eaton et al. and Spotts are consistent with research by Liao and Fu (2014) showing that older adults are less likely to carefully scrutinize the credibility of health information they encounter online. In order to bolster their resistance to persuasion, Liao and Fu suggest that older adults should be trained in the techniques necessary to evaluate the credibility of online health information. In addition, they suggest that websites that provide such information should be designed with features that remind users to pay attention to relevant website features to "help older adults naturally adopt more effective credibility judgment strategies" (Liao & Fu, 2014, p. 18).

Extant literature reveals important relationships between chronological age and persuasion, but what does it say about cognitive age? As Chang (2008) notes, cognitive age is the age a person believes themselves to be (i.e., the age a person feels, looks, and acts). Chang's study demonstrates that ads that use models that are congruent with receivers' cognitive age are far more persuasive than ads featuring models congruent with receivers' chronological age. Further, Chang found that when the models matched receivers' cognitive age, they elaborated more about the benefits of the advertised product and were more likely to relate ad messages to their own personal experiences. As a result, persuaders would be wise to carefully consider their receivers' cognitive age in addition to their chronological age.

Gender

Do women and men respond differently to persuasive messages? Jacks and Lancaster (2015) examined gender differences in persuasive exercise messages based on delivery style and message framing. Their results show that women responded more positively, in terms of source credibility and message effectiveness, when the message fit a prevention focus. In this scenario, the message was framed to encourage exercise as a way to prevent harmful health outcomes (i.e., loss framed). In contrast, men in their sample responded more favorably to messages that fit a promotion focus. In sum, men were most persuaded by messages that stressed the benefits of regular exercise (i.e., gain framed).

Scholars have also examined gender differences in terms of consumers' decision-making processes. For example, Killgore et al. (2010) found that men tended to be more risk seeking in their decision making, while women tended to be more risk averse. Further, Richard et al. (2010) found that women tend to spend more time evaluating relevant persuasive purchase information, while men tend to collect information and make decisions quickly. Similarly, Papyrina's (2019) research indicates that women engage in detailed evaluation of advertising messages, while males rely more on heuristic cues.

In terms of persuasion via word of mouth (WOM), Swanson et al. (2003) found that men were persuaded to attend a sporting event based on eustress motivation (i.e., the emotional stimulation that arouses the senses compelling fans to take the additional effort to become a spectator). The women in their study did not report the same effect. Further, Asada and Ko (2019) found three gender differences for persuasive WOM recommendations regarding sport-watching behavior: (a) women were more persuaded by WOM than men, (b) trustworthiness had a positive relationship with WOM only for women, and (c) strength of message delivery was positively correlated with WOM only for men.

Recent research demonstrates some interesting gender difference when persuasion is conveyed through technology. For example, Ghazali et al. (2018) examined how robot characteristics influence the way individuals experience human-robot interactions and their compliance with the persuasive attempts of robots. Their study used a robot that could display different faces and social cues. In addition, participants were guided by a robot through a trust game. Specifically, the robot advisor used persuasive messages to influence the choices participants made as they navigated through the game. Ghazali et al.'s results indicated that participants experienced high psychological reactance when interacting with a robot of the opposite gender. Further, the reactance was strongest with the female face even though the male and female robots delivered exactly the same persuasive message using the same facial expressions. Ghazali et al. conclude that social robots will be most persuasive if they are personalized to match the gender of the user.

Importantly, gender roles influence how women and men are perceived as persuasive communicators. For example, Matthews's (2016) research shows that female debaters are perceived as significantly more verbally aggressive than their male counterparts. When it comes to advancing persuasive arguments, women face a double bind. In other words, they are expected to be as aggressive as men in order to win the debate, but they are punished for violating stereotypical gender roles. These stereotypes hold that we expect males to be more aggressive persuaders than females (Deturck, 1987). Further, Jordan-Jackson et al. (2008) explain that "even though men and women may not actually differ on aggressiveness in a particular situation, they may be perceived and evaluated differently because of the cultural belief that men are usually more aggressive" (p. 253).

Can persuasion theory and research be used to combat sexism? Gervais and Hillard (2014) sought to answer this question. Participants in their study received vignettes describing organizational leaders using persuasive messages to confront sexist remarks. In addition, the vignettes described confrontations occurring in public and private contexts. Their findings showed that confronters were perceived as more likely to stop future sexist events when they confronted publicly rather than privately. However, when female leaders in the study confronted sexism publicly, participants evaluated them less favorably than their male counterparts. In fact, participants evaluated female confronters as more charismatic when they confronted acts of sexism privately. While Gervais and Hillard's study suggests that persuasion can be employed to deter future sexist acts, it also reveals important differences in the ways male and female confronters are perceived. We agree with their conclusion that, hopefully, "confronting eventually will stop everyday sexism from occurring in the first place, eliminating this trade-off for women" (Gervais & Hillard, 2014, p. 665).

Engaged Persuasion Activity: Using Persuasion to Combat Sexism

The study by Gervais and Hillard (2014) described in this chapter provides hope that confronting sexism publicly can deter future sexist acts. Their study also demonstrated that participants perceived biased statements as more sexist when the confrontation occurred in a public rather than private context. However, the results of the study showed a double bind for female confronters who were evaluated more negatively than their male counterparts when they confronted sexism publicly. Given this finding, what do you think can be done to eliminate this double bind? What other persuasion research or theories might be useful in combatting sexism?

Culture

Culture plays an important role in the production and consumption of persuasive messages. One of the most popular lenses for understanding the influence of culture, individualism-collectivism, was developed by Dutch social psychologist Gerard Hofstede. According to Hofstede (1990), members of individualistic cultures (e.g., Australia, Canada, and the United States) tend to emphasize separateness and the uniqueness of individuals. On the other hand, members of collectivistic cultures (e.g., Hong Kong, Japan, and Taiwan) emphasize connectedness, social context, and group relationships.

Kitirattarkarn et al. (2019) examined differences between members of individualistic and collectivistic cultures in terms of consumers' engagement (i.e., liking, commenting on, and sharing social media posts) with brand-related user-generated content (Br-UGC). Their findings suggest that social relationships within social media networks are more important for members of collectivistic cultures than for consumers from individualistic cultures. The study also revealed that members of individualistic cultures like to interact with their peers to express their opinions or help others more than members of collectivistic cultures. Ultimately, Kitirattarkarn et al. suggest that marketers should emphasize the benefits of social relations when attempting to persuade consumers from collectivistic cultures. In other words, marketers should realize that collectivistic consumers value the opinions of friends in their social network and will follow their brand and product recommendations. In contrast, they suggest that marketers should build social media strategies that provide opportunities for individualistic consumers to freely express their ideas about products and brands.

In the context of health care, Uskul and Oyserman (2010) examined the persuasive effects of tailored health messages for members of collectivistic (Asian Americans) and individualistic (European Americans) cultures. Their results demonstrate that culturally relevant messages are more persuasive if they come after receivers are reminded of their cultural frame. Specifically, individualistic participants, induced to focus on individualism, were more persuaded by health messages associating health behavior with negative consequences for the self. In contrast, collectivistic participants, induced to focus on collectivism, were more persuaded by health messages associating health behavior with negative social consequences. Uskul and Oyserman (2010) conclude that "message effectiveness can be increased by reminding potential listeners of their chronically relevant cultural-orientation by making it momentarily salient" (p. 330).

At this point, you may have reached the conclusion that persuasive messages must always be tailored to the receiver's cultural frame to be effective. Research by Agrawal (2015) indicates that there are circumstances where individuals from individualistic cultures can be induced to adopt a collectivistic frame. For example, members of individualistic cultures can be primed to think about family obligations before being presented with a persuasive appeal to those obligations. The same effect has been observed for members of collectivistic cultures. In addition, research by Lau-Gesk (2003) shows that biculturals, or individuals who have been equally influenced by the individualistic and collectivistic cultural frames, can switch frames and react favorably to persuasive appeals grounded in either approach.

Beyond the individualistic-collectivistic approach, Huang and Shen (2016) conducted a meta-analysis to examine the persuasive impact of culturally tailored persuasive messages in cancer communication. Their findings show that tailoring cancer messages based on the ethnicity and culture of receivers resulted in a small, but statistically significant, effect on persuasion (i.e., behavioral intentions and actual behaviors). More importantly, deep tailoring, which includes references to cultural values, norms, and religious beliefs of the target group, was far more persuasive than surface tailoring, which only includes references to cultural features like language, diet, and risk factors. Huang and Shen (2016) argue that employing "cultural tailoring in cancer communication can generate an appreciable influence on persuasion outcomes" (p. 708).

Psychological States and Traits

Beyond demographic variables, we need to consider psychological factors that influence how receivers respond to persuasive messages. Specifically, persuaders need to understand how receivers' self-esteem, self-monitoring, ego involvement, cognitive style, verbal aggression and argumentativeness, and visual

FIGURE 10.2 Psychological factors influence responses to persuasive messages.

processing style affect how messages are processed and how receivers respond to such messages.

Self-Esteem

How does **self-esteem** influence the way individuals process persuasive messages? Rhodes and Wood (1992) attempted to answer this question in their study examining individuals with high, low, and moderate self-esteem. Rhodes and Wood found that individuals with high and low self-esteem were the most resistant to persuasion. They argue that individuals with high self-esteem are so confident in their opinions that they are highly resistant to persuasion. In contrast, individuals with low self-esteem are often too distracted or withdrawn to receive persuasive messages. As Rhodes and Wood note, those with moderate self-esteem are the best able to attend to, comprehend, and yield to persuasive messages.

Self-Monitoring

According to Synder (1974), **self-monitoring** refers to the fact that receivers of persuasive messages "differ in the extent to which they monitor (observe and control) their expressive behavior and self-presentation" (p. 536). Low self-monitors tend to be less sensitive to the expression and self-presentation of others in social settings. Low self-monitors are also more individualistic and less concerned with what others think of them compared to high self-monitors. As Leone (2006) notes, low self-monitors "derive a sense of satisfaction from being perceived in ways that preserve their reputation as genuine, sincere individuals" (p. 653). In other words, low self-monitors do not feel pressure to conform to the expectations of others in their social environment.

In contrast, high self-monitors are concerned about social appropriateness and are sensitive to the expression and self-presentation of others in social settings. High self-monitors pay close attention to the social situation and use appropriateness cues as guidelines for their behavior. According to Leone (2006), high self-monitors "derive a sense of satisfaction from being perceived in ways that entitle them to favorable social outcomes" (p. 652). Put another way, high self-monitors will modify their behavior and appearance in order to receive the rewards that come with fitting in with others.

Extant research demonstrates that high and low self-monitors are persuaded differently. For example, research by Evans and Clark (2012) shows that self-monitoring affects the way that individuals respond to appeals to source credibility. Specifically, low self-monitors in their study were found to be more influenced by the expertise rather than the attractiveness of the source. In contrast, high self-monitors were found to be more confident in their thoughts when the source was found to be attractive rather than expert.

Other research demonstrates that social monitoring influences the ways consumers process persuasive messages in advertising. Myers and Sar (2013) examined the persuasive effects of social approval cues in visual and textual formats in print advertising. Participants in the high-visual, high-social cues condition viewed an ad for a fictitious champagne product endorsed by four individuals. Participants in the textual, high-social cues condition viewed an ad for the same product with the following accompanying tagline: "When it comes to champagne, everybody can taste the difference" (Myers & Sar, 2013, p. 173). Myers and Sar found that high self-monitors reported significantly higher brand evaluations and purchase intentions when they received social approval cues compared to low self-monitors. In addition, they found that social approval cues were more persuasive when presented visually rather than textually.

Engaged Persuasion Research: Personality Profiles and Susceptibility to Persuasion

Wall et al. (2019) examined relationships between personality profiles and susceptibility to persuasion. Participants in this study completed several personality measures as well as a Susceptibility to Persuasion Scale based on Cialdini's model of influence (i.e., scarcity, liking, reciprocation, commitment, social proof, and authority). The research revealed three distinct personality profiles that the authors labeled "malevolent" (participants who scored above average on measures of extraversion and negative affectivity), "socially apt" (participants who scored above average on measures of agreeableness and conscientiousness), and "fearful" (participants who reported higher scores on measures of neuroticism and social inhibition). Participants in the malevolent profile self-reported as more susceptible to scarcity appeals and were the least susceptible to reciprocity and authority appeals. Those in the socially apt group were most susceptible to appeals that activated commitment. Finally, participants in the fearful group were more likely to report obeying those in authority and going along with the crowd.

Ego Involvement

Recall our discussion of Social Judgment Theory in Chapter 9. This theory highlights the role that ego involvement plays in the processing of persuasion messages. Sherif et al. (1965) define **ego involvement** as the "arousal, singly or in combination, of the individual's commitments or stands in the context of appropriate situations" (p. 65). Individuals are ego involved when they perceive that the issue under discussion addresses their core values, attitudes, and beliefs.

As we noted in Chapter 9, highly involved individuals are much more difficult to persuade than their lesser involved counterparts for three key reasons. First, ego-involved individuals have large latitudes of rejection compared to their latitudes of acceptance and noncommitment. As a result, such individuals are likely to reject any persuasive recommendation that is not consistent with their position. Second, highly ego-involved individuals will experience assimilation effects only when the persuasive recommendations are perceived to be consistent with their attitudes. Third, as we will discuss further in later sections of this chapter, highly ego-involved individuals engage in selective perception. Taken together, these factors make it extremely difficult to change the minds of ego-involved individuals. We suggest that you consult the strategies for changing strong attitudes presented in Chapter 9 for more information regarding persuading ego-involved individuals.

Cognitive Style

According to Tinajero and Páramo (1997), **cognitive styles** are characteristic modes of information processing that can be observed in an individual's perceptual or intellectual activities, and they develop relationships between cognitive and personal/affective spheres. Cognitive styles guide our interactions with information in our environment. For example, some individuals prefer visual representations of concepts, while others prefer to receive information verbally. Similarly, some individuals like to focus on the details of the persuasive arguments they encounter by scrutinizing the arguments. Others focus on more global characteristics and are influenced by those in their social network. How individuals perceive, organize, and remember information is a function of their cognitive style.

Although there are many approaches to the study of cognitive style (e.g., authoritarianism, dogmatism, cognitive complexity, etc.), this section focuses on the work of renowned psychologist Herman Witkin. Witkin (1978) examined cognitive style in relation to an individual's tendency toward more or less differentiated cognitive processing. Thought based on increased differentiation is field-independent (FI), while thought based on lower levels of differentiation is field-dependent (Pithers, 2002).

Cognitive styles have important implications for persuasion. According to Witkin et al. (1977), FD individuals tend to prefer discussion and discovery approaches that nurture interpersonal relationships. On the other hand, FI individuals prefer to receive information verbally or textually and are more adept at impersonal analysis. As Hunt et al. (2006) have argued, FI thinkers adapt better to Toulmin's argument model presented in Chapter 6 compared to their FD counterparts. FI thinkers also tend to prefer persuasion through facts and statistics, while FD thinkers are more influenced by personal examples (Hunt et al., 2006).

In a study examining cognitive style and source credibility, Heesacker et al. (1983) found that credibility did not affect the attitudes of FI participants. Instead, FI individuals were more persuaded by the quality of the message arguments they received. In contrast, source credibility was found to be an important factor for FD participants.

Verbal Aggression and Argumentativeness

Extant research suggests that individuals may resort to antisocial persuasion techniques, such as verbal aggression, if they lack the skills to argue effectively (Infante, 1995; Lippert et al., 2005). According to Infante and Wigley (1986), verbal aggressiveness refers to the predisposition to attack the "self-concept of another person instead of, or in addition to, the person's position on a topic of communication" (p. 61). Several types of verbally aggressive messages have been identified in the literature, including character attacks, competence attacks, background attacks, maledictions, teasing, ridicule, threats, profanity, nonverbal emblems, blame, personality attacks, disconfirmations, negative comparisons, and sexual harassment (Infante et al., 1992; Infante & Wigley, 1986).

The effects of verbal aggression are severe. Infante (1995) notes that the research clearly establishes that the "effects of verbal aggression are negative, supporting the ethical stance that verbal aggression should be discouraged" (p. 55). Scholars have documented that verbal aggression can lead to damage to self-concept (Infante, 1988), physical violence in families (Gelles, 1974), and even criminal violence (Infante & Rancer, 1996). Verbal aggression also negatively influences students' academic performance. Students who employ verbally aggressive messages alienate themselves from their peers and instructors, which may place them at risk for academic failure (Lippert et al., 2005).

As we noted in Chapter 6, persuasion scholars have long embraced training in effective, prosocial argumentation. In fact, such training has been viewed as a means of ameliorating the destructive effects of verbal aggressiveness (Lippert et al., 2005). According to Infante and Rancer (1982), argumentativeness is a "generally stable trait which predisposes the individual in communication situations to advocate positions on controversial issues and to attack verbally the positions which other people take on these issues" (p. 72). In short, individuals who score high on measures of argumentativeness are generally highly motivated to engage in debates about controversial issues in a positive fashion using the tools of argumentation and critical thinking (Colbert, 1993).

Visual Processing Style

There is no doubt we are bombarded by persuasive images every day. In fact, Gurri et al. (2010) argue that "billions of human beings are seeing the world differently. The wholesale transformation of the media information landscape during the last decade in fact represents the triumph of the image over the printed word" (p. 101). We define visual persuasion as the use of graphics, photographs, illustrations, and other images to create, alter, reinforce, or extinguish and audience's values, beliefs, or behaviors. Visuals have been shown to be persuasive in a wide range of contexts, including as a means to increase consumers' product expectations and purchase intentions (Fenko et al., 2018), users' favorable first impressions of nutritional websites (Lazard et al., 2017), effectiveness of messages promoting help-seeking behaviors related to mental health (Sontag, 2018), effectiveness of antismoking messages (Ooms et al., 2020), and recall and informative value of vaccination messages as well as intentions to vaccinate (Avery & Park, 2018).

What characteristics make visuals so persuasive to some individuals? DeRosia and McQuarrie (2019) conceptualize propensity to process visuals as an individual difference construct. Importantly, this conceptualization differentiates between an individual's propensity to process visual and verbal messages. In other words, individuals' preferences for these two mediums are independent of each other (i.e., an individual high in propensity to process visuals could also be high in propensity to process verbal messages). DeRosia and McQuarrie's research demonstrates that individuals with a high propensity to process visuals respond well to persuasive attempts that utilize images. In contrast, those with a low propensity to process visuals respond poorly to visual persuasion.

Priming and Piquing Receivers

In general, we could say that persuaders try to place messages on receivers' radars to either gain their attention or influence their behavior. On the one hand, persuaders may try to prime receivers, perhaps in ways that receivers are not fully conscious of, to influence their behavior. Alternatively, persuaders may pique receivers to prevent automatic rejection of a persuasive message and encourage mindful consideration of a request. How conscious are we about the persuasive messages with which we are bombarded? Do we notice that the actors in a movie we are watching are all using iPhones? And how attentive are we to the plethora of requests we receive to donate money? Do we really stop and consider the request carefully before declining to contribute? Certainly, persuaders will employ various persuasive strategies to try and influence our behavioral reactions.

Priming Effect

Priming involves providing audiences with preliminary cues to influence their behavior. Could persuasive messages or advertisements persuade you without you being consciously aware that a message is even present? "A main assumption in priming research is that behavior is not always guided by conscious intentions or acts of will" (Yoo et al., 2015, p. 63). Though subliminal advertising remains illegal in many countries, including the United States, product placement that is subtle and brief is often present in various entertainment media, such as video games, movies, websites, and sports programs (Bustin et al., 2015). Several scholars argue that subliminal messages are morally objectionable (Hausman & Welch, 2010; Thaler & Sunstein, 2009). As Legal et al. (2012) problematize the issue, subliminal messages could be used in public health campaigns to promote the public good but could also be used by advertisers to manipulate consumers into buying products they were not previously interested in purchasing. Still, meta-analysis evidence suggests subliminal persuasion produces only weak effect sizes, meaning that **subliminal priming**, which occurs at the subconscious level where we may perceive a message without being aware of it, is not as effective as we might otherwise think (Trappey, 1996). Consequently, the meta-analysis of 23 individual studies indicates that "subliminal advertising has little influence on consumer's decision to select between alternatives" (Trappey, 1996, p. 528). An additional criticism leveled against the effectiveness of subliminal advertising is that most studies have been conducted under carefully controlled laboratory settings that do not reflect the clutter and distractions of our real lives. Nevertheless, peripheral cues and suggestions such as smells and sounds are often believed to influence us. Moore (1988) argued that no data exists to verify that subliminal messages can either influence our implicit motivations or complex behaviors. With music, in particular, Egermann et al. (2006) found no behavioral effects for subliminal worded messages in music.

It sounds like subliminal priming does not work, right? Well, more recent studies have found evidence supporting the subliminal priming effect. "There is now growing acceptance of external influences on mental processing and recognition that we may not have conscious access to the reasons underlying our behaviors" (Nelson, 2008, p. 123). Karremans et al. (2006) ran two experiments that affirmed the effectiveness of subliminal priming in advertising. More specifically, they found that priming participants subliminally with the brand name of a drink resulted in participants choosing and intending to drink the primed brand. However, only participants who were thirsty showed these effects. The researchers also noted that it is possible that subliminal brand priming will only work when audiences actually have immediate access to that brand. For instance, when sitting on your couch at home, you may not have the brand drink in your refrigerator; thus, the priming is not highly salient and is unlikely to alter your behavior. Priming that is relevant and applicable to individuals' motivations is likely to affect their actions (Karremans et al., 2006). Strahan et al. (2002) agree that "subliminal priming can enhance persuasion" by stimulating goal-relevant cognitions and motives (p. 566). Fatigue and sensation seeking are two other factors that have been shown to have some moderating effect on people's sensitivity to subliminal priming (Bustin et al., 2015). Thus, situational and dispositional factors may alter the success of subliminal priming. The findings for sensation seeking, a dispositional factor, lend support to claims that personality may moderate the effectiveness of subliminal priming (Bustin et al., 2015). Milyavsky et al. (2012) conducted two experiments that showed how subliminal priming can directly affect choice and is enhanced by implicit motivation. Yoo et al.'s (2015) study demonstrated that participants operating an elderly avatar were unconsciously primed to walk slower, choose particular products, and assimilate other social constructs, especially when they scored low in ageism prior to the study. Ruijten et al. (2011) found that ambient subliminal messages lead to improved performance. More specifically, they found that participants who were unconsciously priming with the goal of performing well were, indeed, able to perform better than participants who were not unconsciously primed with goal-striving messages. Thus, the researchers concluded that behavior-relevant goal priming demonstrated the effectiveness of subliminal persuasion. Finally, their results also demonstrated that persuasive technology can persuaded people subliminally. Legal et al. (2012) found that subliminal goal priming produced more positive evaluations of the message and source and also increased behavioral intentions.

Engaged Persuasion Research: Priming Resistance to Persuasion

In Chapter 9, we discussed metainoculation research. One extension of that research is that priming can aid in fostering resistance to persuasion (Bonetto et al., 2018). More specifically, Bonetto et al. conducted a series of three studies showing that priming resistance to persuasion can successfully decrease participants' agreement with conspiracy theories. The researchers found this effect even when the priming of resistance to persuasion was not accompanied by specific counterarguments. Thus, similar to metainoculation, priming resistance to persuasion can promote vigilance against conspiracy theories. Verwijmeren et al. (2013) found similar results. Specifically, both of their experiments demonstrated that warning people about subliminal advertising reduced the effects of subliminal priming on consumer choice. And the warnings were effective whether the participants were warned before or after the subliminal priming. "Informing participants of the presence and influence of subliminal advertisements—and instructing them to not be influenced—eliminates their effect" (Verwijmeren et al., 2013, p. 1127).

Pique Technique

You have likely received several requests to donate money in your lifetime. Have you ever received a request to donate an unusual amount of money, such as "Can you contribute 17 cents?" Are these requests effective? The **pique technique** persuades by arousing the receiver's curiosity and thus reducing the likelihood that the receiver will respond to the persuasive message with an automatic refusal or denial. The idea behind the pique technique is that unconventional requests may promote fascination and lead to compliance. Put another way, an unusual request may lead to receivers letting down their guard and abandoning refusal scripts. The technique is similar to the disrupt then reframe approach. In fact, one study found that using the pique technique followed by a reframing sentence increased donation amounts (Gueguen et al., 2015).

In a meta-analysis of six studies examining the pique technique, Lee and Feeley (2017) found a statistically significant effect for the pique technique on increasing compliance with persuasive requests. In fact, the effect size for the pique technique was larger than other meta-analyses have found for various compliance gaining strategies, such as the foot-in-the-door tactic, door-in-the-face tactic, and legitimization of paltry favors tactic. "An effect of this magnitude suggests that the pique technique is an effective message strategy in gaining compliance" (Lee & Feeley, 2017, p. 24). Interestingly, the meta-analysis revealed that the pique technique was more effective at generating monetary donations and time when a smaller amount of money was requested and when the rationale for the request was included in the message. In fact, requests for unusual monetary donations are more effective, such as a charity organization asking for 17 cents rather than a quarter. Would a panhandler be more successful asking for $5.00 or $1.17? Would a business meeting scheduled at 7:57 a.m. encourage more punctuality than one scheduled for 8:00 a.m.? The atypical requests tend to arouse curiosity and focus attention on the unusual request, which can work in the favor of those making persuasive requests (Lee & Feeley, 2017). "The unique request amount causes targets to pause and take notice of what is being asked and perhaps why it is needed, rather than mindlessly declining to help or refusing to respond altogether" (Lee & Feeley, 2017, p. 26). The meta-analysis data showed that the pique technique worked significantly better when a reason for the request was included in the message. Finally, Lee and Feeley found that participants given the pique technique asked significantly more questions than did those in the control conditions, thus reflecting greater curiosity and less propensity to revert to mindless refusal scripts. However, while Burger et al.'s (2007) experiments found that unusual requests generated greater compliance and questions about the request, the participants in their experiments did so without giving mindful consideration to the request. Whether participants were provided "a reasonable answer or an uninformative answer" to inquiries

FIGURE 10.3 Requesting sharp numbers piques receivers.

regarding the reason for the request, they still complied and gave money (Burger et al., 2007, p. 2094). Thus, piquing may succeed, but not necessarily because it increases mindful consideration.

Individual experiments have demonstrated that the pique technique increases compliance with the persuasive request, generates greater donations, increases verbal inquiries about the request, and improves perceptions of the person making the request (Santos et al., 1994). Why is it that piqued receivers are more compliant with donation requests? It could be that requesting a specific amount, a "sharp number," such as 17 cents, conveys "a very specific need" as compared to requesting a "round amount of money," which conveys "there is no specific need—rather the requestor just wants money" (Schindler & Yalch, 2006, p. 589). Piquing the receiver's attention is particularly effective when combined with a legitimate reason for the request and when informing the receiver that one is close to raising the total amount of money needed—thus adding pressure to comply with the request (Gueguen & Lamy, 2016). Zawisza et al. (2006) found that nontraditional advertising, which inverted gender role expectations, was more effective than traditional advertising. They concluded the study data was consistent with the pique technique, but noted that differences existed among participants. More specifically, progressive participants responded better to the nontraditional adverts, whereas those with conservative beliefs preferred

FIGURE 10.4 Emotions impact persuasion.

the traditional adverts. The researchers argue these results supported the pique technique since "cognitive response that follows the disruption of the reluctance script is more positive in Liberal than in Traditional participants" (Zawisza et al., 2006, p. 296).

Mood and Persuasion

"Emotions can exert a powerful impact on persuasion" (Dillard & Peck, 2000, pp. 489–490). In a meta-analysis of 14 studies, Hullett (2005) examined the impact that mood has on persuasion. His findings supported the hedonic contingency model, meaning that the motivation to attain or maintain positive moods affects the processing of persuasive messages. In other words, we try to manage our mood to either achieve or maintain a positive mood state. **Mood** is conceptually defined as a lasting or enduring state, ranging from positive to negative affect on a continuum, that are generalizable and different than emotions (Hullett, 2005). Hullett concluded that while recipients in a positive mood state can still scrutinize persuasive messages, positive mood reduced systematic processing. Those in a positive mood state were able to process positive persuasive messages but tended to avoid negative messages. Recipients form rather quick impressions of messages as being either positive or negative. They then process those messages in a manner that attempts to enhance pleasant thoughts and minimize unpleasant cognitions by expending effort to alleviate negative moods. Ultimately, the meta-analysis showed that "hedonically motivated selectivity processes are called on more to protect positive affect than to alleviate negative states" (Hullet, 2005, p. 437). The results also indicated:

> Strong arguments will be more effective than weak arguments when message recipients are in a negative mood or when the advanced position is one with which the happy recipients are predisposed to agree. Therefore, strong arguments directed toward people in positive moods probably would be more effective for attitude shaping (i.e., the initial formation of new attitudes) or reinforcement than attitude change. Attitude change resulting from strong arguments may be best accomplished when targeting people in bad moods. (Hullet, 2005, p. 439)

Banas et al.'s (2012) experimental study confirmed that argument strength was more strongly associated with persuasion for those in negative moods than for those in positive moods. Bless et al. (1990) explained that "subjects in a good mood are less likely to engage in message elaboration than subjects in a bad mood" (p. 331). Those in a good mood are not as likely to show differences between message content and behavior, processing messages systematically, and are not influenced by the content or context of the information, while those in a bad mood process information through the central route, scrutinize information more carefully, and elaborate on the implications (Bohner et al., 1992). More specifically, those in an angry mood show greater reliance on heuristic cues (Bodenhausen et al., 1994).

FIGURE 10.5 Mood affects persuasive processing. Those in a positive mood state, such as the woman shown in this photo, tend to avoid negative messages.

So what are the implications for persuasion? One takeaway is that message recipients in certain positive moods show greater acceptance of weak persuasive messages, whereas other positive moods demonstrate reduced acceptance of weak persuasive messages (Griskevicius et al., 2010). Thus, not all positive moods are the same, and the reactions to persuasive messages differ by particular moods. Specific emotions have been found to affect the impact of persuasive messages through the emotional framing of persuasive appeals that match the emotional state of receivers (DeSteno et al., 2004). In a study exploring organ donation, Wang (2011) found that anticipated guilt predicted intentions to discuss organ donation with family members and to register as an organ donor. Thus, Wang concluded that health campaign messages should include guilt appeals. Graton et al. (2016) also concluded that guilt, when coupled with reparation suggestions, can promote prosocial behavior. Additionally, a meta-analysis, conducted by Xu and Guo (2019), confirmed that viewers' emotional responses are more persuasive than their cognitive judgments in particular situations.

Scholars have also examined the use of anger as a persuasive appeal. In a meta-analysis of 55 studies, Walter et al. (2019) found a weak impact of anger on behavior and nonsignificant effects on attitudes and behavioral intent. However, a closer inspection of the data revealed positive effects of anger when accompanied by strong arguments and efficacy appeals. Perhaps most importantly, the meta-analysis demonstrated that the use of anger must be deemed relevant to the issue. The study further showed that anger intensity is an important consideration, as low to moderate levels of anger were most persuasive.

Raghunathan and Trope (2002) found support for the mood-as-a-resource hypothesis in their study of mood and caffeine consumption. For consumers high in the consumption of caffeine, the induction of a positive mood state improved their recall as well as the impact of negative information about caffeine, thus altering their attitudes and intentions about future consumption. The results indicated that "positive mood states may enable people to focus on the long-term value" of negative health-related information and "better cope with its immediate emotional costs," which means that, "positive mood should enhance search, processing, and integration of negative self-relevant information" (Raghunathan & Trope, 2002, p. 522). Meanwhile, those in a negative mood may lack the resources to adapt to or cope with negative information and feedback that could threaten their future well-being. "Compared with negative mood, positive mood led our participants not only to attend to negative self-relevant information but also to change their prior belief in line with its implications" (Raghunathan & Trope, 2002, p. 523). Clore and Huntsinger (2007) would seem to echo these results when they explain that positive emotions validate, whereas negative emotions invalidate, accessible cognitions.

Engaged Persuasion Research: Emotional Appeals in Political Advertisements

Can emotional appeals promote democratically desirable behavior? According to Brader (2005), the answer is yes. He tested whether political advertisements could get citizens more involved and alter their choices. The results of two experiments Brader conducted suggest that cueing enthusiasm can generate participation and activate existing loyalties. Meanwhile, he discovered that cueing fear will foster reliance on contemporary evaluations, trigger vigilance, and enhance persuasion. Thus, political campaign advertisements that employ emotional appeals can influence the political behavior of voters.

Motivated Reasoning Theory

Like Social Judgment Theory discussed in the last chapter, Motivated Reasoning Theory posits that receivers do not act as blank slates when they process persuasive information. As Kunda (1990) argued, **Motivated Reasoning Theory** stipulates that motivation affects reasoning through a series of biased cognitive processes. In other words, individuals are biased by the existing attitudes, values, and beliefs they hold and are thus motivated to protect them. For example, if you are an ardent advocate of second amendment rights, you are likely to accept information that supports your attitudes and reject crosscutting information. According to this approach, when individuals engage in motivated reasoning, they "are more likely to arrive at those conclusions they want to arrive at" (Kunda, 1990, p. 495). As we will see, this theory has significant implications for senders and receivers of persuasive communication and for the functioning of our democracy. In order to better understand the cognitive processes that are engaged during motivated reasoning, we turn first to the literature on selective exposure.

FIGURE 10.6 Selective exposure drives motivated reasoning. We often seek out information online, like the man in this photo, that is consistent with our existing attitudes, values, and beliefs.

Selective Exposure

Empirical research clearly demonstrates that individuals engage in motivated reasoning. Selective exposure is one cognitive mechanism that allows individuals to create and sustain positive illusions (Garrett, 2009; Iyengar et al., 2008). Specifically, selective exposure refers to the fact that individuals actively seek out information that is consistent with their existing attitudes, values, and beliefs and avoid crosscutting information (Hart et al., 2009). In their meta-analysis of selective exposure research, Hart et al. (2009) found that people are nearly twice as likely to "select information congenial rather than uncongenial to their pre-existing attitudes, beliefs, and behaviors" (p. 579).

What drives individuals' motives to select pro- or counterattitudinal information? According to Hart et al. (2009), individuals may be motivated to select information that is congenial to preexisting attitudes in order to defend those attitudes. Hart et al. also found that individuals seek out crosscutting information when they are motivated to find accurate information; however, the mean effect sizes in their study demonstrate that defense is a much stronger predictor of information-seeking behavior. In other words, we have the capacity to seek accurate information and find the truth, but we tend to be more motivated to select information consistent with our attitudes, values, and beliefs.

Engaged Persuasion Research: Political Partisanship and Selective Exposure

Do liberals and conservatives differ in their tendency to avoid crosscutting information? Frimer et al. (2017) set out to answer this question and found similar selective exposure motives for liberals and conservatives on a wide variety of controversial issues. For example, on the topic of same-sex marriage, Frimer et al. found that people on both sides of the political spectrum were willing to give up a chance to win money to avoid hearing from the other side. Importantly, the motive to avoid counterattitudinal information was not driven by a lack of interest or fatigue. Instead, Frimer et al. found that participants anticipated that hearing from the other side would induce cognitive dissonance and potentially threaten interpersonal relationships. Unfortunately, the tendency for people to avoid crosscutting information has serious implications for democracy. Frimer et al. (2017) conclude that the outcome of this desire to avoid counterattitudinal information is that "liberals and conservatives live in ideological information bubbles, and what could ultimately be a contest of ideas is being replaced by two, non-interacting monopolies" (p. 11).

Biased Assimilation

Beyond the strategies we employ to seek or avoid information, research demonstrates that we are prone to confirmation and disconfirmation biases when we process persuasive information. In other words, we tend to accept claims that support our preexisting attitudes, values, and beliefs (confirmation bias) and reject claims that counter our attitudes, values, and beliefs (disconfirmation bias; Edwards & Smith, 1996).

In a seminal study of biased assimilation, Lord et al. (1979) established that individuals process information and evidence in ways that bolster preexisting attitudes. Participants in Lord et al.'s study were split into two groups—one group that believed the death penalty is an effective deterrent and one group known to believe it is not an effective deterrent. Both groups of participants were presented with information supporting the deterrent effect of the death penalty as well as information indicating the death penalty is an ineffective deterrent. In other words, both groups received evidence that supported and challenged their position on the death penalty. As you might expect, Lord et al. found that both groups of participants became more polarized as a result of reading the two arguments. This study vividly demonstrates how confirmation and disconfirmation biases influence the way we process persuasive information. Participants who supported the death penalty accepted the study supporting their preexisting views. Participants in the group against the death penalty employed similar biases in evaluating the research.

Can the process of biased assimilation be used to predict racist behavior? Saucier and Miller (2003) created a measure called the Racial Argument Scale (RSA) to explore this question. Across eight studies they demonstrated that the process of biased assimilation of positive and negative arguments about race provide an indirect measure of racism. Specifically, their findings revealed that participants "who report that pro-Black arguments are low in supportiveness, whereas anti-Black arguments are high in supportiveness, are also more likely to exhibit racist behavior" (Saucier & Miller, 2003, p. 1312).

In a more recent study, Mattes and Redlawsk (2020) found receivers are more likely to seek fact-checks for political opponents, thereby avowing challenges to

FIGURE 10.7 Protests are an example of political communication.

their own preexisting political preferences. This research clearly demonstrates biased assimilation, as receivers of political communication actively search for information consistent with their preferences for political candidates.

Motivated Reasoning in the Post-Truth Era

Motivated Reasoning Theory has received renewed attention by scholars interested in the spread of persuasive misinformation. As we have noted throughout this text, the post-truth era establishes the conditions for the spread of misinformation and viral deception. For example, we noted in Chapter 3 that the transmission bias makes individuals prone to spreading conspiracy theories and persuasive misinformation (Bøggild et al., 2020). Further, we noted in Chapter 6 that the death of expertise phenomenon challenges the way many assess source credibility, making it difficult to employ experts in efforts to correct persuasive misinformation. Also, individuals are able to use the internet and social media to quickly drive the spread of misinformation to large numbers of receivers. Nyhan and Reifler (2012) capture the challenges of the current situation when they argue that "individuals may be more likely to be exposed to false or unsupported information that conforms with their pre-existing views and to accept such information as true when exposed to it" (pp. 9–10).

As we noted in Chapter 1, belief perseverance dynamics further complicate efforts to correct false beliefs. Kavanagh and Rich (2018) describe the situation in the following terms:

> If people were readily willing to update prior beliefs when presented with contradictory facts or relied more heavily on objective facts and analysis in decision-making than on social cues, emotions, and heuristics, it would be easier to correct misinformation and disinformation, prevent or break up the formation of echo chambers, and train people to evaluate news media objectively. (pp. 81–82)

Unfortunately, scholarship is this area makes it abundantly clear that merely providing corrective information is rarely effective because of the **continued-influence effect** (Lewandowsky et al., 2017). In other words, "Despite being corrected, and despite acknowledging the correction, people by and large continue to rely at least partially on information they know to be false" (Lewandowsky et al., 2017, p. 355). In fact, research indicates that providing corrective information may backfire and make individuals even more confident in their false beliefs (Nyhan & Reifler, 2012).

According to Jacks and Cameron (2003), individuals engage in several processes to resist accepting counterattitudinal information, including counterarguing (directly refute the claim in question), attitude bolstering (recalling reasons supporting why the initial belief was correct), source derogation (dismissing the credibility of the source), negative affect (becoming angry or upset), message distortion (selectively interpreting the claim to support the initial belief), social validation (thinking of others who hold the same view), and selective exposure (ignoring or avoiding counterattitudinal information).

Our tendency to engage in motivated reasoning has serious implications for civic engagement, policymaking, and decision making, especially during a crisis. As Hameleers et al. (2020) argue, "Disinformation can pose vexing problems on democratic decision-making as falsehoods related to politics and society can be perceived as credible when they rely on heuristic cues" (p. 298). Consider the way American policymakers and the public have responded to crises like the COVID-19 pandemic and climate change. Weber (2020) argues that biased processing and selective attention fuel political partisanship and division on these issues. More specifically, Weber (2020) notes that we have become more polarized, with "Democrats more likely to subscribe to science-based explanations of both crises and express great concern and Republicans more likely to agree with conspiracy theories that downplay the risks" (p. 25). This claim is consistent with research by Stein et al. (2020) indicating that conservatives view nonscientific experiential evidence as persuasive as scientific evidence, while liberals view scientific evidence as more credible. This polarization drives the spread of persuasive misinformation, hinders policymaking, and jeopardizes timely and effective responses to a crisis.

FIGURE 10.8 Disinformation in the post-truth era is dangerous.

We have discussed several strategies for overcoming the challenges to persuasive communication posed by the post-truth era in previous chapters. Beyond these strategies, the following recommendations account for some of the problems described by Motivated Reasoning Theory:

- *Early corrections are essential.* Persuaders should strive to correct any errors they make as early as possible and quickly notify any other individuals, media outlets, or organizations that disseminated them.
- *Avoid the information deficit fallacy.* Remember that merely providing corrective information may not be effective and could even backfire. In addition, Nyhan and Reifler (2012) note that corrections "may also increase the prevalence of a misperception among members of the most vulnerable group if they provoke them to defend their prior beliefs" (p. 18). Also, persuaders should consider test marketing the messages they use to ensure they are effective. Further, a recent meta-analysis indicates that corrective messages may be more successful when they are delivered by the source of the misinformation itself (Walter & Tukachinsky, 2020).
- *Minimize repetition of false claims.* As Nyhan and Reifler (2012) note, the more times misinformation is repeated, the more people are exposed to it. In addition, the fluency effect means that people are more likely to judge familiar claims as correct (Weisbuch & Mackie, 2009).
- *Use credible sources to support your claims.* As we noted in Chapter 6, source credibility matters when receivers evaluate persuasive claims. Make sure to establish your credibility on the topic and provide evidence credibility statements for any evidence you use.
- *Carefully consider the context of communication.* A meta-analysis by Walter and Murphy (2018) revealed that corrective messages can be effective; however, it was more difficult to correct misinformation in the context of politics and marketing compared to health. In addition, the research revealed that correction of real-world misinformation is more difficult than correction of constructed misinformation. Finally, the results revealed that rebuttals were more effective than forewarnings while appeals to coherence were more effective than fact-checking and appeals to credibility.
- *Use graphics and images to correct misperceptions.* In a recent study, Nyhan and Reifler (2019) found that providing participants with graphical information significantly decreased false beliefs compared to equivalent textual information. Nyhan and Reifler argue that graphs help receivers understand complex information and relationships.
- *Use inoculating messages to limit the effects of misinformation.* Recall our discussion of Inoculation Theory in Chapter 9. Research by Cook et al. (2017) on climate change suggests that inoculating messages that explain the flawed argumentation in the misinformation and highlight scientific consensus on the issue are effective in neutralizing the effects of misinformation.

- *Providing alternative news stories via social media may help slow the spread of misinformation.* Although the algorithms social media platforms utilize to curate content have been broadly criticized for reinforcing current beliefs, Bode and Vraga (2015) found positive effects when users received related stories designed to correct misinformation. Encouraging such platforms to intentionally curate content to combat misinformation may hold promise going forward. Further, research by Clayton et al. (2020) demonstrates that adding tags like "disputed" and "rated false" to false news stories on social media can modestly reduce beliefs in misinformation.
- *Fact checking and journalistic arbitration can correct misinformation in certain circumstances.* Research by Thorson (2018) demonstrates that citizens' opinions and beliefs are influenced by more factors than party identification. Fact-checking can help correct persuasive misinformation and boost individuals' positive evaluations of mass media. In addition, research demonstrates some promise in correcting misperceptions encountered in social media using logic- and humor-based corrections (Vraga et al., 2019). Further, research by Amazeen and Bucy (2019) suggests that knowledge of how the news media operate increases news consumers' resistance to persuasive misinformation. Finally, York et al. (2020) suggest that journalists should offer brief facts checks that are easy to understand and boost receiver's confidence that they can locate objective political truth.

Summary

In this chapter we have covered the individual characteristics that influence how persuasive messages are received as well as the cognitive and emotional responses of receivers. You have learned that certain demographic variables (such as age, gender, and culture) as well as psychological variables (such as self-esteem, self-monitoring, ego involvement, cognitive style, and verbal aggression and argumentativeness) are important factors to consider when analyzing how persuasive messages are received. We also explored subliminal priming, the pique technique, and how mood and emotion affect receivers of persuasive messages. Finally, you learned about Motivated Reasoning Theory and how receivers' existing positions on issues influence their reception of persuasive messages and information.

The next chapter introduces theories vital to understanding the behavioral reactions and responses of receivers to persuasive messages.

Check Your Understanding Review Questions

1. How do demographic variables (e.g., age, gender, and culture) influence the reception of persuasive messages?
2. How do psychological factors (e.g., self-esteem, self-monitoring, ego involvement, cognitive style, and verbal aggression and argumentativeness) affect the processing of persuasive messages?
3. What is subliminal priming? And is subliminal priming effective?
4. How does the pique technique work? How can persuaders pique receivers most effectively to obtain compliance?
5. How does mood and emotion affect responses to persuasive messages?
6. What is the hedonic contingency model?
7. What does the mood-as-a-resource hypothesis say?
8. What is Motivated Reasoning Theory?
9. How does Motivated Reasoning Theory apply to the post-truth era?

Key Terms

cognitive style (p. 253)
continued-influence effect (p. 266)
culture (p. 249)
demographics (p. 246)
ego involvement (p. 253)
mood (p. 260)
Motivated Reasoning Theory (p. 263)
pique technique (p. 258)
self-esteem (p. 251)
self-monitoring (p. 251)
subliminal priming (p. 256)

Credits

CHAPTER 11

Theories of Behavioral Reactions

Chapter Objectives

After reading this chapter, you should be able to:

- Define Psychological Reactance Theory and explain its importance
- Appreciate how boomerang effects may cause persuasion attempts to backfire
- Explain Diffusion of Innovations Theory and its various components
- Understand how the S-curve is driven by adopter categories and the rate of adoption
- Understand Cognitive Dissonance Theory and its applications
- Explain how counterattitudinal advocacy can result in attitude change

This chapter introduces three theories vital to understanding how receivers react and respond to persuasive messages. Each of these theories has a long, rich history and vast body of accompanying research literature testing the theoretical premises. In short, these are extremely important theories for a persuasion scholar to know, understand, and be able to apply. As you will read in this chapter, each of these theories is still alive and well today—in some cases after more than 50 years of research. While each of these theories is certainly unique, the majority of these theories address the cognitive processes that individuals go through when exposed to persuasive stimuli. Furthermore, each theory addresses how receivers respond to persuasive messages—whether that means behavioral responses to a message, adopting an innovation, or rationalizing changes in attitudes or behaviors.

Psychological Reactance Theory

Psychological Reactance Theory, developed by psychologist Jack Brehm while at Duke University, provides an explanation of how people respond to messages that they perceive to restrict their freedoms or choices. Often referred to as *reverse psychology*, the theory posits that people believe they have free will and are thus free to make decisions, which means they value choice and freedom behaviors (Brehm, 1966). **Freedom behaviors**, which refer only to actions that are realistically possible for individuals, are sometimes as simple as exercising choice or picking among alternatives (Brehm, 1966). When threats to our freedoms or the elimination of our freedom behaviors occur, our reactance is aroused (Brehm, 1966), which may reduce compliance (Ghazali et al., 2018). "Reactance is best understood as an intermingling of negative cognition and anger" (Dillard & Shen, 2005, p. 160). In fact, Rains's (2013) meta-analysis concurred that anger and counterarguments are indicators of reactance. Notice that mere threats to our freedoms are positively correlated with reactance (Quick et al., 2017), meaning that freedoms do not actually have to be removed or eliminated to trigger reactance. Our reactance is aroused when we perceive implied threats (Brehm & Brehm, 1981) or social influence attempts (Wicklund, 1974) that might threaten a specific behavioral freedom. Importantly, Brehm's theory (1989) argues that a specific behavioral freedom can be threatened or lost without necessarily affecting other freedoms.

Reactance can vary in intensity based on the perceived value of the freedom, the proportion of the freedom in comparison to other freedoms, and the ability to restore the freedom (Brehm, 1966; Brehm & Brehm, 1981; Wicklund, 1974). Essentially, we will attempt to recover the freedom that has been lost or threatened, value the freedom more than we did previously, or engage in related freedom behaviors (Brehm, 1966, 1989; Brehm & Brehm, 1981; Wicklund, 1974). When we respond in these ways, our response is called a **boomerang effect** (Quick & Stephenson, 2007).

Ironically enough, psychological reactance can even occur when freedoms we have chosen not to exercise in the past are threatened. In other words, a persuader might think they are removing a freedom people do not use or care about, only to discover that people react negatively when the previously unexercised freedom is removed as an option. Do you like the idea that you could eat a bowl of cold, leftover chili for breakfast if you wanted (being an independent college student in charge of your own nutritional choices, who may have even indulged in the notorious breakfast of cold pizza upon occasion), even though you have never done so? Now, imagine the university announces that students are prohibited from eating chili during morning hours on any campus grounds or while participating in an off-campus university-related event. How would you feel about this breakfast option having been eliminated from your potential menu? It's not hard to imagine the resulting sit-ins, protests, and student newspaper editorials demanding chili rights be restored, is it?

Ultimately, threats to freedom reduce the persuasiveness of messages (Reinhart & Anker, 2012). If the university's health and wellness office truly believed that chili was a bad breakfast choice for students, wouldn't they find greater receptivity to their message if it were delivered in some manner other than an outright ban on the activity? Of course, some individuals are more prone to experiencing particularly high levels of reactance than others (Dillard & Shen, 2005).

FIGURE 11.1 It is not just children who experience reactance arousal.

Not everyone will sign the "Save our chili rights" petition, right? Still, it is easy to imagine some students taking the issue very seriously even if for no other reason than thinking the university might continue to restrict other freedoms until one they truly care about is taken away. Psychological reactance can be measured along the four dimensions of freedom of choice, conformity reactance, behavioral freedom, and reactance to advice and recommendations (Hong, 1992; Hong & Page, 1989). Reactance to advice and recommendations? Yes, we may even react when we perceive simple advice and recommendations to have the potential of threatening our freedom of choice.

Boomerang Effects

Parents of toddlers soon discover that one of the quickest and surest ways to get a child to do something is to tell them not to do that exact behavior. In fact, parents quickly learn to take advantage of this reverse psychology. As Silvia (2006) explains, "People may change their attitudes simply because they are motivated to restore their freedom, and disagreement is the most direct way to do so" (p. 674). Thus, "Boomerang effects represent built-in responses to threats—all else equal, a threat to freedom is sufficient for negative attitude change" (Silvia, 2006, p. 674). In other words, a receiver's attitude may change—but in a direction opposite of the stated message.

Three Forms of Boomerang Effects

Boomerang effects come in three forms: direct boomerang, related boomerang, and vicarious boomerang (see Table 11.1). A direct boomerang implies doing the opposite of what we are told not to do. An example of this would be the toddler doing exactly what the parent has told them not to do. Some speculation even exists about stereotype reactance, in which one would defy stereotypes placed upon them by acting in a manner contrary to the stereotype (Miron & Brehm, 2006). The related boomerang, on the other hand, plays out in a scenario wherein one would not defy a policy restricting their freedom but would exhibit related behaviors that essentially demonstrate defiance or push the boundaries of the restrictive policy. Rather than violating a campus smoking ban, for example, students and employees may smoke just across the street, take up smokeless tobacco or vaping, or carry cigarette cartons around visibly in their pockets or backpacks. The vicarious boomerang effect may be akin to experiencing empathetic reactance on behalf of another person (Miron & Brehm, 2006). For instance, a student might protest that a classroom policy is unfair to other students, even though they themselves are not directly affected by the policy. Alternatively, a vicarious boomerang is manifested by an individual not directly violating a policy restricting their freedom but aligning themselves with those who do defy the restriction. For example, a student may not take up smoking but may hang out with the smokers who still do so despite a campus ban on the behavior.

TABLE 11.1 Boomerang Effects

Effect	Explanation	Example
1. Direct Boomerang	Exercising the exact freedom that has been threatened or restricted	A child doing exactly what they have been told not to do
2. Related Boomerang	Exercising a freedom or behavior similar or related to the one that has been threatened or restricted	A person wearing a scarf on their head to work when the dress code has outlawed hats
3. Vicarious Boomerang	Expressing solidarity with or showing alliance with those who exercise the freedom that has been threatened or restricted	A person hanging out with smokers, but not smoking, when smoking has been banned in an area

Triggers of Reactance

So what triggers psychological reactance? And what strategies can persuasive campaigns utilize to avoid creating reactance? Whereas high-controlling language has been found to be perceived as reducing freedom, thereby triggering reactance, anger, and negative cognitions, the use of low-controlling language and concrete, direct, or plain language in restoration postscripts (i.e., a short message added at the end of the main persuasive message) can avoid detrimental effects as demonstrated in studies of promotional health messages with young audiences (Miller et al., 2007). Not only were restorative postscripts with concrete language given more attention by consumers of these messages but Miller et al. also found these messages to be more persuasive while minimizing reactance. Postscript messages could, for example, inform recipients that the choice to comply with or follow the prescribed behavior is up to them, thus restoring their sense of freedom (Reinhart & Anker, 2012).

Meanwhile, fear appeal messages have been shown to increase perceptions of freedom threats (Quick et al., 2017). However, high efficacy appeals have also been found to mitigate perceptions by reducing fear-control processing of freedom threats among underage students in a study of messages discouraging excessive alcohol consumption (Quick et al., 2017). Additionally, the message source may matter. In a study encouraging organ donation, Reinhart and Anker (2012) discovered that research participants tended to strongly agree with a message source that they deemed as similar to themselves even when they perceived a threat to their freedom.

FIGURE 11.2 Freedom and choice lie at the heart of psychological reactance.

Freedom and Choice

Freedom and choice are essential to preserve, lest persuaders risk triggering reactance. According to Psychological Reactance Theory, freedoms are beliefs about what one can and cannot do in specific situations (Miron & Brehm, 2006). Threats to freedom can be real or implied, explicit or implicit (Miron & Brehm, 2006). However, for a person to feel that their freedom is threatened and thus experience **reactance arousal**, a person must possess and value the freedom in the first place (Quick, 2012), meaning that reactance is not proactive, but rather it is reactive (Miron & Brehm, 2006). A threat to freedom precedes and galvanizes psychological reactance (Quick, 2012). Freedoms represent behaviors that one is able to engage in at any given moment or in the future (Miron & Brehm, 2006). If the freedom is either threatened or eliminated, then reactance is aroused (Miron & Brehm, 2006). Even threats to attitudinal freedom, or one's freedom to disagree, can provoke reactance (Silvia, 2006). What crosses your mind when you see the "Do not cross" police tape in front of the White House? Did something stir inside of you? Admit it; you want to cross now, don't you?

As Silvia (2006) demonstrated, "There are several ways in which the motivation to restore threatened freedoms can cause resistance to persuasion," including sleeper effects (p. 683). A case in point would be a choice that presents relatively equal reasons for agreeing or disagreeing. However, "The same levels of initial disagreement can change into different levels of long-term agreement, depending on why people disagreed in the first place" (Silvia, 2006, p. 683). In other words, a threat to freedom alone is ample reason to react. But if the initial reactance is merely an artifact of the source of the message, then removal of the threat will eventually lead to agreement and diffuse reactance (Silvia, 2006).

FIGURE 11.3 Threats to attitudinal freedom can evoke reactance.

We previously discussed how people may experience reactance in reaction to persuasive health campaign messages in Chapter 3. In one study examining how people both high and low in trait reactance, as well as high and low in sensation seeking, responded to persuasive health messages, Quick and Stephenson (2008) found that people commonly perceive vivid and dogmatic language as threatening their freedom of choice. Trait reactance refers to an individual's general tendency to experience reactance in response to perceived threats, whereas state reactance refers to an individual's reactance in a given situation or in response to a particular message. Being prone to reactance is reflective of trait reactance, although individuals vary in their level of reactance depending on the particular persuasive message and topic (Dillard & Shen, 2005). Thus, "Dogmatic language is not likely to make a message persuasive" (Quick & Stephenson, 2008, p. 465). Vivid language was similarly unpersuasive (Quick & Stephenson, 2008). Quick and Stephenson also found that trait reactance predicted all three types of boomerang effects (direct, related, and vicarious). Additionally, individuals high in trait reactance were "more prone to experience reactance following a perceived threat to an established freedom" (Quick & Stephenson, 2008, p. 466). Both trait reactance and sensation seeking were associated with state reactance (Quick & Stephenson, 2008). In the case of organ donation messages, research participants who reported feeling their freedom of choice was threatened by a persuasive message attempt were more likely to experience negative reactions to the message (Reinhart & Anker, 2012).

Another situation in which we need to be concerned with reactance is within organizations. As Olison and Roloff (2012) point out, organizations occasionally create policies that restrict the freedoms of their members, thus risking psychological reactance and dissent. Olison and Roloff wondered if having a representative voice in the decision-making process would quell dissent and mitigate reactance. Indeed, their findings revealed that "a decision-making process that does not afford voice to those affected by the decision runs the risk of creating psychological reactance and, consequently, dissent" (Olison & Roloff, 2012, p. 213). In fact, they reasoned that dissent is one means through which people express their reactance. Additionally, their results indicated that providing a voice in the decision-making process produces less reactance.

Restrictions of Freedom

Are there times when freedoms are restricted but reactance does not occur? According to Miron and Brehm (2006), reactance may initially be experienced but will ultimately disappear if the freedom has clearly been lost as opposed to simply threatened. In other words, if a person realizes that the freedom cannot be restored or recovered, then their reactance would be low. When comparing absolute restrictions of freedom in the workplace, where the constraints on the behavioral freedom were certain to come into effect, to nonabsolute restrictions, where there was a slight chance of the constraint on freedom not coming to fruition, Laurin et al. (2012) found that people responded to absolute restrictions with rationalization (similar to Cognitive Dissonance Theory, which we will discuss later in this chapter), whereas they responded to nonabsolute restrictions with reactance. More specifically, when freedom restrictions are definitive, people will minimize the importance of the freedom and respond positively via rationalization (Laurin et al., 2012). Meanwhile, if there is even a small chance that the constraint on freedom will not actually occur, people will respond negatively via reactance and exaggerate the importance of the freedom (Laurin et al., 2012). Thus, we can conclude that if one were to take away a behavioral freedom, they are best off making it clear that the freedom will be definitively restricted, as leaving any wiggle room only invites reactance. Parents often experience just such a pattern with young children and soon learn to be clear and definitive when saying "no" or denying requests.

Mitigating Reactance

In addition, there are certain conditions in which reactance may be mitigated. For instance, Miron and Brehm (2006) explain that freedom threats from powerful communicators or pressure from group members may diffuse reactance. However, in an experimental study manipulating the social cues of robots, Ghazali et al. (2018) found that robots utilizing more social cues triggered higher levels of reactance. Relatedly, as levels of psychological involvement and social agency increase, so too does reactance (Ghazali et al., 2018).

FIGURE 11.4 Some innovations take off, while others never do.

Ultimately, Psychological Reactance Theory holds important practical applications for persuaders and persuasive campaigns (Reynolds-Tylus, 2019). As Rains (2013) notes, "A pervasive challenge faced by campaign message designers is balancing the need to offer directives for behavior change with the potential consequences of threatening and audience's freedom" (p. 67). Directives employ phrases, such as "You have to" or "You must," or use dogmatic or controlling language. Thus, directives ought to be avoided by persuaders hoping to avoid triggering reactance arousal in receivers. Similarly, verbally aggressive language has been found to trigger reactance in debates about issues like climate change and should therefore be avoided (Yuan & Lu, 2020).

Diffusion of Innovations Theory

Diffusion of Innovations Theory, codified by the late Everett Rogers while he was working on his dissertation at Iowa State University, explains how ideas, innovations, and practices spread throughout a population. The diffusion of technological as well as ideological innovations, for example, is a social process that involves communication networks and personal influence or persuasion (Rogers, 2003). Rogers was initially intrigued by his own experiences growing up on his family's farm. He noticed that his father was slow to adopt hybrid corn seed, while he noticed that neighboring farmers who were quicker to adopt these changes benefited from higher crop yields. Thus, Rogers wondered how innovations spread and why some individuals adopted innovations at different rates. What made the early adopters different than the late adopters?

Knowledge informs the positive or negative attitudes one forms toward an innovation, at which point the persuasion step in the diffusion process occurs (Sahin, 2006). Diffusion itself is a communicative process, leading to the decision to either adopt or reject the innovation (Rogers, 2003; Sahin, 2006). In a study examining the utilization of information technology after adoption, Moore and Benbasat (1996) found that perceptions of ease of use, relative advantage, and compatibility had the most significant effects on diffusion.

The **rate of adoption**, or speed at which the adoption of an innovation spreads throughout a social system, is also critical (Sahin, 2006). Diffusion proceeds by reaching certain categories of adopters in a particular community. See Figure 11.5 for the categories of adopters. For instance, early adopters will take to an innovation noticeably earlier than others, and perhaps more eagerly. The child using the virtual reality player in Figure 11.4 seems like an eager early adopter. Once opinion leaders influence others in their communication networks and the innovation takes off, or reaches a critical mass, the early majority helps to spur the spread of the adoption in an S-curve type pattern. While Figure 11.5 shows a bell curve because it reflects how many adopters fall into each category, if this same data were mapped on a line graph, the curve would start slowly, then take off rapidly at the point where the opinion leaders get the early majority on board with the innovation, before the line would eventually level out. After the innovation has taken off, the late majority joins in. Laggards, however, are particularly slow to adopt the innovation and usually do so only after nearly everyone else has, and they may have little choice but to adopt in order to keep up.

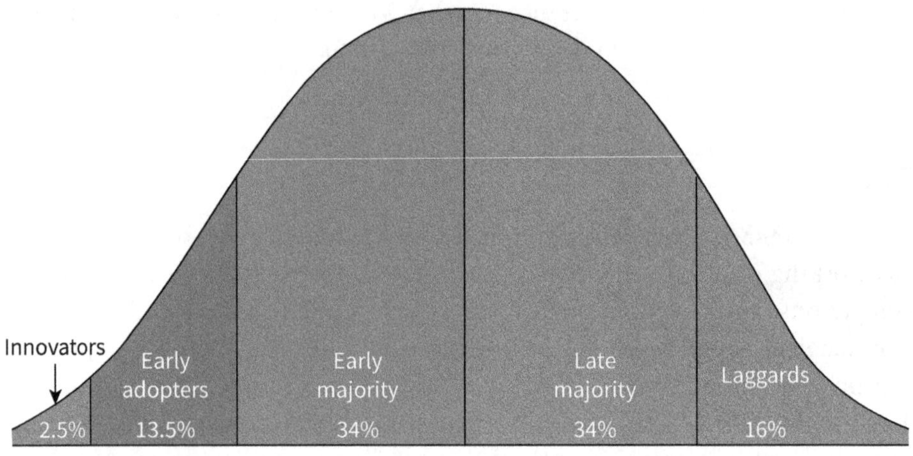

FIGURE 11.5 Adopter categories in the Diffusion of Innovations (Rogers, 2003).

As Dearing and Meyer (2006) note, "Different people take different amounts of time to adopt innovations" (p. 34). The adoption of cell phones provides a fairly good example of the diffusion of innovations. When mobile phone technologies blossomed in the late 1990s and early 2000s, some users were quick to adopt the new technology. Opinion leaders helped to spread the word about this new technology, and its benefits, by talking about and demonstrating the capabilities of cell phones to those within their social networks. Eventually, more and more users in the early majority began switching to cell phones. It was at this point that the tipping point was reached, wherein the number of cell phone users expanded exponentially. The late majority were slow to make the switch and typically preferred to also maintain landline phones in their homes. Laggards, however, clung to the older phone technology, preferring to not be reached by phone when they were on the go. But even the laggards eventually adopted mobile phone technology once it was clear everyone else had done so, and they were being left behind. When the iPhone first came out, our friend Jeff acquired one immediately. Shortly after, another friend in our social circle, Scott, purchased an iPhone. Unlike Jeff, who we always knew to seek out the newest invention, Scott would talk to and show the iPhone's features to those he knew; and he knew and influenced quite a few others. Eventually, one of the authors of this textbook purchased an iPhone only when his phone company informed him that they no longer supported plans for phones that did not have data services (making him the laggard).

According to Backer and Rogers (1998), during the early stages of the diffusion process, adoption rates for an innovation or new idea occur very slowly. If early adopters perceive the innovation as relatively advantageous, however, Backer and Rogers explain that the rate of adoption speeds up as early adopters and opinion leaders share their favorable impressions and experiences with other, potential adopters. Since diffusion is a social process wherein people talk to others about the innovation, the beginning stages of a diffusion process proceed relatively slowly (Backer & Rogers, 1998). It is not until a critical mass is reached that the innovation takes off and spreads rapidly.

S-Curve

As Backer and Rogers (1998) explain, the rate of adoption speeds up once the critical mass is reached and follows an S-curve pattern:

> An S-shaped rate of adoption of the innovation over time is typically formed by the relatively slow initial diffusion, which then speeds up when a critical mass has occurred and, finally, levels off in the rate of adoption as fewer and fewer individuals (or organizations) remain to adopt. (p. 17)

In some cases, it takes years for an innovation to diffuse across communication networks (Dearing & Meyer, 2006). The **S-curve** is a visual depiction, as shown in Figure 11.6, of how ideas or innovations take off and go viral. Compare Figures 11.5 and 11.6, imagining that the two figures overlap. Recall in Figure 11.5 that most people fall into the early majority and late majority—which would be the area in Figure 11.6 labelled "diffusion." This is also the area of the figure where you would describe an innovation as having taken off or gone viral since the rate of diffusion accelerates at this point. The key juncture at which innovations begin to spread rapidly is what Rogers (2003) referred to as the critical mass that "occurs at the point at which enough individuals in a system have adopted an innovation so that the innovation's further rate of adoption becomes self-sustaining" (p. 343). Importantly, though, Rogers (2003) noted that "the critical mass can also affect *discontinuance* of an interactive innovation" (p. 353). **Critical mass** "is the point after which further rates of adoption occur rapidly in a self-sustaining process" (Backer & Rogers, 1998, p. 17). Finding an opinion leader or "champion" for the innovation or new idea could be the key factor in reaching a critical mass (Backer & Rogers, 1998).

Opinion Leaders

Opinion leaders greatly influence other adopters, thus driving the S-curve. Opinion leadership is defined by Rogers (2003) as the ability to informally influence

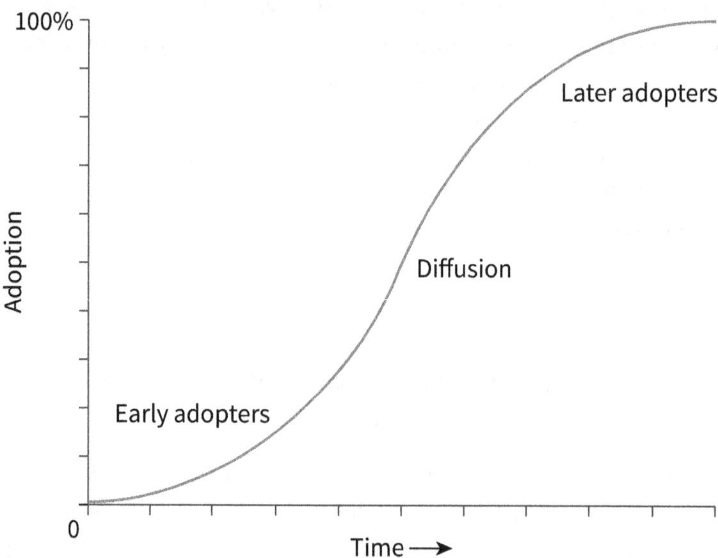

FIGURE 11.6 The S-curve rate of adoption in the Diffusion of Innovations (Dearing & Meyer, 2006).

the attitudes or behaviors of others. Roughly 5% of a communication network can be considered opinion leaders (Dearing & Meyer, 2006). Valente and Davis (1999) discovered that diffusion occurs at a much faster rate when initiated by opinion leaders. "In most organizations and communities, different individuals will be seen as opinion leaders in different domains" (Valente & Davis, 1999, p. 64). While some opinion leaders may enjoy their influence, others may find the role of being an opinion leader intrusive (Valente & Davis, 1999).

Due to the central role of communication networks in the diffusion process, networks represent an important concern for diffusion practitioners and researchers. Importantly, networks should be harnessed and used to create diffusion campaigns, whereas ignoring networks can jeopardize the success of the campaign (Rogers, 2003). Rogers noted that cluster studies have demonstrated the vital role that network influences play on individuals. "The fact that certain innovations are adopted by clusters of individuals suggests that interpersonal networks among neighbors are powerful influences on individual decisions to adopt" (Rogers, 2003, p. 335). Edwards (2014) argues that personal social networks, including weak ties, have the most influence over decisions to adopt new ideas or innovations. However, more communication about an innovation does not necessarily increase the rate of adoption, and adopters are not merely passive receivers who adapt to innovations without careful thought and decision making (Dearing & Meyer, 2006).

Engaged Persuasion Research: Opinion Leaders and Political Persuasion on Facebook

How do opinion leaders persuade others about politics on social network sites like Facebook? Carpenter and Averbeck (2020) sought to answer this question by exploring opinion leader types and motives for producing persuasive political messages on Facebook. They found that certain types of opinion leaders called mavens (i.e., people whose networks recognize them as particularly credible sources of information and therefore network members seek their advice) act as superdiffusers. Mavens were the most likely opinion leaders to produce messages aimed at persuading members in their network through status updates and sharing links. Further, moderation analysis revealed that mavens were most likely to engage in online persuasion when they perceived that doing so would be fun. Their results have significant implications for anyone interested in persuading others to support online political causes, campaigns, and movements.

Implications

According to Ma et al. (2014), the combination of Diffusion of Innovations Theory and the Theory of Reasoned Action can explain how news is shared through social media. Opinion leaders were found to exert exceptionally strong influence over intentions to share news via social media (Ma et al., 2014). Independently, sharing news on social media can enhance self-perceptions of opinion leadership (Ma et al., 2014). Overall, their study demonstrated that the strength of ties within a diffusion network exerts substantial influence on intentions to disseminate news over social media platforms, particularly when members of the network are nonhomophilous. In other words, if the members of your social network are relatively homophilous, or similar to you, you may only consume news rather than share it. However, if the members of your social network have interests that vary from your own, you may perceive yourself to have greater influence over them if you share news stories that they may not otherwise encounter.

Interestingly, Ma et al. (2014) found that news credibility was not significantly related to sharing intentions. In other words, because the credibility of online news content is difficult to verify, participants in the study indicated they would share news content they perceived as interesting, relevant, attention grabbing, and able to initiate interactions. Such a scenario would certainly explain how rumors spread quickly in social media environments, as news stories are diffused through opinion leaders.

Persuasive campaigns can use Diffusion of Innovations Theory to guide **entertainment-education** efforts to affect positive social changes. Slater and Rouner (2002) explain that entertainment-education, which takes advantage of narrative persuasion as well as the audience's empathy with and emotional investment in fictional characters, can increase the likelihood that similar attitudes and behaviors will be adopted by audience members. Entertainment-education persuades counterattitudinal audiences to adopt new ideas or innovations because it suppresses counterarguments, which is consistent with the Elaboration Likelihood Model's conceptualization of deep processing (Slater & Rouner, 2002).

Cognitive Dissonance Theory

Cognitive Dissonance Theory, developed by Leon Festinger, a social psychologist at Stanford University, has served as a staple for understanding persuasion for decades and has spawned other theories. According to the theory, if an individual holds two pieces of knowledge that are relevant to each other but inconsistent, the individual will experience a state of discomfort—or dissonance (Bem, 1967; Harmon-Jones & Harmon-Jones, 2007). Under this negative and unpleasant state of dissonance, Festinger (1957) posited that individuals will work to psychologically reduce the inconsistency by supporting the cognition that requires the least change. Indeed, the psychological discomfort of experiencing dissonance is alleviated by attitude change that reduces dissonance (Elliot & Devine, 1994). Dissonance will increase in magnitude "as the number and importance of dissonant cognitions relative to consonant cognitions increase" (Harmon-Jones, 2002, p. 100).

Cognitive dissonance can be misattributed and can be affected by past experiences (Cooper, 1998). Cooper (1998) found that the cognitive dissonance effect was weaker following misattribution. In other words, if participants had misattributed their dissonance in the past, then there was less likelihood of cognitive dissonance being aroused in the future. One implication of this study is that dissonance can be unlearned, which could help people deal with issues that affect how they function (i.e., anxiety, emotional pain, depression). Cooper argues that **dissonance arousal** is a negative state, so unlearning dissonance would be helpful.

Over the years, several revisions to Festinger's original conceptualization of cognitive dissonance theory have been proposed. However, a relatively recent meta-analysis of decades of research on the theory supports the original version of the theory and concludes that revisions to the theory are not superior to Festinger's original model: "Several experiments have challenged the revisions of dissonance theory and have provided support for Festinger's original conception of dissonance" (Harmon-Jones & Harmon-Jones, 2007, p. 13). A vast body of research provides strong support that "dissonance produces genuine and lasting attitude, belief, and behavior changes," and most proposed revisions concur with Festinger's original theory (Harmon-Jones, 2002, p. 106). A host of experimental research has shown that cognitive dissonance has the potential to change future behaviors (McDonald et al., 2015).

While Festinger suggested that people can reduce their dissonance in multiple ways, relatively little attention has been paid to the avenues of **dissonance reduction** (McGrath, 2017). Some of the means that people may use to reduce their cognitive dissonance involve distraction and forgetting, trivialization and self-affirmation, denial of responsibility, adding consonant cognitions, behavior change, or act rationalization (McGrath, 2017). Seeking social support may also

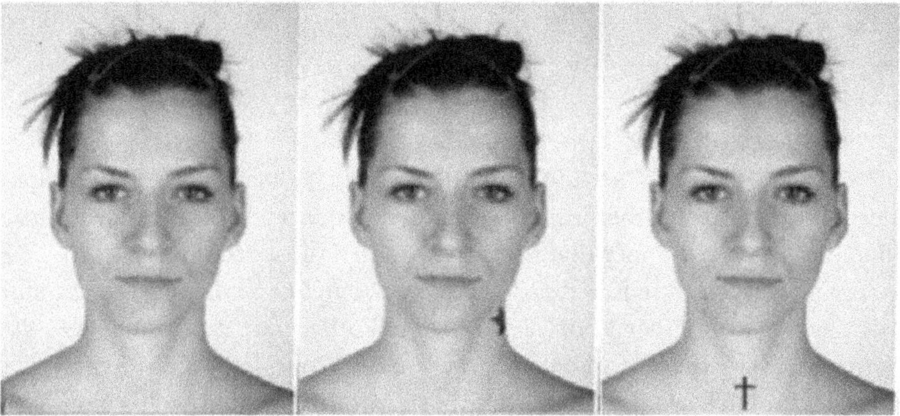

FIGURE 11.7 Timming and Perrett (2016) examined how Christian-themed tattoos may send mixed signals, creating cognitive dissonance. Participants were randomly assigned to view one of these three headshots. The headshot on the right-hand side sends a mixed message in that it shows a Christian-themed tattoo.

> **Engaged Persuasion Activity: Tattoos and Trust**
>
> Researchers from the University of St. Andrews in the United Kingdom investigated whether the presence of a Christian-themed tattoo would send a mixed signal to participants. Participants were randomly assigned to view either a headshot photo without a tattoo, photo with a tattoo, or photo with a Christian-themed tattoo. The presence of a tattoo in the photo lowered participants' perceptions of trustworthiness across the board. However, among Christian participants, the presence of a Christian-themed tattoo sent a mixed signal of trustworthiness, thus creating a potential state of cognitive dissonance (Timming & Perrett, 2016). How would you perceive the trustworthiness of the individual represented in the three photographs shown in Figure 11.7? Why do you think some people might experience cognitive dissonance in this situation? Now, try your hand at conducting research, and do an informal replication study! Show one of the pictures in Figure 11.7 to your friends and family members to see their reactions regarding trustworthiness. But be sure to randomly assign your acquaintances to just one of the three pictures and then ask them how much they would trust the individual in the picture.

be a means of dissonance reduction (Maikovich, 2005). Independently, an experimental lab study by Vaidis and Oberle (2014) showed that participants arranged chairs farther apart when meeting with another person who disagreed with their position, indicating that proximity may be used to reduce dissonance. Dissonance reduction may depend on one's habits, as behaviors that are satisfying can create resistance to change and coping through simple distraction, as well as whether the behavior change will be painful or result in some loss—which can also be met with resistance (McGrath, 2017). Maikovich (2005) even theorizes that dissonance reduction plays a role in people who initially would prefer nonviolent alternatives gradually accepting violent options and committing terrorism. As McGrath (2017) points out, "Individuals can experience dissonance in a wide range of situations and the context in which dissonance occurs" will probably be a critical factor "in terms of how it will be reduced" (p. 12). Unfortunately, most experimental research that tests dissonance reduction fails to include multiple reduction modes and thus do not provide accurate reflections of realistic or naturalistic choices people make (McGrath, 2017).

Rationalization Strategies

In 1959, Festinger and Carlsmith conducted their now famous forced-compliance study to test whether an individual will experience dissonance arousal when they act in a manner that is contrary to their attitudes. In the study, Festinger and Carlsmith required participants to complete a boring and mundane task, paying them either $1 or $20 to then tell other participants the task was interesting. As expected, those who were paid $20 to lie did not experience much dissonance arousal. However, those who lied for only $1 experienced dissonance and ended up changing their attitudes as a way of rationalizing their behavior. In other words, the greater attitude change occurred when the compensation was less (Festinger & Carlsmith, 1959). Further, "Dissonance can be reduced by exaggerating the desirability of the outcome, which would

FIGURE 11.8 Attitude changes are greater when participants are paid less to write counterattitudinal essays.

add consonant cognitions" (Harmon-Jones & Harmon-Jones, 2007, p. 8). In the end, Cognitive Dissonance Theory helps explain postdecisional processing (Harmon-Jones & Harmon-Jones, 2007).

Due to the cognitive dissonance effect—that people will avoid information that is inconsistent with their thoughts and perceptions—it is likely that they will avoid information about risky behaviors, thus making persuasive risk communication campaigns less effective (Gaspar et al., 2016). In fact, when risk communication messages expose people to information that is inconsistent with their attitudes and cognitions, people will avoid such information (Gaspar et al., 2016). And we would expect that these persuasive attempts would fail. However, in an experimental study examining exposure to the risks of red meat, Gaspar et al. (2016) found that even those people who have favorable attitudes toward red meat and try to avoid information about the risks ended up with less favorable attitudes toward red meat and increased perceived knowledge of the risks. In fact, the experiment found that this effect lasted over time. Even 2 weeks later, those high in information avoidance about red meat risks demonstrated the same positive effects of the messaging as those low in information avoidance. Gaspar et al. explained this ironic result through the suppression of unwanted thoughts and the rebound effect. In other words, attempting to suppress unwanted thoughts can trigger greater unconscious activation of the unwanted thoughts when the suppression ceases. Thus, the evidence suggested that those who avoid information about red meat risks ultimately end up being swayed.

One group that may be important to target in persuasive campaigns is exemplified in a study about climate change and water conservation behaviors by Taylor et al. (2017). The researchers discovered that hypocrites need directed messages that arm them with more information about the consequences of their behavior. "Hypocrites held different perspectives on climate change than the general public," and "they believed climate change was real and caused by humans but are doing little to curb their personal water use and are not taking personal action to mitigate the effects of climate change" (Taylor et al., 2017, p. e1).

Act rationalization, which has been proposed as a way of reducing dissonance, refers to the need to rationalize one's problematic or inconsistent behavior (McGrath, 2017). Attitude change, for instance, is a likely act of rationalization (McGrath, 2017). Memory may also be altered as attitudes change. More specifically, Rodriguez and Strange (2015) found that people may misremember their initial attitudes as a result of cognitive dissonance. These distortions in their memories occur through dissonance reduction and are called dissonance-induced memory distortion. "Human beings tend to reduce experienced cognitive dissonance by assimilating their post-behavior perceptions toward their prior expectations" (Steelman & Soror, 2017, p. 209).

In Chapter 1, we noted that persuasion theory and research can be employed to address prejudice and systematic racism. The extant literature does provide evidence that an understanding of Cognitive Dissonance Theory can be helpful in that regard. For example, research by McFalls and Cobb-Roberts (2001) shows that cognitive dissonance can be used to reduce resistance to diversity training for teacher education majors at predominately White public universities. Specifically, their research demonstrates that metadissonance, or the idea that the student is cognitively aware of discomfort they experience due to dissonance, can prevent the rejection or selective processing of diversity information. According to McFalls and Cobb-Roberts (2001), when students developed "an understanding of metadissonance before discussing diversity issues, fewer responses were labeled as denial, compared with responses of students who were not exposed to the theory" (p. 170). We will discuss additional applications of Cognitive Dissonance Theory to efforts to reduce prejudice in the next section of this chapter.

Counterattitudinal Advocacy

"The dominant paradigm used to test dissonance theory is the induced compliance paradigm in which participants are asked to write counterattitudinal essays" (McGrath, 2017, p. 6). Bem (1967) proposed an interpersonal model of self-perception as a means of explaining attitudes that emerged from the forced-compliance studies, which is often referred to as the induced-compliance paradigm. Later, Elliot and Devine (1994) produced experimental data that ruled out the self-perception based explanation. The free-choice paradigm, championed by Brehm (1956), which holds that people enhance their perceptions of a chosen alternative while downplaying the features of alternatives they did not choose, is the other method of examining dissonance theory (Bem, 1967).

Elliot and Devine (1994) provided empirical evidence to support Festinger's dissonance-reduction postulate, revealing that attitude change alleviates the psychological discomfort of dissonance "generated by a freely chosen counterattitudinal behavior" (p. 387). Participants "who reported their affect immediately after freely consenting to compose a counterattitudinal essay reported greater levels of discomfort than control group subjects" (Elliot & Devine, 1994, p. 391). Greater discomfort means that our brains work harder to alleviate that discomfort by changing our attitudes. Because counterattitudinal behavior leads to psychological discomfort, attitude change is necessary to reduce that discomfort (Elliot & Devine, 1994).

Meta-analysis evidence also supports the effectiveness of **counterattitudinal advocacy** (CAA) induction (Kim et al., 2014). CAA is conceptually defined as a situation in which an individual performs a communicative action that runs counter to their attitudes (Kim et al., 2014). Ultimately, when we hold an attitude that is inconsistent with our behavior, we require a cognitive adjustment to restore consistency (Kim et al., 2014). As opposed to classical theories that posit that attitudes predict behavior through passive message reception, CAA views attitude change as an active and engaged process whereby message behavior is a predictor of attitude change (Kim et al., 2014). "The publicity of a counterattitudinal act may also have consequences for dissonance reduction" (McGrath, 2017, p. 12).

Several specific studies have found interesting results associated with CAA. For instance, writing tasks with students have been found to be more effective in prompting CAA than reading and other tasks (Miller et al., 1996). Independently, Vraga (2015) discovered that after writing a CAA essay promoting the benefits of membership in the opposing political party, only the Republican participants demonstrated increased dissonance, polarization, and selective exposure—meaning that dissonance responses may vary by political ideology in some tasks. On the other hand, distraction has been found to reduce advocacy-favorable attitudes, which can unravel positive CAA outcomes (Eisenstadt et al., 2003).

In one study by Martinie et al. (2017) that had participants write counterattitudinal essays, the researchers discovered that mood induction affected attitude change. More specifically, following a mood induction manipulation (positive, negative, or neutral), participants high in dissonance affected attitude change after writing the CAA essay for those who received either positive or neutral mood induction; the negative incidental mood induction group who rated high in dissonance did not experience attitude change. Additionally, research subjects experienced attitude change when they freely produced the CAA essay in all of the mood conditions. However, those in the positive mood condition produced the strongest essays, while those in the negative mood condition produced the weakest essays. Thus, inducing positive or neutral mood before CAA can produce attitude changes that alter negative health behaviors and promote positive health behaviors (Martinie et al., 2017). Of note, the results of this study did not support the misattribution and distraction hypothesis.

Heitland and Bohner (2010) explored whether prejudice can be reduced through the development of CAA, using the theoretical framework of cognitive dissonance. In their study of German adults, they found that participants who were initially high in prejudice toward Turks and high in preference for consistency were able to change their perceptions when asked to generate counterattitudinal arguments supporting integrated housing of Turks and Germans. "Dissonance was reduced by replacing dissonant cognitions with consonant ones, which allowed participants to reduce the inconsistency between their prior attitude and their subsequent actions (favoring multicultural living situations)" (Heitland & Bohner, 2010, pp. 176–177). In other words, the findings indicate that German adults who initially scored high in prejudice and preference for consistency were more likely to alter their prejudiced attitudes after engaging in CAA.

Engaged Persuasion Research: Partisan Bias in News Coverage

Mark Tremayne, an assistant professor of communication at the University of Texas at Arlington, conducted a content analysis of 323 news stories about the 2012 U.S. presidential election and found that news websites showed partisan bias, providing partial support for Cognitive Dissonance Theory. His findings revealed that journalists tended to write stories about political polling when the results reflected their preferred election outcomes. The story headlines and introductory paragraphs reflected partisan bias, and conservative writers were more prone to discuss criticism of polling when President Obama had a larger lead in the race while liberal writers behaved similarly when Mitt Romney was leading. Tremayne concludes that the media writers were attempting to reduce their cognitive dissonance and achieve consonance when polls showed their candidate behind by explaining away the poll results.

Summary

This chapter covered three landmark theories that explain attitude change and behavioral reactions in response to persuasive messages. Each of these theories have demonstrated staying power, in that each is supported by decades of academic research. Scholars and practitioners of persuasion often employ one of these theories to guide their inquiry, testing, and implementation of persuasive campaign messages. As you might imagine, these theories can certainly be utilized to advance the common good. For instance, persuasive efforts that are driven by civic engagement objectives might find Psychological Reactance

Theory, Diffusion of Innovations Theory, or Cognitive Dissonance Theory to be particularly useful in guiding and crafting their persuasive efforts.

In the next chapter, we turn our attention to the role of language and nonverbal communication in persuasion.

Check Your Understanding Review Questions

1. What is reactance arousal?
2. How do restrictions on behavioral freedoms and choices trigger reactance arousal?
3. What is a boomerang effect, according to Psychological Reactance Theory?
4. What are the differences among the three types of boomerang effects?
5. How do innovations diffuse throughout a population?
6. Which roles do each of the adopter categories play in the diffusion of an innovation?
7. Why is the tipping point, or critical mass, important in the successful diffusion of an innovation?
8. How does the S-curve explain the success of a diffusion?
9. Why are people uncomfortable with dissonant thoughts and feelings? And how do people attempt to reduce dissonance?
10. What effect does counterattitudinal advocacy play in attitude change?

Key Terms

boomerang effect (p. 273)
Cognitive Dissonance Theory (p. 284)
counterattitudinal advocacy (p. 289)
critical mass (p. 282)
Diffusion of Innovations Theory (p. 279)
dissonance arousal (p. 285)
dissonance reduction (p. 285)
entertainment-education (p. 284)
freedom behaviors (p. 272)
opinion leaders (p. 282)
Psychological Reactance Theory (p. 272)
rate of adoption (p. 280)
reactance arousal (p. 276)
S-curve (p. 282)

Credits

Fig. 11.3: Copyright © 2017 by Jacob Morch. Reprinted with permission.

Fig. 11.4: Copyright © 2019 by Jessica Lewis. Reprinted with permission.

Fig. 11.5: Everett Rogers, from *Diffusion of innovations*, p. 247. Copyright © 2003 by Free Press.

Fig. 11.6: James Dearing and Gary Meyer, from "Revisiting Diffusion Theory," *Communication of Innovations: A Journey With Ev Rogers*, ed. Arvind Singhal and James W. Dearing, p. 33. Copyright © 2006 by SAGE Publications.

Fig. 11.7: Andrew Timming and David Perrett, "[image]: Tattoes, from "Trust and Mixed Signals: A Study of Religion, Tattoos, and Cognitive Dissonance"," *Personality and Individual Differences*, vol. 97, pp. 235. Copyright © 2016 by Elsevier B.V.

Fig. 11.8: Copyright © 2018 by Sharon McCutcheon. Reprinted with permission.

CHAPTER 12

Language and Nonverbal Persuasion

Chapter Objectives

After reading this chapter, you should be able to:

- Understand the ways that language influences persuasion
- Articulate the implications of persuasive language use in a post-truth era
- Understand the role that nonverbal behaviors play in persuasive communication
- Identify the types of nonverbal influence behaviors
- Ponder how silence affects persuasion

What persuades us more easily? Does the speaker who demonstrates a solid grasp of language and a large vocabulary sway us? Is the fast-talking salesperson able to influence us more effectively than one who is slower? Or does the authority figure who merely stares us down influence our behavior better than if they had opened their mouth? This chapter will address various language factors, or elements of verbal persuasion, as well as nonverbal persuasion and paralinguistic cues. Though we may be quick to think of persuasion as a verbal act—meaning that we communicate through language—whether written or spoken—there is more to it than that. Given that we communicate both verbally and nonverbally, it seems obvious that persuasion is affected by verbal and nonverbal characteristics and behaviors. Take a close look at the opening photograph of this chapter. The language a persuader utilizes affects us, such as the protestor with the "I can't breathe" sign at a Black Lives Matter protest, but so too do their nonverbal cues, such as the protestors kneeling. Furthermore, consider that even silence may influence us.

Language Factors

Before discussing the extant research on language and persuasion, it is important that you understand that language is symbolic. As a symbol, language is something that represents something else. Consider the word "dog." What immediately comes to mind when you think about that word? Perhaps you envision a West Highland terrier? Or you have an image of yourself throwing a ball to your dog? Or you conjure up an image of an instructor showing a dog to students in an online lecture during the coronavirus pandemic? As symbols, words have no meaning in and of themselves. Instead, words are conventional and therefore get their meaning from the people who use them. In order for language to be persuasive, the sender and receiver must agree on the meanings of the words used. Importantly, persuasion scholars differentiate between denotative and connotative meaning. **Denotative meaning** is the literal dictionary definition of the word. In contrast, **connotative meaning** refers to the emotions and thoughts associated with the word.

One powerful example of the persuasiveness of language can be found in the words "I can't breathe" displayed on the poster of a protester in the opening photograph of this chapter. This phrase came to popularity following the death of Eric Garner after he was placed in an illegal chokehold by a New York City police officer in 2014. The denotative meanings of the words in this phrase are straightforward. However, as Fulton-Babicke (2018) notes, the connotative meanings elicit the "recurring phenomenon of black Americans' deaths at the hands of law enforcement" (p. 443). Fulton-Babicke (2018) argues further that members of the Black Lives Matter (BLM) movement have "mobilized his embodied and verbal argument to assert his right to agency, to justice" (p. 444).

Ultimate Terms

Although connotative meanings are more subjective than denotative meanings, there are some connotative meanings that carry special persuasive power, as they are shared and recognized widely in society. Famed rhetorician and educator at the University of Chicago Richard Weaver (1953) labeled such words as **ultimate terms**. Weaver identified three subsets of ultimate terms: god, devil, and charismatic. As Hart et al. (2018) argue, **god terms** "cause people to genuflect when hearing them" (p. 163). Put another way, these terms require deference and subservience. God terms include phrases like "real American," "family values," and "equal rights."

In contrast to god terms, **devil terms** communicate malevolence and disgust. Weaver (1953) argued that devil terms are persuasive because they represent what is evil to society and provide a mechanism for its members to vent. He suggested that, throughout time, societies have been compelled to identify enemies. Further, he noted that if a nation did not have an enemy, one would have to be invented. According to Weaver (1953), when a political state is not available as an enemy, "then a class will be chosen, or a race, or a type, or a political faction" to receive the scorn, hatred, and repudiation of society (p. 222). Examples of devil terms include phrases like "Islamic terrorism," "illegal immigrants," and "hate crime."

According to Weaver (1953), charismatic terms differ from god and devil terms in that they are not associated with something observable. Weaver (1953) further argued that the "charismatic term is given its load of impulsion without reference, and it functions by convention" (p. 228). Weaver was particularly concerned about terms like "freedom" and "democracy" that require great sacrifice (e.g., military service, abridgement of rights, increased taxes, etc.) but are difficult to define.

In their summary of ultimate terms, Hart et al. (2018) outlined five concerning characteristics that have important implications for ethical persuasion. First, ultimate terms are abstract, which means their definitions can be twisted. Consider, for example, the use of the phrase "right to work," which is used to advocate against unions. Second, ultimate terms are extremely efficient in triggering emotions. For example, some radical activists used the word "pig" to refer to police in the 1960s, a label that still endures today. For instance, in Figure 12.1, a protester in 2020 holds up a sign reading "Demilitarize the pigs." In addition to using an ultimate term like pigs, the sign also makes the argument that law enforcement funding should be cut due to racially biased policing and disturbing tendencies for Black or African American individuals to be shot and killed by police. Thus, the sign is evoking another ultimate term that is not visible—that

FIGURE 12.1 This "Demilitatize the Pigs" protest sign uses an ultimate term that is visible ("pigs") as well as one that is not visible ("racist").

Engaged Persuasion Research: Judicious Swearing and Persuasion

Does a speaker's use of obscenity hamper or facilitate persuasion? Scherer and Sagarin (2006) sought to answer this question through an experiment that examined the effects of judicious swearing in a proattitudinal speech. In this study, participants were exposed to one of three versions of a speech in which the speaker advocated for lower tuition. Scherer and Sagarin manipulated where the use of the word "damn" appeared in the speech (beginning of the speech, end of the speech, or nowhere in the speech). Their results demonstrated that the use of obscenity at the beginning or the end of the speech significantly increased perceived persuasiveness and intensity of the speaker. Interestingly, they found that obscenity had no effect on perceptions of speaker credibility. As the authors note, caution should be taken in generalizing these results, as the experiment was executed in an optimal setting (e.g., participants had a favorable attitude toward the message) and used a single, mild swear word.

of "racist." As Hart et al. (2018) note, this three letter word "evoked images of filthy individuals doing the bidding of corrupt politicians" (pp. 163–164). Third, ultimate terms are hierarchical and subsume all lesser terms. As Hart et al. (2018) note, such ultimate terms "can be used to pull rank, making an opponent's case seem small and expedient in contrast" (p. 164). Fourth, ultimate terms allow the persuader to preempt counterarguments and seal off the grounds for argument. Consider the USA Patriot Act, which was passed by Congress in response to the September 11, 2001, terrorist attacks on the United States. The shortened title of the legislation references the United States and incorporates the term "patriot." Perhaps supporters of the bill thought nobody would oppose the legislation because of the name they used? Incidentally, the full name of the legislation is "Uniting and Strengthening America by Providing Appropriate Tools Required to Intercept and Obstruct Terrorism Act of 2001." Fifth, ultimate terms have unstable meanings. In other words, the meaning of terms like "freedom" can vary vastly over time but retain the same form.

Beyond these ethical concerns, the language persuaders use has significant implications for attitudes and behaviors. Without question, audience members will draw conclusions about the attitudes of speakers who consistently use racist or sexist language. But does that language use really reflect the attitudes and behaviors of the speaker? The Sapir-Whorf hypothesis posits that people's understanding of the world, thoughts, and behaviors correspond to the language they use (Sapir, 1949; Whorf, 1956). As Whorf (1956) noted, language is the vehicle by which humans communicate personality, analyze the world, notice or neglect relationships and phenomena, channel reasoning, and ultimately "build the house of consciousness" (p. 252). Sapir (1929) further described this hypothesis in the following terms:

> Human beings do not live in the objective world alone, nor alone in the world of social activity as ordinarily understood, but are very much at the mercy of the particular language which has become the medium of expression for their society. It is quite an illusion to imagine that one adjusts to reality essentially without the use of language and that language is merely an incidental means of solving particular problems of communication or reflection. The fact of the matter is that the "real world" is to a large extent unconsciously built up on the language habits of the group. (p. 209)

Put another way, the Sapir-Whorf hypothesis suggests that a choice of words is also a choice of worlds. Although the notion that language determines reality has been met with skepticism, scholars have persuasively argued for a less deterministic view that language influences thought and behavior (Regier & Xu, 2017).

Intensity

Bowers (1963) defines language **intensity** as the "quality of language which indicates the degree to which the speaker's attitude toward a concept deviates from neutrality" (p. 345). Intense language is emotional and extreme. For example, the statement that "the Chicago Bears are the best team in the NFL" is far less intense than the statement that "the Chicago Bears will destroy every other stupid team in the NFL." The later statement clearly employs extreme and emotional language, and it departs significantly from neutrality. However, is such language use persuasive? In the sections that follow, we examine several theories that have been applied to understand the persuasive effects of language intensity.

Communication Accommodation Theory

Communication Accommodation Theory proposes that individuals attempt to converge toward the speech styles of their message recipients as a strategy to bolster persuasion (Giles & Coupland, 1991). Aune and Kikuchi (1993) used this theory to examine language intensity and found that senders who accommodate to their receivers' preferences are perceived as more persuasive than senders who do not accommodate to their receivers' language intensity preferences. Specifically, Aune and Kikuchi found that similarities in language intensity between senders and receivers were positively related to perceptions of the speaker's competence, sociability, composure, immediacy, and intimacy. In addition, speakers who matched their receivers' preference for language intensity produced greater message agreement than speakers who did not converge to the preferences of their audience. Further, instructional communication research demonstrates that teachers who converge to students' communication preferences are perceived more favorably (Mazer & Hunt, 2008a) and produce higher levels of learning (Mazer & Hunt, 2008b) than teachers who do not converge their communication.

Information Processing Theory

Hamilton and Stewart (1993) extended Information Processing Theory to the study of the persuasive effects of language intensity. **Information Processing Theory** posits that when exposed to a persuasive message, receivers compare their position on an issue with the position advocated by the source (McGuire, 1968). Some discrepancy between the two positions is advantageous to the sender to the extent that it causes the receiver to think more carefully about the message. Consistent with this approach, Hamilton and Stewart found that language intensity enhanced attitude change by increasing receivers' perceptions of the strength of the message as well as increasing message discrepancy.

Craig and Blankenship (2011) explored the persuasiveness of language intensity through the lenses of Information Processing Theory and the Elaboration Likelihood Model (ELM). Through two studies, the authors found that linguistic extremity increased message processing relative to a control message. They also found that extremity positively influenced participants' willingness to sign a petition, indicating increased intention to comply with the message. Craig and Blankenship posit that language intensity fosters persuasion by increasing involvement in the message. Specifically, participants likely experienced a discrepancy between their initial position on the topic and

Engaged Persuasion Research: Using Intense Language to Boost Survey Response Rates

Think of the last time you received a request to complete a survey through email. Did you complete the survey? Why, or why not? Determining how to boost response rates to surveys is an important concern for corporations, nonprofit organizations, and survey researchers. Andersen and Blackburn (2004) used Information Processing Theory to examine the effects of language intensity on persuasive targets' actual behavior. Specifically, they measured survey response rates to low- and high-intensity persuasive messages conveyed via email. Their results showed that the response rate in the high language intensity condition exceeded the low language intensity condition by an impressive 12.6%.

the position created by the use of extreme language. This discrepancy created interest and involvement with the message, which motivated receivers to engage in deeper information processing.

Language Expectancy Theory

Language Expectancy Theory stipulates that language is a rule-governed system, and individuals develop expectations and preferences for what is competent communication (Burgoon et al., 2002). Negative violations of receivers' expectations for persuasive communication occur when speakers use message strategies that fall outside of the bandwidth of socially accepted behavior. As you might expect, such violations have little persuasive value and may even trigger a boomerang effect. In contrast, positive violations occur when the persuasive behavior is better than was expected or conforms to expected norms. Positive violations are most likely to result in attitude and behavior change.

Jensen et al. (2013) applied Language Expectancy Theory to explore participants' perceptions of the credibility of anonymous online product reviews. They found that consumers afford a very narrow bandwidth of acceptable persuasion to anonymous reviewers. As a result, such reviewers are limited in the amount of intense language they can use to discuss products. Jensen et al. (2013) conclude that "high affect intensity in product reviews negatively violates expectations, and these violations negatively affect credibility" (p. 314).

Clementson et al. (2016) employed Language Expectancy Theory to examine language intensity in presidential campaign communication. They found significant interactions between language intensity and economic conditions. Specifically, during bad economic times, people perceive presidential candidates to be more trustworthy and presidential when they use high-intensity language rather than low-intensity language. Their research demonstrates that our expectations for language intensity shift during stable economic times, as we perceive candidates to be more trustworthy and presidential when they use low-intensity language.

Vividness

Nisbett and Ross (1980) describe vivid language as "likely to attract and hold our attention and to excite the imagination to the extent that it is emotionally interesting, concrete and imagery-provoking, and proximate in a sensory, temporal, or spatial way" (p. 45). Vivid language has been operationalized in the extant literature in several ways, including manipulations of concrete and abstract words (Smith & Shaffer, 2000), narrative and statistical evidence (de Wit et al., 2008), and direct versus indirect transmission of information (Herr et al., 1991).

The research on the persuasive effects of **vividness** has been mixed with some studies finding positive effects (Adaval & Wyer, 1998; Amos & Spears, 2010;

Engaged Persuasion Research: Examining the Effects of Threat Vividness in Health Communication

Blondé and Girandola (2018) compared the persuasive effects of vivid and pallid (i.e., language lacking vitality or interest) threats in the context of health communication. Threatening health messages are defined as a persuasive strategy that combines relevant threats (e.g., poor eating habits will kill you) with protective information (e.g., eating fruits and vegetables will help you live longer). Their findings demonstrate that, compared to pallid threats, vivid threats caused participants to respond more positively toward protective health recommendations. Blondé and Girandola (2018) conclude that "exposing threats in a clear and concrete manner leads people to accept more information that can guarantee their protection" (p. 43).

Fennis et al., 2012; Miller & Marks; 1992; Sherer & Rogers, 1984), while others demonstrate no effect (Edell & Staelin, 1983; Hong & Park, 2012). To complicate matters further, research by Frey and Eagly (1983) suggests that vividness can actually undermine the persuasiveness of messages.

In an effort to better understand research in this area, Blondé and Girandola (2016) conducted a meta-analysis of 43 studies exploring vividness. Their results demonstrate that vividness can have a significant, positive impact on receivers' attitudes and behavioral intentions in three ways. First, vivid messages are persuasive when receivers are able to easily recall the information from memory. Second, receivers will elaborate on vivid information when it is positive. As we learned from the ELM, cognitive elaboration facilitates longer lasting attitude change. Third, the effects of vividness are much greater when the valence of the topic at hand is positive rather than negative.

Powerless Language

According to O'Barr and Atkins (1980), **powerless language** conveys a lack of certainty and control and is marked by the speech forms listed in Table 12.1 (also see Blankenship & Craig, 2007a; Frandrich & Beck, 2012; Hosman & Siltanen, 2006). Powerless language communicates that the speaker is tentative, hesitant, and unsure.

TABLE 12.1 Forms of Powerless Language

Form of Powerless Language	Example
Hedges	I sort of like that movie.
Hesitation Forms	Ah, the university should, uhm, have better, uhm, parking for students.
Polite Forms	Excuse me, I hate to bother you, but would you please consider my request? Thank you.
Tag Questions	This is the best way to solve the problem, don't you think?
Verbal Fillers	This policy is, like, the only way to, like, solve the problem.

The use of powerless language has several important implications for how audiences evaluate persuasive speakers. For example, Parton et al. (2002) found that powerless language negatively affects receivers' judgments of a speaker's dynamism, social attractiveness, competence, and employability. Similarly, Areni and Sparks (2005) found a significant, negative relationship between powerless language use and perceptions of the speaker's persuasive abilities.

In contrast to powerless language, powerful language lacks hesitations and qualifiers and is more assertive, dominant, and certain (Grob et al., 1997). In a meta-analysis of 16 studies, Burrell and Koper (1998) found that powerful language was perceived as significantly more credible and persuasive than powerless language. In the context of education, Haleta (1996) found that teachers who employed powerful language were perceived as more dynamic and credible by students than teachers who used powerless language. In a study of a salesperson's use of language power, Gadzhiyeva and Sager (2017) found that participants evaluated the use of powerful language as significantly more persuasive than powerless language.

Should powerless language be avoided in every context? Jensen (2008) set out to explore this question in the context of scientific uncertainty about cancer research. In contrast to many of the studies referred to earlier, Jensen found that scientists who used hedges in describing the limitations of their own research were evaluated as more trustworthy than those using powerful language. According to Jensen, communication norms in the scientific community favor a more self-critical style of communication than other contexts.

Rubin (2017) found that certain types of tag questions can be persuasive in the context of crisis negotiations. For example, facilitative tag questions are employed to show interest in and solidarity with a persuasive target in negotiations (e.g., "Let's see if we can handle this situation, okay?"). Softening tag questions are designed to mitigate speech that might otherwise seem commanding or critical in negotiations (e.g., "I'll get her on the phone and you talk to her, okay?"). Rubin concludes that these types of tag questions are persuasive, as they reinforce a collaborative problem-solving mindset, minimize the target's negative actions, and reframe orders or commands as requests.

Beyond the context of persuasive communication, research demonstrates that perceptions of speaker credibility influence how receivers process powerless language. Blankenship and Craig (2007b) found that credible sources who paired tag questions with strong arguments stimulated more favorable attitudes than credible sources who did not use tag questions. In contrast, the authors found that low credible sources who used tag questions were evaluated as less persuasive. In other words, the use of tag questions confirmed the participants' perceptions of the source's lack of credibility.

Finally, recall our discussion of gender and persuasion in Chapter 10. We noted that women face a double bind when advancing persuasive arguments.

FIGURE 12.2 This protest sign the woman in the photo is holding, which reads "Rage against the machine," uses powerful language that is assertive, dominant, and certain.

In other words, they are expected to be as aggressive as men when advocating a persuasive argument but may be punished for violating stereotypical gender roles. Such stereotypes hold that we expect men to be more aggressive and powerful persuaders than women (Deturck, 1987). So what can you do to address this double bind for female persuaders? A report by Catalyst (2007) suggests that persuaders should actively interrupt bias. In other words, you should speak up if you notice that others are advancing negative gender stereotypes. In the workplace, employers should use the same standards for women and men when formally evaluating productivity. Finally, it is important that we all embrace being visible champions for women. As a champion for the accomplishments of women, you will serve as a powerful role model for others.

Persuasive Language in a Post-Truth Era

We have discussed the implications of the post-truth era for persuasion throughout this textbook. We introduced the concept in Chapter 2 and defined it as "relating to or denoting circumstances in which objective facts are less influential in shaping public opinion than appeals to emotion and personal belief" (Oxford University Press, 2017, para. 1). We noted further that the post-truth era is characterized by deliberate deception, fake news, uncertainty, and persuasive misinformation. These characteristics are made more problematic by tools like social media that allow persuasive misinformation to spread quickly to large audiences. The implications of this "truth decay" include widespread disagreement about facts, a blurring of the distinction between fact and opinion, the increasing persuasiveness of opinion over fact, and declining trust in previously respected sources of information (Kavanagh & Rich, 2018).

In Chapter 3, we discussed the implications of the post-truth era for persuasion and civic engagement. We noted that polarizing political language dominates our conversations about civics and politics (Zompetti, 2018). In fact, we presented research showing that fear-based language in news reports contributes to political polarization along party lines (Jang, 2018). We further noted that language expressing outrage (i.e., outrage discourse) permeates the television, radio, online blogs, and newspapers we consume (Sobieraj & Berry, 2011). We also noted that the consumption of divisive language via social media fuels political polarization (Hong & Kim, 2016).

In Chapter 6, we noted that persuasive argumentation in the post-truth era is subject to a Műnchausen effect that involves the intentional distortion of truth through emotional and fallacious language for the purpose of persuading others (Vasile, 2018).

In Chapter 7, we discussed source credibility in a post-truth era, noting that the death of expertise challenges conceptualizations of credibility and threatens democracy (Nichols, 2017). In Chapter 10, we noted that motivated reasoning makes it difficult to correct persuasive misinformation (Nyhan & Reifler, 2012).

In what other ways do persuaders use language intentionally to obfuscate the truth and create political polarization in the post-truth era? Cervi and Andrade (2019) explored this question by examining political speeches during Brexit. They found that politicians used language to create conflict with opponents, delegitimize others, juxtapose meanings, tap into the feelings and emotions of their audience, and select or ignore facts. Cervi and Andrade (2019) conclude that the goal of politicians on both sides of the Brexit debate was to be provocative, as the "more provocative an argument is, the most probable that people will repeat it" (p. 145).

Using President Trump's Twitter activity as a case study, Bratslavsky et al. (2019) examined the implications of the use of rude and impolite language on political discourse and decision making. They define strategic incivility as the use of impolite language with the intent to elicit unquestioned and emotional responses from a target audience for the purpose of establishing, maintaining, and communicating power. Bratslavsky et al. offer four propositions regarding the use of incivility as a mechanism to persuade and maintain power. First, they argue that strategic incivility persuades and shapes cognition. One of President Trump's most frequent targets is the media who he often refers to as "fake" and "dishonest." According to Bratslavsky et al., the use of such language is potentially persuasive to supporters, as it allows him to distract from and deflect other concerns about his positions, behaviors, and policies.

Bratslavsky et al.'s (2019) second proposition is that Trump's use of Twitter inverts private–public communication and amplifies shifts in the standards of appropriate communication that we apply to elected officials. Consider the language in the following tweet from 2017:

> I heard poorly rated @Morning_Joe speaks badly of me (don't watch anymore). Then how come low I.Q. Crazy Mika, along with Psycho

> Joe came to Mar-a-Lago 3 nights in a row around New Year's Eve, and insisted on joining me. She was bleeding badly from a face-lift. I said no! (Trump, 2017)

As Bratslavsky et al. (2019) note, tweets like this convey language not typically used in public and fall "far outside the normative codes of president's communicative actions" (p. 20).

Bratslavksy et al.'s (2019) third proposition is that strategic incivility exploits Twitter's technological architecture and subverts meaningful discussion. In other words, by taking advantage of the connected networks of Twitter, President Trump uses the platform to spread conflict, confusion, and disinformation to large audiences.

The fourth proposition stipulates that the use of strategic incivility on Twitter illustrates how the platform can be used as a means of domination. According to Bratslavsky et al. (2019), President Trump's use of capital letters, language, and "declarations of how to feel (e.g., despicable, shameful, disgusting, etc.) evoke not only emotion, but also an intensity of feelings" (p. 23). Ultimately, the authors conclude that the use of strategic incivility plays an important role in the current landscape of divisive discourse and hinders political decision making.

Moving beyond politicians, scholars have examined the manipulation of persuasive language in fake news. For example, Alba-Juez and Mackenzie (2019) examined fake news reports in politics and science. They found that authors of fake news reports use language to manipulate readers' emotions. Further, Alba-Juez and Mackenzie (2019) note this language features "subtle blends of truths and lies, often designed more to entertain than to inform" (p. 41). They also argue that this strategy is related to Frankfurt's (2005) Theory of Bullshit, which refers to the use of language that is intended to persuade without regard for the truth. Alba-Juez and Mackenzie conclude that authors of fake news accounts willfully abuse language to create content that resonates with the prejudices of their anticipated readers.

Building on post-truth scholarship and Frankfort's Theory of Bullshit, Hyvömen (2018) developed a conceptual framework of careless speech. For Hyvömen, truth-telling is a form of caring for the world given its contributions to the existence of shared reality. In contrast to truth-telling through caring speech, Hyvömen (2018) defines careless speech as the use of language that is "unconcerned not only with the truth but also with the world as a common space in which things become public" (p. 33). Hyvömen argues that in the current era, media and citizens have adopted the view that there are always multiple perspectives on any issue, and therefore, definitive truth does not exist. In this environment, practitioners of post-truth persuasion capitalize on the use of social and legacy media as channels for entertainment. Ultimately, purveyors of careless speech seek to create uncertainty and confusion and halt democratic debate. This perspective echoes Weaver's concerns about the use of ultimate terms to obfuscate the truth, trigger receivers' emotions, and seal off the grounds of debate.

Nonverbal Behaviors

Although we are often prone to conjure images of a person speaking when imagining what persuasion looks like, we should carefully consider the various nonverbal elements that are involved in persuasive attempts. Nonverbal communication refers to all those aspects of communication that do not involve spoken or written language. Research suggests that a variety of nonverbal behaviors affect persuasion (Burgoon et al., 1990). Burgoon et al. (1990) argued that "nonverbal behaviors exert their greatest influence indirectly by affecting source credibility which, in turn, affects persuasion" (p. 141). Further, Burgoon and Bacue (2003) have noted that nonverbal communication can be used to project power, status, and authority; maximize attractiveness; develop relationships; apply rewards and punishments; and signal expectancy violations. Although a full review of the nonverbal literature is beyond the scope of this chapter, the next sections provide an overview of some of the most important research in this area.

FIGURE 12.3 Social distancing might appear on the surface to be at odds with nonverbal immediacy in a physical sense, yet could actually demonstrate nonverbal immediacy in a psychological sense since social distancing is meant to protect others' health.

Nonverbal Immediacy

Nonverbal immediacy refers to communication behaviors that reduce the physical or psychological distance between communicators (Mehrabian, 1971). Albert Mehrabian, professor emeritus of psychology at the University of California, Los Angeles, grounded immediacy in the approach/avoidance construct, which suggests that individuals generally approach things they like and avoid things they dislike. Though immediacy was originally thought to spring from both verbal and nonverbal immediacy cues, Andersen et al. (1979) suggested that most research supported the conclusion that nonverbal immediacy was more persuasive than verbal immediacy. As a result, immediacy cues include nonlinguistic approach behaviors, signals of availability for communication, and communication of interpersonal closeness. Further, Mehrabian (1969) identified a range of nonverbal immediacy cues, including reducing physical distance, displaying relaxed body posture, using gestures, smiling, and engaging in eye contact during interactions. Gorham (1988) added that immediacy is connected to vocalics and delivery, among other factors.

So what are the benefits of greater perceptions of nonverbal immediacy? Previous studies have found that nonverbal behaviors exhibit a substantial impact on persuasiveness (Burgoon et al., 1990). Among married couples, nonverbal immediacy has been associated with greater liking of partners (Hinkle, 1999). Nonverbal immediacy also preserves the credibility of workplace supervisors (Teven, 2007) and classroom instructors (Zhu & Anagondahalli, 2017). In the context of sales, nonverbal immediacy has been found to be essential to cultivating relationships with customers (Limbu et al., 2016). In a meta-analysis of 49 studies, Segrin (1993) found positive effects for nonverbal immediacy and compliance-gaining effectiveness. Segrin concluded that nonverbal behavioral effects on compliance gaining are as strong or stronger than the effects of the verbal compliance-gaining strategies we discussed in Chapter 8.

Consider the power that immediacy has in the classroom context. Instructors who are perceived as more nonverbally immediate by their students, as compared to those who are rated as less immediate, have been shown to be more effective as instructors (Henning, 2012), perceived as more credible (Thweatt & McCroskey, 1998), and perceived as better able to generate affective learning (Katt et al., 2009) and motivation in their students (Christophel, 1990; Frymier et al., 2019). Thus, we can conclude that instructors who are perceived as more immediate may be in a better position to persuade their students to learn (Comadena et al., 2007).

The study of immediacy is not limited to face-to-face interactions. In fact, O'Sullivan et al. (2004) define mediated immediacy as "communicative cues in mediated channels that can shape perceptions of psychological closeness between interactants" (p. 471). Their research examined the use of mediated immediacy cues (e.g., instructor self-disclosure, personalness, and engagement) on an instructional website. Overall, the results indicated that participants rated the instructor in the high immediacy condition as significantly more credible than the instructor in the low immediacy condition. Enskat et al. (2017) found that instructors could establish mediated immediacy and credibility through Facebook.

Types of Nonverbal Persuasion

Over the years, communication scholars have examined several types of nonverbal persuasion. In this section, we focus on research related to artifacts, chronemics, haptics, kinesics, and paralinguistics.

Artifacts

Artifacts as well as the overall context or appearance in which artifacts reside influence how we regard those who may wish to persuade us. Artifacts can include such nonverbal indicators as tattoos, clothing, cosmetics, and accessories (e.g., sunglasses, jewelry, personal electronics, or backpacks). Even a face mask is an artifact. And wearing a face mask in the COVID-19 era could be viewed as a persuasive statement.

How would you approach a job interview? Would you dress in professional clothes or bring a briefcase? It is likely that you would select your nonverbal artifacts carefully for the interview, believing that they might help your chances—or, at least, would not hurt your chances. These impression management strategies on your part would make sense if you were seeking to sway recruiters. Goldberg and Cohen (2004) found that during interviews nonverbal skills impacted assessments of candidates more than verbal skills. Stroe (2015) argued that nonverbal artifacts, such as your clothing and appearance, improve selection chances in interview situations since recruiters form impressions about your confidence level within the first 407 seconds of the interview based on your appearance.

So should applicants visibly display a tattoo during their interview? Whether fair or not, research has shown that visible tattoos and piercings depress hireability ratings, especially for positions in which the applicant would interact with customers face to face (Seiter & Sandry, 2003; Timming et al., 2015). Now, before you write this off to recruiters not understanding kids today, check this out—Martino and Lester (2011) found that undergraduate students exhibited similar biases. In particular, undergraduates judged pictures of pierced individuals to be less intelligent, attractive, normal, honest, caring, religious, and generous than pictures of nonpierced individuals. And before you say things have changed since 2011, consider that Broussard and Harton (2018) found essentially the same results among college students years later. Speaking of college students, both men and women rate women who dress in less revealing and less tight clothing more positively for professionalism and competence (Gurung et al., 2017), thus betraying sexist perceptions of clothing expectations. In addition, women who engage in beauty work that substantially alters their appearance or only lasts for a short time—such as tanning, hair styling, or cosmetics—were judged to possess poorer moral character (Samper et al., 2017).

Fashion and clothing also make a difference in student perceptions of classroom teachers (Gorham et al., 1999). Is this why your instructors tend to dress up the first few weeks of the semester? Specifically, Gorham et al. (1999) found that attire showed moderate effects for perceptions of competence and extroversion but only minimal effects for perceptions of credibility and approachability. In fact, Dunbar and Segrin (2012) recommended that teachers should adopt a relatively formal style of attire.

Remember when your parents told you to clean up your bedroom? There may have been some wisdom in that advice! Teven and Comadena's (1996) experiment demonstrated that college students rated professors whose offices were of high aesthetic quality (e.g., neat, organized, and attractive) as being more credible and possessing a better communication style than professors with low quality office aesthetics (e.g., messy). The more pleasing-looking office led to greater perceptions of trustworthiness and authority. And since we already know that credibility leads to enhanced persuasive capacity, it is reasonable to conclude that organized and tidy office spaces present a better homefield advantage for persuaders.

Chronemics

Chronemics refers to the study of how time is used to communicate. One line of persuasion research in this area examines appeals based on limited or scarce time. As we noted in Chapter 1, the scarcity principle stipulates that "opportunities seem more valuable to us when they are less available" (Cialdini, 2009, p. 200). Cialdini (2009) argues that one of the most popular appeals based on time is the deadline tactic, where an official time limit is given for a target's action (e.g., "This exclusive, limited offer ends soon" or "Customers who act in the next 10 minutes will receive 50% off").

What makes appeals to scarcity so effective? Initially, we invoke a simple heuristic that things that are difficult to obtain are better than things that are easy to obtain (Lynn, 1991). Another explanation for the effectiveness of scarcity can be found in the literature on Psychological Reactance Theory presented in Chapter 11. Scarcity triggers reactance, as it threatens and limits our freedoms. Further, the reactance we experience causes us to want the items or goods and services more.

Importantly, research has demonstrated that scarcity appeals are especially effective under certain conditions. For example, Mukherjee and Lee (2016) found that the effect of scarcity is moderated by consumers' expectations of scarcity. Specifically, scarcity appeals had a positive effect when participants' expectation of scarcity was high but not when their expectation of scarcity was low.

Shen's (2016) research demonstrated that scarcity had a positive impact on product evaluation when the value inferred from scarcity was congruent with the worth derived from the product message. Participants in the congruent condition were exposed to high time restriction and strong product messages or low time restriction and weak product messages. In contrast, participants in the incongruent condition were exposed to high time restriction and weak product messages or low time restriction and strong product messages. Why was scarcity effective for those in the congruent condition but not for those in the incongruent condition? Shen argued that those in the congruent condition processed scarcity as a simple judgmental heuristic. However, those in the incongruent condition carefully scrutinized the message, resulting in lower evaluations of the product.

Research on chronemics also reveals certain situations in which it can be persuasive to provide consumers with more time to take advantage of promotions. Garnefeld et al. (2018) examined the persuasive effects of ex post time extensions of sales promotions. This strategy involves the extension of an initial deadline of a promotion shortly before or directly after the previously announced deadline. Garnefeld et al. found mixed results for this strategy across four studies. Generally, participants found ex post promotions less attractive, and it decreased their purchase intentions. However, a positive effect emerged for potential and emerging consumers of frequently bought products. Garnefeld et al. conclude that companies can offset the negative effects of ex post promotions by offering extensions that last for a brief time or offering an explanation for the extension that emphasizes the popularity of the initial promotion.

Does the way you consume time influence how others perceive you? Bellezza et al. (2017) conducted a study to examine how individuals perceive others' consumption of paid work time, unpaid work time, and leisure time. The central research question examined the impact of signaling busyness and lack of leisure time on participants' perceptions of status. Across four studies, Bellezza et al. found those who display busyness and lack of leisure time are perceived as significantly more competent and ambitious than those who display a lack of busyness and a wealth of leisure time. Beyond the persuasive implications of status associated with busy individuals, the authors conclude that persuaders and marketers should appeal to a target's lack of time because the appeal will be interpreted as a sign of flattery. In other words, such appeals should make targets feel that their time is valuable.

Scholars have also examined the persuasiveness of messages with different temporal frames (i.e., present- versus future-framed messages). Zhuang et al. (2018) explored the perceptions of and reactions to temporal framed persuasive messages regarding water conservation. In addition, the study employed a cross-cultural lens by comparing reactions of participants from the United States and China. Overall, Zhuang et al. found that present-framed messages resulted in more positive attitudes toward water conservation than future-framed messages. In addition, they found a significant interaction between message framing and country in that future-framed messages were more persuasive for

Chinese participants compared to their American counterparts. They found no differences between the groups for present-framed messages.

Haptics

Persuasion scholars have examined haptics, or touch, in several contexts. For example, touch has been found to enhance the effectiveness of the foot-in-the-door (FITD) compliance-gaining technique, increase acceptance of requests to dance in a nightclub (Guéguen, 2007), improve consumers' evaluations of brands (Leo et al., 2016) and products (Marlow & Jansson-Boyd, 2011; Peck & Childers, 2003; Peck & Wiggins, 2006), increase willingness of individuals to donate time or money to a nonprofit (Peck & Johnson, 2011), and increase willingness of individuals to complete questionnaires (Vaidis & Halimi-Falkowicz, 2008).

Interestingly, scholars have even examined how consumers react when retailers engage in interpersonal haptic blocking. Ringler et al. (2019) conducted four experiments, including a retail field experiment, in which employees were instructed to ask customers not to touch a product on display. They found that haptic blocking engendered feelings of psychological reactance and increased compensatory touching of subsequently encountered products. Perhaps most surprisingly, they found that haptic blocking actually increased spending when consumers left the reactance-inducing encounter. Further, haptic blocking did not increase negative attitudes toward the retailer.

FIGURE 12.4 COVID-19 precautions have changed our understanding of haptics.

One of the most common forms of haptic behavior, especially in Western cultures, is the handshake. Research by Bernieri and Petty (2011) demonstrates that handshakes influence the first impressions we form of others, especially in male-male dyads. More recent research by Katsumi et al. (2017) shows that culture plays an important role in the persuasive effects of handshakes. Specifically, they found that the effect of handshakes on appraisals of social interactions was more positive in Caucasian than in East Asian participants. Similarly, the effect of a handshake on appraisals of those interactions was more positive for men than women.

The persuasiveness of touch depends on several factors. As Green (2017) notes, touch is a complex issue because it may be ambiguous and difficult to interpret. Further, touch may be intentional or unintentional. Although it can be used to express affection, reassurance, and solidarity, it can also be used in "threatening ways to demonstrate control or dominance" (Green, 2017, p. 774). In addition, Green argues that there are significant cultural, gender, relational, age, class, and sexuality issues that have implications for how individuals respond to touch. As a result, touch that is perceived as inappropriate may backfire and reduce the likelihood of successful persuasion.

Engaged Persuasion Activity: Haptics in the Time of a Global Pandemic

The research we reviewed in this section clearly highlights the importance of touch to human communication. Social distancing guidelines that were put into place in response to the coronavirus pandemic obviously limited our ability to employ haptics. Consider how the precautions, such as wearing masks and gloves, as depicted in Figure 12.4, influence our new understanding about touch. For this activity, reflect on how social distancing influenced your use of touch. Did these guidelines fundamentally alter the way you communicate? Also, if touch is not an option, what other nonverbal behaviors can persuaders rely on?

Kinesics

What role does eye contact play in the process of persuasion? What about the gestures and body movements you use when delivering a persuasive message? Would you be persuaded to help the woman shown in Figure 12.5 based on her eye contact and gestures? Scholars have devoted significant attention to these questions in a line of research on kinesics, or the study of eye contact, body movement, and gestures. We begin this section with a review of relevant literature on eye contact and persuasion.

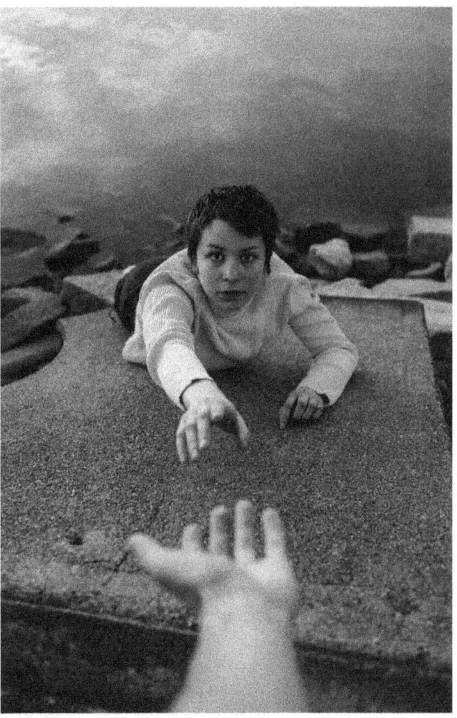

FIGURE 12.5 Kinesics includes eye contact, body movement, and gestures.

Research by Murphy (2007) shows that eye contact influences impression management and receivers' judgments of the speaker's intelligence. Murphy found that participants in the study who established eye contact while speaking and listening were judged as more intelligent than those who did not employ the same level of eye contact. Similarly, research by Napieralski et al. (1995) demonstrates that maintaining eye contact is an essential way that communicators can convey competence, confidence, and composure. Direct eye contact has also been shown to increase compliance with a request. For example, Guéguen and Jacob (2002) found that more participants complied with a request to complete a survey when the research participant used direct eye contact (66% compliance) compared to the use of an evasive gaze (34% compliance; participant initially established eye contact and then looked away).

If direct eye contact facilitates positive evaluations of speakers, how do receivers respond to those who intentionally avert eye contact? Research by Wirth et al. (2010) suggests that averting eye contact leads to feelings of ostracism and relational devaluation. The authors note that averting eye contact is the most common nonverbal cue to indicate the silent treatment. Across three studies, Wirth et al. found that, compared to receiving direct eye contact, participants who received averted eye contact felt ostracized and reported increased intentions to act aggressively toward their interaction partner.

Does direct eye contact always facilitate persuasion? Chen et al. (2013) conducted two studies to answer this question. In the first study, participants viewed videos of speakers advocating positions on controversial topics. They found that direct eye contact was associated with less attitude change in the direction advocated by the speaker. In the second study, Chen et al. directed participants to look at either the eyes or mouths of speakers presenting counterattitudinal arguments. Again, they found that maintaining direct eye contact led to less persuasion. Chen et al. conclude that direct eye contact may increase resistance to persuasion when receivers interpret it as a hostile cue that is used to assert dominance and intimidate others. These findings are consistent with research indicating that direct eye contact exerts a causal influence on

FIGURE 12.6 Example of expressive nonverbal behavior.

dominance-related responding (Tang & Schmeichel, 2015) and leads to more competitive behavior (Giacomantonio et al., 2018).

In terms of body movement, Ekman and Friesen (1969) identified the following five categories of nonverbal behavior important to persuasive communication: emblems, illustrators, affect displays, regulators, and adaptors. Which behaviors are the individuals in Figures 12.6 and 12.7 displaying?

According to Ekman and Friesen (1969), emblems are nonverbal behaviors, usually gestures, that serve as a substitute for words. Consider some of the words that we use emblems for, such as "stop," "peace," "I don't know," "shame on you," "move back," and "come to me." Research suggests that the appropriate use of gestures can enhance persuasion by facilitating recall of the persuasive message (Woodall & Folger, 1981) and bolstering the motivation of receivers (Cesario & Higgins, 2008). In the context of investment judgments, Clarke et al. (2019) found that the positive use of hand gestures persuaded prospective investors by evoking mental imagery of ventures that were pitched to them.

Ekman and Friesen (1969) define illustrators as nonverbal behaviors that illustrate and emphasize verbal messages. Importantly, illustrators can complement or contradict verbal information. For example, you might complement your verbal message that you are stuffed after eating a big dinner by patting your stomach. In contrast, you might contradict your verbal message that you are not angry by simultaneously pounding your fist on a table. In terms of persuasion, research shows that illustrators used during speech enhance receivers' attention and accuracy of understanding (Graham & Argyle, 1975) as well as message recall (Beattie & Shovelton, 2006). Further, research by Maricchiolo et al. (2009) shows that receivers judge speakers who employ ideational (i.e., gestures that make discourse more understandable) and conversational (i.e., gestures that add emphasis to speech) illustrators as more persuasive, composed, and competent than persuasive speakers who do not use illustrators. Importantly, research also indicates that nonverbal behaviors are more persuasive when they match, rather than mismatch, verbal behaviors (Fennis & Stel, 2011).

FIGURE 12.7 Another example of expressive nonverbal behavior.

Affect displays refer to movements of the face and body that communicate emotions like happiness, disgust, anger, sadness, fear, surprise, and interest (Ekman & Friesen, 1969). According to Ekman and Friesen (1969), the face is the primary site of affect displays, while body movements occur largely as a reaction to the affect. Although affect displays are temporally dynamic and some displays are more relevant to decision making than others, extant research demonstrates that they can be persuasive. For example, Jiang et al. (2019) found that entrepreneurs who displayed positive emotions like joy during a funding pitch were more successful than their counterparts who did not employ similar affect displays. Further, the affect displays were most effective when used in the introduction and conclusion of the pitch.

Engaged Persuasion Activity: Affect Displays and Customer Loyalty

Think about a recent interaction you had with an employee in the service industry (e.g., buying lunch at Chick-fil-A). Was your interaction with the person pleasant? Did the employee smile at you or employ other nonverbal movements to communicate positive emotions? Further, is it even possible that affect displays can be used strategically to enhance customers' loyalty intentions in the service industry? Wang et al. (2017) addressed this question through two studies. They found that the use of intense affect displays (i.e., displays that communicate positive emotions but are not authentically felt by the communicator) work particularly well for consumers low in epistemic motivation (i.e., an individual's motivation to develop an accurate understanding of the current situation). For such individuals, intense affect displays boost loyalty intentions by heightening their positive affective reactions (i.e., customers reported being more pleased and contented after the interaction). In contrast, authentic affect displays (i.e., positive emotions that the communicator authentically feels) were more effective for individuals high in epistemic motivation. According to Wang et al., these individuals tend to reflect more critically on the quality of customer service interactions and are therefore more influenced by authentic displays of emotions. Are you able to differentiate between authentic and inauthentic affect displays? If so, how do these displays affect your interactions with employees?

Regulators are nonverbal acts that maintain and regulate speaking and listening between communicators (Ekman & Friesen, 1969). For example, audience members might use nonverbal behaviors to signal that the speaker should continue, repeat a point, or hurry up. Conversely, speakers can use regulators to signal that the audience should pay attention to a specific point. Importantly, the frequency and type of regulators vary with the context of the situation as well as the role and demographic characteristics of the communicator. Also, regulators are culturally bound and may be misinterpreted, which could dramatically decrease the persuasiveness of the speaker.

Finally, adaptors are nonverbal behaviors that satisfy self or bodily needs, perform bodily actions, and manage emotions. Scratching your arm, bouncing your leg while sitting, stroking your hair, and picking your nose are all examples of adaptors. Importantly, research by Maricchiolo et al. (2009) shows that self-touching behaviors negatively influence receivers' perceptions of the composure of persuasive speakers. Similarly, Carli et al. (1995) found that adaptors often serve as cues of anxiety and nervousness.

Paralinguistics

Paralinguistics is the study of the acoustic properties of speech (e.g., fluency, pitch, rate, and volume). Put simply, paralinguistics concern not what persuaders say but how they say it. For example, when you imagine a persuasive speaker, does a smooth talker come to mind? If so, you would not be wrong. Rarely is the speaker who frequently stumbles, pauses, or speaks haltingly accused of being persuasive. Speech fluency has been found to significantly impact persuasion. Burgoon et al. (1990) define **fluent speech** as typically "free of lengthy pauses, hesitations, repetitions, sentence changes, interruptive vocalizations, and the like" (p. 146). Burgoon et al. investigated several nonverbal behaviors and found that speech fluency had the greatest impact on perceived speaker competence and persuasiveness. This finding is largely consistent with Carpenter's (2012) meta-analysis of the speaker disfluency literature that found a "consistently negative impact on speaker credibility and a weaker, possibly more distal negative impact on persuasiveness" (p. 565).

Pitch refers to variations in the intonation of speech (i.e., highness and lowness). Pitch can be used strategically to emphasize particular ideas or words. For example, in the phrase "Smoking can cause *serious* health problems, including cancer" (where "serious" is spoken at a different pitch than the other words), attention is drawn to the severity of the health risks of smoking. The research on the persuasiveness of pitch is mixed. For example, pitch has been shown to be positively related to persuasion and source credibility (Pittam, 1990) as well as purchase intention (Gélinas-Chebat et al., 1996). Other studies suggest excessively high pitch decreases persuasion (Chebat et al., 2007). In that vein, research by Elbert and Dijkstra (2014) suggested that high pitch lowered participants' intentions to engage in healthy behavior compared to moderate and low pitch.

Speech rate, quite simply, refers to the rate of speech that a speaker uses in their communication. Speech rate is an important source of information that receivers use to make judgments about the source of a message (Ray, 1986). Previous studies have consistently found that moderate and fast speakers are described as more intelligent, competent, confident, credible, socially attractive, and effective as compared to slow speakers (Buller et al., 1992; Putnam & Street, 1984; Skinner et al., 1999).

Is the fast-talking persuader unfairly maligned by stereotypical depictions of car salespeople or advertising spokespersons who rapidly list disclaimers or side effects at the end of a commercial, for example? We may typically associate fast talkers with those who are trying to pull one over on us. Perhaps the more accurate image would be the debater who is a quick thinker on their feet or the auctioneer who easily commands language at rates our ears may feel they can barely keep up with. You might be surprised to learn that most academic studies about speech rate have demonstrated the positive perceptions, associations, and effects of fast talkers. Simonds et al.'s (2006) experiment found that college instructors who spoke at moderate or fast rates of speech were perceived more positively by students than were slow-speaking instructors. More specifically, student perceptions of instructor's credibility and nonverbal immediacy as well as self-reports of affective learning were significantly higher for moderate- and fast-speaking instructors as compared to slow-speaking instructors. The connection to nonverbal immediacy, a variable we discussed earlier in this chapter, is particularly noteworthy, as speech rate may help to reap the benefits of nonverbal immediacy for fast-talking persuaders. However, perceptions of instructor clarity and students' information recall did not differ significantly due to speech rate (Simonds et al., 2006). The researchers speculated that a faster rate of speech may suggest the speaker is more knowledgeable, thus triggering the peripheral or heuristic processing hypothesized by dual processing models. Overall, these results suggest that the worst choice for a persuader would be to slow their speech rate down to a crawl, as they would risk damaging their credibility and reducing their nonverbal immediacy.

From childhood, many have learned that slow and steady wins the race. After all, the tortoise ended up crossing the finish line before the hare! If the race had been a speech contest, however, the tortoise would have been toast. Smith and Shaffer's (1995) research demonstrated that increased speech rate was associated with higher perceptions of source credibility. Consistent with the ELM, speech rate was found to be most persuasive in the condition where receivers were moderately involved. In this condition, rapid speech rate increased persuasion by "enhancing subjects' perceptions of the source's credibility" (Smith & Shaffer, 1995, p. 1058). Smith and Shaffer reasoned that fast speaking reduces listeners' ability to distinguish weak from strong arguments.

Volume refers to the loudness or quietness of speech. Across four experiments, Van Zant and Berger (2020) found that manipulations of speakers' volume and volume variability significantly enhanced persuasion. The authors also found evidence to support the claim that the paralinguistic manipulations made communicators appear more confident. When attempting to vocally persuade, speakers may speak louder and with more variety in volume. According to Van Zant and Berger (2020), these nonverbal behaviors "make them seem confident, which enhances persuasion by making them appear to hold more extreme attitudes consistent with the stance they take" (pp. 676–677). Further, the authors found that naturally occurring attempts to persuade through volume did not undermine receivers' perceptions of the speaker's sincerity.

Silence

Does silence communicate? Often, we tend to think of communication as an oral and verbal construct that is connected to and reliant upon words and language.

However, **silence** can communicate. Although silence is often misinterpreted by others, such as when instructors may attribute student silence for lack of interest or poor preparation (Meyer, 2009). So, if we broaden our understanding of communication and recognize that it also includes silence, how exactly should we classify silence? Is silence verbal or nonverbal communication? To the extent that we commonly define the difference between verbal and nonverbal communication by whether words or language is utilized in messages, silence would be considered a nonverbal communication behavior. Unlike oral or written language, which are commonly accepted forms of verbal communication, silence involves a lack of oral or written language and thus would be relegated to the realm of nonverbal communication. For instance, we often consider pauses to be a facet of paralanguage and, therefore, nonverbal communication. Similarly, silence involves the absence of language. But that does not mean that silence is the absence of communication. In fact, silence can communicate a great deal. Can silence also be persuasive? Before answering this question directly, consider a few of the other concepts we discussed earlier in this chapter. For instance, silence is powerful (Picard, 1948/1952, 1963). A person in power may chose not to respond to a question or email from a subordinate, in essence, using silence to exercise their power over others. Conversely, a subordinate may not be able to speak up or protest (at least not without consequences), thus suggesting that their silence represents a lack of power—or what we might deem to be powerlessness. Consider also the various gender and cultural differences that may accompany silent behaviors, inclinations, and preferences as well as interpretations of what silence means, or is communicating.

Engaged Persuasion Research: Nonverbal Persuasion and Leadership

How do leaders use nonverbal behaviors to influence their subordinates? Bellou and Gkorezis (2016) conducted two studies to answer this question. Specifically, they examined the effects of leaders' use of positive kinesics and paralanguage on perceived leader effectiveness. Their findings demonstrate that trust mediates the impact positive nonverbal behaviors have on perceptions of leader effectiveness. Further, they found that highly suspicious subordinates mitigate the positive effect of nonverbal communication on trust toward the leader. They conclude that, given that subordinates associate the use of nonverbal communication with trust, "consistency by supervisors and managers throughout their personal and public interactions is vital" (Bellou & Gkorezis, 2016, p. 325). As a result, it is essential that leaders receive training to ensure their verbal messages are accompanied by appropriate nonverbal cues.

So does silence persuade? If I ask you if I should continue with a lecture or if you have any questions about what we have just covered, and you say nothing in response, how will I interpret your silence? Often, teachers will take your silence to that question as a signal that they may proceed to the next set of notes. In other words, your silence has persuaded the teacher to continue. Silence may also communicate a lack of resistance to persuasion. Or it may communicate resistance to persuasion (Li Li, 2005). For instance, if I were to ask you to register to vote and impress upon you the importance of voting in the election but you were to remain silent when I finished speaking, what would your silence be communicating? Did my persuasive message succeed, or not?

Verbal communication can be used to inveigle (e.g., using flattery or deception to persuade) others into participating or behaving in a particular way. Silence, on the other hand, can persuade through cognitions and interpretation. Jaworski (1993) argued that silence "does not imply the absence of communication," and therefore, "instead of treating silence as a negative phenomenon with respect to speech, it is more plausible to place silence and speech on a communicative continuum" (p. 46). In political situations, silence can serve a strategic function (Jaworski, 1993). As Dauenhauer (1980) explained, "Our ability to use silence appropriately in our own speech and the adequate interpretation of the silence of others are indispensable for successful communication," (p. 4) or we might say persuasion. At a constitutional level, Johannesen (1974) observed that silence is sometimes recommended as a form of social protest. Recognizing the critical role that silence can play in political discourse, Donofrio (2020) defines tactical silence as a "form of silence employed by groups who seek to wrestle power from the dominant by directing audiences' attentions toward a silence with a function" (p. 551). Consider how the protestors in the opening photograph of this chapter use silence to persuade.

Engaged Persuasion Research: Visual Framing

Do visual message components enhance persuasive attempts? Sontag (2018) found that visual frames accompanying persuasive messages can be effective in motivating college students with depression to seek help. Specifically, Sontag found that recovery-related visual frames elicited greater positive emotions and encouraged message consumers to be more like the models in the messages as compared to suffering-related visual frames, which elicited negative emotions. Although the messages tested in Sontag's study included verbal text, the images in the messages were found to be particularly effective. Thus, it would stand to reason that the nonverbal images hold persuasive appeal.

Summary

In this chapter, we addressed the language factors and nonverbal characteristics that affect persuasion. Perhaps it is not surprising that both verbal and nonverbal behaviors affect the persuasion process. However, we noted that several specific verbal factors related to language use as well as a variety of nonverbal behaviors related to paralinguistic delivery and perceptions of the speaker can affect persuasion. We also discussed the role that silence plays in persuasion. Overall, the information in this chapter ought to help you appreciate how language choices and nonverbal behaviors play into the persuasion process.

Now that all the primary content of this textbook has been covered in the chapters, we turn our attention to a couple of other issues noted in the appendices.

Appendix A, which appears next, addresses practical issues of constructing persuasive presentations as well as effective means of delivery. Following that, Appendix B will address issues of research methods and theory.

Check Your Understanding Review Questions

1. What does language intensity mean? How does intensity affect persuasion?
2. Why does vivid language affect persuasion?
3. What is the difference between verbal and nonverbal persuasion?
4. How do god and devil terms differ? Why are god and devil terms considered ultimate terms?
5. What are the differences between powerless language and powerful language?
6. How do Communication Accommodation Theory, Information Processing Theory, and Language Expectancy Theory enhance our understanding of the persuasive effects of language?
7. Why is nonverbal immediacy persuasive? What is mediated immediacy?
8. In what ways is speech fluency related to persuasion?
9. How does speech rate affect persuasion?
10. How is silence related to persuasion?

Key Terms

Communication Accommodation Theory (p. 297)
connotative meaning (p. 294)
denotative meaning (p. 294)
fluent speech (p. 315)
god and devil terms (p. 295)
Information Processing Theory (p. 298)
intensity (p. 297)
Language Expectancy Theory (p. 299)
nonverbal immediacy (p. 305)
powerless language (p. 300)
silence (p. 317)
speech rate (p. 315)
ultimate terms (p. 295)
vividness (p. 299)

Credits

Appendix A

Persuasive Public Speaking

Chapter Objectives

After reading this appendix, you should be able to:

- Understand the nature of persuasive public speaking
- Identify strategies to develop persuasive topics
- Locate and incorporate support for your persuasive speech
- Effectively organize a persuasive speech
- Understand the dynamics of small group presentations

This appendix addresses the range of topics that persuasive speakers must consider when developing a persuasive presentation, including topic selection, locating and incorporating supporting material, organizing persuasive claims, and strategies for facilitating group-led discussions. Throughout this appendix, we make cross applications to previous content that will help you develop robust persuasive arguments. In addition, we discuss the skills necessary for you to develop fluency in navigating and evaluating information. The first step in developing a persuasive speech is topic selection.

Topic Selection

Selecting a topic for a persuasive speech can seem daunting; however, it is obviously a critical step in the process of creating the speech. In this section, we discuss strategies for generating topic ideas as well as the process of narrowing your topic through the creation of purpose and thesis statements.

Generating Ideas

There are multiple options available to you to generate ideas for your persuasive speech. We suggest that you begin by considering topics that are of significance and relevance to your audience. Recall that the Elaboration Likelihood Model (ELM) suggests that receivers of persuasive messages will expend more energy to think carefully about messages they find relevant and personally meaningful (Robert & Dennis, 2005).

You can generate numerous persuasive topics quickly through brainstorming. Give yourself 15 to 20 minutes to jot down as many ideas as possible. You can even organize your ideas into a personal inventory of topics in categories like current events, social issues, and campus issues (you can develop as many categories as you like). Table A.1 provides a sample personal inventory of brainstormed topics. Once you have this list, we suggest consulting with your instructor and other members of the class to determine which topics resonate with them.

TABLE A.1 Sample Personal Inventory of Persuasive Speech Topics

Current Events	Social Issues	Campus Issues
Climate Change	Poverty	Campus Safety
Gun Safety Legislation	Health Care	Free Speech Zones
Vaping Bans	Immigration	Funding of Higher Education
Election Reform	Food Insecurity	Cost of Textbooks

Purpose Statements

When you deliver a persuasive speech, you act as an advocate. In other words, the purpose is to create, alter, reinforce, or extinguish an audience's attitudes, values, beliefs, or behaviors related to some topic. **General purpose statements** outline the overall intent of the message (e.g., to persuade the audience to support action on the student loan debt crisis).

In contrast, your **specific purpose statement** will focus on one aspect of the topic you selected. What specifically will you be persuading your audience to think, believe, or do? The process of crafting a specific purpose statement is important, as it allows you to narrow the topic and identify exactly what you will cover in your presentation. Returning to the student loan debt example in Chapter 6, the specific purpose statement on that topic could be worded as follows:

> To persuade the audience that cancellation of all student loan debt would benefit the U.S. economy.

Notice how the specific purpose statement presents a directional version (benefits of cancellation to the U.S. economy) of the more general topic area (student loan debt).

As you write your specific purpose statement, make sure it encompasses your general purpose, the focus of your topic, and your audience. Written this way, the specific purpose statement will outline the topics you will cover and what the audience should think, believe, or do at the end of your speech. As noted previously, the specific purpose should be crafted to be significant and relevant to your audience.

Thesis Statements

The **thesis statement** provides a single sentence containing the main points that you will advance in your persuasive speech. Returning to the student loan debt example, the thesis statement could be worded as follows:

General Purpose:	To persuade the audience to support action on the student loan debt crisis.
Specific Purpose:	To persuade the audience that cancellation of all student loan debt would benefit the U.S. economy.
Thesis Statement:	Cancellation of all student loan debt would boost the U.S. economy by increasing the gross domestic product (GDP) and decreasing the unemployment rate.

In terms of guidelines for writing thesis statements, Simonds et al. (2018) suggest that you write the statement in as few words as possible, develop the thesis as a declarative statement rather than a question, and avoid being too general or broad.

FIGURE A.1 This speaker attempts to persuade the audience by acting as an advocate.

Locating and Incorporating Supporting Material

Once you have selected a topic for your persuasive speech, you need to develop a strategy for locating and incorporating **supporting material.** Importantly, the ability to develop and execute a research strategy for locating and evaluating information is essential to becoming a competent persuasive speaker and participant in our democracy (Simonds et al., 2018). In addition, as we noted in Chapter 6, an effective strategy for bolstering your credibility is to cite credible evidence to support your persuasive arguments (Reynolds & Reynolds, 2002; Stiff, 1986). In this section, we discuss how to develop a research strategy, explore different types of supporting material, and present strategies for evaluating the supporting material you find.

Developing a Research Strategy

Think for a moment about how you typically approach conducting research for course assignments. Do you start by diving into Wikipedia or Google Scholar or by going to the library? Without question, students today have access to more information than any other generation in history; however, navigating all those sources can be tricky. Further, as we have noted throughout this textbook, it is critical that the research strategy you develop results in reliable, credible, and timely information for your persuasive speech.

According to Biddix et al. (2011), college students indicate that they desire to find credible sources for course projects but often default to research strategies that allow them to access information quickly and efficiently. The result is that students often do not find the most credible information available on their topic. To develop a more robust research strategy, we suggest that you begin by developing a set of research questions that stem directly from your thesis statement. Consider the following examples of research questions related to the student loan debt topic:

- How many individuals in the United States face hardships because of student loan debt?
- What are the effects of student loan debt on the U.S. economy?
- Would the cancellation of student loan debt benefit the U.S. economy?
- How is student loan debt related to the unemployment rate?

Developing research questions will provide you with a roadmap for navigating the myriad of sources (i.e., internet, library catalogs and databases, etc.) available to you. Also, you may find that your research questions evolve as you work through different sources. That evolution is to be expected, but remember to keep your specific purpose and audience in mind as you modify your research strategy. You can find more information about academic research questions in Appendix B.

Types of Supporting Material

As you collect research related to your topic, you will encounter many forms of supporting material. As you gather information, we encourage you to think strategically about using a mix of sources and data. It is easy to imagine how frustrated an audience might become with an unending barrage of statistics. Using an optimal mix of supporting material will add vitality to the speech and keep the audience engaged. For example, a persuasive speaker might use statistics and personal examples together to establish the scope of the topic and provide a real-word example that deepens the audience's understanding of the issue. In the following section we focus on a few of the common types of supporting material, including statistics, examples, and testimony.

Statistics

Statistics provide a numerical method for summarizing data and can take such forms as means, medians, ratios, and percentages. Although statistics can provide rich support for your persuasive claims, they can also be confusing, overwhelming if overused, and misleading. Your chances of using statistics successfully improve dramatically if you follow a few practical guidelines.

Initially, as suggested previously, you should not rely on statistics exclusively as support for your persuasive arguments. Similarly, you should round off statistics to help your audience understand and retain key information. For example, it will be much easier for your audience to remember that the United States spent nearly $700 billion on national defense in 2018 than it would be to remember the spending was $678,055,000,000.00. Finally, it is important that you translate obscure and/or difficult-to-understand numbers into comprehensible, relatable, and vivid terms. Consider the following example:

> According to recent statistics posted on the Dehydration Project website, one of the leading advocacy groups for the elimination of world hunger, 40 million people die every year from hunger and hunger-related illnesses. This number is equivalent to more than 300 jumbo jet crashes every day with no survivors.

You can find more information about statistics and quantitative research in Appendix B.

Examples

Examples are specific instances developed at varying lengths and are used by persuasive speakers to make abstract ideas more concrete or relatable. You can use brief, extended, or hypothetical examples to support your persuasive claims.

A brief example is a specific case used to support a claim. For instance, if you wanted to support the claim that the federal government does not respond quickly enough to disasters, you might reference the slow response to the victims of the Flint, Michigan, water crisis starting in 2014.

Extended examples, also referred to as narratives, stories, metaphors, or anecdotes, are substantially more developed and lengthy than brief examples. Extended examples can be an especially effective way to help your audience visualize, relate to, and identify with your topic (Alam & So, 2020; Thibodeau, 2016). Returning to the example of the Flint water crisis, a persuasive speaker could tell a compelling story about a resident's struggle to locate lead-free drinking water for their children. The speaker could also describe the rancid water conditions faced by residents as well as the illnesses that ravaged the community because of lead exposure.

Hypothetical examples describe imaginary situations that could conceivably take place in the way described. Although hypothetical examples are fictitious, you should avoid exaggerating or distorting the scenarios you develop. One advantage of hypothetical examples is that they allow the audience to imagine themselves in a specific situation. Consider the following example highlighting the Flint water crisis.

> Imagine that the water in your city was unsafe to drink. Suppose further that you could not use the water in your home for everyday tasks like cooking or bathing. Now imagine spending more than 5 years dealing with the serious health effects of lead poisoning in your children. How would this situation affect you and your family?

This example is likely to help listeners imagine the difficulties of navigating everyday activities that require clean water as well as the possibility of becoming very ill as a result of exposure to contaminated water. A persuasive speaker could use this example to help the audience understand the importance of a timely response by the federal government to future environmental crises.

Testimony

Persuasive speakers use testimony when they quote from or paraphrase an authoritative and credible source. When you use testimony, you are relying on someone else's judgment and expertise. As we noted in Chapter 6, testimonial evidence will be more persuasive if you employ an evidence credibility statement (Kim et al., 2012). Consider the following example:

> In a 2018 report posted on the New Deal blog, Dr. Marshall Steinbaum (Ph.D. in economics from the University of Chicago), who is a Fellow and Research Director at the Roosevelt Institute, concludes that cancellation of all student loan debt would increase annual GDP in the U.S. by $22 billion and decrease the unemployment rate. (Steinbaum, 2018)

When employed effectively, testimony can provide support for your persuasive claims and bolster the audience's perception of your credibility. On

FIGURE A.2 A speaker at a rally in 2020 uses persuasive testimony to support his claims.

the other hand, relying on testimony from sources that your audience deems unreliable or incompetent will have negative implications for their assessment of your credibility.

Evaluating Supporting Material

As a critical consumer and producer of persuasive information, it is essential to carefully evaluate your supporting material. As an ethical persuader, you should locate and utilize credible and reliable information and scrutinize how you will use it in your persuasive speech. We encourage you to consider the following questions as you select and incorporate supporting material.

Is the source of information identified and credible? Members of your audience are likely to consider the credibility of the sources you utilize. As we noted in Chapters 5 and 7, supporting material is most persuasive when it is judged as legitimate and credible (Dong et al., 2018; Reynolds & Reynolds, 2002; Stiff, 1986). As you select supporting material, keep the following questions in mind: What special training and/or qualifications does the author possess that enable them to speak on this topic? Is the author recognized as an authority on the subject? If you are unable to answer these questions, you should look for other sources to support your claims.

Are the facts verifiable? As you collect facts for your speech, you should evaluate the verifiability of your information. Are you able to find the same fact in more than one source? Cross checking your facts with multiple sources is one way to verify your information.

Is the source biased? An information source is biased when it provides an opinion that is so slanted to one perspective that it is not objective or fair. Imagine that you are conducting research on the effects of carbon dioxide on the environment. Suppose you find testimony stating that there is no evidence that the global climate is warming. Further, assume that you find additional testimony from the same source indicating that increasing levels of carbon dioxide are actually good for the planet. Setting aside other questions about the verifiability of this evidence, can you think of any reason an individual would advance such claims? One explanation could be that such advocates are paid by large oil and gas companies to undermine consensus in the scientific community that humans are causing climate change. In other words, oil and gas companies actively seek out and pay for this kind of testimony to lobby politicians to limit expensive constraints on the production of carbon dioxide (Ball, 2015). Clearly, such sources are biased and should not be used to support your persuasive claims. Examples like this demonstrate the need for you to evaluate what your sources have to gain or lose by advocating certain positions.

Are the statistics representative? A representative sample is a critical indication of the reliability and validity of statistics. To be representative, the sample must be similar to the population from which it was taken. Consider the other students in this persuasion class. To what extent to do they represent the entire population of students on your campus? Are they representative of the wide range of majors at your institution? Do they accurately reflect the range of demographics on your campus, including age, cultural background, and socioeconomic status? Also, the students in your class were likely not drawn randomly from the entire student body. As a result, they do not constitute a representative sample for your campus. Although a full discussion of sampling procedure is beyond the scope of this text, you should carefully consider how the samples were drawn for the statistics you incorporate into your speech.

Are the items being compared in analogies similar? Any analogies that you use to support your ideas should compare cases that share similar characteristics.

Are the examples you use relevant, typical, and vivid? Any example you incorporate should be relevant to the claim it is supporting. Further, if the connection between the example and claim is unclear, the example will not be persuasive. You should also apply the test of typicality to any examples you use. Typicality refers to the extent to which your example is normal. Your audience will easily recognize atypical examples and evaluate your credibility negatively. For example, the argument that your classmates should wager their tuition money on video poker because you won big last weekend likely will not be taken seriously, as it is atypical.

As we noted in Chapter 12, the examples you use should also vividly illustrate the claims you advance. In a recent meta-analysis exploring the relationship between vividness and persuasion, Blondé and Girandola (2016) found that the use of vivid stimuli facilitates acceptance of the advocated attitude and intention to change. Importantly, their research also demonstrates that vividness is most persuasive when the valence of the topic is positive rather than negative.

Is the supporting material timely? The information you use in your speech should be recent enough to account for the laws, regulations, attitudes, and so on that currently exist in the status quo. For example, a speaker advocating action in response to salmonella infections linked to contact with pig ear dog treats would need to know exactly what actions have already been taken to propose a novel solution. How might the audience react to a speaker who advocates that the Centers for Disease Control and Prevention (CDC) should immediately issue a warning about the dangers of pig ear dog treats if they know the CDC has already issued that warning? As you might imagine, audience members are likely to question the credibility of the speaker and their ability to conduct detailed research.

Organizing Persuasive Claims

Presenting your speech in an organized and strategic manner is essential if you expect to persuade your audience. In order to organize your speech, you first need to consider whether you will advocate claims of fact, value, or policy.

Claims of Fact, Value, and Policy

As you will see in the sections that follow, the type of persuasive claims you advance has significant implications for the way you organize and outline your speech.

Claims of Fact

When persuasive speakers address **claims of fact**, they are concerned with what is or is not true, what does or does not exist, or what did or did not happen. Importantly, factual claims may address whether something did or did not happen in the past (past fact), whether something is true or not true in the present (present fact), or whether something will be true or not in the future (future fact). It is obviously impossible to know with certainty what will happen in the future. As a result, speakers advocating future fact claims need to provide sufficient evidence regarding the probability or likelihood that specific events will occur in the future. The following list contains examples of persuasive claims of fact:

- Elizabeth Holmes deceived investors about the efficacy of her blood testing technology (past fact).
- Hillary Clinton received millions more popular votes in the 2016 presidential election than Donald Trump (past fact).
- Colleges and universities do not do enough to advance diversity, equity, and inclusion (present fact).
- Food insecurity is prevalent among college students (present fact).
- Climate change will result in a four-foot increase in global sea level by 2100 (future fact).
- The national debt will double from 78% of GDP today to 160% by 2050 (future fact).

One of the important considerations for speakers advocating factual claims is to select a topic that is controversial enough for a meaningful conversation. In other words, some factual claims are so narrow in scope or so widely accepted as truth that the audience will likely agree with them before hearing from you, which leaves little room for persuasion.

Claims of Value

Does the security of a society outweigh the personal freedoms of individuals? Is democracy overvalued by the U.S. government? Is animal experimentation justifiable? These questions go well beyond an assessment of facts to a judgment about values. **Claims of value** address what you deem to be right or wrong, moral or immoral, just or unjust, or good or bad. The following list provides several examples of persuasive claims of value:

- Embryonic stem cell research is morally wrong.
- It is less important to value religious freedom in the classroom than to protect against it.
- National security is more important than freedom of expression.
- Civil disobedience in a democracy is morally justified.
- The benefits of the U.S. federal government's use of offensive cyber operations outweigh the harms.
- The intergenerational accumulation of wealth is antithetical to democracy.

As you can see, some of these topics examine one action (e.g., stem cell research), while others are comparative (e.g., national security versus freedom of expression).

Claims of Policy

Claims of policy address what should be done, what law should be changed, or what policy should be followed. Policy claims are easily identifiable by the inclusion of the word "should" as well as the existence of an agent of action, or entity that is tasked with taking action. Consider the following persuasive policy topics:

- The university (agent of action) should lower tuition by 25%.
- The U.S. government (agent of action) should increase market-based regulations requiring reductions in greenhouse gas emissions.
- The U.S. government (agent of action) should enact substantial criminal justice reform.
- The U.S. government (agent of action) should increase its regulation of campaign financing in federal elections.
- College students (agent of action) should engage in individual action to address discrimination against members of the LGBTQ community.
- The NCAA (agent of action) should allow student athletes to share in revenue generated by sales of merchandise.

We explore strategies for organizing persuasive claims of fact, value, and policy in the following section.

Organizing Claims of Fact, Value, and Policy

Organizing your speech is vital, as it helps your audience better comprehend and understand your arguments. Organization also helps you as a speaker to stay on point and craft a persuasive argument that will sway your audience.

Organizing Claims of Fact

The majority of speeches that advance claims of fact will likely follow a topical (organized by subtopics of the larger topic), chronological (organized by a time sequence), or spatial (organized by physical space or geographic location) organizational pattern. The following example follows a topical organizational pattern:

Specific Purpose: To persuade my audience to believe that Elizabeth Holmes deceived Theranos investors.

Thesis Statement: Elizabeth Holmes deceived Theranos investors by promoting devices that did not work and endangered lives.

Main Points:

A. Elizabeth Holmes lied about the efficacy of the blood testing devices she invented.

B. The inaccurate test results produced by Theranos devices endangered lives.

If you are attempting to persuade your audience that climate change is dangerous, you could present your claims chronologically.

Specific Purpose: To persuade my audience to believe that climate change will be disastrous for the planet.

Thesis Statement: Data from climatologists indicate that the effects of climate change will become significantly more devastating over time.

Main Points:

A. Climate change will result in an additional 100 million people living in extreme poverty by 2030.

B. Climate change will result in the loss of $10 billion in annual revenue for global fisheries by 2050.

C. Climate change will cause global sea levels to rise four feet by 2100.

It is also possible to organize a speech on a claim of fact spatially. Consider the following example:

Specific Purpose: To persuade my audience to believe that food insecurity is a serious national problem.

Thesis Statement: Food insecurity causes serious health problems across the nation.

Main Points:

A. In New Mexico, nearly 17% of the population faces food insecurity.

B. In Oklahoma, 15.6% of the population faces food insecurity.

C. In West Virginia, 15.7% of the population faces food insecurity.

The examples in this section demonstrate several ways to organize and outline persuasive claims of fact. The next section examines techniques for organizing persuasive claims of value.

Organizing Claims of Value

As we noted in Chapter 1, values represent abstract goals that individuals use as guiding principles in their lives. Speakers advancing claims of value should identify some criterion or standard by which the value judgment is to be made. Consider the following claim: "National security is more important than freedom of expression." How should the speaker advocating this claim arrive at the ultimate conclusion? How can the audience determine the conditions under which national security is more important than freedom of expression? The persuasive speaker could argue that protection of human life is the most important value. It would be hard to argue against that fact that the dead do not have freedom of expression. In this case, the speaker would need to prove that national security should be prioritized over freedom of expression to protect human life. As you can see, the criterion of life becomes the measuring stick by which the value judgment is made.

Claims of value are organized topically; however, the speaker can choose to weave the criteria into the main points of the speech or separate them into different subpoints. The following example illustrates how the criteria can be integrated into the main points of the speech:

Specific Purpose: To persuade my audience that civil disobedience in a democracy is morally justified.

Thesis Statement: Civil disobedience is morally justified against unjust laws and when the protestors' motives include advancing the common good.

Main Points:

A. Acts of civil disobedience are justified as a response to unjust laws.

B. Acts of civil disobedience are morally justified when they advance the common good.

Alternatively, persuasive speakers may choose to devote the first main point to establishing the criteria for the value judgment and subsequent points to applying those criteria to the topic.

Specific Purpose: To persuade my audience to believe that colleges and universities ought not consider standardized tests in admissions decisions.

Thesis Statement: Colleges and universities ought not consider standardized tests in admissions decisions, as they are inaccurate and racially biased.

Main Points:

A. Standardized tests must meet two major criteria to be used in admissions decisions.

1. The results must accurately predict an individual's potential in higher education.
2. The results must not be biased against any particular race.

B. Colleges and universities ought not consider standardized tests in admissions decisions, because they fail to meet these criteria.

1. Several studies demonstrate that standardized tests do not accurately predict college potential.
2. Recent research shows that the process of question selection is biased against non-White test takers.

As you can see, claims of value "assess the worth or merit of an idea, object, or practice according to standards or criteria supplied by the arguer" (Inch & Warnick, 1998, p. 139). Recall from Chapter 1 that persuaders that provide cognitive support for the values held by the audience are more likely to induce attitude and behavior change (Maio & Olson, 1998). When advancing claims of value, it is therefore important to provide strong and compelling reasons for why the value you are advocating is important.

Organizing Claims of Policy

The following **organizational patterns** are particularly well-suited for organizing policy speeches: problem-solution, problem-cause-solution, and comparative advantage.

When using the problem-solution order, the first main point in the body of the speech should be devoted to establishing the problem you have identified. You will introduce your specific plan and explain how it solves the problem in the second main point. The following speech demonstrates the problem-solution order:

Specific Purpose: To persuade my audience to support market-based strategies to combat climate change.

Thesis Statement: The U.S. government should increase market-based regulations requiring reductions in greenhouse gas emissions.

Main Points:

A. The dangers of climate change are significant.

1. The U.S. government has failed to take meaningful action to address climate change.
2. The range of published scientific evidence indicates that the dangers of climate change are significant and will increase over time.

B. Market-based strategies are an effective way to decrease greenhouse gas emissions.

    1. The U.S. government should set a price that emitters must pay for each ton of greenhouse gasses they emit.

    2. Market-based strategies address the problems of climate change by putting an explicit price on carbon emissions and encouraging business to find cost-effective ways to reduce those emissions.

If you want to highlight the causes associated with a problem, you should consider using the problem-cause-solution format. Consider the following example:

Specific Purpose: To persuade the audience to support criminal justice reform.

Thesis Statement: The U.S. government should enact substantial reforms to address the problems and causes that exist in the criminal justice system.

Main Points:

A. The U.S. criminal justice system is marred by vast racial discrimination.

    1. Over the last 40 years, our nation's incarceration rate has quadrupled.

    2. The criminal justice system stigmatizes and targets young Black men, unfairly punishes communities of color, and exacts a significant social cost.

B. There are several causes of these racial disparities.

    1. The decades-long war on drugs has contributed to the racial disparities in our criminal justice system.

    2. Mandatory minimum sentencing policies transfer power to prosecutors who are twice as likely to charge Black defendants compared to their White counterparts.

C. The U.S. government should enact several reforms to address the problems in the criminal justice system.

    1. The U.S. government should pass legislation that ends racial profiling.

    2. The U.S. government should strengthen the Department of Justice's pattern or practice unit to better monitor civil rights violations.

    3. The U.S. government should provide funding to make body cameras available in every police department in the country.

If your audience already agrees that a problem exists in the status quo, you should consider using the comparative advantages organizational pattern. This pattern requires that you present arguments through the main points, establishing why your solution is preferable to other options.

Specific Purpose: To persuade my audience that the United States should provide subsidies for renewable energy production.

Thesis Statement: Renewable energy is friendlier to the environment and less costly compared to coal power.

Main Points:

A. Renewable energy sources produce far less CO_2 emissions compared to coal power.

B. Subsidized renewable energy sources provide cheaper electricity compared to coal power.

Once you have a topic, research to support your claims, and a strategy for organizing and outlining your arguments, you should carefully consider how you will deliver your persuasive speech. Although a full discussion of delivery is beyond the scope of this appendix, we recognize that effective delivery is essential to persuasive speaking (Carpenter, 2012). You will find an explanation of several methods of delivery in Table A.2. We advocate that persuasive speakers employ the extemporaneous delivery style for most classroom speeches. Extemporaneous speaking allows you to analyze the reaction of the audience and adjust your speech accordingly on the fly. In addition, the extemporaneous style is more like an informal conversation, especially compared to speakers who read from a manuscript, which allows you to build rapport and immediacy with the audience. Ultimately, this style best facilitates liking, which enhances persuasion.

TABLE A.2 Methods of Delivery

Method of Delivery	Characteristics of Delivery Style
Manuscript	The speaker reads the presentation word for word from a prepared manuscript. This style is appropriate when time limits are important and when what you have to say needs to be precise.
Memorized	The speaker delivers a memorized speech. This style is appropriate when the speech is brief. This style may also be appropriate for special occasions like introducing other speakers or making a toast.
Impromptu	This delivery style is used when speakers are given very limited time to prepare content and are asked to speak off the cuff. For example, you employ the impromptu style when you participate in classroom discussions.
Extemporaneous	The speaker delivers the presentation from a prepared outline or brief speaking notes. This style is appropriate for most classroom speeches, as it is more conversational than other methods of delivery.

Group Persuasive Presentations

We noted in Chapter 3 that groups are complex, and many variables influence their performance. Although many react to group assignments negatively, communication scholars have demonstrated that working in small groups can facilitate the development of a range of skills, including organization, teamwork, time management, peer tutoring, creative thinking, conflict management, and communication competence (Rothwell, 2019). Further, research by Gaudet et al. (2010) demonstrates that small group learning, when done well, can increase academic achievement and improve students' attitudes toward group work. Similarly, a meta-analysis by Pai et al. (2015) demonstrates that working in small groups facilitates better transfer of skills and knowledge to new contexts compared to working individually. Over the course of your life, you are likely to work in many groups, and you will probably have to work with others to deliver a persuasive presentation or facilitate a discussion. In this final section of the appendix, we explore strategies for overcoming the challenges of working in groups and offer tips for facilitating group-led discussions.

Overcoming the Challenges of Working in Groups

There are several challenges of working in groups compared to working individually (Abril, 2016). In terms of how groups make decisions, we noted in Chapter 3 that groups are susceptible to **polarization effects**, or the tendency to make extreme decisions (Sunstein, 2002). As Hastie and Sunstein (2015) note, polarization is particularly likely when members of the group feel social pressure to conform to positions they perceive to be proper in the context of that group. Being aware that groups may experience polarization can help you combat its effects. In addition, Rothwell (2019) suggests that groups can further minimize polarization and facilitate effective decision making by ensuring that a wide range of issues are discussed by the group, encouraging members to act as a devil's advocate to challenge popular positions, and thoroughly discussing all issues before taking a firm position.

Social loafing is yet another challenge to working in groups. Recall that we defined **social loafing** in Chapter 3 as the "reduction in motivation and effort when individuals work collectively compared with when they work individually or coactively" (Karau & Williams, 1993, p. 681). There are several strategies for reducing social loafing, including providing members of the group with feedback about their performance, monitoring individual performance, and assigning meaningful and unique tasks to group members (Karau & Williams, 1993). In addition, students in Shak's (2016) study on free riding suggested that groups should impose penalties on free riders and directly confront them with the problems that slacking presents to group performance. Of course, we would also advocate that you notify your instructor of any social loafing problems as early as possible.

According to Yamane (1996), one of students' most significant concerns about working in groups relates to the transaction costs they incur. **Transaction costs** result from having to interact and collaborate with group members and include time spent scheduling and attending meetings, negotiating differences of opinion, managing conflict, and completing group work (Yamane, 1996). Transaction costs can be reduced by establishing a fair division of labor for all group members and exchanging contact information and schedules as soon as the group forms. If possible, we also suggest that you join groups that have members that share your interest in the topic for the group presentation.

Facilitating Group Discussions

There are many different forms of group presentations; however, traditional group presentations often mirror individual presentations with the exception that they are performed by more than one person. As a result, the suggestions for developing a persuasive speech provided in previous sections of this appendix can be applied to the traditional group presentation assignment. In this final section, we discuss strategies for facilitating group-led instructional discussions.

FIGURE A.3 This group of students appears to enjoy working with teammates. When all group members contribute and social loafing is avoided, members are more satisfied and have positive attitudes.

Working in a group to facilitate a discussion related to persuasion content differs significantly from the traditional group presentation. Therefore, this section outlines several guidelines to follow if your group is tasked with facilitating an instructional discussion. Initially, **instructional discussions** feature in-depth conversations about the course content that provide participants opportunities to hone their communication skills and knowledge (Simonds et al., 2015). These group-facilitated discussions are characterized by high participant interaction where the participants provide the reasoning, rather than having it presented to them, so that concepts can be systematically discovered. Instructional discussions produce greater learning and recall of information than other techniques because participants, including the group facilitators, are provided the opportunity to articulate and verbalize concepts and link them to prior experiences (van Blankenstein et al., 2011). In addition, these discussions give facilitators the opportunity to clarify flaws in reasoning in real time as they are exposed. Consider the following tips for facilitating group-led discussions:

- *Carefully consider prediscussion variables.* Have a plan for how the room should be set up to facilitate the discussion. In addition, you should assess the psychological climate for the discussion. In other words, are the participants prepared to be actively engaged in the discussion? Do they have the stimulus material needed to engage in a meaningful and substantive discussion?
- *Grab the attention of your audience in the introduction.* The introduction of your discussion should capture attention and establish the relevance of the material you will cover to your participants. In addition, you should clearly articulate the goals of your discussion in the introduction.
- *Develop a question strategy.* Your group members should think strategically about your question strategy. Start with questions on material that is comfortable for your participants. Once they are warmed up, ask them higher order questions that require them to explain relationships among concepts. Ultimately, your strategy should move participants to application and evaluation of relevant concepts. Also, make sure to provide sufficient wait time after asking a question. Facilitators that immediately provide answers to their own questions communicate that participation from the audience is not really expected. A guide to constructing questions that facilitate discussion can be found in Table A.3.
- *Engage in behaviors that facilitate discussion.* Keep in mind that your role as a facilitator is to encourage rather than to dominate the discussion. At times, you may also need to mediate differences of opinion and resolve conflicts. In addition, remember that all members of your group have a responsibility for facilitating the discussion and should remain nonverbally

engaged at all times. Nonverbal behaviors that signal boredom or hostility will have a chilling effect on the discussion. As a result, group members should remain engaged and positively reinforce participants for responding. Finally, your effort should be a group effort rather than a series of individual monologues. This requires careful planning in advance and a degree of interactivity among group members during the discussion.

- *Develop a compelling conclusion.* Your group should summarize and synthesize the content of the discussion in the conclusion. Also, you should revisit the goals of the discussion and provide a memorable close that leaves participants wanting to know more about your topic.

TABLE A.3 Guide to Asking Questions That Provoke Discussion

Questions That Tend Not to Provoke Discussion

Type	Example
Yes/No	"Is persuasion always unethical?"
Factual	"Who created Interpersonal Deception Theory?"
Elliptical	"So how about terrorism as persuasion?"
Leading	"I think the Hunt and Meyer textbook is the best ever, don't you?"
Guessing	"Why do you think deception is so jacked up?"

Questions That Provoke Discussion

Type	Example
Analytic	"How can learning about persuasion make you a more informed consumer of information?"
Evaluative	"Do cue theories of deception offer better explanations than noncue theories?"
Compare/Contrast	"How are the ELM and HSM similar and different?"
Descriptive	"How would you describe the role attitudes play in predicting behavior?"
Personalized	"How would you describe what you are learning in this class to your friends?"

Summary

As this appendix makes clear, persuasive speakers must consider several issues in the process of developing a compelling presentation. Initially, selecting a topic that you find interesting but that also relates to the interests and needs of your audience is essential. Also, you should take the necessary time to develop and execute a robust research strategy in order to locate and integrate information to support your persuasive arguments. In addition, it is critical that you select an organizational pattern that is appropriate to the type of persuasive claim you will advance in your speech. Finally, we discussed strategies for overcoming the challenges of group work as well as tips for facilitating instructional discussions.

Check Your Understanding Review Questions

1. How can you generate persuasive speech topics through brainstorming?
2. What are the differences between general, specific, and thesis statements?
3. Why is it important to develop research questions as a part of your research strategy?
4. What are the strategies you can employ to evaluate supporting material?
5. What are the differences between persuasive claims of fact, value, and policy?
6. What organizational pattern(s) are appropriate for each type of claim?
7. What are the main methods of delivery available to persuasive speakers?
8. What are the challenges of working in groups, and how can you overcome them?
9. How does instructional discussion differ from other types of group presentations?
10. What are the guidelines for generating questions that facilitate discussion?

Key Terms

claims of fact, value, and policy (p. 330, 331)
general purpose statements (p. 323)
instructional discussion (p. 339)
organizational patterns (p. 334)
polarization effects (p. 337)
social loafing (p. 337)
specific purpose statements (p. 323)
supporting material (p. 324)
thesis statements (p. 323)
transaction costs (p. 338)

Credits

Fig. A.0: Copyright © 2019 by Wonderlane. Reprinted with permission.

Fig. A.1: Copyright © 2018 by Miguel Henriques. Reprinted with permission.

Fig. A.2: Copyright © 2020 by Edward Howell. Reprinted with permission.

Fig. A.3: Copyright © 2018 by Brooke Cagle. Reprinted with permission.

Appendix B

Academic Research and Theory

Objectives

After reading this appendix, you should be able to:

- Describe the basic components of academic research
- Understand the differences between quantitative and qualitative research methods
- Appreciate the difference between a meta-analysis and a single research study
- Describe the basic components of metatheory
- Describe the basic components of theory

A relatively extensive body of scholarly research and theory building related to the study of persuasion has emerged over time in multiple academic disciplines. The roots of interest in persuasion can be traced from ancient Greece and Rome to contemporary homes in communication and psychology departments across the globe. In the past 100 years, there has been an explosion of research studies and theoretical frameworks that address the nature of persuasion, influence, and behavior change. Obviously, we will cover a fairly sizeable chunk of that body of literature in this textbook. However, this text is not meant to be a chronical of the history of persuasion or a comprehensive treatment of the subject. Rather, we believe that a focus on the theories and research that still guide our thinking on persuasion is the better path to venture down. We have intentionally chosen to focus our attention on understanding the research and theory that scholars across academic units and professional practitioners should understand and utilize. In other words, the academic literature that has survived the rigor of scientific inquiry and is still guiding our thinking about persuasion is privileged in this textbook. Of course, to fully grasp that research and theory, readers must have some familiarity with the nature of scientific inquiry, research design, and theory building. While our purpose is not to comprehensively review all the material that falls within the purview of research methodology and theory courses, we do think it would be helpful to highlight some basic concepts and terms that ought to enable readers to journey with us through what is an exciting body of literature on persuasion.

Academic Source Citations

As you read this textbook, you are bound to notice a plethora of **academic source citations**. We have included these citations within the chapters for a couple of reasons. First, these citations should give you an indication that the claims we make are supported by academic research studies, which is important because you certainly want to know that research supports these claims. Second, the citations are provided within the chapters, rather than as footnotes, to make it easy for you to look up those sources and explore the original studies in more detail. While we follow the American Psychological Association's (APA) 7th edition style guide for citing sources within the chapters, which often means you see the last names of authors and the year of publication, this information will enable you to turn to our references list at the end of each chapter to locate the full APA citation for each study. Nearly all the sources we cite in this textbook are prominent scholars who are experts in the subject matter. However, you will notice that we only provide first names and credentials (or author qualifications) for a few of the most notable names. Rather than providing first names and credentials for each and every scholar we cite, which would disrupt the flow of the chapter for readers, we have intentionally chosen to provide details for only the most essential names you would need to know and remember.

Reading Academic Research

Academic **research methods** are tools that scientists employ to answer research questions and hypotheses addressing particular topics of inquiry. When social scientists concerned with answering questions about persuasion endeavor to do so, they are compelled to follow rigorous and appropriate methods to design investigative studies, collect data, analyze data, and draw conclusions about the implications of those findings. While you might be tempted to think that you can pose and answer research questions by simply speculating about a topic and then asking a few people you know to confirm your suspicions, scientists take an entirely different approach. Initially, researchers will consult the existing body of academic literature to determine which previous scientific studies and theories have already addressed the topic or related topics. From this body of research and theory, scientists will pose either research questions where the answers are not apparent or hypotheses where the answers appear to be better developed.

Research Studies

To test those research questions and hypotheses, scholars design research studies using appropriate, rigorous, and scientifically accepted methodologies. For instance, there are times when it may be appropriate to ask participants directly to report their perceptions, what would be considered a self-report of data, usually collected through **surveys**. Often, though, it may be better to survey people and have them report about how other individuals behave, what we would call an other-report. On the other hand, we may find that a lab or field **experiment** is needed to collect data about how people really respond to particular stimuli. In Chapter 4, we addressed measurement issues in persuasion research, or how we ask survey questions and collect participants' responses.

As researchers consult existing studies and theory, they identify **variables** that seem to be important factors in the topic area. So, you might be wondering, what do variables do? Quite simply, they vary. How much do variables vary? In quantitative terms, variables can vary by up to 100%. This is why **quantitative research**, which deals with numeric data and employs statistical tests, is concerned with explaining as much variance accounted for with statistical models as possible. While you will likely notice when a research study reports that the results have **statistical significance**, you should also pay attention to the effect sizes or magnitude of the effect observed. Typically, scholars who conduct empirical studies develop theories to explain, predict, and control variables and test theories through methods and data that permits them to make generalizable claims. For instance, if quantitative scholars draw random samples of research participants that are representative of the population from which the sample is drawn, then they can make generalizations—within certain limits—about the conclusions they reach. However, if researchers use convenience samples, then their ability to make generalizable claims is severely restricted. The caveat, though, is that experimental research studies might employ a convenience sample and then use **random assignment** to distribute those participants to control groups or experiment groups. So, when you read research studies, you should pay careful attention to the methods section of the research report to see if the scholars used either random sampling or random assignment; if they do not, then you should read their results with the understanding that those results are not generalizable.

Qualitative research, which is concerned with nonnumeric data, takes an approach that is quite different. For example, qualitative scholars typically seek to understand phenomena rather than predict and control. A researcher who

FIGURE B.1 There are many specific terms to know about conducting academic research.

employs qualitative methods might collect data through in-depth interviews, focus group interviews, or ethnographic observation. The data yielded by such methods is often the words of the participants or the behaviors that are observed. In other words, qualitative researchers are not seeking to count anything or convert their data into numeric form. They are also not trying to generalize their results. Instead, they wish to provide rich and thick descriptions of their data and, perhaps, privilege the voice of their participants to produce results they think might be transferable to other situations or groups.

Meta-Analysis

As you might imagine, quite a collection of research studies about a particular topic may build up over a period of time. After all, the scientific process is premised on the acknowledgement that any single research study is unable to bring resolution to the subject at hand. Instead, scientists will replicate studies and explore similar topics through various research projects addressing slightly different questions or sampling different groups of participants. Once a collection of similar studies has accumulated, some researchers will conduct meta-analyses to determine if the quantitative data all points toward a bottom-line conclusion that cuts across the various studies. A **meta-analysis** is an analysis of other analyses, or a study of other studies. Thus, meta-analyses are potentially important works because they offer us insight into what research across a variety of studies, perhaps within various disciplines, says over a period of time.

Some persuasion instructors may require students to read not only a textbook on persuasion but also selected examples of original research studies published in peer-reviewed academic journals. It is quite common for these journal articles to be 25 pages or more and be written in a manner that requires the reader to understand research methodology at an advanced level. This is why textbooks are helpful tools for both instructors and students. For instance, in writing this textbook, we have reviewed and read hundreds of original research studies published in academic peer-reviewed journals to glean what we actually know about persuasion. While we cannot go into much detail about any of those particular studies, we can provide students a general understanding of the bottom-line findings, conclusions, and implications contained in those studies. In other words, when you read a textbook, such as this one, you are reading a synopsis of the vast body of academic research that exists on the subject. Textbooks also provide the advantage of being written in a language that permits a lay audience to understand academic research. Nevertheless, it is important that you pay special attention to the methodological details that we relay in summarizing the research studies we cite. For example, if we say that a team of researchers conducted a meta-analysis, then you ought to pay special attention to that information and recognize that an additional layer of credibility would accompany those results.

Measurement

If you ever attempt to tackle a do-it-yourself home improvement project or simply want to build something yourself (like that new bookshelf you have always wanted to hold all your college textbooks), you will encounter the sage advice to "measure twice, cut once" (see Figure B.2). In academic research, measurement is also an issue of primary concern. When it comes to measuring attitudes and behaviors, social scientists should use carefully designed and pilot-tested means of collecting data from participants. Then they should use sound sampling procedures while employing research designs that permit replication of findings. Most introductory research methods classes emphasize these three points: One's data merely reflects the questions that we asked, the data is only as good as the sample from which it was drawn, and findings need to be replicated if we are to have confidence in the conclusions.

Survey Instruments

Persuasion researchers are especially interested in collecting data from human participants. Some researchers are interested in observational data, while others are interested in self-reports or other-reports. And this data may be collected through experiments, survey instruments, interviews, focus groups, or ethnographies, among other methods. In persuasion research, surveys requiring self-report or other-report data are quite common, so we will use this method as an example for the moment.

Let's say that a researcher is interested in asking participants to respond to survey questions about their intentions to sign up to be organ donors. The responses that participants provide are a reflection of the questions they are asked, the wording of the questions, and the response options provided. What

FIGURE B.2 The adage "measure twice, cut once" is a good way to think about quantitative survey scales. Data is only as good as the measurement instrument we employ to collect data. Scales must be both valid and reliable.

questions should the researcher ask? How should those questions be worded? And how should participants be asked to respond? When measuring attitudes, for instance, self-reports are more accurate for reporting perceptions than other-reports (Gibson et al., 2018). Wording survey items in the first-person as opposed to third-person language more accurately yields reports of feelings, especially with regard to risky behaviors (Gibson et al., 2018). After all, you might be able to tell us about your own attitudes toward organ donation on a survey; but can you accurately tell us about the attitudes of another person? You know your own thoughts on the subject but can only tell us what another person may have said about organ donation. You cannot really tell us what they think.

So how would we measure behavior? We could observe a person's past or present behavior. Or we could ask them to report that behavior to us. But can we observe their future behavior? At best, we can only ask them to tell us how they intend to behave in the future. While we are at it, do you think one's attitudes might determine future behavior? Perhaps, but can we establish that connection through survey responses? We could ask a series of questions in which participants tell us their attitudes about signing up to become an organ donor. On the behavioral side, however, our survey would only be able to tell us about either the participant's past behavior or how they intend to behave in the future. You get the point, right? Measurement issues are tricky and need to be carefully planned to yield the sort of data we are interested in knowing. Unlike using a tape measurer before cutting that board for the bookshelf we are making, where

FIGURE B.3 Measurement error should be reduced in quantitative research. Scale development helps to minimize measurement errors.

we might know precisely where to cut if the board needs to be 27 inches long, survey questions are more likely to result in measurement error.

Writing Survey Questions

What about that whole "measure twice, cut once" analogy? Often, we only have one chance to collect data from participants, so if we ask the wrong questions or fail to provide participants with the appropriate response options, then we have missed our opportunity. Additionally, we may want to ask the same basic question in multiple ways so that we know the information participants are providing is accurate. For instance, if a researcher is interested in measuring job satisfaction, they could simply ask participants if they are satisfied with their job. However, survey respondents will not always answer such questions honestly or accurately, especially if they are concerned their boss might see the responses or they don't want to seem disgruntled. Even though most research surveys are completed anonymously, rather than linking personally identifiable information with the survey answers, and study findings are reported in aggregate totals, rather than by individual participant, people may forget that we won't know who provided which response. And participants often have a social desirability bias that results in them providing the responses they think we want to hear or are socially acceptable answers. Sure, you could tell me you like your job. But what if I also asked you if you were currently monitoring new job postings or even applying for other jobs? Are you keeping your resume up to date? Do you arrive to work early? Do you stay late? Do you often socialize with coworkers on your own time? Do you like your boss? Do you feel valued by the company? It is possible that someone might tell us they like their job but then answer those other survey questions in a manner that appears as if they really are not satisfied with their current job. This is why researchers often ask a series of questions that attempt to measure the same general construct or variable. The series of questions might appear redundant to participants, but that battery of questions that is known as a scale will yield better data.

We have already discussed whether to word survey questions in the first-person (e.g., self-report) or third-person (e.g., other-report) form. Are there other wording tips to follow? Yes, survey questions should be clear, use language that participants understand, avoid emotionally charged terms, avoid asking more than one thing at a time, and not be leading. More specifically, if we asked you "Do you support the troops and agree with our military involvement?" how would you respond? In an interview, focus group, or on an open-ended survey question, you could respond to both parts of that double-barreled question. But, if the survey only provides closed-ended response options, such as yes/no or rate your agreement on a 1 to 5 Likert scale, then it would be much tougher for you to respond. And it would be nearly impossible for researchers to later determine if you were responding favorably to both parts of the question or just one part of the question. What if you took an online survey and encountered the following question: Given that many college students work minimum wage jobs, do you think professors make too much money? This sort of a leading question taints the responses participants provide by pointing them in a particular direction. The next time you receive a survey in the mail from a political party, carefully examine how many of the questions are double-barreled, leading questions, or use emotionally loaded words. We suspect the people who create those surveys are less interested in discovering what your attitudes are than they are with trying to influence you through the questions themselves.

Validity and Reliability

While we are at it, let's talk briefly about validity and reliability. Validity refers to accuracy. Are we really measuring what we think we are measuring? If you were playing darts and hit what you were aiming at, then you would be accurate (bullseye!). Reliability refers to consistency. Will our survey questions yield consistent results? If you throw three darts at the board, and they land in a tight cluster in the same area of the board, then you are consistent. You might miss what you are aiming at, but at least you do so consistently. In survey research, we want measures to be both valid and reliable.

After all, we might think we have constructed a series of survey questions about job satisfaction only to later discover that those questions were really measuring workplace culture. In that case, our survey instrument, or questionnaire, would not be accurate. Or what if a participant would respond to a question differently each time they take the survey? If you have ever asked a 6-year-old their favorite color and received a different answer depending on the day you asked, then you know what we are talking about! Perhaps different participants do not respond to the same questions similarly because the questions are too ambiguous? A 6-year-old might interpret your question to mean their favorite color at this given moment rather than a more static preference. In this case, our survey instrument would not be consistent. Again, it is important for persuasion researchers to develop survey instruments that are both valid and reliable.

Sampling Issues

Okay, so now that we know what to include in our survey, who should get to respond to it? Twenty of your friends? The first five people that pass by you on the college green? As we discussed in Chapter 1, quantitative researchers are interested in results that are generalizable. Thus, random sampling techniques are better than convenience samples. From what population, though, should researchers draw their samples?

Much of what we know from academic research is based on a fairly narrow sampling of participants. In fact, over 90% of studies published in top psychology journals consist of research subjects from Western, industrialized nations and represent just over 10% of the world's population (Henrich et al., 2010). Other academic disciplines, communication included, are prone to similar biases. In other words, our research is a reflection of WEIRD populations (meaning Western, educated, industrialized, rich, and democratic; Rad et al., 2018), leading Henrich et al. (2010) to conclude:

> Much research on human behaviour and psychology assumes that everyone shares most fundamental cognitive and affective processes, and that findings from one population apply across the board. A growing body of evidence suggests that this is not the case. (p. 29)

Yet, different human populations can vary considerably in their attitudes, behaviors, values, and beliefs. The result is often that what we think we know is extremely difficult to generalize across cultures. Some findings have simply not been replicated when participants from non-Western cultures have been studied (Rad et al., 2018). Thus, we should always remember that our ability to generalize findings is limited by the sampling procedures employed as well as the representativeness of study participants to the general population. In essence, this means that we should always ask ourselves if the research and theory we read would hold true if investigated in another culture.

Replication Studies

Peer-reviewed academic journals represent the gold standard for scholars to share their findings with the scientific community. However, journals have a strong tendency to publish studies that produce statistically significant findings that are novel, what is known as a publication bias (Yong, 2012). See Figure B.4 for a breakdown of publication bias by academic discipline. Notice that all the disciplines represented in Figure B.4 heavily favor studies with significant findings. In fact, over 70% of the published research in each discipline are studies with statistically significant findings. The problem with the trend you see in this graph is that some of those significant findings might be false positives, or what we call Type I errors. And some of the nonsignificant findings that are never published may be false negatives, or Type II errors. It certainly does not look as if the nonsignificant findings are being given fair attention, does it? Many of these studies are never repeated, and replication studies that fail to confirm the original studies tend not to published (Yong, 2012). Recently, psychologists have struggled to succeed in reproducing experiments (Yong, 2018). One project, called Many Labs 2, has only been able to reproduce previous classic experiments in half the cases—even with much larger sample sizes (Yong, 2018).

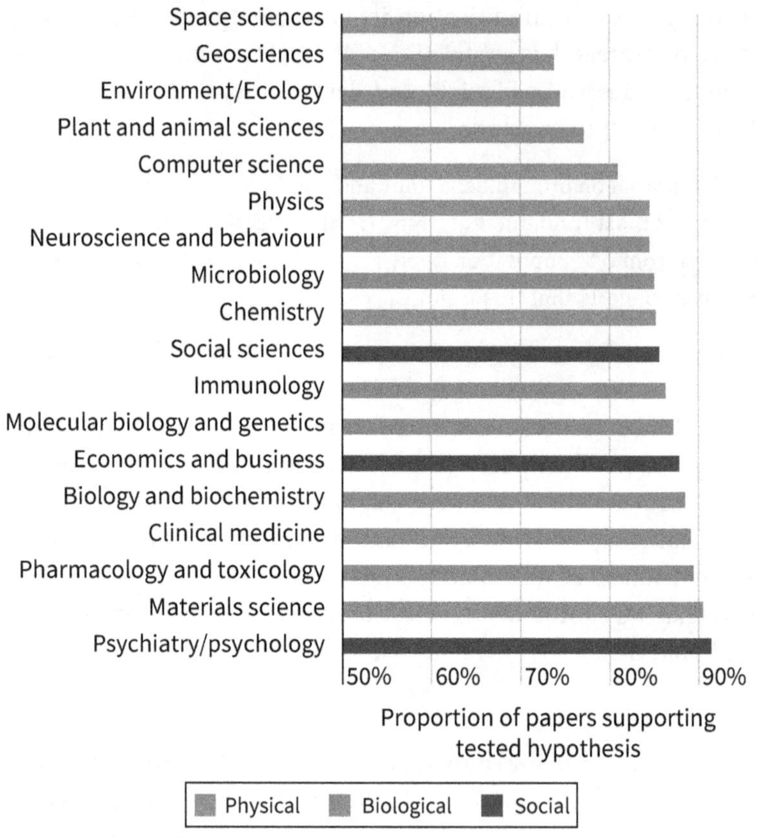

FIGURE B.4 Yong (2012) found publication bias exists in academic journals from various disciplines. Publication bias means that non-significant results are often unpublished, which can hamper the scientific process.

Understanding Theory

Theory Building

Scholarly theory building is an attempt to understand and explain phenomena within a particular area of inquiry. The nature of persuasion crosses academic boundaries, necessitating an examination of theoretical frameworks that have emerged from disparate "silos" or academic departments. In fact, to be properly understood, persuasion ought to be viewed as an interdisciplinary subject of interest. While disciplines like communication and psychology may develop theory in different ways, there are many shared beliefs about how theories should be built, tested, and refined. Put simply, **theories** are sensemaking devices that explain why phenomena occurs and how variables are related.

> **Engaged Persuasion Activity: Replication Studies**
>
> How confident can we be about the academic research that is published in peer-reviewed journals? In recent years, social scientists have become increasingly concerned with replicating classic experiments. Check out two such projects: the Many Labs 2 project (see https://osf.io/ux3eh/) and the Social Sciences Replication Project (see http://www.socialsciencesreplicationproject.com/). How important do you think replication is in the social sciences? What are the arguments both in favor of and against the need for replication?

As you have already read in this chapter, dual process models theorize that persuasive messages are cognitively processed in distinct ways, which produces different end results. While anyone can come up with a theory about why things work the way they do—what is known as armchair theorizing—scientists approach theory from the perspective that theories need to be tested, and theoretical propositions, or assumptions, must be subjected to academic scrutiny. Some scholars begin with theory and then collect data to test that theory, which is known as deductive theory building. You already saw how this approach works with the ELM and HSM. Others collect data and then develop inductive theory, or grounded theory, as data emerge to formulate theoretical frameworks.

FIGURE B.5 Research and theory go hand-in-hand. Studies are conducted to test existing theories while data may also lead to the development of new theories. It is important to connect the dots between theory and research.

Metatheoretical Assumptions

Any specific theory that is developed comes with certain metatheoretical assumptions. **Metatheory** means theory about theory, so it is not concerned with any particular theory. Theorists bring their metatheoretical assumptions to their theory building, which means any particular theory is packed with certain **metatheoretical considerations** that underlie the theory. There are three metatheoretical considerations: ontological, epistemological, and axiological concerns. Ontology refers to assumptions about the nature of reality or what is real. For example, realists assume that reality exists independent of human consciousness, nominalists believe that language creates reality, and social constructionists believe that reality results from the cocreation of meaning among individuals. Epistemology refers to assumptions about what counts as knowledge. For instance, objectivists believe that we must separate the known from the known, while subjectivists believe that we can only know something through interaction between the knower and the known (e.g., the researcher and the participants). Axiology refers to assumptions about the role of values in the research process. Some believe that theory should be value "free" or value neutral, while others believe that theory should embrace or embed values.

Theorists also approach theory building from particular **metatheoretical perspectives**, or paradigms. The three metatheoretical perspectives are post-positivism, interpretivism, and critical. Post-positivist theorists value empirical or scientific inquiry, which often means they privilege quantitative research, objectivist epistemology, and value free or value neutral axiology. Interpretive theorists value humanist principles, which means they often embrace qualitative methods and subjectivist epistemology. Critical theorists wish to question existing power structures, ideologies, and hierarchies, which means they privilege subjectivist epistemology and value embedded axiology.

In this textbook, we address a variety of theories about persuasive communication. Not all of these theories share the same metatheoretical assumptions and perspectives. Thus, each of the theories that we write about may approach our understanding of persuasion in vastly different ways. It is certainly important for you to keep this in mind when reading about a particular theory and the research studies that have tested that theory. We should also note that we have intentionally and deliberately decided to highlight those theories that we believe will help you to best understand persuasive communication, are well-supported by the body of academic research or would be important to know to appreciate the context of thinking about persuasion, and are currently in use by practitioners or scholars. In other words, we are not trying to comprehensively cover every theory that addresses persuasion.

Summary

In this appendix, we explained academic research methods and theory. Although this textbook is not meant to provide a comprehensive account of research methods or theory building, as separate courses in those subjects would, we have introduced you to some methodology and metatheory in order to help you better understand the sources and evidence we cite throughout the textbook chapters.

Check Your Understanding Review Questions

1. In what ways do scholars conduct research about persuasive communication phenomena?
2. What research methods do persuasion scholars employ in their studies?
3. What are variables?
4. How do quantitative and qualitative research methods differ?
5. How does a meta-analysis differ from a typical research study?
6. How do scholars build individual theories of persuasion?
7. What is metatheory?
8. What three metatheoretical considerations do theories address?
9. What are the three metatheoretical perspectives that describe theorists?
10. What measurement issues should researchers be concerned with?

Key Terms

academic source citations (p. 343)
experiments (p. 344)
meta-analysis (p. 346)
metatheoretical considerations (p. 354)
metatheoretical perspectives (p. 354)
metatheory (p. 354)
qualitative research (p. 345)
quantitative research (p. 344)
random assignment (p. 345)
research methods (p. 344)
statistical significance (p. 344)
surveys (p. 344)
theories (p. 353)
variables (p. 344)

Credits

Glossary

academic source citations: involves citing sources in text to support claims

anchor point: refers to the receiver's stance on a particular issue or message

assimilation effect: occurs when the positionality of the persuasive message is relatively close to the advocated position of the receiver

attitude: consists of positive or negative evaluations of some object (e.g., person, issue, or oneself)

attitude toward the behavior: "people's attitude toward personally performing the behavior—that is, their positive or negative evaluation of their performing the behavior in question" (Fishbein & Ajzen, 2010, p. 20)

Attribution Theory: posits that receivers of persuasive messages are skeptical and actively develop explanations for why communicators advocate certain positions

behavior(s): consists of the action performed, target toward which the action is directed, context in which the action is performed, and time

behavioral intention: an individual's projection of what their future behavior will be

belief(s): an individual's acceptance that a particular statement is true

belief perseverance dynamics: when information is "encoded in memory, it can be very difficult to eliminate its effects on subsequent attitudes and beliefs" (Nyhan & Reifler, 2012, p. 3)

boomerang effect(s): receivers will attempt to recover the freedom that has been lost or threatened, value the freedom more than we did previously, or engage in related freedom behaviors

"but you are free" tactic: involves informing the persuasive target that they are free to refuse the request

central route: attitude change as stems from careful scrutiny of information and weighing of the pros and cons related to message itself

civic agency: the "capabilities of people and communities to solve problems and to generate cultures that sustain such agency" (Boyte, 2009, p. 3)

civic engagement: "acting upon a heightened sense of responsibility to one's community" (Jacoby, 2009, p. 9)

claim: represents the assertion or point that a persuader advocates

claim of fact: concerned with what is or is not true, what does or does not exist, or what did or did not happen

claim of policy: addresses what should be done, what law should be changed, or what policy should be followed

claim of value: addresses what you deem to be right or wrong, moral or immoral, just or unjust, or good or bad

coercion: involves the invocation of some threat to force the target to act as the coercer desires

Cognitive Dissonance Theory: stipulates that if an individual holds two pieces of knowledge that are relevant to each other but inconsistent, the individual will experience a state of discomfort—or dissonance

cognitive misers: receivers who are not involved with the message and less likely to engage cognitively with it

cognitive style: characteristic modes of information processing that can be observed in an individual's perceptual or intellectual activities and they develop relationships between cognitive and personal/affective spheres

Collective Effort Model: posits that social loafing occurs when individuals in a group perceive that their work will not be rewarded or that they will not accomplish their individual goals

Commitment-Communication Model: posits that getting the public to commit to solve a problem must attempt to get others to recognize there is a problem, provide a means for the target audience to become educated on the problem, and provide opportunities for the target audience to actively participate in efforts to alleviate and solve problems

Communication Accommodation Theory: proposes that individuals attempt to converge toward the speech styles of their message recipients as a strategy to bolster persuasion

compliance gaining: the "communicative behavior in which an agent engages so as to elicit from a target some agent-selected behavior" (Wheeless et al., 1983, p. 111)

conformity: social influence based on the belief that it is desirable to fit in with a group

confrontational persuasion: can include nonviolent resistance and civil disobedience as well as militant confrontational strategies

connotative meaning: refers to the emotions and thoughts associated with the word

continued-influence effect: "despite being corrected, and despite acknowledging the correction, people by and large continue to rely at least partially on information they know to be false" (Lewandowsky et al., 2017, p. 355)

contrast effect: occurs when the persuasive message and the receiver's stated position are far apart

counterattitudinal advocacy: an individual performs a communicative action that runs counter to their attitudes

counterfactual thinking: the process of imagining alternative outcomes when reflecting on past events

credibility: refers to the "judgments made by a perceiver (e.g., a message recipient) concerning the believability of a communicator" (O'Keefe, 2002, p. 181)

critical mass: refers to "the point after which further rates of adoption occur rapidly in a self-sustaining process" (Backer & Rogers, 1998, p. 17)

culture: a shared system of knowledge, attitudes, values, and beliefs that individuals use to make sense of the world

deception: "intentionally, knowingly, and/or purposely misleading another person" (Levine, 2014, p. 379)

democratic engagement: is "based upon reciprocity and co-creation of knowledge. From this perspective, community members and organizations and those affiliated with institutions of higher education have shared authority for knowledge production. In addition, students, faculty, and members of the community work collaboratively to address community problems" (Hunt & Woolard, 2016, p. 545)

demographics: individual variables like age, gender, and culture that influence the consumption and production of persuasive messages

denotative meaning: the literal dictionary definition of the word

descriptive normative beliefs: involve an assessment of the likelihood that referents are or are not performing a behavior

devil terms: words that communicate malevolence and disgust

Differential Decay Hypothesis: holds that a sleeper effect is observed when the message and discounting cue have a similar initial influence on attitudes; however, the cue decays more quickly than the message

Diffusion of Innovations Theory: explains how ideas, innovations, and practices spread throughout a population

Discrepancy Motives Model: stipulates that when individuals encounter counterattitudinal messages, they are motivated to defend their existing opinion by counterarguing and refuting the message

disrupt-then-reframe tactic: involves employing a small disruption, such as asking for 100 pennies rather than saying one dollar, followed by a direct reframing of the request, such as noting that 100 pennies is a bargain

Dissociative Cue Hypothesis: stipulates that the immediate impact of a message is reduced when it is associated with a disclaimer, counterattitudinal message, or negative information about the source

dissonance arousal: occurs when an individual experiences a negative and unpleasant state of dissonance

dissonance reduction: strategies used by individuals to reduce cognitive dissonance, such as distraction and forgetting, trivialization and self-affirmation, denial of responsibility, adding consonant cognitions, behavior change, or act rationalization

door-in-the-face tactic: this technique involves making an extreme request, that likely will be rejected, followed by a legitimate concession that results in a subsequent request for that which is truly desired

dual process models of persuasion: the models (e.g., ELM and HSM) delineate between deliberative and intuitive information processing, judgment, and decision making

dump-and-chase tactic: this compliance-gaining technique involves making repeated requests of a target until they comply

Dunning-Kruger effect: stipulates that unskilled and incompetent people are often so confident in their beliefs that they lack the ability to recognize they are incompetent

Dyadic Power Theory: examines factors that cause individuals to feel powerful relative to others

efficacy statement: a statement that tells us that we can take actions to avoid the problem described in the message

ego involvement: refers to the receiver's perception of the importance of the persuasive message to their life

Elaboration Likelihood Model: proposes that persuasive messages are processed via central or peripheral routes

emotional appeal: appeals that target the feelings of receivers

engaged persuasion: ethical persuasion that is aimed at advancing the common good

entertainment-education: used to spread innovations by taking advantage of narrative persuasion as well as the audience's empathy with and emotional investment in fictional characters

ethics: the study of what ought to be the grounds for determining right and wrong human behavior and the commitment to do what is right

ethical persuasion: persuasion that is truthful, authentic, respectful, fair, and concerned about the common good

evidence: used to substantiate a persuader's claim and can take several forms, including statistics, analogies, facts, examples, testimony, and narrative

evidence credibility statement: brief statements that establish the quality of the information you use to support your claims

evoking-freedom tactic: a compliance-gaining strategy that uses the phrase "You are free to refuse" to preserve the freedom of the target

experiment: research conducted in a lab or in the field to collect data about how people really respond to particular stimuli

expertise: refers to the receiver's perceptions of the communicator's intelligence, competence, and overall knowledge related to the position advocated

Extended Parallel Process Model: examines how fear appeals are coupled with efficacy statements to spur behavioral changes

fake news: false or misleading information that is presented as truthful

fear appeal: an appeal designed to scare or threaten targets into doing what a persuasive message recommends

firehose of falsehood: technique based on information warfare techniques employed by the Russian government to use "high numbers of channels and messages and a shameless willingness to disseminate partial truths or outright fictions" (Paul & Matthews, 2016, p. 1)

fluent speech: speech that is typically "free of lengthy pauses, hesitations, repetitions, sentence changes, interruptive vocalizations, and the like" (Burgoon et al., 1990, p. 146)

foot-in-the-door tactic: this technique involves an initial small request that is followed by a larger, related request

foot-in-the-hand tactic: involves requesting money while the requester is holding a few coins in one hand

forewarning: designed to generate resistance to future influence by bolstering current attitudes or increasing counterarguing to the anticipated persuasive message

Four Factor Model: stipulates that attempted control, arousal, felt emotion, and cognitive processing play significant roles in deceptive communication

free sample technique: consumers feel compelled to purchase goods and services in response to a perceived need to reciprocate for receiving a free sample

freedom behaviors: refer only to actions that are realistically possible for individuals, sometimes as simple as exercising choice or picking among alternatives

fringe persuasion: persuasion that is characterized by manipulation, subliminal messages, coercion, intimidation, torture, or indoctrination

functional theory: positions "candidate statements in a political campaign as functional, or as a means to an end: obtaining sufficient votes to win the office sought in the campaign" (Benoit, 2017, p. 5)

gain-framed messages: typically "present the benefits that are accrued through adopting the behavior" (Salovey et al., 2002, p. 392)

general purpose statements: outline the overall intent of the message (e.g., to persuade the audience to support action on the student loan debt crisis)

god terms: require deference and subservience and "cause people to genuflect when hearing them" (Hart et al., 2018, p. 163)

goodwill: reflects the extent to which an audience perceives that the communicator has their best interests in mind

group polarization: deliberating groups make a decision that is more extreme in the direction of group members' prediscussion preferences

guilt appeals: appeals that seeks to elicit feelings of guilt in receivers and stresses the personal responsibility of the individual to engage in the recommended behavior

halo effect: one positive characteristic of a person dominates the way that person is viewed by others

Health Belief Model: proposes that an individual's health behaviors are a result of their perceptions of threat perception and an evaluation of behaviors

Heuristic Systematic Model: proposes that persuasive messages are processed via systematic processing and heuristic processing

humorous appeal: an appeal designed to stimulate a psychological state associated with amusement

Image Repair Theory: offers five broad categories of image repair strategies that persuaders can employ to respond to a crisis: denial, evasion of responsibility, reducing offensiveness of the event, corrective action, and mortification

information deficit fallacy: stipulates that the assumption that more information will correct misperceptions is false and cautions that providing corrective information may even backfire

informational incongruity assumption: incongruent expertise and certainty information "violate expectations, stimulate involvement, and foster persuasion as long as message arguments were strong" (Karmarkar & Tormala, 2010, p. 1044)

Information Manipulation Theory: posits that deceptive messages derive from violations of conversational norms

Information Processing Theory: posits that when exposed to a persuasive message, receivers compare their position on an issue with the position advocated by the source

injunctive normative beliefs: "subjective probabilities that particular referents prescribe or proscribe performance of a behavior" (Fishbein & Ajzen, 2010, p. 221)

Inoculation Theory: posits that small doses, or exposure, to a message can help people build immunity to the message and learn to resist being persuaded by such messages

instructional discussion: features in-depth conversations about the course content that provide participants opportunities to hone their communication skills and knowledge

Interpersonal Deception Theory: positions deception as an interaction process that entails strategic management of information, behavior, and image

intensity: the "quality of language which indicates the degree to which the speaker's attitude toward a concept deviates from neutrality" (Bowers, 1963, p. 345)

knowledge bias: refers to a receiver's belief that a communicator has a biased view of an issue

judgmental heuristics: mental shortcuts we use when making decisions

"just-one-more tactic": involves variations of the phrase "I just need one more person to help" and creates the impression that the compliance of the target is more valuable than others who have been approached

Language Expectancy Theory: stipulates that language is a rule-governed system, and individuals develop expectations and preferences for what is competent communication

legitimization of paltry contributions tactic: involves adding the phrase "Even a penny helps" to a direct message request, which activates the target's sense of social responsibility as well as feelings of duty and obligation

logical appeal: appeals based on evidence and reasoning

loss-framed messages: "convey the costs of not adopting the requested behavior" (Salovey et al., 2002, p. 392)

lowball tactic: the persuader seeks commitment to an initial offer, then follows with less favorable terms

message design logics: individuals hold different definitions of communication that manifest in a range of ways of constructing and consuming persuasive messages

meta-analysis: an analysis of other analyses, or a study of other studies

metatheoretical considerations: refers to the ontological, epistemological, and axiological concerns that underlie theory

metatheoretical perspectives: refers to the paradigms of post-positivism, interpretivism, and critical scholarship

metatheory: refers to a theory about a theory

misperceptions: "factual beliefs that are false or contradict the best available evidence in the public domain" (Flynn et al., 2017, p. 128)

MODE (Motivation and Opportunity as Determinants of Behavior) Model: stipulates that attitudes guide behavior through one of two processes—"a fairly spontaneous process based on the automatic activation of a relevant attitude or a more effortful, deliberative process involving careful consideration of the available information" (Schuette & Fazio, 1995, p. 704)

mood: a lasting or enduring state, ranging from positive to negative affect on a continuum

Motivated Reasoning Theory: stipulates that motivation affects reasoning through a series of biased cognitive processes

nasty effect: posits that those exposed to uncivil user comments online develop more negative perceptions of the media sources that house the comments

nonverbal immediacy: refers to communication behaviors that reduce the physical or psychological distance between communicators

nudges: involves shaping the choices or actions of persuasive targets

one-sided message: presents arguments in favor of the speaker's position on the issue

opinion leaders: individuals who possess the ability to informally influence the attitudes or behaviors of others

organizational patterns: strategic method of organizing a persuasive speech based on the types of claims advocated

outrage discourse: persuasive communication designed to "provoke visceral responses (e.g., anger, righteousness, fear, moral indignation) from the audience through the use of overgeneralizations, sensationalism, misleading or patently inaccurate information, ad hominem attacks, and partial truths about opponents" (Sobieraj & Berry, 2011, p. 20)

perceived behavioral control: encompasses the ability, or behavioral control, one perceives to have over one's behavior

peripheral route processing: attitude change results from simple inferences made about positive and negative cues attendant to the message

persuasive communication: the process of employing symbolic communication to create, alter, reinforce, or extinguish an audience's attitudes, values, beliefs, or behaviors in a given situation

persuasive public communication campaigns: involve intentional efforts to influence attitudes and behaviors in large audiences within a specific time frame using media messages in several channels with the intent of benefiting individuals and society

pique technique: persuades by arousing the receiver's curiosity and thus reducing the likelihood that the receiver will respond to the persuasive message with an automatic refusal or denial

polarization effects: the tendency to make extreme decisions when deliberating in groups

political engagement: includes direct participation in electoral politics, such as "voting, participating in campaigns or political parties, contacting elected officials, running for office, and the like" (Colby et al., 2007, p. 29)

political ideology: a set of assumptions, beliefs, principles, and values that outline how society should work

post-truth persuasion: characterized by "massive dissemination of blatant lies, new forms of propaganda and deception facilitated by the digital revolution, public opinion completely unsupported by facts, and publics uninterested in the fact-grounded truth and relatively impermeable to correction" (Waisbord, 2018, p. 19)

power: involves the use of different prosocial and/or antisocial bases of power to influence a target

power bases: includes reward, coercive, referent, legitimate, and expert power

powerless language: conveys a lack of certainty and control and is marked by the speech forms

principle of association: we like people and objects that are linked to positive things

principle of authority: people generally obey authorities and defer to the recommendations of experts

principle of consistency: the desire to be consistent with what we have said and done in the past

principle of liking: we are more prone to the persuasive attempts of people we like

principle of reciprocation: holds that "we should try to repay, in kind, what another person has provided us" (Cialdini, 2009, p. 19)

principle of scarcity: "opportunities seem more valuable to us when they are less available" (Cialdini, 2009, p. 200)

principle of social proof: we determine what is correct behavior by modeling the behavior of others

propaganda: control, manipulation, and perhaps even coercion that dehumanizes targets through a power imbalance between the propagandist and the audience

Psychological Reactance Theory: examines how messages that threaten perceived freedoms or choices can trigger boomerang effects that flaunt desired behavioral outcomes

qualifier: express the degree of certainty you have in the claims you advance

qualitative research: concerned with nonnumeric data, typically seeks to understand phenomena rather than predict and control

quantitative research: deals with numeric data and employs statistical tests, is concerned with explaining as much variance accounted for with statistical models as possible

random assignment: a technique used to randomly assign participants to the control or experimental groups

rate of adoption: the speed at which the adoption of an innovation spreads throughout a social system

reactance arousal: occurs when an individual perceives that their freedom and choice is threatened

reasoned action approach: extends the theory of planned behavior by dividing each of the constructs (attitude toward behavior, perceived norm, and perceived behavioral control) into two subcomponents

rebuttals: responses to arguments that run counter to your positions or claims

recognition involvement: refers to the degree to which individuals view a problem "as needing to be addressed and is based on perceived level of personal salience and involvement" with the problem (Hill & Thompson-Hayes, 2017, p. 113)

reporting bias: refers to the belief that the source is unwilling to report or disclose certain points of view on an issue

repulsion effect: occurs in group discussion when members who are outnumbered are driven further to their ideology and preferences

research methods: tools that scientists employ to answer research questions and hypotheses addressing particular topics of inquiry

S-curve: a visual depiction of how ideas or innovations take off and go viral

self-esteem: the degree of confidence an individual has in their own abilities

self-monitoring: refers to the fact that receivers of persuasive messages "differ in the extent to which they monitor (observe and control) their expressive behavior and self-presentation" (Synder, 1974, p. 536)

sequential persuasion: persuasive requests are sequenced in a specific order to gain the compliance of receivers

service learning: a "form of experiential education in which students engage in activities that address human and community needs together with structured opportunities intentionally designed to promote student learning and development" (Jacoby, 1996, p. 5)

silence: absence of oral and written language and sound

sleeper effect: a "delayed persuasive impact following a communication accompanied by a discounting cue (i.e., information indicating that the communication is untrustworthy)" (Greenwald et al., 1986, p. 217)

Social Impact Theory: posits that the work load imposed on individuals decreases as the size of the group increases

Social Judgment Theory: aims to predict the direction and extent of attitude changes based on the positionality of the persuasive message in relation to the target's current attitude

social loafing: the "reduction in motivation and effort when individuals work collectively compared with when they work individually or coactively" (Karau & Williams, 1993, p. 681)

social movement: entities that are organized, uninstitutionalized, large in scope, promote or oppose changes in societal norms and values, encounter opposition in a moral struggle, and rely primarily on persuasion to achieve goals

social validation: the notion that we can see that others have either supported or rejected an idea

specific purpose statement: focuses on one aspect of the topic you selected

speech rate: refers to the rate of speech that a speaker uses in their communication

statistical significance: refers to the claim that the result generated from analyzing data is not likely to occur randomly

Strength Model of Self-Control: posits that self-control is a finite resource and that acts of self-control result in short-term reductions in subsequent self-control in related and unrelated areas

strong attitudes: characterized by attributes like extremity, intensity, certainty, importance, and accessibility

subjective norm: the perception that those who are important to the individual in question wish, expect, or recommend the individual to either engage in or refrain from a specific behavior

subliminal priming: occurs at the subconscious level where receivers may perceive a message without being aware of it

sufficiency principle: individuals require sufficient information to change attitudes or behaviors, but no more or less

supporting material: materials like statistics, examples, and testimony that a persuasive speaker uses to support their claims

surveys: conducted to ask participants directly to report their perceptions

that's-not-all tactic: the persuader follows an initial offer by immediately sweetening the deal

theories: sensemaking devices that explain why phenomena occurs and how variables are related

Theory of Planned Behavior: "places the construct of self-efficacy belief or perceived behavioral control within a more general framework of the relations among beliefs, attitudes, intentions, and behavior" (Ajzen, 1991, p. 184)

Theory of Reasoned Action: posits that behavioral intentions lead to actual behaviors

thesis statement: provides a single sentence containing the main points that you will advance in your persuasive speech

Toulmin Argument Model: a model of argumentation containing claims, evidence, evidence credibility statements, warrants, qualifiers, and rebuttals

transaction costs: result from having to interact and collaborate with group members and include time spent scheduling and attending meetings, negotiating differences of opinion, managing conflict, and completing group work

trustworthiness: refers to the receiver's perception of the communicator's character, honesty, and sincerity

truth bias: individuals assume others are truthful, leaving them unable to detect deceptive communication

truth decay: a set of four related trends: (a) widespread disagreement about facts and interpretations of data, (b) a blurring of the distinction between fact and opinion, (c) the increasing persuasiveness of opinion over fact, and (d) declining trust in previously respected sources of information

Truth Default Theory: assumes that when "humans communicate with other humans, we tend to operate on a default presumption that what the other person says is basically honest" (Levine, 2014, p. 378)

two-sided message: presents arguments in favor of the speaker's position as well as counterarguments to the position

ultimate terms: connotative meanings that carry special persuasive power, as they are shared and recognized widely in society

Uses and Gratifications Theory: posits that the effects of exposure to political communication on voters depends on their needs and motivations

values: abstract goals that individuals use as guiding principles in their lives

variable: an element or feature that is likely to change

vividness: language that is "likely to attract and hold our attention and to excite the imagination to the extent that it is emotionally interesting, concrete and imagery-provoking, and proximate in a sensory, temporal, or spatial way" (Nisbett & Ross, 1980, p. 45)

volitional control: the perception that an individual has conscious control of their behaviors

warrant: provides the justification and reasoning to connect the evidence with the claim

References

Abramowitz, A. I., & Webster, S. W. (2018). Negative partisanship: Why Americans dislike parties but behave like rabid partisans. *Advances in Political Psychology, 39,* 119–135. https://doi.org/10.1111/pops.12479

Abril, P. S. (2016). Reimagining the group project of the business law classroom. *Journal of Legal Studies Education, 33*(2), 235–262. https://doi.org/10.1111/jlse.12047

Adaval, R., & Wyer, R. S. (1998). The role of narratives in consumer information processing. *Journal of Consumer Psychology, 7*(3), 207–245. https://doi.org/10.1207/s15327663jcp0703_01

Agrawal, N. (2015). Culture and persuasion. In S. Ng & A. Y. Lee (Eds.), *Handbook of culture and consumer behavior* (pp. 121–134). Oxford University Press.

Aguirre-Rodriguez, A. (2013). The effect of consumer persuasion knowledge on scarcity appeal effectiveness. *Journal of Advertising, 42*(4), 371–379. https://doi.org/10.1080/00913367.2013.803186

Ajzen, I. (1991). The theory of planned behavior. *Organizational Behavior and Human Decision Processes, 50,* 179–211. https://doi.org/10.1016/0749-5978(91)90020-t

Ajzen, I. (2001). Nature and operation of attitudes. *Annual Review of Psychology, 52*(1), 27–58. https://doi.org/10.1146/annurev.psych.52.1.27

Ajzen, I. (2002). Perceived behavioral control, self-efficacy, locus of control, and the theory of planned behavior. *Journal of Applied Social Psychology, 32,* 665–683. https://doi.org/10.1111/j.1559-1816.2002.tb00236.x

Ajzen, I. (2011). The theory of planned behaviour: Reactions and reflections. *Psychology and Health, 26,* 1113–1127. https://doi.org/10.1080/08870446.2011.613995

Ajzen, I. (2012). Martin Fishbein's legacy: The reasoned action approach. *The ANNALS of the American Academy of Political and Social Science, 640,* 11–27. https://doi.org/10.1177/0002716211423363

Ajzen, I., & Fishbein, M. (1977). Attitude-behavior relations: A theoretical analysis and review of empirical research. *Psychological Bulletin, 84*(5), 888–918. https://doi.org/10.1037//0033-2909.84.5.888

Ajzen, I., & Fishbein, M. (2004). Questions raised by a reasoned action approach: Comment on Ogden (2003). *Health Psychology, 23,* 431–434. https://doi.org/10.1037/0278-6133.23.4.431

Alam, N., & So, J. (2020). Contributions of emotional flow in narrative persuasion: An empirical test of the emotional flow framework. *Communication Quarterly, 68,* 161–182. https://doi.org/10.1080/01463373.2020.1725079

Alba-Juez, L., & Mackenzie, J. L. (2019). Emotion, lies, and "bullshit" in journalistic discourse: The case of fake news. *Ibérica, 38,* 17–50.

Albanese, R., & Van Fleet, D. D. (1985). Rational behavior in groups: The free-riding tendency. *The Academy of Management Review, 10*(2), 244–255. https://doi.org/10.5465/amr.1985.4278118

Albarracin, D., Johnson, B. T., Fishbein, M., & Muellerleile, P. A. (2001). Theories of reasoned action and planned behavior as models of condom use: A meta-analysis. *Psychological Bulletin, 127,* 142–161. https://doi.org/10.1037/0033-2909.127.1.142

Albarracín, D., Kumkale, G. T., & Poyner-Del Vento, P. (2017). How people can become persuaded by weak messages presented by credible communicators: Not all sleeper effects are created equal. *Journal of Experimental Social Psychology, 68,* 171–180. https://doi.org/10.1016/j.jesp.2016.06.009

Allen, M., & Stiff, J. B. (1989). Testing three models for the sleeper effect. *Western Journal of Speech Communication, 53,* 411–426. https://doi.org/10.1080/10570318909374318

Allen, M., Adamski, L., Bates, M., Bernhagen, M., Callendar, A., Casey, M., Czerwinski, A., Decker, L., Howard, G., Jordan, B., Kujawski, E., May, K., Olson, P., Parenteau, A., Reilly, S., Schmidt, J., Stebnitz, S., Thau, S., Tollefson, M., Zindler, D., & Zirbel, C. (2002). Effect of timing of communicator identification and level of source credibility on attitude. *Communication Research Reports, 19,* 46–55. https://doi.org/10.1080/08824090209384831

Allison, T. H., Davis, B. C., Webb, J. W., & Short, J. C. (2017). Persuasion in crowdfunding: An elaboration likelihood model of crowdfunding performance. *Journal of Business Venturing, 32,* 707–725. https://doi.org/10.1016/j.jbusvent.2017.09.002

Al-Sibai, N. (2018, October 4). Former CIA interrogator: I've never seen an interview subject as 'deceptive' as Brett Kavanaugh. *Raw Story.* https://www.rawstory.com/2018/10/former-cia-interrogator-ive-never-seen-interview-subject-deceptive-brett-kavanaugh/

Alves, H., Kock, A., Unkelbach, C. (2016). My friends are all alike—the relation between liking and perceived similarity in person perception. *Journal of Experimental Social Psychology, 62,* 103–117. https://doi.org/10.1016/j.jesp.2015.10.011

Amazeen, M., & Bucy, E. P. (2019). Conferring resistance to digital disinformation: The inoculating influence of procedural news knowledge. *Journal of Broadcasting & Electronic Media, 63,* 415–432. https://doi.org/10.1080/08838151.2019.1653101

Amichai-Hamburger, Y., Gazit, T., Bar-Ilan, J., Perez, O., Aharony, N., Bronstein, J., & Dyne, T. S. (2016). Psychological factors behind the lack of participation in online discussions. *Computers in Human Behavior, 55,* 268–277. https://doi.org/10.1016/j.chb.2015.09.009

Amos, C., & Spears, N. (2010). Generating a visceral response: The effects of visceral cues in weight loss advertising. *Journal of Advertising, 39*(3), 25–38. https://doi.org/10.2753/joa0091-3367390302

Ancu, M., & Cozma, R. (2009). MySpace politics: Uses and gratifications of befriending candidates. *Journal of Broadcasting & Electronic Media, 53*(4), 567–583. https://doi.org/10.1080/08838150903333064

Andersen, J. F., Andersen, P. A., & Jensen, A. D. (1979). The measurement of nonverbal immediacy. *Journal of Applied Communication Research, 7*(2), 153–180. https://doi.org/10.1080/00909887909365204

Andersen, P. A., & Blackburn, T. R. (2004). An experimental study of language intensity and response rate in e-mail surveys. *Communication Reports, 17,* 73–84. https://doi.org/10.1080/08934210409389377

Anderson, A. A., Yeo, S. K., Brossard, D., Scheufele, D. A., & Xenos, M. A. (2018). Toxic talk: How online incivility can undermine perceptions of media. *International Journal of Public Opinion Research, 30*(1), 156–168. https://doi.org/10.1093/ijpor/edw022

Anderson, S. (2017, Winter). Coercion. In E. N. Zalta (Ed.), *The Stanford encyclopedia of philosophy.* Center for the Study of Language and Information at Stanford University. https://plato.stanford.edu/archives/win2017/entries/coercion/

André, A., Deneuve, P., & Louvet, B. (2011). Cooperative learning in physical education and acceptance of students with learning disabilities. *Journal of Applied Sport Psychology, 23,* 474–485. https://doi.org/10.1080/10413200.2011.580826

Anker, A. E., Feeley, T. H., McCracken, B., & Lagoe, C. A. (2016). Measuring the effectiveness of mass-mediated health campaigns through meta-analysis. *Journal of Health Communication, 21,* 439–456. https://doi.org/10.1080/10810730.2015.1095820

Antonetti, P., & Baines, P. (2015). Guilt in marketing research: An elicitation-consumption perspective and research agenda. *International Journal of Management Reviews, 17,* 333–355. https://doi.org/10.1111/ijmr.12043

Antonetti, P., Baines, P., & Jain, S. (2018). The persuasiveness of guilt appeals over time: Pathways to delayed compliance. *Journal of Business Research, 90,* 14–25. https://doi.org/10.1016/j.jbusres.2018.03.030

Arendt, C., LaFleche, M., & Limperopulos, M. A. (2017). A qualitative meta-analysis of apologia, image repair, and crisis communication: Implications for theory and practice. *Public Relations Review, 43,* 517–526. https://doi.org/10.1016/j.pubrev.2017.03.005

Areni, C. S. (2003). The effects of structural and grammatical variables on persuasion: An elaboration likelihood model perspective. *Psychology & Marketing, 20*(4), 349–375. https://doi.org/10.1002/mar.10077

Areni, C. S., & Sparks, J. R. (2005). Language power and persuasion. *Psychology & Marketing, 22*(6), 507–525. https://doi.org/10.1002/mar.20071

Aristotle. (1960). *The rhetoric of Aristotle* (L. Cooper, Trans.). Appleton-Century-Crofts. (Original translation published 1932)

Armitage, C. J. (2015). Time to retire the theory of planned behaviour? A commentary on Sniehotta, Presseau, and Araújo-Soares. *Health Psychology Review, 9,* 151–155. https://doi.org/10.1080/17437199.2014.892148

Armitage, C. J., & Conner, M. (2001). Efficacy of the theory of planned behaviour: A meta-analytic review. *British Journal of Social Psychology, 40,* 471–499. https://doi.org/10.1348/014466601164939

Arnett, R. C., Arneson, P., & Bell, L. M. (2006). Communication ethics: The dialogic turn. *The Review of Communication, 6*(1–2), 62–92. https://doi.org/10.1080/15358590600763334

Asada, A., & Ko, Y. J. (2019). Perceived influence of word-of-mouth recommendation on sport-watching behavior: A gender difference perspective. *Sport Marketing Quarterly, 28*, 135–147. https://doi.org/10.32731/smq.283.092019.02

Asemah, E. S., & Nwammuo, A. N. (2017). Implications of social judgement theory for persuasive advertising campaigns. *Journal of Research in National Development, 15*, 75–82. www.ajol.info/journals/jorind

Atkin, R. E., & Rice, C. K. (2013). Theory and principles of public communication campaigns. In R. E. Atkin & C. K. Rice (Eds.), *Public communication campaigns* (4th ed., pp. 3–19). SAGE.

Aune, R. K., & Kikuchi, T. (1993). Effects of language intensity similarity on perceptions of credibility, relational attributions, and persuasion. *Journal of Language and Social Psychology, 12*(3), 224–237. https://doi.org/10.1177/0261927x93123004

Avery, E. J., & Park, S. (2018). HPV vaccination campaign fear visuals: An eye-tracking study exploring effects of visual attention and type on message information value, recall, and behavioral intentions. *Public Relations Review, 44*, 321–330. https://doi.org/10.1016/j.pubrev.2018.02.005

Ayeh, J. K. (2015). Travelers' acceptance of consumer-generated media: An integrated model of technology acceptance and source credibility theories. *Computers in Human Behavior, 48*, 173–180. https://doi.org/10.1016/j.chb.2014.12.049

Backer, T. E., & Rogers, E. M. (1998). Diffusion of innovations theory and work-site AIDS programs. *Journal of Health Communication, 3*, 17–28. https://doi.org/10.1080/108107398127481

Bail, C. A., Argyle, L. P., Brown, T. W., Bumpus, J. P., Chen, H., Fallin Hunzaker, M. B., Lee, J., Mann, M., Merhout, F., & Volfovsky, A. (2018). Exposure to opposing views on social media can increase political polarization. *Proceedings of the National Academy of Sciences, 00*, 1–6. https://doi.org/10.1073/pnas.1804840115

Baker, L. A., Meyer, K. R., & Hunt, S. K. (2005). First-year students' perception of power and use of persuasive techniques: A comparison of learning community versus traditional classes. *Journal of the First-Year Experience and Students in Transition, 17*(2), 23–48. http://fyesit.metapress.com/content/mum2301651698606/

Baker, S., & Martinson, D. L. (2001). The TARES test: Five principles for ethical persuasion. *Journal of Mass Media Ethics, 16*(2–3), 148–175. https://doi.org/10.1080/08900523.2001.9679610

Bakir, V., & McStay, A. (2018). Fake news and the economy of emotions. *Digital Journalism, 6*(2), 154–175. https://doi.org/10.1080/21670811.2017.1345645

Ball, J. (2015, February 3). Facing the truth about climate change. *The New Republic*. https://newrepublic.com/article/120914/how-congress-can-compromise-climate-change-legislation

Banas, J. A., & Miller, G. (2013). Inducing resistance to conspiracy theory progaganda: Testing inoculation and metainoculation strategies. *Human Communication Research, 39*, 184–207. https://doi.org/10.1111/hcre.12000

Banas, J. A., & Rains, S. A. (2010). A meta-analysis of research on inoculation theory. *Communication Monographs, 77*, 281–311. https://doi.org/10.1080/03637751003758193

Banas, J. A., & Richards, A. S. (2017). Apprehension or motivation to defend attitudes? Exploring the underlying threat mechanism in inoculation-induced resistance to persuasion. *Communication Monographs, 84*, 164–178. https://doi.org/10.1080/03637751.2017.1307999

Banas, J., Turner, M. M., & Shulman, H. (2012). A test of competing hypotheses of the effects of mood on persuasion. *Communication Quarterly, 60*, 143–164. https://doi.org/10.1080/01463373.2012.668845

Barbour, J. B., Jacocks, C. W., & Wesner, K. J. (2013). The message design logics of organizational change. *Communication Monographs, 80*, 354–378. https://doi.org/10.1080/03637751.2013.78825

Barton, M. H., & Stein, K. A. (2017). Diabetes, patient care and compliance: The role of message design in doctor-patient interactions. *The Pennsylvania Communication Annual, 73*, 11–26.

Basil, D. Z., Ridgway, N. M., & Basil, M. D. (2006). Guilt appeals: The mediating effect of responsibility. *Psychology & Marketing, 23*(12), 1035–1054. https://doi.org/10.1002/mar.20145

Baumeister, R. F., Vohs, K. D., & Tice, D. M. (2007). The strength model of self-control. *Current Directions in Psychological Science, 16*, 351–355. https://doi.org/10.1111/j.1467-8721.2007.00534.x

Beard, F. K. (2005). One hundred years of humor in American advertising. *Journal of Macromarketing, 25*(1), 54–65. https://doi.org/10.1177/0276146705274965

Beattie, G. W., & Shovelton, H. K. (2006). When size really matters: How a single semantic feature is represented in the speech and gesture modalities. *Gesture, 6*, 63–84. https://doi.org/10.1075/gest.6.1.04bea

Beaumont, E., Colby, A., Ehrlich, T., & Torney-Purta, J. (2006). Promoting political competence and engagement in college students: An empirical study. *Journal of Political Science Education, 2*, 249–270. https://doi.org/10.1080/15512160600840467

Beck, L., & Ajzen, I. (1991). Predicting dishonest actions using the theory of planned behavior. *Journal of Research in Personality, 25*, 285–301. https://doi.org/10.1016/0092-6566(91)90021-h

Becker, A. B. (2014). Playing with politics: Online political parody, affinity for political humor, anxiety reduction, and implications for political efficacy. *Mass Communication and Society, 17*, 424–445. https://doi.org/10.1080/15205436.2014.891134

Bègue, L., Beauvois, J. L., Courbet, D., Oberlé, D., Lepage, J., & Duke, A. A. (2015). Personality predicts obedience in a Milgram paradigm. *Journal of Personality, 83*, 299–306. https://doi.org/10.1111/jopy.12104

Bellezza, S., Paharia, N., & Keinan, A. (2017). Conspicuous consumption of time: When busyness and lack of leisure time become a status symbol. *Journal of Consumer Research, 44*, 118–138. https://doi.org/10.1093/jcr/ucw076

Bellou, V., & Gkorezis, P. (2016). Unveiling the link between facets of positive nonverbal communication and perceived leader effectiveness: A moderated mediation model. *Human Performance, 29*(4), 310–330. https://doi.org/10.1080/08959285.2016.1157597

Bem, D. J. (1967). Self-perception: An alternative interpretation of cognitive dissonance phenomena. *Psychological Review, 74*(3), 183–200. https://doi.org/10.1037/h0024835

Bench-Capon, T. J. M. (2003). Persuasion in practical argument using value-based argumentation frameworks. *Journal of Logic and Computation, 13*, 429–448. https://doi.org/10.1093/logcom/13.3.429

Benoit, W. L. (1998). Forewarning and persuasion. In M. Allen & R. Preiss (Eds.), *Persuasion: Advances through meta-analysis* (pp. 159–184). Hampton.

Benoit, W. L. (2014). A functional analysis of 2008 and 2012 presidential nomination acceptance addresses. *Speaker & Gavel, 51*(1), 50–59.

Benoit, W. L. (2015). *Accounts, excuses, apologies: Image repair theory and research* (2nd ed.). State University of New York Press.

Benoit, W. L. (2016). Effects of image repair strategies. In J. R. Blaney (Ed.), *Putting image repair to the test: Quantitative applications of image restoration theory* (pp. 16–37). Lexington.

Benoit, W. L. (2017). The functional theory of political campaign discourse. In R. E. Denton (Ed.), *Political campaign communication: Theory, method, and practice* (pp. 3–32). Lexington.

Benoit, W. L. (2019). A functional analysis of visual and verbal symbols in presidential campaign posters, 1828–2012. *Presidential Studies Quarterly, 49*(1), 4–22. https://doi.org/10.1111/psq.12503

Benoit, W. L., & Compton, J. L. (2014). A functional analysis of 2012 presidential primary TV spots. *American Behavioral Scientist, 58*(4), 497–509. https://doi.org/10.1177/0002764213506209

Benoit, W. L., & Harthcock, A. (1999). Functions of the great debates: Acclaims, attacks, and defenses in the 1960 presidential debates. *Communication Monographs, 66*, 341–357. https://doi.org/10.1080/03637759909376484

Benoit, W. L., Blaney, J. R., & Pier, P. M. (2000). Acclaiming, attacking, and defending: A functional analysis of U.S. nominating convention keynote speeches. *Political Communication, 17*, 61–84. https://doi.org/10.1080/105846000198512

Berger, I. E., & Mitchell, A. A. (1989). The effect of advertising on attitude accessibility, attitude confidence, and the attitude-behavior relationship. *Journal of Consumer Research, 16*, 269–279. https://doi.org/10.1086/209213

Berlo, D. K., Lemert, J. B., & Mertz, R. J. (1969). Dimensions for evaluating the acceptability of message sources. *Public Opinion Quarterly, 33*, 563–576. https://doi.org/10.1086/267745

Bernieri, F. J., & Petty, K. N. (2011). The influence of handshakes on first impression accuracy. *Social Influence, 6*(2), 78–87. https://doi.org/10.1080/15534510.2011.566706

Biddix, J. P., Chung, C. J., & Park, H. W. (2011). Convenience or credibility? A study of college student online research behaviors. *Internet and Higher Education, 14*, 175–182. https://doi.org/10.1016/j.iheduc.2011.01.003

Biernat, M. (1990). Stereotypes on campus: How contact and liking influence perceptions of group distinctiveness. *Journal of Applied Social Psychology, 20*, 1485–1513. https://doi.org/10.1111/j.1559-1816.1990.tb01489.x

Black, J. (2001). Semantics and ethics of propaganda. *Journal of Mass Media Ethics, 16*(2–3), 121–137. https://doi.org/10.1080/08900523.2001.9679608

Black, L. W. (2008). Deliberation, storytelling, and dialogic moments. *Communication Theory, 18*, 93–116. https://doi.org/10.1111/j.1468-2885.2007.00315.x

Blair, J. P., Reimer, T. O., & Levine, T. R. (2018). The role of consistency in detecting deception: The superiority of correspondence over coherence. *Communication Studies, 69*, 483–498. https://doi.org/10.1080/10510974.2018.1447492

Blanchard, S. J., Carlson, K. A., & Hyodo, J. D. (2016). The favor request effect: Requesting a favor from consumers to seal the deal. *Journal of Consumer Research, 42*, 985–1001. https://doi.org/10.1093/jcr/ucw005

Blankenship, K. L., & Craig, T. Y. (2007a). Powerless language markers and the correspondence bias: Attitude confidence mediates the effects of tag questions on attitude attributions. *Journal of Language and Social Psychology, 26*(1), 28–47. https://doi.org/10.1177/0261927x06296470

Blankenship, K. L., & Craig, T. Y. (2007b). Language and persuasion: Tag questions as powerless speech or as interpreted in context. *Journal of Experimental Social Psychology, 43*, 112–118. https://doi.org/10.1016/j.jesp.2005.12.012

Bless, H., Bohner, G., Schwarz, N., & Strack, F. (1990). Mood and persuasion: A cognitive response analysis. *Personality and Social Psychology Bulletin, 16*, 331–345. https://doi.org/10.1177/0146167290162013

Bligh, M. C., & Kohles, J. C. (2009). The enduring allure of charisma: How Barack Obama won the historic 2008 presidential election. *The Leadership Quarterly, 20*, 483–492. https://doi.org/10.1016/j.leaqua.2009.03.013

Blondé, J., & Girandola, F. (2016). Revealing the elusive effects of vividness: A meta-analysis of empirical evidences assessing the effect of vividness on persuasion. *Social Influence, 11*(2), 111–129. https://doi.org/10.1080/15534510.2016.1157096

Blondé, J., & Girandola, F. (2016). Revealing the elusive effects of vividness: A meta-analysis of empirical evidences assessing the effect of vividness on persuasion. *Social Influence, 11*(2), 111–129. https://doi.org/10.1080/15534510.2016.1157096

Blondé, J., & Girandola, F. (2018). Are vivid (vs. pallid) threats persuasive? Examining the effects of threat vividness in health communications. *Basic and Applied Social Psychology, 40*(1), 36–48. https://doi.org/10.1080/01973533.2017.1412969

Blumler, J. G., & McQuail, D. (1969). *Television in politics: Its uses and influence*. University of Chicago Press.

Bode, L., & Vraga, E. K. (2015). In related news, that was wrong: The correction of misinformation through related stories functionality in social media. *Journal of Communication, 65*, 619–638. https://doi.org/10.1111/jcom.12166

Bodenhausen, G. V., Sheppard, L. A., & Kramer, G. P. (1994). Negative affect and social judgment: The differential impact of anger and sadness. *European Journal of Social Psychology, 24*, 45–62. https://doi.org/10.1002/ejsp.2420240104

Bøggild, T., Aarøe, L., & Petersen, M. B. (2020, September). Citizens as complicits: Distrust in politicians and biased social dissemination of political information. *American Political Science Review*, 1–17. https://doi.org/10.1017/s0003055420000805

Bohner, G., Crow, K., Erb, H.-P., & Schwarz, N. (1992). Affect and persuasion: mood effects on the processing of message content and context cues and on subsequent behaviour. *European Journal of Social Psychology, 22*, 511–530. https://doi.org/10.1002/ejsp.2420220602

Bohner, G., Ruder, M., & Erb, H. P. (2002). When expertise backfires: Contrast and assimilation effects in persuasion. *British Journal of Social Psychology, 41*, 495–519. https://doi.org/10.1348/014466602321149858

Bolkan, S., & Rains, S. A. (2017). The legitimization of paltry contributions as a compliance-gaining technique: A meta-analysis testing three explanations. *Communication Research, 44*(7), 976–996. https://doi.org/10.1177/0093650215602308

Bond, C. F., & DePaulo, B. M. (2006). Accuracy of deception judgments. *Personality and Social Psychology Review, 10*(3), 214–234. https://doi.org/10.1207/s15327957pspr1003_2

Bonetto, E., Troian, J., Varet, F., Lo Monaco, G., & Girandola, F. (2018). Priming resistance to persuasion decreases adherence to conspiracy theories. *Social Influence, 13*(3), 125–136. https://doi.org/10.1080/15534510.2018.1471415

Borah, P. (2016). Political Facebook use: Campaign strategies used in 2008 and 2012 presidential elections. *Journal of Information Technology & Politics, 13*(4), 326–338. https://doi.org/10.1080/19331681.2016.1163519

Boren, J. P., & McPherson, M. B. (2018). Is coming out in the classroom still an occupational hazard? A replication of Russ, Simonds, and Hunt (2002). *Communication Studies, 69*, 242–250. https://doi.org/10.1080/10510974.2018.1466719

Boster, F. J., & Stiff, J. B. (1984). Compliance gaining message selection behavior. *Human Communication Research, 10*, 539–556. https://doi.org/10.1111/j.1468-2958.1984.tb00031.x

Boster, F. J., Shaw, A. S., Hughes, M., Kotowski, M. R., Strom, R. E., & Deatrick, L. M. (2009). Dump-and-chase: The effectiveness of persistence as a sequential request compliance-gaining strategy. *Communication Studies, 60*(3), 219–234. https://doi.org/10.1080/10510970902955976

Bouder, S. (2013, January). Critical components for public awareness campaigns. *Advocacy Unleashed*. https://advocacyunleashed.kontribune.com/articles/1371

Boudewyns, U., Turner, M. M., & Paquin, R. S. (2013). Shame-free guilt appeals: Testing the emotional and cognitive effects of shame and guilt appeals. *Psychology and Marketing, 30*(9), 811–825. https://doi.org/10.1002/mar.20647

Boudry, M., & Braeckman, J. (2012). How convenient! The epistemic rationale of self-validating belief systems. *Philosophical Psychology, 25*(3), 341–364. https://doi.org/10.1080/09515089.2011.579420

Bowers, J. W. (1963). Language intensity, social introversion, and attitude change. *Speech Monographs, 30*, 345–352. https://doi.org/10.1080/03637756309375380

Boyte, H. C. (2009). *Civic agency and the cult of the expert*. Kettering Foundation.

Brader, T. (2005). Striking a responsive chord: How political ads motivate and persuade voters by appealing to emotions. *American Journal of Political Science, 49*, 388–405. https://doi.org/10.1111/j.0092-5853.2005.00130.x

Bratslavsky, L., Carpenter, N., & Zompetti, J. (2019). Twitter, incivility, and presidential communication: A theoretical incursion into spectacle and power. *Cultural Studies*, 1–32. https://www.tandfonline.com/doi/full/10.1080/09502386.2019.1656760

Brehm, J. W. (1956). Postdecision changes in the desirability of alternatives. *Journal of Abnormal and Social Psychology, 52*, 384–389. https://doi.org/10.1037/h0041006

Brehm, J. W. (1966). *A theory of psychological reactance*. Academic Press.

Brehm, J. W. (1989). Psychological reactance: Theory and applications. *Advances in Consumer Research, 16*, 72–75.

Brehm, S. S., & Brehm, J. W. (1981). *Psychological reactance: A theory of freedom and control*. Academic Press.

Brooks, C. M., & Ammons, J. L. (2003). Free riding in group projects and the effects of timing, frequency, and specificity of criteria in peer assessments. *Journal of Education for Business, 78*(5), 268–272. https://doi.org/10.1080/08832320309598613

Broussard, K. A., & Harton, H. C. (2018). Tattoo or taboo? Tattoo stigma and negative attitudes toward tattooed individuals. *The Journal of Social Psychology, 158*(5), 521–540. https://doi.org/10.1080/00224545.2017.1373622

Brown, A. (2017). *5 key findings about LGBT Americans. Pew Research Center.* http://www.pewresearch.org/fact-tank/2017/06/13/5-key-findings-about-lgbt-americans/

Brown, P., & Levinson, S. C. (1987). *Politeness: Some universals in language usage*. Cambridge University.

Bruchmann, K., Koopmann-Holm, B., & Scherer, A. (2018). Seeing beyond political affiliations: The mediating role of perceived moral foundations on the partisan similarity-liking effect. *PLoS ONE, 13*(8), e0202101. https://doi.org/10.1371/journal.pone.0202101

Buchs, C., Gilles, I., Dutrévis, M., & Butera, F. (2011). Pressure to cooperate: Is positive reward interdependence really needed in cooperative learning? *British Journal of Educational Psychology, 81*, 135–146.

Buller, D. B., & Burgoon, J. K. (1996). Interpersonal deception theory. *Communication Theory, 6*, 203–243. https://doi.org/10.1111/j.1468-2885.1996.tb00132.x

Buller, D. B., LePoire, B. A., Aune, R. K., & Eloy, S. V. (1992). Social perceptions as mediators of the effect of speech rate similarity on compliance. *Human Communication Research, 19*, 286–311. https://doi.org/10.1111/j.1468-2958.1992.tb00303.x

Burger, J. M., Hornisher, J., Martin, V. E., Newman, G., & Pringle, S. (2007). The pique technique: Overcoming mindlessness or shifting heuristics? *Journal of Applied Social Psychology, 37,* 2086–2096. https://doi.org/10.1111/j.1559-1816.2007.00252.x

Burger, J. M., Messian, N., Patel, S., del Prado, A., & Anderson, C. (2004). What a coincidence! The effects of incidental similarity on compliance. *Personality and Social Psychology Bulletin, 30,* 35–43. https://doi.org/10.1177/0146167203258838

Burgoon, J. K. (2009). Interpersonal deception theory. In S. W. Littlejohn & K. A. Foss (Eds.), *Encyclopedia of communication theory* (pp. 552–554). SAGE.

Burgoon, J. K., & Bacue, A. E. (2003). Nonverbal communication skills. In J. O. Greene & B. R. Burleson (Eds.), *Handbook of communication and social interaction skills* (pp. 179–219). Erlbaum.

Burgoon, J. K., Birk, T., & Pfau, M. (1990). Nonverbal behaviors, persuasion, and credibility. *Human Communication Research, 17*(1), 140–169. https://doi.org/10.1111/j.1468-2958.1990.tb00229.x

Burgoon, M., Denning, V. P., & Roberts, L. (2002). Language expectancy theory. In J. P. Dillard, & M. Pfau (Eds.), *The persuasion handbook: Developments in theory and practice* (pp. 117–136). SAGE.

Burnell, P., & Reeve, A. (1984). Persuasion as a political concept. *British Journal of Political Science, 14,* 393–410. https://doi.org/10.1017/s0007123400003690

Burrell, N. A., & Koper, R. J. (1998). The efficacy of powerful/powerless language on attitudes and source credibility. In M. Allen & R. W. Preiss (Eds.), *Persuasion: Advances through meta-analysis* (pp. 203–215). Hampton.

Bustin, G. M., Jones, D. N., Hansenne, M., & Quoidbach, J. (2015). Who does Red Bull give wings to? Sensation seeking moderates sensitivity to subliminal advertisement. *Frontiers in Psychology, 6,* article 825. https://doi.org/10.3389/fpsyg.2015.00825

Cacioppo, J. T., Petty, R. E., & Quintanar, L. R. (1982). Individual differences in relative hemispheric alpha abundance and cognitive responses to persuasive communications. *Journal of Personality and Social Psychology, 43,* 623–636. https://doi.org/10.1037/0022-3514.43.3.623

Cai, D. A., & Wilson, S. R. (2000). Identity implications of influence goals: A cross-cultural comparison of interaction goals and facework. *Communication Studies, 51,* 307–328. https://doi.org/10.1080/10510970009388529

Cameron, K. A., Campo, S., & Brossard, D. (2003). Advocating for controversial issues: The effect of activism on compliance-gaining strategy likelihood of use. *Communication Studies, 54*(3), 265–281. https://doi.org/10.1080/10510970309363286

Cantarero, K., Gamian-Wilk, M., & Dolinski, D. (2017). Being inconsistent and compliant: The moderating role of the preference for consistency in the door-in-the-face technique. *Personality and Individual Differences, 115,* 54–57. https://doi.org/10.1016/j.paid.2016.07.005

Carcioppolo, N., Dunleavy, V. O., & Yang, Q. (2017). How do perceived descriptive norms influence indoor tanning intentions? An application of the theory of normative social behavior. *Health Communication, 32,* 230–239. https://doi.org/10.1080/10410236.2015.1120697

Carli, L. L., LaFluer, S. J., & Loeber, C. C. (1995). Nonverbal behavior, gender, and influence. *Journal of Personality and Social Psychology, 68,* 1030–1041. https://doi.org/10.1037/0022-3514.68.6.1030

Carpenter, C. J. (2012). A meta-analysis and experiment investigating the effects of speaker disfluency on persuasion. *Western Journal of Communication, 76,* 552–569. https://doi.org/10.1080/10570314.2012.662307

Carpenter, C. J. (2012a). A meta-analysis and an experiment investigating the effects of speaker disfluency on persuasion. *Western Journal of Communication, 76,* 552–569. https://doi.org/10.1080/10570314.2012.662307

Carpenter, C. J. (2012b). A meta-analysis of the functional matching effect based on functional attitude theory. *Southern Communication Journal, 77,* 438–451. https://doi.org/10.31235/osf.io/jqvhn

Carpenter, C. J. (2013). A meta-analysis of the effectiveness of the "but you are free" compliance-gaining technique. *Communication Studies, 64*(1), 6–17. https://doi.org/10.1080/10510974.2012.727941

Carpenter, C. J. (2014). Making compliance seem more important: The "just-one-more" technique of gaining compliance. *Communication Research Reports, 31*(2), 163–170. https://doi.org/10.1080/08824096.2014.907144

Carpenter, C. J. (2015). A meta-analysis of the ELM's argument quality x processing type predictions. *Human Communication Research, 41,* 501–534. https://doi.org/10.1111/hcre.12054

Carpenter, C. J., & Averbeck, J. M. (2020). What do superdiffusers do when they want to persuade someone about politics on Facebook? *Communication Quarterly, 68*, 54–72. https://doi.org/10.1080/01463373.2019.1671886

Carpenter, C. J., & Pascual, A. (2016). Testing the reactance vs. The reciprocity of politeness explanations for the effectiveness of the "but you are free" compliance-gaining technique. *Social Influence, 11*(2), 101–110. https://doi.org/10.1080/15534510.2016.1156569

Carty, V., & Reynoso Barron, F. G. (2019). Social movements and new technology: The dynamics of cyber activism in the digital age. In B. Berberoglo (Ed.), *The Palgrave handbook of social movements, revolutions, and social transformation* (pp. 373–397). Palgrave MacMillian.

Catalyst. (2007). *The double-bind dilemma for women in leadership: Damned if you do, doomed if you don't.* https://www.catalyst.org/wp-content/uploads/2019/01/The_Double_Bind_Dilemma_for_Women_in_Leadership_Damned_if_You_Do_Doomed_if_You_Dont.pdf

Cavazza, N. (2016). When political candidates "go positive": The effects of flattering the rival in political communication. *Social Influence, 11*, 166–176. https://doi.org/10.1080/15534510.2016.1206962

Cavazza, N., & Guidetti, M. (2018). *Captatio benevolentiae*: Potential risks and benefits of flattering the audience in a public political speech. *Journal of Language and Social Psychology, 37*, 706–720. https://doi.org/10.1177/0261927x18800132

Cerejo, L. (2018, June 5). The ethics of persuasion. *Smashing Magazine.* https://www.smashingmagazine.com/2018/06/ethics-of-persuasion/

Cervi, L., & Andrade, A. C. (2019). Post-truth and disinformation: Using discourse analysis to understand the creation of emotional and rival narratives in Brexit. *Revista ComHumanities, 10*(2), 125–149.

Cesario, J., & Higgins, E. T. (2008). Making message recipients "feel right": How nonverbal cues can increase persuasion. *Psychological Science, 19*, 415–420. https://doi.org/10.1111/j.1467-9280.2008.02102.x

Chaiken, S., & Maheswaran, D. (1994). Heuristic processing can bias systematic processing: Effects of source credibility, argument ambiguity, and task importance on attitude judgment. *Journal of Personality and Social Psychology, 66*, 460–473. https://doi.org/10.1037/0022-3514.66.3.460

Chang, C. (2008). Chronological age versus cognitive age for younger consumers: Implication for advertising persuasion. *Journal of Advertising, 37*(3), 19–32. https://doi:org/10.2753/joa0091-3367370302

Chang, C. T. (2011). Guilt appeals in cause-related marketing: The subversive roles of product type and donation magnitude. *International Journal of Advertising, 30*(4), 587–616. https://doi.org/10.2501/ija-30-4-587-616

Chang, M. K. (1998). Predicting unethical behavior: A comparison of the theory of reasoned action and the theory of planned behavior. *Journal of Business Ethics, 17*, 1825–1834. https://doi.org/10.1023/A:1005721401993

Chebat, J. C., Hedhli, K. E., Gélinas-Chebat, C., & Boivin, R. (2007). Voice and persuasion in a banking telemarketing context. *Perceptual and Motor Skills, 104*, 419–437. https://doi.org/10.2466/pms.104.2.419-437

Chen, F. S., Minson, J. A., Schöne, M., & Heinrichs, M. (2013). In the eye of the beholder: Eye contact increases resistance to persuasion. *Psychological Science, 24*(11), 2254–2261. https://doi.org/10.1177/0956797613491968

Chen, G. M., Murray, C., Newton, E., Gillmor, D., Roschke, K., & Stroud, N. (2018, November 19). How the public, news sources, and journalists think about the news in three communities. *News Co/Lab.* https://newscollab.org/wp-content/uploads/2018/11/How-the-Public_News-Sources_and-Journalists.pdf

Chen, H. C., Reardon, R., Rea, C., & Moore, D. J. (1992). Forewarning of content and involvement: Consequences for persuasion and resistance to persuasion. *Journal of Experimental Social Psychology, 28*, 523–541. https://doi.org/10.1016/0022-1031(92)90044-k

Chidambaram, V., Chiang, Y-H., & Mutlu, B. (2012). Designing persuasive robots: How robots might persuade people using vocal and nonverbal cues. *Proceedings of the seventh annual ACM/IEEE international conference on human-robot interaction.* https://doi.org/10.1145/2157689.2157798

Christophel, D. M. (1990). The relationships among teacher immediacy behaviors, student motivation, and learning. *Communication Education, 39*(4), 323–340. https://doi.org/10.1080/03634529009378813

Cialdini, R. B. (2001). Harnessing the science of persuasion. *Harvard Business Review, 284*(2), 72–79. https://doi.org/10.1038/scientificamerican0201-76

Cialdini, R. B. (2009). *Influence: Science and practice* (5th ed.). Pearson.

Cialdini, R. B., & Goldstein, N. J. (2004). Social influence: Compliance and conformity. *Annual Review of Psychology, 55*, 591–621. https://doi.org/10.1146/annurev.psych.55.090902.142015

Cialdini, R. B., Wosinska, W., Barrett, D. W., Butner, J., & Gornik-Durose, M. (1999). Compliance with a request in two cultures: The differential influence of social proof and commitment/consistency on collectivists and individualists. *Personality and Social Psychology Bulletin, 25,* 1242–1253. https://doi.org/10.1177/0146167299258006

Clark, J. K., & Evans, A. T. (2014). Source credibility and persuasion: The role of message position in self-validation. *Personality and Social Psychology Bulletin, 40*(8), 1024–1036. https://doi.org/10.1037/e527772014-350

Clark, J. K., & Wegener, D. T. (2013). Message position, information processing, and persuasion: The discrepancy motives model. *Advances in Experimental Social Psychology, 47,* 189–232. https://doi.org/10.1016/b978-0-12-407236-7.00004-8

Clarke, J. S., Cornelissen, J. P., & Healey, M. P. (2019). Actions speak louder than words: How figurative language and gesturing in entrepreneurial pitches influences investment judgments. *Academy of Management Journal, 62*, 335–360. https://doi.org/10.5465/amj.2016.1008

Clayton, K., Blair, S., Busam, J. A., Forstner, S., Glance, J., Green, G., Kawata, A., Kovvuri, A., Martin, J., Morgan, E., Sandhu, M., Sang, R., Scholz-Bright, R., Welch, A. T., Wolff, A. G, Zhou, A., & Nyhan, B. (2020). Real solutions for fake news? Measuring the effectiveness of general warnings and fact-check tags in reducing belief in false stories on social media. *Political Behavior, 42,* 1073–1095. https://doi.org/10.1007/s11109-019-09533-0

Clementson, D. E. (2018). Susceptibility to deception in a political news interview: Effects of identification, perceived cooperativeness, and ingroup vulnerability. *Communication Studies, 69,* 522–544. https://doi.org/10.1080/10510974.2018.1454486

Clementson, D. E., Pascual-Ferrá, P., & Beatty, M. J. (2016). When does a presidential candidate seem presidential and trustworthy? Campaign messages through the lens of language expectancy theory. *Presidential Studies Quarterly, 46*(3), 592–617. https://doi.org/10.1111/psq.12299

Clore, G. L., & Huntsinger, J. R. (2007). How emotions inform judgment and regulate thought. *Trends in Cognitive Sciences, 11*, 393–399. https://doi.org/10.1016/j.tics.2007.08.005

Clyne, L., Fellers, M., & Richards, A. S. (2020). Metacognitive inoculation reduces the persuasiveness of sarcastic attack messages. *Communication Reports, 33*, 68–81. https://doi.org/10.1080/08934215.2020.1755876

Cobb, M. D., Nyhan, B., & Reifler, J. (2013). Beliefs don't always persevere: How political figures are punished when positive information about them is discredited. *Political Psychology, 34*(4), 307–326. https://doi.org/10.1111/j.1467-9221.2012.00935.x

Cody, M. J., McLaughlin, M. L., & Jordan, W. J. (1980). A multidimensional scaling of three sets of compliance-gaining strategies. *Communication Quarterly, 28*, 34–46. https://doi.org/10.1080/01463378009369373

Cody, M. J., Woelfel, M. L., & Jordan, W. J. (1983). Dimensions of compliance-gaining situations. *Human Communication Research, 9,* 99–113. https://doi.org/10.1111/j.1468-2958.1983.tb00686.x

Coffman, J. (2002). *Public communication campaign evaluation: An environmental scan of challenges, criticisms, practice, and opportunities.* Harvard Family Research Project.

Cohen, G. L. (2003). Party over policy: The dominating impact of group influence on political beliefs. *Journal of Personality and Social Psychology, 85,* 808–822. https://doi.org/10.1037/0022-3514.85.5.808

Colbert, K. R. (1993). The effects of debate participation on argumentativeness and verbal aggression. *Communication Education, 42*, 206–214. https://doi.org/10.1080/03634529309378928

Colby, A., Beaumont, E., Ehrlich, T., & Corngold, J. (2007). *Educating for democracy: Preparing undergraduates for responsible political engagement.* Jossey-Bass.

Colby, A., Beaumont, E., Ehrlich, T., & Stephens, J. (2003). *Educating citizens: Preparing America's undergraduates for lives of moral and civic responsibility.* Jossey-Bass.

Collisson, B., & Howell, J. L. (2014). The liking-similarity effect: Perceptions of similarity as a function of liking. *The Journal of Social Psychology, 154*, 384–400. https://doi.org/10.1080/00224545.2014.914882

Comadena, M. E., Hunt, S. K., & Simonds, C. J. (2007). The effects of teacher clarity, nonverbal Immediacy, and caring on student motivation, affective and cognitive learning. *Communication Research Reports, 24*(3), 241–248. https://doi.org/10.1080/08824090701446617

Compton, J. (2016). Image prepare: Image repair, inoculation theory, and anticipated attacks on credibility. *The International Journal of the Image, 8*(1), 1–9. https://doi.org/10.18848/2154-8560/cgp/v08i01/1-9

Compton, J., & Ivanov, B. (2012). Untangling threat during inoculation-conferred resistance to influence. *Communication Reports, 25,* 1–13. https://doi.org/10.1080/08934215.2012.661018

Compton, J., & Kaylor, B. (2013). Inoculating for small pox inoculation objections in Reverend Cooper's *Letter to a Friend in the Country. Journal of Communication and Religion, 36*(1), 92–107. http://www.americanrhetoric.com/rca/rcajournals.html

Condit, C. M. (1997). In praise of eloquent diversity: Gender and rhetoric as public persuasion. *Women's Studies in Communication, 20*(2), 91–116. https://doi.org/10.1080/07491409.1997.10162405

Conner, M., & Armitage, C. J. (1998). Extending the theory of planned behavior: A review and avenues for further research. *Journal of Applied Social Psychology, 28,* 1429–1464. https://doi.org/10.1111/j.1559-1816.1998.tb01685.x

Cook, J., Ellerton, P., & Kinkead, D. (2018). Deconstructing climate misinformation to identify reasoning errors. *Environmental Research Letters, 13*(2), 024018. https://iopscience.iop.org/article/10.1088/1748-9326/aaa49f/meta doi:10.1088/1748-9326/aaa49f

Cook, J., Lewandowsky, S., & Ecker, U. K. H. (2017). Neutralizing misinformation through inoculation: Exposing misleading argumentation techniques reduces their influence. *PLoS ONE, 12,* e0175799. https://doi.org/10.1371/journal.pone.0175799

Cook, T. D., Gruder, C. L., Hennigan, K. M., & Flay, B. R. (1979). History of the sleeper effect: Some logical pitfalls in accepting the null hypothesis. *Psychological Bulletin, 86*(4), 662–679. https://doi.org/10.1037/0033-2909.86.4.662

Cooper, J. (1998). Unlearning cognitive dissonance: Toward an understanding of the development of dissonance. *Journal of Experimental Social Psychology, 34,* 562–575. https://doi.org/10.1006/jesp.1998.1365

Corn, D. (2016, November). The NSA chief says Russia hacked the 2016 election. Congress must investigate. *Mother Jones.* https://www.motherjones.com/politics/2016/11/will-congress-investigate-russian-interference-2016-campaign/

Cos, G., Worrell, T. R., & Blosenhouser, J. D. (2016). An empirical test of image restoration strategies. In J. R. Blaney (Ed.), *Putting image repair to the test: Quantitative applications of image restoration theory* (pp. 93–105). Lexington.

Craig, T. Y., & Blankenship, K. L. (2011). Language and persuasion: Linguistic extremity influences message processing and behavioral intentions. *Journal of Language and Social Psychology, 30*(3), 290–310. https://doi.org/10.1177/0261927x11407167

Crawford, M. T., & McCrea, S. M. (2004). When mutations meet motivations: Attitude biases in counterfactual thought. *Journal of Experimental Social Psychology, 40*(1), 65–74. https://doi.org/10.1016/S0022-1031(03)00062-3

Crowley, A. E., & Hoyer, W. D. (1994). An integrative framework for understanding two-sided persuasion. *Journal of Consumer Research, 20,* 561–574. https://doi.org/10.1086/209370

Cvancara, K. E., Youngvorst, L., Otto, V., & Brown, C. (2016). Testing role models' differential effect on use of aggressive compliance gaining strategies. *Communication Quarterly, 64,* 36–54. https://doi.org/10.1080/01463373.2015.1078829

Cyr, D., Head, M., Lim, E., & Stibe, A. (2018). Using the elaboration likelihood model to examine online persuasion through website design. *Information and Management, 55,* 807–821. https://doi.org/10.1016/j.im.2018.03.009

Dadipoor, S., Mehraban, M., Aghamolaei, T., Ramezankhani, A., & Safari-Moradabadi, A. (2017). Prediction of birth type based on the health belief model. *Journal of Family and Reproductive Health, 11*(3), 159–164. http://jfrh.tums.ac.ir

Dahl, D. W., Honea, H., & Manchanda, R. V. (2005). Three Rs of interpersonal consumer guilt: Relationship, reciprocity, reparation. *Journal of Consumer Psychology, 15,* 307–315. https://doi.org/10.1207/s15327663jcp1504_5

Dailey, W. O., Hinck, S. S., Hinck, R. S., & Hinck, E. A. (2017). Intensity of face threats in the 2008, 2012, and 2016 U.S. presidential debates. In R. E. Denton (Ed.), *Political campaign communication: Theory, method, and practice* (pp. 77–102). Lexington.

Dallinger, J. M., & Hample, D. (1994). The effects of gender on compliance gaining strategy endorsement and suppression. *Communication Reports, 7*(1), 43–49. https://doi.org/10.1080/08934219409367582

Dalton, R. J. (2009). *The good citizen: How a younger generation is reshaping American politics.* CQ Press.

Das, E., Galekh, M., & Vonkeman, C. (2015). Is sexy better than funny? Disentagling the persuasive effects of pleasure and arousal across sex and humor appeals. *International Journal of Advertising, 34*(3), 406–420. https://doi.org/10.1080/02650487.2014.997423

Dauenhauer, B. P. (1980). *Silence: The phenomenon and its ontological significance.* Indiana University Press.

Davis, B. P., & Knowles, E. S. (1999). A disrupt-then-reframe technique of social influence. *Journal of Personality and Social Psychology, 76*(2), 192–199. https://doi.org/10.1037/0022-3514.76.2.192

de Graaf, A. (2014). The effectiveness of adaptation of the protagonist in narrative impact: Similarity influences health beliefs through self-referencing. *Human Communication Research, 40,* 73–90. https://doi.org/10.1111/hcre.12015

de Vreese, C. H. (2004). The effects of frames in political television news on issue interpretation and frame salience. *Journalism & Mass Communication Quarterly, 81*(1), 36–52. https://doi.org/10.1177/107769900408100104

de Wit, J. B. F., Das, E., & Vet, R. (2008). What works best: Objective statistics or a personal testimony? An assessment of the persuasive effects of different types of message evidence on risk perception. *Health Psychology, 27*(1), 110–115. https://doi.org/10.1037/0278-6133.27.1.110

Dearing, J. W., & Meyer, G. (2006). Revisiting diffusion theory. In A. Singhal & J. W. Dearing, *Communication of innovations: A journey with Ev Rogers* (pp. 29–60). SAGE.

Demarque, C., Apostolidis, T., & Joule, R. V. (2013). Consideration of future consequences and pro-environmental decision making in the context of persuasion and binding commitment. *Journal of Environmental Psychology, 36,* 214–220. https://doi.org/10.1016/j.jenvp.2013.07.019

Dempster, N. R., Wildman, B. G., Masterson, T. L., & Omlor, G. J. (2018). Understanding treatment adherence with the health belief model in children with cystic fibrosis. *Health Education and Behavior, 45,* 435–443. https://doi.org/10.1177/1090198117736346

Denton, R. E. (Ed.) (2017). *Political campaign communication: Theory, method, and practice.* Lexington.

DePaulo, B. M., & Kirkendol, S. E. (1989). The motivational impairment effect in the communication of deception. In J. C. Yuille (Ed.), *Credibility assessment* (pp. 51–70). Kluwer.

DeRosia, E. D., & McQuarrie, E. F. (2019). Lost and found: Individual differences in propensity to process visual elements of persuasion. *Psychology of Marketing, 36,* 266–275. https://doi.org/10.1002/mar.21177

DeSante, C. D., & Smith, C. W. (2020). Fear, institutionalized racism, and empathy: The underlying dimensions of whites' racial attitudes. *Political Science & Politics, 53,* 639–645. https://doi.org/10.1017/s1049096520000414

Descheemaeker, M., Spruyt, A., & Hermans, D. (2014). On the relationship between indirectly measured attitude towards beer and beer consumption: The role of attitude accessibility. *PLoS ONE, 9*(4), e95302. https://doi.org/10.1371/journal.pone.0095302

Desforges, D. M., Lord, C. G., Ramsey, S. L., Mason, J. A., Van Leeuwen, M. D., West, S. C., & Lepper, M. R. (1991). Effects of structured cooperative contact on changing negative attitudes toward stigmatized social groups. *Journal of Personality and Social Psychology, 60,* 531–544. https://doi.org/10.1037/0022-3514.60.4.531

DeSteno, D., Petty, R. E., Rucker, D. D., Wegener, D. T., & Braverman, J. (2004). Discrete emotions and persuasion: The role of emotion-induced expectancies. *Journal of Personality and Social Psychology, 86,* 43–56. https://doi.org/10.1037/0022-3514.86.1.43

Deturck, M. A. (1987). When communication fails: Physical aggression as a compliance-gaining strategy. *Communication Monographs, 54*(1), 106–112. https://doi.org/10.1080/03637758709390219

Dillard, J. P. (1994). Rethinking the study of fear appeals: An emotional perspective. *Communication Theory, 4,* 295–323. https://doi.org/10.1111/j.1468-2885.1994.tb00094.x

Dillard, J. P. (1998). Compliance-gaining message-selection: What is our dependent variable? *Communication Monographs, 55,* 162–183. https://doi.org/10.1080/03637758809376164

Dillard, J. P. (2014). Language, style and persuasion. In P. E. Nathan (Ed.), *The Oxford handbook of language and social psychology* (pp. 177–187). Oxford University Press.

Dillard, J. P., & Peck, E. (2000). Affect and persuasion: Emotional responses to public service announcements. *Communication Research, 27,* 461–495. https://doi.org/10.1177/009365000027004003

Dillard, J. P., & Shen, L. (2005). On the nature of reactance and its role in persuasive health communication. *Communication Monographs, 72,* 144–168. https://doi.org/10.1080/03637750500111815

Dillard, J. P., Plotnick, C. A., Godbold, L. C., Freimuth, V. S., & Edgar, T. (1996). The multiple affective outcomes of AIDS PSAs: Fear appeals do more than scare people. *Communication Research, 23*(10), 44–72. https://doi.org/10.1177/009365096023001002

Dillard, J. P., Segrin, C., & Harden, J. M. (1989). Primary and secondary goals in the production of interpersonal influence messages. *Communication Monographs, 56*, 19–38. https://doi.org/10.1080/03637758909390247

Dillard, J. P., Shen, L., & Vail, R. G. (2007). Does perceived message effectiveness cause persuasion or vice versa? 17 consistent answers. *Human Communication Research, 33*, 467–488. https://doi.org/10.1111/j.1468-2958.2007.00308.x

Dillingham, L. L., & Ivanov, B. (2015). Boosting inoculation's message potency: Loss framing. *Communication Research Reports, 32*, 113–121. https://doi.org/10.1080/08824096.2015.1016152

Dolinski, D., Grzyb, T., Olejnik, J., Prusakowski, S., & Urban, K. (2005). Let's dialogue about penny: Effectiveness of dialogue involvement and legitimizing paltry contribution techniques. *Journal of Applied Social Psychology, 35*(6), 1150–1170. https://doi.org/10.1111/j.1559-1816.2005.tb02164.x

Dong, Y., Hu, S., & Zhu, J. (2018). From source credibility to risk perception: How and when climate information matters to action. *Resources, Conservation, & Recycling, 136*, 410–417. https://doi.org/10.1016/j.resconrec.2018.05.012

Dong, Y., Hu, S., & Jhu, J. (2018). From source credibility to risk perception: How and when climate information matters to action. *Resources, Conservation & Recycling, 136*, 410–417. https://doi.org/10.1016/j.resconrec.2018.05.012

Donofrio, A. R. (2020). "If you don't want to be silenced, be silent: Tactical silence & Jeffco Students for Change." *Western Journal of Communication, 84*, 550–567. https://doi.org/10.1080/10570314.2020.1780303

Douglas, K. M., & Sutton, R. M. (2015). Climate change: Why the conspiracy theories are dangerous. *Bulletin of the Atomic Scientists, 71*(2), 98–106. https://doi.org/10.1177/0096340215571908

Duck, J. M., Hogg, M. A., & Terry, D. J. (1999). Social identity and perceptions of media persuasion: Are we always less influenced than others? *Journal of Applied Social Psychology, 29*, 1879–1899. https://doi.org/10.1111/j.1559-1816.1999.tb00156.x

Duhachek, A., Agrawal, N., & Han, D. (2012). Guilt versus shame: Coping, fluency, and framing in the effectiveness of responsible drinking messages. *Journal of Marketing Research, 49*(6), 928–941. https://doi.org/10.1509/jmr.10.0244

Dunbar, N. E., & Segrin, C. (2012). Clothing and teacher credibility: An application of expectancy violations theory. *ISRN Education*, 1–12. https://doi.org/10.5402/2012/140517

Dunbar, N. E., Jensen, M. L., Bessarabova, E., Burgoon, J. K., Bernard, D. R., Harrison, K. J., Kelley, K. M., Adame, B. J., & Eckstein, J. M. (2014). Empowered by persuasive deception: The effects of power and deception on dominance, credibility, and decision making. *Communication Research, 41*, 852–876. https://doi.org/10.1177/0093650212447099

Dykstra, P., Jager, W., Elsenbroich, C., Verbrugge, R., & de Lavalette, G. R. (2015). An agent-based dialogical model with fuzzy attitudes. *Journal of Artificial Societies and Social Simulation, 18*(3), article 3. https://doi.org/10.18564/jasss.2813

Eagly, A. H., & Chaiken, S. (1993). *The psychology of attitudes.* Harcourt Brace Jovanovich College Publishers.

Eagly, A. H., Wood, W., & Chaiken, S. (1978). Causal inferences about communicators and their effect on opinion change. *Journal of Personality and Social Psychology, 36*(4), 424–435. https://doi.org/10.1037/0022-3514.36.4.424

Eaton, A. A., Visser, P. S., Krosnick, J. A., & Anand, S. (2009). Social power and attitude strength over the life course. *Personality and Social Psychology Bulletin, 35*(12), 1646–1660. https://doi.org/10.1037/e657582007-001

Edell, J. A., & Staelin, R. (1983). The information processing of pictures in print advertising. *Journal of Consumer Research, 10*, 45–61. https://doi.org/10.1037/e541882009-002

Edwards, G. (2014). Infectious innovations? The diffusion of tactical innovation in social movement networks, the case of suffragette militancy. *Social Movement Studies, 13*, 48–69. https://doi.org/10.1080/14742837.2013.834251

Edwards, K., & Smith, E. E. (1996). A disconfirmation bias in the evaluation of arguments. *Journal of Personality and Social Psychology, 71*, 5–24. https://doi.org/10.1037//0022-3514.71.1.5

Effron, D. A. (2018). It could have been true: How counterfactual thoughts reduce condemnation of falsehoods and increase political polarization. *Personality and Social Psychology Bulletin, 44,* 729–745. https://doi.org/10.1177/01461672177461

Egermann, H., Kopiez, R., & Reuter, C. (2006). Is there an effect of subliminal messages in music on choice behavior. *Journal of Articles in Support of the Null Hypothesis, 4,* 29–45. www.jasnh.com

Eisend, M. (2004). Is it still worth it to be credible? A meta-analysis of temporal patterns of source credibility effects in marketing. *Advances in Consumer Research, 31,* 352–357. http://acrwebsite.org/volumes/8916/volumes/v31/NA-31

Eisend, M. (2009). A meta-analysis of humor in advertising. *Journal of the Academy of Marketing Science, 37,* 191–203. https://doi.org/10.1007/s11747-008-0096-y

Eisend, M. (2011). How humor in advertising works: A meta-analytic test of alternative models. *Marketing Letters, 22,* 115–132. https://doi.org/10.1007/s11002-010-9116-z

Eisenstadt, D., Leippe, M. R., Rivers, J. A., & Stambush, M. A. (2003). Counterattitudinal advocacy on a matter of prejudice: Effects of distraction, commitment, and personal importance. *Journal of Applied Social Psychology, 33,* 2123–2152. https://doi.org/10.1111/j.1559-1816.2003.tb01878.x

Ekman, P., & Friesen, W. V. (1969). The repertoire of nonverbal behavior: Categories, origins, usage, and coding. *Semiotica, 1,* 49–98. https://doi.org/10.1515/semi.1969.1.1.49

Ekman, P., & Friesen, W. V. (1974). Detecting deception from the body or face? *Journal of Personality and Social Psychology, 54,* 414–420. https://doi.org/10.1037/h0036006

Elbert, S. P., & Dijkstra, A. (2014). An experimental test of the relationship between voice intonation and persuasion in the domain of health. *Psychology & Health, 29,* 1014–1031. https://doi.org/10.1080/08870446.2014.903482

Elliot, A. J., & Devine, P. G. (1994). On the motivational nature of cognitive dissonance: Dissonance as psychological discomfort. *Journal of Personality and Social Psychology, 67,* 382–394. https://doi.org/10.1037/0022-3514.67.3.382

Enskat, A. Hunt, S. K., & Hooker, J. F. (2017). A generational examination of instructional Facebook use and the effects on perceived instructor immediacy, credibility and student affective learning. *Technology, Pedagogy and Education, 26*(5), 545–557. https://doi.org/10.1080/1475939X.2017.1354065

Entman, R. M., & Usher, N. (2018). Framing in a fractured democracy: Impacts of digital technology on ideology, power, and cascading network activation. *Journal of Communication, 68,* 298–308. https://doi.org/10.1093/ct/jqx019

Evans, A. T., & Clark, J. K. (2012). Source characteristics and persuasion: The role of self-monitoring in self-validation. *Journal of Experimental Social Psychology, 48,* 383–386. https://doi.org/10.1016/j.jesp.2011.07.002

Fall, E., Izaute, M., & Chakroun-Baggioni, N. (2018). How can the health belief model and self-determination theory predict both influenza vaccination and vaccination intention? A longitudinal study among university students. *Psychology and Health, 33,* 746–764. https://doi.org/10.1080/08870446.2017.1401623

Fârte, G. I. (2016). How to change people's beliefs? Doxastic coercion vs. evidential persuasion. *Argumentum: Journal of the Seminar of Discursive Logic, Argumentation Theory and Rhetoric, 14*(2), 49–78.

Fawkes, J. (2007). Public relations models and persuasion ethics: A new approach. *Journal of Communication Management, 11,* 313–331. https://doi.org/10.1108/13632540710843922

Fazeli, N., Moradi, M., Khadivzadeh, T., & Esmaily, H. (2018). Effect of preconception care education by health volunteers on knowledge and attitudes of women: Application of the health belief model. *Evidence Based Care Journal, 8*(1), 76–81. https://doi.org/10.22038/ebcj.2018.28654.1709

Fazio, R. H. (1990). Multiple processes by which attitudes guide behavior. The MODE model as an integrative framework. In M. P. Zanna (Ed.), *Advances in experimental social psychology* (Vol. 23, pp. 75–109). Academic Press.

Fazio, R. H., & Powell, M. C. (1997). On the value of knowing one's likes and dislikes: Attitude accessibility, stress, and health in college. *Psychological Science, 8,* 430–436. https://doi.org/10.1111/j.1467-9280.1997.tb00456.x

Federal Bureau of Investigation. (2017). *2017 internet crime report.* https://pdf.ic3.gov/2017_IC3Report.pdf

Feeley, T., Fico, A. E., Shaw, A. Z., Lee, S., & Griffin, D. J. (2017). Is the door-in-the-face a concession? *Communication Quarterly, 65*(1), 97–123. https://doi.org/10.1080/01463373.2016.1187186

Fenko, A., de Vries, R., & van Rompay, T. (2018). How strong is your coffee? The influence of visual metaphors and textual claims on consumers' flavor perception and product evaluation. *Frontiers in Psychology, 9.* https://doi.org/10.3389/fpsyg.2018.00053

Fennis, B. M., & Stel, M. (2011). The pantomime of persuasion: Fit between nonverbal communication and influence strategies. *Journal of Experimental Social Psychology, 47,* 806–810. https://doi.org/10.1016/j.jesp.2011.02.015

Fennis, B. M., Das, E., & Fransen, M. L. (2012). Print advertising: Vivid content. *Journal of Business Research, 65,* 861–864. https://doi.org/10.1016/j.jbusres.2011.01.008

Ferguson, D. P., Wallace, J. D., & Chandler, R. C. (2018). Hierarchical consistency of strategies in image repair theory: PR practitioners' perceptions of effective and preferred crisis communication strategies. *Journal of Public Relations Research, 30,* 251–272. https://doi.org/10.1080/1062726x.2018.1545129

Festinger, L. & Carlsmith, J. M. (1959). Cognitive consequences of forced compliance. *Journal of Abnormal and Social Psychology, 58,* 203–210. https://doi.org/10.1037/h0041593

Festinger, L. (1957). *A theory of cognitive dissonance.* Stanford University Press.

Finlay, A. K., Wray-Lake, L., Warren, M., & Maggs, J. (2015). Anticipating their future: Adolescent values for the future predict adult behaviors. *International Journal of Behavior Development, 39*(4), 359–367. https://doi.org/10.1177/0165025414544231

Finn, A. N., Schrodt, P., Witt, P. L., Elledge, N., Jernberg, K. A., & Larson, L. M. (2009). A meta-analytical review of teacher credibility and its associations with teacher behaviors and student outcomes. *Communication Education, 58,* 516–537. https://doi.org/10.1080/03634520903131154

Fishbein, M. (2008). A reasoned action approach to health promotion. *Medical Decision Making, 28,* 834–844. https://doi.org/10.1177/0272989X08326092

Fishbein, M., & Ajzen, I. (2010). *Predicting and changing behavior: The reasoned action approach.* Psychology Press.

Fleming, P., & Zyglidopoulos, S. C. (2007). The escalation of deception in organizations. *Journal of Business Ethics, 81,* 837–850. https://doi.org/10.1007/s10551-007-9551-9

Flynn, D. J. (2016, September). *The scope and correlates of political misperceptions in the mass public* [Paper presentation]. American Political Science Association Annual Meeting, Philadelphia, PA, United States.

Flynn, D. J., Nyhan, B., & Reifler, J. (2017). The nature and origins of misperceptions: Understanding false and unsupported beliefs about politics. *Advances in Political Psychology, 38*(1), 127–150. https://doi.org/10.1111/pops.12394

Foos, A. E., Keeling, K., & Keeling, D. (2016). Redressing the sleeper effect: Evidence for the favorable persuasive impact of discounting information over time in a contemporary advertising context. *Journal of Advertising, 45*(1), 19–25. https://doi.org/10.1080/00913367.2015.1085820

Francesconi, R. A. (1982). James Hunt, The Wilmington 10, and institutional legitimacy. *Quarterly Journal of Speech, 68,* 47–59. https://doi.org/10.1080/00335638209383591

Frandrich, A. M., & Beck, S. J. (2012). Powerless language in health media: The influence of biological sex and magazine type on health language. *Communication Studies, 63,* 36–53. https://doi.org/10.1080/10510974.2011.598600

Frank, M. G., Paolantonio, N., Feeley, T. H., & Servoss, T. J. (2004). Individual and small group accuracy in judging truthful and deceptive communication. *Group Decision and Negotiation, 13,* 45–59. https://doi.org/10.1023/B:GRUP.0000011945.85141.af

Frankfurt, H. (2005). *On bullshit.* Princeton University Press.

Fransen, M. L., & Fennis, B. M. (2014). Comparing the impact of explicit and implicit resistance induction strategies on message persuasiveness. *Journal of Communication, 64,* 915–934. https://doi.org/10.1111/jcom.12118

French, J. R. P., Jr., & Raven, B. H. (1959). The bases of social power. In D. Cartwright (Ed.), *Studies in social power* (pp. 150–167). Institute for Social Research.

Frey, K. P., & Eagly, A. H. (1993). Vividness can undermine the persuasiveness of messages. *Journal of Personality and Social Psychology, 65*(1), 32–44. https://doi.org/10.1037/0022-3514.65.1.32

Frimer, J. A., Skitka, L. J., & Motyl, M. (2017). Liberals and conservatives are similarly motivated to avoid exposure to one another's opinions. *Journal of Experimental Social Psychology, 72,* 1–12. https://doi.org/10.1016/j.jesp.2017.04.003

Fulton-Babicke, H. (2018). "I can't breathe": Eric Garner and in/out-group rhetorics. *Rhetoric Review, 37*, 434–446. https://doi.org/10.1080/07350198.2018.1497888.

Funk, C., Kennedy, B., & Hefferon, M. (2017). Vast majority of Americans say benefits of childhood vaccines outweigh risks. *Pew Research Center.* http://www.pewinternet.org/2017/02/02/public-opinion-about-childhood-vaccines-for-measles-mumps-and-rubella/

Fymier, A. B., Goldman, Z. W., & Claus, C. J. (2019). Why nonverbal immediacy matters: A motivation explanation. *Communication Quarterly, 67*, 526–539. https://doi.org/10.1080/01463373.2019.1668442

Gadzhiyeva, N. M., & Sager, K. L. (2017). Maximizing the persuasiveness of a salesperson: An exploratory study of the effects of nonverbal immediacy and language power on the extent of persuasion. *Journal of Work and Organizational Psychology, 33*, 83–93. https://doi.org/10.1016/j.rpto.2017.03.001

Galston, W. A. (2003). Civic education and political participation. *Phi Delta Kappan, 85*, 29–33. https://doi.org/10.1017/s1049096504004202

Garnefeld, I., Böhm, E., Klimke, L., & Oestreich, A. (2018). I thought it was over, but now it is back: Customer reactions to *ex post* time extensions of sales promotions. *Journal of the Academy of Marketing Science, 46*, 1133–1147. https://doi.org/10.1007/s11747-018-0600-y

Garrett, R. K. (2009). Echo chambers online?: Politically motivated selective exposure among internet news users. *Journal of Computer-Mediated Communication, 14*, 265–285. https://doi.org/10.1111/j.1083-6101.2009.01440.x

Gaspar, R., Luis, S., Seibt, B., Lima, M. L., Marcu, A., Rutsaert, P., Fletcher, D., Verbeke, W., & Barnett, J. (2016). Consumers' avoidance of information on red meat risks: Information exposure effects on attitudes and perceived knowledge. *Journal of Risk Research, 19*, 533–549. https://doi.org/10.1080/13669877.2014.1003318

Gastil, J., Black, L., & Moscovitz, K. (2008). Ideology, attitude change, and deliberation in small face-to-face groups. *Political Communication, 25*, 23–46. https://doi.org/10.1080/10584600701807836

Gaube, S., Fischer, P., Windl, V., & Lermer, E. (2020). The effect of persuasive messages on hospital visitors' hand hygiene behavior. *Health Pyschology, 39*, 471–481. https://doi.org/10.31234/osf.io/w28s5

Gaudet, A. D., Ramer, L. M., Nakonechny, J., Cragg, J. J., & Ramer, M. S. (2010). Small-group learning in an upper-level university biology class enhances academic performance and student attitudes toward group work. *PLoS ONE, 5*(12), 1–10. https://doi.org/10.1371/journal.pone.0015821

Gavilan, D., Avello, M., & Martinez-Navarro, G. (2018). The influence of online ratings and reviews on hotel booking consideration. *Tourism Management, 66*, 53–61. https://doi.org/10.1016/j.tourman.2017.10.018

Gélinas-Chebat, C., Chebat, J. C., & Vaninsky, A. (1996). Voice and advertising: Effects of intonation and intensity of voice on source credibility, attitudes toward the advertised service and the intent to buy. *Perceptual and Motor Skills, 83*, 243–262. https://doi.org/10.2466/pms.1996.83.1.243

Gelles, R. J. (1974). *The violent home.* SAGE.

Gerlach, P., Teodorescu, D., & Hertwig, R. (2019). The truth about lies: A meta-analysis on dishonest behavior. *Psychological Bulletin, 145*(1), 1–44. https://doi.org/10.1037/bul0000174

Gervais, S. J., & Hillard, A. L. (2014). Confronting sexism as persuasion: Effects of a confrontation's recipient, source, message, and context. *Journal of Social Issues, 70*(4), 653–667. https://doi.org/10.1111/josi.12084

Ghazali, A. S., Ham, J., Barakova, E. I., & Markopoulos, P. (2018a). Effects of robot facial characteristics and gender in persuasive human-robot interaction. *Frontiers in Robotics and AI, 5*, 1–16. https://doi.org/10.3389/frobt.2018.00073

Ghazali, A. S., Ham, J., Barakova, E. I., & Markopoulos, P. (2018b). The influence of social cues in persuasive social robots on psychological reactance and compliance. *Computers in Human Behavior, 87*, 58–65. https://doi.org/10.1016/j.chb.2018.05.016

Giacomantonio, M., Jordan, J., Federico, F., van den Assem, M. J., & van Dolder, D. (2018). The evil eye: Eye gaze and competitiveness in social decision making. *European Journal of Social Psychology, 48*, 388–396. https://doi.org/10.1002/ejsp.2336

Gibson, L. A., Creamer, M. R., Breland, A. B., Giachello, A. L., Kaufman, A., Kong, G., Pechacek, T. F., Pepper, J. K., Soule, E. K., & Halpern-Felsher, B. (2018). Measuring perceptions related to e-cigarettes: Important principles and next steps to enhance study validity. *Addictive Behaviors, 79*, 219–225. https://doi.org/10.1016/j.addbeh.2017.11.017

Giles, H., & Coupland, N. (1991). *Language: Contexts and consequences.* Brooks/Cole.

Gillig, P. M., & Greenwald, A. G. (1974). Is it time to lay the sleeper effect to rest? *Journal of Personality and Social Psychology, 29*(1), 132–139. https://doi.org/10.1037/h0035744

Glockner, A., & Witteman, C. (2010). Beyond dual-process models: A categorisation of processes underlying intuitive judgement and decision making. *Thinking and Reasoning, 16*(1), 1–25. https://doi.org/10.1080/13546780903395748

Godbold, L. C., & Pfau, M. (2000). Conferring resistance to peer pressure among adolescents. *Communication Research, 27,* 411–437. https://doi.org/10.1177/009365000027004001

Godin, G., & Kok, G. (1996). The theory of planned behavior: A review of its applications to health-related behaviors. *American Journal of Health Promotion, 11*(2), 87–98. https://doi.org/10.4278/0890-1171-11.2.87

Goei, R., Roberto, A., Meyer, G., & Cralyle, K. (2007). The effects of favor and apology on compliance. *Communication Research, 34,* 575–595. https://doi.org/10.1177/0093650207307896

Goldberg, C., & Cohen, D. J. (2004). Walking the walk and talking the talk: Gender differences in the impact of interviewing skills on applicant assessments. *Group & Organization Management, 29*(3), 369–384. https://doi.org/10.1177/1059601103257408

Goldman, M., Kiyohara, O., & Pfannensteil, D. A. (1985). Interpersonal touch, social labeling, and the foot-in-the-door effect. *Journal of Social Psychology, 125,* 143–147. https://doi.org/10.1080/00224545.1985.9922866

Goldner, L., & Golan, D. (2017). The long-term effects of youth mentoring on student mentors' civic engagement attitudes and behavior. *Journal of Community Psychology, 45,* 691–703. https://doi.org/10.1002/jcop.21886

Goldstein, N. J., Cialdini, R. B., & Griskevicius, V. (2008). A room with a viewpoint: Using social norms to motivate environmental conservation in hotels. *Journal of Consumer Research, 35,* 472–482. https://doi.org/10.1086/586910

Golish, T. D. (1999). Students' use of compliance-gaining strategies with graduate teaching assistants: Examining the other end of the power spectrum. *Communication Quarterly, 47,* 12–32. https://doi.org/10.1080/01463379909370121

Golish, T. D., & Olson, L. N. (2000). Students' use of power in the classroom: An investigation of student power, teacher power, and teacher immediacy. *Communication Quarterly, 48,* 293–310. https://doi.org/10.1080/01463370009385598

Goodman-Delahunty, J., & Howes, L. M. (2016). Social persuasion to develop rapport in high-stakes interviews: Qualitative analyses of Asian-Pacific practices. *Policing and Society, 26,* 270–290. https://doi.org/10.1080/10439463.2014.942848

Gorham, J. (1988). The relationship between verbal teacher immediacy behaviors and student learning. *Communication Education, 37*(1), 40–53. https://doi.org/10.1080/03634528809378702

Gorham, J., Cohen, S. H., & Morris, T. L. (1999). Fashion in the classroom III: Effects of instructor attire and immediacy in natural classroom interactions. *Communication Quarterly, 47*(3), 281–299. https://doi.org/10.1080/01463379909385560

Graham, J. A., & Argyle, M. (1975). A cross-cultural study of the communication of extra-verbal meaning by gestures. *International Journal of Psychology, 10,* 57–67. https://doi.org/10.1080/00207597508247319

Grant, J. A., King, P. E., & Behnke, R. R. (1994). Compliance-gaining strategies, communication satisfaction, and willingness to comply. *Communication Reports, 7*(2), 99–108. https://doi.org/10.1080/08934219409367592

Grant, N. K., Fabrigar, L. R., & Lim, H. (2010). Exploring the efficacy of compliments as a tactic for securing compliance. *Basic and Applied Social Psychology, 32,* 226–233. https://doi.org/10.1080/01973533.2010.497456

Graton, A., Ric, F., & Gonzalez, E. (2016). Reparation or reactance? The influence of guilt to persuasive communication. *Journal of Experimental Social Psychology, 62,* 40–49. https://doi.org/10.1016/j.jesp.2015.09.016

Green, L. (2017). The trouble with touch? New insights and observations on touch for social work and social care. *British Journal of Social Work, 47,* 773–792. https://doi.org/10.1093/bjsw/bcw071

Greenwald, A. G., Pratkanis, A. R., Leippe, M. R., & Baumgardner, M. H. (1986). Under what conditions does theory obstruct research progress? *Psychological Review, 93*(2), 216–229. https://doi.org/10.1037//0033-295x.93.2.216

Gribas, J., DiSanza, J., Legge, N., Hartman, R., & Santee, C. (2016). Exploring the alignment of image repair tactics to audience type. In J. R. Blaney (Ed.), *Putting image repair to the test: Quantitative applications of image restoration theory* (pp. 49–70). Lexington.

Griffin, R. J., Neuwirth, K., Giese, J., & Dunwoody, S. (2002). Linking the heuristic-systematic model and depth of processing. *Communication Research, 29,* 705–732. https://doi.org/10.1177/009365002237833

Griskevicius, V., Shiota, M. N., & Neufeld, S. L. (2010). Influence of different positive emotions on persuasion processing: A functional evolutionary approach. *Emotion, 10,* 190–206. https://doi.org/10.1037/a0018421

Grob, L. M., Meyers, R. A., & Schuh, R. (1997). Powerful/powerless language use in group interactions: Sex differences or similarities? *Communication Quarterly, 45,* 282–303. https://doi.org/10.1080/01463379709370066

Guadagno, R. E., Muscanell, N. L., Rice, L. M., & Roberts, N. (2013). Social influence online: The impact of social validation and likeability on compliance. *Psychology of Popular Media Culture, 2*(1), 51–60. https://doi.org/10.1037/a0030592

Guéguen, N. (2007). Courtship compliance: The effect of touch on women's behavior. *Social Influence, 2*(2), 81–97. https://doi.org/10.1080/15534510701316177

Gueguen, N. (2015). The effect of requesting money with a few coins in one hand: The foot-in-the-hand technique. *Social Influence, 10*(4), 193–201. https://doi.org/10.1080/15534510.2015.1045935

Guéguen, N., & Jacob, C. (2002). Direct look versus evasive glance and compliance with a request. *Journal of Social Psychology, 142,* 393–396. https://doi.org/10.1080/00224540209603907

Gueguen, N., & Lamy, L. (2016). The pique technique: A goal-oriented effect? *Communication Reports, 29,* 115–125. https://doi.org/10.1080/08934215.2015.1050120

Gueguen, N., Meineri, S., Pascual, A., & Girandola, F. (2015). The pique then reframe technique: Replication and extension of the pique technique. *Communication Research Reports, 32,* 143–148. https://doi.org/10.1080/08824096.2015.1016151

Guilford, K., McKinley, E., & Turner, L. (2017). Breast cancer knowledge, beliefs, and screening behaviors of college women: Application of the health belief model. *American Journal of Health Education, 48,* 256–263. https://doi.org/10.1080/19325037.2017.1316694

Gulas, C. S., McKeage, K. K., & Weinberger, M. G. (2010). It's just a joke: Violence against males in humorous advertising. *Journal of Advertising, 39*(4), 109–120. https://doi.org/10.2753/joa0091-3367390408

Gurri, M., Denny, C., & Harms, A. (2010). Our visual persuasion gap. *The US Army War College Quarterly: Parameters, 40*(1), 101–109.

Gurung, R. A. R., Brickner, M., Leet, M., & Punke, E. (2017). Dressing "in code": Clothing rules, propriety, and perceptions. *The Journal of Social Psychology, 158*(5), 553–557. https://doi.org/10.1080/00224545.2017.1393383

Guttman, N., Siegal, G., Appel, N., & Bar-On, G. (2016). Should altruism, solidarity, or reciprocity be used as prosocial appeals? Contrasting conceptions of members of the general public and medical professionals regarding promoting organ donation. *Journal of Communication, 66,* 909–936. https://doi.org/10.1111/jcom.12267

Hagger, M. S., Chatzisarantis, N. L. D., & Biddle, S. J. H. (2002). A meta-analytic review of the theories of reasoned action and planned behavior in physical activity: Predictive validity and the contribution of additional variables. *Journal of Sport and Exercise Psychology, 24,* 3–32. https://doi.org/10.1123/jsep.24.1.3

Haleta, L. L. (1996). Student perceptions of teachers' use of language: The effects of powerful and powerless language on impression formation and uncertainty. *Communication Education, 45,* 16–28. https://doi.org/10.1080/03634529609379029

Hall, C. C., & Oppenheimer, D. M. (2015). Error parsing: An alternative method of implementing social judgment theory. *Judgment and Decision Making, 10,* 469–478. http://journal.sjdm.org/

Hall, M. P., & Raimi, K. T. (2018). Is belief superiority justified by superior knowledge? *Journal of Experimental Social Psychology, 76,* 290–306. https://doi.org/10.1016/j.jesp.2018.03.001

Hameleers, M., Powell, T. E., Van Der Meer, T. G. L. A., & Bos, L. (2020). A picture paints a thousand lies? The effects and mechanisms of multimodal disinformation and rebuttals disseminated via social media. *Political Communication, 37,* 281–301. https://doi.org/10.1080/10584609.2019.1674979

Hamilton, M. A., & Stewart, B. L. (1993). Extending an information processing model of language intensity effects. *Communication Quarterly, 41,* 231–246. https://doi.org/10.1080/01463379309369882

Hampton, A. J., Fisher Boyd, A. N., & Sprecher, S. (2019). You're like me and I like you: Mediators of the similarity-liking link assessed before and after a getting-acquainted social interaction. *Journal of Social and Personal Relationships, 36,* 2221–2244. https://doi.org/10.1177/0265407518790411

Han, J-T., Chen, Q., Liu, J.-G., Luo, X.-L., & Fan, W. (2018). The persuasion of borrowers' voluntary information in peer to peer lending: An empirical study based on elaboration likelihood model. *Computers in Human Behavior, 78,* 200–214. https://doi.org/10.1016/j.chb.2017.09.004

Hancock, J. T., Woodworth, M. T., & Goorha, S. (2010). See no evil: The effect of communication medium and motivation on deception detection. *Group Decision and Negotiation, 19,* 327–343. https://doi.org/10.1007/s10726-009-9169-7

Happ, C., Melzer, A., & Steffgen, G. (2016). Trick with treat—Reciprocity increases willingness to communicate personal data. *Computers in Human Behavior, 61,* 372–377. https://doi.org/10.1016/j.chb.2016.03.026

Harmon-Jones, E. (2002). A cognitive dissonance theory perspective on persuasion. In J. P. Dillard & M. Pfau (Eds.), *The persuasion handbook: Developments in theory and practice* (pp. 99–116). SAGE.

Harmon-Jones, E., & Harmon-Jones, C. (2007). Cognitive dissonance theory after 50 years of development. *Zeitschrift für Sozialpsychologie, 38,* 7–16. https://doi.org/10.1024/0044-3514.38.1.7

Hart, R. P., Daughton, S., & LaVally, R. (2018). *Modern rhetorical criticism* (4th ed.). Routledge.

Hart, W., Albarracín, D., Eagly, A. H., Brechan, I., Lindberg, M. J., & Merrill, L. (2009). Feeling validated versus being correct: A meta-analysis of selective exposure to information. *Psychological Bulletin, 135*(4), 555–588. https://doi.org/10.1037/a0015701

Hartley, E. M., Hoch, M. C., & Cramer, R. J. (2018). Health belief model and theory of planned behavior: A theoretical approach for enhancing lower extremity injury prevention program participation. *International Journal of Athletic Therapy and Training, 23,* 16–20. https://doi.org/10.1123/ijatt.2017-0016

Hass, R. G., & Grady, K. (1975). Temporal delay, type of forewarning, and resistance to influence. *Journal of Experimental Social Psychology, 11,* 459–469. https://doi.org/10.1016/0022-1031(75)90048-7

Hastie, R., & Sunstein, C. R. (2015, July 21). Polarization: One reason groups fail. *Chicago Booth Review.* https://review.chicagobooth.edu/magazine/spring-2015/one-reason-groups-fail-polarization

Hausenblas, H. A., Carron, A. V., & Mack, D. E. (1997). Application of the theories of reasoned action and planned behavior to exercise behavior: A meta-analysis. *Journal of Sport and Exercise Psychology, 19,* 36–51. https://doi.org/10.1123/jsep.19.1.36

Hausman, D. M., & Welch, B. (2010). Debate: To nudge or not to nudge. *The Journal of Political Philosophy, 18*(1), 123–136. https://doi.org/10.1111/j.1467-9760.2009.00351.x

Heesacker, M., Petty, R. E., & Cacioppo, J. T. (1983). Field dependence and attitude change: Source credibility can alter persuasion by affecting message-relevant thinking. *Journal of Personality, 51*(4), 653–666. https://doi.org/10.1111/j.1467-6494.1983.tb00872.x

Heinback, D., Ziegele, M., & Quiring, O. (2018). Sleeper effect from below: Long-term effects of source credibility and user comments on the persuasiveness of news articles. *New Media & Society, 20*(12), 4765–4786. https://doi.org/10.1177/1461444818784472

Heitland, K., & Bohner, G. (2010). Reducing prejudice via cognitive dissonance: Individual differences in preference for consistency moderate the effects of counterattitudinal advocacy. *Social Influence, 5*(3), 164–181. https://doi.org/10.1080/15534510903332261

Henning, Z. T. (2012). From barnyards to learning communities: Student perceptions of teachers' immediacy behaviors. *Qualitative Research Reports in Communication, 13*(1), 37–43. https://doi.org/10.1080/17459435.2012.719207

Henrich, J., Heine, S. J., & Norenzayan, A. (2010). Most people are not WEIRD. *Nature, 466*(7302), 29. https://doi.org/10.1038/466029a

Herr, P. M., Kardes, F. R., & Kim, J. (1991). Effects of word-of-mouth and product-attribute information on persuasion: An accessibility-diagnosticity perspective. *Journal of Consumer Research, 17,* 454–462. https://doi.org/10.1086/208570

Hibbert, S., Smith, A., Davies, A., & Ireland F. (2007). Guilt appeals: Persuasion knowledge and charitable giving. *Psychology and Marketing, 24,* 723–742. https://doi.org/10.1002/mar.20181

Hildenbrand, G. M., & Houser, M. L. (2020). An investigation of college student learner orientation impact on perceptions of instructor behavior alteration techniques/messages. *Educational Research Quarterly, 43*(3), 3–23.

Hill, M. D., & Thompson-Hayes, M. (2017). *From awareness to commitment in public health campaigns: The awareness myth.* Lexington.

Hillygus, D. S. (2005). The missing link: Exploring the relationship between higher education and political engagement. *Political Behavior, 27,* 25–47. https://doi.org/10.1007/s11109-005-3075-8

Hinkle, L. L. (1999). Nonverbal immediacy communication behaviors and liking in marital relationships. *Communication Research Reports, 16*(1), 81–90. https://doi.org/10.1080/08824099909388704

Hirsh, J. B., Kang, S. K., & Bodenhausen, G. V. (2012). Personalized persuasion: Tailoring persuasive appeals to recipients' personality traits. *Psychological Science, 23,* 578–581. https://doi.org/10.1177/0956797611436349

Hofstede, G. (1990). *Cultures and organizations: Software of the mind.* McGraw Hill.

Hong, S., & Kim, S. K. (2016). Political polarization on Twitter: Implications for the use of social media in digital governments. *Government Information Quarterly, 33,* 777–782. https://doi.org/10.1016/j.giq.2016.04.007

Hong, S., & Park, H. S. (2012). Computer-mediated persuasion in online reviews: Statistical versus narrative evidence. *Computers in Human Behavior, 28,* 906–919. https://doi.org/10.1016/j.chb.2011.12.011

Hong, S.-M. (1992). Hong's Psychological Reactance Scale: A further factor analytic validation. *Psychological Reports, 70,* 512–514. https://doi.org/10.2466/pr0.1992.70.2.512

Hong, S.-M., & Page, S. (1989). A psychological reactance scale: Development, factor structure and reliability. *Psychological Reports, 64,* 1323–1326. https://doi.org/10.2466/pr0.1989.64.3c.1323

Hornick, J., Ofir, C., & Rachamim, M. (2017). Advertising appeals, moderators, and impact on persuasion: A quantitative assessment creates a hierarchy of appeals. *Journal of Advertising Research, 57*(3), 305–318. https://doi.org/10.2501/jar-2017-017

Hosman, L. A., & Siltanen, S. A. (2006). Powerful and powerless language forms: Their consequences for impression formation, attributions of control of self and control of others, cognitive responses, and message memory. *Journal of Language and Social Psychology, 25*(1), 33–46. https://doi.org/10.1177/0261927x05284477

Hovland, C. I., Irving, J. L., & Kelley, H. H. (1953). *Communication and persuasion: Psychological studies of opinion change.* Yale University Press.

Hovland, C. I., Lumsdaine, A. A., & Sheffield, F. D. (1949). *Experiments in mass communication.* Princeton University Press.

Hrubes, D., Ajzen, I., & Daigle, J. (2001). Predicting hunting intentions and behavior: An application of the theory of planned behavior. *Leisure Sciences, 23,* 165–178. https://doi.org/10.1080/014904001316896855

Hu, S., Li, Z., Zhang, J., & Zhu, J. (2018). Engaging scientists in science communication: The effect of social proof and meaning. *Journal of Cleaner Production, 170,* 1044–1051. https://doi.org/10.1016/j.jclepro.2017.09.210

Huang, Y., & Shen, F. (2016). Effects of cultural tailoring on persuasion in cancer communication: A meta-analysis. *Journal of Communication, 66,* 694–715. https://doi.org/10.1111/jcom.12243

Hullett, C. R. (2005). The impact of mood on persuasion: A meta-analysis. *Communication Research, 32,* 423–442. https://doi.org/10.1177/0093650205277317

Hullman, G. A. (2004). Interpersonal communication motives and message design logic: Exploring their interaction on perceptions of competence. *Communication Monographs, 71,* 208–225. https://doi.org/10.1080/0363775042000250411

Hullman, G. A., & Behbehani, A. (2018). Message design logic, tactics, and message goals of first and second requests in romantic relationships. *The Northwest Journal of Communication, 46*(1), 9–32.

Hunt, K. (1972). Source effects, message effects, and general effects in counteradvertising. In M. Venkatesan (Ed.), *Proceedings of the third annual conference of the Association for Consumer Research* (pp. 370–381). Association for Consumer Research.

Hunt, S. K. (2010). Curricular activities for political engagement. In J. Goldfinger & J. Presley (Eds.), *Educating students for political engagement: A guide to implementation and assessment for colleges and universities* (pp. 46–62). American Association of State Colleges and Universities.

Hunt, S. K., & Woolard, C. E. (2016). Service learning and innovative pedagogies. In P. L. Witt (Ed.), *Handbooks of communication science: Vol. 16. Communication and learning* (pp. 527–552). DeGruyter Mouton.

Hunt, S. K., Meyer, K. R., & Lippert, L. R. (2006). Implications of students' cognitive styles for the development of argumentation skills. *Argumentation and Advocacy, 42,* 157–163. https://doi.org/10.1080/00028533.2006.11821648

Hunt, S. K., Meyer, K. R., Hooker, J. F., Simonds, C. J., & Lippert, L. R. (2016). Implementing the political engagement project in an introductory communication course: An examination of the effects on students' political knowledge, efficacy, skills, behavior, and ideology. *eJournal of Public Affairs, 5*(2), 115–151. https://doi.org/10.21768/ejopa.v5i2.111

Hunt, S. K., Simonds, C. J., & Simonds, B. K. (2009). Uniquely qualified, distinctively competent: Delivering 21st century skills in the basic course. *Basic Communication Course Annual, 21*, 1–29. https://ecommons.udayton.edu/bcca/

Hunter, A. (2018). Towards a framework for computational persuasion with applications in behaviour change. *Argument and Computation, 9*, 15–40. https://doi.org/10.3233/ACC-170032

Hyvömen, A. E. (2018). Careless speech: Conceptualizing post-truth politics. *New Perspectives, 26*(3), 31–55. https://doi.org/10.1177/2336825x1802600303

Inch, E. S., & Warnick, B. (1998). *Critical thinking and communication: The use of reason in argument.* Allyn and Bacon.

Infante, D. A. (1988). *Arguing constructively.* Waveland.

Infante, D. A. (1995). Teaching students to understand and control verbal aggression. *Communication Education, 44*, 51–63. https://doi.org/10.1080/03634529509378997

Infante, D. A., & Rancer, A. S. (1982). A conceptualization and measure of argumentativeness. *Journal of Personality Assessment, 46*(1), 72–80. https://doi.org/10.1207/s15327752jpa4601_13

Infante, D. A., & Rancer, A. S. (1996). Argumentativeness and verbal aggressiveness: A review of recent theory and research. *Communication Yearbook, 19*, 319–351. https://doi.org/10.1080/23808985.1996.11678934

Infante, D. A., & Wigley, C. J. (1986). Verbal aggressiveness: An interpersonal model and measure. *Communication Monographs, 53*, 61–69. https://doi.org/10.1080/03637758609376126

Infante, D. A., Riddle, B. L., Horvath, C. L., & Tumlin, S. A. (1992). Verbal aggressiveness: Messages and reasons. *Communication Quarterly, 40*, 116–126. https://doi.org/10.1080/01463379209369827

Ismagilova, E., Slade, E., Rana, N. P., & Dwivedi, Y. K. (in press). The effect of characteristics of source credibility on consumer behaviour: A meta-analysis. *Journal of Retailing and Consumer Services.* https://doi.org/10.1016/j.jretconser.2019.01.005

Ivanov, B., Burns, W. J., Sellnow, T. L., Petrun Sayers, E. L., Veil, S. R., & Mayorga, M. W. (2016). Using inoculation message approach to promote public confidence in protective agencies. *Journal of Applied Communication Research, 44*, 381–398. https://doi.org/10.1080/00909882.2016.1225165

Ivanov, B., Parker, K. A., & Dillingham, L. L. (2018). Testing the limits of inoculation-generated resistance. *Western Journal of Communication, 82*, 648–665. https://doi.org/10.1080/10570314.2018.1454600

Ivanov, B., Rains, S. A., Geegan, S. A., Vos, S. C., Haarstad, N. D., & Parker, K. A. (2017). Beyond simple inoculation: Examining the persuasive value of inoculation for audiences with initially neutral or opposing attitudes. *Western Journal of Communication, 81*, 105–126. https://doi.org/10.1080/10570314.2016.1224917

Ivanov, B., Sims, J. D., Compton, J., Miller, C. H., Parker, K. A., Parker. J. L., Harrison, K. J., & Averbeck, J. M. (2015). The general content of postinoculation talk: Recalled issue-specific conversations following inoculation treatments. *Western Journal of Communication, 79*, 218–238. https://doi.org/10.1080/10570314.2014.943423

Iyengar, S., Hahn, K. S., Krosnick, J. A., & Walker, J. (2008). Selective exposure to campaign communication: The role of anticipated agreement and issue public membership. *The Journal of Politics, 70*(1), 186–200. https://doi.org/10.1017/s0022381607080139

Jacks, J. Z., & Devine, P. G. (2000). Attitude importance, forewarning of message content, and resistance to persuasion. *Basic and Applied Social Psychology, 22*(1), 19–29. https://doi.org/10.1207/s15324834basp2201_3

Jacks, J. Z., & Lancaster, L. C. (2015). Fit for persuasion: The effects of nonverbal delivery style, message framing, and gender on message effectiveness. *Journal of Applied Social Psychology, 45*, 203–213. https://doi.org/10.1111/jasp.12288

Jacks, J., & Cameron, K. A. (2003). Strategies for resisting persuasion. *Basic and Applied Social Psychology, 25*, 145–161. https://doi.org/10.1207/s15324834basp2502_5

Jackson, B., Compton, J., Thornton, A. L., & Dimmock, J. A. (2017). Re-thinking anxiety: Using inoculation messages to reduce and reinterpret public speaking fears. *PLoS ONE, 12*(1), e0169972. https://doi.org/10.1371/journal.pone.0169972

Jackson, J. M., & Harkins, S. G. (1985). Equity in effort: An explanation of the social loafing effect. *Journal of Personality and Social Psychology, 49*(5), 1199–1206. https://doi.org/10.1037//0022-3514.49.5.1199

Jacoby, B. (1996). *Service-learning in higher education: Concepts and practices.* Jossey-Bass.

Jacoby, B. (2009). *Civic engagement in higher education: Concepts and practices.* Jossey-Bass.

Jager, W. (2017). Enhancing the realism of simulation (EROS): On implementing and developing psychological theory in social simulation. *Journal of Artificial Societies and Social Simulation, 20*(3), article 14. https://doi.org/10.18564/jasss.3522

Jang, S. M. (2018). Mass shootings backfire: The boomerang effects of death concerns on policy attitudes. *Media Psychology, 22,* 1–25. https://doi.org/10.1080/15213269.2017.1421471

Janssen, L., Fennis, B. M., & Pruyn, A. T. H. (2010). Forewarned is forearmed: Conserving self-control strength to resist social influence. *Journal of Experimental Social Psychology, 46,* 911–921. https://doi.org/10.1016/j.jesp.2010.06.008

Jarman, J. W. (2016). Influence of political affiliation and criticism on the effectiveness of political fact-checking. *Communication Research Reports, 33*(1), 9–15. https://doi.org/10.1080/08824096.2015.1117436

Jaworski, A. (1993). *The power of silence: Social and pragmatic perspectives.* SAGE.

Jensen, J. D. (2008). Scientific uncertainty in news coverage of cancer research: Effects of hedging on scientists' and journalists' credibility. *Human Communication Research, 34,* 347–369. https://doi.org/10.1111/j.1468-2958.2008.00324.x

Jensen, M. L., Averbeck, J. M., Zhang, Z., & Wright, K. B. (2013). Credibility of anonymous online product reviews: A language expectancy perspective. *Journal of Management Information Systems,* 30(1), 293–323. https://doi.org/10.2753/mis0742-1222300109

Jian, L., Yin, D., & Liu, D. (2019). Can joy buy you money? The impact of the strength, duration, and phases of an entrepreneur's peak displayed joy on funding performance. *Academy of Management Journal, 62,* 1848–1871. https://doi.org/10.5465/amj.2017.1423

Johannesen, R. L. (1974). The functions of silence: A plea for communication research. *Western Speech, 38*(1), 25–35. https://doi.org/10.1080/10570317409373806

Johannesen, R. L., Valde, K. S., & Whedbee, K. E. (2008). *Ethics in human communication* (6th ed.). Waveland.

Johnson, D. W., & Johnson, R. T. (2009). An educational psychology success story: Social independent theory and cooperative learning. *Educational Researcher, 38,* 365–379. https://doi.org/10.3102/0013189x09339057

Jordan-Jackson, F. F., Lin, Y., Rancer, A. S., & Infante, D. A. (2008). Perceptions of males and females' use of aggressive affirming and nonaffirming messages in an interpersonal dispute: You've come a long way baby? *Western Journal of Communication, 72,* 239–258. https://doi.org/10.1080/10570310802210122

Jowett, G. S., & O'Donnell, V. J. (2019). *Propaganda and persuasion* (7th ed.). SAGE.

Jung, J. M., & Kellaris, J. J. (2006). Responsiveness to authority appeals among young French and American consumers. *Journal of Business Research, 59,* 735–744. https://doi.org/10.1016/j.jbusres.2006.01.011

Kahlor, L., Dunwoody, S., Griffin, R. J., Neuwirth, K., & Geise, J. (2003). Studying heuristic-systematic processing of risk communication. *Risk Analysis, 23,* 355–368. https://doi.org/10.1111/1539-6924.00314

Kahne, J., Middaugh, E., & Chi, B. (2003, August). *Democratic education: The untapped potential of high school government courses [Paper presentation].* Annual Meeting of the American Political Science Association, Philadelphia, PA, United States.

Kahneman, D., & Tversky, A. (1979). Prospect theory: An analysis of decision under risk. *Econometrica, 47*(2), 263–292. https://doi.org/10.21236/ada045771

Kamalski, J., Lentz, L., Sanders, T., & Zwaan, R. A. (2008). The forewarning effect of coherence markers in persuasive discourse: Evidence from persuasion and processing. *Discourse Processes, 45,* 545–579. https://doi.org/10.1080/01638530802069983

Kandaurova, M., & Lee, S. H. (2019). The effects of virtual reality (VR) on charitable giving: The role of empathy, guilt, responsibility and social cohesion. *Journal of Business Research, 100,* 571–580. https://doi.org/10.1016/j.jbusres.2018.10.027

Kao, D. T. (2007). Conclusion explicitness in message communication: The roles of NFC and knowledge in attitude formation. *Social Behavior and Personality, 35*(6), 819–826. https://doi.org/10.2224/sbp.2007.35.6.819

Karau, S. J., & Williams, K. D. (1993). Social loafing: A meta-analytic review and theoretical implications. *Journal of Personality and Social Psychology, 65*(4), 681–706. https://doi.org/10.1037//0022-3514.65.4.681

Karau, S. J., & Williams, K. D. (1993). Social loafing: A meta-analytic review and theoretical implications. *Journal of Personality and Social Psychology, 65*(4), 681–706. https://doi.org/10.1037//0022-3514.65.4.681

Kardes, F. R., Kim, J., & Lim, J. S. (1994). Moderating effects of prior knowledge on the perceived diagnosticity of beliefs derived from implicit versus explicit product claims. *Journal of Business Research, 29*, 219–224. https://doi.org/10.1016/0148-2963(94)90006-x

Karlsen, R., & Aardal, B. (2016). Political values count but issue ownership decides? How stable and dynamic factors influence party set and vote choice in multiparty systems. *International Political Science Review, 37*, 261–276. https://doi.org/10.1177/0192512114558456

Karmarkar, V. R., & Tormala, Z. L. (2010). Believe me, I have no idea what I'm talking about: The effects of source certainty on consumer involvement and persuasion. *Journal of Consumer Research, 36*, 1033–1049. https://doi.org/10.1086/648381

Karremans, J. C., Stroebe, W., & Claus, J. (2006). Beyond Vicary's fantasies: The impact of subliminal priming and brand choice. *Journal of Experimental Social Psychology, 42*, 792–798. https://doi.org/10.1016/j.jesp.2005.12.002

Katsumi, Y., Kim, S., Sung, K., Dolcos, F., & Dolcos, S. (2017). When nonverbal greetings "make it or break it": The role of ethnicity and gender in the effect of handshake on social appraisals. *Journal of Nonverbal Behavior, 41*, 345–365. https://doi.org/10.1007/s10919-017-0257-0

Katt, J. A., McCroskey, J. C., Sivo, S. A., Richmond, V. P., & Valencic, K. M. (2009). A structural equation modeling evaluation of the general model of instructional communication. *Communication Quarterly, 57*, 239–258. https://doi.org/10.1080/01463370903107196

Katz, D. (1960). The functional approach to the study of attitudes. *Public Opinion Quarterly, 24*(2), 163–204. https://doi.org/10.1086/266945

Kavanagh, J., & Rich, M. D. (2018). *Truth decay: An initial exploration of the diminishing role of facts and analysis in American public life.* Rand Corporation.

Kaye, B. K., & Johnson, T. J. (2002). Online and in the know: Uses and gratifications of the web for political information. *Journal of Broadcasting & Electronic Media, 46*(1), 54–71. https://doi.org/10.1207/s15506878jobem4601_4

Kearney, P., Plax, T. G., Richmond, V. P., & McCroskey, J. C. (1984). Power in the classroom IV: Alternatives to discipline. In R. N. Bostrom (Ed.), *Communication yearbook 8* (pp. 724–746). SAGE.

Kearney, P., Plax, T. G., Richmond, V. P., & McCroskey, J. C. (1985). Power in the classroom III: Teacher communication techniques and messages. *Communication Education, 34*, 19–28. https://doi.org/10.1080/03634528509378579

Kellermann, K. (2004). A goal-directed approach to gaining compliance: Relating differences among goals to differences in behaviors. *Communication Research, 31*(4), 397–445. https://doi.org/10.1177/0093650204266093

Kellermann, K., & Shea, B. C. (1996). Threats, suggestions, hints, and promises: Gaining compliance efficiently and politely. *Communication Quarterly, 44*, 145–165. https://doi.org/10.1080/01463379609370007

Kelley, H. H. (1973). The processes of causal attribution. *American Psychologist, 28*(2), 107–128. https://doi.org/10.1037/h0034225

Kelley, T. M. (2014). Motivational impairment effect. In T. R. Levine (Ed.), *Encyclopedia of deception* (pp. 682–684). SAGE.

Kendi, I. X. (2019). *How to be an antiracist.* One World.

Killgore, W. D., Grugle, N. L., Killgore, D. B., & Balkin, T. J. (2010). Sex differences in self-reported risk-taking propensity on the evaluation of risks scale. *Psychological Reports, 106*, 693–700. https://doi.org/10.2466/pr0.106.3.693-700

Kim, S. (2013). Does corporate advertising work in a crisis? An examination of inoculation theory. *Journal of Marketing Communications, 19*, 293–305. https://doi.org/10.1080/13527266.2011.634430

Kim, S., & So, J. (2018). How message fatigue toward health messages leads to ineffective persuasive outcomes: Examining the mediating roles of reactance and inattention. *Journal of Health Communication, 23*, 109–116. https://doi.org/10.1080/10810730.2017.1414900

Kim, S., Allen, M., Gattoni, A., Grimes, D., Herrman, A. M., Huang, H., Kim, J., Lu, S., Maier, M., May, A., Omachinski, K., Omori, K., Tenzek, K., LaPlant Turkiewicz, K., & Zhang, Y. (2012). Testing an additive model for the effectiveness of evidence on the persuasiveness of a message. *Social Influence, 7*(2), 65–77. https://doi.org/10.1080/15534510.2012.658285

Kim, S., Allen, M., Gattoni, A., Grimes, D., Herrman, A. M., Huang, H., Kim, J., Lu, S., Maier, M., May, A., Omachinski, K., Omori, K., Tenzek, K., LaPlant Turkiewicz, K., & Zhang, Y. (2012). Testing an additive model for the effectiveness of evidence on the persuasiveness of a message. *Social Influence, 7*(2), 65–77. https://doi.org/10.1080/15534510.2012.658285

Kim, S.-Y., Allen, M., Preiss, R. W., & Peterson, B. (2014). Meta-analysis of counterattitudinal advocacy data: Evidence for an additive cues model. *Communication Quarterly, 62,* 607–620. https://doi.org/10.1080/01463373.2014.949385

Kistler, D., Thöni, C., & Welzel, C. (2017). Survey response and observed behavior: Emancipative and secular values predict prosocial behaviors. *Journal of Cross-Cultural Psychology, 48*(4), 461–489. https://doi.org/10.1177/0022022117696799

Kittirattarkarn, G. P., Araujo, T., & Neijens, P. (2019). Challenging traditional culture? How personal and national collectivism-individualism moderates the effects of content characteristics and social relationships on consumer engagement with brand-related user-generated content. *Journal of Advertising, 48,* 197–214. https://doi.org/10.1080/00913367.2019.1590884

Koch, T. (2017). Again and again (and again): A repetition-frequency-model of persuasive communication. *Studies in Communication and Media, 6*(3), 218–239. https://doi.org/10.5771/2192-4007-2017-3-218

Kolyesnikova, N., & Dodd, T. H. (2009). There is no such thing as a free wine tasting: The effect of a tasting fee on obligation to buy. *Journal of Travel & Tourism Marketing, 26,* 806–819. https://doi.org/10.1080/10548400903356228

Krispenz, A., Dickhauser, O., & Reinhard, M.-A. (2016). Assessing task difficulty for other people: When deeper evaluation means "it's more about me!" *Social Psychology of Education, 19,* 865–877. https://doi.org/10.1007/s11218-016-9341-2

Kristofferson, K., McFerran, B., Morales, A. C., & Dahl, D. W. (2016). The dark side of scarcity promotions: How exposure to limited-quantity promotions can induce aggression. *Journal of Consumer Research, 43,* 683–706. https://doi.org/10.1093/jcr/ucw056

Krosnick, J. A., Boninger, D. S., Chaung, Y. C., Berent, M. K., & Carnot, C. G. (1993). Attitude strength: One construct or many related constructs? *Journal of Personality and Social Psychology, 65,* 1132–1151. https://doi.org/10.1037/0022-3514.65.6.1132

Kruger, J., & Dunning, D. (1999). Unskilled and unaware of it: How difficulties in recognizing one's own incompetence lead to inflated self-assessments. *Journal of Personality and Social Psychology, 77,* 1121–1134. https://doi.org/10.1037//0022-3514.77.6.1121

Kruglanski, A. W., Jasko, K., Chernikova, M., Milyavsky, M., Babush, M., Baldner, C., & Pierro, A. (2015). The rocky road from attitudes to behaviors: Charting the goal systemic course of actions. *Psychological Review, 122,* 598–620. https://doi.org/10.1037/a0039541

Kühberger, A., & Gradl, P. (2013). Choice, rating, and ranking: Framing effects with different response modes. *Journal of Behavioral Decision Making, 26,* 109–117. https://doi.org/10.1002/bdm.764

Kuiper, N. A., McKenzie, S. D., & Belanger, K. A. (1995). Cognitive appraisals and individual differences in sense of humor: Motivational and affective implications. *Personality and Individual Differences, 19*(3), 359–372. https://doi.org/10.1016/0191-8869(95)00072-e

Kumkale, G. T., & Albarracín, D. (2004). The sleeper effect in persuasion: A meta-analytic review. *Psychological Bulletin, 130*(1), 143–172. https://doi.org/10.1037/0033-2909.130.1.143

Kumkale, G. T., Albarracín, D., & Seignourel, P. J. (2010). The effects of source credibility in the presence or absence of prior attitudes: Implications for the design of persuasive communication campaigns. *Journal of Applied Social Psychology, 40*(6), 1325–1356. https://doi.org/10.1111/j.1559-1816.2010.00620.x

Kunda, Z. (1990). The case for motivated reasoning. *Psychological Bulletin, 108*(3), 480–498. https://doi.org/10.1037/0033-2909.108.3.480

Kussart, N. J., Hunt, S. K., & Simonds, C. J. (2007). Learning communities in the basic communication course: Exploring students' perception of power and use of compliance-gaining strategies. *Basic Communication Course Annual, 19,* 72–103. http://ecommons.udayton.edu/bcca/vol19/iss1/8

Küçük, M. (2010). Lurking in online asynchronous discussion. *Procedia Social and Behavioral Sciences, 2,* 2260–2263. https://doi.org/10.1016/j.sbspro.2010.03.319

Lambert, B. L., & Gillespie, J. L. (1994). Patient perceptions of pharmacy students' hypertension compliance-gaining messages: Effects of message design logic and content themes. *Health Communication, 6*(4), 311–325. https://doi.org/10.1207/s15327027hc0604_6

Lammers, H. B., Leibowitz, L., Seymour, G. E., & Hennessey, J. E. (1983). Humor and cognitive responses to advertising stimuli: A trace consolidation approach. *Journal of Business Research, 11*, 173–185. https://doi.org/10.1016/0148-2963(83)90026-7

Lamy, L., Fischer-Lokou, J., Gueguen, N., & Guegan, J. (2015). Sequential love priming as a compliance-gaining technique. *North American Journal of Psychology, 17*(3), 607–615.

Landau, M. J., Arndt, J., & Cameron, L. D. (2018). Do metaphors in health messages work? Exploring emotional and cognitive factors. *Journal of Experimental Social Psychology, 74*, 135–149. https://doi.org/10.1016/j.jesp.2017.09.006

Langlois, J. H., Kalakanis, L., Rubenstein, A. J., Larson, A., Hallam, M., & Smoot, M. (2000). Maxims or myths of beauty? A meta-analytic and theoretical review. *Psychological Bulletin, 126*, 390–423. https://doi.org/10.1037/0033-2909.126.3.390

Lariscy, R. A. W., & Tinkham, S. F. (1999). The sleeper effect and negative political advertising. *Journal of Advertising, 28*(4), 13–30. https://doi.org/10.1080/00913367.1999.10673593

Lariscy, R. W., Tinkham, S. F., & Sweetser, K. D. (2011). Kids these days: Examining differences in political uses and gratifications, Internet political participation, political information efficacy, and cynicism on the basis of age. *American Behavioral Scientist, 55*(6), 749–764. https://doi.org/10.1177/0002764211398091

Latané, B., Williams, K., & Harkins, S. (1979). Many hands make light the work: The causes and consequences of social loafing. *Journal of Personality and Social Psychology, 37*(6), 822–832. https://doi.org/10.1037//0022-3514.37.6.822

Lau-Gesk, L. G. (2003). Activating culture through persuasion appeals: An examination of the bicultural consumer. *Journal of Consumer Psychology, 13*(3), 301–315. https://doi.org/10.1207/s15327663jcp1303_11

Laurin, K., Kay, A. C., & Fitzsimons, G. J. (2012). Reactance versus rationalization: Divergent responses to policies that constrain freedom. *Psychological Science, 23*, 205–209. https://doi.org/10.1177/0956797611429468

Lawless, J. L. (2011). *Becoming a candidate: Political ambition and the decision to run for office*. Cambridge University Press.

Lazard, A. J., Dudo, A., Dennis, T., Ewald, M. G., & Love, B. (2017). Making a visual impression (or not): Current design practices of nutritional websites. *Health Communication, 32*, 470–482. https://doi.org/10.1080/10410236.2016.1140267

Lee, S. A., & Liang, Y. (2019). Robotic foot-in-the-door: Using sequential-request persuasive strategies in human-robot interaction. *Computers in Human Behavior, 90*, 351–356. https://doi.org/10.1016/j.chb.2018.08.026

Lee, S. Y. (2010). Ad-induced affect: The effects of forewarning, affect intensity, and prior brand attitude. *Journal of Marketing Communications, 16*, 225–237. https://doi.org/10.1080/13527260902869038

Lee, S., & Feeley, T. H. (2017). A meta-analysis of the pique technique of compliance. *Social Influence, 12*(1), 15–28. https://doi.org/10.1080/15534510.2017.1305986

LeFebvre, R. K., & Armstrong, C. (2018). Grievance-based social movement mobilization in the #Ferguson Twitter storm. *New Media & Society, 20*(1), 8–28. https://doi.org/10.1177/1461444816644697

Legal, J. B., Chappe, J., Coiffard, V., & Villard-Forest, A. (2012). Don't you know that you want to trust me? Subliminal goal priming and persuasion. *Journal of Experimental Social Psychology, 48*, 358–360. https://doi.org/10.1016/j.jesp.2011.06.006

Leo, L., Swinstead, E. H., Crous, F., & de Bruin, G. P. (2016). The influence of incidental haptic sensations in evaluating consumer brands. *Communicare, 35*(2), 1–15.

Leon, D. T., Rotunda, R. J., Sutton, M. A., & Schlossman, C. (2003). Internet forewarning effects on ratings of attraction. *Computers in Human Behavior, 19*, 39–57. https://doi.org/10.1016/s0747-5632(02)00017-1

Leone, C. (2006). Self-monitoring: Individual differences in orientations to the social world. *Journal of Personality, 74*(3), 632–657. https://doi.org/10.1111/j.1467-6494.2006.00387.x

Levesque, A., & Li, H. Z. (2016). Verbal compliance-gaining strategies used by male physicians and patient healthcare experience. *Communication and Medicine, 12*(2), 185–202. https://doi.org/10.1558/cam.17143

Levin, J. (2014, August). Who invented the ice bucket challenge? A search for the fundraising phenomenon's cold, soaked patient zero. *Slate*. http://www.slate.com/articles/technology/technology/2014/08/who_invented_the_ice_bucket_challenge_a_slate_investigation.html

Levine, K. J., Muenchen, R. A., & Brooks, A. M. (2010). Measuring transformational and charismatic leadership: Why isn't charisma measured? *Communication Monographs, 77,* 576–591. https://doi.org/10.1080/03637751.2010.499368

Levine, P. (2019). Another time for freedom? Lessons from the civil rights era for today's campuses. *Liberal Education,* 6–11.

Levine, T. R. (2014). Truth-default theory (TDT): A theory of human deception and deception detection. *Journal of Language and Social Psychology, 33*(4), 378–392. https://doi.org/10.1177/0261927x14535916

Levine, T. R., & Boster, F. J. (2001). The effects of power and message variables on compliance. *Communication Monographs, 68*(1), 28–48. https://doi.org/10.1080/03637750128049

Levine, T. R., & McCornack, S. A. (2014). Theorizing about deception. *Journal of Language and Social Psychology, 33*(4), 431–440. https://doi.org/10.1177/0261927x14536397

Lewandowsky, S., Ecker, U. K. H., & Cook, J. (2017). Beyond misinformation: Understanding and coping with the "post-truth" era. *Journal of Applied Research in Memory and Cognition, 6,* 353–369. https://doi.org/10.1016/j.jarmac.2017.07.008

Lewin, M., & Phau, I. (2014). An exploratory study of existential guilt appeals in charitable advertisements. *Journal of Marketing Management, 30,* 1467–1485. https://doi.org/10.1080/0267257x.2014.939215

Lewis, I., Watson, B., & White, K. M. (2013). Extending the explanatory utility of the EPPM beyond fear-based persuasion. *Health Communication, 28,* 84–98. https://doi.org/10.1080/10410236.2013.743430

Li Li, H. (2005). Rethinking silencing silences. In M. Boler (Ed.), *Democratic dialogue in education: Troubling speech, disturbing silence* (pp. 69–86). Peter Lang.

Liang, Y., Lee, S. A., & Jang, J. (2013). Mindlessness and gaining compliance in computer-human interaction. *Computers in Human Behavior, 29,* 1572–1579. https://doi.org/10.1016/j.chb.2013.01.009

Liao, Q. V., & Fu, W. T. (2014). Age differences in credibility judgments of online health information. *ACM Transactions on Computer-Human Interaction, 21*(1), 1–23. https://doi.org/10.1145/2534410

Lilleker, D. G., & Liefbroer, M. (2018). "Searching for something to believe in": Voter uncertainty in a post-truth environment. *International Journal of Media & Cultural Politics, 14,* 351–366. https://doi.org/10.1386/macp.14.3.351_1

Limbu, Y. B., Jayachandran, C., Babin, B. J., & Peterson, R. T. (2016). Empathy, nonverbal immediacy, and salesperson performance: The mediating role of adaptive selling behavior. *Journal of Business & Industrial Marketing, 31,* 654–667. https://doi.org/10.1108/jbim-03-2015-0048

Lin, X., Spence, P. R., & Lachlan, K. A. (2016). Social media and credibility indicators: The effect of influence cues. *Computers in Human Behavior, 63,* 264–271. https://doi.org/10.1016/j.chb.2016.05.002

Lipman, S. A., & Burt, S. A. (2017). Self-reported prevalence of pests in Dutch households and the use of the health belief model to explore householders' intentions to engage in pest control. *PLoS ONE, 12*(12), e0190399. https://doi.org/10.17605/OSF.IO/YG5KB

Lippert, L. R., Titsworth, B. S., & Hunt, S. K. (2005). The ecology of academic risk: Relationships between communication apprehension, verbal aggression, supportive communication, and students' academic risk status. *Communication Studies, 56,* 1–21. https://doi.org/10.1080/0008957042000332223

Lippert. L. R., & Hunt, S. K. (2005). *An ethnographic study of the role of humor in health care transactions.* Edwin Mellen Press.

Lokhorst, A. M., Werner, C., Staats, H., van Dijk, E., & Gale, J. L. (2013). Commitment and behavior change: A meta-analysis and critical review of commitment-making strategies in environmental research. *Environment and Behavior, 45,* 3–34. https://doi.org/10.1177/0013916511411477

Lopes, G. S., Sela, Y., & Shackelford, T. K. (2017). Endorsement of existence values predicts mate retention behaviors. *Personality and Individual Differences, 113,* 184–186. https://doi.org/10.1016/j.paid.2017.03.038

Lord, C. G., Ross, L., & Lepper, M. R. (1979). Biased assimilation and attitude polarization: The effects of prior theories on subsequently considered evidence. *Journal of Personality and Social Psychology, 37,* 2098–2190. https://doi.org/10.1037/0022-3514.37.11.2098

Lott, A. J., & Lott, B. E. (1965). Group cohesiveness as interpersonal attraction: A review of relationships with antecedent and consequent variables. *Psychological Bulletin, 64,* 259–309. https://doi.org/10.1037/h0022386

Lou, Y., Burley, H., Moe, A., & Sui, M. (2019). A meta-analysis of news media's public agenda-setting effects, 1972–2015. *Journalism & Mass Communication Quarterly, 96*(1), 150–172. https://doi.org/10.1177/1077699018804500

Lynn, M. (1991). Scarcity effects on value: A quantitative review of the commodity theory literature. *Psychology & Marketing, 8*(1), 43–57. https://doi.org/10.1002/mar.4220080105

Lyttle, J. (2001). The effectiveness of humor in persuasion: The case of business ethics training. *The Journal of General Psychology, 128*(2), 206–216. https://doi.org/10.1080/00221300109598908

Ma, L., Sian Lee, C., & Hoe-Lian Goh, D. (2014). Understanding news sharing in social media: An explanation from the diffusion of innovations theory. *Online Information Review, 38*, 598–615. https://doi.org/10.1108/OIR-10-2013-0239

Madden, T. J., Ellen, P. S., & Ajzen, I. (1992). A comparison of the theory of planned behavior and the theory of reasoned action. *Personality and Social Psychology Bulletin, 18*(1), 3–9. https://doi.org/10.1177/0146167292181001

Maertens, R., Anseel, F., & van der Linden, S. (2020). Combatting climate change misinformation: Evidence for longevity of inoculation and consensus messaging effects. *Journal of Environmental Psychology, 70*, 101455. https://doi.org/10.1016/j.jenvp.2020.101455

Maertens, R., Roozenbeek, J., Basol, M., & van der Linden, S. (2020). Long-term effectiveness of inoculation against misinformation: Three longitudinal experiments. *Journal of Experimental Psychology Applied.* https://doi.org/10.1037/xap0000315

Maikovich, A. K. (2005). A new understanding of terrorism using cognitive dissonance principles. *Journal for the Theory of Social Behaviour, 35*, 373–397. https://doi.org/10.1111/j.1468-5914.2005.00282.x

Maio, G. R., & Olson, J. M. (1998). Values as truisms: Evidence and implications. *Journal of Personality and Social Psychology, 74*(2), 294–311. https://doi.org/10.1037/0022-3514.74.2.294

Maio, G. R., Roese, N., Seligman, C., & Katz, A. (1996). Ratings, rankings, and the measurement of values: Evidence for the superior validity of ratings. *Basic and Applied Social Psychology, 18*, 171–181. https://doi.org/10.1207/s15324834basp1802_4

Maloney, E. K., Lapinski, M. K., & Witte, K. (2011). Fear appeals and persuasion: A review and update of the extended parallel process model. *Social and Personality Psychology Compass, 5*(4), 206–219. https://doi.org/0.1111/j.1751-9004.2011.00341.x

Manis, M., Cornell, S. D., & Moore, J. C. (1974). Transmission of attitude-relevant information through a communication chain. *Journal of Personality and Social Psychology, 30*, 81–94. https://doi.org/10.1037/h0036639

Mann, T., Sherman, D., & Updegraff, T. (2004). Dispositional motivations and message framing: A test of the congruency hypothesis in college students. *Health Psychology, 23*(3), 330–334. https://doi.org/10.1037/0278-6133.23.3.330

Maricchiolo, F., Gnisci, A., Bonaiuto, M., & Ficca, G. (2009). Effects of different types of hand gestures in persuasive speech on receivers' evaluations. *Journal of Cognitive Processes, 24*, 239–266. https://doi.org/10.1080/01690960802159929

Marlow, N., & Jansson-Boyd, C. V. (2011). To touch or not to touch: That is the question. Should consumers always be encouraged to touch products, and does it always alter product perception? *Psychology & Marketing, 28*(3), 256–266. https://doi.org/10.1002/mar.20391

Martin, B. A. S., & Strong, C. A. (2016). The trustworthy brand: Effects of conclusion explicitness and persuasion awareness on consumer judgments. *Marketing Letters, 27*, 473–485. https://doi.org/10.1007/s11002-014-9343-9

Martin, B. A. S., Lange, B., & Wong, S. (2003). Conclusion explicitness in advertising: The moderating role of need for cognition (NFC) and argument quality (AQ) on persuasion. *Journal of Advertising, 32*(4), 57–65. https://doi.org/10.1080/00913367.2003.10639148

Martinie, M.-A., Almecija, Y., Ros, C., & Gil, S. (2017). Incidental mood state before dissonance induction affects attitude change. *PLoS ONE, 12*(7), e0180531. https://doi.org/10.1371/journal.pone.0180531

Martino, S., & Lester, D. (2011). Perceptions of visible piercings: A pilot study. *Psychological Reports, 109*(3), 755–758. https://doi.org/10.2466/07.pr0.109.6.755-758

Marwell, G., & Schmitt, D. R. (1967). Dimensions of compliance-gaining behavior: An empirical analysis. *Sociometry, 30*(4), 350–364. https://doi.org/10.2307/2786181

Matsa, K. E., & Shearer, E. (2018, September 10). *News use across social media platforms 2018. Pew Research Center.* http://www.journalism.org/2018/09/10/news-use-across-social-media-platforms-2018/

Mattes, K., & Redlawsk, D. P. (2020). Voluntary exposure to political fact checks. *Journalism & Mass Communication Quarterly, 97,* 913–935. https://doi.org/10.1177/1077699020923603

Matthews, N. C. (2016). The influence of biological sex on perceived aggressive communication in debater-judge conflicts in parliamentary debate. *Western Journal of Communication, 80,* 38–59. https://doi.org/10.1080/10570314.2015.1114140

Matusitz, J., & Breen, G.-M. (2010). Inoculation theory: A framework for the reduction of skin cancer. *Journal of Evidence-Based Social Work, 7,* 219–234. https://doi.org/10.1080/19371910902911172

Matusitz, J., & Breen, G.-M. (2013). Applying inoculation theory to the study of recidivism reduction in criminal prison inmates. *Journal of Evidence-Based Social Work, 10,* 455–465. https://doi.org/10.1080/15433714.2012.760929

Mazer, J. P., & Hunt, S. K. (2008a). "Cool" communication in the classroom: A preliminary examination of student perceptions of instructor use of positive slang. *Qualitative Research Reports in Communication, 9,* 20–28. https://doi.org/10.1080/17459430802400316

Mazer, J. P., & Hunt, S. K. (2008b). The effects of instructor use of positive and negative slang on student motivation, affective learning, and classroom climate. *Communication Research Reports, 25,* 44–55. https://doi.org/10.1080/08824090701831792

McCornack, S. A. (1992). Information manipulation theory. *Communication Monographs, 59,* 1–16. https://doi.org/10.1080/03637759209376245

McCornack, S. A., Morrison, K., Paik, J. E., Wisner, A. M., & Zhu, X. (2014). Information manipulation theory 2: A propositional theory of deceptive discourse production. *Journal of Language and Social Psychology, 33*(4), 348–377. https://doi.org/10.1177/0261927x14534656

McCright, A. M., & Dunlap, R. E. (2011). The politicization of climate change and polarization in the American public's views of global warming, 2001–2010. *Sociological Quarterly, 52*(2), 155–194. https://doi.org/10.1111/j.1533-8525.2011.01198.x

McCroskey, J. C. (1966). Scales for the measurement of ethos. *Speech Monographs, 33,* 65–72. https://doi.org/10.1080/03637756609375482

McCroskey, J. C., & Teven, J. J. (1999). Goodwill: A reexamination of the construct and its measurement. *Communication Monographs, 66,* 90–103. https://doi.org/10.1080/03637759909376464

McCroskey, J. C., Richmond, V. P., Plax, T. G., & Kearney, P. (1985). Power in the classroom V: Behavior alteration techniques, communication training and learning. *Communication Education, 34,* 214–226. https://doi.org/10.1080/03634528509378609

McDermott, K. C. P., & Lachlan, K. A. (2020). Polarizing organizations and image repair: The effects of extreme disposition and ego-involvement on ELM processing routes for organizational responses. *Communication Studies, 71,* 332–350. https://doi.org/10.1080/10510974.2020.1733039

McDonald, S., Oates, C. J., Thyne, M., Timmis, A. J., & Carlile, C. (2015). Flying in the face of environmental concern: Why green consumers continue to fly. *Journal of Marketing Management, 31,* 1503–1528. https://doi.org/10.1080/0267257X.2015.1059352

McEachan, R., Taylor, N., Harrison, R., Lawton, R., Gardner, P., & Conner, M. (2016). Meta-analysis of the reasoned action approach (RAA) to understanding health behaviors. *Annals of Behavioral Medicine, 50,* 592–612. https://doi.org/10.1007/s12160-016-9798-4

McFalls, E. L., & Cobb-Roberts, D. (2001). Reducing resistance to diversity through cognitive dissonance instruction: Implications for teacher education. *Journal of Teacher Education, 52,* 164–172. https://doi.org/10.1177/0022487101052002007.

McGinnies, E., & Ward, C. (1980). Better liked than right: Trustworthiness and expertise as factors in credibility. *Personality and Social Psychological Bulletin, 6,* 467–472. https://doi.org/10.1177/014616728063023

McGrath, A. (2017). Dealing with dissonance: A review of cognitive dissonance reduction. *Social and Personality Psychology Compass, 11,* e12362. https://doi.org/10.1111/spc3.12362

McGuire, W. J. (1968). Personality and attitude change: An information-processing theory. In A. Greenwald, T. Brock, & T. Ostrum (Eds.), *Psychological foundations of attitudes.* Academic Press.

McGuire, W. J., & Papageorgis, D. (1962). Effectiveness of forewarning in developing resistance to persuasion. *Public Opinion Quarterly, 26*(1), 24–34. https://doi.org/10.1086/267068

McKeever, R., & McKeever, B. W. (2017). Moms and media: Exploring the effects of online communication on infant feeding practices. *Health Communication, 32,* 1059–1065. https://doi.org/10.1080/10410236.2016.1196638

McLean, R. (2018, September 5). Theranos is shutting down for good. *CNN Tech.* https://money.cnn.com/2018/09/05/technology/theranos-elizabeth-holmes/index.html

McLeod, J. M., & Becker, L. B. (1981). The uses and gratifications approach. In D. D. Nimmo & K. R. Sanders (Eds.), *Handbook of political communication* (pp. 67–99). SAGE.

Meadows, C. Z., Meadows, C. W., & Tang. L. (2020). The CDC and state health department Facebook messages: An examination of frames and the extended parallel processing model. *Communication Studies, 71,* 740–752. https://doi.org/10.1080/10510974.2020.1819839

Mehrabian, A. (1969). Some referents and measures of nonverbal behavior. *Behavioral Research Methods and Instrumentation, 1,* 203–207. https://doi.org/10.3758/bf03208096

Mehrabian, A. (1971). *Silent messages.* Wadsworth.

Metzger, M. J., Flanagin, A. J., & Medders, R. B. (2010). Social and heuristic approaches to credibility evaluation online. *Journal of Communication, 60,* 413–439. https://doi.org/10.1111/j.1460-2466.2010.01488.x

Meyer, J. C. (2000). Humor as a double-edged sword: Four functions of humor in communication. *Communication Theory, 10*(3), 310–331. https://doi.org/10.1111/j.1468-2885.2000.tb00194.x

Meyer, K. R. (2009). *Student classroom engagement: Rethinking participation grades and student silence* [Unpublished doctoral dissertation]. Ohio University. https://etd.ohiolink.edu/

Meyer, K. R., Kurtz, R. R., Hines, J. L., Simonds, C. J., & Hunt, S. K. (2010). Assessing preemptive argumentation in students' persuasive speech outlines. *Basic Communication Course Annual, 22,* 6–38.

Miceli, M., de Rosis, F., & Poggi, I. (2006). Emotional and non-emotional persuasion. *Applied Artificial Intelligence, 20,* 849–879. https://doi.org/10.1080/08839510600938193

Milgram, S. (1963). Behavioral study of obedience. *Journal of Abnormal and Social Psychology, 67,* 371–378. https://doi.org/10.1037/h0040525

Miller, C. H., Ivanov, B., Sims, J., Compton, J., Harrison, K. J., Parker, K. A., Parker, J. L., & Averbeck, J. M. (2013). Boosting the potency of resistance: Combining the motivational forces of inoculation and psychological reactance. *Human Communication Research, 39,* 127–155. https://doi.org/10.1111/j.1468-2958.2012.01438.x

Miller, C. H., Lane, L. T., Deatrick, L. M., Young, A. M., & Potts, K. A. (2007). Psychological reactance and promotional health messages: The effects of controlling language, lexical concreteness, and the restoration of freedom. *Human Communication Research, 33,* 219–240. https://doi.org/10.1111/j.1468-2958.2007.00297.x

Miller, D. W., & Marks, L. J. (1992). Mental imagery and sound effects in radio commercials. *Journal of Advertising, 21*(4), 83–93. https://doi.org/10.1080/00913367.1992.10673388

Miller, G. R. (1983). Telling it like it isn't and not telling it like it is: Some thoughts on deceptive communication. In J. I. Sisco (Ed.), *The Jensen lectures: Contemporary communication studies* (pp. 91–116). University of South Florida Press.

Miller, G. R., Boster, F., Roloff, M., & Seibold, D. (1977). Compliance-gaining message strategies: A typology and some findings concerning effects of situational differences. *Communication Monographs, 44,* 37–51. https://doi.org/10.1080/03637757709390113

Miller, R. L., Wozniak, W. J., Rust, M. R., Miller, B. R., & Slezak, J. (1996). Counterattitudinal advocacy as a means of enhancing instructional effectiveness: How to teach students what they do not want to know. *Teaching of Psychology, 23*(4), 215–219. https://doi.org/10.1207/s15328023top2304_2

Milyavsky, M., Hassin, R. R., & Schul, Y. (2012). Guess what? Implicit motivation boosts the influence of subliminal information on choice. *Consciousness and Cognition, 21,* 1232–1241. https://doi.org/10.1016/j.concog.2012.06.001

Miron, A. M., & Brehm, J. W. (2006). Reactance theory—40 years later. *Zeitschrift Für Sozialpsychologie, 37*(1), 9–18. https://doi.org/10.1024/0044-3514.37.1.3

Monahan, D. M. (2014). Eye contact. In T. R. Levine (Ed.), *Encyclopedia of deception* (pp. 351–353). SAGE.

Monahan, J. L., Murphy, S. T., & Zajonc, R. B. (2000). Subliminal mere exposure: Specific, general, and diffuse effects. *Psychological Science, 11,* 462–466. https://doi.org/10.1111/1467-9280.00289

Montanaro, E. A., Kershaw, T. S., & Bryan, A. D. (2018). Dismantling the theory of planned behavior: Evaluating the relative effectiveness of attempts to uniquely change attitudes, norms, and perceived behavioral control. *Journal of Behavioral Medicine, 41,* 757–770. https://doi.org/10.1007/s10865-018-9923-x

Montoya, R. M., & Pittinsky, T. L. (2011). When increased group identification leads to outgroup liking and cooperation: The role of trust. *The Journal of Social Psychology, 151,* 784–806. https://doi.org/10.1080/00224545.2010.538762

Moore, G. C., & Benbasat, I. (1996). Integrating diffusion of innovations and theory of reasoned action models to predict utilization of information by end-users. In K. Kautz & J. Pries-Heje (Eds.), *Diffusion and adoption of information technology* (pp. 132–146). Springer.

Moore, K. P., & Richards, A. S. (2019). The effects of instructor credibility, grade incentives, and framing of a technology policy on students' intent to comply and motivation to learn. *Communication Studies, 70,* 394–411. https://doi.org/10.1080/10510974.2019.1617761

Moore, T. E. (1988). The case against subliminal manipulation. *Psychology and Marketing, 5,* 297–316. https://doi.org/10.1002/mar.4220050403

Morley, D. D., & Walker, K. B. (1987). The role of importance, novelty, and plausibility in producing belief change. *Communication Monographs, 54,* 436–442. https://doi.org/10.1080/03637758709390243

Morrison, K. (2005). Motivating women and men to take protective action against rape: Examining direct and indirect persuasive fear appeals. *Health Communication, 18,* 237–256. https://doi.org/10.1207/s15327027hc1803_3

Morrison, K., & McCornack, S. A. (2015). Rethinking susceptibility: Examining the cognitive and emotional processing of other-directed persuasive fear appeal messages. *Communication Reports, 28*(2), 103–114. https://doi.org/10.1080/08934215.2014.980436

Mottet, T. P., Frymier, A. B., & Beebe, S. A. (2006). Theorizing about instructional communication. In T. P. Mottet, V. P. Richmond, & J. C. McCroskey (Eds.), *Instructional communication: Rhetorical and relational perspectives* (pp. 255–282). Allyn Bacon.

Mukherjee, A., & Lee, S. Y. (2016). Scarcity appeals in advertising: The moderating role of expectation of scarcity. *Journal of Advertising, 45*(2), 256–268. https://doi.org/10.1080/00913367.2015.1130666

Munch, J. M., Buller, G. W., & Swasy, J. L. (1993). The effects of argument structure and affective tagging on product attitude formation. *Journal of Consumer Research, 20,* 294–302. https://doi.org/10.1086/209350

Murphy, N. A. (2007). Appearing smart: The impression management of intelligence, person perception accuracy, and behavior in social interaction. *Personality and Social Psychology Bulletin, 33,* 325–339. https://doi.org/10.1177/0146167206294871

Mwagwabi, F., McGill, T., & Dixon, M. (2018). Short-term and long-term effects of fear appeals in improving compliance with password guidelines. *Communications of the Association for Information Systems, 42,* 147–182. https://doi.org/10.17705/1CAIS.04207

Myers, J. R., & Sar, S. (2013). Persuasive social approval cues in print advertising: Exploring visual and textual strategies and consumer self-monitoring. *Journal of Marketing Communications, 19*(3), 168–181. https://doi.org/10.1080/13527266.2011.581303

Nabi, R. L., & Myrick, J. G. (2018). Uplifting fear appeals: Considering the role of hope in fear-based persuasive messages. *Health Communication,* 1–12. https://doi.org/10.1080/10410236.2017.1422847

Namkoong, K., Nah, S., Record, R. A., & Van Stee, S. K. (2017). Communication, reasoning, and planned behaviors: Unveiling the effect of interactive communication in an anti-smoking social media campaign. *Health Communication, 32,* 41–50. https://doi.org/10.1080/10410236.2015.1099501

Nan, X. (2012). Relative persuasiveness of gain- versus loss-framed human papillomavirus vaccination messages for the present- and future-minded. *Human Communication Research, 38,* 72–94. https://doi.org/10.1111/j.1468-2958.2011.01419.x

Napieralski, L. P., Brooks, C. I., & Droney, J. M. (1995). The effect of duration of eye contact on American college students' attributions of state, trait, and test anxiety. *Journal of Social Psychology, 135,* 273–280. https://doi.org/10.1080/00224545.1995.9713957

NCA Legislative Council. (2017). *Credo for ethical communication.* https://www.natcom.org/sites/default/files/Public_Statement_Credo_for_Ethical_Communication_2017.pdf

Nelson, M. R. (2008). The hidden persuaders. *Journal of Advertising, 37*(1), 113–126. https://doi.org/10.2753/JOA0091-3367370109

Nera, K., Pantazi, M., & Klein, O. (2018). "These are just stories, Mulder": Exposure to conspiracist fiction does not produce narrative persuasion. *Frontiers in Psychology, 9,* article 684. https://doi.org/10.3389/fpsyg.2018.00684

Nettel, A. L., & Roque, G. (2012). Persuasive argumentation versus manipulation. *Argumentation, 26,* 55–69. https://doi.org/10.1007/s10503-011-9241-8

Neuwirth, K., Frederick, E., & Mayo, C. (2002). Person-effects and heuristic-systematic processing. *Communication Research, 29,* 320–359. https://doi.org/10.1177/0093650202029003005

Nichols, T. (2017). *The death of expertise: The campaign against established knowledge and why it matters.* Oxford University Press.

Niederdeppe, J., Gollust, S. E., & Barry, C. L. (2014). Inoculation in competitive framing examining message effects on policy preferences. *Public Opinion Quarterly, 78,* 634–655. https://doi.org/10.1093/poq/nfu026

Nisbett, R. E., & Ross, L. (1980). *Human inference: Strategies and shortcomings of social judgment.* Prentice Hall.

Nyhan, B., & Reifler, J. (2010). When corrections fail: The persistence of political misperceptions. *Political Behavior, 32,* 303–330. https://doi.org/10.1007/s11109-010-9112-2

Nyhan, B., & Reifler, J. (2012, February). *Misinformation and fact-checking: Research findings from social science.* New American Foundation. http://newamerica.net/sites/newamerica.net/files/policydocs/Misinformation_and_Fact-checking.pdf

Nyhan, B., & Reifler, J. (2012, November). *Misinformation and fact-checking: Research findings from social science.* New American Foundation.

Nyhan, B., & Reifler, J. (2019). The roles of information deficits and identity threat in the prevalence of misperceptions. *Journal of Elections, Public Opinion and Parties, 29*(2), 222–244. https://doi.org/10.1080/17457289.2018.1465061

O'Barr, W. M., & Atkins, B. (1980). "Women's language" or "powerless language?" In S. MConnell-Ginet, R. Borker, & N. Furman (Eds.), *Women and language in literature and society* (pp. 93–110). Praeger.

O'Keefe, B. J. (1988). The logic of message design: Individual differences in reasoning about communication. *Communication Monographs, 55,* 80–103. https://doi.org/10.1080/03637758809376159

O'Keefe, B. J., & McCornack, S. A. (1987). Message logic and message goal structure: Effects on perceptions of message quality in regulative communication situations. *Human Communication Research, 14,* 68–92. https://doi.org/10.1111/j.1468-2958.1987.tb00122.x

O'Keefe, D. J. (1987). The persuasive effects of delaying identification of high- and low-credibility communicators: A meta-analytic review. *Central States Communication Journal, 38,* 64–72. https://doi.org/10.1080/10510978709368231

O'Keefe, D. J. (1998). Justification explicitness and persuasive effects: A meta-analytic review of the effects of varying support articulation in persuasive messages. *Argumentation and Advocacy, 35,* 61–75. https://doi.org/10.1080/00028533.1998.11951621

O'Keefe, D. J. (2002). *Persuasion: Theory and research* (2nd ed.). SAGE.

O'Keefe, D. J., & Jensen, J. D. (2007). The relative persuasiveness of gain-framed loss-framed messages for encouraging disease prevention behaviors: A meta-analytic review. *Journal of Health Communication, 12,* 623–644. https://doi.org/10.1080/10810730701615198

O'Keefe, D. J., & Jensen, J. D. (2009). The relative persuasiveness of gain-framed and loss-framed messages for encouraging disease detection behaviors: A meta-analytic review. *Journal of Communication, 59,* 296–316. https://doi.org/10.1111/j.1460-2466.2009.01417.x

O'Sullivan, P. B., Hunt, S. K., & Lippert, L. R. (2004). Mediated immediacy: A language of affiliation in a technological age. *Journal of Language and Social Psychology, 23,* 464–490. https://doi.org/10.1177/0261927x04269588

Oates, C., Blades, M., & Gunter, B. (2002). Children and television advertising: When do they understand persuasive intent? *Journal of Consumer Behavior, 1*(3), 238–245. https://doi.org/10.1002/cb.69

Oates, C., Blades, M., Gunter, B., & Don, J. (2003). Children's understanding of television advertising: A qualitative approach. *Journal of Marketing Communications, 9,* 59–71. https://doi.org/10.1080/1352726032000080858

Ogden, J. (2003). Some problems with social cognition models: A pragmatic and conceptual analysis. *Health Psychology, 22,* 424–428. https://doi.org/10.1037/0278-6133.22.4.424

Olison, W. O., & Roloff, M. E. (2012). Responses to organizational mandates: How voice attenuates psychological reactance and dissent. *Communication Research Reports, 29,* 204–216. https://doi.org/10.1080/08824096.2012.684984

Olson, M. K., Vos, S. C., & Sutton, J. (2020). Threat and efficacy in television news: Reporting on an emerging infectious disease. *Western Journal of Communication, 84,* 623–640. https://doi.org/10.1080/10570314.2020.1755721

Oni, A. A., Oni, S., Mbarika, V., & Ayo, C. K. (2017). Empirical study of user acceptance of online political participation: Integrating civic voluntarism model and theory of reasoned action. *Government Information Quarterly, 34,* 317–328. https://doi.org/10.1016/j.giq.2017.02.003

Ooms, J. A., Jansen, C. J. M., & Hoeks, J. C. J. (2020). The story against smoking: An exploratory study into the processing and perceived effectiveness of narrative visual smoking warnings. *Health Education Journal, 79,* 166–179. https://doi.org/10.1177/0017896919867436

Orji, R., Mandryk, R. L., & Vassileva, J. (2015). Gender, age, and responsiveness to Cialdini's persuasive strategies. In T. MacTavish & S. Basapur (Eds.), *Persuasive Technology* (pp. 147–159). Springer. https://doi.org/10.1007/978-3-319-20306-5_14

Oxford University Press. (2017). *Word of the year 2016.* https://global.oup.com/academic/content/word-of-the-year/?cc=us&lang=en

Pai, H. H., Sears, D. A., Maeda, Y. (2015). Effects of small-group learning on transfer: A meta-analysis. *Educational Psychology Review, 27,* 79–102. https://doi.org/10.1007/s10648-014-9260-8

Palczewski, C. H., Ice, R., & Fritch, J. (2012). *Rhetoric in civic life.* Strata.

Palmer, C. L., & Peterson, R. D. (2016). Halo effects and the attractiveness premium in perceptions of political expertise. *American Politics Research, 44,* 353–382. https://doi.org/10.1177/1532673x15600517

Papyrina, V. (2019). The trade-off between quantity and quality of information in gender responses to advertising. *Journal of Promotion Management, 25*(1), 1–19. https://doi.org/10.1080/10496491.2018.1427652

Paquin, R. S., & Keating, D. M. (2017). Fitting identity in the reasoned action framework: A meta-analysis and model comparison. *The Journal of Social Psychology, 157,* 47–63. https://doi.org/10.1080/00224545.2016.1152217

Park, H. S., Levine, T. R., Kingsley Westerman, C. Y., Orfgen, T., & Foregger, S. (2007). The effects of argument quality and involvement type on attitude formation and attitude change: A test of dual-process and social judgment predictions. *Human Communication Research, 33,* 81–102. https://doi.org/10.1111/j.1468-2958.2007.00290.x

Park, N., Kee, K. F., & Valenzuela, S. (2009). Being immersed in social networking environment: Facebook groups, uses and gratifications, and social outcomes. *CyberPsychology & Behavior, 12,* 729–733. https://doi.org/10.1089/cpb.2009.0003

Parker, K. A., Geegan, S., Ivanov, B., Slone, A., Silberman, W., Martin, J., Hester, E., Goatley-Soan, S., Anderson, A., Herrington, T., & Riker, S. (2020). Defending democracy: Inoculation's efficacy in protecting first amendment attitudes. *Communication Studies, 71,* 22–39. https://doi.org/10.1080/10510974.2019.1671889

Parker, K. A., Rains, S. A., & Ivanov, B. (2016). Examining the "blanket of protection" conferred by inoculation: The effects of inoculation messages on the cross-protection of related attitudes. *Communication Monographs, 83,* 49–68. https://doi.org/10.1080/03637751.2015.1030681

Parton, S. R., Siltanen, S. A., Hosman, L. A., & Langenderfer, J. (2002). Employment interview outcomes and speech style effects. *Journal of Language and Social Psychology, 21*(2), 144–161. https://doi.org/10.1177/02627x02021002003

Pascual, A., Carpenter, C. J., Gueguen, N., & Girandola, F. (2016). A meta-analysis of the effectiveness of the low-ball compliance-gaining procedure. *European Review of Applied Psychology, 66*(5), 261–267. https://doi.org/10.1016/j.erap.2010.06.004

Paul, C., & Matthews, M. (2016). *The Russian "firehose of falsehood" propaganda model: Why it might work and options to counter it.* RAND Corporation. https://www.rand.org/pubs/perspectives/PE198.html

Peachey, A. A., Sutton, D. L., & Cathorall, M. L. (2016). Helmet ownership and use among skateboarders. *Health Education Journal, 75,* 565–576. https://doi.org/10.1177/0017896915607912

Peck, J., & Childers, T. L. (2003). To have and to hold: The influence of haptic information on product judgments. *Journal of Marketing, 67,* 35–48. https://doi.org/10.1509/jmkg.67.2.35.18612

Peck, J., & Johnson, J. W. (2011). Autotelic need for touch, haptics, and persuasion: The role of involvement. *Psychology & Marketing, 28*(3), 222–239. https://doi.org/10.1002/mar.20389

Peck, J., & Wiggins, J. (2006). It just feels good: Customers' affective response to touch and its influence on persuasion. *Journal of Marketing, 70*, 56–69. https://doi.org/10.1509/jmkg.70.4.56

Perloff, R. M. (2017). *The dynamics of persuasion: Communication and attitudes in the 21st century* (6th ed.). Routledge.

Peters, G.-J. Y., Ruiter, R. A. C., & Kok, G. (2013). Threatening communication: a critical re-analysis and a revised meta-analytic test of fear appeal theory. *Health Psychology Review, 7*(supl), S8–S31. https://doi.org/10.1080/17437199.2012.703527

Petty, R. E., & Cacioppo, J. T. (2018). *Attitudes and persuasion: Classical and contemporary approaches*. Routledge.

Petty, R. E., & Wegener, D. T. (1998). Matching versus mismatching attitude functions: Implications for scrutiny of persuasive messages. *Personality and Social Psychology Bulletin, 24*(3), 227–240. https://doi.org/10.1177/0146167298243001

Petty, R. E., Cacioppo, J. T., & Schumann, D. (1983). Central and peripheral routes to advertising effectiveness: The moderating role of involvement. *Journal of Consumer Research, 10*(2), 135–146. https://doi.org/10.1086/208954

Petty, R. E., Priester, J. R., & Wegener, D. T. (1994). Cognitive processes in attitude change. In R. S. Wyer & T. K. Srull (Eds.), *Handbook of social cognition* (2nd ed., pp. 69–142). Erlbaum.

Petty, R. E., Schumann, D. W., Richman, S. A., & Strathman, A. J. (1993). Positive mood and persuasion: Different roles for affect under high- and low-elaboration conditions. *Journal of Personality and Social Psychology, 64,* 5–20. https://doi.org/10.1037/0022-3514.64.1.5

Petty, R. E., Wegener, D. T., & Fabrigar, L. R. (1997). Attitudes and attitude change. *Annual review of Psychology, 48*, 609–647. https://doi.org/10.1146/annurev.psych.48.1.609

Pew Research Center. (2018, July 11). *Activism in the social media age.* https://www.pewinternet.org/2018/07/11/public-attitudes-toward-political-engagement-on-social-media/

Pfau, M., Roskos-Ewoldsen, D., Wood, M., Yin, S., Cho, J., Lu, K., & Shen, L. (2003). Attitude accessibility as an alternative explanation for how inoculation confers resistance. *Communication Monographs, 70*, 39–51. https://doi.org/10.1080/03637750302474

Picard, M. (1952). *The world of silence* (S. Godman, Trans.). Henry Regnery Company. (Original work published 1948)

Picard, M. (1963). *Man and language* (S. Godman, Trans.). Henry Regnery Company.

Pithers, R. T. (2002). Cognitive learning style: A review of the field dependent-field independent approach. *Journal of Vocational Education and Training, 54*(1), 117–132. https://doi.org/10.1080/13636820200200191

Pittam, J. (1990). The relationship between perceived persuasiveness of nasality and source characteristics for Australian and American listeners. *Journal of Social Psychology, 130*, 81–87. https://doi.org/10.1080/00224545.1990.9922937

Platt, G. M., & Williams, R. H. (2002). Ideological language and social movement mobilization: A sociolinguistic analysis of segregationist's ideologies. *Sociological Theory, 20*(3), 328–359. https://doi.org/10.1111/1467-9558.00167

Plax, T. G., Kearney, P., & Tucker, L. K. (1986). Prospective teachers' use of behavior alteration techniques on common student misbehaviors. *Communication Education, 35*, 43–53. https://doi.org/10.1080/03634528609388317

Pornpitakpan, C. (2004). The persuasiveness of source credibility: A critical review of five decades' evidence. *Journal of Applied Social Psychology, 34*(2), 243–281. https://doi.org/10.1111/j.1559-1816.2004.tb02547.x

Pratkanis, A. R., Greenwald, A. G., Leippe, M. R., & Baumgardner, M. H. (1988). In search of reliable persuasion effects: III. The sleeper effect is dead. Long live the sleeper effect. *Journal of Personality and Social Psychology, 54*(2), 203–218. https://doi.org/10.1037//0022-3514.54.2.203

Pressgrove, G., & Kim, C. (2018). Stewardship, credibility, and political communications: A content analysis of the 2016 election. *Public Relations Review, 44*, 247–255. https://doi.org/10.1016/j.pubrev.2018.01.003

Price, P. C., & Stone, E. R. (2004). Intuitive evaluation likelihood judgment producers: Evidence for a confidence heuristic. *Journal of Behavioral Decision Making, 17*, 39–57. https://doi.org/10.1002/bdm.460

Priester, J., Wegener, D., Petty, R., & Fabrigar, L. (1999). Examining the psychological process underlying the sleeper effect: The elaboration likelihood model explanation. *Media Psychology, 1*(1), 27–48. https://doi.org/10.1207/s1532785xmep0101_3

Putnam, W. B. & Street, R. L., Jr. (1984). The conception and perception of noncontent speech performance: Implications for speech-accommodation theory. *International Journal of Social Language, 46,* 97–114. https://doi.org/10.1515/ijsl.1984.46.97

Quaschning, K., Körner, M., & Wirtz, M. (2013). Analyzing the effects of shared decision-making, empathy, and team interaction on patient satisfaction and treatment acceptance in medical rehabilitation using a structural equation modeling approach. *Patient Education and Counseling, 91,* 167–175. https://doi.org/10.1016/j.pec.2012.12.007

Quick, B. L. (2012). What is the best measure of psychological reactance? An empirical test of two measures. *Health Communication, 27,* 1–9. https://doi.org/10.1080/10410236.2011.567446

Quick, B. L., & Stephenson, M. T. (2007). The reactance restoration scale (RRS): A measure of direct and indirect restoration. *Communication Research Reports, 24,* 131–138. https://doi.org/10.1080/08824090701304840

Quick, B. L., & Stephenson, M. T. (2008). Examining the role of trait reactance and sensation seeking on perceived threat, state reactance, and reactance restoration. *Human Communication Research, 34,* 448–476. https://doi.org/10.1111/j.1468-2958.2008.00328.x

Quick, B. L., LaVoie, N. R., Reynolds-Tylus, T., Martinez-Gonzalez, A., & Skurka, C. (2017). Examining mechanisms underlying fear-control in the extended parallel process model. *Health Communication, 33,* 379–391. https://doi.org/10.1080/10410236.2016.1266738

Rad, M. S., Martingano, A. J., & Ginges, J. (2018). Toward a psychology of homo sapiens: Making psychological science more representative of the human population. *Proceedings of the National Academy of Sciences of the United States of America, 115*(45), 11401–11405. https://doi.org/10.1073/pnas.1721165115

Raghunathan, R., & Trope, Y. (2002). Walking the tightrope between feeling good and being accurate: Mood as a resource in processing persuasive messages. *Journal of Personality and Social Psychology, 83,* 510–525. https://doi.org/10.1037//0022-3514.83.3.510

Rains, S. A. (2013). The nature of psychological reactance revisited: A meta-analytic review. *Human Communication Research, 39,* 47–73. https://doi.org/10.1111/j.1468-2958.2012.01443.x

Rao, H., Greve, H. R., & Davis, G. F. (2001). Fool's gold: Social proof in the initiation and abandonment of coverage by Wall Street analysts. *Administrative Science Quarterly, 46,* 502–526. https://doi.org/10.2307/3094873

Rauch, J. (2020, November 18). Trump's firehose of falsehood: His refusal to concede is more than sour grapes. It's an information-warfare tactic to leave the public bewildered and cynical. *Persuasion.* https://www.persuasion.community/p/trumps-firehose-of-falsehood

Ray, G. B. (1986). Vocally cued personality prototypes: An implicit personality theory approach. *Communication Monographs, 53,* 266–276. https://doi.org/10.1080/03637758609376141

Record, R. A., Helme, D., Savage, M. W., & Harrington, N. G. (2017). *Let's Clear the Air*: A campaign that effectively increased compliance with a university's tobacco-free policy. *Journal of Applied Communication Research, 45,* 79–95. https://doi.org/10.1080/00909882.2016.1248471

Regier, T., & Xu, Y. (2017). The Sapir-Whorf hypothesis and inference under uncertainty. *WIREs Cognitive Science, 8,* e1440. https://doi.org/10.1002/wcs.1440

Reinard, J. C. (1998). The persuasive effects of testimonial assertion evidence. In M. Allen & R. W. Preiss (Eds.), *Persuasion: Advances through meta-analysis* (pp. 69–86). Hampton.

Reinhart, A. M., & Anker, A. E. (2012). An exploration of transportation and psychological reactance in organ donation PSAs. *Communication Research Reports, 29,* 274–284. https://doi.org/10.1080/08824096.2012.704601

Reynolds, R. A., & Reynolds, J. L. (2002). Evidence. In J. P. Dillard & M. Pfau (Eds.), *The persuasion handbook: Developments in theory and practice* (pp. 427–444). SAGE.

Reynolds-Tylus, T. (2019). An examination of message elaboration as a moderator of psychological reactance. *Communication Research Reports, 36,* 158–169. https://doi.org/10.1080/08824096.2019.1580567

Reznitskaya, A., & Wilkinson, A. G. (2017). Truth matters: Teaching young students to search for the most reasonable answer. *Phi Delta Kappan, 99,* 33–38. https://doi.org/10.1177/0031721717745550

Rhodes, N., & Wood, W. (1992). Self-esteem and intelligence affect influenceability: The mediating role of message reception. *Psychological Bulletin, 111*(1), 156–171. https://doi.org/10.1037/0033-2909.111.1.156

Rhodes, N., Roskos-Ewoldsen, D. R., Edison, A., & Bradford, M. B. (2008). Attitude and norm accessibility affect processing of anti-smoking messages. *Health Psychology, 27,* S224–S232. https://doi.org/10.1037/0278-6133.27.3(suppl.).s224

Rice, R. E., & Atkin, C. K. (2009). Public communication campaigns: Theoretical principles and practical applications. In J. Bryant & M. Oliver (Eds.), *Media effects: Advances in theory and research* (3rd ed., pp. 436–468). Erlbaum.

Rich, P. R., & Zaragoza, M. S. (2016). The continued influence of implied and explicitly stated misinformation in news reports. *Journal of Experimental Psychology: Learning, Memory, and Cognition, 42*(1), 62–74. https://doi.org/10.1037/xlm0000155

Richard, M. O., Chebat, J. C., Yang, Z., & Putrevu, S. (2010). A proposed model of online consumer behavior: Assessing the role of gender. *Journal of Business Research, 63,* 926–934. https://doi.org/10.1016/j.jbusres.2009.02.027

Richards, A. S., & Banas, J. A. (2015). Inoculating against reactance to persuasive health messages. *Health Communication, 30,* 451–460. https://doi.org/10.1080/10410236.2013.867005

Richards, A. S., Banas, J. A., & Magid, Y. (2017). More on inoculating against reactance to persuasive health messages: The paradox of threat. *Health Communication, 32,* 890–902. https://doi.org/10.1080/10410236.2016.1196410

Richards-Schuster, K., Espitia, N., & Rodems, R. (2019). Exploring values and actions: Definitions of social justice and the civic engagement of undergraduate students. *Journal of Social Work Values & Ethics, 16*(1), 27–38.

Richmond, V. P., McCroskey, J. C., Kearney, P., & Plax, T. G. (1987). Power in the classroom VII: Linking behavior alteration techniques to cognitive learning. *Communication Education, 36,* 1–12. https://doi.org/10.1080/03634528709378636

Ringler, C., Sirianni, N. J., Gustafsson, A., & Peck, J. (2019). Look but don't touch! The impact of active interpersonal haptic blocking on compensatory touch and purchase behavior. *Journal of Retailing, 95,* 186–203. https://doi.org/10.1016/j.jretai.2019.10.007

Roach, K. D. (1991). Graduate teaching assistants' use of behavior alteration techniques in the university classroom. *Communication Quarterly, 39,* 178–188. https://doi.org/10.1080/01463379109369795

Robbins, R., & Niederdeppe, J. (2015). Using the integrative model of behavioral prediction to identify promising message strategies to promote healthy sleep behavior among college students. *Health Communication, 30,* 26–38. https://doi.org/10.1080/10410236.2013.835215

Robert, L. P., & Dennis, A. R. (2005). Paradox of richness: A cognitive model of media choice. *IEEE Transactions on Professional Communication, 48*(1), 10–21. https://doi.org/10.1109/TPC.2003.843292

Robinson, T. (2000). Service learning as justice advocacy: Can political scientists do politics? *PS: Political Science and Politics, 33*(3), 605–612. https://doi.org/10.1017/s1049096500061631

Robson, D. (2019, September 16). How to be a human lie detector of fake news, according to the latest science. *CNN.* https://www.cnn.com/2019/09/16/health/human-lie-detector-fake-news-wellness/index.html

Rocklage, M. D., & Fazio, R. H. (2018). Attitude accessibility as a function of emotionality. *Personality and Social Psychology Bulletin, 44,* 508–520. https://doi.org/10.1177/0146167217743762

Rodriguez, D. N., & Strange, D. (2015). False memories for dissonance inducing events. *Memory, 23,* 203–212. https://doi.org/10.1080/09658211.2014.881501

Rogers, E. M. (2003). *Diffusion of innovations* (5th ed.). Free Press.

Rokeach, M. (1968). *Beliefs, attitudes, and values.* Jossey-Bass.

Rokeach, M. (1973). *The nature of human values.* Free Press.

Roozenbeek, J., & van der Linden, S. (2019). The fake news game: Actively inoculating against the risk of misinformation. *Journal of Risk Research, 22,* 570–580. https://doi.org/10.1080/13669877.2018.1443491

Roozenbeek, J., Maertens, R., McClanahan, W., & van der Linden, S. (2020). Disentangling item and testing effects in inoculation research on online misinformation: Solomon revisited. *Educational and Psychological Measurement,* 1–23. https://doi.org/10.1177/0013164420940378

Rosenstock, I. M., Strecher, V. J., & Becker, M. H. (1988). Social learning theory and the health belief model. *Health Education Quarterly, 15*(2), 175–183. https://doi.org/10.1177/109019818801500203

Rothwell, J. D. (2019). *In mixed company: Communicating in small groups and teams* (10th ed.). Oxford University Press.

Rozendaal, E., Buijs, L., & van Reijmersdal, E. A. (2016). Strengthening children's advertising defenses: The effects of forewarning of commercial and manipulative intent. *Frontiers in Psychology, 7,* article 1186. https://doi.org/10.3389/fpsyg.2016.01186

Rubin, A. M., & Rubin, R. B. (1985). Interface of personal and mediated communication: A research agenda. *Critical Studies in Mass Communication, 2,* 36–53. https://doi.org/10.1080/15295038509360060

Rubin, G. B. (2017). Power, solidarity and tag questions in crisis negotiations. *International Journal of Speech, Language, and the Law, 24*(1), 45–65. https://doi.org/10.1558/ijsll.31003

Ruijten, P. A. M., Midden, C. J. H., & Ham, J. (2011, June). Unconscious persuasion needs goal-striving: The effect of goal activation on the persuasive power of subliminal feedback. *Proceedings of the 6th International Conference on Persuasive Technology: Persuasive Technology and Design: Enhancing Sustainability and Health,* United States, article 4. https://doi.org/10.1145/2467803.2467807

Ruiter, R. A. C., Kessels, L. T. E., Peters, G.-J. Y., & Kok, G. (2014). Sixty years of fear appeal research: Current state of the evidence. *International Journal of Psychology, 49*(2), 63–70. https://doi.org/10.1002/ijop.12042

Rulffes, A. M. (2017). *Privacy vs. security: Fear appeals, terrorism and the willingness to allow increased government surveillance* [Unpublished doctoral dissertation]. Syracuse University.

Rumble, J., Lundy, L., Xu, B., & Anderson, S. (2017). Gender and GMOs: Understanding Floridians attitudes toward GMOs through the lens of social judgment theory. *Journal of Applied Communications, 101*(4), 1–12, article 1. https://doi.org/10.4148/1051-0834.1845

Russ, T. L., Simonds, C. J., & Hunt, S. K. (2002). Coming out in the classroom ... an occupational hazard?: The influence of sexual orientation on teacher credibility and perceived student learning. *Communication Education, 51,* 311–324. https://doi.org/10.1080/03634520216516

Ruth, T. K., & Rumble, J. N. (2019). Consumers' evaluations of genetically modified food messages. *Journal of Applied Communications, 103*(1), article 5. https://doi.org/10.4148/1051-0834.2193

Sahin, I. (2006). Detailed review of Rogers' diffusion of innovations theory and educational technology-related studies based on Rogers' theory. *The Turkish Online Journal of Educational Technology, 5*(2), 14–23.

Salovey, P., Schneider, T. R., & Apanovitch, A. M. (2002). Message framing in the prevention and early detection of illness. In J. P. Dillard & M. Pfau (Eds.), *The persuasion handbook: Developments in theory and practice* (pp. 391–406). SAGE.

Saltmarsh, J., & Hartley, M. (2011). *To serve a larger purpose: Engagement for democracy and the transformation of higher education.* Temple University Press.

Samper, A., Yang, L. W., & Daniels, M. E. (2017). Beauty, effort, and misrepresentation: How beauty work affects judgments of moral character and consumer preferences. *Journal of Consumer Research, 45*(1), 126–147. https://doi.org/10.1093/jcr/ucx116

Samson-Secrieru, L., & Carpenter, C. J. (2017). Examining mindlessness and friendliness in the evoking-freedom compliance-gaining technique. *Communication Research Reports, 34*(4), 368–375. https://doi.org/10.1080/08824096.2017.1368473

Sangalang, A., & Bloomfield, E. F. (2018). Mother Goose and mother nature: Designing stories to communicate information about climate change. *Communication Studies, 69,* 583–604. https://doi.org/10.1080/10510974.2018.1489872

Santos, M. D., Leve, C., & Pratkanis, A. R. (1994). Hey buddy, can you spare seventeen cents? Mindful persuasion and the pique technique. *Journal of Applied Social Psychology, 24,* 755–764. https://doi.org/10.1111/j.1559-1816.1994.tb00610.x

Sapir, E. (1929). The status of linguistics as a science. *Language, 5,* 207–214. https://doi.org/10.2307/409588

Sapir, E. (1949). *Culture, language, and personality.* University of California Press.

Sas-Nowosielski, K., Hadzik, A., Gorna, J., & Grabara, M. (2016). Applying the health belief model in explaining the stages of exercise change in older adults. *Polish Journal of Sport and Tourism, 23*(4), 221–225. https://doi.org/10.1515/pjst-2016-0029

Saucier, D. A., & Miller, C. T. (2003). The persuasiveness of racial arguments as a subtle measure of racism. *Personality and Social Psychology Bulletin, 29,* 1303–1315. https://doi.org/10.1177/0146167203254612.

Sawyer, A. G., & Howard, D. J. (1991). Effects of omitting conclusions in advertisements to involved and uninvolved audiences. *Journal of Marketing Research, 28,* 467–474. https://doi.org/10.2307/3172786

Scheibe, S., Notthoff, N., Menkin, J., Ross, L., Shadel, D., Deevy, M., & Cartensen, L. L. (2014). Forewarning reduces fraud susceptibility in vulnerable consumers. *Basic and Applied Social Psychology, 36*, 272–279. https://doi.org/10.1080/01973533.2014.903844

Scherer, C. R., & Sagarin, B. J. (2006). Indecent influence: The positive effects of obscenity on persuasion. *Social Influence, 1*(2), 138–146. https://doi.org/10.1080/15534510600747597

Schindler, R., & Yalch, R. (2006). It seems factual, but is it? Effects of using sharp versus round numbers in advertising claims. *Advances in Consumer Research, 33*, 586–590. www.acrwebsite.org/volumes/13117/volumes/v33/NA-33

Schindler, S., & Reinhard, M. A. (2015). When death is compelling: Door-in-the-face compliance under mortality salience. *Social Psychology, 46*, 352–360. https://doi.org/10.1027/1864-9335/a000252

Schnake, M. E. (1991). Equity in effort: The "sucker effect" in co-acting groups. *Journal of Management, 17*(1), 41–55. https://doi.org/10.1177/014920639101700104

Schneider, K. T., & Carpenter, N. J. (2020). Sharing #MeToo on Twitter: Incidents, coping responses, and social reactions. *Equity, Diversity and Inclusion: An International Journal, 39*, 87–100. https://doi.org/10.1108/edi-09-2018-0161

Schuette, R. A., & Fazio, R. H. (1995). Attitude accessibility and motivation as determinants of biased processing: A test of the MODE model. *Personality and Social Psychology Bulletin, 21*, 704–710. https://doi.org/10.1177/0146167295217005

Schulman, G. I., & Worrall, C. (1970). Salience patterns, source credibility, and the sleeper effect. *Public Opinion Quarterly, 34*(3), 371–382. https://doi.org/10.1086/267813

Schweiger, S., & Cress, U. (2019). Attitude confidence and source credibility in information foraging with social tags. *PLoS One, 14*(1), e0210423. https://doi.org/10.1371/journal.pone.0210423

Scott, A. M., Caughlin, J. P., Donovan-Kicken, E., & Mikucki-Enyart, S. L. (2013). Do message features influence responses to depression disclosure? A message design logics perspective. *Western Journal of Communication, 77*(2), 139–163. https://doi.org/10.1080/10570314.2012.694007

Segrin, C. (1993). The effects of nonverbal behavior on outcomes of compliance gaining attempts. *Communication Studies, 44*, 169–187. https://doi.org/10.1080/10510979309368393

Seiter, J. S., & Dutson, E. (2007). The effect of compliments on tipping behavior in hairstyling salons. *Journal of Applied Social Psychology, 37*, 1999–2007. https://doi.org/10.1111/j.1559-1816.2007.00247.x

Seiter, J. S., & Sandry, A. (2003). Pierced for success?: The effects of ear and nose piercing on perceptions of job candidates' credibility, attractiveness, and hirability. *Communication Research Reports, 20*(4), 287–298. https://doi:10.1080/08824090309388828

Seiter, J. S., & Weger, H. (2010). The effect of generalized compliments, sex of server, and size of dining party on tipping behavior in restaurants. *Journal of Applied Social Psychology, 40*, 1–12. https://doi.org/10.1111/j.1559-1816.2009.00560.x

Seiter, J. S., & Weger, H. (2014). The principle of reciprocity in hospitality contexts: The relationship between tipping behavior and food servers' approaches to handling leftovers. *Journal of Hospitality & Tourism Research, 42*, 287–294. https://doi.org/10.1177/1096348014562425

Semetko, H. A., & Tworzecki, H. (2018). Campaign strategies, media, and voters: The fourth era of political communication. In J. Fisher, E. Fieldhouse, M. N. Franklin, R. Gibson, M. Cantijoch, & C. Wlezien (Eds.), *The Routledge handbook of elections, voting behavior, and public opinion* (pp. 441–457). Routledge.

Seo, Y., Li, X., Choi, Y. K., & Yoon, S. (2018). Narrative transportation and paratextual features of social media in viral advertising. *Journal of Advertising, 47*(1), 83–95. https://doi.org/10.1080/00913367.2017.1405752

Shadish, W. R., Cook, T. D., & Campbell, D. T. (2002). *Experimental and quasi-experimental designs for generalized causal inference*. Houghton Mifflin.

Shak, P. (2016). Taken for a ride: Students' coping strategies for free-riding in group work. *Social Sciences & Humanities, 24*(1), 401–414.

Shak, P. (2016). Taken for a ride: Students' coping strategies for free-riding in group work. *Pertanika Journal of Social Sciences & Humanities, 24*(1), 401–414. http://www.pertanika.upm.edu.my/index.php

Shaw, A. Z., Dolan, E. A., Yurgalite, L., Walton, J. A., & Underwood, K. (2017). Using regulatory fit theory to examine how the communication context of compliance-gaining interactions influences compliance. *Social Influence, 12*(2–3), 80–89. https://doi.org/10.1080/15534510.2017.1365759

Shen, F. (2016). Information congruity in scarcity appeal: A structural equation modeling study of time-limited promotions. *Journal of Marketing Communications, 22*(2), 135–154. https://doi.org/10.1080/13527266.2013.828770

Sheppard, B. H., Hartwick, J., & Warshaw, P. R. (1988). The theory of reasoned action: A meta-analysis of past research with recommendations for modifications and future research. *Journal of Consumer Research, 15,* 325–343. https://doi.org/10.1086/209170

Sherer, M., & Rogers, R. W. (1984). The role of vivid information in fear appeals and attitude change. *Journal of Research in Personality, 18,* 321–337. https://doi.org/10.1016/0092-6566(84)90016-3

Sherif, C. W., & Sherif, M. (Eds.). (1967). *Attitude, ego-involvement, and change.* Greenwood.

Sherif, C. W., Sherif, M., & Nebergall, R. E. (1965). *Attitude and attitude change: The social judgment-involvement approach.* Saunders.

Sherif, M., & Hovland, C. (1961). *Social judgment: Assimilation and contrast effects in communication and attitude change.* Yale University Press.

Shobeiri, F., Hesami, E., Khodakarami, B., & Soltarian, A. (2016). Effect of nutritional counseling based on health belief model for osteoporosis prevention in women: A quasi-experimental research. *Journal of Postgraduate Medical Institute, 30,* 345–351. http://www.pakmedinet.com/JPMI

Sidelinger, R. J., Bolen, D. M., Frisby, B. N., & McMullen, A. L. (2012). Instructor compliance to student requests: An examination of student-to-student connectedness as power in the classroom. *Communication Education, 61,* 290–308. https://doi.org/10.1080/03634523.2012.666557

Silverman, C. (2016, November 16). *This analysis shows how fake election news stories outperformed real news on Facebook. BuzzFeed News.* https://www.buzzfeednews.com/article/craigsilverman/viral-fake-election-news-outperformed-real-news-on-facebook#.edLdEVoz5E

Silvia, P. J. (2006). Reactance and the dynamics of disagreement: Multiple paths from threatened freedom to resistance to persuasion. *European Journal of Social Psychology, 36,* 673–685. https://doi.org/10.1002/ejsp.309

Simonds, B. K., Meyer, K. R., Quinlan, M. M., & Hunt, S. K. (2006). Effects of instructor speech rate on affective learning and student perceptions of instructor immediacy, credibility, and clarity. *Communication Research Reports, 23,* 187–197. https://doi.org/10.1080/08824090600796401

Simonds, C. J., Hooker, J. F., & Wright, A. M. (2015). Instructional discussion: The most important area of training for new basic course instructors. *Basic Communication Course Annual, 27,* 32–42. https://ecommons.udayton.edu/bcca/

Simonds, C. J., Hunt, S. K., Simonds, B. K. (2018). *Engaging communication.* Fountainhead Press.

Sjastad, H., & Baumeister, R. F. (2018). The future and the will: Planning requires self-control, and ego-depletion leads to planning aversion. *Journal of Experimental Social Psychology, 76,* 127–141. https://doi.org/10.1016/j.jesp.2018.01.005

Skinner, C. H., Robinson, D. H., Robinson, S. L., Sterling, H. E., & Goodman, M. A. (1999). Effects of advertisement speech rates on feature recognition, and product and speaker ratings. *International Journal of Listening, 13,* 97–110. https://doi.org/10.1080/10904018.1999.10499029

Slater, M. D., & Rouner, D. (1996). How message evaluation and source attributes may influence credibility assessment and belief change. *Journalism and Mass Communication Quarterly, 73*(4), 974–991. https://doi.org/10.1177/107769909607300415

Slater, M. D., & Rouner, D. (2002). Entertainment-education and elaboration likelihood: Understanding the processing of narrative persuasion. *Communication Theory, 12,* 173–191. https://doi.org/10.1093/ct/12.2.173

Smith, S. M., & Shaffer, D. R. (1995). Speed of speech and persuasion: Evidence for multiple effects. *Personality and Social Psychology Bulletin, 21*(10), 1051–1060. https://doi.org/10.1177/01461672952110006

Smith, S. M., & Shaffer, D. R. (2000). Vividness can undermine or enhance message processing: The moderating role of vividness congruency. *Personality and Social Psychology Bulletin, 26*(7), 769–779. https://doi.org/10.1177/0146167200269003

Smith, S. W., Atkin, C. K., Martell, D., Allen, R., & Hembroff, L. (2006). A social judgment theory approach to conducting formative research in a social norms campaign. *Communication Theory, 16,* 141–152. https://doi.org/10.1111/j.1468-2885.2006.00009.x

Sniehotta, F. F., Presseau, J., & Araújo-Soares, V. (2014). Time to retire the theory of planned behaviour. *Health Psychology Review, 8*(1), 1–7. https://doi.org/10.1080/17437199.2013.869710

Snyder, L. B., Hamilton, M. A., Mitchell, E. W., Kiwanuka-Tondo, J., Fleming-Milici, F., & Proctor, D. (2004). A meta-analysis of the effect of mediated health communication campaigns on behavior change in the United States. *Journal of Health Communication*, *9*, 71–96. https://doi.org/10.1080/10810730490271548

Snyder, M. (1974). Self-monitoring and expressive behavior. *Journal of Personality and Social Psychology*, *30*(4), 526–537. https://doi.org/10.1037/h0037039

Snyder, T. (2021, January 9). The American abyss: A historian of fascism and political atrocity on Trump, the mob and what comes next. *The New York Times Magazine*. https://www.nytimes.com/2021/01/09/magazine/trump-coup.html?referringSource=articleShare

So, J. (2013). A further extension of the extended parallel process model (E-EPPM): Implications of cognitive appraisal theory of emotion and dispositional coping style. *Health Communication*, *28*, 72–83. https://doi.org/10.1080/10410236.2012.708633

So, J., Kim, S., & Cohen, H. (2017). Message fatigue: Conceptual definition, operationalization, and correlates. *Communication Monographs*, *84*, 5–29. https://doi.org/10.1080/03637751.2016.1250429

Sobieraj, S., & Berry, J. M. (2011). From incivility to outrage: Political discourse in blogs, talk radio, and cable news. *Political Communication*, *28*, 19–41. https://doi.org/10.1080/10584609.2010.542360

Sontag, J. M. (2018). Visual framing effects on emotion and mental health message effectiveness. *Journal of Communication in Healthcare*, *11*, 30–47. https://doi.org/10.1080/17538068.2018.1435017

Sorochan, C. (2016). Participation as ideology in Occupy Wall Street. In B. Barney, G. Coleman, C. Ross, J. Sterne, & T. Tembeck (Eds.), *The participatory condition in the digital age* (pp. 22–43). University of Minnesota Press.

Spahn, A. (2012). And lead us (not) into persuasion ...? Persuasive technology and the ethics of communication. *Science and Engineering Ethics*, *18*, 633–650. https://doi.org/10.1007/s11948-011-9278-y

Spartz, J. T., Su, L. Y-F., Griffin, R., Brossard, D., & Dunwoody, S. (2017). YouTube, social norms and perceived salience of climate change in the American mind. *Environmental Communication*, *11*(1), 1–16. https://doi.org/10.1080/17524032.2015.1047887

Spiezio, K. E., Baker, K. Q., & Boland, K. (2005). General education and civic engagement: An empirical analysis of pedagogical possibilities. *Journal of General Education*, *54*, 273–292. https://doi.org/10.1353/jge.2006.0012

Spotts, H. (1994). Evidence of a relationship between need for cognition and chronological age: Implications for persuasion in consumer research. *Advances in Consumer Research*, *21*, 238–243.

Sprinkle, R., Hunt, S., Simonds, C., & Comadena, M. (2006). Fear in the classroom: An examination of teachers' use of fear appeals and students' learning outcomes. *Communication Education*, *55*, 389–402. https://doi.org/10.1080/03634520600879170

Spry, A., Pappu, R., & Cornwell, T. B. (2011). Celebrity endorsement, brand credibility and brand equity. *European Journal of Marketing*, *45*, 882–909. https://doi.org/10.1108/03090561111119958

Staats, B. R., KC, D. S., & Gino, F. (2018). Maintaining beliefs in the face of negative news: The moderating role of experience. *Management Science*, *64*(4), 804–824. https://doi.org/10.1287/mnsc.2016.2640

Steelman, Z. R., & Soror, A. A. (2017). Why do you keep doing that? The biasing effects of mental states on IT continued usage intentions. *Computers in Human Behavior*, *73*, 209–223. https://doi.org/10.1016/j.chb.2017.03.027

Stefanone, M. A., Hurley, C. M., Egnoto, M. J., & Covert, J. M. (2015). Information asymmetry and social exchange: Exploring compliance gaining online. *Information, Communication and Society*, *18*, 376–389. https://doi.org/10.1080/1369118X.2014.952658

Stein, R., Swan, A. B., & Sarraf, M. (2020). Hearing from both sides: Differences between liberal and conservative attitudes toward scientific and experiential evidence. *Political Psychology*. Advance online publication. https://doi.org/10.1111/pops.12706

Steinbaum, M. (2018). A radical solution to the student debt crisis. *Next new deal: The blog of the Roosevelt Institute*. http://rooseveltinstitute.org/radical-solution-student-debt-crisis/

Steiner, S. D., & Watson, M. A. (2006). The service learning component in business education: The values linkage void. *Academy of Management Learning & Education*, *5*(4), 422–434. https://doi.org/10.5465/amle.2006.23473203

Stewart, C. J. (1999). Championing the rights of others and challenging evil: The ego function in the rhetoric of other-directed social movements. *Southern Journal of Communication*, *64*(2), 91–105. https://doi.org/10.1080/10417949909373125

Stewart, C. J., Smith, C. A., & Denton, R. E. (2012). *Persuasion and social movements* (6th ed.). Waveland.

Stiff, J. B. (1986). Cognitive processing of persuasive message cues: A meta-analytic review of the effects of supporting information on attitudes. *Communication Monographs, 53,* 75–89. https://doi.org/10.1080/03637758609376128

Stiff, J. B., & Mongeau, P. A. (2016). *Persuasive communication* (3rd ed.). Guilford.

Stiff, J., Corman, S., Krizek, B., & Snider, E. (1994). Individual differences and changes in nonverbal behavior: Unmasking the changing faces of deception. *Communication Research, 21,* 555–581. https://doi.org/10.1177/009365094021005001

Strahan, E. J., Spencer, S. J., & Zanna, M. P. (2002). Subliminal priming and persuasion: Striking while the iron is hot. *Journal of Experimental Social Psychology, 38,* 556–568. https://doi.org/10.1016/s0022-1031(02)00502-4

Strict, M., van Baaren, R. B., Holland, R. W., & van Knippenberg, A. (2009). Humor in advertisements enhances product liking by mere association. *Journal of Experimental Psychology, 15,* 35–45. https://doi.org/10.1037/2160-4134.1.s.16

Stroe, M. (2015). Persuasion through artifacts: Sociological and psychological dimensions. *International Review,* (3–4), 67–74. https://doi.org/10.5937/intrev1504067s

Stroud, N. J. (2008). Media use and political predispositions: Revisiting the concept of selective exposure. *Political Behavior, 30,* 341–366. https://doi.org/10.1007/s11109-007-9050-9

Stroup, J. T., Bunting, H., Dodson, K., Horne, M., & Portilla, J. (2013). Promoting a deliberative and active citizenry: Developing traditional first year college student political engagement. *College Teaching, 61,* 116–126. https://doi.org/10.1080/87567555.2013.809327

Suleiman, J., & Watson, R. T. (2008). Social loafing in technology-supported teams. *Computer Supported Cooperative Work, 17,* 291–309. https://doi.org/10.1007/s10606-008-9075-6

Sundstrom, B., Ferrara, M., DeMaria, A. L., Gabel, C., Booth, K., & Cabot, J. (2018). It's Your Place: Development and evaluation of an evidence-based bystander intervention campaign. *Health Communication, 33,* 1141–1150. https://doi.org/10.1080/10410236.2017.1333561

Sunstein, C. R. (2002). The law of group polarization. *The Journal of Political Philosophy, 10*(2), 175–195. https://doi.org/10.1111/1467-9760.00148

Swanson, S. R., Gwinner, K., Larson, B. V., & Janda, S. (2003). Motivations of college student game attendance and word-of-mouth behavior: The impact of gender differences. *Sport Marketing Quarterly, 12*(3), 151–162.

Tang, D., & Schmeichel, B. J. (2015). Look me in the eye: Manipulated eye gaze affects dominance mindsets. *Journal of Nonverbal Behavior, 39,* 181–194. https://doi.org/10.1007/s10919-015-0206-8

Tangney, J. P., Stuewig, J., & Mashek, D. J. (2007). Moral emotions and moral behavior. *Annual Review of Psychology, 58,* 345–372. https://doi.org/10.1146/annurev.psych.56.091103.070145

Tantiseneepong, N., Gorton, M., & White, J. (2012). Evaluating responses to celebrity endorsements using projective techniques. *Qualitative Market Research: An International Journal, 15,* 57–69. https://doi.org/10.1108/13522751211191991

Taylor, M. R., Lamm, A. J., & Lundy, L. K. (2017). Using cognitive dissonance to communicate with hypocrites about water conservation and climate change. *Journal of Applied Communications, 101*(3), article 5. https://doi.org/10.4148/1051-0834.1843

Teven, J. J. (2007). Effects of supervisor social influence, nonverbal immediacy, and biological sex on subordinates' perceptions of job satisfaction, liking, and supervisor credibility. *Communication Quarterly, 55*(2), 155–177. https://doi.org/10.1080/01463370601036036

Teven, J. J., & Comadena, M. E. (1996). The effects of office aesthetic quality on students' perceptions of teacher credibility and communicator style. *Communication Research Reports, 13*(1), 101–108. https://doi.org/10.1080/08824099609362076

Thaler, R. H., & Sunstein, C. R. (2009). *Nudge: Improving decisions about health, wealth, and happiness.* Penguin.

Thibodeau, P. H. (2016). Extended metaphors are the home runs of persuasion: Don't fumble the phrase. *Metaphor and Symbol, 31,* 53–72. https://doi.org/10.1080/10926488.2016.1150756

Thorson, E. A. (2018). Comparing approaches to journalistic fact checking. In B. G. Southwell, E. A. Thorson, & L. Sheble (Eds.), *Misinformation and mass audiences* (pp. 249–262). University of Texas Press.

Thweatt, K., & McCroskey, J. C. (1998). Impact of teacher immediacy and misbehaviors on teacher credibility. *Communication Education, 47*(4), 348–358. https://doi.org/10.1080/03634529809379141

Timming, A. R., & Perrett, D. (2016). Trust and mixed signals: A study of religion, tattoos, and cognitive dissonance. *Personality and Individual Differences, 97,* 234–238. https://doi.org/10.1016/j.paid.2016.03.067

Timming, A. R., Nickson, D., Re, D., & Perrett, D. (2015). What do you think of my ink?: Assessing the effects of body art on employment chances. *Human Resource Management, 56*(1), 133–149. https://doi.org/10.1002/hrm.21770

Tinajero, C., & Páramo, M. F. (1997). Field dependence-independence and academic achievement: A re-examination of their relationship. *British Journal of Educational Psychology, 67,* 199–212. https://doi.org/10.1111/j.2044-8279.1997.tb01237.x

Tormala, Z. L., & Petty, R. E. (2004). Source credibility and attitude certainty: A metacognitive analysis of resistance to persuasion. *Journal of Consumer Psychology, 14*(4), 427–442. https://doi.org/10.1207/s15327663jcp1404_11

Tormala, Z. L., Briñol, P., & Petty, R. E. (2006). When credibility attacks: The reverse Impact of source credibility on persuasion. *Journal of Experimental Social Psychology, 42,* 684–691. https://doi.org/10.1016/j.jesp.2005.10.005

Tormala, Z. L., Briñol, P., & Petty, R. E. (2007). Multiple roles for source credibility under high elaboration: It's all about the timing. *Social Cognition, 25*(4), 536–552. https://doi.org/10.1521/soco.2007.25.4.536

Toulmin, S. E. (2003). *The uses of argument.* Cambridge University Press.

Trappey, C. (1996). A meta-analysis of consumer choice and subliminal advertising. *Psychology & Marketing, 13,* 517–530. https://doi.org/10.1002/(SICI)1520-6793(199608)13:5<517::AID-MAR5>3.0.CO;2-C

Tremayne, M. (2015). Partisan media and political poll coverage. *Journal of Information Technology and Politics, 12,* 270–284. https://doi.org/10.1080/19331681.2015.1063366

Trumbo, C. W. (1999). Heuristic-systematic information processing and risk judgment. *Risk Analysis, 19*(3), 391–400. https://doi.org/10.1111/j.1539-6924.1999.tb00415.x

Trumbo, C. W. (2002). Information processing and risk perception: An adaptation of the heuristic-systematic model. *Journal of Communication, 52,* 367–382. https://doi.org/10.1093/joc/52.2.367

Tsipursky, G., Votta, F., & Mulick, J. A. (2018). A psychological approach to promoting truth in politics: The pro-truth pledge. *Journal of Social and Political Psychology, 6*(2), 271–290. https://doi.org/10.5964/jspp.v6i2.856

Tskhay, K. O., Zhu, R., Zou, C., & Rule, N. O. (2018). Charisma in everyday life: Conceptualization and validation of the general charisma inventory. *Journal of Personality and Social Psychology, 114*(1), 131–152. https://doi.org/10.1037/pspp0000159

Tufekci, Z. (2014). Social movements and governments in the digital age: Evaluating a complex landscape. *Journal of International Affairs, 68*(1), 1–18. https://jia.sipa.columbia.edu/

Turner, M. M., & Underhill, J. C. (2012). Motivating emergency preparedness behaviors: The differential effects of guilt and actually anticipating guilty feelings. *Communication Quarterly, 60,* 545–559. https://doi.org/10.1080/01463373.2012.705780

Turner, M. M., Mabry-Flynn, A., Shen, H., Jiang, H., Boudewyns, V., & Payne, D. (2018). The effects of guilt-appeal intensity on persuasive and emotional outcomes: The moderating role of sponsor motive. *Journal of Nonprofit & Public Sector Marketing, 30,* 134–150. https://doi.org/10.1080/10495142.2017.1326345

Tversky, A., & Kahneman, D. (1981). The framing of decisions and the psychology of choice. *Science, 211*(4481), 453–458. https://doi.org/10.1007/978-1-4613-2391-4_2

Tweneboah-Koduah, E. Y. (2018). Social marketing: Using the health belief model to understand breast cancer protective behaviours among women. *International Journal of Nonprofit and Voluntary Sector Marketing, 23*(2), 1–7. https://doi.org/10.1002/nvsm.1613

Unsworth, C., Harries, P., & Davies, M. (2015). Using social judgment theory method to examine how experienced occupational therapy driver assessors use information to make fitness-to-drive recommendations. *British Journal of Occupational Therapy, 78,* 109–120. https://doi.org/10.1177/0308022614562396

Uskul, A. K., & Oyserman, D. (2010). When message-frame fits salient cultural-frame, messages feel more persuasive. *Psychology and Health, 25*(3), 321–337. https://doi.org/10.1080/08870440902759156

Vaidis, D. C. F., & Halimi-Falkowicz, S. G. M. (2008). Increasing compliance with a request: Two touches are more effective than one. *Psychological Reports, 103,* 88–92. https://doi.org/10.2466/pr0.103.1.88-92

Vaidis, D. C., & Oberle, D. (2014). Approaching opponents and leaving supporters: Adjusting physical proximity to reduce cognitive dissonance. *Social Behavior and Personality, 42,* 1091–1098. https://doi.org/10.2224/sbp.2014.42.7.1091

Valente, T. W., & Davis, R. L. (1999). Accelerating the diffusion of innovations using opinion leaders. *The ANNALS of the American Academy of Political and Social Science, 566*(1), 55–67. https://doi.org/10.1177/000271629956600100 5

van Blankenstein, F. M., Dolmans, D. H. J. M., van der Vlueten, C. P. M., & Schmidt, H. G. (2011). Which cognitive processes support learning during small-group discussion? The of providing explanations and listening to others. *Instructional Science, 39,* 189–204. https://doi.org/10.1007/s11251-009-9124-7

van der Land, S. F., Schouten, A. P., Feldberg, F., Husyman, M., & van den Hooff, B. (2015). Does avatar appearance matter? How team visual similarity and member-avatar similarity influence virtual team performance. *Human Communication Research, 41,* 128–153. https://doi.org/10.1111/hcre.12044

van der Linden, S., Leiserowitz, A., Rosenthal, S., & Maibach, E. (2017). Inoculating the public against misinformation about climate change. *Global Challenges, 1,* 160008. https://doi.org/10.1002/gch2.201600008

Van Stee, S. K. (2018). Meta-analysis of the persuasive effects of metaphorical vs. literal messages. *Communication Studies, 69,* 545–566. https://doi.org/10.1080/10510974.2018.1457553

Van Zant, A. B., & Berger, J. (2020). How the voice persuades. *Journal of Personality and Social Psychology, 118,* 661–682. https://doi.org/10.1037/pspi0000193

Vasile, A. A. (2018). The Münchausen effect and the post-truth era advertising messages. Critical analysis on fallacious and enthymematic advertising slogan argumentation. *ESSACHESS. Journal for Communication Studies, 11,* 51–66.

Vergeer, M. (2018). Incorrect, fake, and false. Journalists' perceived online source credibility and verification behavior. *Observatorio(OBS*), 12*(1). https://doi.org/10.15847/obsobs12120181126

Verwijmeren, T., Karremans, J. C., Bernritter, S. F., Stroebe, W., & Wigboldus, D. H. J. (2013). Warning: You are being primed! The effect of a warning on the impact of subliminal ads. *Journal of Experimental Social Psychology, 49,* 1124–1129. https://doi.org/10.1016/j.jesp.2013.06.010

Vraga, E. K. (2015). How party affiliation conditions the experience of dissonance and explains polarization and selective exposure. *Social Science Quarterly, 96,* 487–502. https://doi.org/10.1111/ssqu.12138

Vraga, E. K., Kim, S. C., & Cook, J. (2019). Testing logic-based and humor-based corrections for science, health, and political misinformation on social media. *Journal of Broadcasting & Electronic Media, 63,* 393–414. https://doi.org/10.1080/08838151.2019.1653102

Wagner, K. P., Widman, L., Nesi, J., & Noar, S. M. (2018). Intentions to use emergency contraception: The role of accurate knowledge and information source credibility. *American Journal of Health Education, 49*(4), 264–270. https://doi.org/10.1080/19325037.2018.1473179

Wagner, T. R. (2011). Resistance to persuasion in committed romantic relationships: Reactance effects of forewarning and message explicitness. *Ohio Communication Journal, 49,* 15–42. https://ohiocomm.org/ohio-communication-journal/

Waisbord, S. (2018). The elective affinity between post-truth communication and populist politics. *Communication Research and Practice, 4,* 17–34. https://doi.org/10.1080/22041451.2018.1428928

Wall, H. J., Campbell, C. C., Kaye, L. K., Levy, A., & Bhullar, N. (2019). Personality profiles and persuasion: An exploratory study investigating the role of the Big-5, Type D personality and the Dark Triad on susceptibility to persuasion. *Personality and Individual Differences, 139,* 69–76. https://doi.org/10.1016/j.paid.2018.11.003

Walter, N., & Tukachinsky, R. (2020). A meta-analytic examination of the continued influence of misinformation in the face of correction: How powerful is it, why does it happen, and how to stop it? *Communication Research, 47,* 155–177. https://doi.org/10.1177/0093650219854600

Walter, N., Cody, M. J., Xu, L. Z., & Murphy, S. T. (2018). A priest, a rabbi, and a minister walk into a bar: A meta-analysis of humor effects on persuasion. *Human Communication Research, 44,* 343–373. https://doi.org/10.1093/hcr/hqy005

Walter, N., Tukachinsky, R., Pelled, A., & Nabi, R. (2019). Meta-analysis of anger and persuasion: An empirical integration of four models. *Journal of Communication, 69,* 73–93. https://doi.org/10.1093/joc/jqy054

Walters, H., & Stout, K. (2019). *Understanding argument in a post-truth world.* Cognella.

Walther, N., & Murphy, S. T. (2018). How to unring the bell: A meta-analytic approach to correction of misinformation. *Communication Monographs, 85,* 423–441. https://doi.org/10.1080/03637751.2018.1467564

Walton, D. (2001). Persuasive definitions and public policy arguments. *Argumentation and Advocacy, 37*(3), 117–132. https://doi.org/10.1080/00028533.2001.11951664

Walton, D. (2005). Deceptive arguments containing persuasive language and persuasive definitions. *Argumentation, 19,* 159–186. https://doi.org/10.1007/s10503-005-2312-y

Wang Erber, M., Hodges, S. D., & Wilson, T. D. (1995). Attitude strength, attitude stability, and the effects of analyzing reasons. In R. E. Petty & J. A. Krosnick (Eds.), *Attitude strength: Antecedents and consequences* (pp. 433–454). Erlbaum.

Wang, K. Y., & Yang, X. (2011). Counterfactual priming effects on advertising persuasion. In D. W. Dahl, G. V. Johar, and S. M. J. van Osselaer (Eds.), *Advances in consumer research* (Vol. 38). Association for Consumer Research.

Wang, L., Qian, D., & Zhu, L. (2018). The effect of system generated cues on microblogging rewarding repost behavior—A source credibility perspective. *Journal of Electronic Commerce Research, 19*(1), 104–118. http://www.jecr.org

Wang, S. W., & Scheinbaum, A. C. (2018). Enhancing brand credibility via celebrity endorsement: Trustworthiness trumps attractiveness and expertise. *Journal of Advertising Research, 58*(1), 16–31. https://doi.org/10.2501/jar-2017-042

Wang, X. (2011). The role of anticipated guilt in intentions to register as organ donors and to discuss organ donation with family. *Health Communication, 26,* 683–690. https://doi.org/10.1080/10410236.2011.563350

Wang, X. (2020). Predictors of organ donation-related cognitions and intentions in China: Communication variables and cultural values. *Communication Quarterly, 68,* 438–456. https://doi.org/10.1080/01463373.2020.1821734

Wang, Z., Singh, S. N., Li, Y. J., Ambrose, M., & Biernat, M. (2017). Effects of employees' positive affective displays on customer loyalty intentions: An emotions-as-social-information perspective. *Academy of Management Journal, 60*(1), 109–129. https://doi.org/10.5465/amj.2014.0367

Wanzer, M. B., Booth-Butterfield, M. B., & Booth-Butterfield, S. (1986). Are funny people popular? An examination of humor orientation, loneliness, and social attraction. *Communication Quarterly, 44*(1), 42–52. https://doi.org/10.1080/01463379609369999

Warner, B. R., Jennings, F. J., Bramlett, J. C., Coker, C. R., Reed, J. L., & Bolton, J. P. (2018). A multimedia analysis of persuasion in the 2016 presidential election: Comparing the unique and complementary effects of political comedy and political advertising. *Mass Communication and Society, 00,* 1–22. https://doi.org/10.1080/15205436.2018.1472283

Warren, C., Barsky, A., & McGraw, A. P. (2018). Humor, comedy, and consumer behavior. *Journal of Consumer Research, 45,* 529–552. https://doi.org/10.1093/jcr/ucy015

Wasike, B. (2017). Persuasion in 140 characters: Testing issue framing, persuasion, and credibility via Twitter and online news articles in the gun control debate. *Computers in Human Behavior, 66,* 179–190. https://doi.org/10.1016/j.chb.2016.09.037

Weaver, R. M. (1953). *The ethics of rhetoric.* Echo Point Books & Media.

Weber, E. U. (2020). Heads in the sand: Why we fail to foresee and contain catastrophe. *Foreign Affairs, 99*(6), 20–26.

Weber, K., Martin, M. M., Members of COMM 401, & Corrigan, M. (2006). Creating persuasive messages advocating organ donation. *Communication Quarterly, 54*(1), 67–87. https://doi.org/10.1080/01463370500270413

Wegener, D. T., Petty, R. E., & Klein, D. J. (1994). Effects of mood on high elaboration attitude change: The mediating role of likelihood judgments. *European Journal of Social Psychology, 24,* 25–43. https://doi.org/10.1002/ejsp.2420240103

Weinberger, M. G., & Gulas, C. S. (1992). The impact of humor in advertising: A review. *Journal of Advertising, 21*(4), 35–59. https://doi.org/10.1080/00913367.1992.10673384

Weisbuch, M., & Mackie, D. (2009). False fame, perceptual clarity, or persuasion? Flexible fluency attribution in spokesperson familiarity effects. *Journal of Consumer Psychology, 19*(1), 62–72. https://doi.org/10.1016/j.jcps.2008.12.009

Wells, C. (2015). *The civic organization and the digital citizen: Communicating engagement in a networked age.* Oxford University Press.

Westheimer, J., & Kahne, J. (2004). What kind of citizen? The politics of educating for democracy. *American Educational Research Journal, 41*(2), 237–269. https://doi.org/10.3102/00028312041002237

Wheeless, L. R., Barraclough, R., & Stewart, R. (1983). Compliance-gaining and power in persuasion. In R. N. Bostrom (Ed.), *Communication yearbook 7* (pp. 105–145). SAGE.

White, H. A., & Dillon, J. F. (2000). Knowledge about others' reaction to a public service announcement: The impact on self-persuasion and third-person perception. *Journalism and Mass Communication Quarterly, 77,* 788–803. https://doi.org/10.1177/107769900007700405

Whitehead, J. L., Jr. (1968). Factors of source credibility. *Quarterly Journal of Speech, 54,* 59–63. https://doi.org/10.1080/00335636809382870

Whorf, B. L. (1956). *Language, thought, and reality.* John Wiley.

Wichmann, B. K., Carter, C. R., Kaufmann, L., & Wilson, J. R. (2016). Making environmental SCM initiatives work—Moving beyond the dyad to gain affective commitment. *Journal of Supply Chain Management, 52,* 21–40. https://doi.org/10.1111/jscm.12095

Wicklund, R. A. (1974). *Freedom and reactance.* Erlbaum.

Wight, C. (2018). Post-truth, postmodernism, and alternative facts. *New Perspectives, 26,* 17–29. https://doi.org/10.1177/2336825x1802600302

Wilcox, B. L., Kunkel, D., Cantor, J., Dowrick, P., Lin, S., & Palmer, E. (2004). *Report of the APA task force on advertising and children.* American Psychological Association.

Wilder, D. A. (1990). Some determinants of the persuasive power of in-groups and out-groups: Organization of information and attribution of independence. *Journal of Personality and Social Psychology, 59,* 1202–1213. https://doi.org/10.1037/0022-3514.59.6.1202

Williams, M. N., & Bond, C. M. C. (2020). A preregistered replication of "inoculating the public against misinformation about climate change." *Journal of Environmental Psychology, 70,* 101456. https://doi.org/10.1016/j.jenvp.2020.101456

Wilson, E. J., & Sherrell, D. L. (1993). Source effects in communication and persuasion research: A meta-analysis of effect size. *Journal of the Academy of Marketing Science, 21*(2), 101–112. https://doi.org/10.1007/bf02894421

Wilson, S. R., & Kunkel, A. W. (2000). Identity implications of influence goals: Similarities in perceived face threats and facework across sex and close relationships. *Journal of Language and Social Psychology, 19*(2), 195–221. https://doi.org/10.1177/0261927x00019002002

Wilson, T. D., Lindsey, S., & Schooler, T. Y. (2000). A model of dual attitudes. *Psychological Review, 107*(1), 101–126. https://doi.org/10.1037//0033-295x.107.1.101

Winterbottom, A., Bekker, H. L., Conner, M., & Mooney, A. (2008). Does narrative information bias individual's decision making? A systematic review. *Social Science and Medicine, 67,* 2079–2088. https://doi.org/10.1016/j.socscimed.2008.09.037

Wirth, J. H., Sacco, D. F., Hugenberg, K., & Williams, K. D. (2010). Eye gaze as relational evaluation: Averted eye gaze leads to feelings of ostracism and relational devaluation. *Personality and Social Psychology Bulletin, 36*(7), 869–882. https://doi.org/10.1177/0146167210370032

Wirtz, J. G., Sar, S., & Ghuge, S. (2015). The moderating role of mood and personal relevance on persuasive effects of gain- and loss-framed health messages. *Health Marketing Quarterly, 32,* 180–196. https://doi.org/10.1080/07359683.2015.1033936

Witkin, H. A. (1978). *Cognitive styles in personal and cultural adaptation.* Clark University Press.

Witkin, H. A., Moore, C. A., Goodenough, D. R., & Cox, P. W. (1977). Field-dependent and field-independent cognitive styles and their educational implications. *Review of Educational Research, 47*(1), 1–64. https://doi.org/10.2307/1169967

Witte, K. (1992). Putting the fear back into fear appeals: The extended parallel process model. *Communication Monographs, 59,* 329–349. https://doi.org/10.1080/03637759209376276

Witte, K., & Allen, M. (2000). A meta-analysis of fear appeals: Implications for effective public health campaigns. *Health Education and Behavior, 27,* 591–615. https://doi.org/10.1177/109019810002700506

Witte, K., Berkowitz, J. M., Cameron, K. A., & McKeon, J. K. (1998). Preventing the spread of genital warts: Using fear appeals to promote self-protective behaviors. *Health Education and Behavior, 25,* 571–585. https://doi.org/10.1177/109019819802500505

Wojcieszak, M. E. (2012). On strong attitudes and group deliberation: Relationships, structure, changes, and effects. *Political Psychology, 33,* 225–242. https://doi.org/10.1111/j.1467-9221.2012.00872.x

Wong, S. H., & Chow, A. Y. M. (2017). An exploratory study on university students' perceptions of posthumous organ donation base on the theory of reasoned action. *OMEGA—Journal of Death and Dying, 75,* 284–299. https://doi.org/10.1177/0030222816633241

Wood, W., & Quinn, J. M. (2003). Forewarned or forearmed? Two meta-analytic syntheses of forewarnings of influence appeals. *Psychological Bulletin, 129,* 119–138. https://doi.org/10.1037/0033-2909.129.1.119

Woodall, W. G., & Folger, J. P. (1981). Encoding specificity and nonverbal cue context: An expansion of episodic memory research. *Communication Monographs, 48,* 39–53. https://doi.org/10.1080/03637758109376046

Woodward, G. C., & Denton, R. E. (2014). *Persuasion and influence in American life* (7th ed.). Waveland.

Woodward, G. C., & Denton, R. E. (2018). *Persuasion and influence in American life* (8th ed.). Waveland.

Woolard, C. (2017). *Engaging civic engagement: Framing the civic education movement in higher education.* Lexington.

Wouters, R. (2019). The persuasive power of protest. How protest wins public support. *Social Forces, 98,* 403–426. https://doi.org/10.1093/sf/soy110

Wrench, J. S., & Booth-Butterfield, M. (2003). Increasing patient satisfaction and compliance: An examination of physician humor orientation, compliance-gaining strategies, and perceived credibility. *Communication Quarterly, 51,* 482–503. https://doi.org/10.1080/01463370309370169

Wróbel, M., Królewiak, K., & Czarna, A. Z. (2015). Do I mirror your mood if we're peas in a pod? Similarity and liking in the social induction of affect. *The Journal of Social Psychology, 155,* 636–649. https://doi.org/10.1080/00224545.2015.1047437

Xu, Z., & Guo, H. (2019). Advantages of anticipated emotions over anticipatory emotions and cognitions in health decisions: A meta-analysis. *Health Communication, 34,* 774–781. https://doi.org/10.1080/10410236.2018.1434738

Yamane, D. (1996). Collaboration and its discontents: Steps toward overcoming barriers to successful group projects. *Teaching Sociology, 24*(4), 378–383. https://doi.org/10.2307/1318875

Yeow, A., Johnson, S. L., & Faraj, S. (2006). Lurking: Legitimate or illegitimate peripheral participation. *ICIS 2006 Proceedings, 62,* 967–982. https://aisel.aisnet.org/cgi/viewcontent.cgi?article=1183&context=icis2006

Yoo, S. C., Pena, J. F., & Drumwright, M. E. (2015). Virtual shopping and unconscious persuasion: The priming effects of avatar age and consumers' age discrimination on purchasing and prosocial behaviors. *Computers in Human Behavior, 48,* 62–71. https://doi.org/10.1016/j.chb.2015.01.042

Yong, E. (2012). Replication studies: Bad copy. *Nature, 485*(7398), 298–300. https://doi.org/10.1038/485298a

Yong, E. (2018, November 19). Psychology's replication crisis is running out of excuses. *The Atlantic.* https://www.theatlantic.com/science/archive/2018/11/psychologys-replication-crisis-real/576223/

Yoon, H. J., & Tinkham, S. F. (2013). Humorous threat persuasion in advertising: The effects of humor, threat intensity, and issue involvement. *Journal of Advertising, 42*(1), 30–41. https://doi.org/10.1080/00913367.2012.749082

York, C., Ponder, J. D., Humphries, Z., Goodall, C., Beam, M., & Winters, C. (2020). Effects of fact-checking political misinformation on perceptual accuracy and epistemic political efficacy. *Journalism & Mass Communication Quarterly, 97,* 958–980. https://doi.org/10.1177/1077699019890119

Young, D. G. (2008). The privileged role of the late-night joke: Exploring humor's role in disrupting argument scrutiny. *Media Psychology, 11,* 119–142. https://doi.org/10.1080/15213260701837073

Yuan, S., & Lu, H. (2020). "It's global warming, stupid": Aggressive communication styles and political ideology in science blog debates about climate change. *Journalism & Mass Communication Quarterly, 97,* 1003–1025. https://doi.org/10.1177/1077699020904791

Zald, M. N. (2000). Ideologically structured action: An enlarged agenda for social movement research. *Mobilization: An International Quarterly, 5*(1), 1–16. http://mobilizationjournal.org/?code=hjdm-site

Zawisza, M., Cinnirella, M., & Zawadzka, A. M. (2006). Non-traditional male gender portrayal as a persuasion tool in advertising. *Social Influence, 1*(4), 288–300. https://doi.org/10.1080/15553451060101 6976

Zha, X., Li, L., Yan, Y., Wang, Q., & Wang, G. (2016). Exploring digital library usage for getting information from the ELM perspective: The moderating effect of information need. *Aslib Journal of Information Management, 68,* 286–305. https://doi.org/10.1108/AJIM-12-2015-0200

Zha, X., Yang, H., Yan, Y., Liu, K., & Huang, C. (2018). Exploring the effect of social media information quality, source credibility and reputation on informational fit-to-task: Moderating role of focused immersion. *Computers in Human Behavior, 79,* 227–237. https://doi.org/10.1016/j.chb.2017.10.038

Zhu, L., & Anagondahalli, D. (2017). Predicting student satisfaction: The role of academic entitlement and nonverbal immediacy. *Communication Reports, 31*(1), 41–52. https://doi.org/10.1080/08934215.2017.1364777

Zhuang, J., Lapinksi, M. K., & Peng, W. (2018). Crafting messages to promote water conservation: Using time-framed messages to boost conservation actions in the United States and China. *Journal of Applied Social Psychology, 48*, 248–256. https://doi.org/10.1111/jasp.12509

Zompetti, J. (2018). *Divisive discourse: The extreme rhetoric of contemporary American politics* (2nd ed.). Cognella.

Zompetti, J. P., Moore, M. A., Smudde, P. M., & Hunt, S. K. (2013). The right to peaceable assembly and social movements: The role of "occupying" space as a way to speak. In N. S. Lind (Ed.), *First Amendment rights: An encyclopedia* (Vol. 2, pp. 237–256). ABC

Zuckerman, M., & Driver, R. E. (1985). Telling lies: Verbal and nonverbal correlates of deception. In A. W. Siegman and S. Feldstein (Eds.), *Multichannel integrations of nonverbal behavior* (pp. 129–147). Erlbaum.

Zuckerman, M., DePaulo, B. M., & Rosenthal, R. (1981). Verbal and non-verbal communication of deception. In L. Berkowitz (Ed.), *Advances in experimental and social psychology* (pp. 1–59). Academic Press.

Zukin, C., Keeter, S., Anolina, M., Jenkins, K., & Delli Carpini, M. X. (2006). *A new engagement? Political participation, civic life, and the changing American citizen.* Oxford University Press.

Index

D

H

I

J

K

L

M

Q

R

S

T

CPSIA information can be obtained
at www.ICGtesting.com
Printed in the USA
LVHW061534091222
734862LV00002B/6

9 781516 548231